Lecture Notes in Computer Science   10316

Commenced Publication in 1973
Founding and Former Series Editors:
Gerhard Goos, Juris Hartmanis, and Jan van Leeuwen

More information about this series at http://www.springer.com/series/7407

Giovanni Pighizzini · Cezar Câmpeanu (Eds.)

Descriptional Complexity of Formal Systems

19th IFIP WG 1.02 International Conference, DCFS 2017
Milano, Italy, July 3–5, 2017
Proceedings

 Springer

Editors
Giovanni Pighizzini (ID)
Università degli Studi di Milano
Milan
Italy

Cezar Câmpeanu
University of Prince Edward Island
Charlottetown, PE
Canada

ISSN 0302-9743   ISSN 1611-3349   (electronic)
Lecture Notes in Computer Science
ISBN 978-3-319-60251-6   ISBN 978-3-319-60252-3   (eBook)
DOI 10.1007/978-3-319-60252-3

Library of Congress Control Number: 2017943006

LNCS Sublibrary: SL1 – Theoretical Computer Science and General Issues

Printed on acid-free paper

This Springer imprint is published by Springer Nature
The registered company is Springer International Publishing AG
The registered company address is: Gewerbestrasse 11, 6330 Cham, Switzerland

Preface

The 19th International Conference of Descriptional Complexity of Formal Systems (DCFS 2017) was held in Milan during July 3–5, 2017. It was jointly organized by the Working Group 1.02 on Descriptional Complexity of the International Federation for Information Processing (IFIP) and by the Department of Computer Science (Dipartimento di Informatica) of the University of Milan (Università degli Studi di Milano).

Descriptional complexity is a field in computer science that deals with the size of all kinds of objects that occur in computational models, such as Turing machines, finite automata, grammars, splicing systems, and others. The topics of this conference are related to all aspects of descriptional complexity and include, but are not limited to:

- Automata, grammars, languages, and other formal systems; various modes of operations and complexity measures
- Succinctness of description of objects, state-explosion-like phenomena
- Circuit complexity of Boolean functions and related measures
- Size complexity of formal systems
- Structural complexity of formal systems
- Trade-offs between computational models and mode of operation
- Applications of formal systems – for instance in software and hardware testing, in dialogue systems, in systems modeling or in modeling natural languages – and their complexity constraints
- Co-operating formal systems
- Size or structural complexity of formal systems for modeling natural languages
- Complexity aspects related to the combinatorics of words
- Descriptional complexity in resource-bounded or structure-bounded environments
- Structural complexity as related to descriptional complexity
- Frontiers between decidability and undecidability
- Universality and reversibility
- Nature-motivated (bio-inspired) architectures and unconventional models of computing
- Blum static (Kolmogorov/Chaitin) complexity, algorithmic information

DCFS became an IFIP working conference in 2016, continuing the former Workshop on Descriptional Complexity of Formal Systems, which was a merger in 2002 of two other workshops: FDSR (Formal Descriptions and Software Reliability) and DCAGRS (Descriptional Complexity of Automata, Grammars and Related Structures). DCAGRS was previously held in Magdeburg (1999), London (2000), and Vienna (2001). FDSR was previously held in Paderborn (1998), Boca Raton (1999), and San Jose (2000). Since 2002, DCFS has been successively held in London, Ontario, Canada (2002), Budapest, Hungary (2003), London, Ontario, Canada (2004), Como, Italy (2005), Las Cruces, New Mexico, USA (2006), Nový Smokovec, High Tatras, Slovakia (2007), Charlottetown, Prince Edward Island, Canada (2008), Magdeburg,

Germany (2009), Saskatoon, Canada (2010), Gießen, Germany (2011), Braga, Portugal (2012), London, Ontario, Canada (2013), Turku, Finland (2014), Waterloo, Ontario, Canada (2015), and Bucharest, Romania (2016).

This volume contains the papers of the four invited talks and 20 contributed papers presented at DCFS 2017.

The invited talks have been given by:

- Jürgen Dassow (Otto von Guericke University, Magdeburg, Germany)
- Dora Giammarresi (University of Rome Tor Vergata, Italy)
- Stavros Konstantinidis (Saint Mary's University, Halifax/NS, Canada)
- Orna Kupferman (The Hebrew University, Jerusalem, Israel)

We are grateful to all invited speakers for accepting our invitation and for their excellent presentations.

The 20 contributed papers were selected by the Program Committee (PC) out of a total of 26 submissions, by a total of 54 authors from 21 countries (76.9% acceptance rate). The selection was made on the basis of at least three reviews per submission, considering originality, quality, significance, and presentation. We thank all authors who submitted their work for consideration to DCFS 2017. We wish to thank all PC members and external reviewers for their competent and timely handling of the submissions. The success of the scientific program is due to their hard work.

During the selection process and the preparation of these proceedings, we used the EasyChair conference management system, which provided excellent support. We wish to thank the editorial team at Springer, in particular Alfred Hofmann and Anna Kramer, for the efficient production of this volume.

We gratefully acknowledge the support of the University of Milan (Università degli Studi di Milano, Dipartimento di Informatica) and of the Italian Chapter of the European Association for Theoretical Computer Science (EATCS).

Special thanks for the website design and maintenance are due to Luca Prigioniero (University of Milan).

We hope that, as in the past, DCFS 2017 will be a scientifically most valuable and exciting event and, in particular, the starting point for new research and co-operations.

We look forward to seeing this year's participants and many others in Halifax at DCFS 2018!

July 2017

Giovanni Pighizzini
Cezar Câmpeanu

Organization

Steering Committee

Cezar Câmpeanu	University of Prince Edward Island, Charlottetown, Canada
Erzsébet Csuhaj-Varjú	Eötvös Loránd University, Budapest, Hungary
Jürgen Dassow	Otto von Guericke University, Magdeburg, Germany
Helmut Jürgensen	Western University, London, Canada
Martin Kutrib	Justus Liebig University, Gießen, Germany
Giovanni Pighizzini (Chair)	University of Milan, Italy
Rogério Reis	University of Porto, Portugal

Program Committee

Suna Bensch	Umeå University, Sweden
Cezar Câmpeanu (Co-chair)	University of Prince Edward Island, Charlottetown, Canada
Erzsébet Csuhaj-Varjú	Eötvös Loránd University, Budapest, Hungary
Michael J. Dinneen	University of Auckland, New Zealand
Henning Fernau	University of Trier, Germany
Viliam Geffert	Pavol Jozef Šafárik University, Košice, Slovakia
Markus Holzer	Justus Liebig University, Gießen, Germany
Szabolcs Iván	University of Szeged, Hungary
Sylvain Lombardy	Institut Polytechnique de Bordeaux, France
Andreas Malcher	Justus Liebig University, Gießen, Germany
Tomáš Masopust	Dresden University of Technology, Germany
Giovanni Pighizzini (Co-chair)	University of Milan, Italy
Rogério Reis	University of Porto, Portugal
Narad Rampersad	University of Winnipeg, Canada
Kai Salomaa	Queen's University, Kingston, Canada
Shinnosuke Seki	The University of Electro-Communications, Tokyo, Japan
Arseny Shur	Ural Federal University, Ekaterinburg, Russia
Lynette van Zijl	Stellenbosch University, South Africa
Abuzer Yakarylmaz	University of Latvia, Rīga, Latvia

Additional Reviewers

Bednárová, Zuzana
Beier, Simon
Charlier, Émilie
Demirci, Gökalp
Fazekas, Szilard Zsolt
Fujiyoshi, Akio
Gazdag, Zsolt
Huang, Nan
Kallmeyer, Laura
Knop, Alexander
Ko, Sang-Ki
Kosolobov, Dmitry
Kutrib, Martin
Lavado, Giovanna

Lázár, Katalin A.
Montoya, Andres
Moreira, Nelma
Ng, Timothy
Okubo, Fumiya
Pribavkina, Elena
Prigioniero, Luca
Say, A.C. Cem
Šebej, Juraj
Szabari, Alexander
Truthe, Bianca
Villagra, Marcos
Watson, Bruce
Wendlandt, Matthias

Contents

Invited Papers

Sensing as a Complexity Measure

Shaull Almagor[1], Denis Kuperberg[2], and Orna Kupferman[3(✉)]

[1] Department of Computer Science, Oxford University, Oxford, UK
[2] CNRS, ENS Lyon, Université de Lyon, LIP, Lyon, France
[3] School of Engineering and Computer Science, The Hebrew University,
Jerusalem, Israel
orna@cs.huji.ac.il

Abstract. The size of deterministic automata required for recognizing regular and ω-regular languages is a well-studied measure for the complexity of languages. We introduce and study a new complexity measure, based on the *sensing* required for recognizing the language. Intuitively, the sensing cost quantifies the detail in which a random input word has to be read in order to decide its membership in the language. We study the sensing cost of regular and ω-regular languages, as well as applications of the study in practice, especially in the monitoring and synthesis of reactive systems.

1 Introduction

Studying the complexity of a formal language, there are several complexity measures to consider. When the language is given by means of a Turing Machine, the traditional measures are time and space demands. Theoretical interest as well as practical considerations have motivated additional measures, such as randomness (the number of random bits required for the execution) [12] or communication complexity (number and length of messages required) [11]. For regular and ω-regular languages, given by means of finite-state automata, the classical complexity measure is the size of a minimal deterministic automaton that recognizes the language.

We introduce and study a new complexity measure, namely the *sensing cost* of the language. Intuitively, the sensing cost of a language measures the detail with which a random input word needs to be read in order to decide membership in the language. Sensing has been studied in several other CS contexts. In theoretical CS, in methodologies such as PCP and property testing, we are allowed to sample or query only part of the input [9]. In more practical applications, mathematical tools in signal processing are used to reconstruct information based on compressed sensing [6], and in the context of data streaming, one cannot store

The paper gives an overview of the technical results in the papers [2,3]. The research leading to these results has received funding from the European Research Council under the European Union's 7th Framework Programme (FP7/2007-2013, ERC grant no. 278410).

G. Pighizzini and C. Câmpeanu (Eds.): DCFS 2017, LNCS 10316, pp. 3–15, 2017.
DOI: 10.1007/978-3-319-60252-3_1

in memory the entire input, and therefore has to approximate its properties according to partial "sketches" [13].

Our interest in regular sensing is motivated by the use of finite-state automata in reasoning about on-going behaviors of reactive systems. In particular, a big challenge in the design of monitors is an optimization of the sensing needed for deciding the correctness of observed behaviors. Our goal is to formalize regular sensing in the finite-state setting and to study the sensing complexity measure for regular and ω-regular languages.

We consider languages over alphabets of the form 2^P, for a finite set P of signals. Consider a deterministic automaton $\mathcal{A}$ over an alphabet 2^P. For a state q of $\mathcal{A}$, we say that a signal $p \in P$ is *sensed* in q if at least one transition taken from q depends on the truth value of p. The *sensing cost* of q is the number of signals it senses, and the sensing cost of a run is the average sensing cost of states visited along the run. We extend the definition to automata by assuming a uniform distribution of the inputs.[1] Thus, the sensing cost of $\mathcal{A}$ is the limit of the expected sensing of runs over words of increasing length.[2] We show that this definition coincides with one that is based on the stationary distribution of the Markov chain induced by $\mathcal{A}$, which enables us to calculate the sensing cost of an automaton in polynomial time. The sensing cost of a language L, of either finite or infinite words, is then the infimum of the sensing costs of deterministic automata for L. In the case of infinite words, one can study different classes of automata, yet we show that the sensing cost is independent of the acceptance condition being used.

We start by studying the sensing cost of regular languages of finite words. For the complexity measure of size, the picture in the setting of finite words is very clean: each language L has a unique minimal deterministic automaton (DFA), namely the *residual automaton* $\mathcal{R}_L$ whose states correspond to the equivalence classes of the Myhill-Nerode right-congruence relation for L. We show that minimizing the state space of a DFA can only reduce its sensing cost. Hence, the clean picture of the size measure is carried over to the sensing measure: the sensing cost of a language L is attained in the DFA $\mathcal{R}_L$. In particular, since DFAs can be minimized in polynomial time, we can construct in polynomial time a minimally-sensing DFA, and can compute in polynomial time the sensing cost of languages given by DFAs.

We then study the sensing cost of ω-regular languages, given by means of deterministic parity automata (DPAs). Recall the size complexity measure.

---

[1] Our study and results apply also to a non-uniform distribution on the letters, given by a Markov chain.

[2] Alternatively, one could define the sensing cost of $\mathcal{A}$ as the cost of its "most sensing" run. Such a worst-case approach is taken in [5], where the sensing cost needs to be kept under a certain budget in all computations, rather than in expectation. We find the average-case approach we follow appropriate for sensing, as the cost of operating sensors may well be amortized over different runs of the system, and requiring the budget to be kept under a threshold in every run may be too restrictive. Thus, the automaton must answer correctly for every word, but the sensing should be low only on average, and it is allowed to operate an expensive sensor now and then.

There, the picture for languages of infinite words is not clean: A language needs not have a unique minimal DPA, and the problem of finding one is NP-complete [15]. It turns out that the situation is challenging also in the sensing measure. First, we show that different minimal DPAs for a language may have different sensing costs. In fact, bigger DPAs may have smaller sensing costs.

To see the intricacy in the case of ω-regular languages, consider a component in a vacuum-cleaning robot that monitors the dust collector and checks that it is empty infinitely often. The proposition *empty* indicates whether the collector is empty and a sensor needs to be activated in order to know its truth value. One implementation of the component would sense *empty* throughout the computation. This corresponds to the classical two-state DPA for "infinitely often *empty*". A different implementation can give up the sensing of *empty* for some fixed number k of states, then wait for *empty* to hold, and so forth. The bigger k is, the lazier is the sensing and the smaller the sensing cost is. As the example demonstrates, there may be a trade-off between the sensing cost of an implementation and its size. Other considerations, like a preference to have eventualities satisfied as soon as possible, enter the picture too.

Our main result is that despite the above intricacy, the sensing cost of an ω-regular language L is the sensing cost of the residual automaton $\mathcal{R}_L$ for L. It follows that the sensing cost of an ω-regular language can be computed in polynomial time. Unlike the case of finite words, it may not be possible to define L on top of $\mathcal{R}_L$. Interestingly, however, $\mathcal{R}_L$ does capture exactly the sensing required for recognizing L. The proof goes via a sequence $(\mathcal{B}_n)_{n=1}^{\infty}$ of DPAs whose sensing costs converge to that of L. The DPA $\mathcal{B}_n$ is obtained from a DPA $\mathcal{A}$ for L by a lazy sensing strategy that spends time in n copies of $\mathcal{R}_L$ between visits to $\mathcal{A}$, but spends enough time in $\mathcal{A}$ to ensure that the language is L.

In the context of formal methods, sensing has two appealing applications. The first is *monitoring*: we are given a computation and we have to decide whether it satisfies a specification. When the computations are over 2^P, we want to design a monitor that minimizes the expected average number of sensors used in the monitoring process. Monitoring is especially useful when reasoning about *safety* specifications [8]. There, every computation that violates the specification has a bad prefix – one all whose extensions are not in L. Hence, as long as the computation is a prefix of some word in L, the monitor continues to sense and examine the computation. Once a bad prefix is detected, the monitor declares an error and no further sensing is required. The second application is *synthesis*. Here, the set P of signals is partitioned into sets I and O of input and output signals, respectively. We are given a specification L over the alphabet $2^{I \cup O}$, and our goal is to construct an *I/O transducer* that realizes L. That is, for every sequence of assignments to the input signals, the transducer generates a sequence of assignments to the output signals so that the obtained computation is in L [14]. Our goal is to construct a transducer that minimizes the expected average number of sensors (of input signals) that are used along the interaction.

The definition of sensing cost described above falls short in the above two applications. For the first, the definition above does not distinguish between words in the language and words not in the language, whereas in monitoring we care only for words in the language. In particular, according to the definition above, the sensing cost of a safety language is always 0. For the second, the definition above considers automata and does not partition P into I and O, whereas synthesis refers to I/O-transducers. Moreover, unlike automata, correct transducers generate only computations in the language, and they need not generate all words in the language – only these that ensure receptiveness with respect to all sequences of inputs.

We thus continue and study sensing in the context of monitoring and synthesis. We suggest definitions that capture the intuition of "required number of sensors" in these settings and solve the problems of generating monitors and transducers that minimize sensing. For both settings, we focus on safety languages.

Consider, for example, a traffic monitor that has access to various sensors on roads and whose goal is to detect accidents. Once a road accident is detected, an alarm is raised to the proper authorities and the monitoring is stopped until the accident has been taken care of. The monitor can read the speed of cars along the roads, as well as the state of traffic lights. An accident is detected when some cars do not move even-though no traffic light is stopping them. Sensing the speed of every car and checking every traffic light requires huge sensing. Our goal is to find a monitor that minimizes the required sensing and still detects all accidents. In the synthesis setting, our goal is extended to designing a transducer that controls the traffic lights according to the speed of the traffic in each direction, and satisfies some specification (say, give priority to slow traffic), while minimizing the sensing of cars.

We revise our definition as follows. Let us start with monitoring. Recall that the definition of sensing above assumes a uniform probability on the assignments to the signals, whereas in monitoring we want to consider instead more intricate probability spaces – ones that restrict attention to words in the language. As we show, there is more than one way to define such probability spaces, each leading to a different measure. We study two such measures. In the first, we sample a word randomly, letter by letter, according to a given distribution, allowing only letters that do not generate bad prefixes. In the second, we construct a sample space directly on the words in the language. We show that in both definitions, we can compute the sensing cost of the language in polynomial time, and that the minimal sensing cost is attained by a minimal-size automaton. Thus, luckily enough, even though different ways in which a computation may be given in an online manner calls for two definitions of sensing cost, the design of a minimally-sensing monitor is the same in the two definitions.

Let us continue to synthesis. Recall that there, given a specification over sets I and O of input and output signals, the goal is to construct a finite-state system that, given a sequence of input signals, generates a computation that satisfies the specification. In each moment in time, the system reads an assignment to the input signals, namely a letter in 2^I, which requires the activation of $|I|$ Boolean sensors. A well-studied special case of limited sensing is synthesis with *incomplete information.* There, the system can read only a subset of the signals in I, and should still generate only computations that satisfy the specification [4,10]. A more sophisticated case of sensing in the context of synthesis is studied in [5], where the system can read some of the input signals some of the time. In more detail, sensing the truth value of an input signal has a cost, the system has a budget for sensing, and it tries to realize the specification while minimizing the required sensing budget.

The main challenge there is that we no longer need to consider all words in the language. This introduces a new degree of freedom, which requires different techniques than those used for the definition above. In particular, while a minimal-size transducer for a safety language can be defined on top of the state space of a minimal-size deterministic automaton for the language, this is not the case when we seek minimally-sensing transducers. In fact, we show that a minimally-sensing transducer for a safety language might be exponentially bigger than a minimal-size automaton for the language. Consequently, the problems of computing the minimal sensing cost and finding a minimally-sensing transducer are EXPTIME-complete even for specifications given by means of deterministic safety automata. On the positive side, a transducer that attains the minimal sensing cost always exists for safety specifications.

2   Preliminaries

Automata. A *deterministic automaton on finite words* (DFA) is $\mathcal{A} = \langle \Sigma, Q, q_0, \delta, \alpha \rangle$, where Q is a finite set of states, $q_0 \in Q$ is an initial state, $\delta : Q \times \Sigma \to Q$ is a total transition function, and $\alpha \subseteq Q$ is a set of accepting states. We sometimes refer to δ as a relation $\Delta \subseteq Q \times \Sigma \times Q$, with $\langle q, \sigma, q' \rangle \in \Delta$ iff $\delta(q, \sigma) = q'$. The run of $\mathcal{A}$ on a word $w = \sigma_1 \cdot \sigma_2 \cdots \sigma_m \in \Sigma^*$ is the sequence of states $q_0, q_1, \ldots, q_m$ such that $q_{i+1} = \delta(q_i, \sigma_{i+1})$ for all $i \geq 0$. The run is accepting if $q_m \in \alpha$. A word $w \in \Sigma^*$ is accepted by $\mathcal{A}$ if the run of $\mathcal{A}$ on w is accepting. The language of $\mathcal{A}$, denoted $L(\mathcal{A})$, is the set of words that $\mathcal{A}$ accepts. For a state $q \in Q$, we use $\mathcal{A}^q$ to denote $\mathcal{A}$ with initial state q. We sometimes refer also to nondeterministic automata (NFAs), where $\delta : Q \times \Sigma \to 2^Q$ suggests several possible successor states. Thus, an NFA may have several runs on an input word w, and it accepts w if at least one of them is accepting.

Consider a language $L \subseteq \Sigma^*$. For two finite words u_1 and u_2, we say that u_1 and u_2 are *right L-indistinguishable*, denoted $u_1 \sim_L u_2$, if for every $z \in \Sigma^*$, we have that $u_1 \cdot z \in L$ iff $u_2 \cdot z \in L$. Thus, $\sim_L$ is the Myhill-Nerode right congruence used for minimizing automata. For $u \in \Sigma^*$, let $[u]$ denote the equivalence class of u in $\sim_L$ and let $\langle L \rangle$ denote the set of all equivalence classes. Each class $[u] \in \langle L \rangle$ is associated with the *residual language* $u^{-1}L = \{w : uw \in L\}$. When L is regular, the set $\langle L \rangle$ is finite, and induces the *residual automaton* of L, defined by $\mathcal{R}_L = \langle \Sigma, \langle L \rangle, \Delta_L, [\epsilon], \alpha \rangle$, with $\langle [u], a, [u \cdot a] \rangle \in \Delta_L$ for all $[u] \in \langle L \rangle$ and $a \in \Sigma$. Also, α contains all classes $[u]$ with $u \in L$. The DFA $\mathcal{R}_L$ is well defined and is the unique minimal DFA for L.

A *deterministic automaton on infinite words* is $\mathcal{A} = \langle \Sigma, Q, q_0, \delta, \alpha \rangle$, where Q, q_0, and δ are as in DFA, and α is an acceptance condition. The run of $\mathcal{A}$

on an infinite input word $w = \sigma_1 \cdot \sigma_2 \cdots \in \Sigma^\omega$ is defined as for automata on finite words, except that the sequence of visited states is now infinite. For a run $r = q_0, q_1, \ldots$, let $inf(r)$ denote the set of states that r visits infinitely often. Formally, $inf(r) = \{q : q = q_i$ for infinitely many i's$\}$. We consider the following acceptance conditions. In a *Büchi* automaton, the acceptance condition is a set $\alpha \subseteq Q$ and a run r is accepting iff $inf(r) \cap \alpha \neq \emptyset$. A *looping* automaton is a special case of the Büchi condition, with $\alpha = Q$. Finally, a parity condition is a mapping $\alpha : Q \to [i, \ldots, j]$, for integers $i \leq j$, and a run r is accepting iff $\max_{q \in inf(r)}\{\alpha(q)\}$ is even. We use the acronyms NBA, DBA, NLA, DLA, NPA, and DPA to denote nondeterministic/deterministic Büchi/looping/parity word automata.

We extend the right congruence $\sim_L$ as well as the definition of the residual automaton $\mathcal{R}_L$ to languages $L \subseteq \Sigma^\omega$. Here, however, $\mathcal{R}_L$ need not accept the language of L, and we ignore its acceptance condition.

Sensing. We study languages over an alphabet $\Sigma = 2^P$, for a finite set P of signals. A letter $\sigma \in \Sigma$ corresponds to a truth assignment to the signals. When we define languages over Σ, we use predicates on P in order to denote sets of letters. For example, if $P = \{a, b, c\}$, then the expression $(\text{True})^* \cdot a \cdot b \cdot (\text{True})^*$ describes all words over 2^P that contain a subword $\sigma_a \cdot \sigma_b$ with $\sigma_a \in \{\{a\}, \{a,b\}, \{a,c\}, \{a,b,c\}\}$ and $\sigma_b \in \{\{b\}, \{a,b\}, \{b,c\}, \{a,b,c\}\}$.

Consider an automaton $\mathcal{A} = \langle 2^P, Q, q_0, \delta, \alpha \rangle$. For a state $q \in Q$ and a signal $p \in P$, we say that p is *sensed in* q if there exists a set $S \subseteq P$ such that $\delta(q, S \setminus \{p\}) \neq \delta(q, S \cup \{p\})$. Intuitively, a signal is sensed in q if knowing its value may affect the destination of at least one transition from q. We use $sensed(q)$ to denote the set of signals sensed in q. The *sensing cost* of a state $q \in Q$ is $scost(q) = |sensed(q)|$.[3]

Consider a deterministic automaton $\mathcal{A}$ over $\Sigma = 2^P$ (and over finite or infinite words). For a finite run $r = q_1, \ldots, q_m$ of $\mathcal{A}$, we define the sensing cost of r, denoted $scost(r)$, as $\frac{1}{m} \sum_{i=0}^{m-1} scost(q_i)$. That is, $scost(r)$ is the average number of sensors that $\mathcal{A}$ uses during r. Now, for a finite word w, we define the sensing cost of w in $\mathcal{A}$, denoted $scost_\mathcal{A}(w)$, as the sensing cost of the run of $\mathcal{A}$ on w. Finally, the sensing cost of $\mathcal{A}$ is the expected sensing cost of words of length that tends to infinity, where we assume that the letters in Σ are uniformly distributed. Thus, $scost(\mathcal{A}) = \lim_{m \to \infty} |\Sigma|^{-m} \sum_{w:|w|=m} scost_\mathcal{A}(w)$. Note that the definition applies to automata on both finite and infinite words.

Two DFAs may recognize the same language and have different sensing costs. In fact, as we demonstrate in Example 1 below, in the case of infinite words two different minimal automata for the same language may have different sensing costs.

For a language L of finite or infinite words, the sensing cost of L, denoted $scost(L)$ is the minimal sensing cost required for recognizing L by a deterministic automaton. Thus, $scost(L) = \inf_{\mathcal{A}:L(\mathcal{A})=L} scost(\mathcal{A})$. For the case of infinite

---

[3] We note that, alternatively, one could define the *sensing level* of states, with $slevel(q) = \frac{|sensed(q)|}{|P|}$. Then, for all states q, we have that $slevel(q) \in [0, 1]$. All our results hold also for this definition, simply by dividing the sensing cost by $|P|$.

words, we allow $\mathcal{A}$ to be a deterministic automaton of any type. In fact, as we shall see, unlike the case of succinctness, the sensing cost is independent of the acceptance condition used.

Example 1. Let $P = \{a\}$. Consider the language $L \subseteq (2^{\{a\}})^\omega$ of all words with infinitely many a and infinitely many $\neg a$. In Fig. 1 below we present two minimal DBAs for L with different sensing costs.

Fig. 1. Two minimal DBAs for L with different sensing costs.

While all the states of the second automaton sense a, thus its sensing cost is 1, the signal a is not sensed in all the states of the first automaton, thus its sensing cost is strictly smaller than 1.   □

Remark 1. Our study of sensing considers deterministic automata. The notion of sensing is less natural in the nondeterministic setting. From a conceptual point of view, we want to capture the number of sensors required for an actual implementation for recognizing the language. Technically, guesses can reduce the number of required sensors. To see this, take $P = \{a\}$ and consider the language $L = \texttt{True}^* \cdot a$. A DFA for L needs two states, both sensing a. An NFA for L can guess the position of the letter before the last one, where it moves to the only state that senses a. The sensing cost of such an NFA is 0 (for any reasonable extension of the definition of cost on NFAs).   □

Probability. Consider a directed graph $G = \langle V, E \rangle$. A *strongly connected component* (SCC) of G is a maximal (with respect to containment) set $C \subseteq V$ such that for all $x, y \in C$, there is a path from x to y. An SCC (or state) is *ergodic* if no other SCC is reachable from it, and is *transient* otherwise.

An automaton $\mathcal{A} = \langle \Sigma, Q, q_0, \delta, \alpha \rangle$ induces a directed graph $G_{\mathcal{A}} = \langle Q, E \rangle$ in which $\langle q, q' \rangle \in E$ iff there is a letter σ such that $q' \in \delta(q, \sigma)$. When we talk about the SCCs of $\mathcal{A}$, we refer to those of $G_{\mathcal{A}}$. Recall that we assume that the letters in Σ are uniformly distributed, thus $\mathcal{A}$ also corresponds to a Markov chain $M_{\mathcal{A}}$ in which the probability of a transition from state q to state q' is $p_{q,q'} = \frac{1}{|\Sigma|} |\{\sigma \in \Sigma : \delta(q, \sigma) = q'\}|$. Let $\mathcal{C}$ be the set of $\mathcal{A}$'s SCC, and $\mathcal{C}_e \subseteq \mathcal{C}$ be the set of its ergodic SCC's.

Consider an ergodic SCC $C \in \mathcal{C}_e$. Let P_C be the matrix describing the probability of transitions in C. Thus, the rows and columns of P_C are associated with states, and the value in coordinate q, q' is $p_{q,q'}$. By [7], there is a unique probability vector $\pi_C \in [0, 1]^C$ such that $\pi_C P_C = \pi_C$. This vector describes the *stationary distribution* of C: for all $q \in C$ it holds that $\pi_C(q) = \lim_{m \to \infty} \frac{E_m^C(q)}{m}$, where $E_m^C(q)$ is the average number of occurrences of q in a run of M_A of length m that starts anywhere in C [7]. Thus, intuitively, $\pi_C(q)$ is the probability that a long run that starts in C ends in q. In order to extend the distribution to the entire Markov chain of A, we have to take into account the probability of reaching each of the ergodic components. The *SCC-reachability distribution* of A is the function $\rho : C \to [0,1]$ that maps each ergodic SCC C of A to the probability that M_A eventually reaches C, starting from the initial state. We can now define the *limiting distribution* $\pi : Q \to [0,1]$, as

$$\pi(q) = \begin{cases} 0 & \text{if } q \text{ is transient,} \\ \pi_C(q)\rho(C) & \text{if } q \text{ is in some } C \in \mathcal{C}_e. \end{cases}$$

Note that $\sum_{q \in Q} \pi(q) = 1$, and that if P is the matrix describing the transitions of M_A and π is viewed as a vector in $[0,1]^Q$, then $\pi P = \pi$. Intuitively, the limiting distribution of state q describes the probability of a run on a random and long input word to end in q. Formally, we have the following.

Lemma 1. *Let $E_m(q)$ be the expected number of occurrences of a state q in a run of length m of M_A that starts in q_0. Then, $\pi(q) = \lim_{m \to \infty} \frac{E_m(q)}{m}$.*

Computing the Sensing Cost of an Automaton. Consider a deterministic automaton $A = \langle 2^P, Q, \delta, q_0, \alpha \rangle$. The definition of $scost(A)$ by means of the expected sensing cost of words of length that tends to infinity does not suggest an algorithm for computing it. In this section we show that the definition coincides with a definition that sums the costs of the states in A, weighted according to the limiting distribution, and show that this implies a polynomial-time algorithm for computing $scost(A)$. This also shows that the cost is well-defined for all automata.

Theorem 1. *For all automata A, we have $scost(A) = \sum_{q \in Q} \pi(q) \cdot scost(q)$, where π is the limiting distribution of A.*

Remark 2. It is not hard to see that if A is strongly connected, then π is the unique stationary distribution of M_A and is independent of the initial state of A. Accordingly, $scost(A)$ is also independent of A's initial state in this special case. □

Theorem 2. *Given an automaton A, the sensing cost $scost(A)$ can be calculated in polynomial time.*

Example 2. Let $P = \{a, b\}$. Consider the DFA A_1 appearing in Fig. 2. Note that $L(A_1) = (\text{True})^* \cdot a \cdot b \cdot (\text{True})^*$. It is easy to see that $sensed(q_0) = \{a\}$, $sensed(q_1) = \{b\}$, and $sensed(q_2) = \emptyset$. Accordingly, $scost(q_0) = scost(q_1) = 1$ and $scost(q_2) = 0$. Since the state q_2 forms the only ergodic SCC, the limiting distribution on the states of A is $\pi(q_0) = \pi(q_1) = 0$ and $\pi(q_2) = 1$. Hence, $scost(A_1) = 0$.

Consider now the DFA A_2, appearing in Fig. 3, with $L(A_2) = (\text{True})^* \cdot a \cdot b$. Here, $sensed(q_0) = \{a\}$, $sensed(q_1) = \{a, b\}$, and $sensed(q_2) = \{a\}$. Accordingly, $scost(q_0) = scost(q_2) = 1$ and $scost(q_2) = 2$.

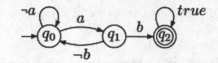

Fig. 2. The DFA $\mathcal{A}_1$.

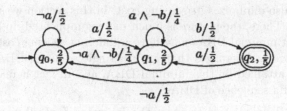

Fig. 3. The DFA $\mathcal{A}_2$ and its corresponding Markov chain.

Since $\mathcal{A}_2$ is strongly connected, its limiting distribution is its unique stationary distribution, which can be calculated by solving the following system of equations, where x_i corresponds to $\pi(q_i)$:

- $x_0 = \frac{1}{2}x_0 + \frac{1}{4}x_1 + \frac{1}{2}x_2.$ • $x_2 = \frac{1}{2}x_1.$
- $x_1 = \frac{1}{2}x_0 + \frac{1}{4}x_1 + \frac{1}{2}x_2.$ • $x_0 + x_1 + x_2 = 1.$

Accordingly, $\pi(q_0) = \pi(q_1) = \frac{2}{5}$ and $\pi(q_2) = \frac{1}{5}$. We conclude that the sensing cost of $\mathcal{A}_2$ is $1 \cdot \frac{2}{5} + 2 \cdot \frac{2}{5} + 1 \cdot \frac{1}{5} = \frac{7}{5}$. $\qquad\square$

3   The Sensing Cost of Regular Languages of Finite Words

In this section we study the setting of finite words. We show that there, sensing minimization goes with size minimization, which makes things clean and simple, as size minimization for DFAs is a feasible and well-studied problem.

Consider a regular language $L \subseteq \Sigma^*$, with $\Sigma = 2^P$. Recall that the residual automaton $\mathcal{R}_L = \langle \Sigma, \langle L \rangle, \Delta_L, [\epsilon], \alpha \rangle$ is the minimal-size DFA that recognizes L. We claim that $\mathcal{R}_L$ also minimizes the sensing cost of L.

Lemma 2. *Consider a regular language $L \subseteq \Sigma^*$. For every DFA $\mathcal{A}$ with $L(\mathcal{A}) = L$, we have that $scost(\mathcal{A}) \geq scost(\mathcal{R}_L)$.*

Since $L(\mathcal{R}_L) = L$, then $scost(L) \leq scost(\mathcal{R}_L)$. This, together with Lemma 2, enables us to conclude the following.

Theorem 3. *For every regular language $L \subseteq \Sigma^*$, we have $scost(L) = scost(\mathcal{R}_L)$.*

Finally, since DFAs can be size-minimized in polynomial time, Theorems 2 and 3 imply we can efficiently minimize also the sensing cost of a DFA and calculate the sensing cost of its language:

Theorem 4. *Given a DFA $\mathcal{A}$, the problem of computing $scost(L(\mathcal{A}))$ can be solved in polynomial time.*

4   The Sensing Cost of ω-Regular Languages

For the case of finite words, we have a very clean picture: minimizing the state space of a DFA also minimizes its sensing cost. In this section we study the case of infinite words. There, the picture is much more complicated. In Example 1 we saw that different minimal DBAs may have a different sensing cost. We start by showing that even for languages that have a single minimal DBA, the sensing cost may not be attained by this minimal DBA, and in fact it may be attained only as a limit of a sequence of DBAs.

Example 3. Let $P = \{p\}$, and consider the language L of all words $w_1 \cdot w_2 \cdots$ such that $w_i = \{p\}$ for infinitely many i's. Thus, $L = (\text{True}^* \cdot p)^\omega$. A minimal DBA for L has two states. The minimal sensing cost for a two-state DBA for L is $\frac{2}{3}$ (the classical two-state DBA for L senses p in both states and thus has sensing cost 1. By taking $\mathcal{A}_1$ in the sequence we shall soon define we can recognize L by a two-state DBA with sensing cost $\frac{2}{3}$). Consider the sequence of DBAs $\mathcal{A}_m$ appearing in Fig. 4. The DBA $\mathcal{A}_m$ recognizes $(\text{True}^{\geq m} \cdot p)^\omega$, which is equivalent to L, yet enables a "lazy" sensing of p. Formally, The stationary distribution π for $\mathcal{A}_m$ is such that $\pi(q_i) = \frac{1}{m+1}$ for $0 \leq i \leq m-1$ and $\pi(q_m) = \frac{2}{m+1}$. In the states $q_0, \ldots, q_{m-1}$ the sensing cost is 0 and in q_m it is 1. Accordingly, $scost(\mathcal{A}_m) = \frac{2}{m+1}$, which tends to 0 as m tends to infinity.   □

Fig. 4. The DBA $\mathcal{A}_m$.

Still we can characterize the sensing cost of an ω-regular language by means of the residual automaton for the language:

Theorem 5. *For every ω-regular language $L \subseteq \Sigma^\omega$, we have $scost(L) = scost(\mathcal{R}_L)$.*

Trade-off Between Sensing and Quality: The key idea in the proof of Theorem 5 is that when we reason about languages of infinite words, it is sometimes possible to delay the sensing and only sense in "sparse" intervals. This sort of lazy sensing is sound, as eventualities are allowed to be satisfied in an unboundedly-far future (see also Example 3). In practice, however, it is often desirable to satisfy eventualities quickly. This is formalized in multi-valued formalisms such as LTL with future discounting [1], where formulas assign higher satisfaction values to computations that satisfy eventualities fast. Our study here suggests that lower sensing leads to lower satisfaction values. An interesting problem is to study and formalize this intuitive trade-off between sensing and quality.

5 Monitoring

As described in Sect. 1, the definition of sensing above takes into an account all words in $(2^P)^\omega$, regardless their membership in the language. In monitoring, we restrict attention to words in the language, as once a violation is detected, no further sensing is required. In particular, in safety languages, violation amounts to a detection of a bad prefix, and indeed safety languages are the prominent class of languages for which monitoring is used [8].

As it turns out, however, there are many approaches to define the corresponding probability space. We suggest here two. We focus on safety languages, namely these recognizable by DLAs. Let $\mathcal{A}$ be a DLA and let $L = L(\mathcal{A})$.

1. [**Letter-based**] At each step, we uniformly draw a "safe" letter – one with which we are still generating a word in $pref(L)$, thereby iteratively generating a random word in L.
2. [**Word-based**] At the beginning, we uniformly draw a word in L.

We denote the sensing cost of $\mathcal{A}$ in the letter- and word-based approaches $lcost(\mathcal{A})$ and $wcost(\mathcal{A})$, respectively. The two definitions yield two different probability measures on L, as demonstrated in Example 4 below.

Example 4. Let $P = \{a\}$ and consider the safety language $L = a^\omega + (\neg a) \cdot (True)^\omega$. That is, if the first letter is $\{a\}$, then the suffix should be $\{a\}^\omega$, and if the first letter is $\emptyset$, then all suffixes result in a word in L. Consider the DLA $\mathcal{A}$ for L in Fig. 5.

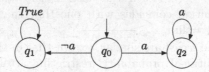

Fig. 5. A DLA for $a^\omega + (\neg a) \cdot (True)^\omega$.

In the letter-based definition, we initially draw a letter from $2^{\{a\}}$ uniformly, i.e., either a or $\neg a$ w.p. $\frac{1}{2}$. If we draw $\neg a$, then we move to q_1 and stay there forever. If we draw a, then we move to q_2 and stay there forever. Since $scost(q_1) = 0$ and $scost(q_2) = 1$, and we reach q_1 and q_2 w.p $\frac{1}{2}$, we get $lcost(\mathcal{A}) = \frac{1}{2}$.

In the word-based definition, we assign a uniform probability to the words in L. In this case, almost all words are not a^ω, and thus the probability of a^ω is 0. This means that we will get to q_1 w.p. 1, and thus $wcost(\mathcal{A}) = 0$.   □

As a more realistic example, recall our traffic monitor in Sect. 1. There, the behavior of the cars is the random input, and the two approaches can be understood as follows. In the letter-based approach, we assume that the drivers do their best to avoid accidents regardless of the history of the traffic and the traffic lights so far. Thus, after every safe prefix, we assume that the next input is also safe. In the word-based approach, we assume that the city is planned well enough to avoid accidents. Thus, we a-priori set the distribution to safe traffic behaviors according to their likelihood.

We now define the two approaches formally.

The Letter-Based Approach. Consider a DLA $\mathcal{A} = \langle \Sigma, Q, q_0, \delta, Q \rangle$. For a state $q \in Q$, let $avail(q)$ be the set of letters available in q, namely letters that do not cause $\mathcal{A}$ to get stuck. Formally, $avail(q) = \{\sigma \in \Sigma : \delta(q, \sigma) \text{ is defined}\}$. We model the drawing of available letters by the Markov chain $\mathcal{M}_{\mathcal{A}} = \langle Q, P \rangle$, where the probability of a transition from state q to state q' in $\mathcal{M}_{\mathcal{A}}$ is $P(q, q') = \frac{|\{\sigma \in \Sigma : \delta(q,\sigma) = q'\}|}{|avail(q)|}$. Let π be the limiting distribution of $\mathcal{M}_{\mathcal{A}}$. We define $lcost(\mathcal{A}) = \sum_{q \in Q} \pi(q) \cdot scost(q)$.

Since computing the limiting distribution can be done in polynomial time, we have the following.

Theorem 6. *Given a DLA $\mathcal{A}$, the sensing cost $lcost(\mathcal{A})$ can be calculated in polynomial time.*

The Word-Based Approach. Consider a DLA $\mathcal{A} = \langle 2^P, Q, q_0, \delta, Q \rangle$ recognizing a non-empty safety language L. From Sect. 2, $scost(\mathcal{A}) = \lim_{n \to \infty} \frac{1}{|\Sigma|^n} \sum_{u \in \Sigma^n} scost_{\mathcal{A}}(u)$, which is proven to coincide with $\mathbb{E}[scost_{\mathcal{A}}(u)]$ where $\mathbb{E}$ is the expectation with respect to the standard measure on Σ^ω. Our goal here is to replace this standard measure with one that restricts attention to words in L. Thus, we define $wcost(\mathcal{A}) = \mathbb{E}[scost(u) \mid u \in L]$. For $n \geq 0$, let $pref(L, n)$ be the set of prefixes of L of length n. Formally, $pref(L, n) = pref(L) \cap \Sigma^n$. As in the case of the standard measure, the expectation-based definition coincides with one that that is based on a limiting process: $wcost(\mathcal{A}) = \lim_{n \to \infty} \frac{1}{|pref(L,n)|} \sum_{u \in pref(L,n)} scost_{\mathcal{A}}(u)$. Thus, the expressions for $scost$ and $wcost$ are similar, except that in the expectation-based definition we add conditional probability, restricting attention to words in L, and in the limiting process we replace Σ^n by $pref(L, n)$.

Note that the term $\frac{1}{|pref(L,n)|}$ is always defined, as L is a non-empty safety language. In particular, the expectation is well defined even if L has measure 0 in Σ^ω.

Theorem 7. *Given a DLW $\mathcal{A}$, we can compute $wcost(\mathcal{A})$ in polynomial time.*

References

1. Almagor, S., Boker, U., Kupferman, O.: Discounting in LTL. In: Ábrahám, E., Havelund, K. (eds.) TACAS 2014. LNCS, vol. 8413, pp. 424–439. Springer, Heidelberg (2014). doi:10.1007/978-3-642-54862-8_37

2. Almagor, S., Kuperberg, D., Kupferman, O.: Regular sensing. In: Proceedings of 34th FST & TCS, LIPIcs, vol. 29, pp. 161–173 (2014)

3. Almagor, S., Kuperberg, D., Kupferman, O.: The sensing cost of monitoring and synthesis. In: Proceedings of 34th FST & TCS, LIPIcs, vol. 35, pp. 380–393 (2015)

4. Chatterjee, K., Majumdar, R.: Minimum attention controller synthesis for omega-regular objectives. In: Fahrenberg, U., Tripakis, S. (eds.) FORMATS 2011. LNCS, vol. 6919, pp. 145–159. Springer, Heidelberg (2011). doi:10.1007/978-3-642-24310-3_11

5. Chatterjee, K., Majumdar, R., Henzinger, T.A.: Controller synthesis with budget constraints. In: Egerstedt, M., Mishra, B. (eds.) HSCC 2008. LNCS, vol. 4981, pp. 72–86. Springer, Heidelberg (2008). doi:10.1007/978-3-540-78929-1_6

6. Donoho, D.L.: Compressed sensing. IEEE Trans. Inform. Theory **52**, 1289–1306 (2006)

7. Grinstead, C., Laurie Snell, J.: Markov chains. In: Introduction to Probability. American Mathematical Society (1997)

8. Havelund, K., Rosu, G.: Efficient monitoring of safety properties. STT&T **6**(2), 18–173 (2004)

9. Kindler, G.: Property testing, PCP, and Juntas. Ph.D. thesis, Tel Aviv University University (2002)

10. Kupferman, O., Vardi, M.Y.: Church's problem revisited. Bull. Symbol. Log. **5**(2), 245–263 (1999)

11. Kushilevitz, E., Nisan, N.: Communication Complexity. Cambridge University Press, Cambridge (1997)

12. Mauduit, C., Sárköz, A.: On finite pseudorandom binary sequences. i. measure of pseudorandomness, the legendre symbol. Acta Arith. **82**(4), 365–377 (1997)

13. Muthukrishnan, S.: Theory of data stream computing: where to go. In: Proceedings of 30th PODS, pp. 317–319 (2011)

14. Pnueli, A., Rosner, R.: On the synthesis of a reactive module. In: Proceedings of 16th POPL, pp. 179–190 (1989)

15. Schewe, S.: Beyond hyper-minimisation—minimising DBAs and DPAs is NP-complete. In: Proceedings of 30th FST & TCS, LIPIcs, vol. 8, pp. 400–411 (2010)

Avoiding Overlaps in Pictures

Marcella Anselmo[1], Dora Giammarresi[2(✉)], and Maria Madonia[3]

[1] Dipartimento di Informatica, Università di Salerno, Via Giovanni Paolo II,
132-84084 Fisciano, SA, Italy
manselmo@unisa.it
[2] Dipartimento di Matematica, Università Roma "Tor Vergata",
via della Ricerca Scientifica, 00133 Roma, Italy
giammarr@mat.uniroma2.it
[3] Dipartimento di Matematica e Informatica, Università di Catania,
Viale Andrea Doria 6/a, 95125 Catania, Italy
madonia@dmi.unict.it

Abstract. In string combinatorics, the sets of strings that have no overlaps (i.e. the prefix of one string does not coincide with the suffix of
another string) are extensively investigated since they play an important
role in the context of string matching and coding. The notion of overlap
can be extended naturally to two dimensions; two pictures p and q have
an overlap if one can put one corner of p on some position in q in such a
way that all symbols in the common positions coincide. A picture with
no self-overlaps is called unbordered and it is a generalization in two
dimensions of an unbordered (or bifix-free) string.

We study the problem of generating all unbordered pictures of fixed
size and present a construction of non-expandable non-overlapping sets
of pictures together with some examples.

Keywords: Two-dimensional language · Overlap · Unbordered picture

1 Introduction

Pictures are a generalization of strings to two dimensions and they are represented by two-dimensional (rectangular) arrays of symbols taken from a finite
alphabet Σ. The *size* of a picture with m rows and n columns is indicated by
(m, n). Single row or column pictures can be always identified with strings.

Extending results from the formal string language theory to two dimensions
is a very challenging task. The intrinsic complexity of two-dimensional structures
is evident even in the generalizations of the basic concepts and definitions. For
example, the definition of "prefix" of a string can be naturally extended to a
picture by considering its rectangular portion in the top-left corner; nevertheless, if one deletes a prefix from a picture, the remaining part is not a picture

Partially supported by INdAM-GNCS Project 2017, FARB Project ORSA138754 of
University of Salerno and FIR Project 375E90 of University of Catania.

G. Pighizzini and C. Câmpeanu (Eds.): DCFS 2017, LNCS 10316, pp. 16–32, 2017.
DOI: 10.1007/978-3-319-60252-3_2

anymore. Despite such difficulties, several results from string language theory have been worthy extended to pictures. Many researchers have investigated how the notion of recognizability by finite state automata can be transferred to two dimensions to accept picture languages [2,6–8,20,25,26,28,31]. Moreover two dimensional codes were studied in different contexts [1,17,21,29] and recently two-dimensional prefix codes were introduced as the two-dimensional counterpart of prefix string codes [3,4,8,10,11].

In the combinatorics of strings, the study of the structure and the special patterns of the strings plays an important role both from the theoretical and the applicative side. Given a string s, a *bifix* or a *border* of s is a substring x that is both prefix and suffix of s. A string s is *bifix-free* or *unbordered* if it has no other bifixes besides the empty string and s itself. Bifix-free strings are connected with the theory of codes [18] and are involved in the data structures for pattern matching algorithms [24,27]. From a more applicative point of view, bifix-free strings are suitable as synchronization patterns in digital communications and similar communications protocols [30]. The combinatorial structure of bifix-free strings over a given alphabet was studied by Nielsen in [30]; he provided an algorithm to enumerate all bifix-free strings of the same length n over a given alphabet. A set of strings X in which no prefix of any string is the suffix of any other string in X is called a *cross-bifix-free code*. Constructive methods for cross-bifix-free codes are widely investigated in [14,19,22].

In this paper we investigate the notion of *overlaps* in pictures. It can be very naturally extended from the string theory since it is not related to any preferred scanning direction. Informally, we say that two pictures p and q overlap when it is possible to place p somewhere on q in such a way that all the superimposed positions hold the same symbol. In other words, two pictures p and q overlap when we can find the same rectangular portion x at one corner of p and at the opposite corner of q. Observe that there are two different kinds of overlaps depending on the pair of opposite corners involved. If such common rectangular part x is found at the top-left corner of p (and bottom-right corner of q) we will say that p and q *tl*-overlap; if x is found at the bottom-left corner of p (and top-right corner of q) we will say that p and q *bl*-overlap. Moreover, special cases of overlaps will occur when such common part x is a "string" (for example there is a prefix of the first row in p that is a suffix of the last row in q). We refer to them as *frame-overlaps*.

The notion of overlap leads easily to the notion of *border*, when we consider overlaps between a picture p and its copy p'. As for overlaps, we can have *tl*- and *bl*-borders. A picture p is *unbordered* if it has no proper borders. Unbordered pictures are connected both to picture codes and to two-dimensional pattern matching. We are interested in computing all the unbordered pictures of a fixed size (m,n) on a given alphabet.

It can be verified that the recursive construction of bifix-free strings given by Nielsen in [30] cannot be directly generalized to generate unbordered pictures. Nevertheless, a bidimensional version of Nielsen's construction produces a bigger set of pictures to which we referred to as *quasi-unbordered* pictures in [5]. The quasi-unbordered pictures can have only certain particular types of borders. The unbordered pictures can then be extracted from this set. In this paper we discuss more in detail the advantages of using quasi-unbordered pictures as an intermediate step in the construction of the unbordered ones. In particular we show that the probability that any quasi-unbordered picture is actually unbordered goes to 1 when the size of the picture grows. Moreover we prove that unbordered pictures can be obtained by intersecting two different sets of quasi-unbordered pictures.

Next we consider particular sets of unbordered pictures where no picture can be overlapped on another one of the same set. We refer to them to as *non-overlapping sets*. They are therefore a generalization of cross-bifix-free codes of strings and they correspond to a family of picture codes. In particular, non-overlapping sets of pictures are two-dimensional comma-free codes (recently studied in [12]) with a stronger property.

Using a naive algorithm, a non-overlapping set of pictures of a fixed size (m, n) can be "extracted" by getting pictures one by one from the set of all unbordered pictures, by checking at each step that the current picture does not overlap with all the previously chosen ones. This procedure can be useful for getting small sets. The major problem is to find *non-expandable non-overlapping (NENO)* sets of pictures, i.e. sets to which it is not possible to add other non-overlapping pictures of the same size.

Very recently, in [15,16], some sets of non-overlapping matrices have been presented by exploiting some techniques from the string case. The problem of finding non-expandable non-overlapping sets was left open. Note that also in the string case the corresponding problem of finding large non-expandable cross-bifix-free sets is difficult [14,19,22]. In [9] a first example of a family of NENO sets of pictures is proposed. It is constructed by exploiting some conditions on the frames of the pictures of NENO sets. (The frame of a picture is the quadruple of strings corresponding to its first and last rows and columns). Once fixed the "right" set of frames $\mathcal{F}$ that avoid frame overlaps, the NENO set is found as subset of all the pictures with frame in $\mathcal{F}$.

The method can be applied to obtain further examples. It was not clear the role of the frame for the selection of the pictures of the NENO set; in particular it was left open the problem whether fixing the frame set could univocally determine the NENO set. In this paper we solve this problem by exhibiting two different NENO sets with the same frame set.

2   Preliminaries

We recall some definitions about two-dimensional languages (see [26]). A *picture* over a finite alphabet Σ is a two-dimensional rectangular array of elements of Σ. Given a picture p, $|p|_{row}$ and $|p|_{col}$ denote the number of rows and columns, respectively, while $size(p) = (|p|_{row}, |p|_{col})$ denotes the picture *size*. We also consider all the empty pictures that correspond to all pictures of size $(m, 0)$ or $(0, n)$. The set of all pictures over Σ of fixed size (m, n) is denoted by $\Sigma^{m,n}$.

The set of all pictures over Σ is denoted by Σ^{**} while Σ^{++} refers to the set Σ^{**} without the empty pictures. A *two-dimensional language* (or *picture language*) over Σ is a subset of Σ^{**}.

In order to locate a position in a picture, it is necessary to put the picture in a reference system. Let p be a picture of size (m, n). The set of coordinates $dom(p) = \{1, 2, \ldots, |p|_{row}\} \times \{1, 2, \ldots, |p|_{col}\}$ is referred to as the *domain* of a picture p. We let $p(i, j)$ denote the symbol in p at coordinates (i, j). We assume the top-left corner of the picture to be at position $(1, 1)$, and fix the scanning direction for a picture from the top-left corner toward the bottom right one. Moreover, to easily detect border positions of pictures, we use initials of words "top", "bottom", "left" and "right"; then, for example the *tl-corner* of p refers to position $(1, 1)$ while the *br-corner* refers to position (m, n). Furthermore, we denote by $r_F(p), r_L(p) \in \Sigma^n$ the first and the last row of p, respectively and by $c_F(p), c_L(p) \in \Sigma^m$ the first and the last column of p, respectively. Then, the *frame* of p is $frame(p) = (r_F(p), r_L(p), c_F(p), c_L(p))$.

For the sequel, it is convenient to extend the notation for the frame of a picture to languages. Let $X \subseteq \Sigma^{m,n}$. Let us denote by $R_F(X) \subseteq \Sigma^n$ the set $R_F(X) = \{r_F(p) \mid p \in X\}$ of the first rows of all pictures in X. In a similar way, $R_L(X), C_F(X)$, and $C_L(X)$ will denote the sets of the last rows, of the first columns, and of the last columns of all pictures in X, respectively. The *frame* of X is the quadruple $frame(X) = (R_F(X), R_L(X), C_F(X), C_L(X))$.

A *subdomain* of $dom(p)$ is a set d of the form $\{i, i+1, \ldots, i'\} \times \{j, j+1, \ldots, j'\}$, where $1 \leq i \leq i' \leq m$, $1 \leq j \leq j' \leq n$, also specified by the pair $[(i, j), (i', j')]$. The portion of p corresponding to positions in subdomain $[(i, j), (i', j')]$ is denoted by $p[(i, j), (i', j')]$. Then, a non-empty picture x is *subpicture of* p if $x = p[(i, j), (i', j')]$, for some $1 \leq i \leq i' \leq m$, $1 \leq j \leq j' \leq n$; we say that x *occurs* at position (i, j) (its tl-corner).

Observe that the notion of subpicture generalizes very naturally to two dimensions the notion of substring. On the other hand, the notions of prefix and suffix of a string implicitly assume the left-to-right reading direction. In two dimensions, there are four corners and four scanning-directions from a corner toward the opposite one. Hence, we introduce the definition of four different "prefixes" of a picture, each one referring to one corner.

Given pictures $p \in \Sigma^{m,n}$, $x \in \Sigma^{h,k}$, with $1 \leq h \leq m$, $1 \leq k \leq n$, we say that x is a *tl-prefix* of p if x is a subpicture of p occurring at position $(1, 1)$; x is a *tr-prefix* of p if x is a subpicture of p occurring at position $(1, n - k + 1)$; x is a *bl-prefix* of p if x is a subpicture of p occurring at position $(m - h + 1, 1)$; x is a *br-prefix* of p if x is a subpicture of p occurring at position $(m - h + 1, n - k + 1)$.

Some operations can be defined on pictures. Let $p, q \in \Sigma^{**}$ be pictures of size (m, n) and (m', n'), respectively. The *column* and the *row concatenation* of p and q are defined by horizontally and vertically juxtaposing p and q and are denoted by $p \ominus q$ and $p \oplus q$, respectively. They are partial operations, defined only if $m = m'$ and if $n = n'$, respectively. The reverse operation on strings can be generalized to pictures and gives rise to two different mirror operations (called *row-* and *col-mirror*) obtained by reflecting with respect to a vertical and a horizontal axis, respectively. Another operation that has no counterpart in one dimension is the *rotation*. The rotation of a picture p of size (m, n), is the clockwise rotation of p by $90°$, denoted by $p^{90°}$. Note that $p^{90°}$ has size (n, m). All the operations defined on pictures can be extended in the usual way to sets of pictures.

We conclude by remarking that any string $s = y_1 y_2 \cdots y_n$ can be identified either with a single-row or with a single-column picture.

3   Overlaps in Strings and in Pictures

In the string theory, patterns and overlaps are widely investigated. Two strings s and s' *overlap* if there exists a string x that is a suffix of s and a prefix of s', or vice versa; we will equivalently say that s overlaps s'. In this framework, the *cross-bifix-free* sets have been introduced in [13] by taking back a notion introduced in early sixties. A set of strings X is cross-bifix-free when no prefix of any string is the suffix of any other string in X (i.e. no two strings in X overlaps); it is *non-expandable* if no other element can be added to X without falsifying the property of the set.

The case when a string overlaps with itself leads to the notions of *border* (or *bifix*) of a string and *unbordered* (or *bifix-free*) strings. A string x that is both prefix and suffix of s is called a *border* or a *bifix* of s. The empty string and s itself are *trivial* borders of s. A string s is *unbordered* or *bifix-free* if it has no borders other than the trivial ones. In [30] Nielsen proposed a procedure to generate all bifix-free strings of a given length that is based on a property of string borders; we will give some details of this procedure in Sect. 4.

This notion of overlap of strings can be extended very naturally to two dimensions by taking into account that now four different corners exist. Informally, we say that two pictures p and q overlap when we can find the same rectangular portion at a corner of p and at the opposite corner of q. Observe that there are two different kinds of overlaps depending on the pair of opposite corners involved. The definitions here reported can be found in [9].

Definition 1. *Let $p \in \Sigma^{m,n}$ and $q \in \Sigma^{m',n'}$.*

The pictures p and q tl-overlap if there exists a picture $x \in \Sigma^{h,k}$, with $1 \leq h \leq \min\{m, m'\}$ and $1 \leq k \leq \min\{n, n'\}$, which is a tl-prefix of p and a br-prefix of q, or vice versa.

The pictures p and q bl-overlap if there exists a picture $x \in \Sigma^{h,k}$, with $1 \leq h \leq \min\{m, m'\}$ and $1 \leq k \leq \min\{n, n'\}$, which is a bl-prefix of p and a tr-prefix of q, or vice versa.

The pictures p and q overlap if they tl-overlap or they bl-overlap.

The picture x is called an overlap *of p and q, and its size (h, k) is the* size *of the overlap.*

For the sequel, it is useful to identify some special cases of picture overlaps and we list them in the definition below. Note that the same overlap can be of different types. Let $p \in \Sigma^{m,n}$ and $q \in \Sigma^{m',n'}$, then

p and q *properly overlap* if they have an overlap x with $x \neq p$ and $x \neq q$
p and q *h-slide overlap* if they have an overlap $x \in \Sigma^{h,k}$ with $h = m = m'$
p and q *v-slide overlap* if they have an overlap $x \in \Sigma^{h,k}$ with $k = n = n'$
p and q *frame-overlap* if they have an overlap $x \in \Sigma^{h,k}$ with $h = 1$ or $k = 1$.

Examples are given in Fig. 1.

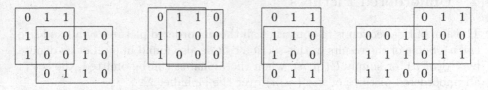

Fig. 1. From left to right: a pair of pictures that tl-overlap, h-slide overlap, v-slide overlap, frame-overlap (and also bl-overlap).

Consider now the case when a picture overlaps with itself; this case leads to the generalization of the notion of border from strings to pictures.

Definition 2. *Given pictures $p \in \Sigma^{m,n}$ and $x \in \Sigma^{m',n'}$, with $1 \leq m' \leq m$ and $1 \leq n' \leq n$, the picture x is a tl-border of p, if x is a subpicture of p occurring at position $(1,1)$ and at position $(m - m' + 1, n - n' + 1)$; picture x is a bl-border of p, if x is a subpicture of p occurring at position $(m - m' + 1, 1)$ and at position $(1, n - n' + 1)$ Moreover x is a border of p if it is either a tl- or a bl-border.*

As special cases, p is a *trivial border* of itself, and x is a *proper border* of p if it is not trivial. A tl-border is called a diagonal border in [23]. Notice that a tl-border x of a picture p of size (m, n) can be univocally detected either by giving the position where it occurs in p (besides position $(1, 1)$) or by giving its size. The same holds for bl-borders. Examples of pictures together with their borders are given below.

0	1 0	0 0 0		1 0 0	1 0				0 1 0 0
1	1 0	1 1 1		1 1 0	1 1				1 1 1 1

Note that if a picture p has a tl-border x, then the rotation $p^{90°}$ has a bl-border (that coincides with $x^{90°}$). In the figure above, the second picture is the rotation of the first one.

Definition 3. *A picture $p \in \Sigma^{m,n}$ is bordered if there exists a picture x that is a proper border of p. Picture p is unbordered (or border-free) if it is not bordered.*

In the next two sections we consider two main problems. Firstly we discuss the problem of generating the set of all unbordered pictures of fixed size and secondly we study sets of unbordered pictures that also do not overlap each others and that are non-expandable. Such sets, we call NENO sets, are the generalization to two dimensions of cross-bifix-free sets of strings.

4 Unbordered Pictures

The aim of this section is to construct all the unbordered pictures of a fixed size (m, n). Some of the results in this section can be also found in [5]. Let us denote by $U_\Sigma(m, n)$, or simply $U(m, n)$, when the alphabet can be omitted, the set of all unbordered pictures of size (m, n) over the alphabet Σ.

Few simple results useful in determining the unbordered pictures can be immediately listed. They hold for any alphabet Σ and integers $m, n \geq 1$.

The set $U_\Sigma(m, n)$ is closed with respect to the col- and row-mirror operations, and with respect to permutation of symbols in Σ. Moreover, $U_\Sigma(m, n)^{90°} = U_\Sigma(n, m)$. The first row (column, resp.) of an unbordered picture p of size (m, n) must be different from its last one, otherwise p would have a border of size $(1, n)$ $((m, 1), \text{respectively})$.

The opposite corners of an unbordered picture p of size (m, n) must contain different symbols otherwise p would have a border of size $(1, 1)$. This last simple remark allows to give a bound on the cardinality of the set of all unbordered pictures, $|U(m, n)| \leq 1/4|\Sigma^{m,n}|$.

The unbordered pictures of size $(1, n)$ or $(m, 1)$ coincide with the unbordered strings, which have been widely investigated in the literature. In particular, as we recalled in the previous section, Nielsen proposed a recursive procedure to generate all bifix-free strings of a given length (cf. [30]). Let us report briefly the main steps of this construction.

The construction is based on the result that a string s of length n is unbordered if and only if it has no "short" border, that is no border of length i for $1 \leq i \leq \lfloor n/2 \rfloor$. Unbordered strings of length n are constructed from unbordered strings of shorter length, by inserting extra symbols in the central positions. The starting set of unbordered strings of length 2 is simply the set of all strings ab with $a, b \in \Sigma$ and $a \neq b$. Then, the unbordered strings of odd length n are obtained by inserting any symbol in the middle of any unbordered string of length $n - 1$. The unbordered strings of even length n are obtained by inserting two symbols in the middle of any unbordered string of length $n - 2$ and excluding those strings that have a border of length $n/2$.

Before studying the general case let us consider the case of the binary alphabet $\Sigma = \{0, 1\}$ and of pictures of "small" size. It is immediate to see that there are no unbordered pictures of size $(2, 2)$, since there is no way to have different opposite corners and different first and last row. For similar reasons there are no unbordered pictures of sizes $(2, 3), (3, 2)$ and $(3, 3)$. The "smallest" unbordered pictures are of size $(4, 2)$ and they all are listed below:

$$
\begin{array}{|cc|}\hline 0 & 0 \\ 1 & 0 \\ 0 & 1 \\ 1 & 1 \\ \hline\end{array}\,,\quad
\begin{array}{|cc|}\hline 0 & 0 \\ 0 & 1 \\ 1 & 0 \\ 1 & 1 \\ \hline\end{array}\,,\quad
\begin{array}{|cc|}\hline 1 & 1 \\ 0 & 1 \\ 1 & 0 \\ 0 & 0 \\ \hline\end{array}\,,\quad
\begin{array}{|cc|}\hline 1 & 1 \\ 1 & 0 \\ 0 & 1 \\ 0 & 0 \\ \hline\end{array}\,.
$$

To generate the 40 unbordered pictures of size $(4,3)$ we can generalize Nielsen's construction, and construct them by inserting a suitable middle row in the unbordered pictures of size $(4,2)$ listed above. Unfortunately, this procedure does not work when the size of pictures grows, as shown by the following example.

Example 4. The following picture of size $(5,4)$ is unbordered but it cannot be obtained by insertion of a row or a column in a middle position of a smaller picture. All the pictures obtained by deleting either the third row or the second column or the third column (or both the second and the third column) are bordered pictures.

$$
\begin{array}{|cccc|}\hline
0 & 1 & 0 & 1 \\
0 & 1 & 0 & 0 \\
0 & 1 & 1 & 1 \\
0 & 0 & 0 & 0 \\
0 & 0 & 1 & 1 \\
\hline
\end{array}
$$

The main reason why Nielsen's construction of unbordered strings can not be directly generalized to pictures (as in Example 4), is that the result that any string with a "long" border has necessarily a "short" border too, does not hold in two dimensions. For pictures we have the following weaker result claiming that if a picture has a "large" border then it necessarily has a "small" or a "middle" border. More precisely, [5], if a picture $p \in \Sigma^{m,n}$ has a border of size (i,j) with $i \geq \lfloor m/2 \rfloor + 1$ and $j \geq \lfloor n/2 \rfloor + 1$ then p has a border of size (h,k) with $h \leq \lfloor m/2 \rfloor$ or $k \leq \lfloor n/2 \rfloor$.

A simple generalization of Nielsen's construction to pictures, presented in [5], produces the family of *quasi-unbordered* pictures, which is a family containing all unbordered pictures. In the sequel, we will recall such construction and then discuss the ways to obtain the set of unbordered pictures of given size from the family of quasi-unbordered pictures of that size. Notice that in the special case of one-row pictures, identifiable with strings, the quasi-unbordered pictures are exactly the unbordered strings and the construction presented below coincides with Nielsen's construction.

Definition 5. *A picture $p \in \Sigma^{m,n}$ is* quasi-unbordered *if p has no border at position (i,j) with $1 \leq i \leq m$ and $\lceil n/2 \rceil + 1 \leq j \leq n$.*

Informally, a picture is quasi-unbordered if it has no border occurring in its right side. The set of all quasi-unbordered pictures of size (m,n) over an alphabet Σ is denoted by $Q_\Sigma(m,n)$, or simply $Q(m,n)$, when the alphabet can be omitted. Observe that $U(m,n) \subseteq Q(m,n)$. Moreover, a quasi-unbordered picture either is an unbordered picture or it necessarily has a border of size (i,j), with $i \leq \lceil m/2 \rceil$ and $j > \lfloor n/2 \rfloor$ (and possibly a large one).

In the following, the set $Q(m,n)$ is constructed in a recursive way by the insertion of one column in the middle of pictures in $Q(m, n-1)$. We introduce first some formal notations. For any picture $p \in \Sigma^{m,n}$, the *left side* of p is the subpicture $p_L = p[(1,1),(m, \lceil n/2 \rceil)]$, containing the first $\lceil n/2 \rceil$ columns of p, and the *right side* of p is the subpicture $p_R = p[(1, \lceil n/2 \rceil + 1),(m,n)]$ containing the remaining columns. Hence $p = p_L \oslash p_R$.

The picture obtained by inserting in the "middle" of p a column $c \in \Sigma^{m,1}$ is denoted $p^{\|c} = p_L \oslash c \oslash p_R$. We also define the inverse operation of removing the central column in a picture. More exactly, if n is odd, then $p^{\|}$ denotes the picture obtained by removing the $\lceil n/2 \rceil$-th column; if n is even, then $p^{\|}$ denotes the picture obtained by removing the $(n/2 + 1)$-th column.

We are now ready to sketch the algorithm that provides the set $Q(m,n)$ of quasi-unbordered pictures of a given size (m,n) (see [5] for more details). It consists in the following two steps.

1. Construct $Q(m,2)$.
2. Recursively construct $Q(m,n)$ from $Q(m,n-1)$ as follows.
   If n is odd then define $Q(m,n)$ as the set of all pictures $p^{\|c}$ for all $p \in Q(m,n-1)$, $c \in \Sigma^{m,1}$.
   If n is even then define $Q(m,n)$ as the set of all pictures $p^{\|c}$ for all $p \in Q(m,n-1)$, $c \in \Sigma^{m,1}$, such that $p^{\|c}$ has no border occurring at a position in c.

A detailed example of this construction can be found in [5].

After having recalled the construction for the quasi-unbordered pictures let us now come back to the unbordered pictures. We discuss here more in detail the advantages of using such construction as an intermediate step in the construction of the unbordered ones.

Recall that $U(m,n) \subseteq Q(m,n)$. In the special case of one-row pictures, identifiable with strings, $Q(1,n) = U(1,n)$, for any $n \geq 1$. In the general case, $Q(m,n)$ contains all unbordered pictures in $U(m,n)$, but it may also contain some bordered pictures which are characterized by the occurrence of a "middle" border in their left side.

In order to estimate the overhead of considering the set $Q(m,n)$ as intermediate step for obtaining $U(m,n)$, note that the difference in size of the two sets sensibly decreases when n grows. This can be easily understood if we think that the probability that a picture has a border with more than $n/2$ columns sensibly decreases when n grows. More precisely, the following result holds.

Proposition 6. *Let m,n,h be positive integers, $1 \leq h \leq \lfloor m/2 \rfloor$, and Σ be an alphabet. The probability $P(m,n,h)$ that a random picture p in $Q_\Sigma(m,n)$ has a border in its left part of size (h,k) for some $\lceil n/2 \rceil \leq k \leq n$ is such that $\lim_{n \to \infty} P(m,n,h) = 0$.*

Proof. Let $p \in Q_\Sigma(m,n)$ and m,n,h,k be fixed as in the statement and let $P(m,n,h,k)$ be the probability that p has a border x in its left part of size (h,k). Since the two occurrences of the border x inside p do not overlap,

$P(m, n, h, k) = \frac{1}{|\Sigma|^{hk}}$. Suppose that n is even (the case of n odd goes similarly). Then, $P(m, n, h) = P(m, n, h, n/2) + P(m, n, h, n/2 + 1) + \cdots + P(m, n, h, n)$.

By simple calculations one obtains that $P(m, n, h) = \frac{1}{|\Sigma|^{hn/2}} \cdot \frac{1 - \frac{1}{|\Sigma|^{h(n/2+1)}}}{1 - \frac{1}{|\Sigma|^h}}$.

Hence, $\lim_{n \to \infty} P(m, n, h) = 0$. $\qquad\qquad\qquad\qquad\qquad\qquad\qquad\qquad\qquad\qquad\qquad\square$

Let us now consider the problem of extracting $U(m, n)$ from $Q(m, n)$.

A first solution consists in considering any picture p in $Q(m, n)$ and test whether it has a "middle" border in its left side. Notice that this procedure is more efficient (at least in terms of the necessary comparisons) than the one of taking any picture in $\Sigma^{m,n}$ and test whether it has a border of any size inside the whole picture. A simple bound on $|Q(m, n)|$ is $|Q(m, n)| \leq 1/4|\Sigma^{m,n}|$, for any $m, n \geq 2$, since opposite corners in quasi-unbordered pictures must be different.

A second way to obtain $U(m, n)$, once $Q(m, n)$ is constructed, is provided by the following result, where $Q(m, n)^{rev}$ denotes the col-mirror of $Q(m, n)$.

Proposition 7. *For any* $m, n \geq 2$, $U(m, n) = Q(m, n) \cap Q(m, n)^{rev}$.

Proof. Recall that by definition $Q(m, n)$ is the set of all pictures with no border in their right sides. Then, $Q(m, n)^{rev}$ is the set of all pictures with no border in their left sides. The intersection of these two sets gives the set of all pictures with no border at all, that is $U(m, n)$. $\qquad\qquad\qquad\qquad\square$

The previous proposition motivates a further investigation to find a clever procedure to generate $Q(m, n)$ and $Q(m, n)^{rev}$ in such a way to easily perform the intersection operation.

5   Non-overlapping Sets of Pictures

In this section we consider the generalization to two dimensions of the notion of cross-bifix-free sets of strings, introduced in [13]. They are special sets of unbordered pictures such that all the pictures do not overlap each others. Moreover, in analogy to the case of cross-bifix-free sets of strings, we will consider sets of pictures of fixed size.

Definition 8. *A set of pictures* $X \subseteq \Sigma^{m,n}$ *is* non-overlapping *if for any* $p, q \in X$, p *and* q *do not properly overlap.*

A set $X \subseteq \Sigma^{m,n}$ *is* non-expandable non-overlapping, *NENO for short, if* X *is non-overlapping and for any* $p \in \Sigma^{m,n} \setminus X$, *there exists* $q \in X$ *such that* p *and* q *overlap.*

We here consider the problem of constructing NENO sets, continuing the investigation in [9] where all the missing proofs can be found.

Notice that a way to obtain a NENO set X of pictures of size (m, n) is to consider the set $U(m, n)$ of all unbordered pictures, constructed following the results in Sect. 4; pick a picture $p \in U(m, n)$ and put in X; then add one by one the other pictures in $U(m, n)$ after checking that they do not cause conflicts.

For example, a NENO set X of pictures of size $(4,2)$, can be obtained from the set $U(4,2)$ shown in Sect. 4. By an exhaustive procedure, one can show that, for any picture $p \in U(4,2)$, the set $\{p\}$ is a NENO set. This kind of technique does not shed light on the structure of NENO sets. Indeed, our aim is to give a description of some families of NENO sets.

In general it seems not too complicate to construct sets of non-overlapping pictures by selecting *ad-hoc* pictures; the hard part is to let them satisfy the non-expandability property. In [9] the problem is tacked in a sort of reverse way. First, it is generated a set of pictures X non-expandable with respect to the non-overlapping property. This set X is defined by imposing particular conditions only on the frames of the pictures. Then, the problem is reduced to finding a non-overlapping set inside such X, by stating some conditions on the internal part of the pictures. We briefly report here the main steps of this procedure (all the proofs can be found in [9]) and subsequently, we discuss some questions related to the choice of the conditions on the internal part of the pictures. Moreover we introduce some significant new examples of NENO sets.

Recall that the frame of a picture language X is the quadruple of the sets of its first and last rows and columns, $frame(X) = (R_F(X), R_L(X), C_F(X), C_L(X))$. Note that not any quadruple (S_1, S_2, S_3, S_4) of string languages $S_1, S_2 \subseteq \Sigma^n$ and $S_3, S_4 \subseteq \Sigma^m$, can be the frame of a set of pictures since the corresponding strings need to match in the corner positions. If there exists a picture language $X \subseteq \Sigma^{m,n}$ such that $frame(X) = (S_1, S_2, S_3, S_4)$ we say that the quadruple is *frame-compatible*.

The following definition captures a *sufficient condition* for a set X to be non-expandable with respect to the overlapping. (Note that pictures inside X could possibly overlap each others).

Definition 9. *Let $X \subseteq \Sigma^{m,n}$. X is* frame-complete *if for any $p, q \in X$, p and q do not frame-overlap, and if for any picture $p \in \Sigma^{m,n} \setminus X$ there exists a picture $q \in X$ such that p and q frame-overlap.*

Frame-complete sets of pictures can be constructed by exploiting the following proposition.

Proposition 10. *Let $S_1, S_2 \subseteq \Sigma^n$, $S_3, S_4 \subseteq \Sigma^m$ and (S_1, S_2, S_3, S_4) be a quadruple of frame-compatible string languages. If for each pair $(M, N) = (S_1, S_2)$ or $(M, N) = (S_3, S_4)$ the following properties hold*

1. $M \cap N = \emptyset$.
2. *for any $u \in M$, $v \in N$, u and v do not overlap.*
3. *for any $w \notin M \cup N$, there exist $u \in M$, $v \in N$ such that w and u overlap, and w and v overlap*

then the set X of all the pictures p with $frame(p) \in S_1 \times S_2 \times S_3 \times S_4$ is frame-complete.

The next proposition states some sufficient conditions for a subset Y of a frame-complete set X to be NENO. The idea is that, providing that Y has the same frame as X, we can choose Y as a maximal non-overlapping set inside X. Moreover, in order to choose the pictures in Y, we need only to check overlaps of size (h, k) with $h, k \geq 2$; that is we do not need to take care of frame-overlaps in this next step.

Proposition 11. *Let $X \subseteq \Sigma^{m,n}$ be a frame-complete set. If a subset Y of X is such that*

(a) $frame(Y) = frame(X)$
(b) Y is non-overlapping
(c) for any $p \in X \setminus Y$ there exists $q \in Y$ such that p and q overlap

then Y is a NENO set.

A first example of a NENO set is given in [9] by exploiting Proposition 11. A particular frame is chosen in a way that the set X of all pictures with that frame is frame-complete and then the NENO set Y is extracted from X. It was not clear the role of the frame in extracting Y. The problem whether, once fixed the frame, the set Y was uniquely determined, was left open. Here, we show that there can be different NENO sets with the same frame. Let us start defining the frame.

Example 12. Let $\Sigma = \{0, 1\}$ and let $\mathcal{F} = (S_1, S_2, S_3, S_4)$ be a quadruple of string languages defined as follows:

- $S_1 = \{1w0 \mid |w| = n - 2, w \neq 0^{n-2}, w \text{ with no suffix in } 110^*\} \subseteq \Sigma^n$
- $S_2 = \{110^{n-2}\} \subseteq \Sigma^n$
- $S_3 = \{1w1 \mid w \in \{0, 1\}^{m-2}\} \subseteq \Sigma^m$
- $S_4 = \{0^m\} \subseteq \Sigma^m$

After comparing the first and last symbols of the strings in S_i, we note that $\mathcal{F}$ is frame-compatible. Let us show that the pairs (S_1, S_2) and (S_3, S_4) verify all the conditions in Proposition 10.

Consider the pair (S_1, S_2). The sets S_1 and S_2 are disjoint and no strings $u \in S_1$ and $v \in S_2$ overlap by definition. Let s be any string $s \notin S_1 \cup S_2$. If $s = 0x$ then s overlaps any string in S_1 and the string in S_2 with an overlap of length 1. If $s = 1y1$ then s overlaps any string in S_1 and the string in S_2 with an overlap of length 1. If $s = 1z0$ then, since $s \notin S_1$, two cases are possible: either $z \in 0^*$ or z has a suffix, say r, in 110^*. In the first case, s overlaps some string in S_1 with an overlap of length 2 and s overlaps the string in S_2 with an overlap of length $|s| - 1$. In the second case s overlaps some string in S_1 with an overlap of length $|r|$ and s overlaps the string in S_2 with an overlap of length $|r| + 1$.

Consider now the pair (S_3, S_4). The sets S_3 and S_4 are disjoint and no strings in S_3 can be overlapped with a string in S_4. Moreover, let s be any string $s \notin S_3 \cup S_4$. Two cases are possible: $s = 0x$ or $s = 1y$. In the first case, s overlaps the string in S_4 with an overlap of length 1. Moreover, since $s \notin S_4$, we can write $s = 0^k 1r$ for some $k \geq 1$, and then s overlaps some string in S_3 with an overlap of length $k + 1$. In the second case, s overlaps any string in S_3 with an overlap of length 1. Moreover, since $s \notin S_3$, we have $s = 1z0$ and therefore s overlaps the string in S_4 with an overlap of length 1.

Finally, by Proposition 10, we can affirm that the set of all the pictures in $\Sigma^{m,n}$ that have frame in (S_1, S_2, S_3, S_4) is frame-complete.

We now define a set $P(m, n)$ of pictures of size (m, n), which have the quadruple (S_1, S_2, S_3, S_4) of Example 12 as their frame, while their internal part is filled with all 0's, apart for the positions in the second column that can hold either 0 or 1. See the leftmost picture in Fig. 2 for a generic picture in $P(m, n)$, where $x, y, w \in \{0, 1\}^*$, $w \neq 0^{n-2}$, and w has no suffix in 110^*.

Definition 13. *Let $\Sigma = \{0, 1\}$ and $m, n \geq 4$. Let $S_1, S_2 \subseteq \Sigma^n$ and $S_3, S_4 \subseteq \Sigma^m$ be the languages $S_1 = \{1w0 \mid |w| = n - 2, w \neq 0^{n-2}, w \text{ with no suffix in } 110^*\}$, $S_2 = \{110^{n-2}\}$, $S_3 = \{1w1 \mid w \in \{0, 1\}^{m-2}\}$ and $S_4 = \{0^m\}$. Let $X(m, n) \subseteq \Sigma^{m,n}$ be the set of all the pictures p with $frame(p) \in S_1 \times S_2 \times S_3 \times S_4$.*

The set $P(m, n) \subseteq X(m, n)$ is the set of all the pictures $p \in X(m, n)$ such that $p(i, j) = 0$ for $2 \leq i \leq m - 1$ and $3 \leq j \leq n - 1$.

Proposition 14. *The language $P(m, n)$ in Definition 13 is a NENO set, for any $m, n \geq 4$.*

Proof. Let $X(m, n)$ and $P(m, n)$ be the languages defined in Definition 13. The set $X(m, n)$ is frame-complete as shown in Example 12. Let us show that $P(m, n)$ satisfies the conditions (a), (b), and (c), of Proposition 11.

(a) $frame(P(m, n)) = frame(X(m, n))$
It is obvious.

(b) $P(m, n)$ *is non-overlapping.*
Let $p, q \in P(m, n)$. The pictures p and q cannot frame-overlap, because the pairs $(R_F(X(m, n)), R_L(X(m, n)))$, $(C_F(X(m, n)), C_L(X(m, n)))$ satisfy condition 2 of Proposition 10 (as shown in Example 12).
The pictures p and q cannot h-slide overlap, because the last row of any picture in $P(m, n)$ is unbordered. The pictures p and q cannot v-slide overlap because, for any $p, q \in P(m, n)$, $p(1, 3)p(1, 4) \ldots p(1, n) \neq q(i, 3)q(i, 4) \ldots q(i, n)$, for $2 \leq i \leq m$.
Moreover, p and q cannot tl-overlap. Indeed, since they cannot h-slide or v-slide overlap, and $p(1, 1) = q(1, 1) = 1$, then p and q could eventually tl-overlap only with an overlap of size $(h, n - 1)$ with $1 < h < m$. But this would imply that the first row of a picture in $P(m, n)$ is of the form $1w0$ with $w = 0^{n-2}$ and this is impossible.
Finally, p and q cannot bl-overlap. Indeed, since they cannot h-slide or v-slide overlap, and $p(m, 1) = q(m, 1) = 1$, we have that p and q could eventually bl-overlap only with an overlap of size $(h, n - 1)$ with $1 < h < m$. But this would imply that position $(h, 3)$ of a picture in $P(m, n)$ carries symbol 1 and this is impossible.

(c) *For any $p \in X(m, n) \setminus P(m, n)$ there exists $q \in P(m, n)$ such that p and q overlap.*

1	w		0
	0...0		0
x y	: : :		:
	0...0		:
1	1	0...0	0

1	0	**0**	1	0
0	1	**0**		0
0	**0**	**0**		0
				0
1	1	0	0	0

1	0	1	0	0
			0	**0**
			0	**0**
1	0	0	**0**	0
1	1	0	0	0

1	1	1	1	0
				0
	1	**1**	**0**	**0**
				0
1	1	0	0	0

Fig. 2. From left to right: a generic picture in $P(m, n)$ and three pictures in $X(5, 5) \setminus T(5, 5)$ that violate condition (1), (2) and (3), respectively, in the positions in bold.

If $p \in X(m, n) \setminus P(m, n)$ then $frame(p) \in S_1 \times S_2 \times S_3 \times S_4$, but there exists (i, j), with $2 \le i \le m - 1$ and $3 \le j \le n - 1$, such that $p(i, j) = 1$. Let (i_0, j_0) be the rightmost among the lowest positions such that $p(i_0, j_0) = 1$. Then, one can find in $P(m, n)$ a picture q such that p and q tl-overlap, since there exists in $P(m, n)$ a picture q with its tl-prefix of size $(m - i_0 + 1, n - j_0 + 1)$ equal to the br-prefix of p of size $(m - i_0 + 1, n - j_0 + 1)$. □

We now define another set of pictures $T(m, n)$ with the same frame as $P(m, n)$. This time the positions in the internal part of the pictures can hold 0 or 1 everywhere, except for some special forbidden configurations. For example, there cannot be rows with a suffix in 110^+, or some particular L-shapes. Here below is the formal definition, while some forbidden configurations are illustrated in Fig. 2.

Definition 15. *Let $X(m, n) \subseteq \Sigma^{m,n}$ be the set given in Definition 13. The set $T(m, n) \subseteq X(m, n)$ is the set of all the pictures $p \in X(m, n)$ such that*

1. *if there exists (i, j), with $2 \le i \le m - 1$ and $2 \le j \le n - 2$, such that $p(i, 1) = p(i, 2) = \ldots = p(i, j) = 0$ and $p(1, j) = p(2, j) = \ldots = p(i-1, j) = 0$, then there exists (i', j'), with $1 \le i' < i$ and $1 \le j' < j - 1$, such that $p(i', j')p(i', j' + 1) \ldots p(i', j) \in 110^+$.*
2. *there exists no index i, $2 \le i \le m - 1$, such that $p(i, 1) = 1$, $p(i, 2) = p(i, 3) = \ldots = p(i, n - 1) = 0$ and $p(1, n - 1) = p(2, n - 1) = \ldots = p(i-1, n-1) = 0$.*
3. *there exists no (i, j), with $1 \le i \le m - 1$ and $1 \le j \le n - 1$, such that $p(i, j)p(i, j + 1) \ldots p(i, n) \in 110^+$.*

Proposition 16. *The language $T(m, n)$ in Definition 15 is a NENO set, for any $m, n \ge 4$.*

Proof. The set $X(m, n)$ is frame-complete (see Example 12). Let us show that $T(m, n)$ satisfies conditions (a), (b), and (c), of Proposition 11. Condition (a) is trivially true.

(b) $T(m, n)$ *is non-overlapping.*

Let $p, q \in T(m, n)$. The pictures p and q cannot frame-overlap, because the pairs $(R_F(X(m, n)), R_L(X(m, n)))$, $(C_F(X(m, n)), C_L(X(m, n)))$ satisfy condition 2. of Proposition 10 (as shown in Example 12).

The pictures p and q cannot h-slide overlap, because the last row of any picture in $T(m, n)$ is unbordered. The pictures p and q cannot v-slide overlap because of condition (3) in the definition of $T(m, n)$.

Moreover, p and q cannot tl-overlap. Indeed, suppose that p and q tl-overlap with an overlap of size (h, k) and w.l.o.g. suppose that the tl-corner of p is inside q.

If $k = n - 1$ then p violates condition (2) with $i = h$.

If $k < n-1$, then we have $p(h, 1) = p(h, 2) = \ldots = p(h, k) = 0$ and $p(1, k) = p(2, k) = \ldots = p(h - 1, k) = 0$. By condition (1), there exists (i', j'), with $1 \le i' < h$ and $1 \le j' < k-1$, such that $p(i', j')p(i', j'+1) \ldots p(i', k) \in 110^+$. Therefore, picture q violates condition (3) in its $(m - h + i' + 1)$-th row.

Finally, p and q cannot bl-overlap. Indeed, suppose that p and q bl-overlap with an overlap of size (h, k) and w.l.o.g. suppose that the bl-corner of p is inside q. In this case q violates condition (3) in position $(h, n - k + 1)$.

(c) *For any $p \in X(m, n) \setminus T(m, n)$ there exists $q \in T(m, n)$ such that p and q overlap.*

If $p \in X(m, n) \setminus T(m, n)$ then $frame(p) \in S_1 \times S_2 \times S_3 \times S_4$, but p does not satisfy at least one condition among (1), (2) and (3) in Definition 15. Let (i_0, j_0) be the highest position of p that violates some condition. If in position (i_0, j_0) condition (1) is violated, then there exists $q \in T(m, n)$ with the br-prefix of q of size (i_0, j_0) equal to the tl-prefix of p of the same size i.e. p and q tl-overlap. Note that the maximality of (i_0, j_0) implies that q does not violate neither condition (1) nor condition (2). Moreover, since there exists no (i', j'), with $1 \le i' < i_0$ and $1 \le j' < j_0 - 1$, such that $p(i', j')p(i', j' + 1) \ldots p(i', j_0) \in 110^+$, then q does not violate condition (3). Similar reasonings show that there exists $q \in T(m, n)$ such that p and q tl-overlap, also when in position (i_0, j_0) condition (2) or (3) is violated. $\square$

We have defined two NENO sets of pictures $P(m, n)$ and $T(m, n)$ with the same frame. Note that the two languages are different, actually they are disjoint. It would be interesting to investigate the relationships among NENO sets with the same frame together with the role of the frame in their definitions.

References

1. Aigrain, P., Beauquier, D.: Polyomino tilings, cellular automata and codicity. Theoret. Comput. Sci. **147**, 165–180 (1995)
2. Anselmo, M., Giammarresi, D., Madonia, M.: Deterministic and unambiguous families within recognizable two-dimensional languages. Fund. Inform. **98**(2–3), 143–166 (2010)
3. Anselmo, M., Giammarresi, D., Madonia, M.: Strong prefix codes of pictures. In: Muntean, T., Poulakis, D., Rolland, R. (eds.) CAI 2013. LNCS, vol. 8080, pp. 47–59. Springer, Heidelberg (2013). doi:10.1007/978-3-642-40663-8_6
4. Anselmo, M., Giammarresi, D., Madonia, M.: Two dimensional prefix codes of pictures. In: Béal, M.-P., Carton, O. (eds.) DLT 2013. LNCS, vol. 7907, pp. 46–57. Springer, Heidelberg (2013). doi:10.1007/978-3-642-38771-5_6

5. Anselmo, M., Giammarresi, D., Madonia, M.: Unbordered pictures: properties and construction. In: Maletti, A. (ed.) CAI 2015. LNCS, vol. 9270, pp. 45–57. Springer, Cham (2015). doi:10.1007/978-3-319-23021-4_5

6. Anselmo, M., Giammarresi, D., Madonia, M., Restivo, A.: Unambiguous recognizable two-dimensional languages. ITA **40**(2), 227–294 (2006)

7. Anselmo, M., Giammarresi, D., Madonia, M.: A computational model for tiling recognizable two-dimensional languages. Theor. Comput. Sci. **410**(37), 3520–3529 (2009)

8. Anselmo, M., Giammarresi, D., Madonia, M.: Prefix picture codes: a decidable class of two-dimensional codes. Int. J. Found. Comput. Sci. **25**(8), 1017–1032 (2014)

9. Anselmo, M., Giammarresi, D., Madonia, M.: Non-expandable non-overlapping sets of pictures. Theor. Comput. Sci. **657**, 127–136 (2017)

10. Anselmo, M., Giammarresi, D., Madonia, M.: Picture codes and deciphering delay. Inf. Comput. **253**, 358–370 (2017)

11. Anselmo, M., Giammarresi, D., Madonia, M.: Structure and properties of strong prefix codes of pictures. Math. Struct. Comput. Sci. **27**(2), 123–142 (2017). http://journals.cambridge.org/article-S0960129515000043

12. Anselmo, M., Madonia, M.: Two-dimensional comma-free and cylindric codes. Theor. Comput. Sci. **658**, 4–17 (2017)

13. Bajic, D.: On construction of cross-bifix-free kernel sets. In: 2nd MCM COST 2100, Lisbon, Portugal (2007)

14. Bajic, D., Loncar-Turukalo, T.: A simple suboptimal construction of cross-bifix-free codes. Crypt. Commun. **6**(1), 27–37 (2014)

15. Barcucci, E., Bernini, A., Bilotta, S., Pinzani, R.: Cross-bifix-free sets in two dimensions. Theor. Comput. Sci. **664**, 29–38 (2017)

16. Barcucci, E., Bernini, A., Bilotta, S., Pinzani, R.: Non-overlapping matrices. Theor. Comput. Sci. **658**, 36–45 (2017)

17. Beauquier, D., Nivat, M.: A codicity undecidable problem in the plane. Theor. Comp. Sci **303**, 417–430 (2003)

18. Berstel, J., Perrin, D., Reutenauer, C.: Codes and Automata. Cambridge University Press, Cambridge (2009)

19. Bilotta, S., Pergola, E., Pinzani, R.: A new approach to cross-bifix-free sets. IEEE Trans. Inf. Theory **58**(6), 4058–4063 (2012)

20. Blum, M., Hewitt, C.: Automata on a 2-dimensional tape. In: SWAT (FOCS), pp. 155–160 (1967)

21. Bozapalidis, S., Grammatikopoulou, A.: Picture codes. ITA **40**(4), 537–550 (2006)

22. Chee, Y.M., Kiah, H.M., Purkayastha, P., Wang, C.: Cross-bifix-free codes within a constant factor of optimality. IEEE Trans. Inf. Theory **59**(7), 4668–4674 (2013)

23. Crochemore, M., Iliopoulos, C.S., Korda, M.: Two-dimensional prefix string matching and covering on square matrices. Algorithmica **20**(4), 353–373 (1998)

24. Crochemore, M., Rytter, W.: Jewels of Stringology. World Scientific, Singapore (2002). http://www-igm.univ-mlv.fr/ mac/JOS/JOS.html

25. Giammarresi, D., Restivo, A.: Recognizable picture languages. Int. J. Pattern Recognit. Artif. Intell. **6**(2–3), 241–256 (1992)

26. Giammarresi, D., Restivo, A.: Two-dimensional languages. In: Rozenberg, G., Salomaa, A. (eds.) Handbook of Formal Languages, vol. III, pp. 215–268. Springer, Heidelberg (1997)

27. Gusfield, D.: Algorithms on Strings, Trees, and Sequences - Computer Science and Computational Biology. Cambridge University Press, Cambridge (1997)

28. Kari, J., Salo, V.: A survey on picture-walking automata. In: Kuich, W., Rahonis, G. (eds.) Algebraic Foundations in Computer Science. LNCS, vol. 7020, pp. 183–213. Springer, Heidelberg (2011). doi:10.1007/978-3-642-24897-9_9

29. Kolarz, M., Moczurad, W.: Multiset, set and numerically decipherable codes over directed figures. In: Arumugam, S., Smyth, W.F. (eds.) IWOCA 2012. LNCS, vol. 7643, pp. 224–235. Springer, Heidelberg (2012). doi:10.1007/978-3-642-35926-2_25

30. Nielsen, P.T.: A note on bifix-free sequences. IEEE Trans. Inf. Theory 19(5), 704–706 (1973)

31. Pradella, M., Cherubini, A., Crespi-Reghizzi, S.: A unifying approach to picture grammars. Inf. Comput. 209(9), 1246–1267 (2011)

Descriptional Complexity and Operations – Two Non-classical Cases

Jürgen Dassow[✉]

Fakultät für Informatik, Otto-von-Guericke-Universität Magdeburg,
PSF 4120, 39016 Magdeburg, Germany
dassow@iws.cs.uni-magdeburg.de

Abstract. For a language family $\mathcal{L}$, a syntactic complexity measure K defined on languages of $\mathcal{L}$, a number $n \geq 1$, and an n-ary operation $\circ$ under which $\mathcal{L}$ is closed, we define $g_\circ^K(m_1, m_2, \ldots, m_n)$ as the set of all integers r such that there are n languages L_i, $1 \leq i \leq n$, with

$$K(L_i) = m_i \text{ for } 1 \leq i \leq n \text{ and } K(\circ(L_1, L_2, \ldots, L_n)) = r.$$

In this paper we study these sets for the operation union, catenation, star, complement, set-subtraction, and intersection and the measure number of accepting states (defined for regular languages) as well as for reversal, union, catenation, and star and the measures number of nonterminals, productions, and symbols (defined for context-free languages).

Moreover, we discuss the change of these sets if one restricts to finite languages, unary languages, and finite unary languages.

1 Introduction

The state complexity $\mathsf{sc}(L)$ of a regular language L is defined as the minimal number of states that are sufficient and necessary for a deterministic finite automaton to accept L. The study of the state complexity of regular languages is a central topic in theoretical computer science, but it has also large importance in applied fields. The first important results by Lupanov, Moore, Meyer, Fischer and others date back to the sixties and seventies, i.e., to the beginning of theoretical computer science.

In the last three decades the following problem was intensively investigated: Given a binary regularity preserving operation $\circ$ and two numbers m and n, determine the maximal number k (denoted by $f_\circ^{\mathsf{sc}}(m, n)$) such that there are languages L_m and L_n with $\mathsf{sc}(L_m) = m$, $\mathsf{sc}(L_n) = n$ and $\mathsf{sc}(L_m \circ L_n) = k$ (we have introduced the concept for binary operations, but the concept can be used for unary, ternary etc. operations as well). Summaries on the study of $f_\circ^{\mathsf{sc}}$ can be found in the papers [8, 25].

As for other problems concerning the state complexity, one has noticed that the behaviour of the complexity under operations can considerably change if one

G. Pighizzini and C. Câmpeanu (Eds.): DCFS 2017, LNCS 10316, pp. 33–44, 2017.
DOI: 10.1007/978-3-319-60252-3_3

Operation	Regular	Finite	Reg. unary	Fin. unary
Union	mn	$mn - (m + n)$	$\sim mn$	$\max\{m, n\}$
Intersection	mn	$mn - 3(m + n) + 12$	$\sim mn$	$\min\{m, n\}$
Complement	m	m	m	m
Kleene plus	$2^{m-1} + 2^{m-2} - 1$	m	$(m - 1)^2$	m
Reversal	2^m	$O(2^{O(m)})$	m	m

restricts to finite or unary or finite unary languages. This can be seen from the following table.

We mention that there are also many papers where other subfamilies of the family of regular languages have been studied, e.g., star-free languages, union-free languages, languages closed under certain subword operations. Examples for such results can be found in [12,18].

There are also some results where instead of the maximal number $f_\circ^{sc}$ the set $g_\circ^{sc}$ of all numbers k such that there are languages L_m and L_n with $sc(L_m) = m$, $sc(L_n) = n$, and $sc(L_m \circ L_n) = k$ is determined. We mention here three such results.

- Complement: $g_C^{sc}(m) = \{m\}$ for $m \geq 1$,
- Union: [16] $g_\cup^{sc}(m, n) = \{1, 2, \ldots, mn\}$ for $m \geq 2$ and $n \geq 2$
- Kleene star: [17] $g_*^{sc}(m) = \begin{cases} \{1, 2\} & \text{for } m = 1 \\ \{1, 2, \ldots, 2^{m-1} + 2^{m-2}\} & \text{for } m \geq 2 \end{cases}$.

Obviously, the problem of the behaviour of syntactic measures of complexity under operations can be discussed in other cases, too, where one can change the complexity measure and/or the considered type of automaton. We mention here the following approaches.

The most natural extension of deterministic finite automata are nondeterministic finite automata. The operational behaviour of the (nondeterministic) state complexity is studied in [14] and summarized in [15].

The number of transitions is not of interest for complete deterministic finite automata, but the situation changes if one allows incomplete finite automata. In the papers [9,19], one can find results on the behaviour of the number of transitions under operations.

In order to cover XML structures one has to extend usual finite automata and comes to nested word automata or visibly pushdown automata or input-driven pushdown automata. The state complexity of these automata under operations is studied in the papers [1,20,21].

Another natural extension of finite automata over strings is given by tree automata. There are also some results for their operational state complexity (see [22,23]).

In this paper we summarize results on the behaviour of some further non-classical measures of descriptional complexity under operations.

First we consider the number of accepting states instead of the number of (all) states. For a regular language L, the number $\mathtt{asc}(L)$ is defined as the minimal number of accepting states that are sufficient and necessary for a deterministic finite automaton to accept L. We mention two points of interest in this measure:

- It was shown that, for two languages L_m and L_n with $\mathtt{sc}(L_m) = m$ and $\mathtt{sc}(L_n) = n$, the relation $\mathtt{sc}(L_m \cdot L_n) \leq m2^n - \mathtt{asc}(L_m) \cdot 2^{n-1}$ holds for $m \geq 2$ and $n \geq 1$, and that the bound is optimal. For the Kleene-closure and the cut-operation, the complexity of the resulting language also depends on the number of accepting states (see [6,8]).
- The complexity of algorithms for the minimization of Büchi automata and for model checking based on Büchi automata depend on the number of accepting states of the Büchi automaton (see [2,7]).

We determine the sets $g_\circ^{\mathtt{asc}}$ for union, complement, set-subtraction, Kleene star, catenation, and intersection. Furthermore, we discuss variants of $g_\circ^{\mathtt{asc}}$ where we restrict the sets L_m and L_n to be finite sets or regular unary sets and or finite unary sets. The comparison shows that, for most operations, the situation is similar for arbitrary regular, finite sets, and regular unary sets, whereas finite unary sets show a completely different behaviour.

Some of these results were already published in [3].

Furthermore, we consider context-free languages and define their syntactic complexity as the minimal number of nonterminals or productions or symbols which is necessary to generate the language by context-free grammars. These measures were introduced and studied by Gruska in [10,11]. We summarize some results obtained in cooperation with Ralf Stiebe and Ronny Harbich (see [4,5, 13]) for the operational behaviour of these measures for arbitrary context-free languages under reversal, union, catenation, and star. Moreover, we add results for the case of finite, unary context-free, and finite unary languages. For the number of variables, there is a large difference which comes from the fact that the complexity for finite and unary context-free languages is bounded by one or two. For the number of productions, it seems that the difference between arbitrary and finite sets is essentially that we miss one or two "large" values.

2   Definitions and Notations

We assume that the reader is familiar with the basic notions of theory of automata and formal languages; for details we refer to [24]. Essentially, we give some notations and define the complexity measures of regular and context-free languages which are considered in this paper.

By $\mathrm{card}(M)$, we denote the cardinality of a set M. The empty word is denoted by λ. By $\mathbb{N}$, we denote the set of all positive integers. If L is a language, then we define the complement $C(L)$ of L as the set of all words $w \in V^*$ which are not contained in L, where V is the minimal set (with respect to inclusion) with $L \subseteq V^*$.

We specify a (deterministic) finite automaton as a tuple $\mathcal{A} = (Q, X, q_0, F, \delta)$ where Q and X are finite sets of states and inputs, respectively, $q_0 \in Q$ is a distinguished state (the initial state), F is a subset of Q (the set of accepting states), and δ is a function from $Q \times X$ into Q. The language accepted by $\mathcal{A}$ is denoted by $L(\mathcal{A})$.

For a finite automaton $\mathcal{A} = (Q, X, q_0, F, \delta)$ and a regular language L, we set

$$\mathtt{asc}(\mathcal{A}) = \mathrm{card}(F),$$
$$\mathtt{asc}(L) = \min\{\mathtt{asc}(\mathcal{A}) \mid L(\mathcal{A}) = L\}.$$

A context-free grammar is specified as a quadruple $G = (N, T, P, S)$ where N and T are two finite and disjoint sets, P is a finite subset of $N \times (v \cup N)^*$, and S is a distinguished element of N. The elements of N, T, and P are called nonterminals, terminals, and productions, respectively, and S is called the axiom. We write $A \rightarrow w$ instead of $(A, w) \in P$. By $L(G)$, we denote the language generated by G.

For a context-free grammar $G = (N, T, P, S)$, we set

$$\mathrm{Var}(G) = \mathrm{card}(N),$$
$$\mathrm{Prod}(G) = \mathrm{card}(P), and$$
$$\mathrm{Symb}(G) = \sum_{A \rightarrow w \in P} (|w| + 2).$$

Let $K \in \{\mathrm{Var}, \mathrm{Prod}, \mathrm{Symb}\}$. For a context-free language L, we set

$$K(L) = \min\{K(G) \mid L(G) = L\}.$$

For a language family $\mathcal{L}$, a syntactic complexity measure K defined on languages of $\mathcal{L}$, a number $n \geq 1$, and an n-ary operation $\circ$ under which $\mathcal{L}$ is closed, we define $g_\circ^K(m_1, m_2, \ldots, m_n)$ as the set of all integers r such that there are n languages L_i, $1 \leq i \leq n$, with

$$K(L_i) = m_i \text{ for } 1 \leq i \leq n \text{ and } K(\circ(L_1, L_2, \ldots, L_n)) = r.$$

If we additional require that the languages L_i, $1 \leq i \leq n$, are finite or unary or finite unary, we use the notations $g_\circ^{K,f}(m_1, m_2, \ldots, m_n)$, $g_\circ^{K,u}(m_1, m_2, \ldots, m_n)$, and $g_\circ^{K,f,u}(m_1, m_2, \ldots, m_n)$.

3   Number of Accepting States

In this section we only consider regular languages; therefore we omit the adjective "regular".

With respect to the measure number of accepting states, we consider the operations complement, union, set-substraction, catenation, star, and intersection.

We start with complement.

Theorem 1. *The following relations hold for the operation complement:*

$$g_C^{\mathrm{asc}}(m) = g_C^{\mathrm{asc},u} \begin{cases} \{1\} & \text{for } m = 0 \\ \{0\} \cup \mathbb{N} & \text{for } m = 1 \\ \mathbb{N} & \text{for } m \geq 2 \end{cases}$$

$$g_C^{\mathrm{asc},f}(m) = g_C^{\mathrm{asc},f,u}(m) = \begin{cases} \{1\} & \text{for } m \in \{0\} \\ \mathbb{N} & \text{for } m \geq 2 \end{cases}.$$

We see that the only difference is that 0 is not in $g_C^{\mathrm{asc},f}(1)$ and not in $g_C^{\mathrm{asc},f,u}(1)$. This difference comes from the following observations:

- $\mathrm{asc}(\emptyset) = 0$ holds, and $\mathrm{asc}(L) \geq 1$ iff L is not empty.
- the complement of the empty set is the non-finite set V^* of all words (and $\mathrm{asc}(V^*) = 1$).

We now give the results for union, set-subtraction, and star and compare them afterwards.

Theorem 2. *The following relations hold for the operation union:*

$$g_\cup^{\mathrm{asc}}(m,n) = g_\cup^{\mathrm{asc},u}(m,n) = \begin{cases} \{m\} & \text{for } n = 0, m \geq 0 \\ \{n\} & \text{for } m = 0, n \geq 0 \\ \mathbb{N} & \text{for } m \geq 1, \ n \geq 1 \end{cases},$$

$$g_\cup^{\mathrm{asc},f}(m,n) = \begin{cases} \{m\} & \text{for } n = 0, m \geq 0 \\ \{n\} & \text{for } m = 0, n \geq 0 \\ \mathbb{N} & \text{for } m = n = 1 \\ \mathbb{N} \setminus \{1\} & \text{for } m \geq 1, n \geq 1, m + n \geq 3 \end{cases},$$

$$g_\cup^{\mathrm{asc},f,u}(m,n) = \{\max\{m,n\}, \max\{m,n\} + 1, \ldots, m + n\}.$$

Theorem 3. *The following relations hold for the operation set-subtraction:*

$$g_\setminus^{\mathrm{asc}}(m,n) = g_\setminus^{\mathrm{asc},u} = \begin{cases} \{0\} & \text{for } m = 0, n \geq 0 \\ \{m\} & \text{for } n = 0, m \geq 0 \\ \mathbb{N} \cup \{0\} & \text{for } m \geq 1, \ n \geq 1 \end{cases},$$

$$g_\setminus^{\mathrm{asc},f}(m,n) = \begin{cases} \{0\} & \text{for } m = 0, n \geq 0 \\ \{m\} & \text{for } n = 0, m \geq 0 \\ \{0,1\} & \text{for } m = 1, n \geq 1 \\ \mathbb{N} \cup \{0\} & \text{for } m \geq 2, \ n \geq 1 \end{cases},$$

$$g_\setminus^{\mathrm{asc},f,u}(m,n) = \{m, m - 1, \ldots, m - n\}.$$

Theorem 4. *The following relations hold for the operation star:*

$$g_*^{\mathrm{asc}}(m) = g_*^{\mathrm{asc},u}(m) = \begin{cases} \{1\} & \text{for } m = 0 \\ \mathbb{N} & \text{for } m \geq 1 \end{cases},$$

$$g_*^{\mathrm{asc},f}(m) = g_*^{\mathrm{asc},f,u}(m) = \begin{cases} \{1\} & \text{for } m \in \{0,1\} \\ \mathbb{N} & \text{for } m \geq 2 \end{cases}.$$

First we mention that, for all these three operations union, set-subtraction, and star, there is no difference between the situations for arbitrary sets and arbitrary unary sets.

Moreover, for all these three operations, a difference between allowing arbitrary sets and restricting to finite sets only occurs for $m = 1$. In all cases, essentially, it comes from the following lemma.

Lemma 1. *Let L be a finite language. Then $\mathtt{asc}(L) = 1$ if and only if L is prefix-free (i.e., no prefix of $w \in L$, which is different from w, is in L).*

If we now assume that $\mathtt{asc}(L \cup L') = 1$, then $L_m \cup L_n$ is prefix-free, and consequently L_m and L_n are prefix-free, too, which gives $\mathtt{asc}(L) = \mathtt{asc}(L') = 1$.

Moreover, if $\mathtt{asc}(L) = 1$ and thus L is prefix-free, we get that $L \setminus L'$ is prefix-free for all languages L'. Therefore, we get

$$\mathtt{asc}(L \setminus L') = \begin{cases} 0 & \text{if } L \subseteq L' \\ 1 & \text{otherwise} \end{cases}.$$

However, we see that there are differences between the situations for finite sets and finite unary sets at one hand and arbitrary unary sets and finite unary sets at the other hand. These differences come from the fact that, for a unary finite set L with n elements, we have $\mathtt{asc}(L) = n$, from which the statements for finite unary sets follow.

We now turn to catenation where we have no results – except for some trivial cases – for unary sets.

Theorem 5. *The following relations hold for the operation catenation:*

$$g_{\cdot}^{\mathtt{asc}}(m, n) = g_{\cdot}^{\mathtt{asc},u}(m, n) = \begin{cases} \{0\} & \text{for } \min\{m, n\} = 0 \\ \mathbb{N} & \text{for } m \geq 1, \ n \geq 1 \end{cases},$$

$$g_{\cdot}^{\mathtt{asc},f}(m, n) = \{0\} \text{ for } \min\{m, n\} = 0$$

$$g_{\cdot}^{\mathtt{asc},f}(m, n) \supseteq \{n + k \mid k \geq 0\} \text{ for } m \geq 2, n \geq 1$$

$$g_{\cdot}^{\mathtt{asc},f,u}(m, n) = \begin{cases} \{0\} & \text{for } \min\{m, n\} = 0 \\ \{k \mid m + n - 1 \leq k \leq m \cdot n\} & \text{for } m \geq 1, \ n \geq 1 \end{cases}.$$

Note that we do not know whether there is a difference for arbitrary and finite sets, since $g^{\mathtt{asc},f}$ is not completely determined.

For all the preceding operations $\circ$, $g_{\circ}^{\mathtt{asc}}(m, n)$ was almost the set of all positive integers. This changes completely, if we consider intersection. Let L and L' be two regular sets accepted by the finite automata $\mathcal{A}$ and $\mathcal{A}'$, respectively. Then the standard construction of an automaton $\mathcal{B}$ accepting $L \cap L'$ gives an upper bound $\mathtt{asc}(\mathcal{A}) \cdot \mathtt{asc}(\mathcal{A}')$ for $\mathtt{asc}(L \cap L')$. Hence $g_{\cap}^{\mathtt{asc}}(m, n)$ contains only numbers $\leq m \cdot n$.

Theorem 6. *The following relation holds for the operation intersection: For $m \geq 0$ and $n \geq 0$,*

$$g_{\cap}^{\mathtt{asc}}(m, n) \supseteq \{(m - k)(n - l) + s \mid 0 \leq k \leq m, 0 \leq l \leq n, 0 \leq s \leq \min\{k, l\}\}.$$

We mention some easy consequences:

- $g_\cap^{\mathrm{asc}}(0,n) = g_\cap^{\mathrm{asc}}(m,0) = \{0\}$ for $m \geq 0$ and $n \geq 0$,
- $m \cdot n \in g_\cap^{\mathrm{asc}}(m,n)$ for $m \geq 0$ and $n \geq 0$,
- for $m \geq 0$, we have $g_\cap^{\mathrm{asc}}(m,m) \supseteq \{r \mid 0 \leq r \leq \frac{4m}{9}\}$, i.e., a large section of small numbers is in $g_\cap^{\mathrm{asc}}(m,m)$.

For the unary case and intersection, we have the following statements:

Theorem 7. *The following relation holds for the operation intersection: For $m \geq 0$ and $n \geq 0$,*

$$g_\cap^{\mathrm{asc},u}(m,m) \supseteq \{(m-k)(m-k) + s \mid 0 \leq k \leq m, 0 \leq s \leq k\} \tag{1}$$

and

$$g_\cap^{\mathrm{asc},f,u}(m,n) = \{0,1,\ldots,\min\{m,n\}\}.$$

By the proof of (1), one can give an extension for $m \neq n$ and numbers k and l with $0 \leq k \leq m$ and $0 \leq l \leq n$, but one has to use in the formulation $\min\{m,n\}$ and $\min\{k,l\}$ which makes the formulae a little bit hard to read.

We have no useful result for $g_\cap^{\mathrm{asc},f}(m,n)$.

We have seen above that there are differences if we considered in general case or the unary case. Thus it is a natural question if there are further differences if we restrict the size of the underlying alphabet, i.e., if we consider the binary, ternary etc. case. We mention that all results presented above for arbitrary regular languages and finite languages already hold for alphabets with at least two letters. Therefore it is not necessary to distinguish by the size of the alphabet.

4 Syntactic Complexity Measures for Context-Free Languages

In this section we only consider context-free languages; therefore we omit the adjective "context-free".

We start with the remark that, $\mathrm{Var}(L) \leq 1$ for any finite language L (the set consisting of the words $w_1, w_2, \ldots, w_n$ is generated by a grammar with the rules $S \to w_1, S \to w_2, \ldots S \to w_n$) and $\mathrm{Var}(L) \leq 2$ for any unary context-free language ($L = \{a^{n_1}, a^{n_2}, \ldots, a^{n_s}\} \cup a^p\{a^{m_1}, a^{m_2}, \ldots, a^{m_t}\}$ is generated by a grammar with the rules $S \to a^{n_1}, S \to a^{n_2}, \ldots, S \to a^{n_s}, S \to S', S' \to a^p S'$, $S' \to a^{m_2} S' \to a^{m_1}, \ldots, S' \to a^{m_t}$). Thus, the sets $g_\circ^{\mathrm{Var},f}(m,n)$ are not defined if $m \geq 2$ or $n \geq 2$, and the sets $g_\circ^{\mathrm{Var},u}(m,n)$ are not defined if $m \geq 3$ or $n \geq 3$.

We now present the results for the reversal operation.

Theorem 8. *For $K \in \{\mathrm{Var}, \mathrm{Prod}, \mathrm{Symb}\}$ and all permissible $m \in \mathbb{N} \cup \{0\}$,*

$$g_R^K(m) = \{m\}, \quad g_R^{K,f}(m) = \{m\}, \quad g_R^{K,u}(m) = \{m\}, \quad g_R^{K,f,u}(m) = \{m\}.$$

From commutativity of union and Theorem 8, it follows that, for the measures $K \in \{\text{Var}, \text{Prod}, \text{Symb}\}$,

$$g_\cup^K(m,n) = g_\cup^K(n,m) \text{ and } g_\cdot^K(m,n) = g_\cdot^K(n,m)$$

and the corresponding relations also hold if we restrict to finite languages, unary languages, and finite unary languages. Therefore we can assume without loss of generality that $m \geq n$, if we discuss union or product.

We have the following results concerning operations and the number of variables.

Theorem 9. *The behaviour of* Var *under union is shown in Fig. 1.*

arbitrary	$g_\cup^{\text{Var}}(m,n) = \{1,2,\ldots,m+n+1\}$ for $m \geq 1, n \geq 1$
finite	$g_\cup^{\text{Var},f}(1,0) = g_\cup^{\text{Var},f}(0,1) = g_\cup^{\text{Var},f}(1,1) = \{1\}, \; g_\cup^{\text{Var},f}(0,0) = \{0\}$
unary	$g_\cup^{\text{Var},u}(m,n) = \{1,2\}$ for $1 \leq m \leq 2, 1 \leq n \leq 2$ $g_\cup^{\text{Var},u}(1,0) = g_\cup^{\text{Var},u}(0,1) = \{1\}, g_\cup^{\text{Var},u}(0,0) = \{0\}$
finite unary	$g_\cup^{\text{Var},f,u}(1,0) = g_\cup^{\text{Var},f,u}(0,1) = g_\cup^{\text{Var},f,u}(1,1) = \{1\}, g_\cup^{\text{Var},f,u}(0,0) = \{0\}$

Fig. 1. Behaviour of the number of variables under union

Theorem 10. *The behaviour of* Var *under catenation is shown in Fig. 2.*

arbitrary	$g_\cdot^{\text{Var}}(m,n) \supseteq \{1\} \cup \{\max\{m,n\}, \max\{m,n\}+1, \ldots, m+n+1\}$ for $m \geq 1, n \geq 1$
finite	$g_\cup^{\text{Var},f}(1,1) = \{1\}, g_\cdot^{\text{Var},f}(1,0) = g_\cdot^{\text{Var},f}(0,1) = g_\cup^{\text{Var},f}(0,0) = \{0\}$
unary	$g_\cdot^{\text{Var},u}(m,n) = \{1,2\}$ for $1 \leq m \leq 2, 1 \leq n \leq 2$ $g_\cdot^{\text{Var},u}(1,0) = g_\cdot^{\text{Var},u}(0,1) = g_\cdot^{\text{Var},u}(0,0) = \{0\}$
finite unary	$g_\cup^{\text{Var},f,u}(1,1) = \{1\}, g_\cdot^{\text{Var},f,u}(1,0) = g_\cdot^{\text{Var},f,u}(0,1) = g_\cup^{\text{Var},f,u}(0,0) = \{0\}$

Fig. 2. Behaviour of the number of variables under catenation

Theorem 11. *The behaviour of* Var *under Kleene star is shown in Fig. 3.*

We see that there is a large difference between arbitrary regular languages on the one side and finite or unary sets on the other hand, but the difference only originates from the restricted domain of $g_\circ^{\text{Var},f}$ and $g_\circ^{\text{Var},u}$. Between finite and finite unary sets, there is no difference.

We now consider the number of productions.

arbitrary	$g_*^{\mathrm{Var}}(n) = \{1, 2, \ldots, n+1\}$ for $n \geq 1$
finite	$g_*^{\mathrm{Var},f}(1) = g_*^{\mathrm{Var},f}(0) = \{1\},$
unary	$g_*^{\mathrm{Var},u}(1) = g_*^{\mathrm{Var},u}(2) = \{1\},\ \ g_*^{\mathrm{Var},u}(0) = \{1\}$
finite unary	$g_*^{\mathrm{Var},f,u}(1) = g_*^{\mathrm{Var},f,u}(0) = \{1\},$

Fig. 3. Behaviour of the number of variables under star

Theorem 12. *Let* $m \geq n \geq 2$.

  (i) The number 1 and all numbers k with $k > m+n+2$ are not in $g_\cup^{\mathrm{Prod}}(m,n)$.
  (ii) If $n \geq 7$, then $\{k \mid 6 \leq k \leq m+n+2\} \subseteq g_\cup^{\mathrm{Prod}}(m,n)$.
(iii) If $n \in \{5,6\}$, then $\{k \mid 4 \leq k \leq m+n+2\} \subseteq g_\cup^{\mathrm{Prod}}(m,n)$.
(iv) If $n = 4$, then $\{2\} \cup \{k \mid 4 \leq k \leq m+n+2\} \subseteq g_\cup^{\mathrm{Prod}}(m,n)$.
  (v) If $n \in \{2,3\}$, then $\{k \mid 2 \leq k \leq m+n+2\} = g_\cup^{\mathrm{Prod}}(m,n)$.

Theorem 13. *(i) For all numbers m with $m \geq 2$, the number 1 and all numbers k with $k > m+2$ are not in $g_\cup^{\mathrm{Prod}}(m,1)$.*
 (ii) For $m \geq 2$, we have $\{k \mid n \leq k \leq m+2\} \subseteq g_\cup^{\mathrm{Prod}}(m,1)$.
  For $m \geq 5$, the relation $n - 1 \in g_\cup^{\mathrm{Prod}}(m,1)$ holds.
  For $n \geq 6$, we have $n - 2 \in g_\cup^{\mathrm{Prod}}(m,1)$.
  Moreover, $g_\cup^{\mathrm{Prod}}(1,1) = \{1,2\}$ is valid.

We notice that the open problems concern only small numbers, i.e., it is open whether or not the following relations hold:

- $2, 3 \in g_\cup^{\mathrm{Prod}}(m,1)$ for $m \in \{4,5\}$ and $2, 3, \ldots, m-2 \in g_\cup^{\mathrm{Prod}}(m,1)$ for $m \geq 6$,
- $3 \in g_\cup^{\mathrm{Prod}}(m,4)$ for $m \geq 4$,
- $2, 3 \in g_\cup^{\mathrm{Prod}}(m,5)$ for $m \geq 5$,
- $2, 3, 4 \in g_\cup^{\mathrm{Prod}}(m,6)$ for $m \geq 6$,
- $2, 3, 4, 5 \in g_\cup^{\mathrm{Prod}}(m,n)$ for $m \geq n \geq 7$.

Theorem 14. *(i) For all numbers $m \geq 1$ and $n \geq 1$, the number 1 and all numbers k with $k > m+n$ are not in $g_\cup^{\mathrm{Prod},f}(m,n)$.*
 (ii) If $m \geq n \geq 1$, then $\{m, m+1, \ldots, m+n\} \subseteq g_\cup^{\mathrm{Prod},f}(m,n)$.
(iii) If $m \geq n \geq 3$, then $\{n, n+1, \ldots m+n\} \subseteq g_\cup^{\mathrm{Prod},f}(m,n)$.
(iv) If $m \geq 6$ and $m \geq n \geq 4$, then $\{6, 7, \ldots, m+n\} \subseteq g_\cup^{\mathrm{Prod},f}(m,n)$.

Theorem 15. *(i) For all numbers $m \geq 1$ and $n \geq 1$, the number 1 and all numbers k with $k > m+n+2$ are not in $g_\cup^{\mathrm{Prod},u}(m,n)$.*
 (ii) If $m \geq n \geq 1$, then $\{m, m+1, \ldots m+n\} \subseteq g_\cup^{\mathrm{Prod},u}(m,n)$.
(iii) If $m \geq n \geq 3$, then $\{n, n+1, \ldots m+n\} \subseteq g_\cup^{\mathrm{Prod},u}(m,n)$.

The essential differences between the cases of arbitrary, finite, and unary sets are:

- If we restrict to finite sets, then $m+n+1$ and $m+n+2$ are not in $g_\cup^{Prod,f}(m,n)$ and not in $g_\cup^{Prod,f,u}(m,n)$.
- If we restrict to the unary case we only know that the numbers $k \geq \min\{m,n\}$ are in $g_\cup^{Prod,u}(m,n)$ and $g_\cup^{Prod,f,u}(m,n)$; for "small" numbers we miss constructions.

For the star operation, we have the following results.

Theorem 16. *The following relations hold:*

(i) $g_*^{\mathrm{Prod}}(0) = g_*^{\mathrm{Prod},f}(0) = \{1\}$,

(ii) $g_*^{\mathrm{Prod}}(1) = g_*^{\mathrm{Prod},f}(1) = \{1,2\}$,

(iii) *For $n \geq 2$, $g_*^{\mathrm{Prod}}(n) = \{2,3,\ldots,n+2\}$ and $g_*^{\mathrm{Prod},f}(n) = \{2,3,\ldots,n+1\}$.*

We see that the only difference between arbitrary context-free and finite sets is that $n+2$ is not contained in $g_*^{\mathrm{Prod},f}(n)$.

We do not have non-trivial results for $g_*^{\mathrm{Prod},u}$ and $g_*^{\mathrm{Prod},f,u}$.

We now discuss the concatenation and restrict to the general case, because all our proofs require infinite languages and languages over an alphabet with at least two letters (i.e., we cannot present results on $g.^{\mathrm{Prod},f}$, $g.^{\mathrm{Prod},u}$, and $g.^{\mathrm{Prod},f,u}$).

Theorem 17. *(i) For all numbers $m \geq n \geq 1$, the number 0 and all numbers k with $k \geq m+n+1$ are not in $g.^{\mathrm{Prod}}(m,n)$. Moreover, if $m \geq 2$, then $m+2 \notin g.^{\mathrm{Prod}}(m,1)$ and $1 \notin g.^{\mathrm{Prod}}(m,n)$.*

(ii) We have $\{1\} = g.^{\mathrm{Prod}}(1,1)$.

(iii) We have $\{2,3,4,5\} = g.^{\mathrm{Prod}}(2,2)$ and $\{m,m+1,m+2,m+3\} \subseteq g.^{\mathrm{Prod}}(m,2)$ for $m \geq 2$.

(iv) We have $\{m+n-1,m+n,m+n+1\} \subseteq g.^{\mathrm{Prod}}(m,n)$ for $m,n \in \{3,4\}$.

(v) We have $\{n+2,n+3,\ldots m+n+1\} \subseteq g.^{\mathrm{Prod}}(m,n)$ for $m \geq n \geq 5$.

With respect to the number of symbols the situation is not very clear for small numbers n and m. We only give the results for "large" numbers; for a proof and further facts we refer to [13].

Theorem 18. *(i) For all numbers $m \geq 23$ and $n \geq 23$, we have*

$$\{k \mid k \geq m+n+7\} \cap g_\cup^{\mathrm{Symb}}(m,n) = \emptyset \text{ and}$$
$$\{23,24,\ldots,n\} \cup \{n+3,n+4,\ldots,m+n-2\} \cup \{m+n+6\} \subseteq g_\cup^{\mathrm{Symb}}(m,n).$$

(ii) For all numbers $m \geq 8$ and $n \geq 5$ with $m \geq n$ we have

$$\{k \mid k \geq m+n+5\} \cap g.^{\mathrm{Symb}}(m,n) = \emptyset \text{ and}$$
$$\{n+4,n+5\ldots,m+n-2\} \cup \{m+n+4\} \subseteq g.^{\mathrm{Symb}}(m,n).$$

(iii) For all numbers $m \geq 10$, we have

$$\{k \mid k \geq m+7\} \cap g_*^{\mathrm{Symb}}(m) = \emptyset \text{ and } \{10,11,\ldots,m\} \cup \{m+6\} \subseteq g_*^{\mathrm{Symb}}(m).$$

5   Conclusion

We have presented a summary of result concerning the operational complexity of the number of accepting states for regular languages and of the number of nonterminals, productions, and symbols for context-free languages.

For the number of accepting states and the operations union, set-subtraction, complement, and star, the results are complete, and we see that there are – essentially – no differences between arbitrary, finite, and unary sets. However, the finite unary sets behave completely differently. With respect to catenation, the situation can be the same, but, for a proof, a complete determination of $g_\circ^{\mathrm{asc},f}$ is necessary (and missing at present). For the intersection, we have not enough information in order to make a statement on the comparison.

The situation is different for the syntactic measures of context-free languages. Concerning the number of nonterminals, we have a difference between arbitrary context-free languages and the restricted versions, but it comes from the very limited domain (of the variables m and n in the case of restrictions). If we restrict to "large" arguments (say $m \geq n \geq 50$, which can be justified by practical reasons), we have a good situation for the number of productions with respect to union and star since the difference between arbitrary context-free sets and finite sets is only in two or one "large" values. For the comparison of unary and finite unary languages, we need more information.

In order to get a more complete picture, it is necessary to determine the sets $g_\circ^{\mathrm{Prod},f}$, $g_\circ^{\mathrm{Prod},u}$, and all sets with a restriction and the measure Symb.

Finally, we mention that it remains open to determine the sets $g_\circ^{\mathrm{asc}}$ and their restricted versions for further operations as reversal (L^R) or squaring (L^2), quotients, etc. as well as the sets $g_\circ^K$ with $K \in \{\mathrm{Var}, \mathrm{Prod}, \mathrm{Symb}\}$ for operations as squaring, quotients, etc.

References

1. Alur, R., Madhusudan, P.: Visibly pushdown languages. In: Proceedings of ACM Symposium on Theory of Computing, pp. 202–211 (2004)
2. Champarnaud, J.-M., Coulon, F.: Büchi automata reduction by means of left and right trace inclusion preorder. Manuscript (2004)
3. Dassow, J.: On the number of accepting states of finite automata. J. Automata Lang. Comb. **21**, 55–67 (2016)
4. Dassow, J., Stiebe, R.: Nonterminal complexity of some operations on context-free languages. Fundam. Inform. **83**, 35–49 (2008)
5. Dassow, J., Harbich, R.: Descriptional complexity of union and star on context-free languages. J. Automata Lang. Comb. **17**, 123–143 (2012)
6. Drewes, F., Holzer, M., Jakobi, S., van der Merwe, B.: Tight bounds for cut-operations on deterministic finite automata. In: Durand-Lose, J., Nagy, B. (eds.) MCU 2015. LNCS, vol. 9288, pp. 45–60. Springer, Cham (2015). doi:10.1007/978-3-319-23111-2_4
7. Edelkamp, S., Jabbar, S.: Large-scale directed model checking LTL. In: Valmari, A. (ed.) SPIN 2006. LNCS, vol. 3925, pp. 1–18. Springer, Heidelberg (2006). doi:10.1007/11691617_1

8. Gao, Y., Moreira, N., Reis, R., Yu, S.: A review on state complexity of individual operations. Technical report series DCC-2011-08, Version 1.1, University of Porto, Faculty of Sciences, Department of Computer Science (2012), September 2012
9. Gao, Y., Salomaa, K., Yu, S.: Transition complexity of incomplete DFAs. Fundam. Inform. **110**, 143–158 (2011)
10. Gruska, J.: Some classifications of context-free languages. Inf. Control **14**, 152–179 (1969)
11. Gruska, J.: On the size of context free grammars. Kybernetika **8**, 213–218 (1972)
12. Han, Y.-S., Salomaa, K.: State complexity of basic operations on suffix-free regular languages. Theoret. Comput. Sci. **410**, 2537–2548 (2009)
13. Harbich, R.: Regel- und Symbolkomplexität kontextfreier Sprachen unter ausgewählten Operationen. Dissertation (2018)
14. Holzer, M., Kutrib, M.: State complexity of basic operations on nondeterministic finite automata. In: Champarnaud, J.-M., Maurel, D. (eds.) CIAA 2002. LNCS, vol. 2608, pp. 148–157. Springer, Heidelberg (2003). doi:10.1007/3-540-44977-9_14
15. Holzer, M., Kutrib, M.: Nondeterministic finite automata - recent results on the descriptional and computational complexity. Int. J. Found. Comput. Sci. **20**, 563–580 (2009)
16. Hricko, M., Jirásková, G., Szabari, A.: Union and intersection of regular languages and descriptional complexity. In: Mereghetti, C., Palano, B., Pighizzini, G., Wotschke, D. (eds.) Proceedings of 7th International Workshop of Descriptional Complexity of Formal Systems, University of Milano, pp. 170–181 (2005)
17. Jirásková, G.: On the state complexity of complements, stars, and reversals of regular languages. In: Ito, M., Toyama, M. (eds.) DLT 2008. LNCS, vol. 5257, pp. 431–442. Springer, Heidelberg (2008). doi:10.1007/978-3-540-85780-8_34
18. Jirásková, G., Krausová, M.: Complexity in prefix-free regular languages. Electron. Proc. Theor. Comput. Sci. **31**, 197–204 (2010)
19. Maia, E., Moreira, N., Reis, R.: Incomplete operational transition complexity of regular languages. Inf. Comput. **244**, 1–22 (2015)
20. Okhotin, A., Salomaa, K.: State complexity of operations on input-driven pushdown automata. J. Comput. Syst. Sci. **86**, 207–228 (2017)
21. Piao, X., Salomaa, K.: Operational state complexity of nested word automata. Theoret. Comput. Sci. **410**, 3250–3260 (2009)
22. Piao, X., Salomaa, K.: State complexity of the concatenation of regular tree automata. Theoret. Comput. Sci. **429**, 273–281 (2012)
23. Piao, X., Salomaa, K.: State complexity of projection and quotient on unranked trees. In: Kutrib, M., Moreira, N., Reis, R. (eds.) DCFS 2012. LNCS, vol. 7386, pp. 280–293. Springer, Heidelberg (2012). doi:10.1007/978-3-642-31623-4_22
24. Rozenberg, G., Salomaa, A. (eds.): Handbook of Formal Languages, vol. I–III. Springer, Berlin (1997)
25. Yu, S.: State complexity of regular languages. J. Automata Lang. Comb. **6**, 221–234 (2001)

Applications of Transducers in Independent Languages, Word Distances, Codes

Stavros Konstantinidis[✉]

Department of Mathematics and Computing Science, Saint Mary's University,
923 Robie Street, Halifax, NS B3H 3C3, Canada
s.konstantinidis@smu.ca

Abstract. A (nondeterministic) transducer t is an operator mapping an input word to a set of possible output words. A few types of transducers are important in this work: input-altering, input-preserving, and input-decreasing. Two words are t-dependent, if one is the output of t when the other one is used as input. A t-independent language is one containing no two t-dependent words. Examples of independent languages are found in noiseless coding theory, noisy coding theory and DNA computing. We discuss how the above transducer types can provide elegant solutions to some cases of the following broad problems: (i) computing two minimum distance witness words of a given regular language; (ii) computing witness words for the non-satisfaction, or non-maximality, of a given regular language with respect to the independence specified by a given transducer t; (iii) computing, for any given t and language L, a maximal t-independent language containing L; (iv) computing, for any given positive integer n and transducer t, a t-independent language of n words. The descriptional complexity cost of converting between transducer types is discussed, when this conversion is possible. We also explore methods of defining more independences in a way that some of the above problems can still be computed.

Keywords: Algorithm · Automata · Codes · Distance · Independence · Language · Maximal · Transducer

1 Introduction

The Abstract already serves as the first part of the introduction to this paper. Our main objective is to survey results related to describing independences and answering algorithmic questions about such independences. In particular, the description of an independence can be part of the input to the algorithms of interest. Many independences are known as *code-related properties*. The paper is organized as follows. Section 2 contains the basic terminology. Section 3 explains the use of transducers to describe the kind of independences we are interested

Research supported by NSERC.

G. Pighizzini and C. Câmpeanu (Eds.): DCFS 2017, LNCS 10316, pp. 45–62, 2017.
DOI: 10.1007/978-3-319-60252-3_4

in. Section 4 presents the algorithmic questions we consider and discusses how to solve some of those questions. Section 5 presents results about embedding a given independent language to a maximal one when the independence is described by an input-decreasing transducer. Section 6 discusses a method of computing minimum distance witnesses of a given regular language. Section 7 discusses some known facts about converting one type of transducer to another. Section 8 explores new ways of describing independences. Section 9 contains a few concluding remarks.

At the end of some sections we also discuss directions for further research.

2   Terminology

We write $\mathbb{N}, \mathbb{N}_0$ for the sets of positive integers and non-negative integers, respectively. If S is a set, then $|S|$ denotes the cardinality of S, and 2^S denotes the set of all subsets of S. When there is no risk of confusion, we write a singleton set $\{x\}$ simply as x. Thus, $S \cup x$ means $S \cup \{x\}$. An *alphabet* is a finite nonempty set of symbols. We write Σ, Δ for arbitrary alphabets. The set of all words, or strings, over Σ is denoted by Σ^*, which includes the *empty* word λ. As usual, Σ^+ denotes $\Sigma^* - \lambda$. A *language* (over Σ) is any set of words. Let L be a language and let u, v, w, x be any words. If $w \in L$ then we say that w is an *L-word*. We use standard operations and notation on words and languages, [14,30,42], in particular $|w|$ denotes the length of w and $\overline{L}$ denotes $\Sigma^* - L$. If w is of the form uv then u is a *prefix* and v is a *suffix* of w. If $u \neq w$ then u is called a *proper* prefix of w—the definition of proper suffix is analogous. A *relation* over Σ and Δ is a subset of $\Sigma^* \times \Delta^*$, that is, a set of pairs (x, y) of words over the two alphabets (respectively). The *inverse* of ρ, denoted by ρ^{-1}, is the relation $\{(y, x) \mid (x, y) \in \rho\}$.

Independent Languages, Code Properties. Consider a fixed, but arbitrary, alphabet Σ containing at least two symbols. A (language) property is any set of languages, that is, subsets of Σ^*. An *independence*, or *code property*, [17], is a property $\mathcal{P}$ such that $L \in \mathcal{P}$, if and only if, $L' \in \mathcal{P}$ for all $L' \subseteq L$ with $0 < |L'| < n$, for some $n \in \mathbb{N} \cup \{\aleph_0\}$. If $L \in \mathcal{P}$ then we say that L *satisfies* $\mathcal{P}$. Thus, L satisfies $\mathcal{P}$ exactly when all nonempty subsets of L with less than n elements satisfy $\mathcal{P}$. In this case, we also say that $\mathcal{P}$ is an *n-independence*. A language $L \in \mathcal{P}$ is called $\mathcal{P}$-*maximal*, or a maximal $\mathcal{P}$ code, if $L \cup w \notin \mathcal{P}$ for any word $w \notin L$. Every language satisfying $\mathcal{P}$ is included in some $\mathcal{P}$-maximal language [17]. To our knowledge, almost all code related properties in the literature [4,8,9,12,15,17,18,20,22,31,34,38,44,45] are independences. Also, any independence with respect to a binary relation in the sense of [39] is a 3-independence. Examples: (i) L is a *prefix code* if no L-word is a prefix of another L-word— this is a 3-independence; (ii) L is *2-substitution error-detecting* if no L-word can result by changing one or two symbols in some other L-word—this again is a 3-independence; (iii) L is a *UD-code*[1], if every word in L^+ can be parsed in exactly one way as a list of words in L—this is an $\aleph_0$-independence.

---

[1] UD means Uniquely Decodable/Decipherable.

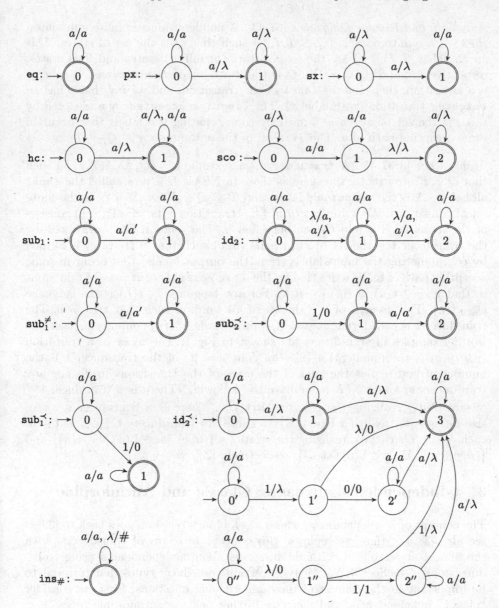

Fig. 1. Various transducers. An arrow with label a/a denotes multiple transitions: one with label a/a for each $a \in \Sigma$, and similarly for labels a/λ. An arrow with label a/a' denotes multiple transitions: one with label a/a' for all $a, a' \in \Sigma$ with $a \neq a'$. Let w be any word. We have: $\mathsf{eq}(w) = \{w\}$; $\mathsf{px}(w)$ = set of proper prefixes of w; $\mathsf{sx}(w)$ = set of proper suffixes of w; $\mathsf{hc}(w)$ = set of words resulting by deleting at least one symbol in w; $\mathsf{sub}_1^{\prec}(w)$ = set of words resulting by substituting exactly one 1 in w with a 0; $\mathsf{sub}_1(w)$ = set of words resulting by substituting at most one symbol in w with another one; $\mathsf{id}_2(w)$ = set of words resulting by inserting and/or deleting at most 2 symbols in w.

Automata and Regular Languages [37,43]. A nondeterministic finite automaton (*NFA*) is a quintuple $\mathbf{a} = (Q, \Sigma, T, I, F)$ such that Q is the set of states, Σ is an alphabet, $I, F \subseteq Q$ are the sets of start (or initial) states and final states, respectively, and $T \subseteq Q \times \Sigma \times Q$ is the finite set of *transitions*. If (p, x, q) is a transition, then x is the *label* of the transition, and we say that p has an *outgoing* transition (with label x). The *language accepted* by $\mathbf{a}$, denoted by $L(\mathbf{a})$, is the set of words w formed by concatenating the labels that occur in some accepting path of $\mathbf{a}$. The *size* $|\mathbf{a}|$ of the automaton $\mathbf{a}$ is $|Q| + |T|$.

Transducers [3,37,43]. A *transducer* is a sextuple $\mathbf{t} = (Q, \Sigma, \Delta, T, I, F)$ such that Q, I, F are exactly the same as those in NFAs, Σ is now called the *input* alphabet, Δ is the *output* alphabet, and $T \subseteq Q \times \Sigma^* \times \Delta^* \times Q$ is the finite set of transitions. We write $(p, x/y, q)$ for a transition—its *label* (x/y) consists of the input label x and the output label y. The relation $R(\mathbf{t})$ *realized* by the transducer $\mathbf{t}$ is the set of word pairs (u, v) such that u (resp. v) is formed by concatenating the input labels (resp. the output labels) that occur in some accepting path of $\mathbf{t}$. We write $\mathbf{t}(u)$ for the set of *possible outputs* of $\mathbf{t}$ on input u, that is, $v \in \mathbf{t}(u)$ iff $(u, v) \in R(\mathbf{t})$. For any language L, $\mathbf{t}(L)$ is the language $\cup_{u \in L} \mathbf{t}(u)$. The *domain* of $\mathbf{t}$ is the set of all words u such that $\mathbf{t}(u) \neq \emptyset$. The transducer $\mathbf{t}$ is called *functional* if, for all words u, $\mathbf{t}(u)$ contains at most one word. Examples of transducers are shown in Fig. 1. The *size* of a transition $(p, x/y, q)$ is the number $1 + |x| + |y|$. The size $|\mathbf{t}|$ of the transducer $\mathbf{t}$ is the number of states plus the sum of the sizes of the transitions in T. For any transducers $\mathbf{s}, \mathbf{t}$ and NFA $\mathbf{a}$, we have the following. There is a transducer $\mathbf{t}^{-1}$ of size $O(|\mathbf{t}|)$ realizing the relation $(R(\mathbf{t}))^{-1}$. There is a transducer $\mathbf{s} \vee \mathbf{t}$ of size $O(|\mathbf{s}| + |\mathbf{t}|)$ realizing $R(\mathbf{s}) \cup R(\mathbf{t})$. There are transducers $\mathbf{t} \downarrow \mathbf{a}$ and $\mathbf{t} \uparrow \mathbf{a}$, each of size $O(|\mathbf{t}| \cdot |\mathbf{a}|)$, realizing the relations $\{(u, v) : u \in L(\mathbf{a}), v \in \mathbf{t}(u)\}$ and $\{(u, v) : u \in \Sigma^*, v \in L(\mathbf{a}) \cap \mathbf{t}(u)\}$, respectively [23].

3   t-Independent Languages: Classic and Antimorphic

The concept of ρ-independence, where ρ is a binary relation, goes back to [39]—see also [38,44]. Here we rephrase this concept in terms of transducers, with the aim of answering *algorithmic questions* about independences using transducer tools—see Sect. 4. We focus on certain transducer types that turn out to be important in the context of those algorithmic questions. First we consider "classic" independences, and then (see further below) "antimorphic" ones.

Definition 1. *Let '$\prec$' be the lexicographic word order^2. A transducer $\mathbf{t}$ is*

input-preserving, if $x \in \mathbf{t}(x)$, for all words x in the domain of $\mathbf{t}$;
input-altering, if $x \notin \mathbf{t}(x)$, for all words x; ·
length-decreasing, if $y \in \mathbf{t}(x)$ implies $|y| < |x|$, for all words x, y;
input-decreasing, if $y \in \mathbf{t}(x)$ implies $y \prec x$, for all words x, y.

---

^{2} In this order, the alphabet Σ is totally ordered. Then, $u \prec v$ if and only if, either $|u| < |v|$, or $|u| = |v|$ and $u = x\sigma_1 y_1, v = x\sigma_2 y_2$ such that $\sigma_1, \sigma_2 \in \Sigma$ and $\sigma_1 \prec \sigma_2$.

Remark 1. Every length-decreasing transducer is input-decreasing and every input-decreasing transducer is input-altering. Moreover, for every transducer t, the transducer $(t \vee eq)$ is input-preserving—see Fig. 1.

Definition 2. *Let t be a transducer. A language L is called t-independent, if the following condition holds for all words u, v:*

$$u, v \in L \ \text{ and } \ v \in t(u) \ \text{ implies } \ u = v. \tag{1}$$

$\mathcal{P}_t$ *denotes the independence described by t; this is the set of all languages satisfying the above condition. In [9], if t is input-preserving then $\mathcal{P}_t$ is called an input-preserving transducer property, and if t is input-altering then $\mathcal{P}_t$ is called an input-altering transducer property. If the transducer t is input-altering, then condition (1) is equivalent to*

$$t(L) \cap L = \emptyset \tag{2}$$

Remark 2. One verifies that condition (1) is equivalent to the one resulting if we replace t with t^{-1}, or with $(t \vee t^{-1})$. Similarly, one verifies that condition (2) is equivalent to "$t^{-1}(L) \cap L = \emptyset$", and also to "$(t \vee t^{-1})(L) \cap L = \emptyset$".

Remark 3. Every independence described by a transducer is a 3-independence. Moreover, for every transducer t, every singleton language $\{w\}$ is t-independent.

Remark 4. The type of transducer used to describe an independence affects the computability and complexity of algorithmic questions about that independence (see subsequent sections). It turns out, however, that limiting (1) to t's that are input-preserving does not constitute any restriction on the describable independences. Indeed, one can confirm that, for any transducer t, we have that

the transducer $(t \vee eq)$ is input-preserving and $\mathcal{P}_t = \mathcal{P}_{t \vee eq}$.

Remark 5. In [25], the independence described by an input-preserving transducer t is called an *error-detecting* property. Specifically, t can be viewed as a communication channel such that, if $v \in t(u)$ and $v \neq u$ then we have a channel error. A language satisfying $\mathcal{P}_t$ is called error-detecting *for* t. This means that the channel t cannot turn an L-word to a different L-word.

Example 1. The transducers px, sx, hc shown in Fig. 1 are input-altering and describe, respectively, prefix codes, suffix codes, and hypercodes. A language L is a *hypercode* if no L-word results by deleting at least one symbol in some other L-word, that is, $hc(L) \cap L = \emptyset$. The transducer sub_1 is input-preserving and describes the 1-substitution error-detecting languages. The transducer id_2 is input-preserving and describes the 2-synchronization error-detecting languages. A language L is k-*synchronization* error-detecting if no L-word results by inserting and/or deleting a total of at most k symbols in some other L-word. For example, $\{0101, 1010\}$ is not 2-synchronization error-detecting as 1010 results by deleting the first 0 of $u = 0101$ and inserting a 0 at the end of u. Using sub_1, id_2, as a guide, one can design input-preserving transducers sub_k, id_k describing the k-substitution and k-synchronization error-detecting languages, for any $k \in \mathbb{N}$.

Remark 6. In [8], 3-independences are defined by trajectories. A regular trajectory expression $\bar{e}$ is any regular expression over $\{0,1\}$ and describes the independence consisting of all languages L such that $(L \sqcup_{\bar{e}} \Sigma^+) \cap L = \emptyset$, where $\sqcup_{\bar{e}}$ is the shuffle operation according to $\bar{e}$. For example, 0^*1^* describes prefix codes because the shuffle inserts symbols at the end of an L-word and the result cannot be an L-word. In [9], it is shown that, for every regular trajectory expression, there is an input-altering transducer describing the same independence. Moreover, there are natural error-detecting properties that cannot be described by regular trajectory expressions. On the other hand, the method of trajectories provides a simple and effective method for describing many independences.

Antimorphic Independences. Independences related to DNA computing cannot be described by transducers as in Definition 2, [20]. This is because such independences involve the antimorphic involution "dna" over the DNA alphabet $\{a, c, g, t\}$. In general, let θ be a permutation on the alphabet Σ. Then, θ is called an *involution* if $\theta^{-1} = \theta$. A *morphic* permutation on Σ^* is a permutation on Σ extended to Σ^* such that $\theta(\lambda) = \lambda$ and $\theta(\sigma x) = \theta(\sigma)\theta(x)$, for all $\sigma \in \Sigma$ and $x \in \Sigma^*$. When θ is extended such that $\theta(\sigma x) = \theta(x)\theta(\sigma)$, then it is called an *antimorphic* permutation. For example, the antimorphic involution "dna" is such that $dna(a) = t$ and $dna(c) = g$. Let θ be any (anti)morphic permutation and let t be any transducer. In [20], the independence *described by* t *and* θ is the set of all languages L such that

$$t(L) \cap \theta(L) = \emptyset. \tag{3}$$

Example 2. A language L is called *strictly θ-compliant*, [19,20], if it contains no two words of the form $x\theta(v)y$ and v. This is equivalent to saying that by deleting a prefix and/or a suffix of an L-word (see transducer sco) the resulting word cannot be in $\theta(L)$, that is, $sco(L) \cap \theta(L) = \emptyset$; hence, strict θ-compliance is described by sco and θ. Now consider the independence $\mathcal{H} = \{L \subseteq \Sigma^* : \delta_H(u, \theta(v)) \geq 2,$ for all $u, v \in L\}$, [20], where $\delta_H(x, y)$ is the Hamming distance between the words x, y. Then, $\mathcal{H}$ is described by sub_1 and θ.

4   Algorithmic Questions About Independent Languages

In the context of the research on languages and independences, we consider the following algorithmic questions.

Satisfaction question. Given the description of an independence $\mathcal{P}$ and the description of a language, decide whether the language satisfies $\mathcal{P}$. In the *witness* version of this problem, a negative answer is also accompanied by an appropriate list of words showing how the property $\mathcal{P}$ is violated.

Maximality question. Given the description of an independence $\mathcal{P}$ and the description of a language L, decide whether the language is $\mathcal{P}$-maximal. In fact we allow the more general problem, where the input includes also the description of a second language M and the question is whether there is no word $w \in M - L$ such that $L \cup w$ satisfies $\mathcal{P}$. The default case is when $M = \Sigma^*$. In error control coding (see also the construction question below) $M = \Sigma^\ell$, for some positive integer ℓ, so all languages of interest are *block codes*, that is, their words are of fixed length ℓ. In the *witness* version of this question, a negative answer is also accompanied by any word $w \in M - L$ that can be added to the language L.

Embedding question. Given the description of an independence $\mathcal{P}$ and the description of a language L satisfying $\mathcal{P}$, compute a $\mathcal{P}$-maximal language containing L. As above, maximality can be considered with respect to a certain language M.

Construction question. Given the description of an independence $\mathcal{P}$ and two positive integers n and ℓ, construct a language that satisfies $\mathcal{P}$ and contains n words of length ℓ (if possible).

Minimum distance question. Given the description of a language L, compute the minimum distance between any two different L-words. In the *witness* version, also return two minimum distance L-words. This question depends on the distance of interest—see Sect. 6.

In this section, we assume that an independence is described by a transducer $\mathbf{t}$, and possibly by a permutation θ, and in the first three problems, the language is given via an NFA $\mathbf{a}$. In the maximality question, the second language M is also given via an NFA $\mathbf{b}$. Answers to the embedding and minimum distance questions are discussed in the next sections.

Remark 7. Next we list a few algorithmic tools used in answering some of the above questions. Occasionally we use *object-oriented notation:* $\mathbf{t}.f(P)$ is the algorithm f of the object $\mathbf{t}$ with list of parameters P.

1. $\mathbf{t}.\mathtt{nEmptyW}()$, where $\mathbf{t}$ is a transducer, returns either a pair of words in $\mathrm{R}(\mathbf{t})$, or $(\mathtt{None}, \mathtt{None})$ if $\mathrm{R}(\mathbf{t}) = \emptyset$. Similarly, for any NFA $\mathbf{a}$, we have that $\mathbf{a}.\mathtt{nEmptyW}()$ returns either a word in $\mathrm{L}(\mathbf{a})$ or $\mathtt{None}$. This algorithm is called non-emptiness witness, and is based on the standard shortest path algorithm from the start states to the final states of $\mathbf{t}$ or $\mathbf{a}$.
2. $\mathbf{t}.\mathtt{nFunctW}()$ returns either a triple (u, v_1, v_2) of words such that $v_1 \neq v_2$ and $v_1, v_2 \in \mathbf{t}(u)$, or a triple of $\mathtt{None}$'s if the transducer $\mathbf{t}$ is functional. This algorithm is a witness version, [25], of the decision algorithm for transducer functionality in [1,2].
3. $(\mathbf{a} \triangleright \mathbf{t})$ is an NFA accepting the language $\mathbf{t}(\mathrm{L}(\mathbf{a}))$, for any given transducer $\mathbf{t}$ and NFA $\mathbf{a}$.

Some results from [9,20,26] are the following.

1. The witness version of the satisfaction question is polynomially computable and, in fact, reasonably efficiently so—see the above references. More specifically we have the following cases: (i) given transducer $\mathbf{t}$ (and possibly a permutation θ) and NFA $\mathbf{a}$, return either $(\mathtt{None}, \mathtt{None})$ if $\mathrm{L}(\mathbf{a})$ satisfies (3), or a pair (u, v) of $\mathrm{L}(\mathbf{a})$-words such that (3) is not satisfied for $L = \{u, v\}$; (ii) given input-preserving transducer $\mathbf{t}$ and NFA $\mathbf{a}$, return as above, either

(None, None), or a pair (u, v) depending on whether (1) is satisfied. Case (i) is solved using the algorithm $(\mathbf{t} \downarrow \mathbf{a} \uparrow \mathbf{a}^\theta).\texttt{nEmptyW}()$, where $\mathbf{a}^\theta$ is an NFA accepting $\theta(L(\mathbf{a}))$. For case (ii), condition (1) is equivalent to whether

$$\text{the transducer } (\mathbf{t} \downarrow \mathbf{a} \uparrow \mathbf{a}) \text{ is functional.} \tag{4}$$

Then, the desired witness version is solved by making use of the algorithm $(\mathbf{t} \downarrow \mathbf{a} \uparrow \mathbf{a}).\texttt{nFunctW}()$.

2. The decision version of the maximality question can be coNP-hard, [26], PSPACE-hard or undecidable, [20]. Specifically, if the given transducer $\mathbf{t}$ is input-preserving, or input-altering, or θ-input-altering[3], then deciding whether $L(\mathbf{a})$ is maximal satisfying, respectively, (1) or (2) or (3), is PSPACE-hard. In fact, the witness version is computable using the algorithm

$$\left(\mathbf{b} \wedge \left((\mathbf{a} \rhd \mathbf{t}) \vee (\mathbf{a}^\theta \rhd \mathbf{t}^{-1}) \vee \mathbf{a}\right)^{\text{co}}\right).\texttt{nEmptyW}(), \tag{5}$$

where we assume that, for any given NFAs $\mathbf{c}$ and $\mathbf{d}$, $\mathbf{c}^{\text{co}}$ is an NFA accepting the complement of $L(\mathbf{c})$, $(\mathbf{c} \wedge \mathbf{d})$ is an NFA accepting $L(\mathbf{c}) \cap L(\mathbf{d})$, and $(\mathbf{c} \vee \mathbf{d})$ is an NFA accepting $L(\mathbf{c}) \cup L(\mathbf{d})$. On the other hand, even for any **fixed** permutation θ, it is undecidable to tell, given $\mathbf{t}$ and $\mathbf{a}$, whether $L(\mathbf{a})$ is maximal satisfying (3), where there is no restriction on $\mathbf{t}$.

3. The approach of [26] for the construction question is as follows: a definition is given of what an $f\%$ $\mathcal{P}$-maximal block code is, and then a simple randomized algorithm is described that is given an input-preserving transducer $\mathbf{t}$ and positive integers n, ℓ, and returns either a $\mathbf{t}$-independent language of n words of length ℓ, or a $\mathbf{t}$-independent language L of **less** than n words of length ℓ such that L is a 95% $\mathcal{P}_\mathbf{t}$-maximal block code.

5   The Embedding Question

The embedding question has been addressed well for several fixed code properties like UD codes [10], bifix codes [46], solid codes [29], and bounded deciphering delay codes [5]. In [40], the question is solved for any independence described by some length-decreasing-and-transitive transducer. In [24], the embedding question is addressed for any independence described by some input-decreasing transducer. We consider maximality with respect to a certain **fixed**, but arbitrary, language M. We discuss next some recent results from [24].

Definition 3. *A (language)* **operator** *is a function* $\text{Op} : 2^{\Sigma^*} \to 2^{\Sigma^*}$. *It is called* **union respecting** *if* $\text{Op}(X) = \cup_{v \in X} \text{Op}(v)$, *for all languages* X. *For any language* X *and nonnegative integer* i, *we define the following operators.*

$$\text{Op}^0(X) = X \quad and \quad \text{Op}^{i+1}(X) = \text{Op}(\text{Op}^i(X))$$

$$\text{Op}^*(X) = \cup_{i=0}^\infty \text{Op}^i(X), \quad \text{Op}^\cap(X) = \cap_{i=1}^\infty \text{Op}^i(X)$$

---

[3] This is when $\theta(w) \notin \mathbf{t}(w)$, for all nonempty words w.

The operator Op *is called **exhaustive**, if* $\mathrm{Op}^{\cap}(X) = \emptyset$, *for all languages* X. *If* Op_1 *is also a language operator then we write* $\mathrm{Op} \subseteq \mathrm{Op}_1$ *to indicate that* $\mathrm{Op}(X) \subseteq \mathrm{Op}_1(X)$ *for all languages* X. *A union respecting operator* Op *is **functional**, if* $\mathrm{Op}(v)$ *contains at most one word, for all words* v.

Example 3. We view a transducer $\mathbf{t}$ as a language operator, which is union respecting. Then, we have that $\mathbf{t}$ is *transitive* if and only if $\mathbf{t}^2 \subseteq \mathbf{t}$.

In the sequel we assume that $\mathbf{t}$ is a *fixed*, but arbitrary, input-altering transducer. We define the following language operators.

$$\mathrm{I}_{\mathbf{t}}(X) = \mathbf{M} - \big(\mathbf{t}(X) \cup \mathbf{t}^{-1}(X)\big) \quad \text{and} \quad \mu_{\mathbf{t}} X = \mathrm{I}_{\mathbf{t}}(X) - \mathbf{t}^{-1}\big(\mathrm{I}_{\mathbf{t}}(X)\big)$$

The above operators are translated to transducer notation from the corresponding ones in [40]. The operator $\mathrm{I}_{\mathbf{t}}(\cdot)$ is the set of all possible words that are either in X or $\mathbf{t}$-independent from X, so in some sense it is the *max*imum set in which X can be embedded. However, two words in $\mathrm{I}_{\mathbf{t}}(X) - X$ might be $\mathbf{t}$-dependent. The operator mapping any Y to $Y - \mathbf{t}^{-1}(Y)$ is the '$\mathbf{t}$-*min*imize' operator which returns all Y-elements that cannot produce another Y-element via $\mathbf{t}$.

Definition 4. *The operator* $\mu_{\mathbf{t}}$ *is called the **max–min operator**. The operator* $\mu_{\mathbf{t}}^*$ *is called the **iterated** max-min operator. We say that it **converges finitely** on a language* L, *if there is* $i \in \mathbb{N}_0$ *such that* $\mu_{\mathbf{t}}^* L = \mu_{\mathbf{t}}^i L$.

In the case of codes defined by length-decreasing-and-transitive transducers, already the language $\mu_{\mathbf{t}} L$ is maximal and constitutes a solution to the embedding question, [40], where L is the given language satisfying $\mathcal{P}_{\mathbf{t}}$. As stated in [40], however, this does not work for other codes like bifix codes, and also for error-detecting codes. The following results about any $\mathbf{t}$-independent language L are shown in [24].

1. If $\mathbf{t}^{-1}$ is exhaustive and there is $i \in \mathbb{N}_0$ such that $\mu_{\mathbf{t}}^{i+1} L = \mu_{\mathbf{t}}^i L$ then $\mu_{\mathbf{t}}^i L$ is $\mathcal{P}_{\mathbf{t}}$-maximal containing L.
2. If $\mathbf{t}^{-1}$ is exhaustive and $\mathbf{t}$ is transitive then $\mu_{\mathbf{t}} L$ is $\mathcal{P}_{\mathbf{t}}$-maximal containing L.
3. If $\mathbf{t}$ is input-decreasing then $\mu_{\mathbf{t}}^* L$ is $\mathcal{P}_{\mathbf{t}}$-maximal containing L. Note that if $\mathbf{t}$ is input-decreasing then $\mathbf{t}^{-1}$ is exhaustive.

Example 4 [24]. Let $\mathbf{M} = \{0,1\}^*$ and let $\mathbf{t} = (\mathbf{px} \vee \mathbf{sx})$, an input-decreasing transducer describing *bifix codes*. We have that $\mu_{\mathbf{t}}(001) = \{001, 000, 10, 11\}$ and $\mu_{\mathbf{t}}^2(001) = 01^*0(0+1) + 10 + 11$, which is maximal. Again, we have $\mu_{\mathbf{t}}^2\big((0+1)^3 11\big) = (0+1)^3(0+10^*1)$, which is maximal—this code is the reverse of what [4] calls the reversible Golomb-Rice code. Now let $\mathbf{M} = \{0,1\}^5$ and $\mathbf{t} = \mathbf{sub}_1^{\prec}$. Then, the following code is maximal and known as the even-parity code of length 5: $\mu_{\mathbf{t}}^3(01111) = \{w \in \{0,1\}^5 \mid w\text{'s count of 1s is even}\}$.

Research Directions. Statement 3 above can be applied to the case where $\mathbf{t}$ describes bifix codes, hence, if L is a bifix code then $\mu_\mathbf{t}^* L$ is a maximal bifix code containing L. An open question stated in [24] is whether in this case $\mu_\mathbf{t}^*$ converges finitely. We believe that the answer here is yes, so this would give an alternate proof of the fact that every regular bifix code can be embedded in a maximal one [4,46]. Computing $\mu_\mathbf{t} L(\mathbf{a})$, for any given transducer $\mathbf{t}$ and NFA $\mathbf{a}$, requires complementing an NFA, which is known to be a hard problem. The question here is whether there is a heuristic that could compute efficiently "chunks" of $\mu_\mathbf{t} L(\mathbf{a})$ containing $L(\mathbf{a})$ and somehow these chunks get "close" to being maximal as $\mu_\mathbf{t}$ gets iterated.

6   The Minimum Distance Question

An *integral difference* is a function δ that maps any pair of words into $\mathbb{N}_0 \cup \{\infty\}$ such that $\delta(x,y) = 0$ if and only if $x = y$. In addition, if $\delta(x,y) = \delta(y,x)$, and $\delta(x,y) \leq \delta(x,z) + \delta(z,y)$, for all words x,y,z, then δ is called a *distance*. The *minimum* difference $\delta(L)$ of a language L containing at least two words is the quantity $\min\{\delta(x,y) : x,y \in L$ and $x \neq y\}$. Here we discuss how to compute $\delta(L(\mathbf{a}))$, for any given NFA $\mathbf{a}$ accepting at least two words, based on the method of [27]. Questions related to the distance between two languages are studied in [13,35].

Definition 5. *Let δ be an integral difference and let $(\mathbf{t}_i)_{i \in \mathbb{N}}$ be a sequence of transducers. We say that δ is* compatible *with $(\mathbf{t}_i)_{i \in \mathbb{N}}$, if the following holds, for any $n \in \mathbb{N}$ and $x,y \in \Sigma^*$ with $x \neq y$,*

$$\delta(x,y) \leq n \qquad \text{if and only if} \qquad y \in \mathbf{t}_n(x) \ \text{or} \ x \in \mathbf{t}_n(y).$$

Example 5. The Hamming distance δ_H is compatible with $(\mathbf{sub}_k)_{k \in \mathbb{N}}$ (see Example 1). In [6], the authors consider the general concept of an additive distance and show that many known distances are additive. For example, for two words x,y, with $|x| \geq |y|$, their prefix Hamming distance $\delta_\mathrm{pH}(x,y)$ is equal to $\delta_\mathrm{H}(x_1,y) + |x_2|$, where $x = x_1 x_2$ and $|x_1| = |y|$. This distance is compatible with $(\mathbf{pH}_k)_{k \in \mathbb{N}}$ (see Fig. 2). The results of [21] imply that the edit distance[4] is compatible with a sequence of input-altering transducers—this can be adapted easily to show that also the Levenshtein distance is compatible with a sequence of input-altering transducers. For any two words x,y, their prefix distance, [32], is $|x_1| + |x_2|$, where $x = ux_1$ and $y = uy_1$ and u is the longest common prefix of x,y. It can be shown that this distance also is compatible with a sequence of input-altering transducers similar to $(\mathbf{pH}_k)_{k \in \mathbb{N}}$.

Lemma 1. *Let δ be an integral difference that is compatible with some sequence $(\mathbf{t}_i)_{i \in \mathbb{N}}$ of input-altering transducers, and let L be a language containing at least two words. Then $\delta(L) = \min\{i \mid \mathbf{t}_i(L) \cap L \neq \emptyset\}$, assuming $\min \emptyset = \infty$.*

---

[4] The *edit distance* $\delta_\mathrm{ed}(x,y)$ is the minimum number of single-symbol substitutions/insertions/deletions in x that turn x to y. The *Levenshtein* distance $\delta_\mathrm{L}(x,y)$ is similar by considering only insertions/deletions.

Remark 8. A classic connection between a distance δ and "error"-detection is that a block code C is a k-"error"-detecting if and only if $\delta(C) > k$. Lemma 1 generalizes this connection when we note that L is error-detecting for $(\mathbf{t}_k \vee \mathbf{eq})$ if and only if $\delta(L) > k$.

Using Lemma 1, we present below an algorithmic method to compute the minimum difference $m = \delta\big(\mathrm{L}(\mathbf{a})\big)$, for any given NFA $\mathbf{a}$, assuming that (i) δ values are not ∞; (ii) $|\mathrm{L}(\mathbf{a})| \geq 2$; (iii) there is an algorithm computing the input-altering transducer $\mathbf{t}_i$, given any $i \in \mathbb{N}$; (iv) there is an algorithm $\mathrm{UB}_\delta(\mathbf{a})$ computing an upper bound for m, that is, $m \leq \mathrm{UB}_\delta(\mathbf{a})$. In addition to m, the method computes two words in $\mathrm{L}(\mathbf{a})$ whose difference is m. Such words are called *witnesses* of minimum difference for $\mathrm{L}(\mathbf{a})$.

> $B :=$ the upper bound on $\delta\big(\mathrm{L}(\mathbf{a})\big)$ returned by $\mathrm{UB}_\delta(\mathbf{a})$;
> Perform binary search for the smallest $m \in \{1, \ldots, 1 + B\}$ such that
> $\quad \big((\mathbf{t}_m \downarrow \mathbf{a}) \uparrow \mathbf{a}\big).\texttt{nEmptyW()} \neq (\texttt{None}, \texttt{None})$
> Return m and the word pair $\big((\mathbf{t}_m \downarrow \mathbf{a}) \uparrow \mathbf{a}\big).\texttt{nEmptyW()}$;

This algorithm works in time $O(|\mathbf{a}|^2 M \log B)$, where $M = \max\{|\mathbf{t}_m| \mid m = 1, \ldots, B + 1\}$. Assuming that $\mathrm{UB}_\delta(\mathbf{a})$ works in time $O(|\mathbf{a}|)$ and B is $O(|\mathbf{a}|)$ and M is polynomially bounded in terms of $|\mathbf{a}|$, which is true in many examples of integral differences, we have that also $|\mathbf{a}|^2 M \log B$ is polynomially bounded.

Remark 9. The above algorithmic method is meant to provide a general approach to addressing the minimum difference question as well as an upper bound for the time complexity of it. In some cases however, with a careful algorithm design the time complexity can be improved. For example when δ is the edit distance, [21], the algorithm can be optimized to work in time $O(m \cdot |\mathbf{a}|^2)$, where m is the computed minimum distance of $\mathrm{L}(\mathbf{a})$. Also in [32], the author discusses computing the minimum prefix distance $\delta_{\mathrm{pd}}(L)$ of a regular language L using weighted transducers in time $O(|\mathbf{a}|^2 \log |\mathbf{a}|)$.

Research Directions. It is interesting to investigate connections between additive distances [6] and their compatible transducer sequences. Also interesting is to investigate the use of weighted transducers in computing the minimum difference of a language, for various differences—recall [32] does this for the prefix distance. To this end, it might be necessary to consider the concept of input-altering weighted transducers.

7   Cost of Converting Between Transducer Types

Describing an independence with an input-altering transducer, or a difference with compatible input-altering transducers, allows us to answer the satisfaction and minimum difference questions using simple and polynomially bounded algorithms. Moreover, if an independence is described by an input-decreasing transducer then the method of the iterated max-min operator can be used to address the embedding question. Ideally we would like to be able to convert any input-preserving transducer to an input-altering one, or even to an input-decreasing one describing the same language independence. We have the following results.

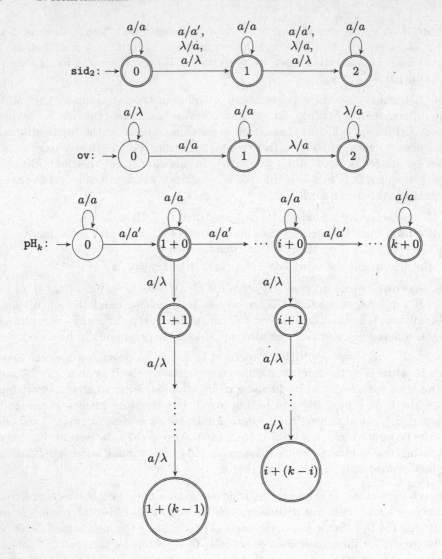

Fig. 2. More transducers. Let w be any word. We have: $\text{sid}_2(w) =$ set of words resulting by substituting and/or inserting and/or deleting a total of at most 2 symbols in w; $\text{ov}(w) =$ set of words (including w) having a nonempty prefix that is equal to a suffix of w; $\text{pH}_k(w) =$ set of words $x \neq w$ such that $|w| \geq |x|$ and the prefix Hamming distance of x, w is at most k—see Example 5.

1. Consider the alphabet $\{0, 1\}$ and the input-preserving transducer sub_k describing the k-substitution error-detecting property. Then there is an input-decreasing transducer $\text{sub}_k^{\prec}$ describing the same property such that $|\text{sub}_k^{\prec}| = |\text{sub}_k| - 1$.

2. Consider the input-preserving transducer sid_k describing the k-sid error-detecting property—see Fig. 2 for the case of $k = 2$. In [21], it is shown that there is an input-altering transducer $\text{sid}_k^{\neq}$ describing the same property such that $|\text{sid}_k^{\neq}| = \Theta(|\text{sid}_k|)$.
3. Consider the input-preserving transducer ov (see Fig. 2) describing the overlap-free property such that no word of an overlap-free language L has a nonempty suffix that is a prefix of another L-word. It can be shown, [28], that there is no input-altering transducer describing the same property.
4. The strictly θ-compliant independence (see Example 2) cannot be described by any input-preserving transducer according to Definition 2, [20].
5. The comma-free code property cannot be described by any transducer (see Remark 10).
6. The transducer $\text{id}_2^{\prec}$ in Fig. 1, [24], is an input-decreasing transducer describing 2-synchronization error-detecting languages over the alphabet $\{0, 1\}$.

Research Directions. A natural question here is to investigate the effect on the size of the transducer when converting from an input-altering transducer to an input-decreasing one (when this is possible). For example, converting id_k to $\text{id}_k^{\prec}$, for any integer $k > 1$. Also interesting is to characterize mathematically when such a conversion is possible for any given input-altering transducer.

8 t-Undescribable Independences and New Directions

Let Σ be the alphabet of independences. In this section we identify some limitations of the transducer method in describing independences (Remark 10), we discuss the method of implicational independence conditions of [16] (Remark 12), and we consider the work of [33] on decision questions related to language equations (Remark 13). These two references provide logical descriptions of language properties. Transducer based methods provide a more operational approach to describing independences, which seems to be a necessary step if one wants to implement objects representing independences [25]. Using all available background information, we explore ways of extending the transducer based method with the aim of describing more independences and at the same time being able to answer related algorithmic questions in a way that some of the algorithms involved can be implemented efficiently in available software systems [11, 41].

Remark 10. No n-independence with $n > 3$ is describable by transducers—see Remark 3. The UD-code property is not an n-independence, for any $n \in \mathbb{N}$, [17]. Dependence theory allows us to give simple proofs of such facts. For example, the comma-free code property is not a 3-independence but it is a 4-independence. A language L is a *comma-free* code, [38], if

$$\Sigma^+ L \Sigma^+ \cap LL = \emptyset. \qquad (6)$$

To see that this is not a 3-independence, it suffices to consider a 3-word language that is not a comma-free code but any two words of that language constitute a comma-free code. This holds for the language $\{01111, 001011, 0110111\}$.

If A is any language and Op is any union respecting operator (e.g., a transducer operator) then we define the union respecting operators $(\mathrm{Op} \downarrow A)$ and $(\mathrm{Op} \uparrow A)$ such that, for all words v, we have

$$(\mathrm{Op} \downarrow A)(u) = \mathrm{Op}(u \cap A) \quad \text{and} \quad (\mathrm{Op} \uparrow A)(u) = \mathrm{Op}(u) \cap A.$$

Remark 11. Let $\#$ be any symbol not in Σ. Using condition (4) as a guide, we can define the UD-code property as the set of languages L satisfying the condition

$$\text{the operator} \quad \mathrm{ins}_\# \uparrow (L\#)^+ \quad \text{is functional.} \tag{7}$$

This says that inserting $\#$'s in any word $u \in \Sigma^*$ results in at most one list of L-words where these words are delimited with $\#$.

Remark 12. In [16], the author uses certain first order logic expressions, called implicational independence conditions, to describe independences. That method is aimed for variable-length type of code properties as opposed to typical error-detecting properties of languages such as block codes. The method provides a very general mechanism for expressing independences and answering the satisfaction question. For example, the first condition below describes prefix codes and the second one describes comma-free codes.

$$\forall u, x : (u \in L \wedge ux \in L) \rightarrow (x = \lambda);$$
$$\forall u, u, w, x, y : (u \in L \wedge v \in L \wedge w \in L \wedge uv = xwy) \rightarrow$$
$$((x = \lambda \wedge y = v) \vee (x = u \wedge y = \lambda));$$

where quantification of variables is over a monoid that is typically equal to Σ^*. Quantification over the number of variables is allowed, so as to express independences like the UD-code property, but the syntax for that capability needs to be worked out.

Remark 13. In [33], the author investigates decision questions about language equations. These equations are based on language expressions. There is a set of variables and a set of constants, both representing languages. A *language expression* φ is defined inductively as follows: it is a variable, or a constant, or one of $\varphi_1\varphi_2, \varphi_1 \cup \varphi_2, \varphi_1 \cap \varphi_2, \overline{\varphi_1}$, where φ_1 and φ_2 are language expressions. When an equation involves only one variable L, then the set of solutions is a set of languages, which does not necessarily constitute an independence. For example, consider the set S of solutions of the following language equation

$$L\Sigma^+ \cap \overline{L} = \emptyset. \tag{8}$$

Then, $0\Sigma^*$ satisfies the equation but the subset $\{0\}$ of $0\Sigma^*$ does not satisfy it, so S cannot be an independence. The cause of this is the presence of the complementation operation $\overline{L}$. On the other hand, the set of solutions of the language Eq. (6) is exactly the comma-free code property.

Considering that Eq. (3) describes an independence and considering also conditions (4) and (7), we are led to define independence expressions involving one variable L. An *independence expression* φ is defined inductively as follows: it is L, or a language constant, or one of $\varphi_1\varphi_2, \varphi_1\cup\varphi_2, \varphi_1\cap\varphi_2, (\varphi)^*, (\varphi)^+,$ $\mathbf{t}(\varphi_1), \theta(\varphi_1)$, where φ_1 and φ_2 are independence expressions, θ is an antimorphic permutation constant, and $\mathbf{t}$ is a transducer constant. We assume here that each language constant is written as a regular expression so it represents a regular language. This implies that when the variable L occurring in φ is replaced with a regular language then also φ evaluates to a regular language. We also note that any regular expression, transducer, or permutation involved might contain symbols outside of Σ (recall Σ is the alphabet of the independences being described).

Definition 6. *Let $\mathbf{t}$ be a transducer and let φ, ψ be independence expressions such that at least one of them contains the variable L. A language L is called $(\mathbf{t}, \varphi, \psi)$-independent if*

$$\text{the operator } \mathbf{t} \downarrow \varphi(L) \uparrow \psi(L) \text{ is functional.} \tag{9}$$

The independence $\mathcal{P}_{\mathbf{t},\varphi,\psi}$ described by $\mathbf{t}, \varphi, \psi$ is the set of all $(\mathbf{t}, \varphi, \psi)$-independent languages. Suppose that φ contains L. A language L is called φ-independent if

$$\varphi(L) = \emptyset \tag{10}$$

Remark 14. It can be shown that the concept of $(\mathbf{t}, \varphi, \psi)$-independence in the above definition is well-defined. Moreover, for every independence expression φ containing L, a language L is φ-independent if and only if it is $(\mathtt{all}_\#, \Sigma^*, \varphi\cup\#)$-independent, where $\mathtt{all}_\#$ is any transducer with input and output alphabet $\Sigma\cup\#$ such that $\mathtt{all}_\#(u) = (\Sigma\cup\#)^*$. It can further be shown that the satisfaction question is decidable, where we assume that, in the given expressions φ and/or ψ, any constant language is represented by a regular expression and the language to be tested is given by an NFA or a regular expression.

Example 6. Any independence described by one of the conditions (2), (3), (6) is a φ-independence for some φ. Any independence described by the condition (1) or (7) is a $(\mathbf{t}, \varphi, \psi)$-independence for some $\mathbf{t}, \varphi, \psi$.

Research Directions. The independences proposed in Definition 6 should be investigated in various ways. (i) In terms of dependence theory: e.g., when φ describes an independence $\mathcal{P}$, find an n such that $\mathcal{P}$ is in fact an n-independence. (ii) Compare the expressibility of the independence method in Definition 6 to that in Remark 12. (iii) In terms of algorithmic questions about these independences: e.g., (a) define, for given language L and given φ and/or ψ describing some independence $\mathcal{P}$, what the witnesses are for the non-satisfaction of L with respect to $\mathcal{P}$; (b) investigate maximality possibly for restricted forms of φ in (10).

9   Concluding Remarks

We have surveyed applications of transducers in questions related to independent languages. Describing independences by transducers is an operational approach that has led to the implementation of related objects and algorithms [25]. At the end of some sections we proposed directions for future research. In the previous section we proposed a possible extension of the transducer method for describing independences. The method allows one to treat in a uniform way many existing independences as well as to deal with a priory unknown independences. We close with an example of combining three independences.

1. From variable-length codes: UD-code relative to some language M, [7]: $\mathtt{ins}_\# \downarrow$ $M \uparrow (L\#)^+$ is functional.
2. From error-control codes: error-detection for $\mathtt{sub}_k$ (see Example 1): $\mathtt{sub}_k^{\neq}(L) \cap L = \emptyset$.
3. From DNA codes: θ-compliance (see Example 2): $\mathtt{sco}(L) \cap \theta(L) = \emptyset$.

Let Σ' be a primed and disjoint copy of the alphabet Σ and let $\mathtt{cp}$ be a transducer that outputs a primed copy of any given input Σ^*-word. The conjunction of the above independences is described by the condition

$$\left(\mathtt{ins}_{\#'}' \vee \mathtt{all}_\# \right) \downarrow \left(\mathtt{cp}M \cup \Sigma^* \right) \uparrow \left(\left(\mathtt{cp}(L\#) \right)^+ \cup \left(\varphi(L) \cup \# \right) \right) \text{ is functional,}$$

where $\varphi(L) = \left(\mathtt{sub}_k^{\neq}(L) \cap L \right) \cup \left(\mathtt{sco}(L) \cap \theta(L) \right)$, and $\mathtt{ins}_{\#'}'$ is the primed version of $\mathtt{ins}_\#$.

References

1. Allauzen, C., Mohri, M.: Efficient algorithms for testing the twins property. J. Automata Lang. Comb. **8**(2), 117–144 (2003)
2. Béal, M.P., Carton, O., Prieur, C., Sakarovitch, J.: Squaring transducers: an efficient procedure for deciding functionality and sequentiality. Theoret. Comput. Sci. **292**(1), 45–63 (2003)
3. Berstel, J.: Transductions and Context-Free Languages. B.G. Teubner, Stuttgart (1979)
4. Berstel, J., Perrin, D., Reutenauer, C.: Codes and Automata. Cambridge University Press, Cambridge (2009)
5. Bruyère, V.: Maximal codes with bounded deciphering delay. Theoret. Comput. Sci. **84**, 53–76 (1991)
6. Calude, C., Salomaa, K., Yu, S.: Additive distances and quasi-distances between words. J. Univ. Comput. Sci. **8**(2), 141–152 (2002)
7. Daley, M., Jürgensen, H., Kari, L., Mahalingam, K.: Relativized codes. Theoret. Comput. Sci. **429**, 54–64 (2012)
8. Domaratzki, M.: Trajectory-based codes. Acta Inf. **40**, 491–527 (2004)
9. Dudzinski, K., Konstantinidis, S.: Formal descriptions of code properties: decidability, complexity, implementation. Int. J. Found. Comput. Sci. **23**(1), 67–85 (2012)
10. Ehrenfeucht, A., Rozenberg, G.: Each regular code is included in a maximal regular code. RAIRO Inform. Théor. Appl. **20**, 89–96 (1985)

11. FAdo: Tools for formal languages manipulation. http://fado.dcc.fc.up.pt/. Accessed Apr 2017
12. Hamming, R.W.: Error detecting and error correcting codes. Bell Syst. Tech. J. **26**(2), 147–160 (1950)
13. Han, Y.-S., Ko, S.-K., Salomaa, K.: Computing the edit-distance between a regular language and a context-free language. In: Yen, H.-C., Ibarra, O.H. (eds.) DLT 2012. LNCS, vol. 7410, pp. 85–96. Springer, Heidelberg (2012). doi:10.1007/978-3-642-31653-1_9
14. Hopcroft, J.E., Ullman, J.D.: Introduction to Automata Theory, Languages, and Computation. Addison-Wesley, Boston (1979)
15. Jonoska, N., Mahalingam, K.: Languages of DNA based code words. In: Chen, J., Reif, J. (eds.) DNA 2003. LNCS, vol. 2943, pp. 61–73. Springer, Heidelberg (2004). doi:10.1007/978-3-540-24628-2_8
16. Jürgensen, H.: Syntactic monoids of codes. Acta Cybern. **14**, 117–133 (1999)
17. Jürgensen, H., Konstantinidis, S.: Codes. In: Rozenberg and Salomaa [36], pp. 511–607 (1997)
18. Kamabe, H.: Outfix-free and intercode constraints for DNA sequences. In: Proceedings of 2011 IEEE International Symposium on Information Theory, pp. 1574–1578 (2011)
19. Kari, L., Kitto, R., Thierrin, G.: Codes, involutions, and DNA encodings. In: Brauer, W., Ehrig, H., Karhumäki, J., Salomaa, A. (eds.) Formal and Natural Computing. LNCS, vol. 2300, pp. 376–393. Springer, Heidelberg (2002). doi:10.1007/3-540-45711-9_21
20. Kari, L., Konstantinidis, S., Kopecki, S.: Transducer descriptions of DNA code properties and undecidability of antimorphic problems. In: Shallit, J., Okhotin, A. (eds.) DCFS 2015. LNCS, vol. 9118, pp. 141–152. Springer, Cham (2015). doi:10.1007/978-3-319-19225-3_12
21. Kari, L., Konstantinidis, S., Kopecki, S., Yang, M.: An efficient algorithm for computing the edit distance of a regular language via input-altering transducers. CoRR abs/1406.1041 (2014). http://arxiv.org/abs/1406.1041
22. Kari, L., Konstantinidis, S., Sosík, P.: On properties of bond-free DNA languages. Theoret. Comput. Sci. **334**, 131–159 (2005)
23. Konstantinidis, S.: Transducers and the properties of error-detection, error-correction and finite-delay decodability. J. Univ. Comput. Sci. **8**, 278–291 (2002)
24. Konstantinidis, S., Mastnak, M.: Embedding rationally independent languages into maximal ones. J. Automata Lang. Comb. (2017, to appear)
25. Konstantinidis, S., Meijer, C., Moreira, N., Reis, R.: Implementation of code properties via transducers. In: Han, Y.-S., Salomaa, K. (eds.) CIAA 2016. LNCS, vol. 9705, pp. 189–201. Springer, Cham (2016). doi:10.1007/978-3-319-40946-7_16
26. Konstantinidis, S., Moreira, N., Reis, R.: Generating error control codes with automata and transducers. In: Bordihn, H., Freund, R., Nagy, B., Vaszil, G. (eds.) Proceedings of NCMA 2016, pp. 211–226. No. 321 in Österreichische Computer Gesellschaft (2016)
27. Konstantinidis, S., Silva, P.V.: Computing maximal error-detecting capabilities and distances of regular languages. Fundam. Inf. **101**(4), 257–270 (2010)
28. Kopecki, S.: Personal communication (2013)
29. Lam, N.H.: Finite maximal solid codes. Theoret. Comput. Sci. **262**, 333–347 (2001)
30. Mateescu, A., Salomaa, A.: Formal languages: an introduction and a synopsis. In: Rozenberg and Salomaa [36], pp. 1–39 (1997)

31. Mercier, H., Bhargava, V.K., Tarokh, V.: A survey of error-correcting codes for channels with symbol synchronization errors. IEEE Commun. Surv. Tutor. **12**, 87–96 (2010)

32. Ng, T.: Prefix distance between regular languages. In: Han, Y.-S., Salomaa, K. (eds.) CIAA 2016. LNCS, vol. 9705, pp. 224–235. Springer, Cham (2016). doi:10. 1007/978-3-319-40946-7_19

33. Okhotin, A.: Decision problems for language equations. J. Comput. Syst. Sci. **76**, 251–266 (2010)

34. Paluncic, F., Abdel-Ghaffar, K., Ferreira, H.: Insertion/deletion detecting codes and the boundary problem. IEEE Trans. Inf. Theory **59**(9), 5935–5943 (2013)

35. Pighizzini, G.: How hard is computing the edit distance? Inf. Comput. **165**, 1–13 (2001)

36. Rozenberg, G., Salomaa, A. (eds.): Handbook of Formal Languages, vol. I. Springer, Berlin (1997)

37. Sakarovitch, J.: Elements of Automata Theory. Cambridge University Press, Berlin (2009)

38. Shyr, H.J.: Free Monoids and Languages, 2nd edn. Hon Min Book Company, Taichung (1991)

39. Shyr, H.J., Thierrin, G.: Codes and binary relations. In: Malliavin, M.P. (ed.) Séminaire d'Algèbre Paul Dubreil Paris 1975–1976 (29ème Année). LNM, vol. 586, pp. 180–188. Springer, Heidelberg (1977). doi:10.1007/BFb0087133

40. Van, D.L., Hung, K., Huy, P.T.: Codes and length-increasing transitive binary relations. In: Hung, D., Wirsing, M. (eds.) ICTAC 2005. LNCS, vol. 3722, pp. 29–48. Springer, Heidelberg (2005). doi:10.1007/11560647_2

41. Vaucanson: The vaucanson project. http://vaucanson-project.org/. Accessed Apr 2017

42. Wood, D.: Theory of Computation. Harper & Row, New York (1987)

43. Yu, S.: Regular languages. In: Rozenberg and Salomaa [36], pp. 41–110 (1997)

44. Yu, S.S.: Languages and Codes. Tsang Hai Book Publishing, Taichung (2005)

45. Zaccagnino, R., Zizza, R., Zottoli, C.: Testing DNA code words properties of regular languages. Theoret. Comput. Sci. **608**, 84–97 (2015)

46. Zhang, L., Shen, Z.: Completion of recognizable bifix codes. Theoret. Comput. Sci. **145**, 345–355 (1995)

Contributed Papers

On the Degree of Nondeterminism of Tree Adjoining Languages and Head Grammar Languages

Suna Bensch[1($\boxtimes$)] and Maia Hoeberechts[2]

[1] Department of Computing Science, Umeå University, Umeå, Sweden
suna@cs.umu.se
[2] Ocean Networks Canada and Department of Computer Science,
University of Victoria, Victoria, Canada
maiah@uvic.ca

Abstract. The degree of nondeterminism is a measure of syntactic complexity which was investigated for parallel and sequential rewriting systems. In this paper, we consider the degree of nondeterminsm for tree adjoining grammars and their languages and head grammars and their languages. We show that a degree of nondeterminism of 2 suffices for both formalisms in order to generate all languages in their respective language families. Furthermore, we show that deterministic tree adjoining grammars (those with degree of nondeterminism equal to 1), can generate non-context-free languages, in contrast to deterministic head grammars which can only generate languages containing a single word.

Keywords: Tree adjoining languages · Head grammar languages · Degree of nondeterminism

1 Introduction

The degree of nondeterminism for tabled Lindenmayer systems and languages has been studied in [8,9] as a measure of syntactic complexity. The degree of nondeterminism has also been considered for sequential rewriting systems in [1–3]. The degree of nondeterminism is usually defined as the maximal number of production rules with the same left-hand side which provides a measure of the amount of choice available during derivations using the grammar. In this paper we consider the degree of nondeterminism for tree adjoining grammars and head grammars. *Tree adjoining grammars* were first introduced in [5] and their formal properties and linguistic relevance have been considered in [4,10]. TAGs are tree-generating grammars which use an *adjoining* operation that generates new trees

---

M. Hoeberechts—This research has been supported in part by an NSERC scholarship and by NSERC grant OGP 249 (Helmut Jürgensen).

G. Pighizzini and C. Câmpeanu (Eds.): DCFS 2017, LNCS 10316, pp. 65–76, 2017.
DOI: 10.1007/978-3-319-60252-3_5

by joining and attaching two different trees at a particular node. *Head Grammars* were first introduced in [7]. The principle feature which distinguishes a Head Grammar (HG) from a context-free grammar is that the head grammar includes a wrapping operation which allows one string to be inserted into another string at a specific point (the head). It is known that for both tree adjoining grammars and head grammars, the class of string languages generated by the grammars is larger than the class of context-free languages (e.g. they are able to define the language $\{a^n b^n c^n d^n | n \geq 0\}$ [10]). In [10] it is shown that the two formalisms generate exactly the same class of string languages, and that these languages are *mildly context-sensitive*.

The notion of mild context-sensitivity tries to capture mathematical and computational properties that formal models for the description and analysis of natural language should possess. The notion of mild context-sensitivity was first mentioned in [4] and sparked active research yielding to many different approaches and definitions thereof (see, for example, [6]). There has been much discussion about the linguistic differences between mildly context-sensitive grammar formalisms, and in general, investigations mainly focus on polynomial parsing algorithms. Formal properties of mild context-sensitive grammar formalisms have not been as extensively considered. The examination of degree of nondeterminism for TAGs and MHGs is a step in that direction. It would be interesting to consider whether there are any linguistic implications for the degree of nondeterminism — for example, are there aspects of natural language modelling which are best done with a grammar having a higher (or lower) degree of nondeterminism than others?

2   Notational Conventions

The reader is assumed to be familiar with the basic notions in formal language theory. We use the following notational conventions and definitions in this paper. $|S|$ denotes the cardinality of the set S, $\emptyset$ denotes the empty set, $\cup$ denotes set union, and $\setminus$ denotes set difference. S is called an *alphabet* if it is a finite non-empty set of symbols. $\mathbb{N}$ denotes the set of natural numbers $\{1, 2, 3, \ldots\}$. For any set X, a *word* over X is a finite sequence of symbols from X. λ will be used to denote the empty word. The *concatenation* of two words x and y is denoted by xy and represents the word formed by the juxtaposition of x and y. The concatenation of a word x and a set S is $xS = \{xy \mid y \in S\}$ (Sx is similarly defined). X^* is the free monoid generated by X with concatenation as binary operation and λ as identity element. $X^+ = X^* \setminus \lambda$.

3   Tree Adjoining Grammars (TAGs)

Tree Adjoining Grammars. (TAGs) are linguistically motivated tree-generating grammars which were originally introduced in [5]. For linguistic applications, TAGs have an advantage over string generating grammars such as context-free grammars because the elementary objects and all the objects generated are trees, which represent syntactic structure explicitly, as opposed to strings, which do not. In what follows, we give an informal description of TAGs first and their formal definition later.

The components of a TAG are a set of *initial trees* and a set of *auxiliary trees*. Each node in an initial tree or an auxiliary tree is labelled by a terminal symbol, by λ, or by a nonterminal symbol and constraints (which serve to restrict adjunction at that node, as will be explained later). The initial trees are the axioms used in the generation of new trees. The only means by which new trees are generated is the adjunction operation, which allows an auxiliary tree to be inserted into an initial tree or a derived (i.e. previously generated) tree. TAGs which include a second operation, substitution, are not discussed here as they are equivalent in generative power to TAGs which use only adjoining.

Tree adjunction is illustrated in Fig. 1 (adapted from [10]). The tree shown on the left, γ, is an initial tree or a derived tree. The root node of γ is labelled by the nonterminal A, and γ contains an interior node n which is labelled by the nonterminal B. The tree in the centre, β, is an auxiliary tree in which both the root node and the *foot node*, a special node on the frontier of the tree, are labelled by B. As the nonterminal labelling n in γ and the nonterminal labelling the root node of β are the same, it is possible to adjoin β at n. Adjunction results in the new tree γ' which is constructed by removing the subtree rooted at n from γ, inserting β into γ at the point where n was removed, and then replacing the foot node in β by the subtree originally rooted at n.

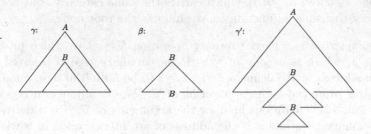

Fig. 1. Tree adjunction

The language defined by a TAG G is the set of all words which are produced as the *yield* of some tree generated through zero or more adjunction operations in G. The yield of a tree is the word obtained by concatenating the terminal symbols on the leaf nodes of the tree, read from left to right. In a TAG, initial trees must have only terminal symbols on their leaf nodes, and auxiliary trees have terminal symbols on all leaf nodes except for the foot node. Thus, every tree generated through adjunction operations in G has a terminal word as its yield, and that word is an element of $L(G)$. All trees discussed in this paper are finite.

In a TAG, a node n in a tree γ is labelled either by a terminal symbol, by λ, or by a triple of the form $\langle A, sa_{(\gamma,n)}, oa_{(\gamma,n)} \rangle$ where A is a nonterminal symbol and

$sa_{(\gamma,n)}$ and $oa_{(\gamma,n)}$ are called the *adjunction constraints* and have the following interpretations[1]:

- $sa_{(\gamma,n)}$ is a set of trees. For a given node, $sa_{(\gamma,n)}$ (*selective adjunction*) is the set of trees from the grammar which are allowed to be adjoined at that node. We assume that for all β in $sa_{(\gamma,n)}$, the root node of β is labelled by the same nonterminal as n. If $sa_{(\gamma,n)} = \emptyset$, then adjunction is not permitted at that node, and we can write NA to indicate a *null adjunction* constraint.
- $oa_{(\gamma,n)} \in \{\text{true}, \text{false}\}$. If $oa_{(\gamma,n)}$ has the value true then we speak about an OA (*obligatory adjunction*) constraint and if $oa_{(\gamma,n)}$ has the value false then this indicates that adjunction is optional.

Definition 1. A *Tree Adjoining Grammar* (TAG) is a quadruple $G = (N, T, \mathcal{I}, \mathcal{A})$, where, N is the alphabet of nonterminal symbols, T the alphabet of terminal symbols, $N \cap T = \emptyset$, $\mathcal{I}$ and $\mathcal{A}$ are given as follows

- $\mathcal{I}$ is a finite set of *initial trees* where each $\alpha \in \mathcal{I}$ satisfies:
  - All interior nodes of α are labelled by $\langle B, sa_{(\alpha,n)}, oa_{(\alpha,n)} \rangle$, $B \in N$, $sa_{(\alpha,n)} \subseteq \mathcal{A}$ and $oa_{(\alpha,n)} \in \{\text{true}, \text{false}\}$.
  - All leaf nodes of α are labelled by some $u \in \{T \cup \{\lambda\}\}$.
- $\mathcal{A}$ is a finite set of *auxiliary trees* where each $\beta \in \mathcal{A}$ satisfies:
  - All interior nodes of β are labelled by $\langle B, sa_{(\beta,n)}, oa_{(\beta,n)} \rangle$, $B \in N$, $sa_{(\beta,n)} \subseteq \mathcal{A}$ and $oa_{(\beta,n)} \in \{\text{true}, \text{false}\}$.
  - All leaf nodes of β are labelled by some $u \in \{T \cup \{\lambda\}\}$, except the foot node, denoted by $ft(\beta)$, which carries the same category (but not necessarily the same adjunction constraints) as the root node.

Tree adjunction is a partial ternary operation $\nabla(\gamma, \beta, n)$ which produces a new tree, γ', which is a copy of γ with the auxiliary tree β inserted at the node with address n. We define a *derived tree* to be an initial tree, an auxiliary tree or a tree produced by an application of ∇. We say adjunction is *permitted* when the following conditions hold for the arguments of ∇: γ is a derived tree, β is an auxiliary tree, and n is the address of an interior node in γ with label $\gamma(n) = \langle B, sa_{(\gamma,n)}, oa_{(\gamma,n)} \rangle$. The root node of β must be labelled by the same nonterminal as n, that is, $\langle B, sa_{(\beta,\lambda)}, oa_{(\beta,\lambda)} \rangle$, and β must be an element of $sa_{(\gamma,n)}$.

After adjunction the labels of the nodes are unchanged from their original labels in γ and β, except for the nodes affected by adjunction: the node at address n which now carries the label from the root node of β, and the foot node of β with the change that the oa constraint on the node is set to false.

For a TAG $G = (N, T, \mathcal{I}, \mathcal{A})$, a derivation in G will be denoted by $\underset{G}{\Longrightarrow}$. The tree γ' can be derived from γ if and only if there exist $\beta \in \mathcal{A}$ and n in *gamma* such that adjunction of β in γ at n is permitted and $\nabla(\gamma, \beta, n) = \gamma'$. Then we write $\gamma \underset{G}{\Longrightarrow} \gamma'$. Let $\underset{G}{\overset{*}{\Longrightarrow}}$ denote the reflexive, transitive closure of $\underset{G}{\Longrightarrow}$.

---

[1] This notation has been changed slightly from [10] to include an index on the sa and oa constraint.

The *tree language* generated by G is the set of all trees which can be generated in zero or more derivation steps from the initial trees of G, and in which no nodes remain which are labelled by an OA (obligatory adjunction) constraint.

$$T(G) = \{\gamma \mid \alpha \overset{*}{\underset{G}{\Longrightarrow}} \gamma \text{ for some } \alpha \in \mathcal{I} \text{ and } \gamma \text{ has no OA nodes}\}$$

The *yield* of a tree is the string one obtains by concatenating the labels on the leaf nodes from left to right.

For a TAG $G = (N, T, \mathcal{I}, \mathcal{A})$ with tree language $T(G)$, the tree adjoining language generated by G is

$$L(G) = \{yield(\gamma) \mid \gamma \in T(G)\}.$$

Let $\mathcal{L}^{\text{TAG}}$ represent the family of tree adjoining languages.

3.1 Degree of Nondeterminism for TAGs

The degree of nondeterminism for tree adjoining grammars will measure the amount of choice between auxiliary trees which can be adjoined within a given TAG. When defining the degree of nondeterminism for TAGs an essential ambiguity in the interpretation has to be taken into account. On the one hand, when defining the degree of nondeterminism for a given node n in a tree γ, one could consider only the auxiliary trees in the set $sa_{(\gamma,n)}$, which can be adjoined at that node. On the other hand, one could consider *all* auxiliary trees in the set $\mathcal{A}$ for the given tree adjoining grammar (even if they are not in the set $sa_{(\gamma,n)}$). We will call these views *weak degree of nondeterminism* and *strong degree of nondeterminism*, respectively. In this section we will define strong and weak degree of nondeterminism, and then show that the two measures are equivalent. For the following definitions, consider a TAG $G = (N, T, \mathcal{I}, \mathcal{A})$. Let γ represent an arbitrary tree in $\mathcal{I} \cup \mathcal{A}$ and $\beta \in \mathcal{A}$ represent an arbitrary auxiliary tree.

Definition 2. Weak degree of nondeterminism

- For a node in γ at address n labelled by $\langle B, sa_{(\gamma,n)}, oa_{(\gamma,n)} \rangle$, the *degree of the node* is denoted by $Deg_G(\gamma, n)$, and is defined as the number of trees in the selective adjunction set for the node. That is, $Deg_G(\gamma, n) = |sa_{(\gamma,n)}|$.
- The *weak degree of nondeterminism of a tree adjoining grammar* G is denoted by $Det_w(G)$, and is defined as the maximal degree of any node in a tree in G: $Det_w(G) = \max\{Deg_G(\gamma, n) \mid \gamma \in \mathcal{I} \cup \mathcal{A}, n \in dom(\gamma)\}$.
- The *weak degree of nondeterminism of a tree adjoining language* L, $Det_w(L)$, is defined as the minimal weak degree of nondeterminism of any TAG capable of generating L: $Det_w(L) = \min\{Det_w(G) \mid G \text{ is a TAG with } L(G) = L\}$.

Definition 3. Strong degree of nondeterminism

- The *degree of a nonterminal* $B \in N$, denoted by $Deg_G(B)$, is the number of auxiliary trees in $\mathcal{A}$ which have B labelling their root node: $Deg_G(B) = |\{\beta \mid \beta \in \mathcal{A}, \beta(\lambda) = \langle B, sa_{(\beta,\lambda)}, oa_{(\beta,\lambda)} \rangle\}|$.

– The *strong degree of nondeterminism for a tree adjoining grammar* G, denoted by $Det_s(G)$, is defined as the maximal degree of a nonterminal in N: $Deg_s(G) = \max\{Deg_G(B) \mid B \in N\}$.
– The *strong degree of nondeterminism of a tree adjoining language* L, $Det_s(L)$, is defined as the minimal strong degree of nondeterminism of any TAG capable of generating L: $Det_s(L) = \min\{Det_s(G) \mid G$ is a TAG with $L(G) = L\}$.

We will now show that strong and weak degree of nondeterminism are equivalent measures for TAGs.

Theorem 1. Given a TAG $G = (N, T, \mathcal{I}, \mathcal{A})$, $Det_w(G) \leq Det_s(G)$.

Proof. By definition, for every node n in a tree $\gamma \in \mathcal{I} \cup \mathcal{A}$ labelled by $\langle B, sa_{(\gamma,n)}, oa_{(\gamma,n)} \rangle$, $sa_{(\gamma,n)} \subseteq \mathcal{A}$. Therefore, $Deg_G(\gamma, n) \leq Deg_G(B)$ for any given node labelled by B in a tree γ at n, and thus $Det_w(G) \leq Det_s(G)$.

Theorem 2. Given a TAG $G = (N, T, \mathcal{I}, \mathcal{A})$ with $Det_w(G) < Det_s(G)$, there effectively exists a TAG $G' = (N', T', \mathcal{I}', \mathcal{A}')$ for which $L(G) = L(G')$ and $Det_w(G') = Det_s(G') = Det_w(G)$.

Proof. The intuitive idea behind the proof is that the set of auxiliary trees which can be adjoined at any given node is determined by two conditions: (i) the nonterminal symbol labelling the node, and (ii) the *sa* constraint which restricts the subset of auxiliary trees which are actually permitted to be adjoined at that node. The Algorithm 1 below works by making copies of the auxiliary trees such that for an *sa* set containing $\{\beta_1, \ldots, \beta_k\}$, k new auxiliary trees are introduced, whose root nodes are labelled by a common nonterminal which is used only for the auxiliary trees in that *sa* set. The result of copying and relabelling is that the strong degree of nondeterminism for the grammar is reduced to the weak degree because the number of auxiliary trees labelled by any given nonterminal is equal to the size of the *sa* set in which the auxiliary trees bearing that nonterminal appear. The algorithm recursively relabels all new auxiliary trees which are created.

An example of the effect of Algorithm 1 for one node is shown in Fig. 2. The trees at the top, α_1, β_1 and β_2, are the trees from the TAG before relabelling takes place. In the new initial tree, α'_1, the relabelled node can be seen. The new auxiliary trees, δ_1 and δ_2, are copies of β_1 and β_2 respectively for which new root and foot nodes have been added, and relabelling has been recursively applied to produce β'_1 and β'_2.

Algorithm 1.
Preconditions: $G = (N, T, \mathcal{I}, \mathcal{A})$ is the TAG which will be relabelled.
Postconditions: A new TAG $G' = (N', T', \mathcal{I}', \mathcal{A}')$ is produced for which $L(G) = L(G')$ and $Det_w(G') = Det_s(G') = Det_w(G)$.
Let $N' = \emptyset$, $T' = T$, $\mathcal{I}' = \emptyset$, $\mathcal{A}' = \emptyset$
For each t in $\mathcal{I}$
    Let t' be a new tree name, $t' \notin (\mathcal{I} \cup \mathcal{A} \cup \mathcal{I}' \cup \mathcal{A}')$
    $t' = Relabel(N', t, \mathcal{A}')$
    Let $\mathcal{I}' = \mathcal{I}' \cup t'$
Function $Relabel(N', t, \mathcal{A}')$
Preconditions: N' is the set of nonterminal symbols defined so far, t is the tree currently being considered, $\mathcal{A}'$ is the set of new auxiliary trees constructed so far

Postconditions: N' has been updated to include any new nonterminals, t is unchanged, $\mathcal{A}'$ has been updated to include any new trees resulting from the relabelling of t

Returns a new tree t' which is the relabelled t

Let t' be a copy of t

For each node n of t labelled by $\langle A, sa_{(t,n)}, oa_{(t,n)}\rangle$, with $sa_{(t,n)} = \{\beta_1, \ldots, \beta_k\}$

Let $A\beta_1 \cdots \beta_k$ be a nonterminal symbol

If $A\beta_1 \cdots \beta_k \notin N'$

Let $N' = N' \cup A\beta_1 \cdots \beta_k$

For each β_i in $sa_{(t,n)}$

Let δ_i be a new tree name, $\delta_i \notin \mathcal{A}'$

Let δ_i be an auxiliary tree constructed as follows:

- label the root node of δ_i by $\langle A\beta_1 \cdots \beta_k, \emptyset, \mathsf{false}\rangle$
- connect the root node of δ_i to the root node of a copy of β_i
- connect the foot node of the copy of β_i to the foot node of δ_i
- label the foot node of δ_i by $\langle A\beta_1 \cdots \beta_k, \emptyset, \mathsf{false}\rangle$

Let $\mathcal{A}' = \mathcal{A}' \cup \delta_i$

For i from 1 to k

$\delta_i = Relabel(N', \delta_i, \mathcal{A}')$

If $sa_{(t,n)} = \emptyset$

Let $sa'_{(t,n)} = \emptyset$

Else

Let $sa'_{(t,n)} = \{\tau \mid \tau \in \mathcal{A}', \tau(\lambda) = \langle A\beta_1 \cdots \beta_k, sa_{(\tau,\lambda)}, oa_{(\tau,\lambda)}\rangle\}$

($sa'_{(t,n)}$ is the set of all trees in $\mathcal{A}'$ whose root nodes are labelled by $A\beta_1 \cdots \beta_k$)

Let the node corresponding to n in t' be labelled by $\langle A\beta_1 \cdots \beta_k, sa'_{(t,n)}, oa_{(t,n)}\rangle$

End Function

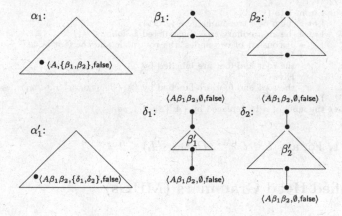

Fig. 2. Effect of Algorithm 1 for one node in α_1

Thus, as the strong degree of nondeterminism can be reduced to the weak degree for any given TAG, one measure of degree of nondeterminism is sufficient. We can omit reference to strong or weak in our notation, and therefore, $Det(G)$ will be used to denote the (weak) degree of nondeterminism for TAGs, and $Det_{TAG}(L)$ will denote the degree of nondeterminism for tree adjoining languages. Finally, we will show that for a TAG G with degree of nondeterminism greater than 2, we can create an equivalent TAG G' with degree of nondeterminism equal to 2. Thus, the degree of nondeterminism for any tree adjoining language is at most 2.

Theorem 3. Given a TAG $G = (N, T, \mathcal{I}, \mathcal{A})$ with $Det(G) > 2$, there effectively exists an TAG G' for which $L(G) = L(G')$ and $Det(G') = 2$.

Proof. The following Algorithm 2 examines all the nodes in the initial trees and auxiliary trees of G. When a node n in a tree γ is found with $Deg(\gamma, n) > 2$, this indicates that there is a choice between more than two auxiliary trees for adjunction at that node. Suppose the selective adjunction set for the node is $sa_{(\gamma,n)} = \{\beta_1, \ldots, \beta_n\}$ with $n > 2$. The algorithm works by introducing new auxiliary trees $\delta_1, \ldots, \delta_{n-2}$ each consisting of only a root node and foot node. The purpose of the δ_i trees is to reduce the choice between auxiliary trees to 2 at any given node. Node n is relabelled such that only β_1 or δ_1 can be adjoined, that is, $sa_{(\gamma,n)} = \{\beta_1, \delta_1\}$. At the root node of δ_1, β_2 or δ_2 can be adjoined, that is, $sa_{(\delta_1,\lambda)} = \{\beta_2, \delta_2\}$. Generally, for δ_i with $1 \leq i < n-2$, $sa_{(\delta_i,\lambda)} = \{\delta_{i+1}, \beta_{i+1}\}$ For δ_{n-2}, the root node is labelled by the sa set $sa_{\delta_{n-2},\lambda} = \{\beta_{n-1}, \beta_n\}$. Introduction of new auxiliary trees and relabelling is done for all nodes in G with degree greater than 2. The resulting TAG G' generates the same language as G, but contains no node with more than 2 trees in its sa set, and therefore $Det(G') = 2$.

Algorithm 2.
Preconditions: $G = (N, T, \mathcal{I}, \mathcal{A})$ is a TAG with $Det(G) > 2$
Postconditions: G has been modified such that $L(G)$ is unchanged and $Det(G) = 2$
For each $\gamma \in \mathcal{I} \cup \mathcal{A}$
    For each n in $dom(\gamma)$ labelled by $\langle A, sa_{(\gamma,n)}, oa_{(\gamma,n)} \rangle$ with $sa_{(\gamma,n)} = \{\beta_1, \ldots, \beta_k\}$
        If $k > 2$
            For i from 1 to $(k-2)$
                Let δ_i be a new tree name $\delta_i \notin (\mathcal{I} \cup \mathcal{A})$
                Let δ_i be an auxiliary tree constructed as follows:
                    • δ_i consists of two nodes: the root node and the foot node
                    • If $i < k - 2$
                    the root and foot are labelled by $\langle A, \{\beta_{i+1}, \delta_{i+1}\}, oa_{(\gamma,n)} \rangle$
                    Else
                    the root and foot are labelled by $\langle A, \{\beta_{i+1}, \beta_{i+2}\}, oa_{(\gamma,n)} \rangle$
                Let $\mathcal{A} = \mathcal{A} \cup \delta_i$
            Let the label of n be replaced by $\langle A, \{\beta_1, \delta_1\}, oa_{(\gamma,n)} \rangle$

Corollary 1. For any $L \in \mathcal{L}^{\mathrm{TAG}}$, $Det_{\mathrm{TAG}}(L) \leq 2$.

4   Modified Head Grammars (MHGs)

We will consider Modified Head Grammars (MHGs) which were proposed in [11], and differ only slightly from the definition in [7]. The strings used in modified head grammars are called *headed strings*. In a headed string, a special position between two symbols, marked by $\uparrow$, is designated as the *head* of the string. MHGs use a wrapping operation to insert one string into another, and the purpose of the head is to designate the insertion point during this operation. For an alphabet X, let $\mathcal{H}_X$ be the set of headed strings over X. $\mathcal{H}_X$ is defined as:

$$\mathcal{H}_X = \{v {\uparrow} w \,|\, v, w \in X^*\}$$

For example, for the alphabet $X = \{a, b, c\}$, $abc{\uparrow}cbacba$, $\lambda{\uparrow}aaa$ and $\lambda{\uparrow}\lambda$ are three of the elements of $\mathcal{H}_X$.

The production rules of an MHG are defined in terms of two types of operations, wrapping and concatenation, which are performed on headed strings.

The *wrapping operation*, $W : \mathcal{H}_X^2 \to \mathcal{H}_X$ is a binary operation which has the effect of inserting one string into another at the head. Given headed strings $v_1 \uparrow w_1$ and $v_2 \uparrow w_2$, the result of applying W is a new headed string comprised of $v_2 \uparrow w_2$ inserted into $v_1 \uparrow w_1$ at its head:

$$W(v_1 \uparrow w_1, v_2 \uparrow w_2) = v_1 v_2 \uparrow w_2 w_1$$

The *concatenation* of headed strings is an n-ary operation denoted by $C_{m,n} : \mathcal{H}_X^n \to \mathcal{H}_X$, where n is the number of headed strings to be concatenated and m is the index of the string whose head becomes the head for the resulting string. The indices must satisfy $n \geq 1$ and $1 \leq m \leq n$. The interpretation of $C_{m,n}$ is as follows:

$$C_{m,n}(v_1 \uparrow w_1, v_2 \uparrow w_2, \ldots, v_m \uparrow w_m, \ldots, v_n \uparrow w_n) = v_1 w_1 v_2 w_2 \cdots v_m \uparrow w_m \cdots v_n w_n$$

Given a nonterminal alphabet N and a terminal alphabet T, a *headed string expression* over N and T is recursively defined as follows:

- Every headed string $\sigma \in \mathcal{H}_T$ is a headed string expression.
- For all $A \in N$, A is a headed string expression.
- If σ_1 and σ_2 are headed strings expressions, then $W(\sigma_1, \sigma_2)$ is a headed string expression.
- If $\sigma_1, \ldots, \sigma_n$ are headed string expressions, then $C_{i,n}(\sigma_1, \ldots, \sigma_n)$ are headed string expressions for $1 \leq i \leq n$.
- There are no other headed string expressions.

Let $\mathcal{E}_{N,T}$ represent the set of headed string expressions over N and T. By convention, we will use σ to represent a headed string expression. If a headed string expression contains no nonterminals, we call it *closed*.

Definition 4. A *Modified Head Grammar (MHG)* is a quadruple, $G = (N, T, P, S)$ where N is a finite set of nonterminal symbols, T is a finite set of terminal symbols, $S \in N$ is the start symbol, P is a set of production rules $\{p_1, \ldots, p_k\}$, where $p_i = A \to \sigma_i$, with $A \in N, \sigma_i \in \mathcal{E}_{N,T}$.

Consider an MHG, $G = (N, T, P, S)$, with $p_i = A \to \sigma_i \in P$. Given a headed string expression $\sigma \in \mathcal{E}_{N,T}$ containing a nonterminal A, we may apply the rule p_i to replace one instance of A in σ by the right hand side of p_i, σ_i. Let σ' denote the resulting string. Then we write $\sigma \underset{G}{\Longrightarrow} \sigma'$ to indicate that σ' can be derived from σ using a production rule in G. If the grammar in use is clear from the context, we write $\Longrightarrow$ rather than $\underset{G}{\Longrightarrow}$. Let $\underset{G}{\overset{*}{\Longrightarrow}}$ denote the reflexive, transitive closure of $\underset{G}{\Longrightarrow}$.

For an MHG $G = (N, T, P, S)$, the *expression language* generated by G, $E(G)$, is the set of all closed headed string expressions which can be derived from S using the rules of G. Formally,

$$E(G) = \{\sigma \mid S \underset{G}{\overset{*}{\Longrightarrow}} \sigma, \sigma \text{ is closed}\}$$

The *head language* generated by G, $H(G)$, is the set of headed strings which result from the evaluation according to the definitions of W and $C_{m,n}$ of the closed headed string expressions in $E(G)$:

$$H(G) = \{v{\uparrow}w \mid v{\uparrow}w \in E(G)\}$$

The *language generated by* G, $L(G)$, is the set of strings one obtains by removing the heads from the strings in $H(G)$:

$$L(G) = \{vw \mid v{\uparrow}w \in H(G)\}$$

Let $\mathcal{L}^{\mathrm{MHG}}$ denote the family of languages which can be defined by MHGs.

4.1   Degree of Nondeterminism for MHGs

Let $G = (N, T, P, S)$ be an MHG. For a nonterminal A, let P_A be the set of production rules with A on the left-hand side.

That is, $P_A = \{p_i \mid p_i \in P, p_i = A \to \sigma\}$.

Definition 5. Degree of nondeterminism

- The *degree of the nonterminal* A, denoted by $Deg_G(A)$, is the number of production rules with A on the left-hand side: $Deg_G(A) = |P_A|$.
- The *degree of nondeterminism* of the MHG G, $Det(G)$, is defined as the maximum degree of a nonterminal in G: $Det(G) = \max\{Deg_G(A) \mid A \in N\}$. Intuitively, the degree of nondeterminism measures how much choice between productions rules there is during a derivation using a specific MHG.
- $Det_{\mathrm{MHG}}(L)$, the *degree of nondeterminism for an MHG language* L, is defined as the minimal degree of nondeterminism of any MHG capable of generating L: $Det_{\mathrm{MHG}}(L) = \min\{Det(G) \mid G \text{ is an MHG for which } L(G) = L\}$.

It will now be shown that the degree of nondeterminism for any MHG language is at most 2. The proof of Theorem 4 contains an algorithm which generates an MHG with degree of nondeterminism equal to 2 from any MHG with degree of nondeterminism greater than 2.

Theorem 4. Given an MHG $G = (N, T, P, S)$ with $Det(G) > 2$, there effectively exists an MHG $G' = (N', T, P', S')$ for which $L(G') = L(G)$ and $Det(G') = 2$.

Proof. An MHG G with $Det(G) > 2$ contains nonterminals $A \in N$ which appear on the left hand side of more than 2 production rules. The Algorithm 3 presented below introduces new nonterminal symbols and production rules so that the choice between production rules at any point in a derivation is always binary. To understand how it works, suppose there is a nonterminal $A \in N$ which appears on the left hand side of 3 rules, $p_1 : A \to \sigma_1$, $p_2 : A \to \sigma_2$ and $p_3 : A \to \sigma_3$. After execution of the algorithm, the nonterminal A would be replaced by three nonterminal, A_1, A_2 and A_3, and the rules p_1, p_2 and p_3 would be replaced by six production rules: $p'_1 = A_1 \rightarrow \sigma'_1$, $p''_1 = A_1 \rightarrow A_2$, $p'_2 = A_2 \rightarrow \sigma'_2$, $p''_2 = A_2 \rightarrow A_3$, $p'_3 = A_3 \rightarrow \sigma'_3$, $p''_3 = A_3 \rightarrow A_1$. The rules are "chained" such that the same strings can be derived but the choice of production rules at any given time is reduced to 2.

Algorithm 3.
Preconditions: $G = (N, T, P, S)$ is an MHG with $Det(G) > 2$
Postconditions: New MHG $G' = (N', T', P', S')$ such that $L(G') = L(G)$ and $Det(G') = 2$
Let $N' = \emptyset$, $T' = T$, $P' = \emptyset$, $S' = S_1$
For each $A \in N$
    Let $P_A = \{p_1, \ldots p_j\}$ be the set of rules with A on the left hand side
    Let A_1 be a new nonterminal, $A_1 \notin (N \cup N')$
    Let $N' = N' \cup A_1$
    For $i = 1$ to j
        From $p_i = A \rightarrow \sigma_i$
        Create rule $p'_i = A_i \rightarrow \sigma'_i$
           where σ'_i is the headed string expression which results
           by replacing all $B \in N$ appearing in σ_i by B_1
        Let $P' = P' \cup p'_i$
        If $i < j$
           Let A_{i+1} be a new nonterminal, $A_{i+1} \notin (N \cup N')$
           Create rule $p''_i = A_i \rightarrow A_{i+1}$
           Let $N' = N' \cup A_{i+1}$, $P' = P' \cup p''_i$
        Else If $j > 1$
           Create rule $p''_i = A_i \rightarrow A_1$
           Let $P' = P' \cup p''_i$

Corollary 2. For any $L \in \mathcal{L}^{\mathrm{MHG}}$, $Det_{\mathrm{MHG}}(L) \leq 2$.

A *deterministic MHG* is an MHG $G = (N, T, P, S)$ for which $Det(G) = 1$. In other words, no nonterminal $A \in N$ appears on the left-hand side of more than one production rule $p_i \in P$.

Theorem 5. A deterministic MHG $G = (N, T, P, S)$ defines a language with $|L(G)| \leq 1$.

Proof. We can observe the following requirements for the production rules of a deterministic MHG with a nonempty language: (i) At least one production rule must have only terminal symbols or λ on the right-hand side. (ii) The same nonterminal symbol may not appear on the left and right-hand side of a given production rule. (iii) There can be no set of production rules $P_{\mathrm{cycle}} \subseteq P = p_1, \ldots, p_k$ which have the following form: $p_1 : A_1 \rightarrow \sigma_1$ where σ_1 contains $A_1 \ldots p_i : A_i \rightarrow \sigma_i$, where σ_i contains $A_{i+1} \ldots p_k : A_k \rightarrow \sigma_k$, where σ_k contains A_1.

(i) is necessary so that it is possible to derive a headed string expression which is closed. (ii) and (iii) are necessary so that the sequence of derivations does not contain a loop. Such a loop would prevent the sequence of derivations from ending since each nonterminal appears on the left hand side of only one rule, and therefore the derivation leading to the loop would be chosen every time. Thus, since the sequence of derivations does not contain a loop and must start from S, if $L(G)$ is nonempty then $|L(G)| = 1$.

5 Conclusions

The relationship between TAGs and MHGs was explored in several papers [10, 11]. In this paper, we have shown that for both TAGs and MHGs, the degree of nondeterminism 2 suffices to generate all languages in their respective language families. Reducing the degree of nondeterminism with our algorithms can increase the number of elementary trees in a TAG or the number of production in a MHG considerably. We note that there is a significant difference between deterministic MHGs and deterministic TAGs. In [10], an example of a TAG appears which has only one auxiliary tree (and is therefore deterministic by our definition), and yet it generates the language $\{a^n b^n c^n d^n \mid n \geq 0\}$ which is noncontext-free. By contrast, deterministic MHGs are only capable of generating languages for which $|L| \leq 1$. Finally, there is a small question which arose concerning TAGs during our work. Although we know that deterministic TAGs are capable of generating noncontext-free languages, we did not identify the class of languages which can be generated by deterministic TAGs.

Acknowledgments. We thank Henning Bordihn for helping us to understand and define Degree of Nondeterminism for TAGs. Thank you to Helmut Jürgensen for his comments on drafts of this paper and for his support and encouragement for this project.

References

1. Aydin, S., Bordihn, H.: Sequential versus parallel grammar formalisms with respect to measures of descriptional complexity. Fundam. Inf. **55**, 243–254 (2003)
2. Bordihn, H.: Über den Determiniertheitsgrad reiner Versionen formaler Sprachen. Ph.D. thesis, Technische Universität "Otto von Guericke" Magdeburg (1992)
3. Bordihn, H.: On the degree of nondeterminism. In: Dassow, J., Kelemenova, A. (eds.) Developments in Theoretical Computer Science, pp. 133–140. Gordon and Breach Science Publishers, Philadelphia (1994)
4. Joshi, A.: Tree adjoining grammars: how much context-sensitivity is required to provide reasonable structural descriptions? In: Dowty, D., Karttunen, L., Zwicky, A. (eds.) Natural Language Parsing, pp. 206–250. Cambridge University Press, Cambridge (1985)
5. Joshi, A., Levi, L.S., Takahashi, M.: Tree adjunct grammars. J. Comput. Syst. Sci. **10**, 136–163 (1975)
6. Marcus, S.: Mild context-sensitivity, after twenty years. Fundam. Inf. **73**, 203–204 (2006)
7. Pollard, C.: Generalized phrase structure grammars, head grammars and natural language. Ph.D. thesis, Stanford University (1984)
8. Rozenberg, G.: Extension of tabled 0L systems and languages. Int. J. Comput. Inform. Sci. **2**, 311–336 (1973)
9. Rozenberg, G.: T0L systems and languages. Inf. Control **23**, 357–381 (1973)
10. Vijay-Shanker, K., Weir, D.: The equivalence of four extensions of context-free grammars. Math. Syst. Theory **87**, 511–546 (1994)
11. Weir, D., Vijay-Shanker, K., Joshi, A.: The relationship between tree adjoining grammars and head grammars. In: Proceedings of the 24th Annual Meeting of Computational Linguistics, New York, NY (1986)

On the Average Complexity of Strong Star Normal Form

Sabine Broda, António Machiavelo, Nelma Moreira, and Rogério Reis[✉]

CMUP & DM-DCC, Faculdade de Ciências da Universidade do Porto,
Rua do Campo Alegre, 4169-007 Porto, Portugal
{sbb,nam,rvr}@dcc.fc.up.pt, ajmachia@fc.up.pt

Abstract. For regular expressions in (strong) star normal form a large
set of efficient algorithms is known, from conversions into finite automata
to characterisations of unambiguity. In this paper we study the average
complexity of this class of expressions using analytic combinatorics. As
it is not always feasible to obtain explicit expressions for the generating
functions involved, here we show how to get the required information for
the asymptotic estimates with an indirect use of the existence of Puiseux
expansions at singularities. We study, asymptotically and on average, the
alphabetic size, the size of the ε-follow automaton and the ratio of these
expressions to standard regular expressions.

1 Introduction

A regular expression α is in strong star normal form (ssnf) if for any subexpression of the form $\beta^\star$ or $\beta + \varepsilon$ the language represented by β does not include the empty word, ε. The star normal form was introduced by Brüggemann-Klein [5] as a step to improve the construction of the position automaton from a regular expression from cubic to quadratic time. Transforming a regular expression into this normal form can be achieved in linear time, and moreover the position automaton resulting from that normal form coincides with the one of the original expression. In the same paper, the star normal form was also used to characterize certain types of unambiguous expressions. The position automaton construction [9] is a basic conversion between regular expressions and ε-free nondeterministic finite automata (NFA), and several other constructions are known to be its quotients. This is the case for the partial derivative automaton [1,7] and the follow automaton [14]. Champarnaud et al. [6] showed that if a regular expression is in star normal form and is normalised modulo some regular expression equivalences, the partial derivative automaton is a quotient of the follow automaton. Many conversions from regular expressions to equivalent

This work was partially supported by CMUP (UID/MAT/00144/2013), which is
funded by FCT (Portugal) with national (MEC) and European structural funds
through the programs FEDER, under the partnership agreement PT2020.

G. Pighizzini and C. Câmpeanu (Eds.): DCFS 2017, LNCS 10316, pp. 77–88, 2017.
DOI: 10.1007/978-3-319-60252-3_6

NFAs consider automata with transitions labelled by the empty word (ε-NFA). Although the most used of these conversions is the Thompson construction (implemented in many UNIX-like string search commands) [18], an older and more thrifty construction in the use of ε-transitions was presented by Ott and Feinstein in 1961 [16]. An improved version of this construction was redefined by Ilie and Yu, and called the ε-follow automaton. Gulan, Fernau and Gruber [10–12] studied the optimal (worst-case) size for all known constructions from regular expressions to ε-NFAs. It turns out that the optimal construction corresponds to the conversion of a regular expression in strong star normal form into an ε-follow automaton.

All this motivated us to study the average-case complexity of regular expressions in strong star normal form, as well as their conversions to NFAs. In previous work, we studied the asymptotic average complexity for some of the above mentioned conversions from regular expressions using the framework of analytic combinatorics [2–4], which relates the enumeration of combinatorial objects to the algebraic and complex analytic properties of generating functions. In particular, generating functions can be seen as complex analytic functions, and the study of their behaviour around their dominant singularities gives access to the asymptotic form of their coefficients. Starting with an unambiguous grammar for the set of regular expressions over a given alphabet, and a non-negative measure, the symbolic method allows to obtain a generating function associated with the sequence of the (finite) number of expressions of measure n. Multivariate generating functions can be used to analyse different measures apart from the size of combinatorial objects, e.g. the number of states of the automaton resulting from a given conversion method applied to a regular expression of given size, and thus allow to obtain estimates for the average values of those measures.

While in previous work we were able to get explicit expressions for the generating functions involved, here that would be unmanageable. Using the existence of a Puiseux expansion at a singularity, we show how to get the required information for the asymptotic estimates from an algebraic equation satisfied by the generating function, without actually computing that expansion. We note that the technique here presented allows to find, for the combinatorial classes considered, the form of the function without knowing beforehand the explicit value of the singularity. This provides a very useful method, at least for some combinatorial classes, that circumvents some of the more cumbersome steps of the *Algebraic Coefficient Asymptotics* algorithm presented by Flajolet and Sedgewick [8, pp. 504–505], as well as the need to know *a priori* the type of the singularity.

We use this method to derive the asymptotic estimates for the number of regular expressions in ssnf of a given size, as well as a parametric function of several related measures, which can give us, in particular, the alphabetic size or the size of the ε-follow automaton, on average. In the next section, we review some basics on regular expressions and ε-NFAs. In Sect. 3, we consider the transformation into strong star normal form and give some characterisations of expressions in this form. Section 4 describes a shortcut to obtain asymptotic estimates of the coefficients of generating functions. This is used in Sect. 5 to obtain the estimates mentioned before. Some experiments corroborating those estimates are presented in Sect. 6. Conclusions are drawn in Sect. 7.

2   Regular Expressions and ε-NFAs

We consider the grammar for regular expressions proposed by Gruber and Gulan in [10,11], which has the major advantage of avoiding many redundant expressions built with the symbols ε and $\emptyset$. Given an alphabet $\Sigma = \{\sigma_1, \ldots, \sigma_k\}$ of size k, the set $\mathcal{R}_k$ of *regular expressions*, α, over Σ is defined by the following grammar,

$$\alpha := \emptyset \mid \varepsilon \mid \beta,$$

$$\beta := \sigma_1 \mid \cdots \mid \sigma_k \mid (\beta + \beta) \mid (\beta \cdot \beta) \mid \beta^? \mid \beta^\star,$$

where the operator $\cdot$ (concatenation) is often omitted. The language associated with α is denoted by $\mathcal{L}(\alpha)$ and is defined as usual, with $\mathcal{L}(\beta^?) = \mathcal{L}(\beta) \cup \{\varepsilon\}$. It is clear that $\alpha^?$ is equivalent to the standard regular expression $\alpha + \varepsilon$.

For the *size* of a regular expression α, denoted by $|\alpha|$, we will consider reverse polish notation length, i.e., the number of symbols in α, not counting parentheses. The number of letters in α is denoted by $|\alpha|_\Sigma$, and usually called *alphabetic size*. The number of occurrences of each operator $c \in \{+, \cdot, \star, ?\}$ is denoted by $|\alpha|_c$.

A *nondeterministic finite automaton* is a tuple $\mathcal{N} = \langle Q, \Sigma, \delta, q_0, F \rangle$, where Q is a finite set of states, Σ is the alphabet, $\delta \subseteq Q \times (\Sigma \cup \{\varepsilon\}) \times Q$ is the transition relation, $q_0 \in Q$ is the initial state, and $F \subseteq Q$ is the set of final states. The *size* of an NFA $\mathcal{N}$ is $|\mathcal{N}| = |Q| + |\delta|$, the number of states $|\mathcal{N}|_Q = |Q|$, and the number of transitions $|\mathcal{N}|_\delta = |\delta|$. An NFA that has transitions labelled with ε is an ε-NFA. The *language* accepted by an automaton $\mathcal{N}$ is $\mathcal{L}(\mathcal{N}) = \{ w \in \Sigma^\star \mid \delta(q_0, w) \cap F \neq \emptyset \}$, where δ is naturally extended to sets of states and words.

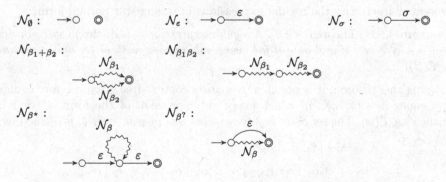

Fig. 1. The ε-follow construction, $\mathcal{A}_{\varepsilon f}$.

Conversion of a regular expression into an equivalent NFA can be defined by induction on the structure of the regular expression. Let $\mathcal{N}_\alpha$ denote the automaton corresponding to a regular expression α. In Fig. 1 we present the construction of the ε-follow automaton, $\mathcal{A}_{\varepsilon f}(\alpha)$ [14]. The size of the $\mathcal{A}_{\varepsilon f}(\alpha)$ for the atomic expressions $\emptyset$, ε, and $\sigma \in \Sigma$ is 2, 3 and 3, respectively. For the remaining constructions, the size of the resulting automaton equals the sum of the sizes of its constituents plus some constant. For instance, for the operator $+$ one has $|\mathcal{N}_{\beta_1+\beta_2}|_Q = |\mathcal{N}_{\beta_1}|_Q + |\mathcal{N}_{\beta_2}|_Q - 2$, $|\mathcal{N}_{\beta_1+\beta_2}|_\delta = |\mathcal{N}_{\beta_1}|_\delta + |\mathcal{N}_{\beta_2}|_\delta$, and thus $|\mathcal{N}_{\beta_1+\beta_2}| = |\mathcal{N}_{\beta_1}| + |\mathcal{N}_{\beta_2}| - 2$. This can be generalised by considering constants $(c_\emptyset, c_\varepsilon, c_\sigma, c_+, c_\bullet, c_\star, c_?)$ that define functions that can be used to compute several interesting measures. For example, using $(2, 2, 2, -2, -1, 1, 0)$ one gets the number of states; the number of transitions are computed using $(0, 1, 1, 0, 0, 2, 1)$, and the combined size corresponds to $(2, 3, 3, -2, -1, 3, 1)$.

We note that the worst-case complexity for this conversion can be reached for expressions with only one letter and $n - 1$ stars. For such an expression of size n, the corresponding $\mathcal{A}_{\varepsilon f}$ automaton has size $3n$.

3   Strong Star Normal Form

A regular expression α is in *star normal form* if for any subexpression of the form $\beta^\star$, $\varepsilon \notin \mathcal{L}(\beta)$ [5]. The original notion of star normal form makes use of two operators on regular expressions. Gulan and Gruber simplified that definition and adapted it to forbid that subexpressions of the form $\beta^?$ could have $\varepsilon \in \mathcal{L}(\beta)$. The resulting form was called *strong star normal form*.

Definition 1. *The operators $\circ$ and $\bullet$ are inductively defined as follows. Let $\varepsilon^\circ = \emptyset^\circ = \emptyset$, $\sigma^\circ = \sigma$ for $\sigma \in \Sigma$, $(\beta_1 + \beta_2)^\circ = \beta_1^\circ + \beta_2^\circ$, $\beta^{?\circ} = \beta^\circ$, $\beta^{\star\circ} = \beta^\circ$; finally $(\beta_1\beta_2)^\circ = \beta_1^\circ + \beta_2^\circ$ if $\varepsilon \in \mathcal{L}(\beta_1\beta_2)$ and $(\beta_1\beta_2)^\circ = \beta_1\beta_2$, otherwise.*

Let $\emptyset^\bullet = \emptyset$, $\varepsilon^\bullet = \varepsilon$, $\sigma^\bullet = \sigma$ for $\sigma \in \Sigma$, $(\beta_1 + \beta_2)^\bullet = \beta_1^\bullet + \beta_2^\bullet$, $(\beta_1\beta_2)^\bullet = \beta_1^\bullet\beta_2^\bullet$, $\beta^{\star\bullet} = \beta^{\circ\bullet\star}$; finally $\beta^{?\bullet} = \beta^\bullet$ if $\varepsilon \in \mathcal{L}(\beta)$, and $\beta^{?\bullet} = (\beta^\bullet)^?$, otherwise.

The expression $\alpha^\bullet$ is the strong star normal form *(ssnf) of α.*

For a regular expression α, $\mathcal{L}(\alpha^\bullet) = \mathcal{L}(\alpha)$ and $|\alpha^\bullet| \le |\alpha|$. The following theorem characterizes the regular expressions in strong star normal form.

Theorem 1 [11, Theorem 3.2.8]. *A regular expression α is in strong star normal form, i.e. $\alpha = \alpha^\bullet$, if and only if for every subexpression $\beta^\star$ or $\beta^?$ of α, one has $\varepsilon \notin \mathcal{L}(\beta)$.*

Using this theorem it is possible to write a context-free grammar for regular expressions in ssnf, i.e., in which every subexpression of the form $\alpha^\star$ or $\alpha^?$, satisfies $\varepsilon \notin \mathcal{L}(\alpha)$. The set $\mathcal{S}_k$ of *regular expressions in ssnf* over Σ is defined by:

$$
\begin{aligned}
\alpha &:= \varepsilon \mid \emptyset \mid \alpha_\varepsilon \mid \alpha_{\overline{\varepsilon}} \\
\alpha_\varepsilon &:= \alpha_\varepsilon \alpha_\varepsilon \mid \alpha_\varepsilon + \alpha_{\overline{\varepsilon}} \mid \alpha_{\overline{\varepsilon}} + \alpha_\varepsilon \mid \alpha_\varepsilon + \alpha_\varepsilon \mid \alpha_{\overline{\varepsilon}}^\star \mid \alpha_{\overline{\varepsilon}}^? \\
\alpha_{\overline{\varepsilon}} &:= \sigma_1 \mid \cdots \mid \sigma_k \mid \alpha_{\overline{\varepsilon}} \alpha_{\overline{\varepsilon}} \mid \alpha_{\overline{\varepsilon}} \alpha_\varepsilon \mid \alpha_\varepsilon \alpha_{\overline{\varepsilon}} \mid \alpha_{\overline{\varepsilon}} + \alpha_{\overline{\varepsilon}},
\end{aligned}
\tag{1}
$$

where α_ε are regular expressions whose language includes ε, while for $\alpha_{\overline{\varepsilon}}$, $\varepsilon \notin \mathcal{L}(\alpha_{\overline{\varepsilon}})$. The following theorem summarizes the results by Gruber and Gulan [10, Theorems 4 and 6] (see also Gulan [11]).

Theorem 2. *Let α be in **ssnf** of size n and alphabetic size m. Then, $\mathcal{A}_{\varepsilon f}(\alpha)$ has size at most* $\min(\frac{22}{15}(n+1)+1, \frac{22}{5}m+1)$.

4   Asymptotic Average Complexity

Let $A(z) = \sum_n a_n z^n$ be the generating function associated with some combinatorial class $\mathcal{A}$ (*cf.* [8]). Given some measure of the objects of the class, the coefficient a_n represents the sum of the values of this measure for all objects of size n. We will use the notation $[z^n]A(z)$ for a_n. The generating function $A(z)$ can be seen as a complex analytic function, and the study of its behaviour around its dominant singularity ρ (when unique) gives us access to the asymptotic form of its coefficients. In particular, if $A(z)$ is analytic in some indented disc neighbourhood of ρ, then one has the following [3,8]:

1. if $A(z) = a - b\sqrt{1 - z/\rho} + o\left(\sqrt{1 - z/\rho}\right)$, with $a, b \in \mathbb{R}$, $b \neq 0$, then

$$[z^n]A(z) \sim \frac{b}{2\sqrt{\pi}}\, \rho^{-n} n^{-3/2};\qquad(2)$$

2. if $A(z) = \frac{c}{\sqrt{1-z/\rho}} + o\left(\frac{1}{\sqrt{1-z/\rho}}\right)$, with $c \in \mathbb{R}^*$, then

$$[z^n]A(z) \sim \frac{c}{\sqrt{\pi}}\, \rho^{-n} n^{-1/2}.\qquad(3)$$

Applying this result for the generating function $R_k(z)$, corresponding to the number of expressions in $\mathcal{R}_k$ of size n, the following asymptotic values were obtained in Broda *et al.* [3]:

$$[z^n]R_k(z) \sim \frac{\sqrt[4]{2k}\sqrt{\rho_k}}{4\sqrt{\pi}}\, \rho_k^{-(n+1)}(n+1)^{-3/2}, \text{ with } \rho_k = \frac{1}{2(\sqrt{2k}+1)}.\qquad(4)$$

In the same paper, the average size of the ε-follow automata construction was studied, and it was shown that, as the alphabet grows, the size of $\mathcal{A}_{\varepsilon f}$ approaches $0.75n$, asymptotically and on average.

Let us now give a generic description of the method used for the combinatorial classes that show up within the present paper. From a grammar one obtains, by the symbolic method expounded in [8], a set of polynomial equations involving the generating function of whose coefficients we want to have an asymptotic estimate. Computing a Gröbner basis for the ideal generated by those polynomials, one gets an algebraic equation for that generating function $w = w(z)$, i.e., an equation of the form

$$G(z, w) = 0,$$

where $G(z, w)$ is a polynomial in $\mathbb{Z}[z][w]$, of which $w(z)$ is a root.

Since $w(z)$ is the generating function of a combinatorial class, thus a series with non-negative integer coefficients, which is not a polynomial, it must have, by

Pringsheim's Theorem [8, Theorem IV.6], a real positive singularity, ρ, smaller than 1. At this singularity two cases may occur: either $\lim_{z \to \rho} w(z) = a$, a positive real number, or $\lim_{z \to \rho} w(z) = +\infty$.

In the first case, after making the change of variable $s = 1 - z/\rho$, one knows that $w = w(s)$ has a Puiseux series expansion at the singularity $s = 0$, i.e., there exists a slit neighbourhood of that point in which $w(s)$ has a representation as a power series with fractional powers [13, Chap. 12]. In particular, w must have the form

$$w(s) = a - g(s)s^{\alpha}, \tag{5}$$

for some $a \in \mathbb{R}$, $\alpha \in \mathbb{Q}^+$, the first positive exponent of that expansion, and $g(s)$ such that $g(s) = b + h(s)s^{\beta}$, $h(0) \neq 0$, $\beta \in \mathbb{Q}^+$, and $b \in \mathbb{R}^*$. We will show that, under some generic conditions that happen to be satisfied in all the cases treated below, one has $\alpha = \frac{1}{2}$ or $\alpha = -\frac{1}{2}$. One then needs to find the values of ρ and of b or c, depending on the case, to use either (2) or (3) to obtain the sought-after asymptotic estimates of the coefficients of $w(z)$.

Using Taylor expansion of $G(z, w)$ at (ρ, a),

$$G(z, w) = G(\rho, a) + \frac{\partial G}{\partial z}(\rho, a)(z - \rho) + \frac{\partial G}{\partial w}(\rho, a)(w - a) +$$
$$+ \frac{1}{2}\frac{\partial^2 G}{\partial z^2}(\rho, a)(z - \rho)^2 + \frac{1}{2}\frac{\partial^2 G}{\partial w^2}(\rho, a)(w - a)^2 +$$
$$+ \frac{\partial^2 G}{\partial z\, \partial w}(\rho, a)(z - \rho)(w - a) + \cdots,$$

and noticing that $G(z, w(z)) = 0$, that $G(\rho, a) = 0$, and using Eq. (5), one has,

$$0 = -\frac{\partial G}{\partial z}(\rho, a)\rho s - \frac{\partial G}{\partial w}(\rho, a)g(s)s^{\alpha} + \frac{1}{2}\frac{\partial^2 G}{\partial z^2}(\rho, a)\rho^2 s^2 +$$
$$+ \frac{1}{2}\frac{\partial^2 G}{\partial w^2}(\rho, a)g(s)^2 s^{2\alpha} - \frac{\partial^2 G}{\partial z\, \partial w}(\rho, a)\rho g(s)s^{1+\alpha} + Q(s)s^{3\alpha}, \tag{6}$$

for some function $Q(s)$, a Puiseux series with non-negative exponents.

In the case under study, the curve defined by G has a shape similar to the one depicted in Fig. 2, and therefore

$$\frac{\partial G}{\partial w}(\rho, a) = 0. \tag{7}$$

This, together with the fact that $G(\rho, a) = 0$, shows that ρ is a root of the discriminant polynomial of G with respect to variable w, which is a polynomial in z (cf. [15, p. 204]). In all the cases studied here, this polynomial has only one root in $]0, 1[$, a fact that allows to numerically get an approximation for the value of ρ. The minimum polynomial in $\mathbb{Q}[z]$ of ρ can be obtained by analysing the greatest common divisor of the polynomials $G(z, w)$ and $\frac{\partial}{\partial w}G(z, w)$ with respect to w: $\gcd_w(G(z, w), \frac{\partial}{\partial w}G(z, w))$. We will denote this polynomial by $m_\rho(z)$. Using now the $\gcd_z(G(z, w), \frac{\partial}{\partial w}G(z, w))$ one can get a polynomial that has a as a root. One can then numerically compute all the real roots of that polynomial, and then check which one is an approximation for the value of a by means of a numerical study of the curve $G(z, w)$.

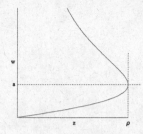

Fig. 2. Generic shape of $G(z,w)$ near its dominant singularity.

Using (7) in (6), and dividing it through by s^α, one gets

$$
\begin{aligned}
0 = &-\frac{\partial G}{\partial z}(\rho,a)\rho s^{1-\alpha} + \frac{1}{2}\frac{\partial^2 G}{\partial z^2}(\rho,a)\rho^2 s^{2-\alpha} \\
&+ \frac{1}{2}\frac{\partial^2 G}{\partial w^2}(\rho,a)g(s)^2 s^\alpha + \\
&+ \frac{\partial^2 G}{\partial z\,\partial w}(\rho,a)\rho g(s)s + Q(s)s^{2\alpha}.
\end{aligned}
\tag{8}
$$

Now, in all cases studied in this paper, one has

$$
\frac{\partial G}{\partial z}(\rho,a) \neq 0, \text{ and } \frac{\partial^2 G}{\partial w^2}(\rho,a) \neq 0.
\tag{9}
$$

This was checked by computing

$$
p_1(z) = \gcd_w(G(z,w), \frac{\partial}{\partial z}G(z,w)), \quad p_2(z) = \gcd_w(G(z,w), \frac{\partial^2}{\partial w^2}G(z,w)),
$$

$\gcd(p_1(z), m_\rho(z))$ and $\gcd(p_2(z), m_\rho(z))$, obtaining a constant depending only on k, that is non-zero for all $k \neq 54$ in all cases dealt with in this paper. The case $k = 54$ was dealt separately. Using the explicit value for ρ, the validity of (9) for this value of k was verified.

It now follows from (8), by noticing that the first and third summands have the smallest degrees in s, that they must have the same degree and cancel each other. Dividing, then, by s^α and letting $s \to 0$, one obtains

$$
\alpha = \frac{1}{2}, \text{ and } b = g(0) = \sqrt{\frac{2\rho\frac{\partial G}{\partial z}(\rho,a)}{\frac{\partial^2 G}{\partial w^2}(\rho,a)}}.
$$

In conclusion, for the case where $\lim_{z\to\rho} w(z) = a$, using (2), one has

$$
[z^n]w(z) \sim \frac{b}{2\sqrt{\pi}}\rho^{-n}n^{-3/2}.
$$

For the case where $\lim_{z\to\rho} w(z) = +\infty$, making $v = 1/w$ one concludes as above that $v = cs^\alpha - g(s)s^{\alpha+\beta}$, for some $0 < \alpha < 1$, $\beta > 0$, and for some Puiseux series $g(s)$, with non-negative exponents. The polynomial satisfied by v is then

$$
H(z,v) = v^n G\left(z, \frac{1}{v}\right),
\tag{10}
$$

which is the reciprocal polynomial of $G(z,w)$ with respect to the variable w. Using the same procedure as above, one computes ρ, and checking that the corresponding derivatives are non-zero, i.e.

$$
\frac{\partial H}{\partial z}(\rho,0) \neq 0, \text{ and } \frac{\partial^2 H}{\partial w^2}(\rho,0) \neq 0,
$$

one gets in the same way that

$$\alpha = \frac{1}{2}, \text{ and } c = \sqrt{\frac{2\rho \frac{\partial H}{\partial z}(\rho, 0)}{\frac{\partial^2 H}{\partial w^2}(\rho, 0)}}. \tag{11}$$

Since

$$w = \frac{1}{cs^\alpha - g(s)s^{\alpha+\beta}} = \frac{1}{c}s^{-\alpha}\frac{1}{1 - \frac{g(s)}{c}s^\beta}$$

$$= \frac{1}{c}s^{-\alpha}\left(1 + \frac{g(s)}{c}s^\beta + \frac{g(s)^2}{c^2}s^{2\beta} + \cdots\right),$$

one sees, using (3), that

$$[z^n]w(z) \sim \frac{1}{c\sqrt{\pi}}\rho^{-n}n^{-1/2}. \tag{12}$$

5   Average Sizes: Concrete Results

Let $A_k(z)$ and $B_k(z)$ be the generating functions for α_ε and $\alpha_{\overline{\varepsilon}}$, respectively. They satisfy the following equations

$$A_k(z) = 2zA_k(z)^2 + 2zA_k(z)B_k(z) + 2zB_k(z) \tag{13}$$
$$B_k(z) = kz + 2zA_k(z)B_k(z) + 2zB_k(z)^2. \tag{14}$$

From (13) one gets

$$B_k(z) = \frac{A_k(z)(1 - 2zA_k(z))}{2z(A_k(z) + 1)},$$

and then substituting $B_k(z)$ in (14) one obtains, after clearing up denominators,

$$4z^2A_k(z)^3 - (2kz^2 + 4z)A_k(z)^2 - (4kz^2 - 1)A_k(z) - 2kz^2 = 0,$$

i.e., $A_k(z)$ is an algebraic function that is a root of

$$G(z, w) = 4z^2w^3 - (2kz^2 + 4z)w^2 - (4kz^2 - 1)w - 2kz^2.$$

Using now (14) to get $A_k(z)$ as a function of $B_k(z)$, and then substituting that into (13), one easily sees that $B_k(z)$ is a root of

$$H(z, w) = 4zw^3 + 2kzw^2 - kw + k^2z.$$

Using the technique described in the previous section, one sees that $A_k(z)$ and $B_k(z)$ have the same singularity, namely the only root in the interval $]0, 1[$ of the polynomial

$$m_\rho(z) = z^3 + \frac{9z^2}{2k + 27} - \frac{z}{8k + 108} - \frac{1}{k(2k + 27)}. \tag{15}$$

Also one gets that $\alpha = \frac{1}{2}$, and that the values of $a_A = A_k(\rho)$ and of $a_B = B_k(\rho)$ are roots of the polynomials $8z^3 - kz^2 + 2kz - k$, and $8z^3 + 2kz^2 - k^2$, respectively. With all this, and writing $S_k(z) = A_k(z) + B_k(z)$ one then gets that

$$[z^n]S_k(z) \sim \frac{b_k}{2\sqrt{\pi}}\rho_k^{-n}n^{-3/2}, \tag{16}$$

where, for example,

$$b_2 = 1.089338906, \quad \rho_2 = 0.1915181504$$
$$b_{10} = 2.313181803, \quad \rho_{10} = 0.09581011247$$
$$b_{50} = 5.054983041, \quad \rho_{50} = 0.4606805763.$$

Using these results and the one mentioned in (4), the ratio of regular expressions in ssnf, $r_{(k,n)} = \frac{[z^n]S_k(n)}{[z^n]R_k(n)}$, can now be computed for any k and n. In particular, one finds that, for example, $r_{(2,1000)} = 4.427117336 \times 10^{-59}$, $r_{(10,1000)} = 2.562752010 \times 10^{-19}$, $r_{(50,1000)} = 1.517513555 \times 10^{-4}$.

5.1 Counting Letters

To obtain the asymptotic average value of several measures for regular expressions of a given size, we consider bivariate generating functions parametrized by weights of the form c_o, with $o \in \{\emptyset, \varepsilon, \sigma, +, \cdot, \star, ?\}$, associated to each regular expression element. Considering the grammar (1), let $A_k(u,z)$ and $B_k(u,z)$ be the bivariate generating functions associated to α_ε and $\alpha_{\overline{\varepsilon}}$, respectively. Then

$$A_k(u,z) = (u^{c_\bullet} + u^{c_+})zA_k(u,z)^2 + 2u^{c_+}zA_k(u,z)B_k(u,z) + (u^{c_?} + u^{c_\star})zB_k(u,z),$$
$$B_k(u,z) = ku^{c_\sigma}z + (u^{c_\bullet} + u^{c_+})zB_k(u,z)^2 + 2u^{c_\bullet}zA_k(u,z)B_k(u,z).$$

Note that A and B depend on the parameters $(c_\emptyset, c_\varepsilon, c_\sigma, c_+, c_\bullet, c_\star, c_?)$, but for sake of simplicity we choose to omit them. For computing the average number of letters those parameters are $(0,0,1,0,0,0,0)$, and analogously for each operator. The generating function $L_k(z)$ for the number of letters is given by

$$L_k(z) = \frac{\partial}{\partial u}\Bigg|_{u=1} (A_k(u,z) + B_k(u,z)).$$

Setting $A = A_k(1,z), B = B_k(1,z), A_1 = \frac{\partial}{\partial u}\Big|_{u=1} A_k(u,z), B_1 = \frac{\partial}{\partial u}\Big|_{u=1} B_k(u,z)$, so that $L_k = A_1 + B_1$, one has:

$$A = 2A^2z + 2ABz + 2Bz,$$
$$B = 2ABz + 2B^2z + kz,$$
$$A_1 = 4AA_1z + 2AB_1z + 2BA_1z + 2B_1z,$$
$$B_1 = 2AB_1z + 2BA_1z + 4BB_1z + kz,$$
$$L_k = A_1 + B_1.$$

Using Gröbner basis, as mentioned above, one gets the following polynomial for $w = L_k$:

$$G(z, w) = \left(\left(8\,k^2 + 108\,k\right) z^3 + 36\,kz^2 - kz - 4\right) w^3 +$$
$$+ \left(\left(k^3 + 12\,k^2\right) z^3 + 4\,k^2 z^2 + kz\right) w - 2\,k^2 z^3 - k^2 z^2.$$

It turns out that, from this, one can deduce that the singularity for this algebraic function w has the same minimal polynomial as in (15), and so it is the same as for the number of regular expressions there considered. One then finds that, in this case, $\alpha = -\frac{1}{2}$, and that

$$[z^n]L_k(z) \sim \frac{1}{c_k\sqrt{\pi}}\rho_k^{-n}n^{-1/2}, \tag{17}$$

where, for example,

$$c_2 = 2.725255757, \quad \rho_2 = 0.1915181504,$$
$$c_{10} = 1.271387537, \quad \rho_{10} = 0.09581011247,$$
$$c_{50} = 0.5749569245, \quad \rho_{50} = 0.04606805763.$$

From this one gets, for any given k, the density of letters in expressions of size n, $\ell_k = \frac{[z^n]L_k(n)}{n[z^n]S_k(n)}$, which is independent of n since the singularities of L_k and S_k are the same. In particular, one finds that, for example, $\ell_2 = 0.4172563448$, $\ell_{10} = 0.4432524170$, $\ell_{50} = 0.4657465002$.

5.2   Size of ε-Follow Automata

Considering the parameters $(2, 3, 3, -2, -1, 3, 1)$, as defined in Sect. 2, the generating function $F_k(z)$ for the size of the $\mathcal{A}_{\varepsilon f}$ automaton is given by

$$F_k(z) = \left.\frac{\partial}{\partial u}\right|_{u=1} (A_k(u, z) + B_k(u, z)).$$

Using the same abbreviations as above, one has:

$$A = 2A^2 z + 2ABz + 2Bz$$
$$B = 2ABz + 2B^2 z + kz$$
$$A_1 = -3A^2 z - 4ABz + 4AA_1 z + 2AA_2 z + 2BA_1 z + 4Bz + 2A_2 z$$
$$A_2 = -2ABz + 2AA_2 z - 3B^2 z + 2BA_1 z + 4BA_2 z + 3kz$$
$$F_k = A_1 + A_2.$$

Proceeding as above, one can verify that the singularity for $F_k(z)$ still has the same minimal polynomial as in (15), that $\alpha = -\frac{1}{2}$, and that

$$[z^n]F_k(z) \sim \frac{1}{c_k\sqrt{\pi}}\rho_k^{-n}n^{-1/2}, \tag{18}$$

where, for example,

$$c_2 = 1.159914873, \quad \rho_2 = 0.1915181504,$$
$$c_{10} = 0.6237795132, \rho_{10} = 0.09581011247,$$
$$c_{50} = 0.3187807970, \rho_{50} = 0.4606805763.$$

For the average ratio, $f_k = \frac{[z^n]F_k(n)}{n[z^n]S_k(n)}$, between the size of the $\mathcal{A}_{\varepsilon f}$ and the size of the respective regular expression (also independent of n) one has, for example, $f_2 = 0.9803566472$, $f_{10} = 0.9034371711$, $f_{50} = 0.8400260553$.

6 Experimental Results

We ran some experiments, using the FAdo package [17], to obtain average sizes of the measures studied above for small values of k and n. For the results to be statistically significant, regular expressions were uniformly random generated using a version of the grammar for $\mathcal{S}_k$ in reverse polish notation. For each size $n \in \{200, 500, 1000\}$, and alphabet size $k \in \{2, 10, 50\}$, samples of 10000 expressions were generated. This is sufficient to ensure a 95% confidence level within a 1% error margin. The results are presented in Table 1, together with the values of ℓ_k and f_k calculated in the previous section. The last column, labeled wc, presents the worst case size of $\mathcal{A}_{\varepsilon f}$ as given in Theorem 2, for expressions of size n.

Table 1. Results for regular expressions in ssnf

k	$|\alpha|$	$|\alpha|_\Sigma$	$|\delta_{\varepsilon f}|$	$|Q_{\varepsilon f}|$	$|\varepsilon f|$	$\frac{|\alpha|_\Sigma}{|\alpha|}$	ℓ_k	$\frac{|\varepsilon f|}{|\alpha|}$	f_k	wc
2	200	83.86	112.20	52.86	165.06	0.42	**0.417**	0.83	**0.98**	1.479
	500	208.99	279.97	129.74	409.71	0.42		0.82		1.472
	1000	417.70	559.04	257.85	816.89	0.42		0.82		1.469
10	200	89.13	111.98	51.80	163.78	0.45	**0.443**	0.82	**0.90**	1.479
	500	222.09	279.11	126.91	406.02	0.44		0.81		1.472
	1000	443.77	557.72	252.30	810.02	0.44		0.81		1.469
50	200	93.63	108.53	51.29	159.82	0.47	**0.466**	0.80	**0.84**	1.479
	500	233.34	270.66	125.80	396.46	0.47		0.79		1.472
	1000	466.20	540.84	249.94	790.78	0.47		0.79		1.469

7 Conclusions

The average complexity results obtained for expressions in ssnf are only slightly smaller than the ones obtained for general regular expressions. Indeed, for the size of $\mathcal{A}_{\varepsilon f}$, and the same values of k, the asymptotic values obtained in [3], were $f_2 = 1.2$, $f_{10} = 1$, and $f_{50} = 0.9$. In that study, we got an explicit expression, depending on k, for the asymptotic size of $\mathcal{A}_{\varepsilon f}$, allowing us to compute its limit of 0.75 as k goes to ∞. Here we were not able to obtain such an expression, but we conjecture that the limit is the same. This would mean that the average size is half the worst-case one. This is corroborated by the experimental results. Furthermore, the ratio between the number of ssnf expressions and the number of general expressions, of a certain size, tends to zero.

References

1. Antimirov, V.M.: Partial derivatives of regular expressions and finite automaton constructions. Theor. Comput. Sci. **155**(2), 291–319 (1996)
2. Broda, S., Machiavelo, A., Moreira, N., Reis, R.: On the average state complexity of partial derivative automata: an analytic combinatorics approach. Int. J. Found. Comput. Sci. **22**(7), 1593–1606 (2011)
3. Broda, S., Machiavelo, A., Moreira, N., Reis, R.: A hitchhiker's guide to descriptional complexity through analytic combinatorics. Theor. Comput. Sci. **528**, 85–100 (2014)
4. Broda, S., Machiavelo, A., Moreira, N., Reis, R.: Average size of automata constructions from regular expressions. BEATCS **116**, 167–192 (2015)
5. Brüggemann-Klein, A.: Regular expressions into finite automata. Theor. Comput. Sci. **48**, 197–213 (1993)
6. Champarnaud, J.M., Ouardi, F., Ziadi, D.: Normalized expressions and finite automata. Int. J. Algebra Comput. **17**(1), 141–154 (2007)
7. Champarnaud, J.M., Ziadi, D.: Canonical derivatives, partial derivatives and finite automaton constructions. Theor. Comput. Sci. **289**, 137–163 (2002)
8. Flajolet, P., Sedgewick, R.: Analytic Combinatorics. CUP, Cambridge (2008)
9. Glushkov, V.M.: The abstract theory of automata. Russ. Math. Surv. **16**(5), 1–53 (1961)
10. Gruber, H., Gulan, S.: Simplifying regular expressions. In: Dediu, A.-H., Fernau, H., Martín-Vide, C. (eds.) LATA 2010. LNCS, vol. 6031, pp. 285–296. Springer, Heidelberg (2010). doi:10.1007/978-3-642-13089-2_24
11. Gulan, S.: On the relative descriptional complexity of regular expressions and finite automata. Ph.D. thesis, Universität Trier (2011)
12. Gulan, S., Fernau, H.: Local elimination-strategies in automata for shorter regular expressions. In: Geffert, V., Karhumäki, J., Bertoni, A., Preneel, B., Návrat, P., Bieliková, M. (eds.) SOFSEM 2008, Vol. II, pp. 46–57 (2008)
13. Hille, E.: Analytic Function Theory, vol. 2. Blaisdell Publishing Company, New York (1962)
14. Ilie, L., Yu, S.: Follow automata. Inf. Comput. **186**(1), 140–162 (2003)
15. Lang, S.: Algebra. Graduate Texts in Mathematics, vol. 211, 3rd edn. Springer, New York (2001)
16. Ott, G., Feinstein, N.H.: Design of sequential machines from their regular expressions. J. ACM **8**(4), 585–600 (1961)
17. Project FAdo: tools for formal languages manipulation. http://fado.dcc.up.pt. Accessed Feb 2017
18. Thompson, K.: Regular expression search algorithm. Commun. ACM **11**(6), 410–422 (1968)

Most Complex Non-returning Regular Languages

Janusz A. Brzozowski[1(✉)] and Sylvie Davies[2]

[1] David R. Cheriton School of Computer Science, University of Waterloo,
Waterloo, ON N2L 3G1, Canada
brzozo@uwaterloo.ca
[2] Department of Pure Mathematics, University of Waterloo, Waterloo,
ON N2L 3G1, Canada
sldavies@uwaterloo.ca

Abstract. A regular language L is non-returning if in the minimal deterministic finite automaton accepting it there are no transitions into the initial state. Eom, Han and Jirásková derived upper bounds on the state complexity of boolean operations and Kleene star, and proved that these bounds are tight using two different binary witnesses. They derived upper bounds for concatenation and reversal using three different ternary witnesses. These five witnesses use a total of six different transformations. We show that for each $n \geqslant 4$ there exists a ternary witness of state complexity n that meets the bound for reversal and that at least three letters are needed to meet this bound. Moreover, the restrictions of this witness to binary alphabets meet the bounds for product, star, and boolean operations. We also derive tight upper bounds on the state complexity of binary operations that take arguments with different alphabets. We prove that the maximal syntactic semigroup of a non-returning language has $(n-1)^n$ elements and requires at least $\binom{n}{2}$ generators. We find the maximal state complexities of atoms of non-returning languages. Finally, we show that there exists a most complex non-returning language that meets the bounds for all these complexity measures.

Keywords: Atom · Boolean operation · Concatenation · Different alphabets · Most complex · Non-returning · Reversal · Regular · Star · State complexity · Syntactic semigroup · Transition semigroup · Unrestricted complexity

1 Introduction

Formal definitions are postponed until Sect. 2; we assume the reader is familiar with basic properties of regular languages and finite automata as described in [11, 13], for example.

This work was supported by the Natural Sciences and Engineering Research Council of Canada grant No. OGP0000871.

G. Pighizzini and C. Câmpeanu (Eds.): DCFS 2017, LNCS 10316, pp. 89–101, 2017.
DOI: 10.1007/978-3-319-60252-3_7

A deterministic finite automaton (DFA) is *non-returning* if there are no transitions into its initial state. A regular language is non-returning if its minimal DFA has that property. The *state complexity* of a regular language L, denoted by $\kappa(L)$, is the number of states in the minimal DFA accepting L. The state complexity of an *operation* on regular languages is the maximal state complexity of the result of the operation, expressed as a function of the state complexities of the operands.

The state complexities of common operations (union, intersection, difference, symmetric difference, Kleene star, reverse and product/concatenation) were studied by Eom et al. [7]. They pointed out that several interesting subclasses of regular languages have the non-returning property; these subclasses include the class of suffix-free languages (suffix codes) and its subclasses (for example, bifix-free languages), and finite languages.

A regular language $L_n(a, b, c)$ of state complexity n is defined for all $n \geqslant 3$ in Fig. 1. It was shown in [2] that the sequence $(L_3(a, b, c), \dots, L_n(a, b, c), \dots)$ of these languages meets the upper bounds (for regular languages) on the complexities of all the basic operations on regular languages as follows: If $L(b, a)$ is $L(a, b)$ with the roles of a and b interchanged, then $L_m(a, b) \circ L_n(b, a)$ meets the bound mn for all binary boolean operations $\circ$ that depend on both arguments; if $m \neq n$, $L_m(a, b) \circ L_n(a, b)$ meets the bound mn; $(L_n(a, b))^*$ meets the bound $2^{n-1} + 2^{n-2}$ for star; $(L_n(a, b, c))^R$ meets the bound 2^n for reversal; and $L_m(a, b, c)L_n(a, b, c)$ meets the bound $(m-1)2^n + 2^{n-1}$ for product.

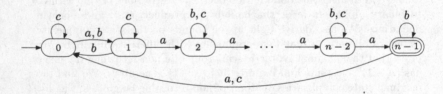

Fig. 1. Most complex regular language $L_n(a, b, c)$

It was proposed in [2] that the size of the *syntactic semigroup* of a regular language is another worthwhile measure of the complexity of the language. The syntactic semigroup is isomorphic to the *transition semigroup* of the minimal DFA of L, that is, the semigroup of transformations of the state set of the DFA induced by non-empty words.

Another complexity measure suggested in [2] is the number and state complexities of the atoms of the language, where an atom is a certain kind of intersection of complemented and uncomplemented quotients of L.

It was shown in [2] that the languages $L_n(a, b, c)$ not only meet the bounds on the state complexities of operations, but also have the largest syntactic semigroups (of size n^n), and the largest number of atoms (2^n), all of which have the maximal possible state complexities. In this sense these are *most complex* regular languages.

In this paper we show that there also exist most complex non-returning languages. For each $n \geqslant 4$, we define a language of state complexity n. We prove that the syntactic semigroup of this language has $(n-1)^n$ elements (the maximal possible for non-returning languages), that it is generated by $\binom{n}{2}$ elements, and that the number of generators cannot be reduced. We also show that this language has 2^n atoms, all of which have maximal state complexity. We demonstrate that the upper bound on the state complexity of reversal is met by a single ternary language, and that no binary language meets this bound. Moreover, restrictions of this language to binary alphabets meet the bounds for star, product and boolean operations. This is in contrast to [7] where several types of witnesses are used to meet the various bounds. We correct an error in [7, Table 1], where it is stated that the upper bound on the complexity of product cannot be reached with binary witnesses. Additionally, we consider both *restricted* and *unrestricted* state complexity [3] of binary operations on non-returning languages. When computing restricted state complexity, one assumes the operation takes in two languages over the same alphabet; for unrestricted state complexity we allow the inputs to be languages over different alphabets.

Omitted proofs can be found at http://arxiv.org/abs/1701.03944.

2 Preliminaries

A *deterministic finite automaton (DFA)* is a quintuple $\mathcal{D} = (Q, \Sigma, \delta, q_0, F)$, where Q is a finite non-empty set of *states*, Σ is a finite non-empty *alphabet*, $\delta: Q \times \Sigma \to Q$ is the *transition function*, $q_0 \in Q$ is the *initial* state, and $F \subseteq Q$ is the set of *final* states. We extend δ to a function $\delta: Q \times \Sigma^* \to Q$ as usual. A DFA $\mathcal{D}$ *accepts* a word $w \in \Sigma^*$ if $\delta(q_0, w) \in F$. The language accepted by $\mathcal{D}$ is denoted by $L(\mathcal{D})$. If q is a state of $\mathcal{D}$, then the language $L_q(\mathcal{D})$ of q is the language accepted by the DFA $(Q, \Sigma, \delta, q, F)$. A state is *empty* if its language is empty. Two states p and q of $\mathcal{D}$ are *equivalent* if $L_p(\mathcal{D}) = L_q(\mathcal{D})$. A state q is *reachable* if there exists $w \in \Sigma^*$ such that $\delta(q_0, w) = q$. A DFA is *minimal* if all of its states are reachable and no two states are equivalent.

We use $Q_n = \{0, \ldots, n-1\}$ as our basic set with n elements. A *transformation* of Q_n is a mapping $t: Q_n \to Q_n$. The *image* of $q \in Q_n$ under t is denoted by qt, and this notation is extended to subsets of Q_n: if $P \subseteq Q_n$, then $Pt = \{qt : q \in P\}$. The *rank* of a transformation t is the cardinality of $Q_n t$. If s and t are transformations of Q_n, their composition is denoted $(qs)t$ when applied to $q \in Q_n$. Let $\mathcal{T}_{Q_n}$ be the set of all n^n transformations of Q_n; then $\mathcal{T}_{Q_n}$ is a monoid under composition.

For $k \geqslant 2$, a transformation t of a set $P = \{q_0, q_1, \ldots, q_{k-1}\} \subseteq Q_n$ is a *k-cycle* if $q_0 t = q_1, q_1 t = q_2, \ldots, q_{k-2} t = q_{k-1}, q_{k-1} t = q_0$. This k-cycle is denoted by $(q_0, q_1, \ldots, q_{k-1})$, and leaves the states in $Q_n \setminus P$ unchanged. A 2-cycle (q_0, q_1) is called a *transposition*. A transformation that sends state p to q and acts as the identity on the remaining states is denoted by $(p \to q)$. If a transformation of Q_n has rank $n-1$, then there is exactly one pair of distinct elements $i, j \in Q_n$ such that $it = jt$. We say a transformation t of Q_n is of *type* $\{i, j\}$ if t has rank $n-1$ and $it = jt$ for $i < j$.

The *syntactic congruence* of a language $L \subseteq \Sigma^*$ is defined on Σ^+ as follows: For $x, y \in \Sigma^+$, $x \approx_L y$ if and only if $wxz \in L \Leftrightarrow wyz \in L$ for all $w, z \in \Sigma^*$. The quotient set $\Sigma^+/\approx_L$ of equivalence classes of $\approx_L$ is a semigroup, the *syntactic semigroup* T_L of L.

Let $\mathcal{D} = (Q_n, \Sigma, \delta, 0, F)$ be a DFA. For each word $w \in \Sigma^*$, the transition function induces a transformation δ_w of Q_n by w: for all $q \in Q_n$, $q\delta_w = \delta(q, w)$. The set $T_\mathcal{D}$ of all such transformations by non-empty words is the *transition semigroup* of $\mathcal{D}$ under composition [12]. Often we use the word w to denote the transformation t it induces; thus we write qw instead of $q\delta_w$. We also write $w: t$ to mean that w induces the transformation t.

If $\mathcal{D}$ is a minimal DFA of L, then $T_\mathcal{D}$ is isomorphic to the syntactic semigroup T_L of L [12], and we represent elements of T_L by transformations in $T_\mathcal{D}$. The size of this semigroup has been used as a measure of complexity [2,6,8,10].

The (left) *quotient* of $L \subseteq \Sigma^*$ by a word $w \in \Sigma^*$ is the language $w^{-1}L = \{x : wx \in L\}$. It is well known that the number of quotients of a regular language is finite and equal to the state complexity of the language.

Atoms are defined by a left congruence, where two words x and y are congruent whenever $ux \in L$ if and only if $uy \in L$ for all $u \in \Sigma^*$. Thus x and y are congruent whenever $x \in u^{-1}L$ if and only if $y \in u^{-1}L$ for all $u \in \Sigma^*$. An equivalence class of this relation is an *atom* of L [5]. Atoms can be expressed as non-empty intersections of complemented and uncomplemented quotients of L (see Sect. 5). The number of atoms and their state complexities were suggested as measures of complexity of regular languages [2] because all quotients of a language and all quotients of its atoms are unions of atoms [4,5,9].

Suppose $\circ$ is a unary operation on languages, and $f(n)$ is an upper bound on the state complexity of this operation. If the state complexity of $(L_n)^\circ$ is $f(n)$, then L_n is called a *witness* to the state complexity of $\circ$ for that n. In general, we need a sequence $(L_k, L_{k+1}, \ldots,)$ of such languages; this sequence is called a *stream*. Often a stream does not start at 1 because the bound may not hold for small values of n. For a binary operation we need two streams. The languages in a stream usually have the same form and differ only in the parameter n.

Sometimes the same stream can be used for both operands of a binary operation, but this is not always possible. For example, for boolean operations when $m = n$, the state complexity of $L_n \cup L_n = L_n$ is n, whereas the upper bound is $mn = n^2$. However, in many cases the second language is a "dialect" of the first, that is, it "differs only slightly" from the first. A *dialect* of $L_n(\Sigma)$ is a language obtained from $L_n(\Sigma)$ by deleting some letters of Σ in the words of $L_n(\Sigma)$ – by this we mean that words containing these letters are deleted – or replacing them by letters of another alphabet Σ'. Here we encounter only two types of dialects:

1. A dialect in which some letters were deleted; for example, $L_n(a, b)$ is a dialect of $L_n(a, b, c)$ with c deleted, and $L_n(a, -, c)$ is a dialect with b deleted.
2. A dialect in which the roles of two letters are exchanged; for example, $L_n(b, a)$ is such a dialect of $L_n(a, b)$.

These two types of dialects can be combined, for example, in $L_n(a, -, b)$ the letter c is deleted, and b plays the role that c played originally. The notion of dialects also extends to DFAs; for example, if $\mathcal{D}_n(a, b, c)$ recognizes $L_n(a, b, c)$ then $\mathcal{D}_n(a, -, b)$ recognizes the dialect $L_n(a, -, b)$.

3   Main Results

From now on by *complexity* we mean *state complexity*.

Let $\Gamma = \{a_{i,j} : 0 \leqslant i < j \leqslant n - 1\}$, where $a_{i,j}$ is a letter that induces any transformation of type $\{i, j\}$ and does not map any state to 0. Let $\Gamma' = \Gamma \setminus \{a_{0,n-1}, a_{0,1}, a_{1,n-1}, a_{0,2}\}$. Let $\Sigma = \{a, b, c, d\} \cup \Gamma'$, where $a : (1, \ldots, n-1)(0 \to 1)$, $b : (1,2)(0 \to 2)$, $c : (2, \ldots, n-1)(1 \to 2)(0 \to 1)$, and $d : (0 \to 2)$. Note that a, b, c and d are transformations of types $\{0, n-1\}$, $\{0, 1\}$, $\{1, n-1\}$ and $\{0, 2\}$, respectively. Note also that a, b and c restricted to $Q_n \setminus \{0\}$ generate all the transformations of $\{1, \ldots, n-1\}$. This follows from the well-known fact that the full transformation semigroup on a set X can be generated by the symmetric group on X together with a transformation of X with rank $|X| - 1$. For $X = \{1, \ldots, n-1\}$, we see that $\{(1, \ldots, n-1), (1,2)\}$ (the restrictions of a and b) generate the symmetric group, and $(2, \ldots, n-1)(1 \to 2)$ (the restriction of c) is a transformation of rank $|X| - 1 = n - 2$.

We are now ready to define a most complex non-returning DFA and language.

Definition 1. *For $n \geqslant 4$, let $\mathcal{D}_n = \mathcal{D}_n(\Sigma) = (Q_n, \Sigma, \delta_n, 0, \{n-1\})$, where $\Sigma = \{a, b, c, d\} \cup \Gamma'$, and δ_n is defined in accordance with the transformations described above. See Fig. 2 for $\mathcal{D}_n(\Sigma)$ restricted to $\{a, b, c, d\}$. Let $L_n = L_n(\Sigma)$ be the language accepted by $\mathcal{D}_n(\Sigma)$.*

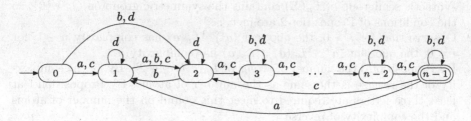

Fig. 2. Most complex non-returning language $L_n(\Sigma)$ of Definition 1. The letters in $\Gamma' = \Sigma \setminus \{a, b, c, d\}$ are omitted

Theorem 1 (Most Complex Non-returning Languages). *For each $n \geqslant 4$, the DFA of Definition 1 is minimal and non-returning. The stream $(L_n(\Sigma) : n \geqslant 4)$ with some dialect streams is most complex in the class of regular non-returning languages in the following sense:*

1. *The syntactic semigroup of $L_n(\Sigma)$ has cardinality $(n-1)^n$, and at least $\binom{n}{2}$ letters are required to reach this bound.*
2. *Each quotient of $L_n(a)$ has complexity $n-1$, except L itself, which has complexity n.*
3. *The reverse of $L_n(a, b, c)$ has complexity 2^n, and at least three letters are needed to meet this bound. Moreover, $L_n(a, b, c)$ has 2^n atoms.*

4. *For each atom A_S of $L_n(\Sigma)$, the complexity $\kappa(A_S)$ satisfies:*

$$\kappa(A_S) = \begin{cases} 2^{n-1}, & \text{if } S \in \{\emptyset, Q_n\}; \\ 2 + \sum_{x=1}^{|S|} \sum_{y=1}^{|S|} \binom{n-1}{x}\binom{n-1-x}{y}, & \text{if } \emptyset \subsetneq S \subsetneq Q_n. \end{cases}$$

Moreover, at least $\binom{n}{2}$ letters are required to meet these bounds.
5. *The star of $L_n(a,b)$ has complexity 2^{n-1}.*
6. *Let $m, n \geqslant 4$.*
   (a) *Restricted product: $\kappa(L_m(a,b)L_n(a,-,b)) = (m-1)2^{n-1} + 1$.*
   (b) *Unrestricted product: $\kappa(L_m(a,b)L_n(a,-,b,d)) = m2^{n-1} + 1$.*
7. *Let $m, n \geqslant 4$.*
   (a) *Restricted boolean operations: $\kappa(L_m(a,b) \circ L_n(b,a)) = mn - (m+n-2)$.*
   (b) *Additionally, when $m \neq n$, we can use the same witness for both arguments: $\kappa(L_m(a,b) \circ L_n(a,b)) = mn - (m+n-2)$.*
   (c) *Unrestricted boolean operations: The complexity of $L_m(a,b,c) \circ L_n(b,a,d)$ is $mn + 1$ if $\circ \in \{\cup, \oplus\}$, that of $L_m(a,b,c) \setminus L_n(b,a)$ is $mn - n + 1$, and that of $L_m(a,b) \cap L_n(b,a)$ is $mn - (m+n-2)$.*

All of these bounds are maximal for non-returning languages.

Proof. From the definition of the letters of Σ it is obvious that the DFA $\mathcal{D}_n$ is non-returning, and that any pair (p,q) of states can be distinguished by the shortest word in a^* accepted by p but not by q.

1. This follows from Propositions 1 and 2 below. In particular, note that the syntactic semigroup of $L_n(\Sigma)$ contains the symmetric group on $Q_n \setminus \{0\}$, so the conditions of Proposition 2 are met.
2. Observe that for $i > 0$, the quotient $(a^i)^{-1}L_n(a)$ has complexity $n - 1$; for $i = 0$, the quotient $(a^0)^{-1}L_n(a) = L_n(a)$ has complexity n.
3. By Proposition 3 the number of atoms of $L_n(a,b,c)$ is 2^n. By [5] the complexity of the reverse is the same as the number of atoms. By Proposition 4 at least three letters are required to meet this bound on the number of atoms and the complexity of reverse.
4. See Propositions 5, 6, and 7.
5. See Proposition 8.
6. See Propositions 9 and 10.
7. See Propositions 11 and 12.

We prove Propositions 1, 2, 3, 4 and 11 below.   □

4   Syntactic Semigroup

For all basic operations on non-returning languages, the complexity bounds can be met with either binary or ternary witnesses [7]. However, to meet the bound for the size of the syntactic semigroup, our most complex stream is forced to use an alphabet that grows quadratically in size.

For $n \geqslant 2$, let N_n denote the semigroup of transformations of Q_n such that it $\neq 0$ for all $i \in Q_n$. We call N_n the *full non-returning semigroup* on Q_n. We give a necessary condition and a sufficient condition for a set G to generate N_n.

Proposition 1. *If G is a generating set for N_n, then G contains a transformation of type $\{i,j\}$ for each $\{i,j\} \subseteq Q_n$. Thus a minimal generating set has exactly one element of type $\{i,j\}$ for each of the $\binom{n}{2}$ sets $\{i,j\} \subseteq Q_n$.*

Proof. Suppose t is a transformation of type $\{i,j\}$, and let t' be an arbitrary transformation. If tt' has rank $n-1$, then tt' has type $\{i,j\}$. Indeed, since $it = jt$, it follows that $itt' = jtt'$. Thus composing a transformation of type $\{i,j\}$ with an arbitrary transformation either preserves the type, or lowers the rank.

Suppose G generates N_n. Observe that N_n does not contain transformations of rank n (since these map some element to 0). Since composition with a transformation of type $\{i,j\}$ either preserves type or lowers rank, the semigroup generated by G contains only transformations that either have the same type as some element of G, or have rank less than $n-1$ and so are typeless. But N_n contains a transformation of type $\{i,j\}$ for each $\{i,j\} \subseteq Q_n$. So if G generates N_n, then G must contain an element of type $\{i,j\}$ for each $\{i,j\} \subseteq Q_n$. $\qquad\square$

Proposition 2. *Let G be a subset of N_n that contains a transformation of type $\{i,j\}$ for each set $\{i,j\} \subseteq Q_n$, $i < j$. Let G' be obtained by restricting every transformation in G to $Q_n \setminus \{0\}$. If G' generates the symmetric group on $Q_n \setminus \{0\}$, then G generates N_n.*

Proof. First, we show that G' in fact generates the full transformation semigroup on $Q_n \setminus \{0\}$. Recall that the full transformation semigroup on X is generated by the symmetric group on X together with a transformation of X of rank $|X| - 1$. By assumption, G' contains generators of the symmetric group on $Q_n \setminus \{0\}$. Transformations in G of type $\{i,j\}$ with $0 < i < j$ have rank $n - 1$, and furthermore their restrictions to $Q_n \setminus \{0\}$ are of rank $n - 2$.

Thus G' contains generators of the symmetric group on $Q_n \setminus \{0\}$, as well as a transformation of rank $|Q_n \setminus \{0\}| - 1 = n - 2$; it follows that G' generates the full transformation semigroup on $Q_n \setminus \{0\}$.

Now, we prove that G generates every transformation in N_n. Let t be an element of N_n; we want to show that t is in the semigroup generated by G. Since N_n does not contain any transformations of rank n, the transformation t has rank less than n, and thus there exist distinct $i,j \in Q_n$ such that $it = jt$. Select a transformation s of type $\{i,j\}$ in G. Then for distinct $q, q' \in Q_n$, we have $qs = q's$ if and only if $\{q, q'\} = \{i, j\}$.

Hence there is a well-defined transformation r' of $Q_n \setminus \{0\}$ given by $(qs)r' = qt$ for all $q \in Q$; it is well-defined since if we have $qs = q's$, then $\{q, q'\} = \{i, j\}$ and is and js get mapped to a common element $it = jt$. The transformation r' lies in the full transformation semigroup on $Q_n \setminus \{0\}$, and so it is in the semigroup generated by G'. Hence there is some transformation r of Q_n in the semigroup generated by G such that r is equal to r' when restricted to $Q_n \setminus \{0\}$.

Since $qs \in Q_n \setminus \{0\}$ for all $q \in Q_n$, it follows that $(qs)r = (qs)r' = qt$ for all $q \in Q_n$, and thus sr and t are equal as transformations. Since s is in G and r is in the semigroup generated by G, it follows $sr = t$ is in the semigroup generated by G. Thus the semigroup generated by G contains all elements of N_n; but G is a subset of N_n, so G generates N_n. $\qquad\square$

5   Number and Complexities of Atoms

Denote the complement of a language L by $\overline{L} = \Sigma^* \setminus L$. Let $Q_n = \{0, \ldots, n-1\}$ and let L_n be a non-empty regular language with quotients $K = \{K_0, \ldots, K_{n-1}\}$. Each subset S of Q_n defines an *atomic intersection* $A_S = \bigcap_{i \in S} K_i \cap \bigcap_{i \in \overline{S}} \overline{K_i}$, where $\overline{S} = Q_n \setminus S$. An *atom* of L is a non-empty atomic intersection; this definition is equivalent to that given in Sect. 2 in terms of a left congruence. Note that if $S \neq T$, then $A_S \cap A_T = \emptyset$; that is, atoms corresponding to distinct subsets of Q_n are disjoint. A language of complexity n can have at most 2^n atoms, since there are 2^n subsets of Q. We show that this bound can be met by non-returning languages. Additionally, we derive upper bounds on the complexities of atoms of non-returning languages, and show that our most complex stream meets these bounds.

We now describe a construction due to Iván [9]. Let L be a regular language with DFA $\mathcal{D} = (Q, \Sigma, \delta, q_0, F)$. For each $S \subseteq Q$, we define a DFA $\mathcal{D}_S = (Q_S, \Sigma, \Delta, (S, \overline{S}), F_S)$ as follows.

- $Q_S = \{(X, Y) : X, Y \subseteq Q, X \cap Y = \emptyset\} \cup \{\bot\}$. State $\bot$ is the *sink state*.
- $\Delta((X, Y), a) = (Xa, Ya)$ if $Xa \cap Ya = \emptyset$, and otherwise $\Delta((X, Y), a) = \bot$; also $\Delta(\bot, a) = \bot$.
- $F_S = \{(X, Y) : X \subseteq F, Y \subseteq \overline{F}\}$.

The DFA $\mathcal{D}_S$ recognizes the atomic intersection A_S of L; if it recognizes a non-empty language, then A_S is an atom. We can determine the complexity of A_S by counting reachable and distinguishable states in $\mathcal{D}_S$.

Proposition 3. *The language $L_n = L_n(a, b, c)$ has 2^n atoms.*

Proof. We want to show that A_S is an atom of L_n for all $S \subseteq Q_n$. It suffices to show for each S that the DFA $\mathcal{D}_S$ recognizes at least one word. Then since atoms corresponding to different subsets of Q_n are disjoint, this proves there are 2^n distinct atoms.

First, we show that from the initial state $(S, \overline{S})$, we can reach some state of the form (X, Y) where $0 \notin X$ and $0 \notin Y$. Consider the set $\{0, 1, n-1\}$. Notice that for each subset $\{i, j\}$ of $\{0, 1, n-1\}$, we have a transformation of type $\{i, j\}$: a has type $\{0, n-1\}$, b has type $\{0, 1\}$, and c has type $\{1, n-1\}$. Additionally, by the pigeonhole principle, either S contains two distinct elements from $\{0, 1, n-1\}$, or $\overline{S}$ contains two distinct elements from $\{0, 1, n-1\}$.

Suppose without loss of generality it is S which contains two distinct elements from $\{0, 1, n-1\}$. Let $\{i, j\} \subseteq S$ for some $\{i, j\} \subseteq \{0, 1, n-1\}$ with $i \neq j$. Let $\sigma \in \Sigma$ be the letter inducing the transformation of type $\{i, j\}$. Then we claim $(S, \overline{S})\sigma \neq \bot$. Indeed, suppose that $q \in S\sigma \cap \overline{S}\sigma$. Then since σ is a transformation of type $\{i, j\}$, we must have $i\sigma = j\sigma = q$, and no other element is mapped to q. But $\{i, j\} \subseteq S$, so we cannot have $q \in \overline{S}\sigma$.

Hence $S\sigma \cap \overline{S}\sigma = \emptyset$. Furthermore, since σ is a non-returning transformation, we have $0 \notin S\sigma$ and $0 \notin \overline{S}\sigma$. Thus starting from the initial state $(S, \overline{S})$, we can apply σ to reach a state of the form (X, Y) with $0 \notin X$ and $0 \notin Y$.

Now, recall that the three transformations $\{a, b, c\}$, when restricted to $Q_n \setminus \{0\}$, generate all transformations of $Q_n \setminus \{0\}$. Since $X \subseteq Q_n \setminus \{0\}$, there exists a transformation of $Q_n \setminus \{0\}$ that maps every element of X to $n - 1$ and every element of $(Q_n \setminus \{0\}) \setminus X$ to 1. Let $w \in \{a, b, c\}^*$ be a word that induces this transformation when restricted to $Q_n \setminus \{0\}$. Since $Y \subseteq Q_n \setminus \{0\}$ and Y is disjoint from X, it follows that w maps every element of Y to 1. Since $F_n = \{n - 1\}$ is the final state set of $\mathcal{D}_n$, we see that $Xw \subseteq F_n$ and $Yw \subseteq \overline{F_n}$. Thus $(Xw, Yw) = (\{n - 1\}, \{1\})$ is a final state of $\mathcal{D}_S$.

This shows that there exists a word $\sigma w \in \{a, b, c\}^*$ that maps the initial state $(S, \overline{S})$ of $\mathcal{D}_S$ to a final state. Thus A_S is an atom. $\square$

Next, we prove that the bound on number of atoms cannot be met by a binary witness. From [5] we know that the number of atoms of a regular language is equal to the state complexity of the reverse of the language. Hence this also proves a conjecture from [7], that a ternary witness is necessary to meet the bound for reversal of non-returning languages.

Proposition 4. *Let L be a non-returning language of complexity n over $\Sigma = \{a, b\}$. Then the number of atoms of L is strictly less than 2^n.*

Proof. Let $\mathcal{D}$ be the minimal DFA of L, with state set Q_n. We introduce some special terminology for this proof, which generalizes the notion of transformations of type $\{i, j\}$. We say that a transformation t *unifies* i and j, or unifies the set $\{i, j\}$, if $it = jt$. For example, transformations of type $\{i, j\}$ unify $\{i, j\}$. But furthermore, every transformation of Q_n of rank $n - 1$ or less unifies at least one pair of elements of Q_n. The transition semigroup of $\mathcal{D}$ cannot have transformations of rank n, since L is non-returning; thus all the transformations in the transition semigroup must unify some pair of states.

Suppose that in $\mathcal{D}$, the letter a induces a transformation that unifies $\{i, j\}$, and b induces a transformation that unifies $\{k, \ell\}$. Assume also that $i \neq j$ and $k \neq \ell$. We will show that at least one atomic intersection A_S of L is empty, and thus is not an atom.

Suppose $\{i, j\} = \{k, \ell\}$. Let $S = \{i\}$ and consider the atomic intersection A_S. The initial state of the DFA for A_S is $(\{i\}, \overline{S})$. Note that $j \in \overline{S}$, so $ja \in \overline{S}a$. But a unifies i and j, so $ja = ia \in \{i\}a$. Thus since $\{i\}a \cap \overline{S}a \neq \emptyset$, the letter a sends the initial state $(\{i\}, \overline{S})$ to the sink state. Since b also unifies i and j, the letter b also sends $(\{i\}, \overline{S})$ to the sink state. Thus A_S is non-empty if and only if $(\{i\}, \overline{S})$ is a final state. In fact, either A_S is non-empty or $A_S = \{\varepsilon\}$, since every non-empty word sends the initial state $(\{i\}, \overline{S})$ to the sink state. If we let $T = \{j\}$, the same argument shows that A_T is either empty or $A_T = \{\varepsilon\}$. But $A_S \cap A_T = \emptyset$, so one of A_S or A_T must be empty.

Now, suppose $\{i, j\} \cap \{k, \ell\} = \emptyset$. Let $S = \{i, k\}$ and consider the atomic intersection A_S. The initial state of the DFA for A_S is $(\{i, k\}, \overline{S})$ with $j, \ell \in \overline{S}$. Thus as before, the transformation a which unifies $\{i, j\}$ and the transformation b which unifies $\{k, \ell\}$ both send A_S to the sink state. So either A_S is empty or $A_S = \{\varepsilon\}$. For $T = \{j, \ell\}$, the same argument shows that either A_T is empty or $A_T = \{\varepsilon\}$. Hence as before, one of A_S or A_T is empty.

Finally, suppose $\{i,j\} \cap \{k,\ell\}$ has exactly one element. Then either $k \in \{i,j\}$ or $\ell \in \{i,j\}$. Assume without loss of generality that $\ell \in \{i,j\}$ and $\ell = i$; otherwise rename the elements so this is the case. Then a unifies $\{i,j\}$, and b unifies $\{i,k\}$. Let $S = \{i\}$ and consider A_S. As before, the initial state of the DFA for A_S is sent to the sink state by both a and b. Thus either A_S is empty or $A_S = \{\varepsilon\}$. For $T = \{j,k\}$, the same argument shows that either A_T is empty or $A_T = \{\varepsilon\}$. Hence one of A_S or A_T is empty. $\qquad\square$

Proposition 5. *Let L be a non-returning language of complexity n, and let Q_n be the state set of its minimal DFA. Let $S \subseteq Q_n$; then we have*

$$\kappa(A_S) \leqslant \begin{cases} 2^{n-1}, & \text{if } S \in \{\emptyset, Q_n\}; \\ 2 + \sum_{x=1}^{|S|} \sum_{y=1}^{|S|} \binom{n-1}{x}\binom{n-1-x}{y}, & \text{if } \emptyset \subsetneq S \subsetneq Q_n. \end{cases}$$

Proposition 6. *The atoms of the language $L_n = L_n(\Sigma)$ meet the complexity bounds of Proposition 5.*

Proposition 7. *Let L be a non-returning language over Σ of complexity n. If the atoms of L meet the bounds of Proposition 5, then Σ has size at least $\binom{n}{2}$.*

6 Other Operations

Proposition 8 (Star). *Let $\mathcal{D}_n(a,b)$ be the DFA of Definition 1 and let $L_n(a,b)$ be its language. Then the complexity of $(L_n(a,b))^*$ is 2^{n-1}.*

When dealing with binary operations, to avoid confusion between the sets of states $\{0,\ldots,m-1\}$ and $\{0,\ldots,n-1\}$ we use $\mathcal{D}'_m(\Sigma) = (Q'_m, \Sigma, \delta'_m, 0', \{(m-1)'\})$, and $\mathcal{D}_n(\Sigma) = (Q_n, \Sigma, \delta_n, 0, \{n-1\})$, where $Q'_m = \{0', \ldots, (m-1)'\}$. We write $L'_m(\Sigma)$ for the language of $\mathcal{D}'_m(\Sigma)$.

Proposition 9 (Restricted Product). *Let $\mathcal{D}_n(a,b,c)$ be the DFA of Definition 1 and let $L_n(a,b,c)$ be its language. Then for $m,n \geqslant 4$ the complexity of $L'_m(a,b)L_n(a,-,b)$ is $(m-1)2^{n-1} + 1$.*

Proposition 10 (Unrestricted Product). *For $m,n \geqslant 4$, let L'_m (respectively, L_n) be a non-returning language of complexity m (respectively, n) over an alphabet Σ', (respectively, Σ). Then the complexity of product is at most $m2^{n+1} + 1$, and this bound is met by $L'_m(a,b)$ and $L_n(a,-,b,d)$.*

A binary boolean operation is *proper* if it is not a constant function or a function of only one argument.

Proposition 11 (Restricted Boolean Operations). *Let $\mathcal{D}_n(a,b)$ be the DFA of Definition 1 and let $L_n(a,b)$ be its language. Then for $m,n \geqslant 4$ and for any proper binary boolean operation $\circ$ the complexity of $L'_m(a,b) \circ L_n(b,a)$ is $mn - (m+n-2)$. If $m \neq n$ then $\kappa(L'_m(a,b) \circ L_n(a,b)) = mn - (m+n-2)$.*

Proof. The upper bound was established in [7]. For the lower bound, Fig. 3 restricted to the alphabet $\{a, b\}$ shows the two argument DFAs. As usual we construct their direct product. State $(0', 0)$ is initial and can never be reached again. If we apply a, we reach state $(1', 2)$, and the states reachable from this state form the direct product of DFA $\mathcal{E}'_{m-1}(a, b) = (\{1, \ldots, (m-1)'\}, \{a, b\}, \delta', 1', \{(m-1)'\})$ and DFA $\mathcal{E}_{n-1}(b, a) = (\{1, \ldots, n-1\}, \{a, b\}, \delta, 2, \{n-1\})$, where δ' and δ are $\delta_{m'}$ and δ_n restricted to $Q'_m \setminus \{0'\}$ and $Q_n \setminus \{0\}$. Since the transition semigroups of $\mathcal{E}'_m$ and $\mathcal{E}_n$ are the symmetric groups S_m and S_n, respectively, the result from [1, Theorem 1] applies, except in the cases where (m, n) is in $\{(4, 5), (5, 4), (5, 5)\}$, which have been verified by computation. Our first claim follows for the remaining cases by [1, Theorem 1]. If $m \neq n$, [1, Theorem 1] applies to $\mathcal{D}'_m(a, b)$ and $\mathcal{D}_n(a, b)$, and the second claim follows. In both cases the direct product of $\mathcal{E}'_m$ and $\mathcal{E}_n$ has $(m-1)(n-1)$ states; hence in the direct product of $\mathcal{D}'_m$ and $\mathcal{D}_n$ there are $(m-1)(n-1) + 1 = mn - (m+n-2)$ states. By [1, Theorem 1] all these states are reachable and pairwise distinguishable for every proper binary boolean operation $\circ$.

Finally, note also that $(0', 0)$ is distinguishable from all other states. Since $(0', 0)a = (1', 2)$ and the preimage of $(1', 2)$ under a is $\{(0', 0), ((m-1)', 1)\}$, we see that $(0', 0)$ is distinguishable from $(p', q) \neq ((m-1)', 1)$ by first applying a, then applying a word that distinguishes $(0', 0)a = (1', 2)$ from $(p', q)a$. It is distinguishable from $((m-1)', 1)$ by first applying b, then applying a word that distinguishes $(0', 0)b = (2', 1)$ from $((m-1)', 1)b = ((m-1)', 2)$.   □

Proposition 12. *For $m, n \geqslant 4$, let $L'_m(\Sigma')$ (respectively, $L_n(\Sigma)$) be a non-returning language of complexity m (respectively, n) over an alphabet Σ', (respectively, Σ). Then the complexity of union and symmetric difference is $mn + 1$ and this bound is met by $L'_m(a, b, c)$ and $L_n(b, a, d)$; the complexity of difference is $mn - n + 1$, and this bound is met by $L'_m(a, b, c)$ and $L_n(b, a)$; the complexity of intersection is $mn - (m+n-2)$ and this bound is met by $L'_m(a, b)$ and $L_n(b, a)$.*

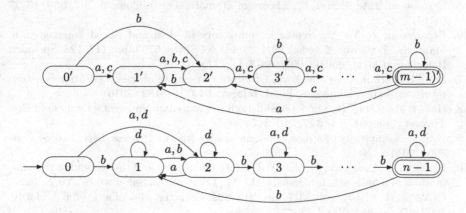

Fig. 3. DFAs $\mathcal{D}'_m(a, b, c)$ and $\mathcal{D}_n(b, a, d)$ for unrestricted boolean operations

7   Conclusions

We have shown that there exists a most complex non-returning language stream $(L_4(\Sigma), \ldots, L_n(\Sigma), \ldots)$. The cardinality of the syntactic semigroup of $L_n(\Sigma)$ is $(n-1)^n$ and its atoms have the highest state complexity possible for non-returning languages; both of these bounds can be reached only if Σ has at least $\binom{n}{2}$ letters. The bounds for the common restricted operations, however, can be met by streams over $\{a, b, c\}$ or $\{a, b\}$: $\kappa(L_m(a, b) \circ L_n(b, a)) = mn - (m + n - 2)$ for all proper boolean operations $\circ$; $\kappa(L_n(a, b))^* = 2^{n-1}$; $\kappa(L_n(a, b, c)^R) = 2^n$; and $\kappa(L'_m(a, b)L_n(a, -, b)) = (m - 1)2^{n-1} + 1$. The bounds for unrestricted boolean operations can be met by $L'_m(a, b, c)$ and $L_n(b, a, d)$, whereas those for the unrestricted product, by $L'_m(a, b)$ and $L_n(a, -, b, d)$.

Acknowledgments. We are very grateful to Corwin Sinnamon and an anonymous reviewer for careful proofreading and constructive comments.

References

1. Bell, J., Brzozowski, J., Moreira, N., Reis, R.: Symmetric groups and quotient complexity of boolean operations. In: Esparza, J., Fraigniaud, P., Husfeldt, T., Koutsoupias, E. (eds.) ICALP 2014. LNCS, vol. 8573, pp. 1–12. Springer, Heidelberg (2014). doi:10.1007/978-3-662-43951-7_1

2. Brzozowski, J.A.: In search of the most complex regular languages. Int. J. Found. Comput. Sci. **24**(6), 691–708 (2013)

3. Brzozowski, J.: Unrestricted state complexity of binary operations on regular languages. In: Câmpeanu, C., Manea, F., Shallit, J. (eds.) DCFS 2016. LNCS, vol. 9777, pp. 60–72. Springer, Cham (2016). doi:10.1007/978-3-319-41114-9_5. Revised version in http://arxiv.org/abs/1602.01387

4. Brzozowski, J.A., Tamm, H.: Complexity of atoms of regular languages. Int. J. Found. Comput. Sci. **24**(7), 1009–1027 (2013)

5. Brzozowski, J.A., Tamm, H.: Theory of átomata. Theor. Comput. Sci. **539**, 13–27 (2014)

6. Brzozowski, J., Ye, Y.: Syntactic complexity of ideal and closed languages. In: Mauri, G., Leporati, A. (eds.) DLT 2011. LNCS, vol. 6795, pp. 117–128. Springer, Heidelberg (2011). doi:10.1007/978-3-642-22321-1_11

7. Eom, H.S., Han, Y.S., Jirásková, G.: State complexity of basic operations on non-returning regular languages. Fund. Inform. **144**, 161–182 (2016)

8. Holzer, M., König, B.: On deterministic finite automata and syntactic monoid size. Theoret. Comput. Sci. **327**, 319–347 (2004)

9. Iván, S.: Complexity of atoms, combinatorially. Inform. Process. Lett. **116**(5), 356–360 (2016)

10. Krawetz, B., Lawrence, J., Shallit, J.: State complexity and the monoid of transformations of a finite set. In: Domaratzki, M., Okhotin, A., Salomaa, K., Yu, S. (eds.) CIAA 2004. LNCS, vol. 3317, pp. 213–224. Springer, Heidelberg (2005). doi:10.1007/978-3-540-30500-2_20

11. Perrin, D.: Finite automata. In: van Leewen, J. (ed.) Handbook of Theoretical Computer Science, vol. B, pp. 1–57. Elsevier, Amsterdam (1990)

12. Pin, J.E.: Syntactic semigroups. In: Rozenberg, G., Salomaa, A. (eds.) Handbook of Formal Languages: Volume 1 Word, Language, Grammar, pp. 679–746. Springer, New York (1997)
13. Yu, S.: Regular languages. In: Rozenberg, G., Salomaa, A. (eds.) Handbook of Formal Languages, pp. 41–110. Springer, Heidelberg (1997)

Uncountable Realtime Probabilistic Classes

Maksims Dimitrijevs[(✉)] and Abuzer Yakaryılmaz

Faculty of Computing, University of Latvia, Raiņa bulvāris 19, Rīga 1586, Latvia
md09032@lu.lv, abuzer@lu.lv

Abstract. We investigate the minimum cases for realtime probabilistic machines that can define uncountably many languages with bounded error. We show that logarithmic space is enough for realtime PTMs on unary languages. On binary case, we follow the same result for double logarithmic space, which is tight. When replacing the worktape with some limited memories, we can follow uncountable results on unary languages for two counters.

1 Introduction

When using uncountable transitions, bounded-error probabilistic and quantum models can recognize uncountably many languages [1,8]. It is interesting to identify the minimum resources that are sufficient to follow this result. Some of the known results [3,8] are as follows:

- Uncountably many unary languages can be defined by poly-time double logspace probabilistic Turing machines (PTMs) and linearithmic ($O(n \log n)$) time log-space one-way PTMs.
- Uncountably many k-ary languages ($k > 1$) can be defined by poly-time constant-space quantum Turing machines, linear-time linear-space two-way probabilistic counter machines, and arbitrarily small but non-constant-space PTMs.

In this paper, we investigate *realtime* probabilistic models that read the input in a streaming mode such that there is no pause on the input symbols. (This is also referred as strict realtime.) On general alphabets, it is known that bounded-error one-way PTMs cannot recognize any nonregular language in space $o(\log \log n)$ [5]. Here we show that $O(\log \log n)$-space is enough for realtime PTMs to define uncountably many languages. Therefore, this bound is tight for general alphabets. On unary alphabet, we follow the same result for $O(\log n)$ space and we leave open whether realtime PTMs can recognize any unary nonregular languages in $o(\log n)$ space. Lastly, we follow the same result for unary realtime probabilistic automata with counters and we show that two counters are sufficient. It is known that one counter is not enough since unary one-way probabilistic automata with one stack can recognize only regular languages with bounded error [6]. On the other hand, the case of two stacks is trivial since

G. Pighizzini and C. Câmpeanu (Eds.): DCFS 2017, LNCS 10316, pp. 102–113, 2017.
DOI: 10.1007/978-3-319-60252-3_8

a work tape can be simulated by two stacks. We leave open to determine the minimum number of counters that use sublinear or sublogarithmic space on the counters.

In the next section, we present some background to follow the rest of the paper and then we present our results in Sect. 3 under two subsections. We first present the results for unary languages (Sect. 3.1), and then for general alphabet languages (Sect. 3.2).

2   Background

We assume the reader is familiar with the basics of complexity theory and automata theory. Throughout the paper, Σ not containing $\textcent$ (the left end-marker) and $\$$ (the right end-marker) denotes the input alphabet, $\tilde{\Sigma}$ is the set $\Sigma \cup \{\textcent, \$\}$, Γ not containing blank symbol denotes the work tape alphabet, $\tilde{\Gamma}$ is the set $\Gamma \cup \{\text{blank symbol}\}$, and Σ^* is set of all strings obtained from the symbols in Σ including the empty string.

Formally, a realtime PTM P is a 7-tuple

$$P = (S, \Sigma, \Gamma, \delta, s_1, s_a, s_r),$$

where S is the set of finite internal states, $s_1 \in S$ is the initial state, $s_a \in S$ and $s_r \in S$ ($s_a \neq s_r$) are the accepting and rejecting states, respectively, and δ is the transition function

$$\delta : S \times \tilde{\Sigma} \times \tilde{\Gamma} \times S \times \tilde{\Gamma} \times \{\leftarrow, \downarrow, \rightarrow\} \to [0,1]$$

that governs the behaviour of P as follows: When P is in state $s \in S$, reads symbol $\sigma \in \tilde{\Sigma}$ on the input tape, and reads symbol $\gamma \in \tilde{\Gamma}$ on the work tape, it enters state $s' \in S$, writes $\gamma' \in \tilde{\Gamma}$ on the cell under the work tape head, and then the work tape head is updated with respect to $d \in \{\leftarrow, \downarrow, \rightarrow\}$ with probability

$$\delta(s, \sigma, \gamma, s', \gamma', d),$$

where "$\leftarrow$" ("$\downarrow$" and "$\rightarrow$") means the head is moved one cell to the left (the head does not move and the head is moved one cell to the right). Note that input head can only perform "$\rightarrow$" moves. To be a well-formed PTM, the following condition must be satisfied: for each triple $(s, \sigma, \gamma) \in S \times \tilde{\Sigma} \times \tilde{\Gamma}$,

$$\sum_{s' \in S, \gamma' \in \tilde{\Gamma}, d \in \{\leftarrow, \downarrow, \rightarrow\}} \delta(s, \sigma, \gamma, s', \gamma', d) = 1.$$

The computation starts in state s_1, and any given input, say $w \in \Sigma^*$, is read as $\textcent w \$$ from the left to the right symbol by symbol, and the computation is terminated and the given input is accepted (rejected) if P enters s_a (s_r). It must be guaranteed that the machine enters a halting state after reading $\$$.

The space used by P on a given input is the number of all cells visited on the work tape during the computation with some non-zero probability. The machine

P is called to be $O(s(n))$ space bounded machine if it always uses $O(s(n))$ space on any input with length n.

If (realtime) P is allowed to spend more than one step on an input symbol, then it is called one-way. Formally, its transition function is extended by the move of the input head with $\{\downarrow, \rightarrow\}$ in each transition, and then, the well-formed condition is updated accordingly.

Moreover, any PTM without work tape is called probabilistic finite automaton (PFA).

A counter is a special type of memory containing only the integers. Its value is set to zero at the beginning. During the computation, its status (whether its value is zero or not) can be read similar to reading blank symbol or non-blank symbol on the work tape, and then its value is incremented or decremented by 1 or not changed similar to the position update of the work head. (A counter can be seen as a unary stack.)

A realtime probabilistic automaton with k counters (PkCA) is a realtime PTM having k counters instead of a working tape. In each step, instead of reading the symbol under the work tape head, it checks the statuses of all counters; and then, it updates the value of each counter by a value from $\{-1, 0, 1\}$ instead of updating the content of the work tape.

The language L is said to be recognized by a PTM with error bound ϵ $(0 \leq \epsilon < 1/2)$ if every member of L is accepted with probability at least $1 - \epsilon$ and every non-member of L ($w \notin L$) is accepted with probability not exceeding ϵ.

We denote the set of integers $\mathbb{Z}$ and the set of positive integers $\mathbb{Z}^+$. The set $\mathcal{I} = \{I \mid I \subseteq \mathbb{Z}^+\}$ is the set of all subsets of positive integers and so it is an uncountable set (the cardinality is $\aleph_1$) like the set of real numbers ($\mathbb{R}$). The cardinality of $\mathbb{Z}$ or $\mathbb{Z}^+$ is $\aleph_0$ (countably many).

The membership of each positive integer in any $I \in \mathcal{I}$ can be represented as a binary probability value:

$$p_I = 0.x_1 01 x_2 01 x_3 01 \cdots x_i 01 \cdots, \quad x_i = 1 \leftrightarrow i \in I.$$

3   Our Results

In our proof we use a fact presented in our previous paper [3].

Fact 1 [3]. *Let $x = x_1 x_2 x_3 \cdots$ be an infinite binary sequence. If a biased coin lands on head with probability $p = 0.x_1 01 x_2 01 x_3 01 \cdots$, then the value x_k can be determined with probability at least $\frac{3}{4}$ after 64^k coin tosses.*

The proof of this fact involves the analysis of probabilistic distributions for the number of heads after tossing 64^k coins that land on the head with probability p. The $(3 \cdot k + 3)$-th bit from the right in obtained number of heads is equal to x_k with probability at least $\frac{3}{4}$.

3.1   Unary Languages

In [9], it was shown that realtime deterministic Turing machines (DTMs) can recognize unary nonregular languages in $O(\log n)$ space. By adopting the technique given there, we can show that bounded-error realtime PTMs can recognize uncountably many unary languages.

Theorem 1. *Bounded-error realtime unary PTMs can recognize uncountably many languages in $O(\log n)$ space.*

Proof. We start with defining a unary nonregular language that can be recognized by bounded-error log-space realtime PTMs:

$$\texttt{ULOG} = \{0^{k_i} \mid k_1 = 64 \cdot 28 \text{ and } k_i = k_{i-1} + 64^i \cdot (18i + 10) \text{ for } i > 1\},$$

where each member is defined recursively. Since it is not a periodic language, ULOG is nonregular.

For any $I \in \mathcal{I}$, we define the following language:

$$\texttt{ULOG(I)} = \{a^{k_i} \mid a^{k_i} \in \texttt{ULOG} \text{ for } i \geq 1 \text{ and } i \in I\}.$$

We describe a bounded-error log-space PTM for ULOG(I), say P_I. Then, we can follow the proof since there is a bijection (one-to-one and onto) between $I \in \mathcal{I}$ and ULOG(I) and $\mathcal{I}$ is an uncountable set.

The PTM P_I uses a coin landing on head with probability

$$p_I = 0.x_1 01 x_2 01 x_3 01 \cdots x_i 01 \cdots,$$

where $x_i = 1$ if and only if $i \in I$. The aim of P_I is iteratively finding the values of $x_1, x_2, \ldots$ with high probability. If all input is read before reaching a decision on one of these values, then the input is always rejected.

During the computation, P_I uses two binary counters on the work tape. At the beginning, the iteration number is one, $i = 1$. The machine initializes the work tape as "#000000#000000#" by reading $15 \ (= 9 \cdot 1 + 5 + 1)$ symbols from the input (after 15-th symbol the working tape head is placed on the first zero to the left from the third #). We name the separator symbols #s for the counters as the first, second, and third ones from the left to the right. The first (second) counter is kept between the last (first) two #s.

By using the first counter, the machine counts up to 64^i and so meanwhile also tosses 64^i coins. By using the second counter, it counts the number of heads. The value of each counter can be easily increased by 1 when the working tape head passes on the counters from right to left once. Thus, when the working tape head is on the third #, it goes to the first #, and meanwhile increases the value of the first counter by 1, then tosses its coin, and, if it is a head, it also increases the value of the second counter. After tossing 64^i coins, the machine uses the leftmost value of the second counter as its answer for x_i. Once this decision is read from the work tape and immediately after the working tape head is placed on the first #, the current iteration is finished. If (i) an iteration is finished,

(ii) there is no more symbol remaining to be read from the input, and (iii) the decision is positive, then the input is accepted, which is the single condition to accept the input. After an iteration is finished, the next one starts and each counter is initialized appropriately and then the same procedure is repeated as long as there are some input symbols to be read.

Since the input is read in realtime mode, the number of computational steps is equal to the length of the input plus two (the end-markers). Now, we provide the details of each iteration step so that we can identify which strings are accepted by P_I.

At the beginning of the i-th iteration, the working tape head is placed in the first # and the contents of the counters are as follows:

$$\# \underbrace{0 \cdots 0}_{3(i-1)+3} \# \underbrace{0 \cdots 0}_{6(i-1)} \#.$$

By reading $9i + 5 + 1$ symbols from the input, the counters are initialized for the current iteration as

$$\# \underbrace{0 \cdots 0}_{3i+3} \# \underbrace{0 \cdots 0}_{6i} \#$$

by shifting the second and third #s to 3 and 9 amounts of cells to the right (after initialization the working head is placed on the first zero to the left from the third #).

After the initialization of the counters, the working head goes to the first # and then comes back on the third # $64^i - 1$ times. In each pass from right to left, the first counter is increased by 1, the coin is flipped, and then the second counter is increased by 1 if the result is head. When all digits of the first counter are 1, which means the number of passes reaches $64^i - 1$, the working tape head makes its last pass from the third # to the first #. During the last pass, P_I flips the coin once more and then determines the leftmost digit of the second counter. Meanwhile, it also sets both counters to zeros.

By also considering the initialization step, P_I makes 64^i passes starting from the first #. So, the total number of steps is $64^i \cdot 2 \cdot (9i + 5)$ during the i-th iteration. One can easily verify that this is valid also for the case of $i = 1$.

Therefore, P_I can deterministically detect the i-th shortest member of ULOG after reading k_i symbols, where $k_1 = 64 \cdot (28)$ and $k_i = k_{i-1} + 64^i \cdot (18i + 10)$ for $i > 1$. Then, by using Fact 1, we can follow that P_I recognizes ULOG(I) with error bound $\frac{1}{4}$. □

It is known that bounded-error unary one-way PFAs with a single stack cannot recognize any nonregular language [6]. Therefore, we can check the case of having two stacks.

Corollary 1. *Bounded-error unary realtime PFA with two stacks using logarithmic amount of space can recognize uncountably many languages.*

Proof. It is a well-known fact that two stacks can easily simulate a worktape of a TMs without any delay on the running time. Therefore, by using Theorem 1, we can follow the result in a straightforward way. □

It is possible to replace stacks with counters by losing the space efficiency. We start with four counters.

Theorem 2. *Bounded-error realtime unary P4CAs can recognize uncountably many languages.*

Proof. We start with describing a realtime P4CA, say P_I, that can use a coin landing head with probability p_I for an $I \in \mathcal{I}$. Let C_i ($1 \leq i \leq 4$) represent the values of counters.

The automaton P_I executes an iterative algorithm. We use m to denote the iteration steps. At the beginning, $m = 1$. In each iteration, 64^m coin tosses are performed. The details are as follows:

- Set $C_1 = 64^m$ and $C_2 = 4 \cdot 8^m$.
- Perform C_1 coin flips and meanwhile increase/decrease the values of C_2 and C_3 by 1. If the coin flip result is head, one of the counters is increased by 1 and the other one is decreased by 1. When one of them hits zero, update strategy is changed. Since C_3 is zero at the beginning, the first strategy is decreasing the value of C_2 and increasing the value of C_3. Thus, after each $4 \cdot 8^m$ heads, the update strategy on the counters is changed.
- When C_1 hits zero, C_2 and C_3 are equal to X and $4 \cdot 8^m - X$, and, the automaton makes its decision on x_m. If the latest strategy is decreasing the value of C_3 or $C_2 = 0$, then x_m is determined as 1. Otherwise, it is determined as 0.

The described algorithm is similar to the one that is used in the proof of Theorem 1. Here changing the update strategy between C_2 and C_3 refers to the change of bit x_m, which is changed after each $4 \cdot 8^m$ heads: it is 0 initially and then changed as $1, 0, 1, \ldots$.

At the end of the m-th iteration, we have $C_1 = 0$, $C_2 = X$, and $C_3 = 4 \cdot 8^m - X$. We initialize $(m + 1)$-th iteration as follows:

- By using C_2 and C_3, we can set $C_1 = 2X + 2(4 \cdot 8^m - X) = 8^{m+1}$. Now $C_2 = C_3 = C_4 = 0$.
- Set $C_2 = C_3 = 8^{m+1}$ by setting $C_1 = 0$. Then, in a loop, until C_2 hits zero: decrease value of C_2 by 1, then transfer C_3 to C_4 (or C_4 to C_3 if at the beginning of loop's iteration $C_3 = 0$) and meanwhile add 8^{m+1} to C_1.
- $C_1 = 8^{m+1}(8^{m+1}) = 64^{m+1}$, $C_2 = 0$, $C_3 = 8^{m+1}$, $C_4 = 0$. Then set $C_2 = 4 \cdot 8^{m+1}$ by setting $C_3 = 0$.

After initializing, we execute the coin-flip procedure. Each iteration is finalized after the coin-flip procedure.

The input is accepted if there is no more input symbol to be read exactly at the end of an iteration, say m-th, and x_m is guessed as 1. Otherwise, the input is always rejected.

The coin tosses part is performed in 64^m steps. The initialization part for m-th iteration is performed in $8^m + 8^m + 64^m + 4 \cdot 8^m = 64^m + 6 \cdot 8^m$ steps, where $m > 1$. The initialization part for $m = 1$ is performed in 64 steps.

Based on this analysis, we can easily formulate the language recognized by P_I, which is subset of the following language

$$\text{UP4CA} = \{0^{k_i} \mid k_1 = 128 \text{ and } k_i = k_{i-1} + 6 \cdot 8^i + 2 \cdot 64^i \text{ for } i > 1\}.$$

For any $I \in \mathcal{I}$, the realtime P4CA P_I can recognize the language

$$\text{UP4CA(I)} = \{a^{k_i} \mid a^{k_i} \in \text{U4PCA for } i \geq 1 \text{ and } i \in I\}$$

with bounded error. The automaton P_I iteratively determines the values of $x_1, x_2, \ldots$ with high probability and the number of steps for each iteration corresponds with the members of U4PCA.

Since $\mathcal{I}$ is an uncountable set and there is a bijection between $I \in \mathcal{I}$ and UP4CA(I), realtime P4CAs can recognize uncountably many unary languages with bounded error.   □

We can establish a similar result also for realtime P2CAs. For this purpose, we can use the well-known simulating technique of k counters by 2 counters.

Theorem 3. *Bounded-error unary realtime P2CAs can recognize uncountably many languages.*

Proof. Let P_I be the realtime P4CA described above and UP4CA(I) be the language recognized by it. Due to the realtime reading mode, the unary inputs to P_I can also be seen as the time steps. For example, P_I can be seen as a machine without any input but still making its transition after each time step. Thus, after each step it can be either in an accepting case or a rejecting case.

It is a well-known fact that two counters can simulate any number of counters with big slowdown [7]. The values of k counters, say $c_1, c_2, \ldots, c_k$, can be stored on a counter as

$$p_1^{c_1} \cdot p_2^{c_2} \cdot \cdots \cdot p_k^{c_k},$$

where $p_1, \ldots, p_k$ are some prime numbers. Then, by the help of the second counter and the internal states, it can be easily detected and stored the status of each simulated counters, and then all updates on the simulated counters are reflected one by one.

Thus, by fixing the above simulation, we can easily simulate P_I by a P2CA, say P'_I. Then, P'_I recognizes a language with bounded error, say UP2CA(I).

It is easy to see that there is a bijection between

$$\{\text{UP4CA(I)} \mid I \in \mathcal{I}\} \text{ and } \{\text{UP2CA(I)} \mid I \in \mathcal{I}\},$$

and so realtime P2CAs also recognize uncountably many languages with bounded error. Remark that for each member of UP4CA(I), the corresponding member of UP2CA(I) is much longer.   □

3.2 Generic Alphabet Languages

Here, we focus on non-unary alphabets and establish our result for double logarithmic space. For this purpose, we use a fact given by Freivalds in [4].

Fact 2. *Let $P_1(n)$ be the number of primes not exceeding $2^{\lceil log_2 n \rceil}$, $P_2(l, N', N'')$ be the number of primes not exceeding $2^{\lceil log_2 l \rceil}$ and dividing $|N' - N''|$, and $P_3(l, n)$ be the maximum of $P_2(l, N', N'')$ over all $N' < 2^n$, $N'' \le 2^n$, $N' \ne N''$. Then, for any $\epsilon > 0$, there is a natural number c such that $\lim_{n \to \infty} \frac{P_3(cn, n)}{P_1(cn)} < \epsilon$.*

Let $bin(i)$ denote the unique binary representation of $i > 0$ that always starts with digit 1. The language LOGLOG is composed by the strings

$$bin(1)2bin(2)2bin(3)2...2bin(s)4,$$

where $|bin(s)| = 64^k$ for some positive integer k. For any $I \in \mathcal{I}$, we define language $\text{LOGLOG(I)} = \{w \mid w \in \text{LOGLOG and } k \in I\}$.

Fact 3. *Denote by $\pi(x)$ the number of primes not exceeding x. The Prime Number Theorem states that $\lim_{x \to \infty} \frac{\pi(x)}{x/\ln x} = 1$ [2].*

Theorem 4. *Bounded–error one–way PTMs can recognize uncountably many languages in $O(\log \log n)$ space.*

Proof. By modifying the one-way algorithm given in [4], we present a PTM, say $P_{c,I}$, shortly P, for language LOGLOG(I) for $I \in \mathcal{I}$ and for a specific c that determines the error bound. P performs different checks by using the separate parts of the work tape.

For each i, P keeps two registers storing $m = |bin(i)|$ and $m_0 = |bin(i-1)|$. After reading $bin(i)$, P checks: if $m = m_0$ or ($m = m_0 + 1$ and $bin(i-1)$ contained only ones), then P continues. Otherwise, P rejects the input.

For each $bin(i)$, P generates a random number of $|m| \cdot c$ bits and tests it for primality. If the generated number is not prime, the same procedure is repeated. Due to Fact 3, we can follow that the probability of picking a prime number of $|m| \cdot c$ bits is $\theta(\frac{1}{|m| \cdot c})$. Therefore, the expected time of finding a prime number is $O(|m| \cdot c)$. Assume that the generated prime number is r_i. For each $bin(i)$, P calculates $bin(i) \mod r_i$ and $bin(i + 1) \mod r_i$. If $(bin(i) \mod r_i) + 1 \ne bin(i + 1) \mod r_i$, P rejects the input. Otherwise, the computation continues.

After reading "4", P checks whether $m = 64^k$ for some integer $k > 0$. If so, m is written on the tape as $1(000000)^k$. If $m \ne 64^k$, then the input is rejected.

If all previous checks are successful, P tosses 64^k coins and meanwhile calculates the number of heads $\mod (8 \cdot 8^k)$, say C. If after all coin tosses, the leftmost bit of C is 1, then the input is accepted, otherwise it is rejected.

The PTM P reaches symbol "4" without rejecting with probability 1 if the input belongs to LOGLOG, and it rejects the input before reaching "4" with probability at least $1 - \epsilon$ if the input is not in LOGLOG due to Fact 2. Due to Fact 1 the membership of $k \in I$ for LOGLOG(I) will be computed with probability at least $\frac{3}{4}$. Therefore language LOGLOG(I) is recognized correctly with probability at least $(1 - \epsilon) \cdot \frac{3}{4}$, which can be arbitrarily close to $\frac{3}{4}$ by picking a suitable c.

The space used on the work tape is linear in the length of the counter for $|bin(i)|$. The value of $bin(i)$ is logarithmic to the length of input word, and so the length of the counter is double logarithmic to the input length. Therefore, the space used is in $O(\log \log n)$ throughout the computation. □

Let $L \subseteq \Sigma^*$ be a language recognized by a one-way DTM, say D, and σ be a symbol not in Σ. We can execute D in realtime reading mode on the inputs defined on $\Sigma \cup \{\sigma\}$ as follows [9]: For each original "wait" move on a symbol from Σ, the machine expects to read symbol σ. If it reads something else or there is no more input symbol, then the input is rejected. If there is more than expected σ symbol, then again the input is rejected. Thus, we can say that this modified machine recognizes a language L' and there is a bijection between L and L'. Moreover, the space and time bounds for both machines are the same.

The question is whether we can apply a similar idea for one-way PTM given above in order to get a realtime PTM. A DTM follows a single path during its computation and so the aforementioned bijection can be created in a straightforward way. On the other hand, PTMs can follow different paths with different lengths in each run. So, in order to follow a similar bijection, we need some modifications. The main modification is necessary for the task of picking the prime numbers. Except this task, the other ones can be executed with the same number of steps (remember the algorithms in the previous subsection) in every execution of the machine.

Now, we modify PTM $P_{c,I}$ in order to guarantee that each computation path uses the same amount of time steps on the same input. We represent the new PTM as $P'_{c,I}$ or shortly P'.

The PTM P' uses some registers on the work tape separated by "#":

$$\#1st\#2nd\# \cdots \#last\#.$$

- The 1st register keeps both the lengths of the counters m and m_0. If $m = x_1x_2x_3 \cdots$ and $m_0 = y_1y_2y_3 \cdots$, then the register keeps the values in the following way: $x_1y_1x_2y_2x_3y_3 \cdots$. After reading symbol "2" it is easy to compare m and m_0 bit by bit with a single pass.
- The 2nd register keeps the number of heads for the coin-tosses, based on which the bit x_k is determined. It is set to $\lceil |m|/2 \rceil + 2$ zeros before any coin-toss procedure and it is updated accordingly when the value of m is changed.
- The 3rd register keeps the track of attempts to generate prime number, it has $|m| \cdot c$ bits.
- The 4th and 5th registers keep the prime numbers with some auxiliary numbers. Each register has $|m| \cdot c \cdot 2$ bits. If the (candidate) prime number is $r = r_1r_2r_3 \cdots$ and the auxiliary number is $q = q_1q_2q_3 \cdots$, then the register keeps both of them as $r_1q_1r_2q_2r_3q_3 \cdots$. The machine uses r to store the prime number that is being checked or computed, and q is used to help to perform tasks with r like storing number modulo r and comparing and copying numbers. For each $j > 0$, the machine uses 4th and 5th registers to work

with prime numbers and then checks the correctness of the candidates for $bin(2 \cdot j - 1)$ and $bin(2 \cdot j)$.

- The 6th and 7th registers are the same as 4th and 5th registers, respectively. Only they are responsible for the correctness of the candidates for $bin(2 \cdot j)$ and $bin(2 \cdot j + 1)$.
- The 8th register has a number to keep track of total number of subtractions performed while checking the divisibility of r by d. It has $|m| \cdot c$ bits.
- The 9th register has twice of $\lceil |m|/2 \rceil \cdot c$ bits to keep numbers d and h (each is $\lceil |m|/2 \rceil \cdot c$ bits). If $d = d_1 d_2 d_3 \cdots$ and $h = h_1 h_2 h_3 \cdots$, then the register keeps them as $d_1 h_1 d_2 h_2 d_3 h_3 \cdots$. Both numbers are used to check whether the generated number r is prime. The machine uses d to check whether d does not divide r, such check is performed for different values d. The check is performed by making subtractions. The value of d is subtracted from r multiple times. For this operation, the machine uses h as auxiliary number.

Each member of LOGLOG(I) has parts $bin(i)$ at least up to $bin(2^{63})$. P' deterministically checks input up to $bin(2^{63})$ and prepares the work tape with 9 registers.

Now, we describe the steps of picking prime numbers.

For number $bin(i)$, the prime number is generated in $(6 - 2 \cdot (i \mod 2))$-th register. The number r is generated by using $|m| \cdot c$ random bits (bit by bit). After this, the primality check is performed. For this purpose, the machine checks whether r is divided by any natural number between 2 and $2^{\lceil |m|/2 \rceil \cdot c} - 1$, where $2^{\lceil |m|/2 \rceil \cdot c} > sqrt(r)$ because $r < 2^{|m| \cdot c}$. Each candidate natural number is denoted by d below. Remark that the number of ds does not depend on r and so for any candidate prime number, the primary test procedure takes the same number of steps.

To begin the check of divisibility of r by d, the value of r is copied to q bit after bit, and the value of d is copied to h bit after bit. The 8th register is initialized with zeros before check for pair r and d. Then, $2^{|m| \cdot c}$ iterations are performed. In each iteration, the values of q and h are decreased by 1, the value of 8th register is increased by 1. If only h reaches zero, d is again copied into h and the machine continues to perform iterations. When q reaches zero, if h reaches zero at the same time, the machine concludes that r is not a prime number, otherwise, r is not divisible by d. After that, P' continues to perform the iterations but without changing q and checks of value of q until the value of the 8th register reaches $2^{|m| \cdot c}$. Then, P' repeats the procedure for the next d.

If r is not divisible by any of these ds, then the procedure of finding prime is terminated successfully since r is prime, otherwise, the machine continues with the next prime candidate number since r is not a prime number.

The 3rd register counts the number of attempts to generate a prime number. It is initialized with zeros and is increased by one after each try. If P' finds a prime number before 3rd register reaches $2^{|m| \cdot c}$, P' continues performing the algorithm until the register reaches $2^{|m| \cdot c}$ by fixing the candidate with the already found prime number. If the register reaches value $2^{|m| \cdot c}$ (all bits become zeros) and P' fails to generate a prime number, P' uses the last generated r for the modular check for pair $bin(i)$ and $bin(i+1)$. P' performs each try to generate (or process already generated) prime number in equal number of steps. For any $bin(i)$ P' performs exactly $2^{|m| \cdot c}$ such operations.

After finding and checking prime r, the machine copies r into $(7 - 2 \cdot (i \bmod 2))$-th register bit by bit. To perform this operation, the machine sets q to zeros in both registers, copies the bits of r one by one, and marks the copied bit by setting the next bit in q to one.

Now, we describe how the machine calculates the value $bin(i) \bmod r$. At the beginning, the register keeps r and zeros for q. Assume that $bin(i) = i_1 i_2 \cdots i_m$. When the machine reads i_j, the value of q is multiplied by 2 and increased by i_j. Therefore, all bits of q are shifted to left by one position, and the machine puts value i_j in leftmost bit. If, after this operation, $q \geq r$, then r is subtracted from q. Because both values are interleaved, it is easy to subtract r from q in one pass. In the case when $q < r$ the machine performs one pass through registers without changing the values. This ensures that each iteration for i_j is performed in equal number of steps. The machine performs the calculation while reading $bin(i)$ for the 5th and the 6th registers if $i \bmod 2 = 0$, and for the 4th and the 7th registers otherwise.

After these, the machine compares the values of two modules: the 4th and the 5th registers if $i \bmod 2 = 0$; the 6th and the 7th registers otherwise. This time machine sets r in both registers to zeros and marks compared bits of q's by setting bits in r to one.

If r in modular check is not prime, P' cannot guarantee that incorrect pair $bin(i)$ and $bin(i+1)$ will be rejected with probability at least $1 - \epsilon$. The probability not to generate a prime number of $|m| \cdot c$ random bits in $2^{|m| \cdot c}$ tries does not exceed $\left(1 - \frac{1}{|m| \cdot c}\right)^{2^{|m| \cdot c}}$ because of Fact 3. Note that $\lim_{n \to \infty} \left(1 - \frac{1}{n}\right)^n = \frac{1}{e}$, therefore $\lim_{m \to \infty} \left(1 - \frac{1}{|m| \cdot c}\right)^{2^{|m| \cdot c}} = \lim_{m \to \infty} \frac{1}{e}^{\frac{2^{|m| \cdot c}}{|m| \cdot c}} = 0$. The smallest $|m|$ for which a prime number is generated is 7. By picking a suitable c, the value $\left(1 - \frac{1}{7 \cdot c}\right)^{2^{7 \cdot c}} = \epsilon_0$ can be arbitrarily close to zero. For each $i > 0$, checking the equality of $bin(i)$ and $bin(i+1)$ by using the generated prime number is performed independently. Therefore, any incorrect pair is accepted with probability at most ϵ due to Fact 2. Since P' can fail to generate a prime number, this probability is increased to at most $\epsilon + \epsilon_0 - \epsilon \cdot \epsilon_0$. If the input belongs to LOGLOG(I), P' is guaranteed to not reject the input before reaching "4" on input tape. If at least one pair $bin(i)$ and $bin(i+1)$ is inacceptable, then P' rejects input right after checking this pair with probability at least $1 - \epsilon - \epsilon_0 \cdot (1 - \epsilon)$. Therefore, the error remains bounded.

The other parts of the algorithm are executed with the same number of steps in every execution of P'.

Theorem 5. *Bounded–error realtime PTMs can recognize uncountably many languages in* $O(\log \log n)$ *space.*

Proof. We can obtain a realtime algorithm from P', say $R_{c,I}$ or shortly R, by using aforementioned technique borrowed from [9]. Let LOGLOG(I)$'$ be the language recognized by R. Then, the language LOGLOG(I)$'$ differs from the language LOGLOG(I) with the presence of symbols "3": for each "wait" move on "0", "1", "2" or "4" by P', R expects to read one symbol of "3". If R fails to read a symbol of "3" when it is expected, the input is rejected.

PTM P' recognizes LOGLOG(I) in $O(\log \log n)$ space, therefore, realtime machine R recognizes LOGLOG(I)$'$ in $O(\log \log n)$ space and there is a bijection between LOGLOG(I) and LOGLOG(I)$'$. $\qquad\qquad\qquad\qquad\qquad\qquad\square$

In [4] Freivalds has proven that only regular languages can be recognized with one-way PTM in $o(\log \log n)$ space and with probability $p > \frac{1}{2}$. Therefore, the presented space bound is tight.

Acknowledgments. Dimitrijevs was partially supported by University of Latvia project AAP2016/B032 "Innovative information technologies". Yakaryılmaz was partially supported by ERC Advanced Grant MQC. We thank to the reviewers for their helpful comments.

References

1. Adleman, L.M., DeMarrais, J., Huang, M.D.A.: Quantum computability. SIAM J. Comput. **26**(5), 1524–1540 (1997)
2. Chandrasekharan, K.: Chebyshev's theorem on the distribution of prime numbers. Springer, Heidelberg (1968). pp. 63–83
3. Dimitrijevs, M., Yakaryılmaz, A.: Uncountable classical and quantum complexity classes. In: Eigth Workshop on Non-Classical Models for Automata and Applications (NCMA2016), vol. 321, pp. 131–146. Austrian Computer Society (2016). books@ocg.at
4. Freivalds, R.: Space and reversal complexity of probabilistic one-way turing machines. In: Karpinski, M. (ed.) FCT 1983. LNCS, vol. 158, pp. 159–170. Springer, Heidelberg (1983). doi:10.1007/3-540-12689-9_101
5. Freivalds, R.: Space and reversal complexity of probabilistic one-way turing machines. Ann. Discrete Math. **24**, 39–50 (1985)
6. Kaņeps, J., Geidmanis, D., Freivalds, R.: Tally languages accepted by Monte Carlo pushdown automata. In: Rolim, J. (ed.) RANDOM 1997. LNCS, vol. 1269, pp. 187–195. Springer, Heidelberg (1997). doi:10.1007/3-540-63248-4_16
7. Minsky, M.: Computation: Finite and Infinite Machines. Prentice-Hall, Upper Saddle River (1967)
8. Say, A.C.C., Yakaryılmaz, A.: Magic coins are useful for small-space quantum machines. Technical report TR14-159, ECCC (2016)
9. Yakaryılmaz, A., Say, A.C.C.: Tight bounds for the space complexity of nonregular language recognition by real-time machines. Int. J. Found. Comput. Sci. **24**(8), 1243–1253 (2013)

A Parametrized Analysis of Algorithms on Hierarchical Graphs

Rachel Faran$^{(\boxtimes)}$ and Orna Kupferman

School of Engineering and Computer Science, Hebrew University, 91904 Jerusalem, Israel
rachelmi@cs.huji.ac.il

Abstract. *Hierarchical graphs* are used in order to describe systems with a sequential composition of sub-systems. A hierarchical graph consists of a vector of subgraphs. Vertices in a subgraph may "call" other subgraphs. The reuse of subgraphs, possibly in a nested way, causes hierarchical graphs to be exponentially more succinct than equivalent flat graphs. Early research on hierarchical graphs and the computational price of their succinctness suggests that there is no strong correlation between the complexity of problems when applied to flat graphs and their complexity in the hierarchical setting. That is, the complexity in the hierarchical setting is higher, but all "jumps" in complexity up to an exponential one are exhibited, including no jumps in some problems.

We continue the study of the complexity of algorithms for hierarchical graphs, with the following contributions: (1) In many applications, the subgraphs have a small, often a constant, number of exit vertices, namely vertices from which control returns to the calling subgraph. We offer a parameterized analysis of the complexity and point to problems where the complexity becomes lower when the number of exit vertices is bounded by a constant. (2) We describe a general methodology for algorithms on hierarchical graphs. The methodology is based on an iterative compression of subgraphs in a way that maintains the solution to the problems and results in subgraphs whose size depends only on the number of exit vertices, and (3) We handle labeled hierarchical graphs, where edges are labeled by letters from some alphabet, and the problems refer to the languages of the graphs.

1 Introduction

Systems are typically constructed in a compositional manner. The two basic types of compositions are *concurrent* and *sequential*. In a concurrent composition, the state space of the composed system is essentially the product of the state spaces of its underlying components. In a sequential composition, the state

The research leading to these results has received funding from the European Research Council under the European Union's 7th Framework Programme (FP7/2007-2013, ERC grant no. 278410).

G. Pighizzini and C. Câmpeanu (Eds.): DCFS 2017, LNCS 10316, pp. 114–127, 2017.
DOI: 10.1007/978-3-319-60252-3_9

space of the composed system consists of copies of the state spaces of its underlying components. Since a component may be reused several times, in particular when nesting is allowed, both types of compositions allow an exponentially more succinct presentation of systems [1]. A natural question is whether one can reason about the succinct presentation in order to answer questions about the composition.

Beyond the theoretical interest in studying this question, the challenge of reasoning about systems in their succinct presentation is of great importance in the context of formal verification. There, we reason about a hardware or software system by translating it to a finite state machine (FSM) [5]. The FSM is a labeled graph, and since it lacks the internal structure of the high-level description of the system, we refer to it as a *flat graph*. The exponential blow-up in the translation of the system to a flat graph is typically the computational bottleneck in model-checking algorithms. For *concurrent graphs*, where components are composed in a concurrent manner [8], there has been extensive research on compositional model checking (cf., [6]). Compositionality methods are successfully applied in practice, but it is a known reality that they cannot always work. Formally, the system complexity of the model-checking problem (that is, the complexity in terms of the system, assuming a specification of a fixed length) for all common temporal logics is exponentially higher in the concurrent setting [14]. This exponential gap is carried over to other related problems such as checking language-containment and bisimulation—all are exponentially harder in the concurrent setting [11].

For sequential compositions, which are common in software systems (reuse of components amounts to calling a procedure), the model used is that of *hierarchical graphs* (HGs, for short). An HG consists of a vector of subgraphs. A subgraph may be used several times in the composition. Technically, this is done via special vertices, termed *boxes*, that are substituted in the composition by subgraphs. Each subgraph has an entry vertex and a set of exit vertices. In order to ensure a finite nesting depth of substitutions, the subgraphs are indexed, and a box of a graph can only *call* (that is, be substituted by) subgraphs with a strictly bigger index. A naive approach to model checking a system with such a sequential composition is to "flatten" its HG by repeatedly substituting references to subgraphs by copies of these subgraphs. This, however, results in a flat graph that is exponential in the nesting depth of the hierarchical system. In [2], it is shown that for LTL model checking, one can avoid this blow-up altogether, whereas for CTL, one can trade it for an exponential blow-up in the (often much smaller) size of the specification and the maximal number of exits of sub-structures. Likewise, μ-calculus model-checking in hierarchical systems is only PSPACE-complete [3].

For general graph algorithms, there is a good understanding that the exponential succinctness of concurrent graphs comes with a computational price. For example, classic NEXPTIME-complete problems (cf., the succinct-Hamiltonian-path problem) are the succinct versions of NP-complete problems [10]. A similar exponential gap exists in other complexity classes. For HGs, the picture is less clear. Indeed, it is shown in [16] that there is no strong correlation between the complexity of problems when applied to flat graphs and their complexity in the hierarchical setting. More specifically, Lengauer and Wagner examine a large number of problems in different complexity classes, and show that while for some, the hierarchical setting makes the problem exponentially harder, for some it does not: problems that are in LOGSPACE, NLOGSPACE, PTIME, NPTIME, and PSPACE in the flat setting, may stay in this complexity or jump to any (at most exponentially harder) class in the hierarchical setting. For example, graph reachability is NLOGSPACE-complete for flat graphs and is PTIME-complete for HGs. On the other hand, alternating graph reachability (that is, where the graph is a two-player game, and the players alternate moves picking a successor vertex) is PTIME-complete for flat graphs and is PSPACE-complete for HGs. Additional examples can be found in [13, 15, 17].

We continue to investigate the complexity of algorithms on HGs. Our contributions are described below.

Parameterized Analysis. In many applications, the subgraph components have a small, often a constant, number of exit vertices. Indeed, these exit vertices form the interface of a procedure or a library component. We offer a *parameterized analysis* of the complexity of algorithms on HGs [7]. In particular, while [16] proves that the problems *Hamiltoniam path*, *3-colorability*, and *independent set* are PSPACE-complete for hierarchical graphs, we show that they are in NP, namely as hard as in the flat setting, for *HGs with a constant number of exits* (CE-HGs, for short). Likewise, while the problem of finding a *maximal flow* in a network jumps from PTIME to PSPACE in the hierarchical setting, we conjecture that it is in PTIME for CE-HGs, and prove that this is indeed the case for HGs with at most 3 exits. As another example, while [16] proves that *alternating reachability* is PSPACE-complete for HGs, we prove it is in PTIME for CE-HGs. We note that analyzing the complexity of the PSPACE algorithms in [16] for a constant number of exit vertices does not lead to improved upper bounds. Thus, our tighter complexity results involve new algorithms, as described below.

Methodology. We define a general methodology for algorithms on HGs. For a problem P, we say that a function f on subgraphs *maintains* P if for every graph G, the graph $f(G)$ has the same entry and exit vertices as G, and every HG that calls G may call $f(G)$ instead without influencing P. Consider, for example, the problem P of finding a shortest path between two vertices in a graph. Consider also the function that maps a subgraph G with entry vertex s and set T of exit vertices to a tree whose vertices are $\{s\} \cup T$, whose edges are $\{s\} \times T$, and in which the weight of an edge $\langle s, t \rangle$ is the length of the shortest path from s to t in G. It is easy to see that f maintains P. Moreover, the size of $f(G)$ depends only on the number of exit points in G. For two complexity functions g_{size} and g_{time}, we say that a problem P is (g_{size}, g_{time})-*compressible* if there is a function f that maintains P, maps graphs G with a set T of exit vertices to graphs whose size is bounded by $g_{size}(|T|)$, and does so in time $g_{time}(|G|, |T|)$. We use the notion of compressibility in order to develop algorithms on HGs that iteratively replace boxes that call internal subgraphs by the compressed version of these subgraphs. In particular, when g_{size} and g_{time} are polynomial, then the complexity of solving P in HGs adds a polynomial factor to the complexity of its solution in flat graphs. Moreover, the fact g_{time} has two parameters, enables the parameterized complexity analysis. In particular, when the number of exit vertices is bounded by a constant, the complexity is induced by g_{time} only. Thus, if g_{time} is linear (or polynomial) in its first parameter, then so is the complexity of solving P in CE-HGs. We extend the notion of compressibility to nondeterministic functions f, where compression of graphs also generates a witness to the soundness of the compression. The witness can be verified in time that is polynomial in the number of exit vertices, and thus nondeterministic compression is used for obtaining NP upper bounds in the hierarchical setting.

Labeled Graphs. We study *labeled hierarchical graphs*, where each edge in the graph is labeled by a letter from some alphabet. In [1], the authors study *communicating hierarchical state machines*, which are similar to labeled hierarchical graphs. The study in [1] extends classical decision problems from automata theory to the hierarchical setting. In particular, the authors study reachability, emptiness, and language inclusion. Here, we study an extension of classical graph-theory problems to the labeled setting. The input to such problems includes, in addition to the graph, a specification that constrains the paths in the graph. For example, [4] studies the problem of finding a shortest path that satisfies regular and even context-free specifications, and shows that the problem stays in polynomial time. On the other hand, research in regular path queries shows that the problem of finding a shortest simple path that satisfies a regular specification is NP-complete [19]. Typical algorithms on labeled graphs are based on a *product* between the graph and an *automaton* for the specification. We show how the compression of subgraphs defined above can be extended to products of labeled HGs and automata, and demonstrate the use of such a compression.

Due to lack of space, the study of labeled graphs as well as some of the proofs are omitted, and can be found in the full version, in the authors' URLs.

2   Preliminaries

A *graph with source and target vertices* is $G = \langle V, s, T, E \rangle$, where V is a set of vertices, $s \in V$ is a source vertex, $T \subseteq V$ is a set of target vertices, and $E \subseteq V \times V$ is an edge relation. A graph may be weighted, in which case the tuple G includes also a weight function $w : E \to \mathbb{R}^+$.

A *hierarchical graph* (HG, for short) consists of a vector of subgraphs that together compose a graph. A subgraph may be used several times in the composition. Technically, this is done via special vertices, called *boxes*, that are substituted in the composition by other subgraphs. In order to ensure a finite nesting depth of substitutions, the subgraphs are indexed, and a box of a graph can only *call* (that is, be substituted by) subgraphs with a strictly bigger index. Formally, an HG $\mathcal{G}$ is a tuple $\langle G_1, \ldots, G_n \rangle$, where each subgraph is $G_i = \langle V_i, B_i, in_i, Exit_i, \tau_i, E_i \rangle$, where V_i and B_i are sets of vertices and boxes, respectively. We assume that $B_n = \emptyset$ and that $V_1, \ldots, V_n, B_1, \ldots, B_{n-1}$ are pairwise disjoint. Then, $in_i \in V_i$ is an entry vertex for G_i, and $Exit_i \subseteq V_i$ is a set of exit vertices for G_i. The function $\tau_i : B_i \to \{i+1, \ldots, n\}$ maps each box of G_i to an index greater than i. If $\tau_i(b) = j$, we say that the box b is *substituted* by G_j in G_i. Finally, E_i is an edge relation. Each edge in E_i is a pair (u,v) with source u and target v. The source u is either a vertex of G_i, or a pair $\langle b,x \rangle$, where $b \in B_i$, and $x \in Exit_{\tau_i(b)}$. That is, u may be a box b coupled with an exit vertex of the subgraph by which b is about to be substituted. The target v is either a vertex or a box of G_i. Formally, $E_i \subseteq (V_i \cup (\cup_{b \in B_i} \{b\} \times Exit_{\tau_i(b)})) \times (V_i \cup B_i)$. We refer to $\{in_i\} \cup Exit_i$ as the set of *interface vertices* of G_i, denoted V_i^{face}. We refer to G_n as the *bottom subgraph* of $\mathcal{G}$.

When $|Exit_i|$ is bounded by a constant for all $1 \le i \le n$, we say that $\mathcal{G}$ is a *hierarchical graph with constant number of exit vertices* (CE-HG, for short). A *weighted HG* is an HG with weight functions $w_i : E_i \to \mathbb{R}^+$ for all $1 \le i \le n$. Note that weights are associated with edges (rather than vertices).

A subgraph without boxes is *flat*. Each HG can be transformed to a flat graph, referred to as its *flat expansion*, by recursively substituting each box by a copy of the suitable subgraph. Formally, given an HG $\mathcal{G}$, for each subgraph G_i we inductively define its flat expansion $G_i^f = \langle V_i^f, in_i, Exit_i, E_i^f \rangle$, where $V_i^f = V_i \cup (\cup_{b \in B_i} \{b\} \times V_{\tau_i(b)}^f)$. Note that different boxes in G_i can be substituted by the same subgraph. By substituting each box b by a set of vertices $\{b\} \times V_{\tau_i(b)}^f$, we preserve b as an identifier. The edge relation E_i^f includes the following edges:

- (u, v) such that $u, v \in V_i$ and $(u,v) \in E_i$,
- $(u, \langle b, v \rangle)$ such that $u \in V_i$, $v = in_{\tau_i(b)}$ and $(u,v) \in E_i$,
- $(\langle b, u \rangle, v)$ such that $u \in Exit_{\tau_i(b)}$, $v \in V_i$ and $(u,v) \in E_i$, and
- $(\langle b, u \rangle, \langle b, v \rangle)$ such that $u, v \in V_{\tau_i(b)}^f$ and $(u,v) \in E_{\tau_i(b)}^f$.

The graph G_1^f is the flat expansion of $\mathcal{G}$, and we denote it by $\mathcal{G}^f$.

Example 1. In Fig. 1 we describe an HG $\mathcal{G} = \langle G_1, G_2 \rangle$, where G_1 includes two boxes, b_1 and b_2, with $\tau_1(b_1) = \tau_1(b_2) = 2$. The bottom subgraph G_2 is flat. The flat graph $\mathcal{G}^f$ is described on the right.   □

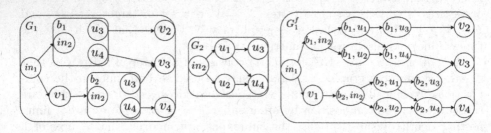

Fig. 1. A hierarchical graph

We define the *size* of a graph $G = \langle V, s, T, E \rangle$, denoted $|G|$, as $|V| + |E|$. For an HG $\mathcal{G} = \langle G_1, \ldots, G_n \rangle$, we define the size of each subgraph $G_i = \langle V_i, B_i, in_i, Exit_i, \tau_i, E_i \rangle$, denoted $|G_i|$, as $|V_i| + |B_i| + |E_i|$. Note that the sizes of the subgraphs that are substituting the boxes in B_i do not affect $|G_i|$. We denote by $|\mathcal{G}|$ the size of all of the subgraphs in $\mathcal{G}$, namely $|G_1| + \cdots + |G_n|$.

It is not hard to see that the hierarchical setting is exponentially more succinct. Formally, we have the following.

Proposition 1 [1]. *Flattening an HG may involve an exponential blow up. That is, $\mathcal{G}^f$ may be exponentially larger than $\mathcal{G}$. The exponential blow-up applies already to the diameter of the graph, and applies even when all the subgraphs in $\mathcal{G}$ have a single exit vertex.*

3   Compression of Hierarchical Graphs

Let $\mathscr{G}$ be the set of all flat graphs with source and target vertices. Let P be a problem on graphs. That is, $P : \mathscr{G} \to \{0, 1\}$ may be a decision problem, say deciding whether all the vertices in T are reachable from s, or $P : \mathscr{G} \to \mathbb{R}$ may be an optimization problem, say finding the length of a shortest path from s to T. For an HG $\mathcal{G}$, solving P on $\mathcal{G}$ amounts to solving P in G_1^f, namely in the flat expansion of $\mathcal{G}$. A naive way to do so is to construct the flat expansion of $\mathcal{G}$ and then solve P on it. By Proposition 1, this may involve an exponential blow-up. In this section we present a general methodology for reasoning about HGs without generating their flat expansions. Essentially, we iteratively replace subgraphs, starting from the innermost ones, by compressed flat versions in a way that maintains $P(\mathcal{G})$. The important fact is that the size of the compressed versions depends only on the number of exit vertices, which enables an analysis of the parametrized complexity of solving P in HGs.

We now formalize this intuition. Consider an HG $\mathcal{G} = \langle G_1, \ldots, G_n \rangle$. A *bottom flatenning* of $\mathcal{G}$, denoted $\mathcal{G}{\downarrow}$, is the HG obtained from $\mathcal{G}$ by removing G_n and replacing all boxes b that call G_n by G_n. Formally, $\mathcal{G}{\downarrow} = \langle G_1', \ldots, G_{n-1}' \rangle$, where for every $1 \leq i \leq n-1$, the subgraph G_i' is obtained from G_i by replacing every box $b \in B_i$ with $\tau_i(b) = n$ by a copy of G_n. As in the case of a flat expansion, the copies preserve b as an identifier. Let $G_i = \langle V_i, B_i, in_i, Exit_i, \tau_i, E_i \rangle$, and let $B_i^n = \{b \in B_i : \tau_i(b) = n\}$. Then, $G_i' = \langle V_i \cup (B_i^n \times V_n), B_i \setminus B_i^n, in_i, Exit_i, \tau_i, E_i \cup (B_i^n \times E_n) \rangle$, where $B_i^n \times E_n$ includes the copies of E_n in the different substitutions. Formally, $\langle u, u' \rangle \in E_n$ iff for all $b \in B_i^n$, we have $(\langle b, u \rangle, \langle b, u' \rangle)$. Note that transitions in E_i that involve a box b with $\tau_i(b) = n$ have end-points in $\langle b, in_n \rangle$ and $\{b\} \times Exit_n$, so the transitions in G_i' are well defined eventhough we remove b.

While $\mathcal{G}{\downarrow}$ has one less subgraph, the boxes in its subgraphs that call G_n have been replaced by G_n, so $|\mathcal{G}{\downarrow}| \geq |\mathcal{G}|$. The key idea behind our methodology is that often we can replace G_n by a subgraph G' of a constant size that retains its properties. We now formalize this intuition. Consider the HG $\mathcal{G} = \langle G_1, \ldots, G_n \rangle$. Given a graph with source and target vertices $G' = \langle V', s, T, E' \rangle$, we say that G_n is *substitutable* by G' if $in_n = s$ and $Exit_n = T$. The HG $\mathcal{G}[G_n \leftarrow G']$ is then $\langle G_1, \ldots, G_{n-1}, G' \rangle$. We say that a function $f : \mathscr{G} \to \mathscr{G}$ *maintains* P if for every graph $G \in \mathscr{G}$, we have that G is substitutable by $f(G)$ and for every HG $\mathcal{G}$ with bottom subgraph G, we have $P(\mathcal{G}) = P(\mathcal{G}[G \leftarrow f(G)])$. Note that, in particular, if $\mathcal{G}$ contains only one flat subgraph G, then solving P in G can be done by solving P in $f(G)$.

Example 2. Let P be the problem of finding the length of a shortest path from s to some vertex in T in a possibly weighted graph. Then a function f_{tree} that maps G to the tree $\{s\} \times T$ in which the weight of an edge $\langle s, t \rangle$ is the length of the shortest path from s to t maintains P. □

Consider two complexity functions $g_s : \mathbb{N} \to \mathbb{N}$ and $g_t : \mathbb{N} \times \mathbb{N} \to \mathbb{N}$, where s and t stand for *size* and *time*, respectively. Note that g_t has two parameters. We say that a problem P is (g_s, g_t)-*compressible* if there is a function $f : \mathscr{G} \to \mathscr{G}$ such that the following hold.

1. f maintains P,
2. For every graph $G = \langle V, s, T, E \rangle$, we have that $|f(G)| \leq g_s(|T|)$, and
3. For every graph $G = \langle V, s, T, E \rangle$, the complexity of calculating $f(G)$ is $g_t(|G|, |T|)$.

We then say that P is (g_s, g_t)-compressible with witness f.

Note that, by Condition 2, the size of $f(G)$ depends only on the number of exit vertices in G. In particular, if G has a constant number of exit vertices, then $f(G)$ is of constant size.

Theorem 1. *Let $\mathcal{G}$ be an HG. If a problem P is (g_s, g_t)-compressible, then we can generate a flat graph G such that $P(\mathcal{G}) = P(G)$, $|G| \leq g_s(|Exit_1|)$, and the complexity of calculating G is $\sum_{i=1}^{n} g_t(|G_i| - |B_i| + \sum_{b \in B_i} g_s(|Exit_{\tau_i(b)}|), |Exit_i|)$.*

Proof. Let $\mathcal{G} = \langle G_1, \ldots, G_n \rangle$, with $G_i = \langle V_i, B_i, in_i, Exit_i, \tau_i, E_i \rangle$. We prove that for every $0 \leq j \leq n - 1$, we can generate an HG $\mathcal{G}'_j = \langle G_1^j, G_2^j, \ldots, G_{n-j}^j \rangle$ such that:

1. $P(\mathcal{G}) = P(\mathcal{G}'_j)$,
2. $|G_{n-j}^j| \leq g_s(|Exit_{n-j}|)$, and
3. The complexity of calculating $\mathcal{G}'_j$ is $\sum_{i=n-j}^{n} g_t(|G_i| - |B_i| + \sum_{b \in B_i} g_s(|Exit_{\tau_i(b)}|), |Exit_i|)$.

The theorem then follows by taking $j = n - 1$. Indeed, $\mathcal{G}'_{n-1} = \langle G_1^{n-1} \rangle$ consists of a single subgraph, which must be flat.

Let $f : \mathscr{G} \to \mathscr{G}$ be such that P is (g_s, g_t)-compressible with witness f. The proof proceeds by an induction on j. For $j = 0$, we define $\mathcal{G}'_0 = \mathcal{G}[G_n \leftarrow f(G_n)]$. The claim follows immediately from the fact P is (g_s, g_t)-compressible with witness f.

Assume the claim holds for $j \in \{0, \ldots, k - 1\}$. We prove it holds for $j = k$. We define $\mathcal{G}'_k = \mathcal{G}'_{k-1} \downarrow [G_{n-k}^k \leftarrow f(G_{n-k}^k)]$. That is, we flatten all boxes that call the bottom subgraph in $\mathcal{G}'_{k-1}$, obtain an HG with $n - k$ subgraphs, and then apply f to the new bottom subgraph, namely on G_{n-k}^k. We prove that all three conditions hold.

1. Since flattening maintains P and so does an application of f, then $P(\mathcal{G}'_k) = P(\mathcal{G}'_{k-1})$. Thus, by the induction hypothesis, $P(\mathcal{G}) = P(\mathcal{G}'_k)$.

2. All subgraphs $G^0_{n-k}, G^1_{n-k}, \ldots, G^k_{n-k}$ have the same set of exit vertices, namely $Exit_{n-k}$. By the definition of (g_s, g_t)-compressibility, $|f(G^k_{n-k})| \leq g_s(|Exit_{n-k}|)$.

3. In particular, note that $|G^k_{n-k}|$ does not depend on the size of internal subgraphs, as f does not change the number of exit vertices. Finally, the calculation of $\mathcal{G}'_k$ involves a calculation of $\mathcal{G}'_j$ for all $j \in \{0, \ldots, k-1\}$. For every $j \in \{0, \ldots, k-1\}$, the calculation of f on G^j_{n-j}, which is required in order to obtain $\mathcal{G}'_j$, is done on a graph of size $|G_{n-j}| - |B_{n-j}| + \sum_{b \in B_{n-j}} g_s(|Exit_{\tau_{n-j}(b)}|)$ with $|Exit_{n-j}|$ exit vertices. Hence, the time complexity of calculating G'_j is $\sum_{i=n-j}^{n} g_t(|G_i| - |B_i| + \sum_{b \in B_i} g_s(|Exit_{\tau_i(b)}|), |Exit_i|)$.

□

We focus on linear, polynomial, and exponential functions. For classes $\gamma_G, \gamma_T \in \{\text{LIN}, \text{POLY}, \text{EXP}\}$, we say that a problem P is (γ_G, γ_T)-compressible if P is (g_s, g_t)-compressible for g_s whose complexity is γ_T in its parameter, and g_t that is γ_G in its first parameter and γ_T in its second parameter. For example, if $g_s(y) = 2^y$ and $g_t(x, y) = x + 2^y$, then P is (LIN, EXP)-compressible.

Theorem 2. *Let P be a (γ_G, γ_T)-compressible problem on graphs.*

1. *If γ_G and γ_T are LIN (respectively, POLY), then the complexity of solving P in HGs is linearly- (polynomially-) reducible to the problem of solving P in flat graphs.*

2. *If γ_G is LIN (respectively, POLY), then the complexity of solving P in CE-HGs is linear (polynomial).*

3.1 Applications

Shortest Path. The problem P from Example 2 is $(\text{POLY}, \text{POLY})$-compressible. Indeed, calculating a tree $\{s\} \times T$ with the length of the shortest path from s to t as the weight of every edge $\langle s, t \rangle$ can be done in polynomial time, and the size of such a tree is clearly linear in $|T|$. Theorem 2 thus implies that the shortest-path problem for HGs can be solved in polynomial time.

Eulerian Cycle. In the full version we present a polynomial function f that maintains the Eulerian cycle problem. Intuitively, f preserves both the parity of the degree of every interface vertex, and the connectivity of the graph. Technically, this is done by maintaining the interface vertices of the bottom subgraph and adding internal vertices for each maximal set of connected interface vertices. The new vertices are connected in a way that preserves connectivity and parity of degrees (parity of both in- and out-degrees, in the case of a connected graph).

Alternating Reachability. A directed AND-OR graph $\langle V, E \rangle$ is a graph whose vertices are partitioned into AND and OR vertices. Thus, $V = V_{and} \cup V_{or}$, with $V_{and} \cap V_{or} = \emptyset$. We say that a set T of vertices is alternating-reachable from a vertex u, denoted $ar(u, T)$, if $u \in T$, $u \in V_{or}$ and T is alternating-reachable from some successor of u, or $u \in V_{and}$ and T is alternating-reachable from all the successors of u. The AR problem is to decide, given G, u, and T, whether $ar(u, T)$. The problem is PTIME-complete [12] for flat graph and PSPACE-complete for HGs [16]. We prove that AR is (LIN, EXP)-compressible, implying it is PTIME-complete for CE-HGs.

We describe a function f that maintains P. Consider an AND-OR graph $G = \langle V, s, T, E \rangle$, with a partition $V_{and} \cup V_{or}$. Let $T_1, \ldots, T_m$ be the subsets of T that are alternating-reachable from s. We define $f(G) = \langle \{s, u_1, \ldots, u_m\} \cup T, s, T, E' \rangle$, where the OR-vertices are $\{s\} \cup (T \cap V_{or})$, and the AND-vertices are $\{u_1, \ldots, u_m\} \cup (T \cap V_{and})$. The edge relation E' consists of edges $\{s\} \times \{u_1, \ldots, u_m\}$ and $\{u_j\} \times T_j$ for every $1 \le j \le m$. That is, there are edges from s to every vertex u_j, and from u_j to every vertex in T_j, where $1 \le j \le m$. It is easy to see that calculating $f(G)$ is polynomial in $|G|$ and exponential in $|T|$, and its size is exponential in $|T|$.

Maximal Flow. A flow network is a weighted directed graph $G = \langle V, s, \{t\}, E, c \rangle$, where the weight function $c : E \to \mathbb{N}$ maps each edge to its capacity, namely the maximum amount of flow that can travel through it, the source edge s has no incoming edges, and the target vertex t has no outgoing edges. A *flow* is a mapping $f : E \to \mathbb{R}^+$ that satisfies the following two constraints: (1) For every edge $(u, v) \in E$, it holds that $f(u, v) \le c(u, v)$, and (2) For every $v \in V \setminus \{s, t\}$, it holds that $\sum_{u:(u,v) \in E} f(u, v) = \sum_{u:(v,u) \in E} f(v, u)$. The *value of flow* is defined by $|f| = \sum_{v:(s,v) \in E} f(s, v)$. The problem of finding a maximal flow (MF, for short) is to find, given a flow network G, the maximal value of a flow for it. For flat graphs, the problem can be solved in polynomial time (cf., the Ford-Fulkerson algorithm [9]). It is shown in [16] that the problem is PSPACE-complete for hierarchical graphs. Here, we conjecture that the problem is $(\text{POLY}, \text{EXP})$-compressible, implying that it can be solved in PTIME for CE-HGs. We prove that for graphs with at most 3 exit vertices, it is even $(\text{POLY}, \text{POLY})$-compressible, implying it can be solved in PTIME for such graphs. For the general case, the problem is strongly related to the problem of polytop optimization (cf., [20]).

Consider a flow graph with source and several target vertices $G = \langle V, s, T, E, c \rangle$. The *characteristic function* $v : 2^T \to \mathbb{R}^+$ of G maps each a set $U \subseteq T$ of target vertices to the maximal flow that can be routed to U. That is, $v(U)$ is the maximal flow in a network $G' = \langle V \cup \{t'\}, s, \{t'\}, E', c' \rangle$, obtained from G by defining a new single sink vertex t' and adding edges with capacity ∞ from every vertex in U to t'. In particular, $v(T)$ is the maximal flow that can be routed to all target vertices together. Also, for a single vertex $t \in T$, we have that $v(t)$ is the maximal flow that can be routed to t. It is known that the characteristic function is necessary and sufficient in order to represent a flow network [18]. Therefore, the equivalence of two flow networks can be proved by proving that their characteristic functions are identical.

We show a function f that maintains the MF problem for flow networks with up to three sink vertices: given a flow network $G = \langle V, s, T, E, w \rangle$, where $|T| \leq 3$, the function $f(G)$ constructs in polynomial time a flow network G' of constant size such that every flow in G is a flow in G', and vice versa. It is easy to see that every flow network with one sink t is equivalent to a flow network with two vertices, s and t, connected by an edge with capacity $v(t)$. Formally, if a given flow network $G = \langle V, s, \{t\}, E, w \rangle$ has one exit vertex, then $f(G) = \langle \{s, t\}, s, \{t\}, \langle s, t \rangle, v(t) \rangle$. In Fig. 2, we describe the flow network that f returns for flow networks with two (left) and three (right) sinks. For the one in the right, it is easy to see that the maximal flow in this network is $v(\{t_1, t_2\})$, while the maximal flow to the sinks t_1 and t_2 is $v(t_1)$ and $v(t_2)$, respectively. In addition, f maintains MF also for three sinks. Note that calculating f requires $2^{|T|} - 1$ polynomial computations, where $|T| \leq 3$.

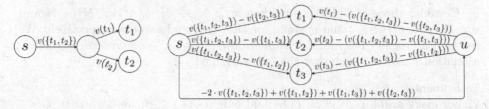

Fig. 2. Compressing flow networks with two and three sinks

Conjecture 1. The problem of maximal flow is (POLY, EXP)-compressible. Thus, by Theorem 2 it can be solved in PTIME for CE-FGs.

3.2 Not All Problems Are Compressible

We conclude this section pointing to a problem for which the exponential penalty cannot be avoided even if the number of exit vertices is constant. The problem of *path of length in a given interval in a tree* (the PI problem, for short) is to decide, given a weighted directed tree $G = \langle V, E, w \rangle$ and an interval $[x, y]$, whether there is a path of length in $[x, y]$ in G. For flat graphs, we can solve the problem by computing the length of the path between every pair of vertices. Since the graph is a directed tree, there is at most one path between every two nodes, and therefore this algorithm is polymonial. A tree HG is an HG all whose subgraphs are trees.

Lemma 1. *The PI problem is NP-complete for CE-HGs.*

4   Nondeterministic Compression of Hierarchical Graphs

In this section we study problems P for which a polynomial verifier is known in the flat setting. We argue that when the number of exit vertices is bounded by a constant, this can be used in order to verify that a suggested compression of the bottom subgraph indeed maintains P. This enables us to show membership in NP for the hierarchical setting for several problems for which membership in NP is known in the flat setting, improving the PSPACE upper bound for the general case (that is, when the number of exit vertices is not a constant).

Consider a decision problem P and a graph with entry and exit vertices G. We say that G is *hopeful with respect to P* if there is an HG in which G is called and $P(\mathcal{G})$ holds. For example, if P is 3-coloring, and G includes a 4-clique, then G is not hopeful. We say that a relation $R : \mathcal{G} \times \mathcal{G}$ *maintains P* if for every graph $G \in \mathcal{G}$ that is hopeful with respect to P there is at least one graph $G' \in \mathcal{G}$ such that $\langle G, G' \rangle \in R$, and for every pair of graphs $\langle G, G' \rangle \in R$, we have that G is substitutable by G' and for every HG $\mathcal{G}$ with bottom subgraph G, we have $P(\mathcal{G}) = P(\mathcal{G}[G \leftarrow G'])$.

Consider three complexity functions $g_s : \mathbb{N} \to \mathbb{N}$, $g_t : \mathbb{N} \times \mathbb{N} \to \mathbb{N}$ and $g_w : \mathbb{N} \to \mathbb{N}$, where s, t and w stand for *size*, *time* and *witness*, respectively. We say that a problem P is *nondeterministically-(g_s, g_t, g_w)-compressible* if there is a relation $R : \mathcal{G} \times \mathcal{G}$ such that the following hold.

1. R maintains P,
2. For every graph $G = \langle V, s, T, E \rangle$ and pair $\langle G, G' \rangle \in R$, we have that $|G'| \leq g_s(|T|)$,
3. There is a verifier $\mathcal{V}$ that runs in time $g_t(|G|, |T|)$ such that whenever $\langle G, G' \rangle \in R$, there is a witness w such that $\mathcal{V}$ returns "yes" on $(\langle G, G' \rangle, w)$, and
4. For every graph $G = \langle V, s, T, E \rangle$, we have $|\{G' : \langle G, G' \rangle \in R\}| \leq g_w(|T|)$.

We then say that P is nondeterministically-(g_s, g_t, g_w)-compressible with witness R.

Theorem 3. *Let $\mathcal{G}$ be an HG. If a problem P is nondeterministically-(g_s, g_t, g_w)-compressible and $P(\mathcal{G})$ holds, then there is a flat graph G such that $|G| \leq g_s(|Exit_1|)$, and there is a verifier $\mathcal{V}$ that runs in time $\sum_{i=1}^{n} g_w(|Exit_i|) \cdot (g_t(|G_i| - |B_i| + \sum_{b \in B_i} g_s(|Exit_{\tau_i(b)}|), |Exit_i|))$ such that if $P(\mathcal{G}) = P(G)$, then there is a witness w such that $\mathcal{V}$ returns "yes" on (G, w).*

Theorem 4. *If a problem P is nondeterministically-(g_s, g_t, g_w)-compressible for g_t polynomial in its first parameter, then P is in NP for CE-HGs.*

4.1   Applications

In this section we describe NP-complete problems that stay in NP for CE-HGs. We rely on Theorem 4, showing that the problems are nondeterministically-(g_s, g_t, g_w)-compressible for g_t that is polynomial in its first parameter in $|G|$.

k-coloring. A valid k-coloring for a graph is a labeling of the vertices of the graph by k colors so that adjacent vertices are mapped to different colors. We define a relation $R : \mathscr{G} \times \mathscr{G}$ such that for every graph $G = \langle V, s, T, E \rangle$, we have that $\langle G, G' \rangle \in R$ iff $G' = \langle \{s, v_1, v_2, \ldots, v_k\} \cup T, s, T, E' \rangle$, there is exactly one valid coloring of G' with k colors, and there is a valid coloring of G that agrees with the coloring of the interface vertices in G'. Note that if there is a valid coloring of the interface vertices in G, then the edge relation E' can force it on the interface vertices in G' using a "k-colors plate" clique $\{v_1, v_2, \ldots, v_k\}$. Namely, the set E' includes an edge between every pair of vertices in $\{v_1, v_2, \ldots, v_k\}$, and in addition it includes edges from every vertex $v \in \{s\} \cup T$ to the colors in $\{v_1, v_2, \ldots, v_k\}$ that v is not colored in. It is easy to see that R maintains P. Note that for every graph $G = \langle V, s, T, E \rangle$ and pair $\langle G, G' \rangle \in R$, $|G'|$ is clearly of size linear in $|T|$, and verifing that $\langle G, G' \rangle \in R$ can be done in polynomial time, given a witness that shows a coloring of G that agrees with G' on the coloring of the interface vertices. Finally, for every graph G, the number of graphs G' such that $\langle G, G' \rangle \in R$ is bounded by $k^{|T|}$, which is constant for CE-HGs.

Independent Set. The independent set problem is to decide, given a graph $G = \langle V, E \rangle$ and number $k \geq 0$, whether G contains an independent set $S \subseteq V$ of size at least k, where S is independent if for all two vertices v and v' in S, we have $(v, v') \notin E$. Note that the input to the problem contains a parameter k. We extend our definition of maintenance to also account for the parameter. Thus, the relation $R : (\mathscr{G} \times \mathbb{N}) \times (\mathscr{G} \times \mathbb{N})$ *maintains* P if for every graph $G \in \mathscr{G}$ and parameter $k \in \mathbb{N}$, such that $\langle G, k \rangle$ is hopeful with respect to P, there is at least one graph $G' \in \mathscr{G}$ and parameter $k' \in \mathbb{N}$, such that $\langle (G, k), (G', k') \rangle \in R$. In addition, we allow R to refer to labeled versions of G and G'. Formally, we rephrase the independent set problem as follows: given $G = \langle V, E \rangle$ and k, decide whether there is a labeling function $l : V \to \{0, 1\}$ such that $l^{-1}(1)$ forms an independent set of size at least k. Now, whenever we compress a graph G, we mark the interface vertices of G' by 0's and 1's, serving as identifiers as to whether these vertices participate in the witness independent set of G. Thus, $\langle (G, k), (G', k - k') \rangle \in R$ iff $G' = \langle \{s\} \cup T, s, T, \emptyset, l \rangle$, where l is such that there is an independent set S in G of size $k' + |(\{s\} \cup T) \cap l^{-1}(1)|$ such that for all $v \in \{s\} \cup T$, we have that $v \in S$ iff $l(v) = 1$. Note that l uniquely defines k', thus for each $l : \{s\} \cup T \to \{0, 1\}$, there is at most one graph G' such that $\langle (G, k), (G', k - k') \rangle \in R$.

Now, when G is replaced by G', the search for a labeling function in $\mathscr{G}$ that serves as a characteristic function of the independent set takes the labels of G' into account. Thus, edges that lead to an interface vertex of G' that is labeled by 1 cannot be labeled by 1. Since there are at most $2^{|T|+1}$ possible labeling functions, all the conditions on R are satisfied.

Hamilton Path. A Hamiltonian path in the graph is a path that traverses all the vertices of the path, each vertex exactly once. For directed graphs, the hierarchical setting is less challenging, as a subgraph may be entered only once.

We consider here also the more challenging undirected case, where a subgraph may be entered via all its interface vertices. There, a Hamiltonian path in an HG may enter a subgraph more than once, and it may visit an interface vertex of a box without entering or leaving it. For an HG $\mathcal{G}$ with a box b that is substituted by G, restricting a Hamiltonian path to b yields a set of paths in G, where every vertex in G appears exactly in one path. This set induces a partition of the interface vertices of G, where the vertices in every subset in the partition are ordered. For a Hamiltonian path with sub-paths $p_1, \ldots, p_m$ in G, we denote this partition as *the restriction of* $p_1, \ldots, p_m$ *to the interface vertices of* G. We define a relation $R : \mathcal{G} \times \mathcal{G}$ such that for every graph $G = \langle V, s, T, E \rangle$, we have that $\langle G, G' \rangle \in R$ iff $G' = \langle \{s\} \cup T, s, T, E' \rangle$, and E' is such that there are two sets of paths $\{p_1, \ldots, p_m\}$ in G and $\{p'_1, \ldots, p'_m\}$ in G' with the same restriction to the interface vertices $\{s\} \cup T$. It is easy to see that this relation maintains the problem of Hamiltonian path both for directed and undirected graphs and for every graph, there is a bounded number of graphs that are in relation R with it. In addition, for every graph $G = \langle V, s, T, E \rangle$ and pair $\langle G, G' \rangle \in R$, $|G'|$ is clearly of size linear in $|T|$. Finally, given a witness that shows set of paths in G that are restricted to the same partition as E' in G', verifing that $\langle G, G' \rangle \in R$ can be easily done in polynomial time.

References

1. Alur, R., Kannan, S., Yannakakis, M.: Communicating hierarchical state machines. In: Wiedermann, J., Emde Boas, P., Nielsen, M. (eds.) ICALP 1999. LNCS, vol. 1644, pp. 169–178. Springer, Heidelberg (1999). doi:10.1007/3-540-48523-6_14
2. Alur, R., Yannakakis, M.: Model checking of hierarchical state machines. ACM TOPLAS **23**(3), 273–303 (2001)
3. Aminof, B., Kupferman, O., Murano, A.: Improved model checking of hierarchical systems. Inf. Comput. **210**, 68–86 (2012)
4. Barrett, C., Jacob, R., Marathe, M.: Formal-language-constrained path problems. SIAM J. Comput. **30**(3), 809–837 (2000)
5. Clarke, E.M., Grumberg, O., Peled, D.: Model Checking. MIT Press, Cambridge (1999)
6. de Roever, W.-P.: The need for compositional proof systems: a survey. In: de Roever, W.-P., Langmaack, H., Pnueli, A. (eds.) COMPOS 1997. LNCS, vol. 1536, pp. 1–22. Springer, Heidelberg (1998). doi:10.1007/3-540-49213-5_1
7. Downey, R.G., Fellows, M.R.: Fundamentals of Parameterized Complexity. Texts in Computer Science. Springer, Heidelberg (2013)
8. Drusinsky, D., Harel, D.: On the power of bounded concurrency I: finite automata. J. ACM **41**(3), 517–539 (1994)
9. Ford, L.R., Fulkerson, D.R.: Maximal flow through a network. Can. J. Math. **8**(3), 399–404 (1956)
10. Galperin, H., Wigderson, A.: Succinct representations of graphs. Inf. Control **56**(3), 183–198 (1983)
11. Harel, D., Kupferman, O., Vardi, M.Y.: On the complexity of verifying concurrent transition systems. Inf. Comput. **173**, 1–19 (2002)
12. Immerman, N.: Length of predicate calculus formulas as a new complexity measure. In: Proceedings of 20th FOCS, pp. 337–347 (1979)

13. Kupferman, O., Tamir, T.: Hierarchical network formation games. In: Legay, A., Margaria, T. (eds.) TACAS 2017. LNCS, vol. 10205, pp. 229–246. Springer, Heidelberg (2017). doi:10.1007/978-3-662-54577-5_13
14. Kupferman, O., Vardi, M.Y., Wolper, P.: An automata-theoretic approach to branching-time model checking. J. ACM **47**(2), 312–360 (2000)
15. Lengauer, T.: The complexity of compacting hierarchically specified layouts of integrated circuits. In: Proceedings of 23rd FOCS, pp. 358–368 (1982)
16. Lengauer, T., Wagner, K.W.: The correlation between the complexities of the non-hierarchical and hierarchical versions of graph problems. JCSS **44**, 63–93 (1990)
17. Lengauer, T., Wanke, E.: Efficient solutions of connectivity problems on hierarchically defined graphs. SIAM J. Comput. **17**(6), 1063–1081 (1988)
18. Megiddo, N.: Optimal flows in networks with multiple sources and sinks. Math. Program. **7**(1), 97–107 (1974)
19. Mendelzon, A.O., Wood, P.T.: Finding regular simple paths in graph databases. SIAM J. Comput. **24**(6), 1235–1258 (1995)
20. Rothvoß, T.: The matching polytope has exponential extension complexity. In: Proceedings of 46th STOC, pp. 263–272 (2014)

Graph-Controlled Insertion-Deletion Systems Generating Language Classes Beyond Linearity

Henning Fernau[1]([⊠]), Lakshmanan Kuppusamy[2], and Indhumathi Raman[3]

[1] Fachbereich 4 – CIRT, Universität Trier, 54286 Trier, Germany
`fernau@uni-trier.de`
[2] SCOPE, VIT University, Vellore 632 014, India
`{klakshma,indhumathi.r}@vit.ac.in`
[3] SITE, VIT University, Vellore 632 014, India

Abstract. A regulated extension of an insertion-deletion system known as graph-controlled insertion-deletion (GCID) system has several components and each component contains some insertion-deletion rules. A rule is applied to a string in a component and the resultant string is moved to the target component specified in the rule. When resources are so limited (especially, when deletion is context-free) then GCID systems are not known to describe the class of recursively enumerable languages. Hence, it becomes interesting to find the descriptional complexity of such GCID systems of small sizes with respect to language classes below RE. To this end, we consider closure classes of linear languages. We show that whenever GCID systems describe LIN with t components, we can extend this to GCID systems with just one more component to describe, for instance, 2-LIN and with further addition of one more component, we can extend to GCID systems that describe the rational closure of LIN.

Keywords: Insertion-deletion systems · Graph-controlled systems · Descriptional complexity measures · Closure classes of linear languages

1 Introduction

The origin of insertion systems comes from linguistics, under the name of semi-contextual grammars [6], as well from biology. In biology, the insertion operation is found in the process of mismatched annealing in DNA strands [14] and in RNA editing, some fragments of messenger RNA are inserted or deleted [1]. Further motivation for insertion operations can be seen in [8]. On the other hand, the deletion operation was introduced independently in [10]. Insertion and deletion operations together were introduced in [11]; the corresponding grammatical mechanism is called *insertion-deletion system* (abbreviated as ins-del system). Informally, insertion means inserting a string η between the strings w_1 and w_2, whereas deletion means deleting a substring δ from the string $w_1 \delta w_2$.

Among the several variants of ins-del systems (e.g., see [15] for this), we focus on graph-controlled ins-del systems (abbreviated as GCID systems). Such a system was introduced in [5] where the concept of components is introduced,

G. Pighizzini and C. Câmpeanu (Eds.): DCFS 2017, LNCS 10316, pp. 128–139, 2017.
DOI: 10.1007/978-3-319-60252-3_10

associated with insertion or deletion rules. The transition is performed by choosing any applicable rule from the set of rules of the current component and by moving the resultant string to the target component specified in the rule. The descriptional complexity measures are based on the size, denoted by $(k; n, i', i''; m, j', j'')$ where the parameters from left to right denote (i) the number of components k (ii) the maximal length of the insertion string n, (iii) the maximal length of the left context and right context used in insertion rules, i' and i'', respectively, (iv) the maximal length of the deletion string m, (v) the maximal length of the left context and right context used in deletion rules, j' and j'', respectively. We will also refer to the last six numbers in the septuple as *ID size*, where *ID* stands for insertion-deletion.

It is known that the class of linear languages LIN is not closed under concatenation and Kleene closure. Let $\mathcal{L}_\circ(\text{LIN})$ and $\mathcal{L}_*(\text{LIN})$ denote the super-classes of LIN closed under concatenation and Kleene closure, respectively. It is shown in [3] that if GCID systems can describe LIN with ID size s and t components, then it can be extended to a GCID system with ID size s and $t + 1$ components to describe $\mathcal{L}_*(\text{LIN})$ and particular cases of GCID systems with ID size s and $t + 2$ components describing $\mathcal{L}_\circ(\text{LIN})$ were reported. In this paper, we generalize these results to show that even the *rational* or *regular closure* of LIN (denoted as $\mathcal{L}_{reg}(\text{LIN})$) can be described by GCID systems with ID size s and $t + 2$ components. We also show that a subclass of $\mathcal{L}_{reg}(\text{LIN})$ containing languages which can be described as concatenation of two languages from $\mathcal{L}_*(\text{LIN})$, can be described by GCID systems with ID size s and $t + 1$ components. For the first result, we employ a new normal form for $\mathcal{L}_{reg}(\text{LIN})$. Due to space restrictions, many illustrations, examples and proofs have been suppressed.

2 Preliminaries

We assume that the readers are familiar with the standard notations used in formal language theory. However, we recall a few notations. Let $\mathbb{N}$ denote the set of positive integers, and $[1 \ldots k] = \{i \in \mathbb{N} : 1 \le i \le k\}$. If Σ is an *alphabet* (finite set), then Σ^* denotes the free monoid generated by Σ. The elements of Σ^* are called *strings* or *words*; λ denotes the empty string. For a string $w \in \Sigma^*$, w^R denotes the reversal (mirror image) of w. Likewise, L^R and $\mathcal{L}^R$ are understood for languages L and language families $\mathcal{L}$. The family of linear, context-free and recursively enumerable languages are denoted by LIN, CF and RE, respectively.

The language class LIN is neither closed under concatenation nor under Kleene closure. This motivates to consider several so-called closure classes of the linear languages. A detailed study of these closure classes is given in [12].

Let $\mathcal{L}_{op}(\mathcal{F})$ be the smallest language class containing $\mathcal{F}$ and being closed under the operation op. Since LIN is not closed under concatenation and Kleene closure, the closure classes $\mathcal{L}_\circ(\text{LIN})$ and $\mathcal{L}_*(\text{LIN})$ are strict supersets of LIN. The class $\mathcal{L}_\circ(\text{LIN})$ is the class of metalinear languages. If $L \in \mathcal{L}_\circ(\text{LIN})$, then $L = L_1 \circ L_2 \circ \cdots \circ L_k$ (in short $L_1 L_2 \ldots L_k$) for some $k \ge 1$, where $L_i \in \text{LIN}$ for each $1 \le i \le k$. Fixing $k \ge 1$, we arrive at the class k-LIN, a subclass of $\mathcal{L}_\circ(\text{LIN})$. In other words, $\mathcal{L}_\circ(\text{LIN}) = \bigcup_{k\geq 1} k\text{-LIN}$ and $\text{LIN} = 1 - \text{LIN}$ by definition. Similarly, if $L \in \mathcal{L}_*(\text{LIN})$, then either $L \in \text{LIN}$ or $L = (L')^*$ for some linear language L'. It is well known that $\mathcal{L}_*(\text{LIN})$ and $\mathcal{L}_\circ(\text{LIN})$ are not closed under concatenation and Kleene closure, respectively; see [12]. The class $\mathfrak{L} := \{L_1^* L_2 \mid L_1, L_2 \in \text{LIN}\}$ is also considered as an extension of $\mathcal{L}_*(\text{LIN})$ in [12].[1] It has a nice characterization in terms of pushdown automata with finite turns. Continuing to play around with the concatenation and Kleene closure operators and extending our notation to lists of operators, we have $\mathcal{L}_{\circ,*}(\text{LIN})$, the smallest language family containing LIN and being closed under concatenation and Kleene closure. Recall that $\mathcal{L}_{reg}(\text{LIN})$ is the smallest language family that contains LIN and is closed under the three regular operators: union, concatenation and Kleene closure. In our notation, this corresponds to $\mathcal{L}_{\cup,\circ,*}(\text{LIN})$.

2.1   Graph-Controlled Insertion-Deletion Systems

We define graph-controlled insertion-deletion systems following [5].

Definition 1. *A graph-controlled insertion-deletion system (GCID system for short) with k components is a construct $\Pi = (k, V, T, A, H, i_0, i_f, R)$, where k is the number of components, V is an alphabet, $T \subseteq V$ is the terminal alphabet and $V \setminus T$ is the non-terminal alphabet, $A \subseteq V$ is a finite set of axioms, H is a set of labels associated (in a one-to-one manner) to the rules in R, $i_0 \in [1 \dots k]$ is the initial component, $i_f \in [1 \dots k]$ is the final component, and R is a finite set of rules of the form (i, r, j) where r is an insertion rule of the form $(u, \eta, v)_{ins}$ or a deletion rule of the form $(u, \delta, v)_{del}$, with $i, j \in [1 \dots k]$. We say that a GCID system handles terminals properly if terminal symbols are only inserted in non-empty contexts containing non-terminals and never get deleted.*

An insertion rule of the form $(u, \eta, v)_{ins}$ means that the string η is inserted between u and v and it corresponds to the rewriting rule $uv \to u\eta v$. Similarly, a deletion rule of the form $(u, \delta, v)_{del}$ means that the string δ is deleted between u and v and this corresponds to the rewriting rule $u\delta v \to uv$. The pair (u, v) is called the *context*, η is called the *insertion string*, δ is called the *deletion string* and $x \in A$ is called an *axiom*. A rule of the form $l : (i, r, j)$, where $l \in H$ is the label associated to the rule, denotes that the string is sent from component i (for short denoted as Ci) to Cj after the application of the insertion or deletion rule r on the string. If the initial component itself is the final component, then we call the system to be a *returning* GCID system.

A graph-controlled ins-del system Π is said to be of size $(k; n, i', i''; m, j', j'')$ if

k is the number of components	
$n = \max\{|\eta| : (i, (u, \eta, v)_{ins}, j) \in R\}$	$m = \max\{|\delta| : (i, (u, \delta, v)_{del}, j) \in R\}$
$i' = \max\{|u| : (i, (u, \eta, v)_{ins}, j) \in R\}$	$j' = \max\{|u| : (i, (u, \delta, v)_{del}, j) \in R\}$
$i'' = \max\{|v| : (i, (u, \eta, v)_{ins}, j) \in R\}$	$j'' = \max\{|v| : (i, (u, \delta, v)_{del}, j) \in R\}$

---

[1] In [12], $\mathfrak{L}$ was called $\mathcal{L}_*$, which we avoid due to possible confusions with our Kleene closure operator notation.

In general, we follow the convention to use rule label names that are carrying some meaning as follows. For instance, if we like to describe the simulation of a rule p, then this is usually done by several rules in several components, so that $pi.j$ would refer to the jth simulation rule in component Ci. The *underlying control graph* of a k-GCID system Π is defined to be a graph with k nodes labelled $C1$ through Ck. There exists a directed edge from Ci to Cj if and only if there exists a rule of the form (i, r, j) in R of Π. We also associate a simple undirected graph on k nodes to a GCID system of k components as follows: There is an undirected edge from a node Ci to Cj $(i \neq j)$ if and only if there exists a rule of the form (i, r_1, j) or (j, r_2, i) in R of Π. If this underlying undirected simple graph is a tree structure, then we call a returning GCID system *tree-structured*. The language class generated by returning GCID systems of size s is denoted by $\mathrm{GCID}(s)$.

We assume the following normal form for linear grammars: $p : X \to aY$, $q : X \to Ya$ and $h : Z \to \lambda$ where $X, Y, Z \in N$, $a \in T$ as in [2–4]. We also call a returning GCID system *simple-deleting* if it contains one rule of the form $h1.1 : (1, (\lambda, Z, \lambda)_{del}, 1)$ intended to simulate $h : Z \to \lambda$ and that this rule is always the last to be applied in order to obtain a terminal string. For simplicity, we will denote the class of simple-deleting GCID systems (of size s), as well as the corresponding language family, by $\mathrm{GCID}_{SD}(s)$. Moreover, we use the subscript SDT if we want to emphasize that the control graph is tree-structured. With these notations, we rephrase the previous LIN results of [2–4] as follows, omitting the situation when even RE could be characterized.

Proposition 1. $\mathrm{LIN} \subsetneq \mathrm{GCID}_{SD}(3; 1, 1, 0; 1, 0, 0) \cap \mathrm{GCID}_{SD}(3; 1, 0, 1; 1, 0, 0)$ *and* $\mathrm{LIN} \subsetneq \mathrm{GCID}_{SDT}(3; 2, 1, 0; 1, 0, 0) \cap \mathrm{GCID}_{SDT}(3; 2, 0, 1; 1, 0, 0)$.

3 Properties of Closure Classes

In this section, we show some auxiliary results needed to describe the closure classes by GCID system and then provide a characterization of the rational closure of LIN which follows directly from a normal form representation for regular expressions which states that each regular expression can be expressed as finite union of union-free expressions; see [13, Theorem 2].

Proposition 2. *The language classes* $\mathcal{L}_*(\mathrm{LIN})$, $\mathcal{L}_\circ(\mathrm{LIN})$, $\mathcal{L} \cup \mathcal{L}^R$, *2-LIN and* $\mathcal{L}_{reg}(\mathrm{LIN})$ *are all closed under reversal, but* $\mathcal{L}$ *and* $\mathcal{L}^R$ *are not.*

Proof. The positive closure properties follow in a straightforward inductive way from what is known about LIN and some algebraic identities.

Suppose $\mathcal{L}$ is closed under reversal. Then $(L_1^* L_2)^R = L_3^* L_4$ for some linear languages L_3, L_4 in particular if $L_1 = \{a^n b^n \mid n \geq 1\}$ and $L_2 = \{c^m d^m \mid m \geq 1\}$. Clearly, $(L_1^* L_2)^R$ is not a linear language. Discuss some $d^j w \in L_3$, where w does not start with d. If $w \neq \lambda$, then $(d^j w)^2 \in L_3$ is not a prefix of any word in $(L_1^* L_2)^R$. Hence, $L_3 \subseteq \{d\}^*$. Consider again $d^j \in L_3$ with $j > 0$. Then, $c^j b^r a^r \in L_4$ for some $r \geq 0$. But then, also $(d^j)^2 c^j b^r a^r \in L_3^* L_4$, but $(d^j)^2 c^j b^r a^r \notin (L_1^* L_2)^R$, contradicting our assumption. $\square$

Proposition 3 [12]. *The following inclusions are true. Moreover, all are strict.*

(i) LIN $\subsetneq \mathcal{L}_*(\text{LIN}) \subsetneq \mathcal{L} \cup \mathcal{L}^R \subsetneq \mathcal{L}_{reg}(\text{LIN}) \subsetneq$ CF.
(ii) LIN $\subsetneq$ 2-LIN $\subsetneq \mathcal{L}_\circ(\text{LIN}) \subsetneq \mathcal{L}_{reg}(\text{LIN})$.

Proposition 4 [12]. *The following pairs of language classes are incomparable.*
(i) 2-LIN *and* $\mathcal{L}_*(\text{LIN})$, *(ii)* 2-LIN *and* $\mathcal{L} \cup \mathcal{L}^R$, *(iii)* $\mathcal{L}_\circ(\text{LIN})$ *and* $\mathcal{L}_*(\text{LIN})$, *(iv)* $\mathcal{L}_\circ(\text{LIN})$ *and* $\mathcal{L} \cup \mathcal{L}^R$.

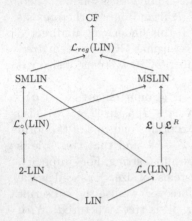

The inter-relationship between the closure classes of LIN stated in Propositions 3 and 4 is shown on the left. A (path of) solid arrow from A to B indicates $A \subsetneq B$ and no arrowed path between A and B tells that A and B are incomparable. We also add MSLIN $= \mathcal{L}_\circ(\mathcal{L}_*(\text{LIN}))$ and SMLIN $= \mathcal{L}_*(\mathcal{L}_\circ(\text{LIN}))$.

The following proposition follows directly from Theorem 2 of [13].

Proposition 5. *Let* $L \subseteq T^*$. *Then* $L \in \mathcal{L}_{reg}(\text{LIN})$ *if and only if* L *is the finite union of languages from* $\mathcal{L}_{\circ,*}(\text{LIN})$.

Let us now consider a small example that illustrates this proposition. Consider the language L described as follows.

$$L = (L_1'(L_2' \cup (L_3')^*)(L_1' \cup L_2')L_3')^*$$

for linear languages $L_1', L_2', L_3' \subseteq T^*$. Then, we find the following representation:

$$L = ((L_1'L_2'L_1'L_3')^* \circ (L_1'L_2'L_2'L_3')^* \circ (L_1'(L_3')^*L_1'L_3')^* \circ (L_1'(L_3')^*L_2'L_3')^*)^*. \quad (1)$$

Due to the previous proposition, we can focus now on expressions that have only concatenation and Kleene star as operations and whose basic elements are linear languages. Recall the well-known equivalence between expressions and (expression) trees about which we talk in the following. So, the term *subexpression* corresponds to a subtree. In this sense, leaf labels can be subexpressions. Also, we consider Kleene star as a unary operation, but concatenation can take any arity of at least two. This allows us to assume that stars and concatenation always alternate on any path in the expression tree.

In order to describe our grammar constructions that show how to generate all languages from the regular closure of LIN by appropriate GCID systems, we need to specify which of the linear grammars (associated to the leaves of the expression trees) should be simulated 'next', i.e., after finishing with the simulation of the 'current' grammar. This is formalized in the following with the notion of continuation points, reminiscent of the Glushkov transformation [7].

Assume that t is an expression tree with inner nodes labeled $*$ or $\circ$, and the leaves be labeled with numbers from $[1 \ldots k]$. For $i \in [1 \ldots k]$, we define the set of

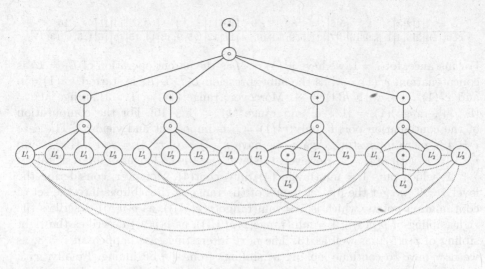

Fig. 1. The expression tree of our example; dotted lines indicate continuation points by joining leaves i and j if $j \in \text{cont}(i)$, suppressing the direction information.

continuation points $\text{cont}(i) \subseteq [1 \ldots k+1]$ as follows. Here, let $\text{subex}(i)$ denote the smallest subexpression to which i belongs, and $r(i)$ be the root label of $\text{subex}(i)$. Moreover, $\text{range}(i)$ be the subinterval of $[1 \ldots k]$ that spans from the first to the last leaf label of $\text{subex}(i)$. Slightly abusing notation, we also write $\text{range}(n)$ for the subinterval of $[1 \ldots k]$ that spans from the first to the last leaf label of the subexpression rooted at some inner node n. Hence, $\text{subex}(i) = \text{subex}(r(i))$. Inductively, we set $\text{subex}^1(i) = \text{subex}(i)$, $r^1(i) = r(i)$ and $\text{range}^1(i) = \text{range}(i)$, as well as $r^j(i) = p(r^{j-1}(i))$, where p is the parent function, $\text{subex}^j(i)$ is the subexpression rooted at $r^j(i)$, and $\text{range}^j(i)$ be the subinterval of $[1 \ldots k]$ that spans from the first to the last leaf label of $\text{subex}^j(i)$. We refer to j also as the *level*. Clearly, at some point $p(r^{j-1}(i))$ is no longer defined, as specified by the *height* $h(i)$. In the following, let $j \leq h(i)$.

- If $r^j(i) = *$ and $i = \max(\text{range}^j(i))$, then $\min(\text{range}^j(i))$ belongs to $\text{cont}(i)$. Moreover, if $j = h(i)$, we include $\max(\text{range}^j(i)) + 1 = k+1$ as a continuation point.
- If $r^j(i) = \circ$ and $i < \max(\text{range}^j(i))$ and either (a) $j = 1$ or (b) $r^{j-1}(i) = *$ and $i = \max(\text{range}^{j-1}(i))$, then let $s_1, \ldots, s_q$ be all the right siblings of (a) i or (b) the root of $\text{subex}^{j-1}(i)$, respectively, such that the labels of $s_1, \ldots, s_q$ are all $*$ but that of s_q, which is $\circ$, or s_q is a leaf; then, $\min(\text{range}(s_o))$ belongs to $\text{cont}(i)$ for all $1 \leq o \leq q$. As a special case, if there is no s_q with label $\circ$ (because all right siblings carry stars), then we have to continue from the beginning, with the left siblings, again from left to right, until we hit the first s'_q with label $\circ$.

Look again at our example to illustrate this definition, calling the 16 linear languages occurring in the leaves of the expression in Eq. (1) as $L_1, \ldots, L_{16}$ from left to right, also cf. Fig. 1. The following table lists the continuation points.

$i =$	1	2	3	4	5	6	7	8	9	10	11	12	13	14	15	16
$\mathrm{cont}(i)$	2	3	4	1, 5, 9, 13	6	7	8	1, 5, 9, 13	10, 11	11	12	1, 5, 9, 13	14, 15	15	16	1, 5, 9, 13, 17

For instance, for $i = 1$, we have $r^1(1) = \circ$, as the parent operation of $L_1 = L_1'$ is concatenation, $r^2(1) = *$, as the subexpression $L_1 L_2 L_3 L_4$ is starred, $r^3(1) = \circ$ and $r^4(1) = *$, with $h(1) = 4$. Moreover, $\mathrm{range}^1(1) = [1 \ldots 1]$, $\mathrm{range}^2(1) = [1 \ldots 4]$, $\mathrm{range}^3(1) = [1 \ldots 4]$ and $\mathrm{range}^4(1) = [1 \ldots 16]$. For the computation of the continuation points, only $r^1(1) = \circ$ is important and yields 2. The case $i = 4$ is more interesting. Again, we have $r^1(4) = \circ$, $r^2(4) = *$, $r^3(4) = \circ$ and $r^4(4) = *$, with $h(4) = 4$. However, the level $j = 1$ is no longer of interest, rather $j = 2$, which puts $1 = \min(\mathrm{range}^2(4))$ into $\mathrm{cont}(4)$. Moreover, considering the level $j = 3$, we get the first elements of the range of the siblings into the set of continuation points, which is $5 = \min(\mathrm{range}(p(p(5))))$, as $p(p(5))$ describes the right sibling of $p(p(4))$, $9 = \min(\mathrm{range}(p(p(9))))$, as $p(p(9))$ describes the right sibling of $p(p(5))$, as well as 13. The next interesting case happens if $i = 8$, as we now have to continue looking at siblings from the beginning. Finally, with $i = 9$, we see something interesting with $j = 1$, as now the starred subexpression $L_{10}^* = (L_3')^*$ that follows $L_9 = L_1'$ can be skipped.

Proposition 6. *Let $L \subseteq T^*$. If $L \in \mathcal{L}_{*,\circ}(\mathrm{LIN})$, given by some expression tree t, then there is a context-free grammar $G = (N, T, S_1', P)$ with $L(G) = L$, together with some integer $k \geq 1$ counting the leaves of t, satisfying the following:*

- *N is partitioned into $N_0, N_1, \ldots, N_k$, where for each $i = 1, \ldots, k$, $S_i \in N_i$;*
- *$N_0 = \{S_1', S_2', S_3', \ldots, S_k', S_{k+1}'\}$;*
- *P can be partitioned into $P_0, P_1, \ldots, P_k$ such that $G_i = (N_i, T, S_i, P_i)$ forms a linear grammar for each $i = 1, \ldots, k$;*
- *$P_0 = \{S_i' \to S_i S_c' \mid c \in \mathrm{cont}(i)\} \cup \{S_{k+1}' \to \lambda\}$.*

If the continuation points satisfy $\mathrm{cont}(i) = \{i + 1\}$ for all $1 \leq i \leq k$, then this gives a characterization of the language class $\mathcal{L}_\circ(\mathrm{LIN})$.

In order to simplify some of our main results in the following sections, the following observations from [4] are helpful.

Proposition 7. *[4]. Let $\mathcal{L}$ be a language class that is closed under reversal and k, n, i', i'', m, j, j'' be non-negative integers. The following statements are true.*

1. *$\mathrm{GCID}(k; n, i', i''; m, j', j'') = [\mathrm{GCID}(k; n, i'', i'; m, j'', j')]^R$*
2. *$\mathcal{L} \subseteq \mathrm{GCID}(k; n, i', i''; m, j', j'')$ iff $\mathcal{L} \subseteq \mathrm{GCID}(k; n, i'', i'; m, j'', j')$*

4   Describing Closure Classes of Linear Languages

Initially, our main objective was to find how much beyond LIN GCID systems (of the four sizes stated in Proposition 1) can lead us. However, we then succeeded to provide a general result showing that if there exists $\mathrm{GCID}_{SD(T)}$ systems of ID size $(n, i', i''; m, j'j'')$ describing LIN, then these constructions can be extended to $\mathrm{GCID}_{SD(T)}$ systems of the same ID size at the expense of two more components to describe $\mathcal{L}_{reg}(\text{LIN})$. Unfortunately, we were not able to describe even CF with GCID systems of these four sizes and this question is left open to the reader.

Describing $\mathcal{L}_{reg}(\text{LIN})$ by GCID systems is rather an immediate consequence of Proposition 6. Here, we slightly extend the notion $\text{cont}(i)$ once more to the case when $i = 0$. This is somehow interesting when $r^{h(1)}(1) = *$ and allows to skip, for instance, to the position $k + 1$ to easily incorporate the empty word.

Theorem 1. *For all integers $t, n, m \geq 1$ and $i', i'', j', j'' \geq 0$ with $i' + i'' \geq 1$, if $\text{LIN} \subseteq \text{GCID}_X(t; n, i', i''; m, j', j'')$ for $X \in \{SD, SDT\}$, then $\mathcal{L}_{reg}(\text{LIN}) \subseteq \text{GCID}_X(t + 2; n, i', i''; m, j', j'')$.*

Proof. Let $L \in \mathcal{L}_{\cup,\circ,*}(\text{LIN})$ for some $L \subseteq T^*$. By Proposition 5, we can assume that L is the finite union of k languages from $\mathcal{L}_{\circ,*}(\text{LIN})$. We first show how to simulate context-free grammars that are given as in Proposition 6, using $\text{GCID}_X(t + 2; n, i', i''; m, j', j'')$ for languages from $\mathcal{L}_{\circ,*}(\text{LIN})$. By using disjoint nonterminal alphabets, we get a GCID system for the finite union of such languages, as well, because we can assume that the constituent systems handle terminals properly.

Since $\text{LIN} \subseteq \text{GCID}_{SD(T)}(t; n, i', i''; m, j', j'')$, each G_i can be simulated by a simple-deleting GCID system $\Pi_i = (t, V_i, T, \{S_i\}, H_i, 1, 1, R_i)$ for $1 \leq i \leq k$, each of size $(t; n, i', i''; m, j', j'')$. We assume, without loss of generality, that $V_i \cap V_j = T$ if $1 \leq i < j \leq k$. Let us first consider the case $i' \geq 1$ and $i'' = 0$. We construct a GCID system Π for G as follows: $\Pi = (t + 2, V, T, \{S_0 S'_c \mid c \in \text{cont}(0)\}, H \cup H', 1, 1, (R \setminus \hat{R}) \cup R' \cup R'')$, where

- $V = \left(\bigcup_{i=1}^{k} V_i \right) \cup \{S_0, S'_1, \ldots, S'_{k+1}\}$

- $H' = \bigcup_{i=1}^{k} \{r_i(t+1).1, r_i(t+1).2, r_i(t+2).1\} \cup \{r_{k+1}(t+1).1\}$

- $H = \bigcup_{i=1}^{k} H_i; \ R = \bigcup_{i=1}^{k} R_i; \ \hat{R} = \bigcup_{i=1}^{k} \{h_i 1.1 : (1, (\lambda, X_i, \lambda)_{del}, 1)\};$

- $R' = \bigcup_{i=0}^{k} \{h_i 1.1 : (1, (\lambda, X_i, \lambda)_{del}, t + 1) \mid X_i \to \lambda \in P_i \vee X_0 = S_0\}$

- R'' is the set with the following rules: for each $1 \leq i \leq k$ and $c \in \text{cont}(i)$,

$$r_i(t+1).1 : (t+1, (S'_i, S_i, \lambda)_{ins}, t+2),$$
$$r_i(t+1).(c+1) : (t+1, (S_i, S'_c, \lambda)_{ins}, 1)$$
$$r_i(t+2).1 : (t+2, (\lambda, S'_i, \lambda)_{del}, t+1);$$
$$\text{Further,} \ r_{k+1}(t+1).1 : (t+1, (\lambda, S'_{k+1}, \lambda)_{del}, 1)$$

Since $L_i = L(G_i)$ is generated by Π_i, respectively, for $1 \leq i \leq k$, the linear rules of Π_i are simulated by rules of R_i in the first t components and there is no interference between rules of different systems Π_i and Π_j, since $V_i \cap V_j = T$ if $1 \leq i < j \leq k$.

We start with the axiom $S_0 S'_c$ for some $c \in \text{cont}(0)$. S_0 is deleted and in $C(t+1)$ and $C(t+2)$, a simulation of G_c is initiated: $(S_0 S'_c)_1 \Rightarrow (S'_c)_{t+1} \Rightarrow (S'_c S_c)_{t+2} \Rightarrow (S_c)_{t+1} \Rightarrow (S_c S'_d)_1$ for some $d \in \text{cont}(c)$. Now, a string $w_1 \in L_c$ is produced by simulating G_c in the first t components of the system Π. In general, the simulation goes from left to right. When the string $w_c \in L_c$ is produced, the terminating rule of L_c, namely $h_c.1$, takes the string to component $t+1$, where we either arrive in configuration $(w_c S'_d)_{t+1}$, and the simulation continues with producing a word according to G_d etc. The whole process ends on applying the rule $r_{k+1}(t+1).1 : (t+1, (\lambda, S'_{k+1}, \lambda)_{del}, 1)$, which deletes the nonterminal S'_{k+1}.

Conversely, any derivation within Π can be split into phases, where each *linear phase* starts and ends in the first component with a string that starts with a terminal string, followed by $S_i S'_c$ for some $c \in \text{cont}(i)$ in the beginning, and by some $X_i v S'_c$ in the end of this phase, where v is some terminal string. Now, on applying $h_i 1.1$, X_i gets deleted and the *transition phase* is initiated, moving a string starting with a terminal string and ending with some S'_c into $C(t+1)$. Now, apart from the special case when S'_{k+1} is the last symbol of the string, by applying rules from $C(t+1)$ or $C(t+2)$, some string is moved back to $C1$ that satisfies the conditions expressed as the beginning of a linear phase. It is now clearly seen that this alternation of linear and transition phases corresponds to generating words from L from left to right, following some concrete instantiation of the expression tree. The case when $i' = 0$ and $i'' \geq 1$ follows from Propositions 2 and 7.   □

5   Reducing Components for Certain Closure Classes

In this section, we show that with GCID systems of ID size s and $t+1$ components we can describe $\mathcal{L}^2_*(\text{LIN}) := \{M_1 M_2 : M_1, M_2 \in \mathcal{L}_*(\text{LIN})\}$. Hence, $\mathcal{L}^2_*(\text{LIN}) = 2\text{-LIN} \cup (\mathfrak{L} \cup \mathfrak{L}^R) \cup \{L_1^* L_2^* : L_1, L_2 \in \text{LIN}\}$. We prove the next theorem by providing three different simulations of its three subsets stated above, in the subsequent theorems.

Theorem 2. *For all integers* $t, n, m \geq 1$ *and* $i', i'', j', j'' \geq 0$ *with* $i' + i'' \geq 1$ *and* $X \in \{SD, SDT\}$, *if* $\text{LIN} \subseteq \text{GCID}_X(t; n, i', i''; m, j', j'')$ *was shown by a simple-deleting simulation, then* $\mathcal{L}^2_*(\text{LIN}) \in \text{GCID}_X(t+1; n, i', i''; m, j', j'')$.

Theorem 3. *For all integers* $t, n, m \geq 1$ *and* $i', i'', j', j'' \geq 0$ *with* $i' + i'' \geq 1$ *and* $X \in \{SD, SDT\}$, *if* $\text{LIN} \subseteq \text{GCID}_X(t; n, i', i''; m, j', j'')$ *was shown by a simple-deleting simulation, then* $2\text{-LIN} \subseteq \text{GCID}_X(t+1; n, i', i''; m, j', j'')$.

Proof. Let $G_1 = (N_1, T, S_1, P_1)$ and $G_2 = (N_2, T, S_2, P_2)$ be linear grammars of L_1 and L_2, respectively, with $N_1 \cap N_2 = \emptyset$ and whose rules are of the form $p_i : X_i \rightarrow a Y_i$, $q_i : X_i \rightarrow Y_i a$ and $h_i : X_i \rightarrow \lambda$, with $X_i, Y_i \in N_i$ for $= 1, 2$. Since $\text{LIN} \subseteq \text{GCID}_{SD}(t; n, i', i''; m, j', j'')$, each of the rule types p_i, q_i, h_i can be simulated by rules of a simple-deleting GCID system $\Pi_i = (t, V_i, T, \{S_i\}, H_i, 1, 1, R_i)$ for $i = 1, 2$, each of size $(t; n, i', i''; m, j', j'')$. Hence, the h_i rule type is simulated by the GCID rules $h_i 1.1 : (1, (\lambda, X_i, \lambda)_{del}, 1)$. First,

consider the case when $i' \geq 1$ and $i'' = 0$. We construct a GCID system
$\Pi_3 = (t+1, V_1 \cup V_2 \cup \{\#\}, T, \{\lambda, S_1\#\}, H_1 \cup H_2 \cup \{r1.1, r(t+1).1\}, 1, 1, R)$
for $L(G_1)L(G_2)$, with $R = ((R_1 \cup R_2) \setminus \{h_11.1 : (1, (\lambda, X_1, \lambda)_{del}, 1)\}) \cup R'$,
where R' has the following three rules: (i) $h_11.1 : (1, (\lambda, X_1, \lambda)_{del}, t+1)$, (ii)
$r(t+1).1 : (t+1, (\#, S_2, \lambda)_{ins}, 1)$, (iii) $r1.1 : (1, (\lambda, \#, \lambda)_{del}, 1)$.

Starting with the axiom $S_1\#$ and using rules of R_1, a string $w_1 \in L_1$ is
produced first with being the last rule applied is $h_11.1$. This leads to $w_1\#$ in
$C(t+1)$. The only rule in $C(t+1)$ is applied which inserts S_2 after $\#$ and moves
back to $C1$. Continuing with $w_1\#S_2$, $w_2 \in L(G_2)$ is generated reaching to the
configuration $(w_1\#w_2)_1$ where $\#$ is deleted by $r1.1$. If $r1.1$ is applied before
$h_11.1$, then the string is stuck at $C(t+1)$ which is not the target component.

Since 2-LIN is closed under reversal (due to Proposition 2), the case when
$i' = 0, i'' \geq 1$ follows from Proposition 7. $\qquad\qquad\qquad\qquad\qquad\qquad\square$

Theorem 4. *For all integers $t, n, m \geq 1$ and $i', i'', j', j'' \geq 0$ with $i' + i'' \geq 1$
and $X \in \{SD, SDT\}$, if $\mathrm{LIN} \subseteq \mathrm{GCID}_X(t; n, i', i''; m, j', j'')$ was shown by a
simple-deleting simulation, then $\mathfrak{L} \cup \mathfrak{L}^R \subseteq \mathrm{GCID}_X(t+1; n, i', i''; m, j', j'')$.*

Proof. Let $G_1 = (N_1, T, S_1, P_1)$ and $G_2 = (N_2, T, S_2, P_2)$ be linear grammars
of L_1 and L_2, respectively, with $N_1 \cap N_2 = \emptyset$. Let $i' \geq 1$, $i'' = 0$ and we will
now show $\mathfrak{L} \subseteq \mathrm{GCID}_{SD}(t+1; n, i', i''; m, j', j'')$. We construct a GCID system
$\Pi_4 = (t+1, V_1 \cup V_2 \cup \{\#\}, T, \{\lambda, \#S_2\}, H_1 \cup H_2 \cup \{r(t+1).1, r(t+1).2\}, 1, 1, R)$
for $(L(G_1))^*L(G_2)$, with $R = ((R_1 \cup R_2) \setminus \{h_11.1 : (1, (\lambda, X_1, \lambda)_{del}, 1), h_21.1 :
(1, (\lambda, X_2, \lambda)_{del}, 1)\}) \cup R'$, where R' has the following rules.

$$h_11.1 : (1, (\lambda, X_1, \lambda)_{del}, t+1) \qquad h_21.1 : (1, (\lambda, X_2, \lambda)_{del}, t+1)$$
$$r(t+1).1 : (t+1, (\#, S_1, \lambda)_{ins}, 1) \qquad r(t+1).2 : (t+1, (\lambda, \#, \lambda)_{del}, 1)$$

If we start with the axiom $\#S_2$, $w_2 \in L_2$ is produced and $\#w_2$ moves to $C(t+1)$.
The rules in $C(t+1)$ initiate the simulation of the rules of G_1 by inserting S_1 after
$\#$ and thereafter continuing with $\#S_1w_2$ from $C1$, the configuration $(\#w_1w_2)_{t+1}$
is reached, with $w_1 \in L_1^*$ and $w_2 \in L_2$. Now if $r(t+1).1$ is applied, the simulation
of G_1 is restarted, and after generating $w_1 \in L(G_1)$ for desired number of times,
the whole derivation stops. With this observation, we conclude that Π_4 generates
$(L(G_1))^*L(G_2) \in \mathfrak{L}$.

Consider the case when $i' = 1$, but we want to prove the inclusion for $\mathfrak{L}^R$.
We aim at constructing a GCID system Π_4' for $L_2L_1^*$. The simulation is identical
to the one just presented except for the axiom, which is $S_2\#$ now.

The case when $i' = 0$ and $i'' \geq 1$ follows from the fact that $\mathfrak{L} \cup \mathfrak{L}^R$ is closed
under reversal and by Propositions 2 and 7. $\qquad\qquad\qquad\qquad\qquad\qquad\square$

Theorem 5. *For all integers $t, n, m \geq 1$ and $i', i'', j', j'' \geq 0$ with $i' + i'' \geq 1$
and $X \in \{SD, SDT\}$, if $L_1, L_2 \in \mathrm{LIN} \subseteq \mathrm{GCID}_X(t; n, i', i''; m, j', j'')$ was shown
by a simple-deleting simulation, then $L_1^*L_2^* \in \mathrm{GCID}_X(t+1; n, i', i''; m, j', j'')$.*

The following proof is a simple extension of Theorem 4. Hence, we give the
simulating rules and refrain from explaining the working.

Proof. For $i' \geq 1$ and $i'' = 0$, we construct a GCID system $\Pi_3 = (t + 1, V_1 \cup V_2 \cup \{\#_1, \#_2\}, T, \{\#_1\#_2\}, H \cup \{r_1(t+1).1, r_2(t+1).1, s_1(t+1).1, s_2(t+1).1\}, t + 1, t + 1, (R \setminus \hat{R}) \cup R' \cup R'')$ such that $L(\Pi_3) = L_1^* L_2^*$, where

- $\hat{R} = \{h_1 1.1 : (1, (\lambda, X_1, \lambda)_{del}, 1), h_2 1.1 : (1, (\lambda, X_2, \lambda)_{del}, 1)\}$;
- $R' = \{h_1 1.1 : (1, (\lambda, X_1, \lambda)_{del}, t + 1), h_2 1.1 : (1, (\lambda, X_2, \lambda)_{del}, t + 1)\}$;

- R'' is the set of the following four rules:

$$r_1(t + 1).1 : (t + 1, (\#_1, S_1, \lambda)_{ins}, 1) \qquad r_2(t + 1).1 : (t + 1, (\#_2, S_2, \lambda)_{ins}, 1)$$
$$s_1(t + 1).1 : (t + 1, (\lambda, \#_1, \lambda)_{del}, t + 1) \qquad s_2(t + 1).1 : (t + 1, (\lambda, \#_2, \lambda)_{del}, t + 1)$$

The case when $i' = 0$ and $i'' \geq 1$ follows from Propositions 2 and 7. □

Remark 1. The proof of Theorem 5 can be extended to describe $\{L_1^* L_2^* \ldots L_k^* : L_i \in \mathrm{LIN} \text{ for } 1 \leq i \leq k\}$. Consider the GCID system Π' as in Theorem 5 with alphabet and label set extended from 2 to k. Let axiom be $\#_1\#_2 \ldots \#_k$. The rules of $\hat{R}, R' \in \Pi_3$ are similarly extended to k rules and there are $2k$ rules in R''. This shows that $L_1^* L_2^* \ldots L_k^* \in \mathrm{GCID}(t + 1; n, i', i''; m, j', j'')$ under the assumptions of Theorem 5. Since there is no control on the number of applications of the rule $r_i(t + 1).1 : (t + 1, (\#_i, S_i, \lambda)_{ins}, 1)$, we cannot enforce it to be applied exactly once; hence $L_1 L_2$ or $L_1^* L_2$ or $L_1 L_2^*$ alone cannot be produced this way.

Remark 2. By Proposition 1, $\mathrm{LIN} \subsetneq \mathrm{GCID}(4; 1, 1, 1; 1, 0, 0)$ and by Theorem 2, $\mathcal{L}_*^2(\mathrm{LIN}) \subsetneq \mathrm{GCID}(5; 1, 1, 1; 1, 0, 0)$. By [4], $\mathrm{RE} = \mathrm{GCID}(5; 1, 1, 1; 1, 0, 0)$. This opens the quest to prove computational incompleteness results, similarly to the conjecture of Ivanov and Verlan [9] which states that $\mathrm{RE} \neq \mathrm{GCID}(s)$ if $k = 2$ in $s = (k; 1, i', i''; 1, j', j'')$, with $i', i'', j', j'' \in \{0, 1\}$ and $i' + i'' + j' + j'' \leq 3$.

6   Summary and Future Challenges

Up to the present, most of the research on the descriptional complexity of (graph-controlled) insertion-deletion systems was about the limits to the resources so that we can still show that such systems are able to describe all recursively enumerable languages. Although we do not have a proof showing that the borderline that we reached is optimal, it might be an idea to look into smaller language classes now. One natural question would be to see with which resources we can still describe all context-free languages. While all results collected in this paper show, in particular, that all linear languages can be described by the corresponding resources, we put it up as a challenge to come up with non-trivial simulations of context-free grammars.

In this paper, we tried to bridge between linear and context-free languages as best as possible. Our main technical contribution is to describe these simulations in quite a general fashion, so that we can save giving similar simulations for each specific case of sizes of the systems.

Acknowledgments. Some part of the work done by the second author was during the author's visits to University of Trier, Germany in June-July and December 2016. The possibility to use some overhead money from a DFG grant to support this stay is gratefully acknowledged.

References

1. Benne, R. (ed.): RNA Editing: The Alteration of Protein Coding Sequences of RNA. Series in Molecular Biology. Ellis Horwood, Chichester (1993)
2. Fernau, H., Kuppusamy, L., Raman, I.: Descriptional complexity of graph-controlled insertion-deletion systems. In: Câmpeanu, C., Manea, F., Shallit, J. (eds.) DCFS 2016. LNCS, vol. 9777, pp. 111–125. Springer, Cham (2016). doi:10.1007/978-3-319-41114-9_9
3. Fernau, H., Kuppusamy, L., Raman, I.: Generative power of graph-controlled insertion-deletion systems with small sizes. J. Automata Lang. Comb. (2017)
4. Fernau, H., Kuppusamy, L., Raman, I.: On the computational completeness of graph-controlled insertion-deletion systems with binary sizes. Theoret. Comput. Sci. (2017). doi:http://dx.doi.org/10.1016/j.tcs.2017.01.019
5. Freund, R., Kogler, M., Rogozhin, Y., Verlan, S.: Graph-controlled insertion-deletion systems. In: McQuillan, I., Pighizzini, G. (eds.) Proceedings of Twelfth Annual Workshop on Descriptional Complexity of Formal Systems, DCFS, EPTCS, vol. 31, pp. 88–98 (2010)
6. Galiukschov, B.S.: Semicontextual grammars (in Russian). Mat. Logica i Mat. Ling., Kalinin Univ. 38–50 (1981)
7. Glushkov, V.M.: The abstract theory of automata (in Russian). Russ. Math. Surv. **16**, 1–53 (1961)
8. Haussler, D.: Insertion languages. Inf. Sci. **31**(1), 77–89 (1983)
9. Ivanov, S., Verlan, S.: About one-sided one-symbol insertion-deletion P systems. In: Alhazov, A., Cojocaru, S., Gheorghe, M., Rogozhin, Y., Rozenberg, G., Salomaa, A. (eds.) CMC 2013. LNCS, vol. 8340, pp. 225–237. Springer, Heidelberg (2014). doi:10.1007/978-3-642-54239-8_16
10. Kari, L.: On insertion and deletion in formal languages. Ph.D. thesis, University of Turku, Finland (1991)
11. Kari, L., Thierrin, G.: Contextual insertions/deletions and computability. Inf. Comput. **131**(1), 47–61 (1996)
12. Kutrib, M., Malcher, A.: Finite turns and the regular closure of linear context-free languages. Discrete Appl. Math. **155**(16), 2152–2164 (2007)
13. Nagy, B.: A normal form for regular expressions. In: Calude, C.S., Calude, E., Dinneen, M.J. (eds.) Supplemental Papers for DLT 2004, CDMTCS, vol. 252, University of Auckland, New Zealand, Centre for Discrete Mathematics and Theoretical Computer Science (2004)
14. Păun, G., Rozenberg, G., Salomaa, A.: DNA Computing: New Computing Paradigms. Springer, Heidelberg (1998)
15. Verlan, S.: Recent developments on insertion-deletion systems. Comput. Sci. J. Moldova **18**(2), 210–245 (2010)

Computational Completeness of Networks of Evolutionary Processors with Elementary Polarizations and a Small Number of Processors

Rudolf Freund[1], Vladimir Rogojin[2], and Sergey Verlan[3(✉)]

[1] Faculty of Informatics, TU Wien, Favoritenstraße 9–11, 1040 Vienna, Austria
rudi@emcc.at
[2] Department of Information Technologies, Åbo Akademi University,
Domkyrkotorget 3, 20500 Turku, Finland
vladimir.rogojin@abo.fi
[3] Laboratoire d'Algorithmique, Complexité et Logique, Université Paris Est Créteil,
61 av. du général de Gaulle, 94010 Créteil, France
verlan@u-pec.fr

Abstract. We improve previous results obtained for networks of evolutionary processors with elementary polarizations $-1, 0, 1$ by showing that only the very small number of seven processors is needed to obtain computational completeness. In the case of not requiring a special output node even only five processors are shown to be sufficient.

1 Introduction

Networks of evolutionary processors (NEPs) consist of cells (processors) each of them allowing for specific operations on strings. Computations in such a network consist of alternatingly performing two steps – an *evolution step* where in each cell all possible operations on all strings currently present in the cell are performed, and a *communication step* in which strings are sent from one cell to another cell provided specific conditions are fulfilled. Examples of such conditions are (output and input) filters which have to be passed, and these (output and input) filters can be specific types of regular languages or permitting and forbidden context conditions. The set of strings obtained as results of computations by the NEP is defined as the set of objects which appear in some distinguished node in the course of a computation. In networks of evolutionary processors with polarizations each symbol has assigned a fixed integer value; the polarization of a string is computed according to a given evaluation function, and in the communication step copies of strings are moved to all cells having the same polarization. As in [12], in this paper we only consider the elementary polarizations $-1, 0, 1$ for the symbols as well as for the cells.

Seen from a biological point of view, networks of evolutionary processors are a collection of cells communicating via membrane channels which makes them

G. Pighizzini and C. Câmpeanu (Eds.): DCFS 2017, LNCS 10316, pp. 140–151, 2017.
DOI: 10.1007/978-3-319-60252-3_11

to be seen as tissue-like P systems (see [11]) considered in the area of membrane computing (see [14]); as in membrane computing, the computations are carried out in a parallel and synchronized way in all cells The operations considered for the processors (cells) in networks of evolutionary processors usually are the point mutations insertion, deletion, and substitution, well-known from biology as operations on DNA.

Networks of Evolutionary Processors (NEPs) were introduced in [7,8] as a model of string processing devices distributed over a graph, with the processors carrying out the operations insertion, deletion, and substitution. NEPs with a very small number of nodes are very powerful computational devices: already with two nodes, they are as powerful as Turing machines, e.g., see [3,4]. For a survey of the main results regarding NEPs the interested reader is referred to [10].

In *hybrid networks of evolutionary processors* (HNEPs), each language processor performs only one of these operations on a certain position of the strings. Furthermore, the filters are defined by some variants of random-context conditions, i.e., they check the presence and the absence of certain symbols in the strings. For an overview on HNEPs and the so far known best results, we refer the reader to [1].

Networks of polarized evolutionary processors were considered in [6] (a new version of that paper is going to appear, [5]), and networks of evolutionary processors with elementary polarizations $-1, 0, 1$ were investigated in [12]. In this paper we consider the same model of networks of evolutionary processors with elementary polarizations $-1, 0, 1$ as in [12], yet we considerably improve the number of processors (cells) needed to obtain computational completeness from 35 to 7, which makes these results already comparable with those obtained in [1] for hybrid networks of evolutionary processors using permitting and forbidden contexts as filters for the communication of strings between cells.

The rest of the paper is structured as follows: In Sect. 2 we give the definitions of the model of a network of evolutionary processors with elementary polarizations $-1, 0, 1$ (*NePEP* for short) and of the variant of a circular Post machine we are going to simulate by the NePEP. In Sect. 3 we show our main result proving that any circular Post machine can be simulated by an NePEP with only seven processors (cells), and in the case of not requiring a special output processor even only five processors are needed. A summary of the results and an outlook to future research conclude the paper.

2   Prerequisites

We start by recalling some basic notions of formal language theory. An alphabet is a non-empty finite set. A finite sequence of symbols from an alphabet V is called a *string* over V. The set of all strings over V is denoted by V^*; the *empty string* is denoted by λ; moreover, we define $V^+ = V^* \setminus \{\lambda\}$. The *length* of a string x is denoted by $|x|$, and by $|x|_a$ we denote the number of occurrences of a letter a in a string x. For a string x, *alph(x)* denotes the smallest alphabet

Σ such that $x \in \Sigma^*$. For more details of formal language theory the reader is referred to the monographs and handbooks in this area, such as [15].

We only remark that in this paper, string rewriting systems as Turing machines, Post systems, etc. are called *computationally complete* if these systems are able to compute any partial recursive relation R on strings over any alphabet U. Computational completeness in the usual sense with respect to acceptance and generation directly follows from this general kind of computational completeness; for more details we refer to [1]. The definitions of the succeeding subsections are mainly taken from [1,12].

2.1   Insertion, Deletion, and Substitution

For an alphabet V, let $a \to b$ be a rewriting rule with $a, b \in V \cup \{\lambda\}$, and $ab \neq \lambda$; we call such a rule a *substitution rule* if both a and b are different from λ; such a rule is called a *deletion rule* if $a \neq \lambda$ and $b = \lambda$, and it is called an *insertion rule* if $a = \lambda$ and $b \neq \lambda$. The set of all substitution rules, deletion rules, and insertion rules over an alphabet V is denoted by Sub_V, Del_V, and Ins_V, respectively.

Given such rules $\pi \equiv a \to b \in Sub_V$, $\rho \equiv a \to \lambda \in Del_V$, and $\sigma \equiv \lambda \to a \in Ins_V$ as well as a string $w \in V^*$, we define the following *actions* of π, ρ, and σ on w:

- If $\pi \equiv a \to b \in Sub_V$, then
$$\pi(w) = \begin{cases} \{ubv : \exists u, v \in V^* \ (w = uav)\}, & \text{if } \mid w \mid_a > 0, \\ \{w\}, & \text{otherwise.} \end{cases}$$
- If $\rho \equiv a \to \lambda \in Del_V$, then
$$\rho^r(w) = \begin{cases} \{u : \exists u \in V^* \ (w = ua)\}, & \text{if } \mid w \mid_a > 0, \\ \{w\}, & \text{otherwise.} \end{cases}$$
$$\rho^l(w) = \begin{cases} \{v : \exists v \in V^* \ (w = av)\}, & \text{if } \mid w \mid_a > 0, \\ \{w\}, & \text{otherwise.} \end{cases}$$
- If $\sigma \equiv \lambda \to a \in Ins_V$, then $\sigma^r(w) = \{wa\}$ and $\sigma^l(w) = \{aw\}$.

The symbol $\alpha \in \{*, l, r\}$ denotes the mode of applying a substitution, insertion or deletion rule to a string, namely, at any position $(\alpha = *)$, on the left-hand end $(\alpha = l)$, or on the right-hand end $(\alpha = r)$ of the string, respectively.

For any rule β, $\beta \in \{\pi, \rho, \sigma\}$, any mode $\alpha \in \{*, l, r\}$, and any $L \subseteq V^*$, we define the α-*action* of β on L by $\beta^\alpha(L) = \bigcup_{w \in L} \beta^\alpha(w)$. For a given finite set of rules M, we define the α-action of M on a string w and on a language L by $M^\alpha(w) = \bigcup_{\beta \in M} \beta^\alpha(w)$ and $M^\alpha(L) = \bigcup_{w \in L} M^\alpha(w)$, respectively. In the following, substitutions will only be used at arbitrary positions, i.e., with $\alpha = *$, which will be omitted in the description of the rule.

2.2   Post Systems and Circular Post Machines

The left and right insertion, deletion, and substitution rules defined in the preceding subsection are special cases of string rewriting rules only working at the ends of a string; they can be seen as restricted variants of Post rewriting rules as already introduced by Post in [13]: for a *simple Post rewriting rule* $\Pi_s \equiv u\$x \rightarrow y\$v$, where $u, v, x, y \in V^*$, for an alphabet V, we define

$$\pi_s(w) = \{yzv \mid w = uzx, \; z \in V^*\}.$$

A *normal Post rewriting rule* $\pi_n \equiv \$x \rightarrow y\$$ is a special case of a simple Post rewriting rule $u\$x \rightarrow y\$v$ with $u = v = \lambda$ (we also assume $xy \neq \lambda$); this normal Post rewriting rule $\$x \rightarrow y\$$ is the mirror version of the normal form rules $u\$ \rightarrow \$v$ as originally considered in [13] for Post canonical systems; yet this variant has already been used several times for proving specific results in the area of membrane computing, e.g., see [9]. A *Post system of type X* is a construct (V, T, A, P) where V is a (finite) set of *symbols*, $T \subseteq V$ is a set of *terminal symbols*, $A \in V^*$ is the *axiom*, and P is a finite set of *Post rewriting rules* of type X; for example, X can mean simple or normal Post rewriting rules. In both cases it is folklore that these Post systems of type X are computationally complete.

The basic idea of the computational completeness proofs for Post systems is the "rotate-and-simulate"-technique, i.e., the string is rotated until the string x to be rewritten appears on the right-hand side, where it can be erased and replaced by the string y on the left-hand side, which in total can be accomplished by the rule $\$x \rightarrow y\$$. By rules of the form $\$a \rightarrow a\$$ for each symbol a the string can be rotated. In order to indicate the beginning of the string in all its rotated versions, a special symbol B (different from all others) is used; B is to be erased at the end of a successful computation.

Circular Post machines are machine-like variants of Post systems using specific variants of simple Post rewriting rules; the variant of $CPM5$ we use in this paper was investigated in [2].

Definition 1. *A (non-deterministic) CPM5 is a construct*

$$M = (\Sigma, T, Q, q_1, q_0, R),$$

where Σ is a finite alphabet, $T \subseteq \Sigma$ is the set of terminal symbols, Q is the set of states, $q_1 \in Q$ is the initial state, $q_0 \in Q$ is the only terminal state, and R is a set of simple Post rewriting rules of the following types (we use the notation $Q' = Q \setminus \{q_0\}$):

- $px\$ \rightarrow q\$$ *(deletion rule) with $p \in Q'$, $q \in Q$, $x \in \Sigma$; we also write $px \rightarrow q$ and, for any $w \in \Sigma^*$, the corresponding computation step is $pxw \xrightarrow{px \rightarrow q} qw$;*
- $p\$ \rightarrow q\$y$ *(insertion rule) with $p \in Q'$, $q \in Q$, $y \in \Sigma$; we also write $p \rightarrow yq$ and, for any $w \in \Sigma^*$, the corresponding computation step is $pw \xrightarrow{p \rightarrow yq} qwy$.*

The CPM5 is called deterministic *if for any two deletion rules $px \rightarrow q_1$ and $px \rightarrow q_2$ we have $q_1 = q_2$ and for any two insertion rules $p \rightarrow q_1y_1$ and $p \rightarrow q_2y_2$ we have $q_1y_1 = q_2y_2$.*

The name circular Post machine comes up from the idea of interpreting the machines to work on circular strings where both deletion and insertion rules have local effects, as for circular strings the effect of the insertion rule $p\$ \to q\$y$ is the same as the effect of $p \to yq$ directly applied to a circular string, which also justifies writing $p\$ \to q\$y$ as $p \to yq$.

For a given input string w, $w \in T^*$, the CPM5 M starts with q_1w and applies rules from R until it eventually reaches a configuration q_0v for some $v \in T^*$; in this case we say that (w, v) is in the relation computed by M.

Definition 2. *A CPM5 $M = (\Sigma, T, Q, q_1, q_0, R)$ is said to be in normal form if*

- $Q \setminus \{q_0\} = Q_1 \cup Q_2$ *where* $Q_1 \cap Q_2 = \emptyset$;
- *for every $p \in Q_1$ and every $x \in \Sigma$, there is exactly one instruction of the form $px \to q$, i.e., Q_1 is the set of states for deletion rules;*
- *for every insertion rule $p \to yq$ we have $p \in Q_2$, i.e., Q_2 is the set of states for insertion rules, and moreover, if $p \to y_1q_1$ and $p \to y_2q_2$ are two different rules in R, then $y_1 = y_2$.*

Theorem 1 *(see [2]). CPM5s in normal form are computationally complete.*

2.3   Networks of Evolutionary Processors with Elementary Polarizations

Definition 3. *A polarized evolutionary processor over V is a triple (M, α, π) where*

- *M is a set of substitution, deletion or insertion rules over the alphabet V, i.e., $(M \subseteq Sub_V)$ or $(M \subseteq Del_V)$ or $(M \subseteq Ins_V)$;*
- *α gives the action mode of the rules of the node;*
- *$\pi \in \{-1, 0, +1\}$ is the polarization of the node (negative, neutral, positive).*

The set M represents the set of evolutionary rules of the processor. It is important to note that a processor is "specialized" in one type of evolutionary operation only as in HNEPs. The set of evolutionary processors over V is denoted by EP_V.

Definition 4. *A network of polarized evolutionary processors (NPEP for short) is a 7-tuple $\Gamma = (V, T, H, \mathcal{R}, \varphi, n_{in}, n_{out})$ where*

- *V is the alphabet of the network;*
- *T is the input/output alphabet, $T \subseteq V$; $T \subseteq V$;*
- *$H = (X_H, E_H)$ is an undirected graph (without loops) with the set of vertices (nodes) X_H and the set of (undirected) edges E_H; H is called the underlying communication graph of the network;*
- *$\mathcal{R} : X_H \longrightarrow EP_V$ is a mapping which with each node $x \in X_H$ associates the polarized evolutionary processor $\mathcal{R}(x) = (M_x, \alpha_x, \pi_x)$;*
- *φ is an evaluation function from V^* into the set of integers;*
- *$n_{in}, n_{out} \in X_H$ are the input and the output node, respectively.*

The number of nodes in X_H, $card(X_H)$, is called the *size* of Γ. If the evaluation mapping φ takes values in the set $\{-1, 0, 1\}$ only, the network is said to be with *elementary polarization* of symbols (an NePEP for short).

A *configuration* of an NPEP Γ, as defined above, is a mapping $C : X_H \longrightarrow 2^{V^*}$ which associates a set of strings over V with each node x of the graph. A component $C(x)$ of a configuration C is the set of strings that can be found in the node x of this configuration, hence, a configuration can be considered as a list of the sets of strings which are present in the nodes of the network at a given moment.

A computation of Γ consists of alternatingly applying an *evolutionary step* and a *communication step*. When changing by an *evolutionary step*, each component $C(x)$ of the configuration C is changed in accordance with the set of evolutionary rules M_x associated with the node x thus yielding the new configuration C', and we write $C \Longrightarrow C'$ if and only if

$$C'(x) = M_x^{\alpha_x}(C(x)) \text{ for all } x \in X_H.$$

In a *communication step*, each node processor $x \in X_H$ sends out copies of all its strings, but keeping a local copy of the strings having the same polarization to that of x only, to all the node processors connected to x, and receives a copy of each word sent by any node processor connected with x providing that it has the same polarization as that of x, thus yielding the new configuration C' from configuration C, and we write $C \vdash C'$,

$$C'(x) = (C(x) \setminus \{w \in C(x) \mid sign(\varphi(w)) \neq \pi_x\}) \cup$$
$$\bigcup_{\{x,y\} \in E_G} (\{w \in C(y) \mid sign(\varphi(w)) = \pi_x\}),$$

for all $x \in X_H$. Here $sign(m)$ is the sign function which returns $+1, 0, -1$, provided that m is a positive integer, is 0, or is a negative integer, respectively. Note that all strings with a different polarization than that of x are expelled. Further, each expelled word from a node x that cannot enter any node connected to x is lost.

In the following, we will only use the evaluation function φ with $\varphi(\lambda) = 0$ and $\varphi(aw) = \varphi(a) + \varphi(w)$ for all $a \in V$ and $w \in V^*$, i.e., the value a string is the sum of the values of the symbols contained in it; we write φ_s for this function.

Given an input word $w \in T^*$, the initial configuration C_0 of Γ for w is defined by $C_0^{(w)}(n_{in}) = \{w\}$ and $C_0^{(w)}(n) = \emptyset$ for all other nodes $x \in X_H \setminus \{n_{in}\}$. The computation of Γ on the input word $w \in V^*$ is a sequence of configurations $C_0^{(w)}, C_1^{(w)}, C_2^{(w)}, \ldots$, where $C_0^{(w)}$ is the initial configuration of Γ on w, $C_{2i}^{(w)} \Longrightarrow C_{2i+1}^{(w)}$ and $C_{2i+1}^{(w)} \vdash C_{2i+2}^{(w)}$, for all $i \geq 0$.

As results we take all terminal strings appearing in the output cell n_{out} during a computation of Γ. In fact, in [1] this variant was called *with terminal extraction*. On the other hand, we may require a special output where *only* the terminal strings appear, which we will consider as the *standard* variant.

3 Main Result

In this section we now show our main result how a given CPM5 can be simulated by an NePEP (with terminal extraction) with only 7 (5) cells provided that for a given input string $w \in T^*$ we start with the initial string $q_1 w$ in the input cell, where q_1 is the initial state of the CPM5. In order to start with the input string w directly we would have to add two more nodes to carry out this initial procedure of adding the initial state q_1.

Theorem 2. *For any CPM5 $M = (\Sigma, T, Q, q_1, q_0, R)$ in normal form there exists a standard NePEP with only seven cells $\Gamma = (V, T, H, \mathcal{R}, \phi_s, i_1, i_0)$ being able to simulate the computations of M.*

Proof. Let $n = |T|$, $m = |Q|$, $0 \le i \le m$ and $0 \le k \le n$. We define

$$V = T \cup \{q_i^0, \hat{q}_i^+, \hat{q}_i^-, X_i^-, D_i^0, D_i^+, \hat{D}_i^+ \mid 0 \le i \le m\}$$
$$\cup \{q_{k,i}^-, \hat{q}_{k,i}^0 \mid 0 \le k \le n, 0 \le i \le m\}$$
$$\cup \{A_{i,k}^-, A_{i,k}^0 \mid 0 \le k \le n, 0 \le i \le m\}$$
$$\cup \{A_k^0, A_k^+, \hat{A}_k^+, \breve{A}_k^+ \mid 0 \le k \le n\} \cup \{\varepsilon^-\}$$

The evaluation ϕ_s for the symbols in V corresponds to the superscript of the symbol, i.e., for $\alpha^z \in V$ with $z \in \{+, 0, -\}$ we define $\phi_s(\alpha^0) = 0$, $\phi_s(\alpha^+) = +1$, $\phi_s(\alpha^-) = -1$, and, moreover, for $a \in T$, we take $\phi_s(a) = 0$.

The communication graph H consists of the set of nodes $\{1, 2, 3, 4, 5, 6, 7\}$ and of the following set of undirected edges:
$\{\{1, 2\}, \{1, 3\}, \{1, 4\}, \{1, 5\}, \{4, 5\}, \{4, 6\}, \{6, 7\}\}$.
Node 1 is the input and node 7 is the output node.

For the seven nodes i, $1 \le i \le 7$, the corresponding evolutionary processors $\mathcal{N}(i)$ are defined as follows:
$\alpha(1) = \alpha(3) = \alpha(4) = \alpha(7) = *$, $\alpha(2) = r$ and $\alpha(5) = \alpha(6) = l$.
$\pi(1) = \pi(7) = 0$, $\pi(2) = \pi(4) = \pi(5) = -$ and $\pi(3) = \pi(6) = +$.
For the types of rules in the rule sets M_i we have $M_1, M_3, M_4 \subset SUB_V$, $M_2 \subset INS_V$, $M_5, M_6 \subset DEL_V$, and $M_7 = \emptyset$, i.e., M_7 could be assumed to be any type of rules.

Processor 1 has polarization (charge) 0 and uses substitution rules to contribute to the simulation of insertion and deletion rules of M:

Insertion : $q_s \to q_j a_k (1 \le l \le k)$	**Deletion** : $q_s a_k \to q_j (1 \le i \le s)$
$1.1 : q_s^0 \to q_{k,j}^-$	$1.7 : q_s^0 \to X_s^-$
$1.2 : q_{l,j}^- \to q_{l-1,j}^0$	$1.8 : A_{i,l}^- \to A_{i+1,l}^0$
$1.3 : A_l^0 \to \hat{A}_l^+$	$1.9 : A_{i,l}^0 \to \hat{A}_{i,l}^0$
$1.4 : A_l^0 \to \breve{A}_l^+$	$1.10 : D_i^0 \to \hat{D}_i^+$
$1.5 : q_{l,j}^0 \to \hat{q}_{l,j}^0$	$1.11 : \hat{D}_i^+ \to D_i^+$
$1.6 : \hat{A}_l^+ \to A_l^+$	$1.12 : A_{i,l}^- \to \hat{q}_j^+$
	$1.13 : \hat{q}_j^+ \to \hat{q}_j^-$

Processor 3 has polarization (charge) $+1$ and uses substitution rules to contribute to the simulation of insertion and deletion rules of M:

Insertion : $q_s \to q_j a_k (1 \le l \le k)$	**Deletion** : $q_s a_k \to q_j (1 \le i \le s)$
$3.1 : A_l^+ \to A_{l+1}^0$	$3.5 : D_i^+ \to D_{i-1}^0, \quad i > 0$
$3.2 : \hat{q}_{l,j}^0 \to q_{l,j}^-, \quad l > 0$	$3.6 : \hat{A}_{i,l}^0 \to A_{i,l}^-$
$3.3 : \hat{q}_{0,j}^0 \to q_j^0$	$3.7 : D_0^+ \to \varepsilon^-$
$3.4 : \hat{A}_l^+ \to a_l^0$	

Processor 4 has polarization (charge) -1 and uses substitution rules to contribute to the simulation of deletion rules of M only:

$$\textbf{Deletion} : q_s a_k \to q_j$$

$$4.1 : a_l^0 \to A_{0,l}^-$$
$$4.2 : X_s^- \to D_s^+$$
$$4.3 : \hat{q}_j^- \to q_j^0, j > 0$$
$$4.4 : \hat{q}_0^- \to q_0^+$$

Processor 2 has polarization (charge) -1 and only contains the single insertion rule 2.1: $\lambda \to A_0^+$.

Processor 5 has polarization (charge) -1 and only contains the single deletion rule 5.1: $\varepsilon^- \to \lambda$.

Processor 6 has polarization (charge) $+1$ and only contains the single deletion rule 6.1: $q_0^+ \to \lambda$.

The proof closely follows the idea from [1] (Theorem 2), which is itself based on the rotate-and-simulate method. We recall the main steps of that proof below.

The configuration of M is represented as $q_s w$, $s \ge 0$, where q_s is the current state. Suppose that $q_s \to q_j a_k$ is the associated instruction. Then the following evolution is performed in Γ (for readability, we omit the superscripts (charges) of the symbols):

$$q_s w \Rightarrow^* q_{k,j} w A_0 \Rightarrow^* q_{k-1,j} w A_1 \Rightarrow^* q_{k-t,j} w A_t \Rightarrow^* q_{0,j} w A_k \Rightarrow^* q_j w a_k$$

As in the classical rotate-and-simulate method, A_0 is appended to the string and then the indices of $q_{k,j}$ (respectively A_0) are decreased (respectively increased) simultaneously. When the first index of $q_{k,j}$ reaches zero, its initial value is stored as an index of A_k, allowing to produce the right symbol a_k afterwards.

The instruction $q_s a_k \to q_j$ is simulated in the following way:

$$q_s a_k w \Rightarrow^* D_s A_{0,k} w \Rightarrow^* D_{i-1} A_{1,k} w \Rightarrow^* D_{i-t} A_{i,k} w A \Rightarrow^*$$
$$\Rightarrow^* D_0 A_{s,k} w \Rightarrow^* \varepsilon A_{s,k} w \Rightarrow^* \varepsilon q_j w \Rightarrow q_j w$$

Here the state symbol q_s is replaced by D_s and the first symbol a_k by $A_{0,k}$. Then in a loop the index of D decreases, while the first index of A increases. At the end of this loop the string $D_0 A_{s,k} w$ is obtained, hence the information about the state s has been transferred to the symbol A, so it now encodes the state and the current symbol of the machine M. Based on this information, the new state q_j is chosen. Finally, symbol D_0 is transformed to symbol ε, which is further deleted.

We remark that it could be possible that another symbol from the string is transformed to $A_{0,k}$ (not necessarily the first one). In this case the computation will not yield a valid result because the state symbol will not be present in the first position and the corresponding symbol ε will never be erased, see [1] for more details.

Now we explain the simulation in more details. We start with the remark that in each step only one symbol of a string w can be changed (by substitution, insertion or deletion) yielding w'. This implies that $|\phi(w) - \phi(w')| \leq 2$. In many cases this allows us to predict the change in the polarization (and thus the communication to another node), based on the above difference and the current node polarization.

Assume that the string $q_s^0 w$ is present in node 1. First, we suppose that there is an instruction $q_s \to q_j a_k$ in M. Then, only the rule 1.1 is applicable, producing the string $q_{k,j}^- w$. Since the initial string had neutral polarization, this rule application changes the polarization of the string to negative and during the communication step this string is sent to nodes 2, 4 and 5. In node 5 there is no rule applicable to this string, so it will never exit this node. In node 4, rule 4.1 can be applied several times, but this will further decrease the value of the string, which will remain negative, so it will never be able to get out of nodes 4 and 5.

In node 2 the insertion rule 2.1 is applied yielding $q_{k,j}^- w A_0^+$. Clearly, this string has a neutral polarization, so it will return back to node 1. Next, we discuss the evolution of strings of form $q_{k-t,j}^- w A_t^+$, $0 \leq t \leq k-2$ in node 1:

$$q_{k-t,j}^- w A_t^+ \Rightarrow_{1.2} q_{k-t-1,j}^0 w A_t^+ \Rightarrow_{3.1} q_{k-t-1,j}^0 w A_{t+1}^0 \Rightarrow_{1.5}$$
$$\Rightarrow_{1.5} \hat{q}_{k-t-1,j}^0 w A_{t+1}^0 \Rightarrow_{1.3} \hat{q}_{k-t-1,j}^0 w \hat{A}_{t+1}^0 \Rightarrow_{3.2}$$
$$\Rightarrow_{3.2} q_{k-t-1,j}^- w \hat{A}_{t+1}^+ \Rightarrow_{1.6} q_{k-t-1,j}^- w A_{t+1}^+$$

During first two steps only rules 1.2 and 3.1 are applicable (and they change the polarization of the string). Next, rules 1.3, 1.4 and 1.5 are applicable. It can be easily seen that if 1.3 is applied yielding the string $q_{k-t-1,j}^0 w \hat{A}_{t+1}^+$, then no more applicable rule is present in node 3. If rule 1.4 is applied then the only possible continuation is the application of the sequence of rules 3.4 and 1.5 yielding the string $\hat{q}_{k-t-1,j}^0 w a_{t+1}^0$ in node 1. Clearly, there are no more applicable rules and this string cannot evolve anymore.

So, rule 1.5 has to be applied. Next, there is a choice between the application of 1.3 and 1.4. In case of the application of 1.4, either 3.4 or 3.2 is applicable. The first application yields to the case discussed before, while the second application produces the following evolution not yielding any result:

$$\hat{q}^0_{k-t-1,j}w\check{A}^+_{t+1} \Rightarrow_{3.2} q^-_{k-t-1,j}w\check{A}^+_{t+1} \Rightarrow_{1.2} q^0_{k-t-2,j}w\check{A}^+_{t+1} \Rightarrow_{3.4}$$

$$\Rightarrow_{3.4} q^0_{k-t-2,j}wa^0_{t+1} \Rightarrow_{1.5} \hat{q}^0_{k-t-2,j}wa^0_{t+1}$$

So, on the fourth step rule 1.3 should be applied. Then the only applicable rule is 3.2. Now, if rule 1.6 is not applied, then on the next step (after the application of 1.2) no more rules will be applicable to the corresponding string in node 3.

Hence, the procedure described above permits to evolve the string $q^-_{k,j}wA^+_0$ into $q^-_{1,j}wA^+_{k-1}$. Now, the sequence described above produces the string $q^-_{0,j}wA^+_k$, which cannot evolve anymore. However, another evolution now becomes possible (by choosing 1.4 instead of 1.3):

$$q^-_{1,j}wA^+_{k-1} \Rightarrow_{1.2} q^0_{0,j}wA^+_{k-1} \Rightarrow_{3.1} q^0_{0,j}wA^0_k \Rightarrow_{1.5} \hat{q}^0_{0,j}wA^0_{t+1} \Rightarrow_{1.4}$$

$$\Rightarrow_{1.4} \hat{q}^0_{0,j}w\check{A}^0_k \Rightarrow_{3.3} q^0_jw\check{A}^+_k \Rightarrow_{3.4} q^0_jwa^0_k$$

We remark that if rule 3.4 is applied instead of 3.3, then corresponding string cannot evolve. This concludes the discussion of the simulation of the rule $q_s \to q_ja_k$ of M.

Now consider that there is an instruction $q_sa_k \to q_j$ in M to be simulated. Then, only rule 1.7 is applicable, producing the string X^-_sw. Since the initial string had neutral polarization, this rule application changes the polarization of the string to negative and during the communication step this string is sent to the nodes 2, 4 and 5. In node 5 there is no rule applicable to this string, so it will never exit this node. In node 2, rule 2.1 can be applied yielding $X^-_swA^+_0$ in node 1 to which no further rule is applicable.

In node 4 rules 4.1 and 4.2 are applicable. If 4.2 is applied, then the polarization of the resulting string is positive and the string will be lost. Hence 4.1 should be applied, yielding $X^-_s A^-_{0,k}w'$ ($w = a_kw$). Now again both rules 4.1 and 4.2 are applicable. This time using rule 4.2 allows to obtain the neutral string $D^+_s A^-_{0,k}w'$ which further goes to node 1. In the other case, the corresponding string will always be negative.

Now let us consider the evolution of strings of type $D^+_{s-t}A^-_{t,k}w'$, $0 \le t \le s-1$ being in node 1. Using the same technique as in the case above the decrement of the index of D and the increment of the index of A is performed, with the rules 1.8, 1.9, 1.10, 1.11, 2.5, and 2.6 now having a similar function as the rules 1.2, 1.5, 1.3, 1.6, 2.1, and 2.2. Hence, we obtain:

$$D^+_{s-t}A^-_{t,k}w' \Rightarrow_{1.8} D^+_{s-t}A^0_{t+1,k}w' \Rightarrow_{2.5} D^0_{s-t-1}A^0_{t+1,k}w' \Rightarrow_{1.9}$$

$$\Rightarrow_{1.9} D^0_{s-t-1}\hat{A}^0_{t+1,k}w' \Rightarrow_{1.10} \hat{D}^+_{s-t-1}\hat{A}^0_{t+1,k}w' \Rightarrow_{2.6}$$

$$\Rightarrow_{2.6} \hat{D}^+_{s-t-1}A^-_{t+1,k}w' \Rightarrow_{1.6} \hat{D}^+_{s-t-1}A^-_{t+1,k}w' \Rightarrow_{1.11} D^+_{s-t-1}A^-_{t+1,k}w'$$

It can easily be verified that the few possible variations of the computation above (not using rule 1.9 or using 1.12 instead of 1.9) immediately yield strings that cannot evolve anymore. Hence, we obtain that from $D_s^+ A_{0,k}^- w'$ only the string $D_0^+ A_{s,k}^- w'$ can be obtained (in node 1). At this point two rules are applicable: 1.8 and 1.12. Using rule 1.8 yields $D_0^+ A_{s+1,k}^0 w'$ in node 3, where only rule 3.7 is applicable, yielding $\varepsilon^- A_{s+1,k}^0 w'$. However, the last string is negative, so it is lost during the communication step. The other possibility gives the following evolution:

$$D_0^+ A_{s,k}^- w' \Rightarrow_{1.12} D_0^+ \hat{q}_j^+ w' \Rightarrow_{3.7} \varepsilon^- \hat{q}_j^+ w' \Rightarrow_{1.13} \varepsilon^- \hat{q}_j^- w' \Rightarrow_{4.3} \varepsilon^- q_j^0 w' \Rightarrow_{5.1} q_j^0 w'$$

We remark that last two operations can be done in a reverse order (if the string first travels to node 5 and then to node 4). The additional application of rule 4.1 traps the string in nodes 4 and 5.

Finally, we show how a terminal string is obtained as a result. We can assume that the last instruction of M is an instruction of type $q_s a_k \to q_0$. Then rule 4.4 produces the word $q_0^+ w'$, which being positive is sent to node 6, where rule 6.1 is applied producing a neutral string w', which further arrives in node 7.

Corollary 1. *For any CPM5 $M = (\Sigma, T, Q, q_1, q_0, R)$ in normal form there exists a NePEP with terminal extraction with five cells $\Gamma = (V, T, H, \mathcal{R}, \phi_s, i_1, i_0)$ being able to simulate the computations of M.*

Proof. The assertion can be easily proved by deleting nodes 6 and 7 from the previous construction, as well as by adding the rule $q_0^0 \to \varepsilon^-$ to processor 1.

4   Conclusion and Future Research

In this paper we have improved the number of cells necessary to obtain computational completeness with networks of polarized evolutionary processors with elementary polarizations $-1, 0, 1$ of symbols to seven. In the case of not requiring a special output node and just taking all terminal strings as results even only five nodes have been shown to be sufficient.

The construction given in this paper, like the previous ones for networks of polarized evolutionary processors makes intensive use of the control given by the structure of the communication graph. On the other hand, in [1] the results were obtained for several specific regular graph structures as complete graphs, starlike and even linear graphs. Hence, an interesting question for future research arises when asking for the ingredients and the number of cells needed to obtain computational completeness for variants of networks of polarized evolutionary processors based on such specific graph structures. Finally, we also may look for reducing the number seven (five for the case of terminal extraction) of cells needed to obtain computational completeness with networks of polarized evolutionary processors with elementary polarizations $-1, 0, 1$ of symbols.

References

1. Alhazov, A., Freund, R., Rogozhin, V., Rogozhin, Y.: Computational completeness of complete, star-like, and linear hybrid networks of evolutionary processors with a small number of processors. Nat. Comput. **15**(1), 51–68 (2016)
2. Alhazov, A., Krassovitskiy, A., Rogozhin, Y.: Circular post machines and P systems with exo-insertion and deletion. In: Gheorghe, M., Păun, G., Rozenberg, G., Salomaa, A., Verlan, S. (eds.) CMC 2011. LNCS, vol. 7184, pp. 73–86. Springer, Heidelberg (2012). doi:10.1007/978-3-642-28024-5_7
3. Alhazov, A., Martín-Vide, C., Rogozhin, Y.: On the number of nodes in universal networks of evolutionary processors. Acta Informat. **43**(5), 331–339 (2006)
4. Alhazov, A., Martín-Vide, C., Rogozhin, Y.: Networks of evolutionary processors with two nodes are unpredictable. In: Loos, R., Fazekas, S.Z., Martín-Vide, C. (eds.) LATA 2007. Proceedings of the 1st International Conference on Language and Automata Theory and Applications. Report, vol. 35/07, pp. 521–528. Research Group on Mathematical Linguistics, Universitat Rovira i Virgili, Tarragona (2007)
5. Arroyo, F., Canaval, S., Mitrana, V.: Popescu, Ş: On the computational power of networks of polarized evolutionary processors. Inf. Comput. **253**(3), 371–380 (2017)
6. Arroyo, F., Gómez Canaval, S., Mitrana, V., Popescu, Ş.: Networks of polarized evolutionary processors are computationally complete. In: Dediu, A.-H., Martín-Vide, C., Sierra-Rodríguez, J.-L., Truthe, B. (eds.) LATA 2014. LNCS, vol. 8370, pp. 101–112. Springer, Cham (2014). doi:10.1007/978-3-319-04921-2_8
7. Castellanos, J., Martín-Vide, C., Mitrana, V., Sempere, J.M.: Solving NP-complete problems with networks of evolutionary processors. In: Mira, J., Prieto, A. (eds.) IWANN 2001. LNCS, vol. 2084, pp. 621–628. Springer, Heidelberg (2001). doi:10.1007/3-540-45720-8_74
8. Castellanos, J., Martín-Vide, C., Mitrana, V., Sempere, J.M.: Networks of evolutionary processors. Acta Inform. **39**(6–7), 517–529 (2003)
9. Freund, R., Rogozhin, Y., Verlan, S.: Generating and accepting P systems with minimal left and right insertion and deletion. Nat. Comput. **13**(2), 257–268 (2014)
10. Manea, F., Martín-Vide, C., Mitrana, V.: Accepting networks of evolutionary word and picture processors: a survey. Sci. Appl. Lang. Methods **2**, 525–560 (2010)
11. Martín-Vide, C., Pazos, J., Păun, G., Rodríguez-Patón, A.: A new class of symbolic abstract neural nets: tissue P systems. In: Ibarra, O.H., Zhang, L. (eds.) COCOON 2002. LNCS, vol. 2387, pp. 290–299. Springer, Heidelberg (2002). doi:10.1007/3-540-45655-4_32
12. Popescu, S.: Networks of polarized evolutionary processors with elementary polarization of symbols. In: NCMA 2016, 275–285 (2016)
13. Post, E.L.: Formal reductions of the general combinatorial decision problem. Am. J. Math. **65**(2), 197–215 (1943)
14. Păun, G., Rozenberg, G., Salomaa, A. (eds.): The Oxford Handbook of Membrane Computing. Oxford University Press, Oxford (2010)
15. Rozenberg, G., Salomaa, A. (eds.): Handbook of Formal Languages, vol. 1-3. Springer, Heidelberg (1997)

Recognizing Union-Find Trees Built Up Using Union-By-Rank Strategy is NP-Complete

Kitti Gelle and Szabolcs Iván[✉]

Department of Computer Science, University of Szeged, Szeged, Hungary
{kgelle,szabivan}@inf.u-szeged.hu

Abstract. Disjoint-Set forests, consisting of Union-Find trees, are data structures having a widespread practical application due to their efficiency. Despite them being well-known, no exact structural characterization of these trees is known (such a characterization exists for Union trees which are constructed without using path compression) for the case assuming union-by-rank strategy for merging. In this paper we provide such a characterization by means of a simple PUSH operation and show that the decision problem whether a given tree (along with the rank info of its nodes) is a Union-Find tree is **NP**-complete, complementing our earlier similar result for the union-by-size strategy.

1   Introduction

Disjoint-Set forests, introduced in [10], are fundamental data structures in many practical algorithms where one has to maintain a partition of some set, which supports three operations: *creating* a partition consisting of singletons, *querying* whether two given elements are in the same class of the partition (or equivalently: *finding* a representative of a class, given an element of it) and *merging* two classes. Practical examples include e.g. building a minimum-cost spanning tree of a weighted graph [4], unification algorithms [17] etc.

To support these operations, even a linked list representation suffices but to achieve an almost-constant amortized time cost per operation, Disjoint-Set forests are used in practice. In this data structure, sets are represented as directed trees with the edges directed towards the root; the CREATE operation creates n trees having one node each (here n stands for the number of the elements in the universe), the FIND operation takes a node and returns the root of the tree in which the node is present (thus the SAME-CLASS(x, y) operation is implemented as FIND(x) == FIND(y)), and the MERGE(x, y) operation is implemented by merging the trees containing x and y, i.e. making one of the root nodes to be a child of the other root node (if the two nodes are in different classes).

In order to achieve near-constant efficiency, one has to keep the (average) height of the trees small. There are two "orthogonal" methods to do that: first, during the merge operation it is advisable to attach the "smaller" tree below the

Research was supported by the NKFI grant no. 108448.

G. Pighizzini and C. Câmpeanu (Eds.): DCFS 2017, LNCS 10316, pp. 152–163, 2017.
DOI: 10.1007/978-3-319-60252-3_12

"larger" one. If the "size" of a tree is the number of its nodes, we say the trees are built up according to the *union-by-size* strategy, if it's the depth of a tree, then we talk about the *union-by-rank* strategy. Second, during a FIND operation invoked on some node x of a tree, one can apply the *path compression* method, which reattaches each ancestor of x directly to the root of the tree in which they are present. If one applies both the path compression method and either one of the union-by-size or union-by-rank strategies, then any sequence of m operations on a universe of n elements has worst-case time cost $O(m\alpha(n))$ where α is the inverse of the extremely fast growing (not primitive recursive) Ackermann function for which $\alpha(n) \leq 5$ for each practical value of n (say, below 2^{65535}), hence it has an amortized almost-constant time cost [22]. Since it's proven [9] that *any* data structure maintaining a partition has worst-case time cost $\Omega(m\alpha(n))$, the Disjoint-Set forests equipped with a strategy and path compression offer a theoretically optimal data structure which performs exceptionally well also in practice. For more details see standard textbooks on data structures, e.g. [4].

Due to these facts, it is certainly interesting both from the theoretical as well as the practical point of view to characterize those trees that can arise from a forest of singletons after a number of merge and find operations, which we call Union-Find trees in this paper. One could e.g. test Disjoint-Set implementations since if at any given point of execution a tree of a Disjoint-Set forest is not a valid Union-Find tree, then it is certain that there is a bug in the implementation of the data structure (though we note at this point that this data structure is sometimes regarded as one of the "primitive" data structures, in the sense that it is possible to implement a correct version of them that needs not be certifying [20]). Nevertheless, only the characterization of Union trees is known up till now [2], i.e. which correspond to the case when one uses one of the union-by- strategies but *not* path compression. Since in that case the data structure offers only a theoretic bound of $\Theta(\log n)$ on the amortized time cost, in practice all implementations imbue path compression as well, so for a characterization to be really useful, it has to cover this case as well.

In this paper we show that the recognition problem of Union-Find trees is **NP**-complete when the union-by-rank strategy is used, complementing our earlier results [13] where we proved **NP**-completeness for the union-by-size strategy. The proof method applied here resembles to that one, but the low-level details for the reduction (here we use the PARTITION problem, there we used the more restricted version 3−PARTITION as this is a very canonical strongly **NP**-complete problem) differ greatly. This result also confirms the statement from [2] that the problem "seems to be much harder" than recognizing Union trees. As (up to our knowledge) in most of the actual software libraries having this data structure implemented the union-by-rank strategy is used (apart from the cases when one quickly has to query the size of the sets as well), for software testing purposes the current result is more relevant than the one applying union-by-size strategy.

Related Work. There is an increasing interest in determining the complexity of the recognition problem of various data structures. The problem was considered for suffix trees [16, 21], (parametrized) border arrays [8, 14, 15, 19], suffix arrays [1, 7, 18], KMP tables [6, 12], prefix tables [3], cover arrays [5], and directed acyclic word- and subsequence graphs [1].

2   Notation

A *(ranked) tree* is a tuple $t = (V_t, \text{ROOT}_t, \text{RANK}_t, \text{PARENT}_t)$ with V_t being the finite set of its *nodes*, $\text{ROOT}_t \in V_t$ its *root*, $\text{RANK}_t : V_t \to \mathbb{N}_0$ mapping a nonnegative integer to each node, and $\text{PARENT}_t : (V_t - \{\text{ROOT}_t\}) \to V_t$ mapping each nonroot node to its parent (so that the graph of PARENT_t is a directed acyclic graph, with edges being directed towards the root). We require $\text{RANK}_t(x) < \text{RANK}_t(\text{PARENT}_t(x))$ for each nonroot node x, i.e. the rank strictly decreases towards the leaves.

For a tree t and a node $x \in V_t$, let $\text{CHILDREN}(t, x)$ stand for the set $\{y \in V_t : \text{PARENT}_t(y) = x\}$ of its children and $\text{CHILDREN}(t)$ stand as a shorthand for $\text{CHILDREN}(t, \text{ROOT}_t)$, the set of depth-one nodes of t. Also, let $x \preceq_t y$ denote that x is a (non-strict) *ancestor* of y in t, i.e. $x = \text{PARENT}_t^k(y)$ for some $k \geq 0$. For $x \in V_t$, let $t|_x$ stand for the *subtree* $(V_x = \{y \in V : x \preceq_t y\}, x, \text{RANK}_t|_{V_x}, \text{PARENT}_t|_{V_x})$ of t rooted at x. As shorthand, let $\text{RANK}(t)$ stand for $\text{RANK}_t(\text{ROOT}_t)$, the rank of the root of t.

Two operations on trees are that of *merging* and *collapsing*. Given two trees $t = (V_t, \text{ROOT}_t, \text{RANK}_t, \text{PARENT}_t)$ and $s = (V_s, \text{ROOT}_s, \text{RANK}_s, \text{PARENT}_s)$ with V_t and V_s being disjoint and $\text{RANK}(t) \geq \text{RANK}(s)$, then their *merge* $\text{MERGE}(t, s)$ (in this order) is the tree $(V_t \cup V_s, \text{ROOT}_t, \text{RANK}, \text{PARENT})$ with $\text{PARENT}(x) = \text{PARENT}_t(x)$ for $x \in V_t$, $\text{PARENT}(\text{ROOT}_s) = \text{ROOT}_t$ and $\text{PARENT}(y) = \text{PARENT}_s(y)$ for each nonroot node $y \in V_s$ of s, and

$$\text{RANK}(\text{ROOT}_t) = \begin{cases} \text{RANK}(t) & \text{if } \text{RANK}(s) < \text{RANK}(t), \\ \text{RANK}(t) + 1 & \text{otherwise,} \end{cases}$$

and $\text{RANK}(x) = \text{RANK}_t(x)$, $\text{RANK}_s(x)$ resp. for each $x \in V_t - \{\text{ROOT}_r\}$, $x \in V_s$ resp.

Given a tree $t = (V, \text{ROOT}, \text{RANK}, \text{PARENT})$ and a node $x \in V$, then $\text{COLLAPSE}(t, x)$ is the tree $(V, \text{ROOT}, \text{RANK}, \text{PARENT}')$ with $\text{PARENT}'(y) = \text{ROOT}$ if y is a nonroot ancestor of x in t and $\text{PARENT}'(y) = \text{PARENT}(y)$ otherwise. For examples, see Fig. 1.

Observe that both operations indeed construct a ranked tree (e.g. the rank remains strictly decreasing towards the leaves).

We say that a tree is a *singleton* tree if it has exactly one node, and this node has rank 0.

The class of Union trees is the least class of trees satisfying the following two conditions: every singleton tree is a Union tree, and if t and s are Union trees with $\text{RANK}(t) \geq \text{RANK}(s)$, then $\text{MERGE}(t, s)$ is a Union tree as well.

Analogously, the class of Union-Find trees is the least class of trees satisfying the following three conditions: every singleton tree is a Union-Find tree, if t and

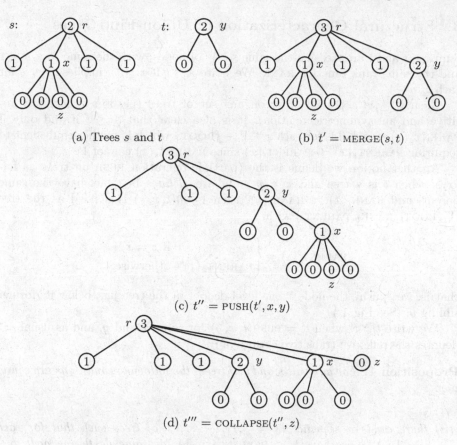

(a) Trees s and t

(b) $t' = \text{MERGE}(s, t)$

(c) $t'' = \text{PUSH}(t', x, y)$

(d) $t''' = \text{COLLAPSE}(t'', z)$

Fig. 1. Merge, collapse and push.

s are Union-Find trees with $\text{RANK}(t) \geq \text{RANK}(s)$, then $\text{MERGE}(t, s)$ is a Union-Find tree as well, and if t is a Union-Find tree and $x \in V_t$ is a node of t, then $\text{COLLAPSE}(t, x)$ is also a Union-Find tree.

We say that a node x of a tree t *satisfies the Union condition* if

$$\{\text{RANK}_t(y) : y \in \text{CHILDREN}(t, x)\} = \{0, 1, \ldots, \text{RANK}_t(x) - 1\}.$$

Then, the characterization of Union trees from [2] can be formulated in our terms as follows:

Theorem 1. *A tree t is a Union tree if and only if each node of t satisfies the Union condition.*

Note that the rank of a Union tree always coincides by its *height*. (And, any subtree of a Union tree is also a Union tree.) In particular, the leaves are exactly those nodes of rank 0.

3   Structural Characterization of Union-Find Trees

Suppose s and t are trees on the same set V of nodes, with the same root ROOT and the same rank function RANK. We write $s \preceq t$ if $x \preceq_s y$ implies $x \preceq_t y$ for each $x, y \in V$.

Clearly, $\preceq$ is a partial order on any set of trees (i.e. is a reflexive, transitive and antisymmetric relation). It is also clear that $s \preceq t$ if and only if $\mathrm{PARENT}_s(x) \preceq_t x$ holds for each $x \in V - \{\mathrm{ROOT}\}$ which is further equivalent to requiring $\mathrm{PARENT}_s(x) \preceq_t \mathrm{PARENT}_t(x)$ since $\mathrm{PARENT}_s(x)$ cannot be x.

Another notion we define is the (partial) operation PUSH on trees as follows: when t is a tree and $x \neq y \in V_t$ are *siblings* in t, i.e. have the same parent, and $\mathrm{RANK}_t(x) < \mathrm{RANK}_t(y)$, then $\mathrm{PUSH}(t, x, y)$ is defined as the tree $(V_t, \mathrm{ROOT}_t, \mathrm{RANK}_t, \mathrm{PARENT}')$ with

$$\mathrm{PARENT}'(z) = \begin{cases} y & \text{if } z = x, \\ \mathrm{PARENT}_t(z) & \text{otherwise,} \end{cases}$$

that is, we "push" the node x one level deeper in the tree just below its former sibling y. (See Fig. 1.)

We write $t \vdash t'$ when $t' = \mathrm{PUSH}(t, x, y)$ for some x and y, and as usual, $\vdash^*$ denotes the reflexive-transitive closure of $\vdash$.

Proposition 1. *For any pair s and t of trees, the following conditions are equivalent:*

(i) $s \preceq t$,
(ii) there exists a sequence $t_0 = s, t_1, t_2, \ldots, t_n$ of trees such that for each $i = 1, \ldots, n$ we have $t_i = \mathrm{PUSH}(t_{i-1}, x, y)$ for some depth-one node $x \in \mathrm{CHILDREN}(t_{i-1})$, moreover, $\mathrm{CHILDREN}(t_n) = \mathrm{CHILDREN}(t)$ and $t_n|_x \preceq t|_x$ for each $x \in \mathrm{CHILDREN}(t)$,
(iii) $s \vdash^* t$.

Proof. **(i)$\Rightarrow$(ii).** It is clear that $\preceq$ is equality on singleton trees, thus $\preceq$ implies $\vdash^*$ for trees of rank 0. Assume $s \preceq t$ for the trees $s = (V, \mathrm{ROOT}, \mathrm{RANK}, \mathrm{PARENT})$ and $t = (V, \mathrm{ROOT}, \mathrm{RANK}, \mathrm{PARENT}')$ and let X stand for the set $\mathrm{CHILDREN}(s)$ of the depth-one nodes of s and Y stand for $\mathrm{CHILDREN}(t)$. Clearly, $Y \subseteq X$ since by $s \preceq t$, any node x of s having depth at least two has to satisfy $\mathrm{PARENT}(x) \preceq_t \mathrm{PARENT}'(x)$ and since $\mathrm{PARENT}(x) \neq \mathrm{ROOT}$ for such nodes, x has to have depth at least two in t as well. Now there are two cases: either $\mathrm{ROOT} = \mathrm{PARENT}(x) = \mathrm{PARENT}'(x)$ for each $x \in X$, or $\mathrm{PARENT}(x) \prec_t \mathrm{PARENT}'(x)$ for some $x \in X$.

If $\mathrm{PARENT}'(x) = \mathrm{ROOT}$ for each $x \in X$, then $X = Y$ and we only have to show that $s|_x \preceq t|_x$ for each $x \in X$. For this, let $u, v \in V(s|_x)$ with $u \preceq_{s|_x} v$. Since $s|_x$ is a subtree of s, this holds if and only if $x \preceq_s u \preceq_s v$. From $s \preceq t$ this implies $x \preceq_t u \preceq_t v$, that is, $u \preceq_{t|_x} v$, hence $s|_x \preceq t|_x$.

Now assume $\mathrm{PARENT}(x) \prec_t \mathrm{PARENT}'(x)$ for some $x \in X$. Then $\mathrm{PARENT}'(x) \neq \mathrm{ROOT}$, thus there exists some $y \in Y$ with $y \preceq_t \mathrm{PARENT}'(x)$. By $Y \subseteq X$, this y is a member of X as well, and $\mathrm{RANK}_s(y) = \mathrm{RANK}_t(y) > \mathrm{RANK}_t(x) = \mathrm{RANK}_s(x)$, thus

$s' = \text{PUSH}(s, x, y)$ is well-defined. Moreover, $s' \preceq t$ since $\text{PARENT}_{s'}(z) \preceq_t z$ for each $z \in V$: either $z \neq x$ in which case $\text{PARENT}_{s'}(z) = \text{PARENT}(z) \preceq_t z$ by $s \preceq t$, or $z = x$ and then $\text{PARENT}_{s'}(z) = y \preceq_t \text{PARENT}'(x) \preceq_t x = z$ also holds. Thus, there exists a tree $s' = \text{PUSH}(s, x, y)$ for some $x \in \text{CHILDREN}(s)$ with $s' \preceq t$; since $\text{CHILDREN}(s') = X - \{x\}$, by repeating this construction we eventually arrive to a tree t_n with $|\text{CHILDREN}(t_n)| = |Y|$, implying $\text{CHILDREN}(t_n) = Y$ by $Y \subseteq \text{CHILDREN}(t_n)$.

(ii)$\Rightarrow$(iii). We apply induction on $\text{RANK}(s) = \text{RANK}(t)$. When $\text{RANK}(s) = 0$, then s is a singleton tree and the condition in ii) ensures that t is a singleton tree as well. Thus, $s = t$ and clearly $s \vdash^* t$.

Now let assume the claim holds for each pair of trees of rank less than $\text{RANK}(s)$ and let $t_0, \ldots, t_n$ be trees satisfying the condition. Then, by construction, $s \vdash^* t_n$. Since $\text{RANK}(t_n|_x) < \text{RANK}(t_n) = \text{RANK}(s)$ for each node $x \in \text{CHILDREN}(t_n)$, by $t_n|_x \preceq t|_x$ we get applying the induction hypothesis that $t_n|_x \vdash^* t|_x$ for each depth-one node x of t_n, thus $t_n \vdash^* t$, hence $s \vdash^* t$ as well.

(iii) $\Rightarrow$ (i). For $\vdash^*$ implying $\preceq$ it suffices to show that $\vdash$ implies $\preceq$ since the latter is reflexive and transitive. So let $s = (V, r, \text{RANK}, \text{PARENT})$ and $x \neq y \in V$ be siblings in s with the common parent z, $\text{RANK}(x) < \text{RANK}(y)$ and let $t = \text{PUSH}(s, x, y)$. Then, since $\text{PARENT}_s(x) = z = \text{PARENT}_t(y) = \text{PARENT}_t(\text{PARENT}_t(x))$, we get $\text{PARENT}_s(x) \preceq_t x$, and by $\text{PARENT}_s(w) = \text{PARENT}_t(w)$ for each node $w \neq x$, we have $s \preceq t$.

$\square$

The relations $\preceq$ and $\vdash^*$ are introduced due to their intimate relation to Union-Find and Union trees (similarly to the case of the union-by-size strategy [13], but there the PUSH operation itself was slightly different):

Theorem 2. *A tree t is a Union-Find tree if and only if $t \vdash^* s$ for some Union tree s.*

Proof. Let t be a Union-Find tree. We show the claim by structural induction. For singleton trees the claim holds since any singleton tree is a Union tree as well. Suppose $t = \text{MERGE}(t_1, t_2)$. Then by the induction hypothesis, $t_1 \vdash^* s_1$ and $t_2 \vdash^* s_2$ for the Union trees s_1 and s_2. Then, for the tree $s = \text{MERGE}(s_1, s_2)$ we get that $t \vdash^* s$. Finally, assume $t = \text{COLLAPSE}(t', x)$ for some node x. Let $x = x_1 \succ x_2 \succ \ldots \succ x_k = \text{ROOT}_{t'}$ be the ancestral sequence of x in t'. Then, defining $t_0 = t$, $t_i = \text{PUSH}(t_{i-1}, x_i, x_{i+1})$ we get that $t \vdash^* t_{k-2} = t'$ and $t' \vdash^* s$ for some Union tree s applying the induction hypothesis, thus $t \vdash^* s$ also holds.

Now assume $t \vdash^* s$ (equivalently, $t \preceq s$) for some Union tree s. We show the claim by induction on the height of t. For singleton trees the claim holds since any singleton tree is a Union-Find tree.

Now assume $t = (V, \text{ROOT}, \text{RANK}, \text{PARENT})$ is a tree and $t \vdash^* s$ for some Union tree s. Then by Proposition 1, there is a set $X = \text{CHILDREN}(s) \subseteq \text{CHILDREN}(t)$ of depth-one nodes of t and a function $f : Y \to X$ with $Y = \{y_1, \ldots, y_\ell\} = \text{CHILDREN}(t) - X$ such that for the sequence $t_0 = t$, $t_i = \text{PUSH}(t_{i-1}, y_i, f(y_i))$ we have that $t_\ell|_x \preceq s|_x$ for each $x \in X$. As each $s|_x$ is a Union tree (since so is s), we have by the induction hypothesis that each $t_\ell|_x$ is a Union-Find tree. Now let

$X = \{x_1, \ldots, x_k\}$ be ordered nondecreasingly by rank; then, as s is a Union tree and $X = \text{CHILDREN}(s)$, we get that $\{\text{RANK}(x_i)\} = \{0, 1, \ldots, \text{RANK}(\text{ROOT}) - 1\}$ by Theorem 1. Hence for the sequence t_i' defined as t_0' being a singleton tree with root ROOT and for each $i \in \{1, \ldots, k\}$, $t_i' = \text{MERGE}(t_{i-1}', t_\ell|_{x_i})$, we get that $t_\ell = t_k'$ is a Union-Find tree. Finally, we get t from t_ℓ by applying successively one COLLAPSE operaton on each node in Y, thus t is a Union-Find tree as well.

$\square$

4   Complexity

In order to show **NP**-completeness of the recognition problem, we first make a useful observation.

Proposition 2. *In any Union-Find tree t there are at least as many rank-0 nodes as nodes of positive rank.*

Proof. We apply induction on the structure of t. The claim holds for singleton trees (having one single node of rank 0). Let $t = \text{MERGE}(t_1, t_2)$ and suppose the claim holds for t_1 and t_2. There are two cases.

- Assume $\text{RANK}(t_1) = 0$. Then, since $\text{RANK}(t_1) \geq \text{RANK}(t_2)$ we have that $\text{RANK}(t_2)$ is 0 as well, i.e. both t_1 and t_2 are singleton trees (of rank 0). In this case t has one node of rank 1 and one node of rank 0.
- If $\text{RANK}(t_1) > 0$, then (since ROOT_{t_1} is the only node in $V_t = V_{t_1} \cup V_{t_2}$ whose rank can change at all, in which case it increases) neither the total number of rank-0 nodes nor the total number of nodes with positive rank changes, thus the claim holds.

Let $t = \text{COLLAPSE}(s, x)$ and assume the claim holds for s. Then, since the COLLAPSE operation does not change the rank of any of the nodes, the claim holds for t as well.

$\square$

In order to define a reduction from the strongly **NP**-complete problem PARTITION we introduce several notions on trees:

An *apple* of weight a for an integer $a > 0$ is a tree consisting of a root node of rank 2, a depth-one node of rank 0 and a depth-one nodes of rank 1.

A *basket* of size H for an integer $H > 0$ is a tree consisting of $H + 4$ nodes: the root node having rank 3, $H + 1$ depth-one children of rank 0 and one depth-one child of rank 1, which in turn has a child of rank 0.

A *flat tree* is a tree t of the following form: the root of t has rank 4. The immediate subtrees of t are:

- a node of rank 0, having no children;
- a node of rank 1, having a single child of rank 0;
- a node of rank 2, having two children: a single node of rank 0 and a node of rank 1, having a single child of rank 0;
- an arbitrary number of apples,

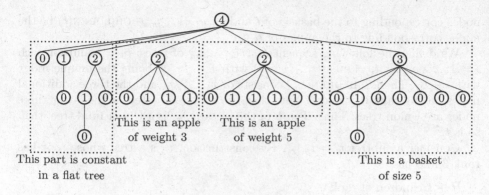

Fig. 2. A flat tree.

– and an arbitrary number of baskets for some fixed size H.

(See Fig. 2.)

At this point we recall that the following problem PARTITION is **NP**-complete in the strong sense [11]: given a list $a_1, \ldots, a_m$ of positive integers and a value $k > 0$ such that the value $B = \frac{\sum_{i=1}^{m} a_i}{k}$ is an integer, does there exist a partition $\mathcal{B} = \{B_1, \ldots, B_k\}$ of the set $\{1, \ldots, m\}$ satisfying $\sum_{i \in B_j} a_i = B$ for each $1 \leq j \leq k$?

(Here "in the strong sense" means that the problem remains **NP**-complete even if the numbers are encoded in unary.)

Proposition 3. *Assume t is a flat tree having k basket children, each having the size H, and m apple children of weights $a_1, \ldots, a_m$ respectively, satisfying $H \cdot k = \sum_{1 \leq i \leq m} a_i$.*

Then t is a Union-Find tree if and only if the instance $(a_1, \ldots, a_m, k)$ is a positive instance of the PARTITION problem.

Proof. (For an example, the reader is referred to Fig. 3.)

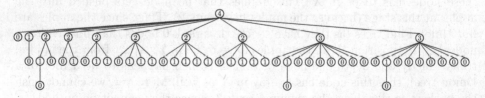

Fig. 3. The initial flat tree t corresponding to the PARTITION instance $(1, 2, 3, 4, 4, k = 2)$. The size of each basket is $(1 + 2 + 3 + 4 + 4)/k = 7$.

Suppose $\mathcal{I} = (a_1, \ldots, a_m, k)$ is a positive instance of the PARTITION problem. Let H stand for the target sum $\frac{\sum a_i}{k}$. Let $\mathcal{B} = \{\mathcal{B}_1, \ldots, \mathcal{B}_k\}$ be a solution of $\mathcal{I}$, i.e., $\sum_{i \in \mathcal{B}_j} a_i = H$ for each $j = 1, \ldots, k$. Let $x_1, \ldots, x_k \in \text{CHILDREN}(t)$ be the nodes corresponding to the baskets of t and let $y_1, \ldots, y_m \in$ CHILDREN(t) be the nodes corresponding to the apples of t.

We define the following sequence $t_0, t_1, \ldots, t_m$ of trees: $t_0 = t$ and for each $i = 1, \ldots, m$, let $t_i =$ PUSH(t_{i-1}, y_i, x_j) with $1 \leq j \leq k$ being the unique index with $i \in \mathcal{B}_j$. Then, CHILDREN(t_m) consists of $x_1, \ldots, x_k$ and the three additional nodes having rank 0, 1 and 2. Note that the subtrees rooted at the latter three nodes are Union trees. Thus, if each of the trees $t_m|_{x_j}$ is a Union-Find tree, then so is t.

Consider a subtree $t' = t_m|_{x_j}$. By construction, t' is a tree whose root has rank 3 and has

- $H + 1$ children of rank 0,
- a single child of rank 1, having a child of rank 0,
- and several (say, ℓ) apple children with total weight H.

We give a method to transform t' into a Union tree. First, we push a_i rank-0 nodes to each apple child of weight a_i. After this stage t' has one child of rank 0, one child of rank 1 and ℓ "filled" apple children, having a root of rank 2, thus the root of the transformed t' satisfies the Union condition. We only have to show that each of these "filled" apples is a Union-Find tree.

Such a subtree has a root node of rank 2, a_i depth-one nodes of rank 1 and $a_i + 1$ depth-one nodes of rank 0. Then, one can push into each node of rank 1 a node of rank 0 and arrive to a tree with one depth-one node of rank 0, and a_i depth-one nodes of rank 1, each having a single child of rank 0, which is indeed a Union tree, showing the claim by Theorem 2.

For an illustration of the construction the reader is referred to Fig. 4.

For the other direction, suppose t is a Union-Find tree. By Theorem 2 and Proposition 1, there is a subset $X \subseteq$ CHILDREN(t) and a mapping $f : Y \to X$ with $Y = \{y_1, \ldots, y_\ell\} =$ CHILDREN$(t) - X$ such that for the sequence $t_0 = t$, $t_i =$ PUSH$(t_{i-1}, y_i, f(y_i))$ we have that each immediate subtree of t_ℓ is a Union-Find tree and moreover, the root of t_ℓ satisfies the Union condition.

The root of t has rank 4, t_ℓ has to have at least one child having rank 0, 1, 2 and 3 respectively. Since t has exactly one child with rank 0 and rank 1, these nodes has to be in X. This implies that no node gets pushed into the apples at this stage (because the apples have rank 2). Thus, since the apples are *not* Union-Find trees (as they have strictly less rank-0 nodes than positive-rank nodes, cf. Proposition 2), all the apples have to be in Y. Apart from the apples, t has exactly one depth-one node of rank 2 (which happens to be a root of a Union tree), thus this node has to stay in X as well. Moreover, we cannot push the baskets as they have the maximal rank 3, hence they cannot be pushed.

Thus, we have to push all the apples, and we can push apples only into baskets (as exactly the baskets have rank greater than 2). Let $x \in X$ be a basket node, let t' stand for $t_\ell|_x$ and let $\{y_1', \ldots, y_j'\} \subseteq Y$ be the set of those apples that get pushed into x during the operation. Then, the total number of nodes having rank 0 in t' is $H + 2 + j$ (j of them coming from the apples and the other ones coming from the basket) while the total number of nodes having a positive rank is $2 + j + A$ where A is the total weight of the apples in $\{y_1', \ldots, y_j'\}$. Applying

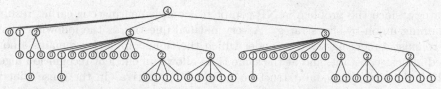

(a) Apples of size 3 and 4 are pushed into the first basket, apples of size 1, 2 and 4 are pushed into the second basket.

(b) The apples get filled from the baskets' surplus rank-0 leaves.

(c) The filling of the apples is pushed a level deeper and we have a Union tree.

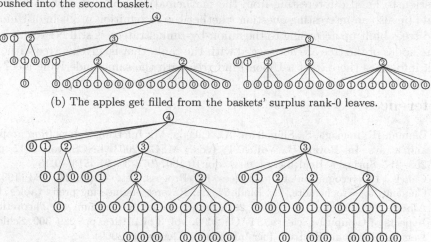

Fig. 4. Pushing t of Fig. 3 into a Union tree according to the solution $3 + 4 = 1 + 2 + 4$ of the PARTITION instance.

Proposition 2 we get that $A \leq H$ for each basket. Since the total weight of all apples is $H \cdot k$ and each apple gets pushed into exactly one basket, we get that $A = H$ actually holds for each basket. Thus, $\mathcal{I}$ is a positive instance of the PARTITION problem. □

Theorem 3. *The recognition problem of Union-Find trees is* **NP**-*complete.*

Proof. By Proposition 3 we get **NP**-hardness. For membership in **NP**, we make use of the characterization given in Theorem 2 and that the possible number of pushes is bounded above by n^2: upon pushing x below y, the depth of x and its descendants increases, while the depth of the other nodes remains the same. Since the depth of any node is at most n, the sum of the depths of all the nodes is at most n^2 in any tree. Hence, it suffices to guess nondeterministically a sequence $t = t_0 \vdash t_1 \vdash \ldots \vdash t_k$ for some $k \leq n^2$ with t_k being a Union tree (which also can be checked in polynomial time). □

5   Conclusion, Future Directions

We have shown that unless $\mathbf{P} = \mathbf{NP}$, there is no efficient algorithm to check whether a given tree is a valid Union-Find tree, assuming union-by-rank strategy, since the problem is **NP**-complete, complementing our earlier results assuming union-by-size strategy. A very natural question is the following: does there exist a merging strategy under which the time complexity remains amortized almost-constant, and at the same time allows an efficient recognition algorithm? Although this data structure is called "primitive" in the sense that it does not really need an automatic run-time certifying system, but we find the question to be also interesting from the mathematical point of view as well. It would be also an interesting question whether the recognition problem of Union-Find trees built up according to the union-by-rank strategy is still **NP**-complete if the nodes of the tree are not tagged with the rank, that is, given a tree without rank info, does there exist a Union-Find tree with the same underlying tree?

References

1. Bannai, H., Inenaga, S., Shinohara, A., Takeda, M.: Inferring strings from graphs and arrays. In: Rovan, B., Vojtáš, P. (eds.) MFCS 2003. LNCS, vol. 2747, pp. 208–217. Springer, Heidelberg (2003). doi:10.1007/978-3-540-45138-9_15
2. Cai, L.: The recognition of Union trees. Inf. Process. Lett. **45**(6), 279–283 (1993)
3. Clément, J., Crochemore, M., Rindone, G.: Reverse engineering prefix tables. In: Albers, S., Marion, J.-Y. (eds.) 26th International Symposium on Theoretical Aspects of Computer Science. STACS 2009, vol. 3 of LIPIcs, pp. 289–300. Schloss Dagstuhl - Leibniz-Zentrum fuer Informatik, Germany (2009)
4. Cormen, T.H., Stein, C., Rivest, R.L., Leiserson, C.E.: Introduction to Algorithms, 2nd edn. McGraw-Hill Higher Education, New York (2001)
5. Crochemore, M., Iliopoulos, C.S., Pissis, S.P., Tischler, G.: Cover array string reconstruction. In: Amir, A., Parida, L. (eds.) CPM 2010. LNCS, vol. 6129, pp. 251–259. Springer, Heidelberg (2010). doi:10.1007/978-3-642-13509-5_23
6. Duval, J.-P., Lecroq, T., Lefebvre, A.: Efficient validation and construction of border arrays and validation of string matching automata. RAIRO - Theor. Inf. Appl. **43**(2), 281–297 (2009)
7. Duval, J.-P., Lefebvre, A.: Words over an ordered alphabet and suffix permutations. Theor. Inf. Appl. **36**(3), 249–259 (2002)
8. Duval, J.-P., Lecroq, T., Lefebvre, A.: Border array on bounded alphabet. J. Autom. Lang. Comb. **10**(1), 51–60 (2005)
9. Fredman, M., Saks, M.: The cell probe complexity of dynamic data structures. In: Proceedings of the Twenty-first Annual ACM Symposium on Theory of Computing, STOC 1989, pp. 345–354. ACM, New York (1989)
10. Galler, B.A., Fisher, M.J.: An improved equivalence algorithm. Commun. ACM **7**(5), 301–303 (1964)
11. Garey, M.R., Johnson, D.S.: Computers and Intractability: A Guide to the Theory of NP-Completeness. W. H. Freeman & Co., New York (1979)
12. Gawrychowski, P., Jez, A., Jez, L.: Validating the Knuth-Morris-Pratt failure function, fast and online. Theory Comput. Syst. **54**(2), 337–372 (2014)
13. Gelle, K., Iván, S.: Recognizing Union-Find trees is NP-complete. CoRR, abs/1510.07462 (2015)
14. I, T., Inenaga, S., Bannai, H., Takeda, M.: Counting parameterized border arrays for a binary alphabet. In: Dediu, A.H., Ionescu, A.M., Martín-Vide, C. (eds.) LATA 2009. LNCS, vol. 5457, pp. 422–433. Springer, Heidelberg (2009). doi:10.1007/978-3-642-00982-2_36

15. Tomohiro, I., Inenaga, S., Bannai, H., Takeda, M.: Verifying and enumerating parameterized border arrays. Theoret. Comput. Sci. **412**(50), 6959–6981 (2011)
16. Tomohiro, I., Inenaga, S., Bannai, H., Takeda, M.: Inferring strings from suffix trees and links on a binary alphabet. Discr. Appl. Math. **163**(Part 3), 316–325 (2014)
17. Knight, K.: Unification: a multidisciplinary survey. ACM Comput. Surv. **21**(1), 93–124 (1989)
18. Kucherov, G., Tóthmérész, L., Vialette, S.: On the combinatorics of suffix arrays. Inf. Process. Lett. **113**(22–24), 915–920 (2013)
19. Weilin, L., Ryan, P.J., Smyth, W.F., Sun, Y., Yang, L.: Verifying a border array in linear time. J. Comb. Math. Comb. Comput. **42**, 223–236 (2000)
20. McConnell, R.M., Mehlhorn, K., Näher, S., Schweitzer, P.: Certifying algorithms. Comput. Sci. Rev. **5**(2), 119–161 (2011)
21. Starikovskaya, T., Vildhøj, H.W.: A suffix tree or not a suffix tree? J. Discr. Algorithms **32**, 14–23 (2015)
22. Tarjan, R.E.: Efficiency of a good but not linear set union algorithm. J. ACM **22**(2), 215–225 (1975)

Self-attraction Removal from Oritatami Systems

Yo-Sub Han[1], Hwee Kim[1], Trent A. Rogers[2], and Shinnosuke Seki[3(✉)]

[1] Department of Computer Science, Yonsei University,
50 Yonsei-Ro, Seodaemun-Gu, Seoul 03722, Republic of Korea
{emmous,kimhwee}@yonsei.ac.kr
[2] Department of Computer Sceince and Computer Engineering,
University of Arkansas, Fayetteville, AR 72701, USA
tar003@uark.edu
[3] Department of Computer and Network Engineering,
University of Electro-Communications,
1-5-1 Chofugaoka, Chofu, Tokyo 1828585, Japan
s.seki@uec.ac.jp

Abstract. RNA cotranscriptional folding refers to the phenomenon in which an RNA transcript folds upon itself while being synthesized (transcribed). Oritatami is a computational model of this phenomenon, which lets its transcript, a sequence of beads (abstract molecules) fold cotranscriptionally via interactions between beads according to its ruleset. In this paper, we study the problem of removing self-attractions, which lets a bead interact with another bead of the same kind, from a given oritatami system without changing its behavior. We provide an algorithm for that with overhead linear in the delay parameter, which should be considerably smaller than the length of its transcript. We also show that this overhead is tight.

1 Introduction

Self-assembly is the process by which relatively simple components coalesce to form intricate and complex structures. Studying self-assembling systems can provide us with insights into everything from designing nanophotonic devices [11] to the origins of life [14]. A number of theoretical models of self-assembly have been proposed [2,12,15] and some models of self-assembly have been implemented in the laboratory to algorithmically build structures out of DNA [3,6,13]. One

---

Y.-S. Han—Supported by International Cooperation Program (2017K2A9A2A08 000270) and Basic Science Research Program (2015R1D1A1A01060097) by NRF of Korea.

Kim was supported by NRF (National Research Foundation of Korea) Grant funded by the Korean Government (NRF-2013-Global Ph.D. Fellowship Program).

T.A. Rogers—This author's research was supported by the National Science Foundation Graduate Research Fellowship Program under Grant No. DGE-1450079, and National Science Foundation grants CAREER-1553166 and CCF-1422152.

S. Seki—In part supported by JST Program to Disseminate Tenure Tracking System No. 6F36 and JSPS KAKENHI Grant-in-Aid for Young Scientists (A) No. 16H05854.

© IFIP International Federation for Information Processing 2017
Published by Springer International Publishing AG 2017. All Rights Reserved
G. Pighizzini and C. Câmpeanu (Eds.): DCFS 2017, LNCS 10316, pp. 164–176, 2017.
DOI: 10.1007/978-3-319-60252-3_13

Fig. 1. RNA origami [9]: the cotranscriptional folding of an RNA tile in a laboratory. The gray spiral is a DNA sequence (template), the orange molecule attaching is the RNA polymerase, and the blue output of the polymerase is the RNA transcript. (Color figure online)

proposed model of self-assembly is called Oritatami (folding in Japanese) [8], which seeks to capture the fundamental dynamics of cotranscriptional folding. Transcription is the first step in gene expression in which an RNA polymerase attaches to a DNA sequence and sequentially produces RNA nucleotides (A, C, G, U) (see Fig. 1). Cotranscriptional folding refers to the folding of RNA during transcription. That is, as the RNA is transcribed, its nucleotides interact with each other via hydrogen bonds, resulting in the folding of the RNA.

Geary, Rothemund, and Andersen harnessed the power of cotranscriptional folding in order to self-assemble nanoscale tiles out of RNA (*RNA origami* [9]). Oritatami is a theoretical model to study the computational aspect of cotranscriptional folding. It models a single strand of RNA as a "strand" of abstract molecules, or *beads*. Each bead is of a certain type taken out of a finite alphabet Σ. The bead types along with a set of attraction rules specify which beads are attracted to one another. In addition, each oritatami system has a parameter called the *delay* δ. It models the speed at which cotranscriptional folding occurs. The folding of an oritatami system proceeds by "looking ahead" at the next δ beads on the strand and folds them so as to create the largest number of bonds. We can see in [1] an oritatami system of delay 3 fold a motif called *glider*.

The class of oritatami systems implementable in the laboratory by the cotranscriptional folding of RNA is limited by the properties of RNA. More specifically, the attraction rules of oritatami systems are limited by the types of allowable interactions between RNA nucleotides. Therefore, laboratory implementation may require to alter the system so that it fits certain criteria required for experimental implementation. For example, a physical implementation of oritatami systems might rely on the Watson-Crick complementarity (G-C and A-U). If we wanted to implement an oritatami system in this setting which had a rule specifying a bead type is attracted to itself, the self-attraction would need to be removed.

In addition to providing tools to make oritatami systems physically realizable, our results are the first set of results to show an oritatami system being "simulated" by another oritatami system with a different set of properties. Simulation has played an important role in determining the relative power of classes of systems in tile assembly and determining how classes of tile systems relate to each other [4,7]. In addition, the notion of simulation in tile assembly has given rise to a rich study of intrinsic universality [5,10,16] which has provided us with a deeper understanding of tile assembly. The results in this paper are a first step towards using "simulation" to develop a better understanding of the model.

In this paper, we examine the removal of rules specifying that a bead type is attracted to itself, which we call self-attraction rules, from Oritatami systems. Given a system Ξ, the goal of self-attraction removal is to create another system Ξ' such that Ξ' behaves in the same way as Ξ, Ξ' produces the same set of conformations as Ξ, and Ξ' does not contain any self-attraction rules.

2   Preliminaries

Let Σ be a finite set of bead types. A bead of type a is called an a-bead. By Σ^* (resp. Σ^ω), we denote the set of finite (one-way infinite) sequences of bead types in Σ. A sequence $w \in \Sigma^*$ can be represented as $w = b_1 b_2 \cdots b_n$ for some $n \geq 0$ and bead types $b_1, b_2, \ldots, b_n \in \Sigma$, where n is the *length* of w and denoted by $|w|$. The sequence of length 0 is denoted by λ. For $1 \leq i, j \leq n$, the subsequence of w ranging from the i-th bead to j-th bead is denoted by $w[i \ldots j]$, that is, $w[i \ldots j] = b_i b_{i+1} \cdots b_j$; $w[i \ldots j] = \lambda$ if $i > j$. This notation is simplified as $w[i]$ when $j = i$, referring to the i-th bead of w. For $k \geq 1$, $w[1 \ldots k]$ is called a *prefix*.

Fig. 2. Triangular lattice.

Oritatami systems fold their transcript, a sequence of beads, over the triangular lattice (Fig. 2) cotranscriptionally by letting nascent beads form as many hydrogen-bond-based interactions (*h-interactions*) as possible according to their own interaction rules. Let $\mathbb{T} = (V, E)$ be the triangular grid graph. A directed path $P = p_1 p_2 \cdots$ in $\mathbb{T}$ is a possibly-infinite sequence of pairwise-distinct points $p_1, p_2, \ldots \in V$ such that $\{p_i, p_{i+1}\} \in E$ for all $i \geq 1$. Its i-th point p_i is referred to as $P[i]$. Provided it is finite, by $|P|$, we denote the number of points in it.

A conformation instance, or *configuration*, is a triple (P, w, H) of a directed path P in $\mathbb{T}$, $w \in \Sigma^* \cup \Sigma^\omega$, and a set $H \subseteq \{(i, j) \mid 1 \leq i, i + 2 \leq j, \{P[i], P[j]\} \in E\}$ of h-interactions. This is to be interpreted as the sequence w being folded in such a manner that its i-th bead $w[i]$ is placed on the i-th point $P[i]$ along the path and the i-th bead interacts with the j-th bead if and only if $(i, j) \in H$. Configurations (P_1, w_1, H_1) and (P_2, w_2, H_2) are *congruent* provided $w_1 = w_2$, $H_1 = H_2$, and P_1 can be transformed into P_2 by a combination of a translation, a reflection, and rotations by 60°. Given a configuration (P, w, H), the set of all configurations congruent to it, denoted by $[(P, w, H)]$, is called its *conformation*. We refer to w as its *primary structure*. A ruleset $\mathcal{H} \subseteq \Sigma \times \Sigma$ is a symmetric relation over the set of pairs of bead types, that is, for all bead types $a, b \in \Sigma$, $(a, b) \in \mathcal{H}$ implies $(b, a) \in \mathcal{H}$. An h-interaction $(i, j) \in H$ is called *valid with respect to $\mathcal{H}$*, or simply *$\mathcal{H}$-valid*, if $(w[i], w[j]) \in \mathcal{H}$. This conformation is *$\mathcal{H}$-valid* if all of its h-interactions are $\mathcal{H}$-valid. For $\alpha \geq 1$, this conformation is *of arity* α if the maximum number of h-interactions per bead is α, that is, if for any $k \geq 1$, $|\{i \mid (i, k) \in H\}| + |\{j \mid (k, j) \in H\}| \leq \alpha$ and the equation holds for some k. By $\mathcal{C}_{\leq \alpha}$, we denote the set of all conformations of arity at most α.

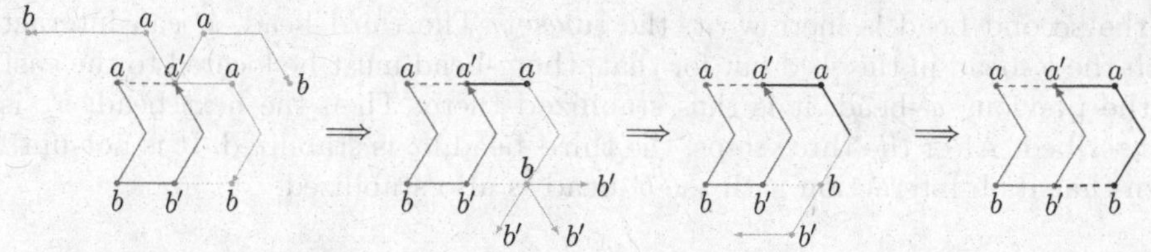

Fig. 3. Folding of a glider motif by a delay-3 deterministic oritatami system. (Color figure online)

Oritatami systems grow conformations by elongating them under their own ruleset. For a finite conformation C_1, another finite conformation C_2 is an *elongation* of C_1 by a bead $b \in \Sigma$ under a ruleset $\mathcal{H}$, written as $C_1 \xrightarrow{\mathcal{H}}_b C_2$, if there exists a configuration (P, w, H) of C_1 such that $(Pp, wb, H \cup H')$ is a configuration of C_2, where $p \in V$ is a point not along the path P and $H' \subseteq \{(i, |P| + 1) \mid 1 \le i \le |P| - 1, \{P[i], p\} \in E, (w[i], b) \in \mathcal{H}\}$. This operation is recursively extended to the elongation by a finite sequence of beads as: for any conformation C, $C \xrightarrow{\mathcal{H}^*}_\lambda C$; and for a finite sequence of beads $w \in \Sigma^*$ and a bead $b \in \Sigma$, a conformation C_1 is elongated to a conformation C_2 by wb, written as $C_1 \xrightarrow{\mathcal{H}^*}_{wb} C_2$, if there is a conformation C' that satisfies $C_1 \xrightarrow{\mathcal{H}^*}_w C'$ and $C' \xrightarrow{\mathcal{H}}_b C_2$.

An *oritatami system* over an alphabet Σ is a 6-tuple $\Xi = (\Sigma, w, \mathcal{H}, \delta, \alpha, \sigma)$, where $\mathcal{H}$ is a *ruleset*, $\delta \ge 1$ is a parameter called *delay*, and σ is an $\mathcal{H}$-valid initial *seed* conformation of arity at most α, upon which its *transcript* $w \in \Sigma^* \cup \Sigma^\omega$ is to be folded by stabilizing beads of w one at a time so as to minimize energy collaboratively with the succeeding $\delta - 1$ nascent beads. The energy $U(C)$ of a conformation $C = [(P, w, H)]$ is defined to be $-|H|$; the more h-interactions a conformation has, the more stable it becomes. The set $\mathcal{F}(\Xi)$ of conformations *foldable* by this system is recursively defined as follows: the seed σ is in $\mathcal{F}(\Xi)$; and provided that an elongation C_i of σ by the prefix $w[1 \ldots i]$ is foldable (i.e., $C_0 = \sigma$), its further elongation C_{i+1} by the next bead $w[i+1]$ is foldable if

$$C_{i+1} \in \underset{\substack{C \in \mathcal{C}_{\le \alpha} \text{ s.t.} \\ C_i \xrightarrow{\mathcal{H}}_{w[i+1]} C}}{\operatorname{argmin}} \min \left\{ U(C') \mid C \xrightarrow{\mathcal{H}^*}_{w[i+2\ldots i+k]} C', k \le \delta, C' \in \mathcal{C}_{\le \alpha} \right\}. \quad (1)$$

The bead $w[i+1]$ and h-interactions it forms are said to have been *stabilized* according to C_{i+1}. A conformation foldable by Ξ is *terminal* if none of its elongations is foldable by Ξ. The oritatami system Ξ is *deterministic* if for all $i \ge 0$, there exists at most one C_{i+1} that satisfies (1). Thus, a deterministic oritatami system folds into a unique terminal conformation.

Example 1 [1]. See Fig. 3 for a delay-3 oritatami system Ξ to fold a motif called glider. Its transcript is a repetition of $a \bullet bb' \bullet a$ and its ruleset is $\{(a, a'), (b, b')\}$. Its seed is colored in red. The first 3 beads, $a \bullet b$, are transcribed and elongate the seed by the seed in all possible ways. The a-bead cannot form any h-interaction or the second bead is inert w.r.t. the ruleset. The third bead, b, can interact with the b'-bead in the seed but for that, the a-bead must be located to the east of the previous a'-bead; it is thus stabilized there. Then the next bead, b', is transcribed. After the three steps, the third bead, b, is stabilized. It is not until then that its h-interaction with the b'-bead is also stabilized.

2.1   Self-attraction-free Oritatami System

A bead type $a \in \Sigma$ is *self-attractive* according to a ruleset $\mathcal{H}$ if $(a, a) \in \mathcal{H}$. An oritatami system is *free from self-attraction*, or *self-attraction-free*, if no bead type in its alphabet is self-attractive according to its ruleset.

We formulate the problem of removing self-attraction from a given oritatami system without changing the behavior in Problem 1. An isomorphism between conformations must be introduced. Conformations C_1 and C_2 are *isomorphic* if there exist an instance (P_1, w_1, H_1) of C_1 and an instance (P_2, w_2, H_2) of C_2 such that $P_1 = P_2$ and $H_1 = H_2$.

Problem 1 (Self-attraction removal). Let $\varXi$ be an oritatami system. Design a self-attraction-free oritatami system $\varXi'$ such that a conformation is foldable by $\varXi$ if and only if the isomorphic conformation is foldable by $\varXi'$.

Replacing the beads in the seed and transcript with pairwise distinct bead types provides a trivial solution, but is not desirable.

The following approach to Problem 1 called *bead type modification* is promising: When a bead type a is found self-attractive, it is modified as $a_1, a_2, \ldots, a_t$. The ruleset is then modified so as not to allow for any self-attraction but to let a bead interact with any of its modifications; for example, if we make three copies a_1, a_2, a_3 of a bead a, none of $(a_1, a_1), (a_2, a_2), (a_3, a_3)$ is in the ruleset but all of (a_1, a_2), (a_2, a_3), and (a_3, a_1) are in it. Moreover, these modifications are to look to non-a beads as if they were identical, or the ruleset should be modified so. More precisely, for any $b \neq a$, the modified ruleset should include the rules $(a_1, b), (a_2, b), (a_3, b)$ if and only if (a, b) is in the original ruleset.

We propose a subproblem of Problem 1 based on this approach and establish the measure for the efficiency of the modification. It employs a *subscript-erasing homomorphism* $h : \Sigma' \to \Sigma$ defined as $h(x_i) = x$ for $x \in \Sigma$ and $i \geq 1$.

Problem 2 (Self-attraction removal by bead type modification). Solve Problem 1 on an oritatami system $\varXi = (\Sigma, w, \mathcal{H}, \delta, \alpha, \sigma)$ so that the resulting self-attraction-free system $\varXi' = (\Sigma', w', \mathcal{H}', \delta, \alpha, \sigma')$ also satisfies the following properties:

1. $\Sigma' = \{x_i \mid x \in \Sigma, 1 \leq i \leq c(x)\}$ for a positive integer $c(x)$ for x.
2. $\mathcal{H}' = \{(x_i, y_j) \mid (x, y) \in \mathcal{H}, x \neq y\} \cup \{(x_i, x_j) \mid (x, x) \in \mathcal{H}, i \neq j\}$.
3. h maps the primary structure of σ' to that of σ and $h(w') = w$.

We use the *copying ratio* $c = \max c(x)$ to measure the efficiency of $\varXi'$.

3 Bead Type Modification Based on the Event Horizon

The bead stabilization is a local optimization. By definition, the stabilization of a bead in a delay-δ system is not affected by any bead outside the circle of radius $\delta + 1$ centered at the bead stabilized previously. The circle is so called the *event horizon*. Beads on its circumference can affect the process not geometrically but energetically by interacting with the bead transcribed most recently. The event horizon can encompass at most $3(\delta + 1)(\delta + 2)$ beads.

The event horizon varies from step to step; in the i-th step is centered at the $i - 1$-th bead a_{i-1}, which was stabilized previously. The nascent fragment $a_i a_{i+1} \cdots a_{i+\delta-1}$ folds so as to stabilize a_i most stably inside the horizon. During this search, the bead $a_{i+\delta-1}$, which was just transcribed and hence is at the tip of the fragment, can observe every point in and on the horizon, if any, unless being hindered by other beads geometrically. The region observable by the bead $a_{i+\delta-1}$ is never widening but just narrowing as steps go by.

We use bead type modification along the transcript to remove self-attraction. Prior to the transcription of a bead of self-attractive type $a \in \Sigma$, an event horizon is queried for another a-bead, and if there is, then modified the bead to be transcribed into $a_1 \notin \Sigma$. Later, if another a-bead is about to be transcribed inside a horizon provided with both an a-bead and an a_1-bead, then modify its type as $a_2 \notin \Sigma$; without any a_1-bead around, the new type a_2 need not be introduced but an a_1-bead can be transcribed next. No more than $3(\delta + 1)(\delta + 2) + 1$ modifications are needed per bead type due to the size of an event horizon.

Algorithm 1 is an implementation of the idea for deterministic oritatami systems that are finite in the sense that their transcript is finite. Transient systems need be simulated in line 16 so that auxiliary rules which let a subscripted bead bind to an unsubscripted one are introduced in line 10 but eliminated in the end.

Lemma 1. *Let $C = [(P, u, H)]$ be a conformation that is not $\mathcal{H}$-valid. For any $v \in h^{-1}(u)$, the isomorphic conformation $C' = [(P, v, H)]$ is not $\mathcal{H}'$-valid.*

Proof. Being $\mathcal{H}$-invalid means that an a-bead interacts with b-bead in C though $(a, b) \notin \mathcal{H}$. Since $v \in h^{-1}(u)$, the corresponding interaction in C' is between an a_i-bead and b_j-bead for some i, j. By definition, $(a_i, b_j) \notin \mathcal{H}'$. $\qquad\square$

Corollary 1. *If an elongation of the seed σ by $w[1 \ldots i]$ is not $\mathcal{H}$-valid, then its isomorphic conformation obtained by elongating σ' by $w'[1 \ldots i]$ is not $\mathcal{H}'$-valid.*

The inverse of the statement in Lemma 1 is not always true. Imagine in the conformation C, an a-bead is bound with another a-bead. Providing these beads with the same subscript results in an $\mathcal{H}'$-invalid conformation. Preventing them from being subscripted identically actually yields a valid conformation.

Lemma 2. *Let $C = [(P, u, H)]$ be an $\mathcal{H}$-valid conformation. For any $v \in h^{-1}(u)$, the conformation $C' = [(P, v, H)]$ is $\mathcal{H}'$-valid if for all $(i, j) \in H$, $h(v[i]) = h(v[j])$ implies $v[i] \neq v[j]$.*

Algorithm 1. Removing self-attractions from a deterministic finite oritatami system

---

Require: A given oritatami system $\Xi = (\Sigma, w, \mathcal{H}, \delta, \alpha, \sigma)$ is deterministic.
1: $c \leftarrow 3(\delta+1)(\delta+2) + 1$
2: $w' \leftarrow w$
3: $\Sigma' \leftarrow \{a_i \mid a \in \Sigma, 1 \leq i \leq c\}$
4: **for all** $(a, a) \in \mathcal{H}$ **do**
5:     $\mathcal{H}_{\text{temp}} \leftarrow \mathcal{H} \cup \{(a_i, a_j), (a_j, a_i) \mid 1 \leq i < j \leq c\}$
6: **end for**
7: **for all** $(a, b) \in \mathcal{H}$ such that $a \neq b$ **do**
8:     $\mathcal{H}_{\text{temp}} \leftarrow \mathcal{H}_{\text{temp}} \cup \{(a_i, b_j), (b_j, a_i) \mid 1 \leq i, j \leq c\}$
9: **end for**
10: **for all** $(a, c) \in \mathcal{H}$ **do**
11:     $\mathcal{H}_{\text{temp}} \leftarrow \mathcal{H}_{\text{temp}} \cup \{(a, c_i), (c_i, a) \mid 1 \leq i \leq c\}$
12: **end for**
13: $\sigma' \leftarrow 3\text{-COLOR}(\sigma)$
14: $\Xi' \leftarrow (\Sigma', w', \mathcal{H}_{\text{temp}}, \delta, \alpha, \sigma')$
15: **for** $i = 1$ to $|w|$ **do**
16:     Simulate Ξ' to compute the event horizon of the $\max(1, i-\delta+1)$-th step, at which the i-th bead is transcribed
17:     $a \leftarrow w'[i]$
18:     $m \leftarrow \min \left\{ k \geq 1 \;\middle|\; \begin{array}{l} \text{no } a_k\text{-bead is in the horizon and} \\ \text{for all } \max(1, i-\delta+1) \leq j < i, w'[i] \neq a_k \end{array} \right\}$
19:     $w'[i] \leftarrow a_m$
20: **end for**
21: $\mathcal{H}' \leftarrow \mathcal{H}_{\text{temp}} \setminus (\mathcal{H} \cup \{(a, c_i), (c_i, a) \mid 1 \leq i \leq c\})$
22: **return** The self-attraction-free oritatami system $(\Sigma', w', \mathcal{H}', \delta, \alpha, \sigma')$

Now we show that the resulting system Ξ' behaves as the given system Ξ does. For $0 \leq i \leq |w|$, let $C_i = [(P_i, w_\sigma w[1 \ldots i], H_i)]$ be the unique conformation foldable by Ξ among all the elongations of the seed σ by the transcript's prefix $w[1 \ldots i]$, where w_σ is the primary structure of σ. That is, $C_0 = \sigma$. The seed σ' of Ξ' is obtained from σ via the function 3-COLOR, which gives subscripts 0, 1, or 2 to beads of a given conformation so as for adjacent beads not to share a common subscript based on the 3-colorability of the triangular grid graph. It is hence $\mathcal{H}'$-valid due to Lemma 2 so that it is foldable by Ξ'. As an inductive hypothesis, assume that C_i' be the unique conformation foldable by Ξ' among all the elongations of the seed σ' by the subscripted transcript's prefix $w'[1 \ldots i]$ and C_i' be isomorphic to C_i. Corollary 1 justifies that the stabilization of the $(i+1)$-th bead in Ξ' counts out any elongation of C_i' by $w'[i+1 \ldots i+\delta]$ or by its prefix that is isomorphic to an $\mathcal{H}$-invalid elongation of C_i. On the contrary, an elongation of C_i' by $w'[i+1 \ldots i+\delta]$ or by its prefix isomorphic to an $\mathcal{H}$-valid elongation of C_i is $\mathcal{H}'$-valid due to Lemma 2 because line 18 of Algorithm 1 prevents any nascent bead in $w'[i+1 \ldots i+\delta]$ from being transcribed in the sight of another bead of identical type. Therefore, only the elongation of σ' by $w'[1 \ldots i+1]$ that is isomorphic to C_{i+1} is foldable by Ξ'. This concludes the inductive proof.

4   On Deterministic Finite Oritatami Systems

The quadratic copying ratio in Algorithm 1 can be reduced to linear. Algorithm 1 is overly cautious; it forbids an a_i-bead to be transcribed inside a horizon with an a_i-bead because an a_i-bead is not self-attractive while its original was. It suffices to guarantee that in at least one of the most stable elongations of each foldable conformation, not both of a beads interacting with each other are modified as a_i. The other elongations may get less stable but it does not affect the behavior of the resulting system because a given system is deterministic so that the next bead is to be stabilized uniquely point-wise and interaction-wise no matter which of the most stable elongations is referred to.

The modified algorithm is implemented as Algorithm 2. A given oritatami system $\Xi = (\Sigma, w, \mathcal{H}, \delta, \alpha, \sigma)$ is deterministic so that, for each $0 \le i \le |w|$, there exists at most one foldable elongation of the seed by the transcript's prefix $w[1 \ldots i]$; let us denote it by C_i. After setting c rather linearly, Algorithm 2 runs as Algorithm 1 up to line 14. It then chooses arbitrarily for each k one representative elongation E_k of C_{k-1}, according to which the next bead $w[k]$ is stabilized in the given system. The i-th bead is transcribed at the $\max(1, i-\delta+1)$-th step and it is involved in the stabilization of the previous at most $\delta - 1$ beads until it is stabilized at the i-th step. By the i-th execution of the outer **for**-loop in line 4, the first $i - 1$ beads of w have been already subscripted somehow; the remaining beads have not been given subscripts yet. The inner **for**-loop examines how the i-th bead is bound to preceding (already-subscripted) beads in the j-th representative for all $\max(1, i - \delta + 1) \le j \le i$ and chooses a proper subscript m out of the set I. All of the representatives $E_{\max(1, i-\delta+1)}, \ldots, E_j$ may have to be considered because the i-th bead may not be bound to the same bead in all of

---

Algorithm 2. Linear-cost self-attraction removal from a deterministic finite oritatami system

---

Require: A given oritatami system $\Xi = (\Sigma, w, \mathcal{H}, \delta, \alpha, \sigma)$ is deterministic.
1: $c \leftarrow 4\delta + 2$
2: Run Algorithm 1 from line 2 up to line 14
3: Simulate Ξ and arbitrarily choose one representative $E_k = (P_k, w_k, H_k)$ among the most stable elongations of C_{k-1} by $w[k \ldots k+\delta-1]$ for all $1 \le k \le |w|$.
4: **for** $i = 1$ **to** $|w|$ **do**
5:     $a \leftarrow w'[i]$
6:     $u_{\text{done}} \leftarrow w_\sigma w'[1 \ldots i-1]$
7:     **for** $j = \max(1, i - \delta + 1)$ **to** i **do**
8:         $I \leftarrow \{1, 2, \ldots, c\} \setminus \{\ell \mid u_{\text{done}}[k] = a_\ell \text{ for some } (k, |w_\sigma| + i) \in H_j\}$
9:     **end for**
10:     $w'[i] \leftarrow a_{\min I}$
11: **end for**
12: $\mathcal{H}' \leftarrow \mathcal{H}_{\text{temp}} \setminus (\mathcal{H} \cup \{(a, c_i), (c_i, a) \mid 1 \le i \le c\})$
13: **return** The self-attraction-free oritatami system $(\Sigma', w', \mathcal{H}', \delta, \alpha, \sigma')$

---

them. Note that the i-th bead can interact with 5 beads in the first representative but with at most 4 beads in the others. Therefore, $4\delta + 2$ subscripts suffice.

Lemma 3. *The following statements hold:*

- *For $1 \leq i \leq |w| + 1$, the elongation C'_{i-1} of σ' by $w'[1\ldots i - 1]$ that is isomorphic to C_{i-1} is foldable by Ξ';*
- *For $1 \leq i \leq |w|$, the elongation E'_i of C'_{i-1} by $w'[i\ldots i + \delta - 1]$ that is isomorphic to the i-th representative chosen in line 3 is $\mathcal{H}'$-valid.*

Theorem 1. *Given a deterministic finite oritatami system Ξ of delay δ, we can solve Problem 2 for Ξ with the copying ratio $c = 4\delta + 2$.*

5   Lower Bounds on Copying Ratio

Having established a linear upper bound on the copying ratio at least for deterministic oritatami systems, now we examine the lower bound. First, we propose a nondeterministic finite oritatami system Ξ_{nd} such that removing self-attraction from it requires a number of new bead types linearly proportional to the length of its transcript (Theorem 2). Based on it, we will design a deterministic finite oritatami system Ξ_{nd} of delay δ, which requires a copying ratio linear in δ to free itself from self-attraction by bead type modification (Theorem 3). This lower bound asymptotically matches the upper bound established in Theorem 1.

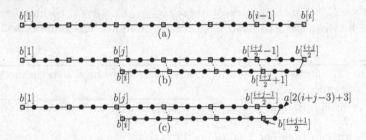

Fig. 4. Three examples of a part of C_j^i for $\delta = 1$. (a) Illustration of a part of C_i^i. (b) The case when $i + j$ is even. (c) The case when $i + j$ is odd.

The transcript of Ξ_{nd} is $w = (b\bullet^{2\delta+1})^t$ for some $t \geq 1$ and the seed of Ξ_{nd} is empty. Its ruleset is a singleton $\{(b, b)\}$, making b-beads self-attractive and $\bullet$-beads inert. By $b[i]$, we denote the i-th b-bead in w. See Fig. 4 for some of the conformations C_j^i foldable by this system, where δ is set to 1, in which $b[i]$ is bound to $b[j]$. Starting from the first bead, $b[1]$, this system can stretch its transcript straight rightward arbitrarily far and switch it back anywhere. The first $\delta + 2$ inert beads after $b[1]$ can be stabilized anyhow because it is not until they are stabilized that the next interactive bead, $b[2]$, is transcribed. Stretching them straight rightward is just one possibility. Being stabilized thus, they keep $b[1]$ out of the event horizon at the transcription of $b[2]$. Otherwise, $b[1]$ can lie in the horizon and pull $b[2]$ next to it and bind. Thus, for arbitrary $i \geq 1$ and $j > i$, this system can fold into a conformation C_j^i in which $b[i]$ is bound to $b[j]$. Consequently, in order to remove the self-attraction (b, b) by bead-type modification, these b-beads must be modified with pairwise-distinct indices, arising the need for the copying ratio $\lfloor |w|/(2\delta + 2) \rfloor$.

Theorem 2. *For a given delay δ and $n \in \mathbb{N}$, there exists a nondeterministic finite oritatami system Ξ_{nd} of delay δ whose transcript is of length n such that any solution Ξ'_{nd} to Problem 2 for Ξ_{nd} requires a copying ratio $c \geq \lfloor |w|/(2\delta+2) \rfloor$.*

The proof of Theorem 2 along with the fact that an oritatami system is only allowed a finite number of unique bead types yield the following result on the impossibility of removing self-attraction from infinite oritatami system.

Corollary 2. *There exists an infinite oritatami system Ξ such that there is no solution to Problem 2 for Ξ.*

Now we give a lower bound for the copying ratio for deterministic systems.

Theorem 3. *For a given delay δ, there exists a deterministic finite oritatami system Ξ_d of delay δ such that any solution Ξ'_d to Problem 2 for Ξ_d requires the copying ratio $c \geq \lfloor \delta/4 \rfloor$.*

We use delay $\delta = 4t$. The transcript of Ξ_d is similar to the transcript of Ξ_{nd} for Theorem 2, having periodic appearance of a self-attractive bead x. Note that conformations in Ξ_{nd} forces the self-attractive bead to have interactions with all other beads of the same type. We want the same phenomenon to happen in Ξ_d. Unlike Ξ_{nd}, a deterministic system stabilizes each bead at a unique point, so it is not possible to force all possible x beads to interact in the final conformation, since the conformation is planar. Instead, we use the most stable elongations during transcription. First, we design elongations to geometrically force all possible x beads to interact. Second, we prove that these elongations are indeed the most stable elongations to stabilize each bead. Third, we prove that all (x, x) interactions in these elongations are necessary for the system.

When we use bead type modification to remove a self-attractive rule (x, x), one (x, x) interaction in the original system may be removed in the resulting system if we modify interacting beads to the same bead type. If we want to maintain the interaction in the resulting system, we need to modify the beads into distinct types, say x_1 and x_2. On the other hand, interactions that are not self-attractive cannot be modified by bead type modification. The fact that we cannot remove unnecessary rules freely makes it challenging to design Ξ_d.

For every $2i - 2$nd bead, we assign an elongation C_i that mimics behaviors of conformations of Ξ_{nd}—proceed straight right, make a single right turn and proceed straight left. In detail, the transcript has two parts: The first part w_h of length δ with the repeated x every fourth bead, and the second part w_t of length $\delta - 5$ with distinct bead types for each bead. Given that x is repeated every fourth bead, it is straightforward to see that the set of these elongations is

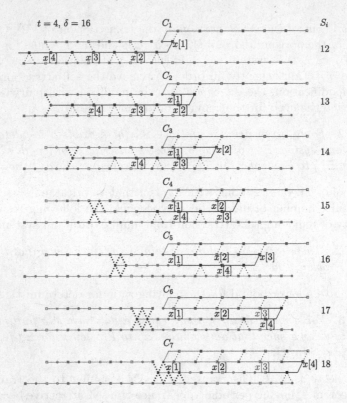

Fig. 5. A list of elongations when $t = 4$ and $\delta = 16$. The seed is given by three conformations $\sigma_b, \sigma_p, \sigma_r$, which are represented by brown, purple and red colors respectively. Two parts w_h and w_t of the transcript are represented by black and cyan colors respectively. The blue line represents beads already stabilized in the transcript. Thick dotted lines represent special interactions. (Color figure online)

sufficient to force all possible x beads to interact. We need basic rules between the primary structure and the seed for the primary structure to proceed straight. In addition, we design the system so that the nascent beads for $2i - 2$nd bead in C_i has interaction strength $S_i = 3t + i - 1$. Figure 5 is an illustration of different elongations C_1 to C_7 when $\delta = 16$ and $t = \delta/4 = 4$. The bead $x[i]$ denotes the ith bead x in the transcript, and the bead $y[i]$ denotes the $i$the bead. To meet the required strength of interactions, we use beads at the very last of each elongation to have special interactions with the seed. Note that a special interaction in one elongation never appears in any other elongations, since the coordinate of a bead in w_t is distinct for all elongations. The last elongation C_{2t-1} is also the final conformation of the system.

First, we claim that each C_i is the most stable elongation while stabilizing $y[2i-2]$. If we compare C_i to C_j where $j < i$, S_j is less than S_i and beads after the primary structure of C_j cannot give additional special interactions. Thus, any elongation from C_j is less attractive than C_i. If we compare C_i to C_j where

$j > i$, special interactions at the end of the primary structure of C_j makes S_j greater than S_i, but these end beads are too far to allow interactions to stabilize $y[2i-2]$. Thus, the part of C_j until the last bead of C_i is less attractive than C_i, which makes C_i most stable.

Second, we claim that all (x,x) interactions are necessary for Ξ_d to fold into the last elongation C_{2t-1}. Suppose we compare C_i to C_{i+1} while stabilizing $y[2i-2]$. Note that the coordinate of $y[2i-2]$ differs in C_i and C_{i+1}. Since C_{2t-1} is the final conformation, $y[2i-2]$ should be stabilized following the coordinate in C_{i+1}. Now, since S_i and S_{i+1} differs just by 1, if we remove some (x,x) interactions in C_{i+1}, either $y[2i-2]$ is stabilized following the coordinate in C_i, or the system becomes nondeterministic. Thus, all (x,x) interactions are necessary. Since there are t different x beads, the lower bound of the copying ratio is $t = \delta/4$.

References

1. dailymotion.com/video/x3cdj35_oritatami-folding-turing-0-abc_school
2. Aggarwal, G., Goldwasser, M.H., Kao, M.Y., Schweller, R.T.: Complexities for generalized models of self-assembly. In: Proceedings of SODA 2004, pp. 880–889 (2004)
3. Barish, R.D., Schulman, R., Rothemund, P.W.K., Winfree, E.: An information-bearing seed for nucleating algorithmic self-assembly. PNAS **106**(15), 6054–6059 (2009)
4. Cannon, S., Demaine, E.D., Demaine, M.L., Eisenstat, S., Patitz, M.J., Schweller, R.T., Summers, S.M., Winslow, A.: Two hands are better than one (up to constant factors): self-assembly in the 2HAM vs. aTAM. In: Proceedings of STACS 2013, vol. 20, pp. 172–184. LIPIcs (2013)
5. Doty, D., Lutz, J.H., Patitz, M.J., Schweller, R.T., Summers, S.M., Woods, D.: The tile assembly model is intrinsically universal. In: Proceedings of FOCS 2012, pp. 302–310 (2012)
6. Evans, C.: Crystals that count! Physical principles and experimental investigations of DNA tile self-assembly. Ph.D. thesis, California Institute of Technology, June 2014
7. Fochtman, T., Hendricks, J., Padilla, J.E., Patitz, M.J., Rogers, T.A.: Signal transmission across tile assemblies: 3D static tiles simulate active self-assembly by 2D signal-passing tiles. Nat. Comp. **14**(2), 251–264 (2015)
8. Geary, C., Meunier, P.E., Schabanel, N., Seki, S.: Programming biomolecules that fold greedily during transcription. In: Proceedings of MFCS 2016, vol. 58, pp. 43:1–43:14. LIPIcs (2016)
9. Geary, C., Rothemund, P.W.K., Andersen, E.S.: A single-stranded architecture for cotranscriptional folding of RNA nanostructures. Science **345**(6198), 799–804 (2014)
10. Hendricks, J., Patitz, M.J., Rogers, T.A.: Universal simulation of directed systems in the abstract tile assembly model requires undirectedness. In: Proceedings of FOCS 2016, pp. 800–809 (2016)
11. Miyazono, A.G.E., Faraon, A., Rothemund, P.W.K.: Engineering and mapping nanocavity emission via precision placement of DNA origami. Nature **535**(7612), 401–405 (2016)

12. Padilla, J.E., Patitz, M.J., Schweller, R.T., Seeman, N.C., Summers, S.M., Zhong, X.: Asynchronous signal passing for tile self-assembly: fuel efficient computation and efficient assembly of shapes. Int. J. Found. Comput. S. **25**(4), 459–488 (2014)
13. Rothemund, P.W.K., Papadakis, N., Winfree, E.: Algorithmic self-assembly of DNA Sierpinski triangles. PLoS Biol. **2**(12), 424 (2004)
14. Schulman, R., Yurke, B., Winfree, E.: Robust self-replication of combinatorial information via crystal growth and scission. PNAS **109**(17), 6405–10 (2012)
15. Winfree, E.: Algorithmic self-assembly of DNA. Ph.D. thesis, California Institute of Technology, June 1998
16. Woods, D.: Intrinsic universality and the computational power of self-assembly. In: Proceedings of MCU 2013, vol. 128, pp. 16–22 (2013)

One-Time Nondeterministic Computations

Markus Holzer and Martin Kutrib[✉]

Institut für Informatik, Universität Giessen, Arndtstr. 2, 35392 Giessen, Germany
{holzer,kutrib}@informatik.uni-giessen.de

Abstract. We introduce the concept of one-time nondeterminism as a new kind of limited nondeterminism for finite state machines and pushdown automata. Roughly speaking, *one-time* nondeterminism means that at the outset the automaton is nondeterministic, but whenever it performs a guess, this guess is fixed for the rest of the computation. We characterize the computational power of one-time nondeterministic finite automata (OTNFAs) and one-time nondeterministic pushdown devices. Moreover, we study the descriptional complexity of these machines. For instance, we show that for an n-state OTNFA with a sole nondeterministic state, that is nondeterministic for only one input symbol, $(n+1)^n$ states are sufficient and necessary in the worst case for an equivalent deterministic finite automaton. In case of pushdown automata, the conversion of a nondeterministic to a one-time nondeterministic as well as the conversion of a one-time nondeterministic to a deterministic one turn out to be non-recursive, that is, the trade-offs in size cannot be bounded by any recursive function.

1 Introduction

The concept of nondeterministic machines was introduced in the seminal paper of Rabin and Scott [13] on finite automata and their decision problems from 1959. Hopcroft [10] writes in his survey "Automata Theory: Its Past and Future" about the nondeterministic finite automaton (NFA) model in the above mentioned paper:

"It was shown that this model was equivalent to the deterministic one. The fact that two models which were so different gave rise to the same sets, along with the fact that both were equivalent to the regular expression notation, indicated that these models were fundamental. This paper was very influential in shaping automata theory ..."

Nondeterminism turned out to be a very fruitful concept in different areas of computer science like, for example, computability theory, complexity theory, automata theory, formal language theory, etc., to mention only a few. Two of the most prominent problems related to nondeterminism are the P *versus* NP problem (see, for example, [5]) and the LBA problem (see, for example [6]). The former problem is listed as one of the ten Millennium Problems from the

© IFIP International Federation for Information Processing 2017
Published by Springer International Publishing AG 2017. All Rights Reserved
G. Pighizzini and C. Câmpeanu (Eds.): DCFS 2017, LNCS 10316, pp. 177–188, 2017.
DOI: 10.1007/978-3-319-60252-3_14

Clay Mathematics Institute, Cambridge, Massachusetts, USA, which is the sole computer science problem in that list.

Although NFAs are as powerful as deterministic one, as already mentioned above, the former model can offer exponential saving in space compared with deterministic finite automata (DFAs), that is, given some n-state NFA one can always construct a language equivalent DFA with at most 2^n states [13]. This so-called powerset construction turned out to be optimal, in general. That is, the bound on the number of states is tight in the sense that for an arbitrary n there is always some n-state NFA which cannot be simulated by any DFA with less than 2^n states [11,12]. It is worth mentioning that Moore's NFA contains a *sole* nondeterministic state, while Meyer and Fischer's nondeterministic automaton has $n-1$ nondeterministic states. In both NFAs the nondeterministic branching, that is, the maximal number of transitions with the same label leaving a state, is bounded by two, thus by a constant. This can be seen as a first indication that not all NFAs make equal use of nondeterminism. In fact, nondeterminism is a resource and its usage can be accurately quantified. There are several possibilities to do so. For instance, one is to count the number of nondeterministic moves during the computation, while another one depends on the number of the successor states and is called branching and guessing. Results on these quantifications are subsumed under the name *limited nondeterminism* in the literature, see, for example, [1] for a survey.

Here we give a new interpretation of nondeterminism. On the one hand, we are still interested in the power of nondeterminism with respect to computations and conciseness, but on the other hand, its usage should be heavily restricted. The restriction we are introducing is that of *one-time* nondeterminism, which means that at the outset the automaton is nondeterministic, but whenever it performs a guess, this guess is fixed for the rest of the computation. This is a clear change on the semantics of nondeterminism. We will study this new concept for finite automata and pushdown machines. Although one-time nondeterminism does not increase the accepting power of ordinary finite state devices, their conciseness is even greater than that of ordinary nondeterministic finite automata compared to deterministic ones. In general, an n-state one time nondeterministic finite automaton (OTNFA) can be simulated by an $(n+1)^{n^{k \cdot n}}$-state deterministic finite automaton, where k is the size of the input alphabet. In general this bound is over-counted. A slightly better estimate is obtained by using the notion of the *degree of nondeterminism* d for finite state devices, which is defined as the product of all non-zero size successor sets of a state. Formally $d(M) = \prod_{\substack{(q,a) \in Q \times \Sigma \\ |\delta(q,a)| \neq 0}} |\delta(q,a)|$, where Q is the set of states, Σ the input alphabet, and δ the nondeterministic transition function of M. A better upper bound on the above mentioned simulation of an OTNFA M is then $(n+1)^{d(M)}$. This bound is tight in a special case, because we can give an example of an n-state OTNFA M of nondeterministic degree $d(M) = n$ such that $(n+1)^n$ states are sufficient and necessary in the worst case for an equivalent deterministic finite automaton. For pushdown automata the results on the descriptional complexity are even more dramatic. First of all it is shown that one-time nondeterministic pushdown automata (OTNPDA) accept exactly the union closure of the deterministic context-free languages. This is a well-known language family which properly lies between the deterministic context-free languages and the context free ones. We utilize this characterization and show that the trade-offs between OTNPDAs and deterministic ones, as well as between ordinary nondeterministic pushdown automata and OTNPDAs are non-recursive. That is, the bound between two equivalent machines of different types cannot be bounded by any recursive function. This is quite exceptional because the use of nondeterminism is highly restricted to the bare necessities.

2   Preliminaries

Let Σ^* denote the set of all words over the finite alphabet Σ. The *empty word* is denoted by λ, and $\Sigma^+ = \Sigma^* \setminus \{\lambda\}$. The *reversal* of a word w is denoted by w^R. For the *length* of w we write $|w|$. For the number of occurrences of a symbol a in w we use the notation $|w|_a$. Set inclusion is denoted by $\subseteq$ and strict set inclusion by $\subset$. We write 2^S for the power set and $|S|$ for the cardinality of a set S.

We recall some notation for descriptional complexity. Following [9] we say that a *descriptional system* S is a set of finite descriptors such that each $D \in S$ describes a formal language $L(D)$, and the alphabet $\mathrm{alph}(D)$ over which D represents a language can be deduced from D. The *family of languages represented* (or *described*) by S is $\mathscr{L}(S) = \{ L(D) \mid D \in S \}$. For every language L, the set $S(L) = \{ D \in S \mid L(D) = L \}$ is the set of its descriptors in S. A *complexity measure* for a descriptional system S is a total recursive mapping $c : S \to \mathbb{N}$.

Finite automata or (deterministic) pushdown automata can be encoded over some fixed alphabet such that their input alphabets can be extracted from the encodings. The sets of these encodings are descriptional systems S_1 and S_2, and $\mathscr{L}(S_1)$ is the family of regular languages and $\mathscr{L}(S_2)$ is the family of (deterministic) context-free languages. Examples for complexity measures for finite automata or pushdown automata are the total number of symbols, that is, the *length of the encoding* (length), or, in the former case, the *number of states* and, in the latter case, the product of the number of transition rules and the maximal number of symbols pushed in one step.

Here we only use complexity measures that are recursively related to length. If there is a total recursive function $g : \mathbb{N} \times \mathbb{N} \to \mathbb{N}$ such that, for all $D \in S$, $\mathrm{length}(D) \leq g(c(D), |\mathrm{alph}(D)|)$, then c is said to be an *s-measure*. If, in addition, for any alphabet Σ, the set of descriptors in S describing languages over Σ is recursively enumerable in order of increasing size, then c is said to be an *sn-measure*. Clearly, the number of states is an sn-measure for finite automata.

Whenever we consider the relative succinctness of two descriptional systems S_1 and S_2, we assume that the intersection $\mathscr{L}(S_1) \cap \mathscr{L}(S_2)$ is non-empty. Let S_1 and S_2 be descriptional systems with complexity measures c_1 and c_2, respectively. A total function $f : \mathbb{N} \to \mathbb{N}$ is an *upper bound* for the increase in complexity when changing from a descriptor in S_1 to an equivalent descriptor in S_2, if for all $D_1 \in S_1$ with $L(D_1) \in \mathscr{L}(S_2)$, there exists a $D_2 \in S_2(L(D_1))$ such that $c_2(D_2) \leq f(c_1(D_1))$. If there is no recursive upper bound, then the *trade-off* for changing from a description in S_1 to an equivalent description in S_2 *is said to be non-recursive*. Non-recursive trade-offs are independent of particular sn-measures.

3   One-Time Nondeterministic Finite Automata

We investigate *one-time nondeterministic* finite automata. The basic idea is that at the outset the automaton is nondeterministic. But whenever it performs a guess, this guess is fixed for the rest of the computation.

A *nondeterministic finite automaton* (NFA) is a system $M = \langle Q, \Sigma, \delta, q_0, F \rangle$, where Q is the finite set of *internal states*, Σ is the finite set of *input symbols*, $q_0 \in Q$ is the *initial state*, $F \subseteq Q$ is the set of *accepting states*, and $\delta : Q \times \Sigma \rightarrow 2^Q$ is the *transition function*. A *configuration* of a finite automaton M is a tuple (q, w), where $q \in Q$ and $w \in \Sigma^*$. If a is in Σ and w in Σ^*, then we write $(q, aw) \vdash_M (p, w)$ if p is in $\delta(q, a)$. As usual, the reflexive transitive closure of $\vdash_M$ is denoted by $\vdash_M^*$. The subscript M will be dropped from $\vdash_M$ and $\vdash_M^*$ if the meaning is clear. Then the *language accepted* by M is defined as

$$L(M) = \{ w \in \Sigma^* \mid (q_0, w) \vdash_M^* (p, \lambda) \text{ for some } p \in F \}.$$

A state q is *nondeterministic on a letter* a in M, if $|\delta(q, a)| \geq 2$, and state q is *nondeterministic in* M, if it is nondeterministic on some letter $a \in \Sigma$. Moreover, a state q is *reachable* in M if there is an input word w with $(q_0, w) \vdash_M^* (q, \lambda)$. Without loss of generality we assume that any state of a (non)deterministic finite automaton is reachable.

A finite automaton M is *partial deterministic* (partial DFA) if and only if $|\delta(q, a)| \leq 1$, for all $q \in Q$ and $a \in \Sigma$, and the device M is *deterministic* (DFA) if and only if $|\delta(q, a)| = 1$, for every $q \in Q$ and $a \in \Sigma$. In these cases we simply write $\delta(q, a) = q'$ for $\delta(q, a) = \{q'\}$ assuming that the transition function is a (partial) mapping $\delta : Q \times \Sigma \rightarrow Q$. Observe, that every partial DFA can be made complete by introducing a non-accepting sink state. So, any DFA is complete, that is, the transition function is total, whereas for partial DFAs and NFAs it is possible that δ maps to the empty set.

Next, the idea of one-time nondeterministic finite automata is formalized as follows: let $M = \langle Q, \Sigma, \delta, q_0, F \rangle$ be an NFA and

$$(q_0, w) = (q_0, a_0 w_0) \vdash_M (q_1, w_0) = (q_1, a_1 w_1) \vdash_M \cdots$$
$$\vdash_M (q_n, w_{n-1}) = (q_n, a_n w_n) \vdash_M (q_{n+1}, w_n) = (q_{n+1}, \lambda),$$

be a computation of M on input $w = a_0 w_0 \in \Sigma^+$. A computation is *permissible* if and only if $(q_i, a_i) = (q_j, a_j)$ implies $q_{i+1} = q_{j+1}$, for all $0 \leq i < j \leq n$, or the computation is *trivial*, that is, it consists of (q_0, λ) only. Now, M is said to be *one-time nondeterministic* if and only if it may only perform permissible computations. In this case we call M a *one-time nondeterministic finite automaton*

(OTNFA). A word w is *permissible acceptable* by M if there is a permissible computation that ends in an accepting state of M. The language accepted by an OTNFA M is

$$L_p(M) = \{\, w \in \Sigma^* \mid \text{word } w \text{ is permissible acceptable by } M \,\}.$$

In order to illustrate the definitions we continue with an example.

Example 1. Consider the NFA M with a single nondeterministic state depicted on the left of Fig. 1. It is easy to see that M accepts all words where the next to last letter is an a, that is, the language $(a+b)^*a(a+b)$. When interpreting M as an OTNFA, then only permissible computations are allowed. This means, that for the sole nondeterministic state either the a-self-loop from state 1 to itself or the a-transition leading form state 1 to 2 can be used during the computation, but not both. Thus, we can think of doing a computation either in the finite automaton M' or M'' shown in the middle of or on the right of Fig. 1. Therefore, the language accepted by the OTNFA M is equal to $b^*a(a+b)$, because the automaton in the middle does not accept anything. ∎

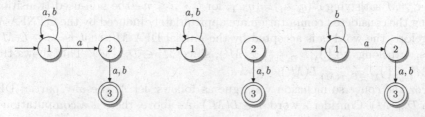

Fig. 1. Left: the NFA M with a sole nondeterministic state accepting the language $(a+b)^*a(a+b)$. Interpreting M as an OTNFA results in accepting $b^*a(a+b)$. Middle: partial DFA M' built from M by choosing the a-self-loop on the state 1 and deleting all other a-transitions leaving state 1. Right: partial DFA M'' built from M by choosing the a-transition from state 1 to 2 and deleting all other a-transitions from state 1.

The following statement is trivial since the permissible computations of an NFA are a subset of all possible computations. The strictness of the inclusion follows by the above given example.

Lemma 2. *Let M be a nondeterministic finite automaton. Then the inclusion $L_p(M) \subseteq L(M)$ holds, and there is a device M such that it is proper.* □

Before we consider the computational power of OTNFAs in more detail, we need some further notation. Let $M = \langle Q, \Sigma, \delta, q_0, F \rangle$ be an NFA. An automaton $M' = \langle Q', \Sigma', \delta', q_0', F \rangle$ is *compatible* with M if and only if (i) $Q' = Q$, (ii) $\Sigma' = \Sigma$, (iii) $q_0' = q_0$, (iv) $F' = F$, and (v) $\delta'(q, a) \subseteq \delta(q, a)$, for every $q \in Q$ and $a \in \Sigma$. If M' is compatible with M, then we write $M' \prec M$. We further define that M' is *non-empty compatible* with M, if and only if M' is compatible with M and $\delta(q, a) \neq \emptyset$ implies $\delta'(q, a) \neq \emptyset$, for every $q \in Q$ and $a \in \Sigma$. If M' is non-empty compatible with M, then we write $M' \prec_{ne} M$. Note that every automaton is (non-empty) compatible with itself. Obviously, $M' \prec_{ne} M$ implies $M' \prec M$, but the converse implication does not hold in general. Both automata M' and M'' depicted in Fig. 1 are non-empty compatible with M shown in the same figure on the left; for short $M' \prec_{ne} M$ and $M'' \prec_{ne} M$. Now we are ready for the next theorem.

Theorem 3. *Let M be an OTNFA. Then $L_p(M) = \bigcup_{M' \in \mathcal{D}_{ne}(M)} L(M')$, where $\mathcal{D}_{ne}(M) = \{ M' \mid M' \text{is a partial DFA with } M' \prec_{ne} M \}$.*

Proof. The inclusion from left to right is seen as follows: let $M = \langle Q, \Sigma, \delta, q_0, F \rangle$. Consider any word $w \in L_p(M)$. Since w belongs to the language in question, there is a permissible computation of the form (q_0, λ), if $w = \lambda$ or

$$(q_0, w) = (q_0, a_0 w_0) \vdash_M (q_1, w_0) = (q_1, a_1 w_1) \vdash_M \cdots$$
$$\vdash_M (q_n, w_{n-1}) = (q_n, a_n w_n) \vdash_M (q_{n+1}, w_n) = (q_{n+1}, \lambda)$$

with $q_{n+1} \in F$, suitable $a_0, a_1, \ldots, a_n$ in Σ, and words $w_0, w_1, \ldots, w_n$ in Σ^*. It is not hard to see that there is a partial DFA $M' = \langle Q, \Sigma, \delta', q_0, F \rangle$ with $M' \prec_{ne} M$ satisfying $\delta'(q_i, a_i) = q_{i+1}$, for $0 \leq i \leq n$—the non-used transitions during the considered computation are appropriately induced by the OTNFA M. Therefore, the word w is accepted by the partial DFA M', that is, $w \in L(M')$. Thus, w belongs to $\bigcup_{M' \in \mathcal{D}_{ne}(M)} L(M')$, since $M' \in \mathcal{D}_{ne}(M)$. This shows that $L_p(M) \subseteq \bigcup_{M' \in \mathcal{D}_{ne}(M)} L(M')$.

For the converse inclusion we argue as follows: let M' be any partial DFA from $\mathcal{D}_{ne}(M)$. Consider a word $w \in L(M')$. As above, there is a computation of the form (q_0, λ), if $w = \lambda$ or

$$(q_0, w) = (q_0, a_0 w_0) \vdash_M (q_1, w_0) = (q_1, a_1 w_1) \vdash_M \cdots$$
$$\vdash_M (q_n, w_{n-1}) = (q_n, a_n w_n) \vdash_M (q_{n+1}, w_n) = (q_{n+1}, \lambda)$$

with $q_{n+1} \in F$, suitable letters $a_0, a_1, \ldots, a_n$ in Σ, and words $w_0, w_1, \ldots, w_n$ in Σ^*. Since this is a deterministic computation one can interpret it as a *permissible* computation of M, since M can simulate every step of the partial DFA M'. Therefore we conclude that $w \in L_p(M)$, hence $L_p(M) \supseteq L(M')$. Note that the given argumentation holds for every $M' \in \mathcal{D}_{ne}(M)$ and therefore $L_p(M) \supseteq \bigcup_{M' \in \mathcal{D}_{ne}(M)} L(M')$. This proves the stated claim. $\qquad \square$

Theorem 3 shows that OTNFAs accept only regular languages, because they are closed under finite union. Although OTNFAs do not improve the computational power of ordinary finite automata, the question on the descriptional complexity of these devices arises. The statement of Theorem 3 give us some hint, that the relative succinctness compared to ordinary finite state devices may be enormous, since the union on the right-hand side of $L_p(M) = \bigcup_{M' \in \mathcal{D}_{ne}(M)} L(M')$ runs over a large number of different M' from $\mathcal{D}_{ne}(M)$. In fact, our intuition is supported by the next result, which states a very large upper bound.

Theorem 4. *Let M be an n-state OTNFA with a k-letter input alphabet. Then $(n+1)^{n^{k \cdot n}}$ states are sufficient for a DFA to accept the language $L_p(M)$.*

Proof. Let $M = \langle Q, \Sigma, \delta, q_0, F \rangle$. Then $L_p(M) = \bigcup_{M' \in \mathcal{D}_{ne}(M)} L(M')$ by Theorem 3, where $\mathcal{D}_{ne}(M) = \{ M' \mid M' \text{ is a partial DFA with } M' \prec_{ne} M \}$. In order to accept the union on the right-hand side by a DFA, we apply the standard cross-product construction [14]. To this end, we complete the involved partial automata from $\mathcal{D}_{ne}(M)$, which results in ordinary DFAs with at most $n + 1$ states. Then the upper bound on the number of states for any DFA accepting $L_p(M)$ is $(n+1)^{|\mathcal{D}_{ne}(M)|}$. Thus, it remains to obtain an upper bound on the size of $\mathcal{D}_{ne}(M)$.

An automaton M' in $\mathcal{D}_{ne}(M)$ is constructed from M by cycling trough all states q and letters a and distinguishing the following cases: (i) if $\delta(q, a) = \emptyset$, then $\delta'(q, a) = \emptyset$, (ii) if $\delta(q, a) = \{p\}$, then $\delta'(q, a) = \{p\}$, and (iii) if $\delta(q, a) = \{p_1, p_2, \ldots, p_k\}$, for $k \geq 2$, then $\delta'(q, a) = \{p_i\}$, for some i with $1 \leq i \leq k$. Since $|\delta(q, a)| \leq n$, for every state q and letter a, we conclude that the size of $\mathcal{D}_{ne}(M)$ is bounded from above by $n^{k \cdot n}$. Hence we get the stated upper bound of $(n+1)^{n^{k \cdot n}}$ states for a DFA accepting the language $L_p(M)$. □

It turns out that the upper bound on the number of states of a DFA accepting $L_p(M)$, for a OTNFA M, is more accurate the better we can determine the size of $\mathcal{D}_{ne}(M)$. A greater precision is obtained by defining the *nondeterministic degree* $d(M)$ of an OTNFA M with state set Q and input alphabet Σ as $d(M) = \prod_{\substack{(q,a) \in Q \times \Sigma \\ |\delta(q,a)| \neq 0}} |\delta(q, a)|$. Then it is easy to see that the following lemma holds.

Lemma 5. *Let M be an OTNFA. Then $|\mathcal{D}_{ne}(M)| = d(M)$.* □

Hence we can reformulate the upper bound given in Theorem 4 as follows:

Corollary 6. *Let M be an OTNFA with nondeterministic degree $d(M)$. Then any DFA that accepts the language $L_p(M)$ needs at most $(n + 1)^{d(n)}$ states.* □

In the remainder of this section we obtain that the bound stated in the previous corollary can be reached already for a OTNFA with a sole nondeterministic state, that is nondeterministic for only one input symbol.

Theorem 7. *There is a n-state OTNFA M with a sole nondeterministic state, that is nondeterministic only for one input symbol, and has nondeterministic degree n, such that $(n + 1)^n$ states are sufficient and necessary in the worst case for a DFA to accept the language $L_p(M)$.*

Proof. The upper bound of $(n + 1)^{d(n)}$ states for a DFA accepting the language $L_p(M)$ follows from Corollary 6. For the lower bound we argue as follows: consider the OTNFA whose transition function δ on the letters a, b, c, and d is depicted in Fig. 2.

By the $\prec_{ne}$-relation the OTNFA M gives rise to several partial DFAs M_j, for $1 \leq j \leq n$, where $M_j = \langle \{1, 2, \ldots, n\}, \{a, b, c, d\}, \delta_j, 1, \{n\} \rangle$ and the transition

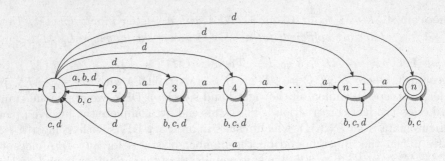

Fig. 2. The transition function δ of the OTNFA M.

function δ_j is equal to δ on the letters a, b, and c, and for the letter d we have $\delta_j(i,d) = \{j\}$, if $i = 1$, $\delta_j(i,d) = \{i\}$, if $2 \le i < n$, and $\delta_j(i,d)$ is undefined otherwise. These partial DFAs $M_1, M_2, \ldots, M_n$ are the basic building blocks in the cross-product construction for the (ordinary) DFA M' accepting the language $L_p(M)$. Define the DFA $M' = \langle Q', \{a,b,c,d\}, \delta', q_0', F' \rangle$, where the set of states is equal to $Q' = (\{1,2,\ldots,n\} \cup \{-\})^n$, the initial state is $q_0' = (1,1,\ldots,1)$, and $F' = \{ f \in Q' \mid f[i] = n, \text{for some } 1 \le i \le n \}$, where $f[i]$ refers to the ith component of $f \in (\{1,2,\ldots,n\} \cup \{-\})^n$. The transition function is given by $\delta'(f,a) = (\delta_1(f[1],a), \delta_2(f[2],a), \ldots, \delta_n(f[n],a))$, for every $f \in Q'$ and $a \in \Sigma$. Here we assume that whenever some $\delta_i(f[i],a)$ is *undefined*, then the component is set to $-$. In order to prove our statement we need to show that the DFA M' is minimal. The proof that every state in M' is reachable and defines a distinct equivalence class utilizes some results from semigroup theory since one can identify the states of M' with partial mappings from $[n]$ to $[n]$. $\square$

4   One-Time Nondeterministic Pushdown Automata

Now we turn to generalize the definitions of OTNFAs to pushdown automata. Nondeterministic pushdown automata are well known for capturing the context-free languages.

Let Σ be an alphabet. For convenience, we use Σ_λ for $\Sigma \cup \{\lambda\}$. A *nondeterministic pushdown automaton* (NPDA) is a system $M = \langle Q, \Sigma, \Gamma, \delta, q_0, \perp, F \rangle$, where Q is a finite set of *internal states*, Σ is the finite set of *input symbols*, Γ is a finite set of *pushdown symbols*, δ is a mapping from $Q \times \Sigma_\lambda \times \Gamma$ to finite subsets of $Q \times \Gamma^*$ called the *transition function*, $q_0 \in Q$ is the *initial state*, $\perp \in \Gamma$ is the so-called *bottom-of-pushdown symbol*, which initially appears on the pushdown store, and $F \subseteq Q$ is the set of *accepting states*.

A *configuration* of a pushdown automaton is a triple (q, w, γ), where q is the current state, w the unread part of the input, and γ the current content of the pushdown store, the leftmost symbol of γ being the top symbol. On input w the initial configuration is defined to be $(q_0, w, \perp)$. If p, q are in Q, a is in Σ_λ, w is in Σ^*, γ and β are in Γ^*, and Z is in Γ, then we write $(q, aw, Z\gamma) \vdash_M (p, w, \beta\gamma)$, if the pair (p, β) is in $\delta(q, a, Z)$. In order to simplify matters, we require that during any computation the bottom-of-pushdown symbol appears only at the bottom of the pushdown store. Formally, we require that if (p, β) is in $\delta(q, a, Z)$, then either β does not contain $\perp$ or $\beta = \beta' \perp$, where β' does not contain $\perp$, and $Z = \perp$. As usual, the reflexive transitive closure of $\vdash_M$ is denoted by $\vdash_M^*$. The subscript M will be dropped whenever the meaning remains clear. The *language accepted* by M with accepting states is

$$L(M) = \{ w \in \Sigma^* \mid (q_0, w, \perp) \vdash^* (q, \lambda, \gamma), \text{ for some } q \in F \text{ and } \gamma \in \Gamma^* \}.$$

An NPDA is a *deterministic pushdown automaton* (DPDA), if there is at most one choice of action for any possible configuration. In particular, there must never be a choice of using an input symbol or of using λ input. Formally, a pushdown automaton $M = \langle Q, \Sigma, \Gamma, \delta, q_0, \perp, F \rangle$ is *deterministic* if (i) $\delta(q, a, Z)$ contains at most one element, for all a in Σ_λ, q in Q, and Z in Γ, and (ii) for all q in Q and Z in Γ: if $\delta(q, \lambda, Z)$ is not empty, then $\delta(q, a, Z)$ is empty for all a in Σ.

Now we turn to *one-time nondeterministic* pushdown automata (OTNPDA). As before, whenever such an automaton performs a guess, this guess is fixed for the rest of the computation. Let $M = \langle Q, \Sigma, \Gamma, \delta, q_0, \perp, F \rangle$ be an NPDA and, for $q_i \in Q$, $a_i \in \Sigma_\lambda$, $0 \leq i \leq n$, and $Z_i \in \Gamma$, $\beta_i \in \Gamma^*$, $1 \leq i \leq n$,

$$(q_0, a_0 w_0, \perp) \vdash_M (q_1, w_0, \beta_1) = (q_1, a_1 w_1, Z_1 \gamma_1) \vdash_M (q_2, w_1, \beta_2 \gamma_1) =$$
$$(q_2, a_2 w_2, Z_2 \gamma_2) \vdash_M^* (q_n, w_{n-1}, \beta_n \gamma_{n-1}) = (q_n, a_n w_n, Z_n \gamma_n)$$

be a computation of M on input $a_0 w_0 \in \Sigma^+$. The computation is defined to be *permissible* if and only if, (i) the equality $(q_i, Z_i) = (q_j, Z_j)$ implies either $a_i = a_j = \lambda$ or $a_i \neq \lambda$ and $a_j \neq \lambda$, and (ii) the equality $(q_i, a_i, Z_i) = (q_j, a_j, Z_j)$ implies $q_{i+1} = q_{j+1}$ and $\beta_{i+1} = \beta_{j+1}$, for all $0 \leq i < j \leq n - 1$. A word w is *permissible acceptable* by M if on input w there is an accepting permissible computation. The language accepted by an OTNPDA M is

$$L_p(M) = \{ w \in \Sigma^* \mid \text{word } w \text{ is permissible acceptable by } M \}.$$

In order to derive the relationships of OTNPDAs, NPDAs, and DPDAs, we generalize the characterization of OTNFAs to pushdown automata. The notation as well as Theorem 3 is straightforwardly adapted. So, we obtain:

Theorem 8. *Let M be a OTNPDA. Then $L_p(M) = \bigcup_{M' \in \mathcal{D}(M)} L(M')$, where $\mathcal{D}_{ne}(M) = \{ M' \mid M' \text{ is a DPDA with } M' \prec_{ne} M \}$.*

So, the family of languages accepted by OTNPDAs is included in the (finite) union closure of the deterministic context-free languages. Conversely, the union of a finite number of languages accepted by DPDAs is accepted by an NPDA whose first transition is a nondeterministic choice of which of the DPDAs is to be simulated. Subsequently, the NPDA simulates the chosen DPDA. In this way, the nondeterministic situation at the beginning is never reached again and, thus, the NPDA is in fact a OTNPDA. We conclude that the union closure of the deterministic context-free languages is included in the family of languages accepted by OTNPDAs.

Corollary 9. *The family of languages accepted by OTNPDAs and the union closure of the deterministic context-free languages are identical.*   □

This characterization together with known results shows that the computational capacity of OTNPDAs is strictly in between the NPDAs and DPDAs.

Theorem 10. $\mathscr{L}(DPDA) \subset \mathscr{L}(OTNPDA) \subset \mathscr{L}(NPDA)$.

For establishing non-recursive trade-offs the following general result is useful that is a slightly generalized and unified form of a result of Hartmanis [4].

Theorem 11 [9]. *Let S_1 and S_2 be two descriptional systems for recursive languages such that any descriptor D in S_1 and S_2 can effectively be converted into a Turing machine that decides $L(D)$, and let c_1 be a measure for S_1 and c_2 be an sn-measure for S_2. If there exists a descriptional system S_3 and a property P that is not semi-decidable for descriptors from S_3, such that, given an arbitrary $D_3 \in S_3$, (i) there exists an effective procedure to construct a descriptor D_1 in S_1, and (ii) D_1 has an equivalent descriptor in S_2 if and only if D_3 does not have property P, then the trade-off between S_1 and S_2 is non-recursive.*

By measuring the amount of ambiguity and nondeterminism in pushdown automata in [7,8] infinite hierarchies in between the deterministic and nondeterministic context-free languages are obtained. Intuitively, the corresponding language families are close together. Nevertheless, there are non-recursive trade-offs between the levels of the hierarchies.

In the following we show non-recursive trade-offs between nondeterministic and OTNPDAs automata as well as between OTNPDAs deterministic pushdown automata by reduction from the non-halting problem for Turing machines on empty tape. To this end, histories of Turing machine computations are encoded into strings, a technique introduced in [3]. It suffices to consider deterministic Turing machines with one single tape and one single read-write head. Without loss of generality and for technical reasons, we assume that the Turing machines cannot print blanks, can halt only after an odd number of moves, accept by halting, and visit an infinite number of squares if they do not halt.

Let Q be the state set of some Turing machine M, where q_0 is the initial state, $T \cap Q = \emptyset$ is the tape alphabet containing the blank symbol, and $\Sigma \subset T$ is the input alphabet. Then a configuration of M can be written as a word of the form T^*QT^* such that $t_1 t_2 \cdots t_i q t_{i+1} \cdots t_n$ is used to express that M is in state q, scanning tape symbol t_{i+1}, and t_1, t_2 to t_n is the support of the tape inscription. Dependent on the Turing machine M we define the following two languages. Let $a, b, \$, \# \notin T \cup Q$, $n \geq 0$, and $w_i \in T^*QT^*$, $0 \leq i \leq 2n+1$ are configurations of M. Then language $L_{M,0}$ contains all words of the form $\$w_0 \$w_1^R \$w_2 \$w_3^R \$ \cdots \$w_{2n} \# w_{2n+1}^R \# a$, where w_0 is an initial configuration with empty tape of the form $w_0 = q_0$ and w_{2i} is the successor configuration of w_{2i-1}, $1 \leq i \leq n$, and language $L_{M,1}$ contains all words of the form

$w_0\$w_1^R\$w_2\$w_3^R\$\cdots\$w_{2n}\#w_{2n+1}^R\#b$, where w_{2i+1} is the successor configuration of w_{2i}, $0 \le i \le n$. As an immediate observation we obtain the next corollary.

Corollary 12. *For any deterministic Turing machine M, both languages $L_{M,0}$ and $L_{M,1}$ are deterministic context-free languages, such that their deterministic pushdown automata can effectively be constructed from M.*   □

In order to apply Theorem 11, we use the family of deterministic one-tape Turing machines as descriptional system $\mathcal{S}_3$, and for the property P we take the property of *not halting on empty tape*. Recall that this property is indeed not semi-decidable for deterministic one-tape Turing machines. Next, given an arbitrary deterministic one-tape Turing machine M, that is, a descriptor $D_3 \in \mathcal{S}_3$, we must construct a nondeterministic pushdown automaton, that is, a descriptor D_1 in $\mathcal{S}_1$, that has an equivalent one-time nondeterministic pushdown automaton, that is, a descriptor in $\mathcal{S}_2$, if and only if M halts on empty tape.

So, given a deterministic one-tape Turing machine M, we use a new symbol c and define $L_M = ((L_{M,0} \cup L_{M,1})c)^*$. By Corollary 12 and the effective closures of the context-free languages under union and marked Kleene star, we derive that L_M is a context-free language, such that its nondeterministic pushdown automaton D_1 can effectively be constructed from M. It remains to be shown that L_M is accepted by a one-time nondeterministic pushdown automaton if and only if M halts on empty tape. The next lemma shows that L_M is accepted even by a deterministic pushdown automaton if M halts on empty tape.

Lemma 13. *Let M be a deterministic Turing machine that* halts *on empty tape. Then language L_M is accepted by some DPDA.*

In order to disprove that L_M is accepted by a OTNPDA if M does not halt on empty tape Ogden's lemma for deterministic context-free languages is used (see, for example, [2]). Then one can show the following result.

Lemma 14. *Let M be a deterministic Turing machine that* does not halt *on empty tape. Then language L_M is not accepted by any OTNPDA.*

So, we have shown the following theorem.

Theorem 15. *The trade-off between nondeterministic pushdown automata and one-time nondeterministic pushdown automata is non-recursive.*   □

The proof of the second non-recursive trade-off between one-time nondeterministic pushdown automata and deterministic pushdown automata follows along the lines of the first non-recursive trade-off. Again, we apply Theorem 11 but now with a simplification of the language L_M. More precisely, given a deterministic one-tape Turing machine M, we define $L'_M = L_{M,0} \cup L_{M,1}$. By Corollary 12, both languages $L_{M,0}$ and $L_{M,1}$ are deterministic context-free languages, such that their deterministic pushdown automata can effectively be constructed from M. So, L'_M is accepted by a one-time nondeterministic pushdown automaton that can effectively be constructed from M. As before, it remains to be shown that L'_M is accepted by a deterministic pushdown automaton if and only if M halts on empty tape. If M halts on empty tape, Lemma 13 says that L_M is accepted by some DPDA. Since the deterministic context-free languages are closed under intersection with regular sets, this implies that L'_M is accepted by some DPDA either.

Lemma 16. *Let M be a deterministic Turing machine that does not halt on empty tape. Then language L'_M is not accepted by any DPDA.*

Thus, we have also shown the following non-recursive trade-off.

Theorem 17. *The trade-off between one-time nondeterministic pushdown automata and deterministic pushdown automata is non-recursive.*   □

References

1. Goldstine, J., Kappes, M., Kintala, C.M.R., Leung, H., Malcher, A., Wotschke, D.: Descriptional complexity of machines with limited resources. J. Univ. Comput. Sci. **8**(2), 193–234 (2002)
2. Harrison, M.A.: Introduction to Formal Language Theory. Addison-Wesley, Reading (1978)
3. Hartmanis, J.: Context-free languages and turing machine computations. Proc. Symp. Appl. Math. **19**, 42–51 (1967)
4. Hartmanis, J.: On Gödel speed-up and succinctness of language representations. Theoret. Comput. Sci. **26**, 335–342 (1983)
5. Hartmanis, J.: Gödel, von Neumann and the P=? NP problem. Bull. EATCS **38**, 101–107 (1989)
6. Hartmanis, J., Hunt III., H.B.: The LBA problem and its importance in the theory of computing. In: Complexity of Computing, SIAM AMS Proceedings, vol. 7, pp. 1–26 (1974)
7. Herzog, C.: Pushdown automata with bounded nondeterminism and bounded ambiguity. Theoret. Comput. Sci. **181**, 141–157 (1997)
8. Herzog, C.: Die Rolle des Nichtdeterminismus in kontextfreien Sprachen. Doctoral dissertation, Universität Frankfurt (1999). (in German)
9. Holzer, M., Kutrib, M.: Descriptional complexity - an introductory survey. In: Scientific Applications of Language Methods, pp. 1–58. Imperial College Press (2010)
10. Hopcroft, J.: Automata theory: its past and future. In: Yu, S. (ed.) A Half-Century of Automata Theory, pp. 37–47. World Scientific (2001)
11. Meyer, A.R., Fischer, M.J.: Economy of description by automata, grammars, and formal systems. In: Proceedings of the 12th Annual Symposium on Switching and Automata Theory, pp. 188–191. IEEE Computer Society Press (1971)
12. Moore, F.R.: On the bounds for state-set size in the proofs of equivalence between deterministic, nondeterministic, and two-way finite automata. IEEE Trans. Comput. **20**, 1211–1219 (1971)
13. Rabin, M.O., Scott, D.: Finite automata and their decision problems. IBM J. Res. Dev. **3**, 114–125 (1959)
14. Yu, S., Zhuang, Q., Salomaa, K.: The state complexity of some basic operations on regular languages. Theoret. Comput. Sci. **125**, 315–328 (1994)

Kuratowski Algebras Generated by Factor-, Subword-, and Suffix-Free Languages

Jozef Jirásek Jr.[1,2], Matúš Palmovský[1], and Juraj Šebej[2(✉)]

[1] Mathematical Institute, Slovak Academy of Sciences,
Grešákova 6, 040 01 Košice, Slovakia
jirasekjozef@gmail.com, palmovsky@saske.sk
[2] Faculty of Science, Institute of Computer Science,
P.J. Šafárik University, Jesenná 5, 040 01 Košice, Slovakia
juraj.sebej@gmail.com

Abstract. We study Kuratowski algebras generated by suffix-, factor-, and subword-free languages under the operations of star and complementation. We examine 12 possible algebras, and for each of them, we provide an answer to the question whether or not it can be generated by a suffix-, factor-, or subword-free language. In each case when an algebra can be generated by such a language, we show that this language may be taken to be regular, and we compute upper bounds on the state complexities of all the generated languages. Finally, we find generators that maximize these complexities.

1 Introduction

The famous Kuratowski's 14-theorem states that, in a topological space, repeatedly applying the operations of closure and complement to any given set can produce at most 14 distinct sets [6,12]. Kuratowski's theorem in the settings of formal languages has been studied by Brzozowski et al. [2]. It has been shown that repeatedly applying Kleene closure and complementation to a given language produces again up to 14 distinct languages. Moreover, all formal languages have been classified according to the structure of the algebras they generate under Kleene closure and complementation. It has been proved that there are precisely 12 such algebras, and even more, each of them can be generated by a binary regular language.

Recently, Kuratowski algebras generated by certain restricted classes of languages have been investigated. Brzozowski et al. [4] proved that prefix-, suffix-, factor-, and subword-closed languages can generate at most 8 languages under the above mentioned operations. They also gave an example of a regular language

M. Palmovský—Research supported by VEGA grant 2/0084/15 and grant APVV-15-0091. This work was conducted as a part of PhD study of Matúš Palmovský at the Faculty of Mathematics, Physics and Informatics of the Commenius University in Bratislava.

J. Šebej—Research supported by VEGA grant 1/0142/15 and grant APVV-15-0091.

G. Pighizzini and C. Câmpeanu (Eds.): DCFS 2017, LNCS 10316, pp. 189–201, 2017.
DOI: 10.1007/978-3-319-60252-3_15

in each of these four classes which generates 8 languages, and also maximizes their state complexities.

In [10], Kuratowski algebras generated by prefix-free languages have been investigated in detail. For each of the 12 possible algebras, the following questions have been answered:

1. Can this algebra be generated by a prefix-free language?
2. Can this algebra be generated by a regular prefix-free language?
3. Can this algebra be generated by a regular prefix-free language of an arbitrary state complexity?
4. What are the maximal state complexities of languages generated in this algebra by a prefix-free regular language?
5. Is there a prefix-free regular generator which maximizes all of these complexities at the same time?

In this paper, we answer the same questions for suffix-, factor-, and subword-free languages. For each of these three classes and each of the 12 algebras, if the algebra can be generated by a language in this class, we give an example of a regular generator. We discuss state complexities of all the generated languages.

If an algebra can be generated by a prefix-free language, then it can also be generated by a suffix-free language, and vice versa. However, we show that there are algebras which are generated by a prefix- (or suffix-) free language, but cannot be generated by any factor-free language. One interesting conclusion is that while in the prefix-free case, if an algebra can be generated by a prefix-free language, the answer to question 5 is always yes, for suffix-free languages this is not always the case.

2   Preliminaries

We assume that the reader is familiar with basic notions in formal languages and automata theory. For details, the reader may refer to [9,13,14].

If Σ is a finite alphabet, then Σ^* is the set of strings over Σ, including the empty string ε. The length of a string w is denoted by $|w|$. A language is any subset of Σ^*. The complement of a language L is the language $L^c = \Sigma^* \setminus L$. The concatenation of languages K and L is $KL = \{uv \mid u \in K \text{ and } v \in L\}$. The Kleene closure, or star, of L is defined as $L^* = \cup_{i \geq 0} L^i$, while the positive closure of L is $L^+ = \cup_{i \geq 1} L^i$, where $L^0 = \{\varepsilon\}$ and $L^{i+1} = L^i L$. To simplify the exposition, we use an exponent notation, so for example, L^{c*} and L^{*c*} stand for $(L^c)^*$ and $((L^*)^c)^*$, respectively.

A *nondeterministic finite automaton* (NFA) is a quintuple $A = (Q, \Sigma, \cdot, s, F)$ defined in a usual way. A state q_d of an NFA A is called a *dead state* if no string is accepted by A from q_d, that is, if $q \cdot w \cap F = \emptyset$ for each string w. We say that (p, a, q) is a transition in NFA A if $q \in p \cdot a$. We also say that the state p has an *out-transition* on a, and the state q has an *in-transition* on a. An NFA is *non-exiting* if its final states have no out-transitions, and it is *non-returning* if its initial state does not have any in-transitions.

An NFA A is a *deterministic finite automaton* DFA if for each state q and each input symbol a, the set $q \cdot a$ has exactly one element. The *state complexity* of a regular language L, sc(L), is the smallest number of states in any DFA for L. It is well known that a DFA is minimal with respect to the number of states if all its states are reachable and pairwise distinguishable.

Every NFA $A = (Q, \Sigma, \cdot, s, F)$ can be converted to an equivalent DFA $A' = (2^Q, \Sigma, \circ, \{s\}, F')$, where $F' = \{S \in 2^Q \mid S \cap F \neq \emptyset\}$ and $S \circ a = S \cdot a$ for each S in 2^Q and each a in Σ. We call the DFA A the *subset automaton* of the NFA A. The subset automaton may not be minimal since some of its states can be unreachable or equivalent to other states. To prove distinguishability of states of the subset automaton, the following notions from [3] are useful.

A state q of the NFA A is said to be *uniquely distinguishable* if there is a string w which is accepted by A from and only from the state q. Next, we say that a transition (p, a, q) is a *unique in-transition* if there is no state r different from p such that (r, a, q) is a transition in A. Finally, we say that a state q is *uniquely reachable* from a state p if there is a sequence of unique in-transitions (p_{i-1}, a_i, q_i) for $i = 1, 2, \ldots, k$ such that $p_0 = p$ and $p_k = q$.

If a uniquely distinguishable state q of an NFA A be uniquely reachable from a state p, then the state p is uniquely distinguishable as well. Next, if two subsets of a subset automaton of an NFA A differ in a uniquely distinguishable state of A, then the two subsets are distinguishable. It follows that if a uniquely distinguishable state of an NFA A is uniquely reachable from any other state of A, then the subset automaton of A does not have equivalents states.

If $u, v, w, x \in \Sigma^*$ and $w = uxv$, then u is a *prefix* of w, x is a *factor* of w, and v is a *suffix* of w. If $w = u_0 v_1 u_1 \cdots v_n u_n$, where $u_i, v_i \in \Sigma^*$, then $v_1 v_2 \cdots v_n$ is a *subword* of w. A prefix v (suffix, factor, subword) of w is *proper* if $v \neq w$.

A language L is *prefix-free* if $w \in L$ implies that no proper prefix of w is in L. Suffix-, factor-, and subword-free languages are defined analogously. A language L is *weakly-prefix-closed* if $w \in L$ implies that each non-empty prefix of w is in L. It is known that a minimal DFA for a prefix-free (suffix-free) language is non-exiting (non-returning) [7,8].

A language is *(positive-)closed* if it is closed under positive closure, that is, if $L = L^+$. It is *open*, if its complement is closed, and it is *clopen* if it is both closed and open. The terms *Kleene-closed* and *Kleene-open* are defined analogously. The *(positive) interior* of a language L is $L^\oplus = L^{c+c}$. The *Kleene interior* is $L^\circledast = L^{c*c}$. Notice that L is open iff $L = L^\oplus$. Next, for every language L, L^+ is closed and $L^\oplus$ is open.

Let $B(L)$ be the family of all languages generated from L by positive closure and positive interior; see [2, Subsect. 4.1]. Let $D(L)$ be the family of all languages generated from L by complementation and Kleene closure. Let $E(L)$ be the family of all languages generated from L by Kleene closure and Kleene interior. It is shown in [2, Lemma 20] that

$$D(L) = E(L) \cup \{M \mid M^c \in E(L)\}. \tag{1}$$

Moreover, if L is neither open nor closed, then by [2, Lemma 22],

$$E(L) = \{L\} \cup \{M \cup \{\varepsilon\} \mid M \in B(L) \text{ and } M \text{ is closed}\}$$
$$\cup \{M \setminus \{\varepsilon\} \mid M \in B(L) \text{ and } M \text{ is open}\}.$$

For each language L, the family $D(L)$ has at most 14 distinct languages, and Table 2 in [2, p. 312] describes 12 possible algebras, each of which is generated by a regular language. Notice that there is an oversight in cases (2a) and (2b): In case (2a) we should have $\varepsilon \notin L$, $|E(L)| = 3$, $|D(L)| = 6$, and it is generated by $\{a\}$. In case (2b) we should have $\varepsilon \in L$, $|E(L)| = 4$, $|D(L)| = 8$, and it is generated by $\{\varepsilon, a\}$ [1]. Here we show a modified table in which we do not display $|D(L)|$, and instead of $|E(L)|$, we display the set $E(L)$. We assume that L is a prefix-free (suffix-, factor-, subword-free) language and use the facts that $M^+ \cup \{\varepsilon\} = M^*$ and $M \setminus \{\varepsilon\} = M$ if $\varepsilon \notin M$. Notice that by (1), we only need to know the state complexities of the languages in $E(L)$.

Table 1. Classification of languages by the structure of $(E(L),^*,^{\oplus})$; cf. [2, p. 312].

Case	Necessary and sufficient conditions	$E(L)$	Regular generator
(1a)	L is clopen; $\varepsilon \in L$	$L, L \setminus \{\varepsilon\}$	a^*
(1b)	L is clopen; $\varepsilon \notin L$	$L, L \cup \{\varepsilon\}$	a^+
(2a)	L is open but not clopen; $\varepsilon \notin L$	L, L^*, L^+	a
(2b)	L is open but not clopen; $\varepsilon \in L$	$L, L \setminus \{\varepsilon\}, L^*, L^+$	$a \cup \varepsilon$
(3a)	L is closed but not clopen; $\varepsilon \notin L$	$L, L^{\oplus}, L^{\oplus} \cup \{\varepsilon\}$	aaa^*
(3b)	L is closed but not clopen; $\varepsilon \in L$	$L, L \cup \{\varepsilon\},$ $L^{\oplus}, L^{\oplus} \cup \{\varepsilon\}$	$aaa^* \cup \varepsilon$
(4)	L is neither open nor closed; L^+ is clopen and $L^{\oplus+} = L^+$	$L, L^*, L^+, L^{\oplus}$	$a \cup aaa$
(5)	L is neither open nor closed; $L^{\oplus}$ is clopen and $L^{+\oplus} = L^{\oplus}$	$L, L^*, L^{\oplus} \cup \{\varepsilon\}, L^{\oplus}$	aa
(6)	L is neither open nor closed; L^+ is open but $L^{\oplus}$ is not closed; $L^{\oplus+} \neq L^+$	$L, L^*, L^+,$ $L^{\oplus}, L^{\oplus*}, L^{\oplus+}$	$G :=$ $a \cup abaa$
(7)	L is neither open nor closed; $L^{\oplus}$ is closed but L^+ is not open; $L^{+\oplus} \neq L^{\oplus}$	$L, L^*, L^{\oplus} \cup \{\varepsilon\}, L^{\oplus},$ $L^{+\oplus} \cup \{\varepsilon\}, L^{+\oplus}$	$(a \cup b)^+ \setminus$ G
(8)	L is neither open nor closed; $L^{\oplus}$ is not closed and L^+ is not open; $L^{+\oplus} = L^{\oplus+}$	$L, L^*, L^{\oplus},$ $L^{+\oplus} \cup \{\varepsilon\}, L^{+\oplus}$	$a \cup bb$
(9)	L is neither open nor closed; $L^{\oplus}$ is not closed and L^+ is not open; $L^{+\oplus} \neq L^{\oplus+}$	$L, L^*, L^{\oplus},$ $L^{+\oplus} \cup \{\varepsilon\}, L^{+\oplus},$ $L^{\oplus*}, L^{\oplus+}$	$a \cup ab \cup bb$

3 Factor-Free and Subword-Free Languages

In this section we investigate Kuratowski algebras generated by factor- and subword-free languages. In [10] we have already shown that algebras in cases (2b), (3a), (3b), (4), and (7) cannot be generated by a prefix-free language. Therefore these cases cannot be generated by a factor- or subword-free language either. We examine all the remaining cases and either show that the algebra cannot be generated by any factor-free (and therefore also any subword-free) language, or we give an example of a subword-free (and therefore also factor-free) regular generator. Moreover, the given generators maximize the state complexities of all the generated languages. We begin by stating several helpful observations.

Proposition 1. *Let $n \geq 3$. If L is a factor free language over Σ with $\mathrm{sc}(L) = n$, then $\mathrm{sc}(L^*) \leq n - 1$ if $|\Sigma| \geq 2$ and $\mathrm{sc}(L^*) = n - 2$ if $|\Sigma| = 1$.*

Proof. Let $A = (\{s, 1, 2, \ldots, n-3, q_f, q_d\}, \Sigma, \cdot, s, \{q_f\})$ be a minimal non-returning and non-exiting DFA for L with the dead state q_d. Construct a DFA for L^* from A by making the state q_f initial and the state s non-initial, and by replacing each transition (q_f, a, q_d) with $(q_f, a, s \cdot a)$. In the resulting DFA, the state s is unreachable, so $\mathrm{sc}(L^*) \leq n - 1$. In the unary case, we must have $L = \{a^{n-2}\}$, so $\mathrm{sc}(L^*) = n - 2$. $\qquad\square$

Since the language $L^\oplus$ contains those strings of L that cannot be expressed as a concatenation of strings of L^c, we get the next proposition.

Proposition 2.
(a) Let $K \subseteq L \subseteq \Sigma^*$ and K be weakly-prefix-closed. Then $K \subseteq L^\oplus$.
(b) Let $L \subseteq \Sigma^*$ and $\Gamma = L \cap \Sigma$. Then $\Gamma \subseteq L^\oplus$.
(c) Let $L \subseteq \Sigma^*$ and $\Gamma = L \cap \Sigma$. If L is a factor-free language different from $\{\varepsilon\}$, then $L^\oplus = \Gamma$ and $L^{+\oplus} = L^{\oplus+} = \Gamma^+$.

Proof. (a) Since K is weakly-prefix-closed, every non-empty prefix of every string in K is in K as well. Therefore, no string in K can be expressed as a concatenation of strings in L^c. Hence $K \subseteq L^\oplus$. Claim (b) follows directly from (a).

(c) We have $\Gamma \subseteq L^\oplus$ by (b). The empty string and strings in $\Sigma \setminus \Gamma$ are not in L, therefore they are not in $L^\oplus$. Let $w \in L$ and $|w| \geq 2$. Since L is factor-free, no symbol occurring in w is in L. It follows that w can be partitioned into one-symbol strings that are in L^c. Hence $w \notin L^\oplus$, so $L^\oplus = \Gamma$ and $L^{\oplus+} = \Gamma^+$. Since $\Gamma^+ \subseteq L^+$ and Γ^+ is weakly-prefix-closed, we have $\Gamma^+ \subseteq L^{+\oplus}$ by (a). Let w be a string in L^+ which contains a symbol in $\Sigma \setminus \Gamma$. Then w must contain at least two such symbols. Therefore we can split w into substrings, each of which contains exactly one symbol in $\Sigma \setminus \Gamma$. These strings cannot be in L^+, therefore $w \in L^{+\oplus}$. Hence $L^{+\oplus} = \Gamma^+$, so $L^{+\oplus} = L^{\oplus+}$. $\qquad\square$

Now we examine the individual cases of possible Kuratowski algebras generated by factor- and subword-free languages. Our aim is to get the results that are summarized in Table 2. In each case we first recall sufficient and necessary conditions from Table 1, and then we discuss the case in detail.

Table 2. Binary subword-free generators of Kuratowski algebras maximizing complexities of generated languages. Cases (2b), (3a), (3b), (4), (6), (7), and (9) cannot be generated by any factor- or subword-free language.

Case	$E(L)$	Upper bounds on state complexities	Subword-free generator
(1a)	$L, L \setminus \{\varepsilon\}$	$2, 1$	$\{\varepsilon\}$
(1b)	$L, L \cup \{\varepsilon\}$	$1, 2$	$\emptyset$
(2a)	L, L^*, L^+	$3, 2, 3$	$\{a\}$ over $\{a, b\}$
(5)	$L, L^*, L^\oplus \cup \{\varepsilon\}$	$n, n-1, 2, 1$	$\{a^{n-2}\}$ over $\{a, b\}$
(8)	$L, L^*, L^\oplus, L^{\oplus *}, L^{\oplus +}$	$n, n-1, 3, 2, 3$	$\{a, b^{n-2}\}$

(1a) L is clopen; $\varepsilon \in L$ **(1b)** L is clopen; $\varepsilon \notin L$

If a factor-free language contains a non-empty string, then it is not closed. It follows that the only two clopen factor-free languages are $\emptyset$ and $\{\varepsilon\}$, which gives the results in the first two rows of Table 2.

(2a) L is open but not clopen; $\varepsilon \notin L$

Let L be a factor-free language over an alphabet Σ such that $\varepsilon \notin L$, $L = L^\oplus$ and $L \neq L^+$. By Proposition 2, we have $L^\oplus = L \cap \Sigma$. Hence, we must have $\emptyset \neq L \subseteq \Sigma$, so $\mathrm{sc}(L) = 3$. Moreover, every such language satisfies the conditions in case (2a). If $L = \Sigma$, then $L^* = \Sigma^*$ and $L^+ = \Sigma^+$, so $\mathrm{sc}(L^*) = 1$ and $\mathrm{sc}(L^+) = 2$. Otherwise, $\mathrm{sc}(L^*) = 2$ and $\mathrm{sc}(L^+) = 3$. The language $\{a\}$ over $\{a, b\}$ mets the upper bounds $(3, 2, 3)$ and $\{a\}$ as a unary language meets the upper bounds $(3, 1, 2)$. Row (2a) in Table 2 displays the binary case.

(5) L is neither open nor closed; $L^\oplus$ is clopen and $L^{+\oplus} = L^\oplus$

Let L be a factor-free language over an alphabet Σ satisfying the conditions in case (5). Then $L \neq \{\varepsilon\}$, and by Proposition 2, we have $L^\oplus = L \cap \Sigma$. Since $L^\oplus$ is closed, we must have $L^\oplus = \emptyset$, so $\mathrm{sc}(L^\oplus) = 1$ and $\mathrm{sc}(L^\oplus \cup \{\varepsilon\}) = 2$. Next, by Proposition 1, $\mathrm{sc}(L^*) \leq n - 1$ if $|\Sigma| \geq 2$, and $\mathrm{sc}(L^*) \leq n - 2$ if $|\Sigma| = 1$. The binary generator $\{a^{n-2}\}$ meets the upper bounds $(n, n - 1, 2, 1)$. In the unary case, the upper bounds $(n, n - 2, 2, 1)$ are met by the unary subword-free generator $\{a^{n-2}\}$. Row (5) in Table 2 displays the binary case.

(6) L is neither open nor closed; L^+ is open but $L^\oplus$ is not closed; $L^{\oplus +} \neq L^+$

Let L be a factor-free language satisfying (6). In particular, we have $L \neq \emptyset, L \neq \{\varepsilon\}$, and L^+ is open. Notice that $ua \in L$ implies $a \in L$ because otherwise we would have $u \in L^{+c}$ and $a \in L^{+c}$, so L^+ would not be open. It follows that L contains no string of length at least two. Hence $L \subseteq \Sigma$. However then $L = L^\oplus$, a contradiction with the assumption that L is not open. Therefore the Kuratowski algebra in case (6) cannot be generated by any factor-free language.

(8) L is neither open nor closed; $L^\oplus$ is not closed; L^+ is not open; $L^{+\oplus} = L^{\oplus +}$

Let L be a factor free language satisfying (8). By Proposition 1, we have $\mathrm{sc}(L^*) \leq n - 1$. Let $\Gamma = L \cap \Sigma$. Then $L^\oplus = \Gamma$ by Proposition 2. Since $L^\oplus$ is not closed, we must have $\Gamma \neq \emptyset$. Therefore $\mathrm{sc}(L^{\oplus}) = \mathrm{sc}(\Gamma) = 3$, $\mathrm{sc}(L^{\oplus*}) = \mathrm{sc}(\Gamma^*) \leq 2$, and $\mathrm{sc}(L^{\oplus+}) = \mathrm{sc}(\Gamma^+) \leq 3$. Next, let $L = \{a, b^{n-2}\}$. Then $L^{\oplus} = \{a\}$, so L is not open. Since we have $aa \in L^+ \setminus L$ and $aa \in L^{\oplus+} \setminus L^{\oplus}$, the languages L and $L^{\oplus}$ are not closed. Since $b^{n-2} \in L^+ \setminus L^{+\oplus}$, the language L^+ is not open. By Proposition 2, $L^{\oplus+} = L^{+\oplus}$. Hence $\{a, b^{n-2}\}$ is a binary subword-free generator of case (8), and notice that it maximizes all the corresponding complexities. In the unary case, we must have $L = \{a^{n-2}\}$. Then $L^{\oplus} = \emptyset$ or $L^{\oplus} = L$, so L does not satisfy (8). Row (8) in Table 2 displays the binary case.

(9) L is neither open nor closed; $L^{\oplus}$ is not closed; L^+ is not open; $L^{+\oplus} \neq L^{\oplus+}$
If L is a factor-free language satisfying (9), then $L \neq \{\varepsilon\}$. However, then $L^{+\oplus} = L^{\oplus+}$ by Proposition 2, so L cannot generate case (9).

4 Suffix-Free Languages

Now we turn our attention to suffix-free languages. Since reversal commutes with complementation and star, whenever an algebra is generated by a prefix-free language, it is also generated by a suffix-free language. However, while the complexities of L^* and L^{*c*} in the prefix-free case are at most n and $2^{n-3} + 2$, respectively, for a suffix-free language, the complexity of L^* may be up to $2^{n-2} + 1$, and the complexity of L^{*c*} is not known. The exact complexity of this combined operation is not known even in the general case of regular languages [11].

Surprisingly, we need the language L^{*c*} only in case (9), and this is the only case which is left open in this paper. In every other case, we are able to compute the maximal complexities of all the generated languages. Next, again surprisingly, the complexities of $L^{\oplus}, L^{\oplus+}$, and $L^{\oplus*}$ are at most n, and a DFA for $L^{\oplus}$ can be obtained from a DFA for L just by omitting the non-final states. Finally, it is interesting that in most cases, all the complexities cannot be maximized by a single generator.

We start with a very useful Cmorik's lemma which helps us easily prove the suffix-freeness of our generators. Then we state and prove some observations concerning suffix-free languages; let us recall that a minimal DFA for a suffix-free language is non-returning.

Lemma 3 [5, Lemma 1]. *Let A be a non-returning DFA that has a unique final state. If each state of A, except for the dead state, has at most one in-transition on every input symbol, then $L(A)$ is suffix-free.*

Lemma 4. *Let $\varepsilon \notin L$ and $L \cap \Sigma = \emptyset$. Then $L^{\oplus} = \emptyset$ and $L^{+\oplus} = \emptyset$.*

Proof. If $L = \emptyset$, then $L^{\oplus} = \emptyset$. Otherwise let w be a non-empty string in L. Then w can be partitioned into one-symbol strings that are in L^c. Thus $w \notin L^{\oplus}$, and we have $L^{\oplus} = \emptyset$. If $L \cap \Sigma = \emptyset$, then also $L^+ \cap \Sigma = \emptyset$, and by the same argument $L^{+\oplus} = \emptyset$. $\square$

Lemma 5. *Let $n \geq 3$ and L be a suffix-free language accepted by a minimal non-returning DFA $A = (\{s, 1, 2, \ldots, n-2, q_d\}, \Sigma, \cdot, s, F)$. Then* *(a)* $\mathrm{sc}(L^{c+}) \leq n$;

(b) $\mathrm{sc}(L^{\oplus}) \leq |F| + 2$;

(c1) L is open if and only if $F = \{1, 2, \ldots, n-2\}$;

(c2) if L is open, then $\mathrm{sc}(L^+) \leq \mathrm{sc}(L)$;

(d) $\mathrm{sc}(L^{\oplus+}) \leq n$;

(e) L^+ is open if and only if L^+ is weakly-prefix-closed;

(f) $\mathrm{sc}(L^+) \leq 2^{n-2} + 1$ and $\mathrm{sc}(L^*) \leq 2^{n-2} + 1$.

Proof. (a) Let $w \in \Sigma^*$. If $w \in L^c$ then $w \in L^{c+}$. If $w \in L$ and some non-empty prefix u of w is in L^c, that is, $w = uv$ with $u \neq \varepsilon$ and $u \in L^c$, then $v \in L^c$ since L is suffix-free. Hence $w \in L^{c+}$. It follows that an n-state DFA for L^{c+} can be constructed from A as follows:

- interchange final and non-final states of A;
- in each final state p of the resulting DFA, except for the initial state, replace each out-transition (p, a, q) with the loop (p, a, p).

(b) Since $L^{\oplus} = L^{c+c}$, we get an n-state DFA for $L^{\oplus}$ by complementing the DFA obtained in case (a). It follows that all non-final states of A, except for the initial state s, are dead in the DFA for $L^{\oplus}$, so $\mathrm{sc}(L^{\oplus}) \leq |F| + 2$.

(c1) The language L is open if and only if $L = L^{\oplus}$. By the construction in case (b), this holds if and only if $F = \{1, 2, \ldots, n-2\}$.

(c2) To get an NFA for L^+, we add the transitions $(q, a, s \cdot a)$ for each final state q and each input symbol a. If $s \cdot a = q_d$, then we can remove the transition (q, a, q_d) since it is not used in any accepting computation. Otherwise, we have $s \cdot a \in F$, and we must have $q \cdot a = q_d$ because otherwise L would not be suffix-free. Hence we can remove the transition (q, a, q_d) for the same reason as above. The resulting automaton is deterministic and has n states.

(d) We have $L^{\oplus} \subseteq L$, so $L^{\oplus}$ is a suffix-free language. Since $L^{\oplus}$ is open, we get $\mathrm{sc}(L^{\oplus+}) \leq n$ by (c2) and (b).

(e) Assume that L^+ is open. Let $w \in L^+, w = uv$ and $u \neq \varepsilon$. If $w \in L$, then $v \notin L$ and also $v \notin L^+$, since is L is suffix-free. Thus $v \in L^{+c}$, and therefore $u \notin L^{+c}$ since L^+ is open. Hence $u \in L^+$. If $w = w_1 w_2 \cdots w_k$ with $k \geq 2$ and $w_i \in L$, and u is a non-empty prefix of w, then $u = w_1 w_2 \cdots w_{i-1} x$ where x is a non-empty prefix of w_i. As shown above, we have $x \in L^+$. Therefore $u \in L^+$. It follows that L^+ is weakly-prefix-closed.

Conversely, assume that L^+ is weakly-prefix-closed. Suppose for a contradiction that there is a string w in L^+ such that $w \notin L^{+\oplus}$. Then $w = w_1 w_2 \cdots w_k$ with $k \geq 2$ and $w_i \in L^{+c}$ and $w_i \neq \varepsilon$. Since L^+ is weakly-prefix-closed, we must have $w_1 \in L^+$, a contradiction.

(f) To get an NFA for L^+ from the DFA A, we first remove the dead state d, and then we add the transition $(q, a, s \cdot a)$ for each final state q and each input symbol a such that $s \cdot a \neq d$. The resulting NFA is non-returning, so its subset automaton is non-returning and it has at most $2^{n-2} + 1$ reachable states. To get a DFA for L^*, we only make the initial state of the subset automaton final. $\square$

Now we inspect the individual cases of possible Kuratowski algebras generated, this time, by suffix-free languages. Our aim is to get the results shown in Table 3. Cases (1a) and (1b) are analogous to the previous section.

Table 3. Suffix-free generators of Kuratowski algebras maximizing complexities of corresponding generated languages. Cases (2b), (3a), (3b), (4), and (7) cannot be generated by any suffix-free language

Case	$E(L)$	Upper bounds on state complexities	Suffix-free generator
(1a)	$L, L \setminus \{\varepsilon\}$	$2, 1$	ε
(1b)	$L, L \cup \{\varepsilon\}$	$1, 2$	$\emptyset$
(2a)	L, L^*, L^+	n, n, n	Fig. 1
(5)	$L, L^*, L^{\oplus} \cup \{\varepsilon\}, L^{\oplus}$	$n, 2^{n-2} + 1, 2, 1$	Fig. 2
(6)	$L, L^*, L^+,$ $L^{\oplus}, L^{\oplus*}, L^{\oplus+}$	$n, 2^{n-3} + 2, 2^{n-3} + 2,$ $n-1, n-1, n-1$	Fig. 3 (top) Fig. 3 (bottom)
(8)	$L, L^*, \; L^{\oplus}, L^{+\oplus} \cup \{\varepsilon\}, L^{+\oplus}$	$n, 2^{n-2} + 1,$ $n-1, n-1, n-1$	Fig. 4 (top) Fig. 4 (bottom)
(9)	$L, L^*,$ $L^{+\oplus} \cup \{\varepsilon\}, L^{+\oplus},$ $L^{\oplus}, L^{\oplus*}, L^{\oplus+}$	$n, 2^{n-2} + 1,$ $2^{3n \log n}, 2^{3n \log n},$ $n-1, n-1, n-1$	Fig. 5 (top) ? Fig. 5 (bottom)

(2a) L is open, L is not closed, $\varepsilon \notin L$

Since L is open, we have $\mathrm{sc}(L^+) \leq n$ by Lemma 5 (c2). To get an n-state DFA for L^*, we only make the initial state s final in the DFA for L^+ obtained in Lemma 5 (c2). Let L be the ternary suffix-free language accepted by the DFA shown in Fig. 1. By Lemma 5 (c1), L is open. Since $aa \in L^+ \setminus L$, L is not closed. Thus L satisfies the conditions (2a). We have $\mathrm{sc}(L) = \mathrm{sc}(L^*) = \mathrm{sc}(L^+) = n$ since the final states in $\{1, 2, \ldots, n-2\}$ can be distinguished by strings in b^*, and in the case of L^*, the final states s and $n-2$ are distinguished by c. This gives the results in row (2a) of Table 3.

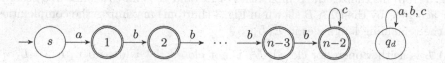

Fig. 1. A suffix-free generator of the Kuratowski algebra in case (2a); the transitions not shown are going to the dead state q_d.

(5) L is neither open nor closed; $L^{\oplus}$ is clopen and $L^{+\oplus} = L^{\oplus}$

Since L is neither open nor closed, we have $L \neq \emptyset$ and $L \neq \{\varepsilon\}$. Thus $\varepsilon \notin L$. Next $L^{\oplus} \subseteq L$, so $L^{\oplus}$ is suffix-free. Moreover $L^{\oplus}$ is assumed to be clopen, therefore $L^{\oplus} = \emptyset$ or $L^{\oplus} = \{\varepsilon\}$. Since $\varepsilon \notin L$, we must have $L^{\oplus} = \emptyset$. Hence $\mathrm{sc}(L^{\oplus} \cup \{\varepsilon\}) = 2$ and $\mathrm{sc}(L^{\oplus} \setminus \{\varepsilon\}) = 1$. Next we have $\mathrm{sc}(L^*) \leq 2^{n-2} + 1$ by Lemma 5 (f). Let

L be the language accepted by the DFA A shown in Fig. 2. By Lemma 3, L is suffix-free. We can show that L is the desired generator.

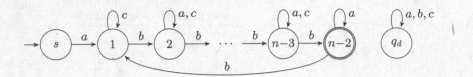

Fig. 2. A suffix-free generator of the Kuratowski algebra in case (5); the transitions not shown are going to the dead state q_d.

(6) L is not open, L is not closed, L^+ is open, $L^\oplus$ is not closed, $L^{\oplus+} \neq L^+$
Let L be accepted by a minimal DFA $A = (\{s, 1, \ldots, n-2, q_d\}, \Sigma, \cdot, s, F)$. First, we prove that $\mathrm{sc}(L^*) \leq 2^{n-3} + 2$ in this case. If L satisfies the conditions in case (6), then L^+ is open. By Lemma 5 (e), L^+ is weakly-prefix-closed. Construct an NFA N for L^+ from A by adding the transitions $(q, a, s \cdot a)$ for each final state q and each input symbol a.

In the subset automaton of the NFA N, each reachable non-final subset, except for the initial subset, must be dead since L^+ is weakly-prefix-closed. We can show that no reachable subset contains two final states of A. Hence the subset automaton has at most $|F| \cdot 2^{n-|F|-2}$ reachable pairwise distinguishable states. This is at most $2^{n-3} + 2$, and to meet this bound, $|F|$ must be 1 or 2. To get a DFA for L^*, we make the initial state final in the subset automaton of the NFA N.

Now consider $L^\oplus$. By Lemma 5 (b), we have $\mathrm{sc}(L^\oplus) \leq |F| + 2$. Thus $\mathrm{sc}(L^\oplus)$ is maximal if $F = \{1, 2, \ldots, n-2\}$. However, then L would be open by Lemma 5 (c1). Therefore we have $\mathrm{sc}(L^\oplus) \leq n - 1$. Notice that if $n \geq 6$, then there is no language that maximizes both the complexities of L^+ and $L^\oplus$.

We can show that the suffix-free generator accepted by the DFA A shown in Fig. 3 (top) maximizes the complexities of L^+ and L^*, and the suffix-free generator accepted by the DFA B shown in Fig. 3 (bottom) maximizes the complexities of the remaining languages in $E(L)$.

(8) L is neither open nor closed; $L^\oplus$ is not closed; L^+ is not open; $L^{+\oplus}=L^{\oplus+}$
Let L be a suffix-free generator in case (8). We can show that the complexities of the generated languages are as in the corresponding row of Table 3. Similarly as in case (6) we can show that the upper bounds on the complexity of L^* and $L^\oplus$ cannot be met by a single generator. The suffix-free generator accepted by the DFA A shown in Fig. 4 (top) maximizes the complexity of L^*, and the suffix-free generator accepted by the DFA B shown in Fig. 4 (bottom) maximizes the complexities of the remaining languages in $E(L)$.

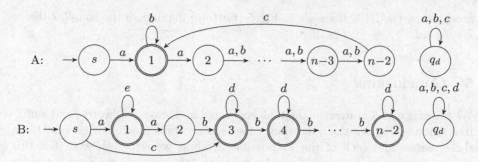

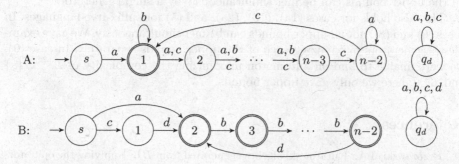

Fig. 3. Suffix-free generators of the Kuratowski algebra in case (6); the transitions not shown are going to the dead state q_d.

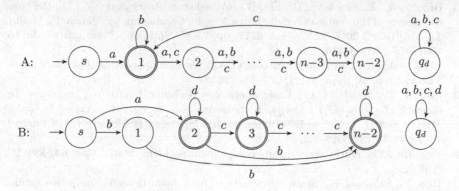

Fig. 4. Suffix-free generators of the Kuratowski algebra in case (8); the transitions not shown are going to the dead state q_d.

Fig. 5. Suffix-free generators of the Kuratowski algebra in case (9); the transitions not shown are going to the dead state q_d.

(9) L is neither open nor closed; $L^\oplus$ is not closed; L^+ is not open; $L^{+\oplus} \neq L^{\oplus+}$ Since the complexity of L^{*c*} is not known for suffix-free languages, this part of case (9) remains open. The suffix-free generator accepted by the DFA A shown in Fig. 5 (top) maximizes the complexity of L^*, and the suffix-free generator accepted by the DFA B shown in Fig. 5 (bottom) maximizes the complexities of $L^\oplus, L^{\oplus *}, L^{\oplus +}$.

5   Conclusions

We investigated Kuratowski algebras generated by factor-, subword-, and suffix-free languages under the operations of star and complement. For each of these three classes and each of the 12 possible algebras we either showed that this algebra cannot be generated by a language in this class, or we gave a regular generator. For each of the possible algebras, we gave upper bounds on the state complexities of the generated languages. For factor- and subword- free languages, all the upper bounds can be met simultaneously by a single generator.

This also holds for cases (1a), (1b), (2a), and (5) for suffix-free languages. In cases (6) and (8), not all upper bounds can be met simultaneously. We gave examples of generators maximizing each of the upper bounds separately. In case (9), we were unable to find an automaton maximizing the complexity of $L^{+\oplus} \cup \{\varepsilon\}$ and $L^{+\oplus}$, here we only gave upper bounds.

References

1. Brzozowski, J.A.: Kuratowski algebras generated from L by applying the operators of Kleene closure and complement. Personal communication (2016)
2. Brzozowski, J.A., Grant, E., Shallit, J.: Closures in formal languages and Kuratowski's theorem. Internat. J. Found. Comput. Sci. **22**(2), 301–321 (2011)
3. Brzozowski, J., Jirásková, G., Liu, B., Rajasekaran, A., Szykuła, M.: On the state complexity of the shuffle of regular languages. In: Câmpeanu, C., Manea, F., Shallit, J. (eds.) DCFS 2016. LNCS, vol. 9777, pp. 73–86. Springer, Cham (2016). doi:10.1007/978-3-319-41114-9_6
4. Brzozowski, J.A., Jirásková, G., Zou, C.: Quotient complexity of closed languages. Theory Comput. Syst. **54**(2), 277–292 (2014)
5. Cmorik, R., Jirásková, G.: Basic operations on binary suffix-free languages. In: Kotásek, Z., Bouda, J., Černá, I., Sekanina, L., Vojnar, T., Antoš, D. (eds.) MEMICS 2011. LNCS, vol. 7119, pp. 94–102. Springer, Heidelberg (2012). doi:10.1007/978-3-642-25929-6_9
6. Fife, J.H.: The Kuratowski closure-complement problem. Math. Mag. **64**, 180–182 (1991)
7. Han, Y., Salomaa, K.: State complexity of basic operations on suffix-free regular languages. Theor. Comput. Sci. **410**(27–29), 2537–2548 (2009)
8. Han, Y., Salomaa, K., Wood, D.: Operational state complexity of prefix-free regular languages. In: Ésik, Z., Fülöp, Z. (eds.) Automata, Formal Languages, and Related Topics, pp. 99–115. Institute of Informatics, University of Szeged, Szeged (2009)
9. Hopcroft, J.E., Ullman, J.D.: Introduction to Automata Theory Languages and Computation. Addison-Wesley, Boston (1979)
10. Jirásek, J., Šebej, J.: Kuratowski algebras generated by prefix-free languages. In: Han, Y.-S., Salomaa, K. (eds.) CIAA 2016. LNCS, vol. 9705, pp. 150–162. Springer, Cham (2016). doi:10.1007/978-3-319-40946-7_13

11. Jirásková, G., Shallit, J.: The state complexity of star-complement-star. In: Yen, H.-C., Ibarra, O.H. (eds.) DLT 2012. LNCS, vol. 7410, pp. 380–391. Springer, Heidelberg (2012). doi:10.1007/978-3-642-31653-1_34
12. Kuratowski, K.: Sur l'operation Ā de l'analysis situs. Fundam. Math. **3**, 182–199 (1922)
13. Sipser, M.: Introduction to the Theory of Computation. Cengage Learning, Boston (2012)
14. Yu, S.: Regular languages. In: Rozenberg, G., Salomaa, A., et al. (eds.) Handbook of Formal Languages, Volume 1 Word, Language, Grammar, pp. 41–110. Springer, Heidelberg (1997)

Branching Measures and Nearly Acyclic NFAs

Chris Keeler and Kai Salomaa[(⊠)]

School of Computing, Queen's University, Kingston, ON K7L 2N8, Canada
{keeler,ksalomaa}@cs.queensu.ca

Abstract. To get a more comprehensive understanding of the branching complexity of nondeterministic finite automata (NFA), we introduce and study the string path width and depth path width measures. The string path width on a string w counts the number of all complete computations on w, and the depth path width on an integer ℓ counts the number of complete computations on all strings of length ℓ. We give an algorithm to decide the finiteness of the depth path width of an NFA. Deciding finiteness of string path width can be reduced to the corresponding question on ambiguity.

An NFA is nearly acyclic if any computation can pass through at most one cycle. The class of nearly acyclic NFAs consists of exactly all NFAs with finite depth path width. Using this characterization we show that the finite depth path width of an m-state NFA over a k-letter alphabet is at most $(k+1)^{m-1}$ and that this bound is tight. The nearly acyclic NFAs recognize exactly the class of constant density regular languages.

1 Introduction

Finite automata are a fundamental model of computation that has been extensively studied since the 1950s. The last decades have seen much work on the descriptional complexity, or state complexity, of regular languages [8,9,25].

The *degree of ambiguity* of a nondeterministic finite automaton (NFA) A on a string w is the number of accepting computations of A on w. Ravikumar and Ibarra [19] have first studied systematically the size-trade-offs between NFAs of different degrees of ambiguity. Leung [15] has shown that general NFAs can be exponentially more succinct than polynomially ambiguous NFAs, and Hromkovič and Schnitger [11] have established a descriptional complexity separation between polynomially ambiguous and finitely ambiguous NFAs.

The degree of ambiguity is defined in terms of the number of accepting computations, and does not directly limit the total amount of nondeterminism in a computation. The computation of an unambiguous NFA may include an unbounded number of nondeterministic steps, as long as at each nondeterministic step, only one choice can lead to acceptance. The *tree width* [1] (a.k.a. leaf size) measure counts the number of leaves of the computation tree [10,17,18]. Other measures of nondeterminism for finite automata have also been considered [6–8,10,18].

---

[1] Note that this is not the same as the graph theory notion of tree width.

© IFIP International Federation for Information Processing 2017
Published by Springer International Publishing AG 2017. All Rights Reserved
G. Pighizzini and C. Câmpeanu (Eds.): DCFS 2017, LNCS 10316, pp. 202–213, 2017.
DOI: 10.1007/978-3-319-60252-3_16

We study a measure called *string path width* that counts the number of complete accepting and non-accepting computations of an NFA on a given string. The string path width can be viewed as a blending between the tree width measure and the degree of ambiguity. For certain NFAs, the string path width is the same as tree width, and for others the same as ambiguity. In fact, Goldstine et al. [6] have defined 'ambiguity' as the number of complete computations, which coincides with our notion of string path width. The *degree automata* [13] extend these notions by considering the ratio of the number accepting computations and the number of all computations on a given string.

To get a more comprehensive understanding of the degree of branching[2] of an NFA, we introduce the *depth path width* measure, which counts the total number of complete computations on all inputs of a given length. We establish necessary and sufficient conditions for an NFA to have infinite depth path width. These conditions are based on the existence of cycles satisfying certain requirements. This characterization yields a polynomial time algorithm to decide whether or not the depth path width of an NFA is bounded. Finiteness of string path width can be decided with existing algorithms from the literature [24].

It is well known that acyclic finite automata characterize exactly the finite languages. We characterize regular languages having bounded depth path width by an extension of acyclic NFAs, called *nearly acyclic* NFAs. An NFA A is said to be nearly acyclic if A, roughly speaking, it does not contain two distinct cycles where a state of one cycle is reachable from the other cycle.

We show that there exists an m-state nearly acyclic NFA over a k-letter alphabet having depth path width $(k+1)^{m-1}$, and that this is an upper bound for all m-state NFAs over a k-letter alphabet having finite depth path width. Finally, we show that nearly acyclic NFAs recognize exactly the regular languages of bounded density [21]. For nearly acyclic DFAs we have a stronger correspondence: any DFA recognizing a bounded density language must be nearly acyclic.

2   Preliminaries

Here we recall and introduce some notation and definitions. More information on finite automata can be found e.g. in [22,25]. The set of strings over a finite alphabet Σ is Σ^*, and ε is the empty string. The cardinality of a finite set F is denoted $|F|$ and $\mathbb{N}$ is the set of non-negative integers.

A *nondeterministic finite automaton* (NFA) is a tuple $A = (Q, \Sigma, \delta, q_0, F)$ where Q is the finite set of states, Σ is the input alphabet, $\delta : Q \times \Sigma \to 2^Q$ is the transition function, $q_0 \in Q$ is the initial state and $F \subseteq Q$ is the set of final states. The transition function δ is in the usual way extended as a function $Q \times \Sigma^* \to 2^Q$, and the language recognized by A is $L(A) = \{w \in \Sigma^* \mid \delta(q_0, w) \cap F \neq \emptyset\}$. If $|\delta(q, b)| \leq 1$ for all $q \in Q$ and $b \in \Sigma$, the automaton A is a *deterministic finite automaton* (DFA). Note that we allow NFAs and DFAs to have undefined

---

[2] Here and in the title of the paper by "branching" we mean an informal notion of path expansion in computations. A specific technical notion called branching is considered by Goldstine et al. [7].

transitions. Our definition does not allow multiple start states or ε−transitions. Unless otherwise mentioned, we always assume that an NFA does not have any unreachable states.

A *(state) path* of the NFA A with underlying string $w = b_1 b_2 \cdots b_k$, $b_i \in \Sigma$, $i = 1, \ldots, k$, $k \geq 0$, is a sequence of states $(p_0, p_1, \ldots, p_\ell)$, where $p_j \in \delta(p_{j-1}, b_j)$, $j = 1, \ldots \ell$, and either $\ell = k$, or, $\ell < k$ and $\delta(p_\ell, b_{\ell+1}) = \emptyset$. That is, the path must read the entire underlying string unless it encounters an undefined transition. Two paths are equal if and only if they have the same sequence of states and underlying string.

A path beginning in the start state q_0, is a *computation* of A on the underlying string w. A computation $(q_0, p_1, \ldots, p_\ell)$ is a *complete computation* on a string $b_1 b_2 \cdots b_k$ if $\ell = k$. An *accepting computation* is a complete computation that ends in an accepting state of F. The set of all (not necessarily complete) computations of A on the string w is denoted $\mathrm{comp}_A(w)$.

Intuitively, a computation of A on a string w is a sequence of states that A reaches when started with the initial state and the symbols of w are read one by one. A complete computation ends with a state reached after consuming all symbols of w. An incomplete computation ends with a state where the transition on the next symbol of w is undefined.

The *length* of a path $C_1 = (p_0, p_1, \ldots, p_\ell)$ is $|C_1| = \ell$ (the number of transitions). The catenation of C_1 and a path $C_2 = (p_\ell, p'_1, \ldots p'_m)$ is $C_1 \cdot C_2 = (p_0, \ldots, p_\ell, p'_1, \ldots p'_m)$. That is, paths C_1 and C_2 can be catenated if C_1 ends with the first state of C_2.

A path $(p_0, p_1, \ldots, p_k)$, $k \geq 1$, with underlying string $b_1 b_2 \cdots b_k$ is a *cycle* if $p_0 = p_k$. A cycle with one transition from a state to itself is called a *self-loop*. (A path of length zero with no transitions is not a cycle.) An NFA with no cycles is called an *acyclic* NFA (aNFA).

Cycles that are obtained from each other by a cyclical shift are said to be *equivalent:* For $0 < i < k$, the above cycle (with $p_0 = p_k$) is equivalent to the cycle $(p_i, \ldots, p_k, p_1, \ldots p_{i-1}, p_i)$ having underlying string $b_{i+1} \cdots b_k b_1 \cdots b_i$.

We define *path trees* that represent all computations of an NFA on all strings of a given length. Note that this is different than the notion of computation trees [10,17], which represent all computations of an NFA on a given string w. For $\ell \in \mathbb{N}$, the *path tree* of an NFA $A = (Q, \Sigma, \delta, q_0, F)$ of depth ℓ, $T_{A,\ell}$, is a finite tree where the nodes are labelled by elements of Q and the edges are labelled by elements of Σ, defined inductively as follows:

- $T_{A,0}$ consists of a single node labelled by q_0.
- Consider $\ell \geq 1$ and let $\mathrm{leaf}(\ell - 1)$ be the set of leaf nodes of $T_{A,\ell-1}$ having distance $\ell - 1$ from the root. If an $x \in \mathrm{leaf}(\ell - 1)$ is labelled by $q \in Q$, then for each $c \in \Sigma$ and $q' \in \delta(q, c)$, in the tree $T_{A,\ell}$ we add to node x a child y labelled by q', and the edge between x and y is labelled with c.

The *pruned path tree* of depth ℓ, $T^p_{A,\ell}$, is obtained from $T_{A,\ell}$ by recursively removing all leaf nodes which have distance smaller than ℓ from the root node.

The *degree of ambiguity* of an NFA A on a string w, $\mathrm{da}(A, w)$ [8,19], is the number of accepting computations of A on w, and the *tree width* of A on w,

$\mathrm{tw}(A, w)$ [10,17], is the number of (not necessarily complete) computations of A on w. Note that Hromkovič et al. [10] call this "leaf size". Tree width is usually defined as the number of leaves of the computation tree of A on w. This quantity is identical to the cardinality of the set $\mathrm{comp}_A(w)$.

For $\ell \geq 0$, the degree of ambiguity (respectively, tree width) of A on strings of length ℓ is defined as $\mathrm{da}(A, \ell) = \max\{\mathrm{da}(A, w) \mid w \in \Sigma^\ell\}$ (respectively, $\mathrm{tw}(A, \ell) = \max\{\mathrm{tw}(A, w) \mid w \in \Sigma^\ell\}$). Strictly speaking, using common practice, we use $\mathrm{da}(A, \cdot)$ (and $\mathrm{tw}(A, \cdot)$) to denote two different functions where one takes a string and the other an integer as argument.

The ambiguity (respectively, the tree width) of the NFA A is said to be finite if the above values are bounded for all $\ell \in \mathbb{N}$, and in this case, the degree of ambiguity (respectively, the tree width) of A is denoted $\mathrm{da}^{\mathrm{sup}}(A)$ (respectively, $\mathrm{tw}^{\mathrm{sup}}(A)$).

3   String Path Width and Depth Path Width

We consider measures that count the number of complete computations on a given string and on all strings of given length, respectively.

In the following, $A = (Q, \Sigma, \delta, q_0, F)$ is always an NFA. The *string path width* of A on a string $w \in \Sigma^*$, $\mathrm{SPW}(A, w)$, is defined as the number of complete computations·of A on w. For $\ell \in \mathbb{N}$, the string path width of A on strings of length ℓ is $\mathrm{SPW}(A, \ell) = \max\{\mathrm{SPW}(A, w) \mid w \in \Sigma^\ell\}$, and when this value is bounded, the *string path width of A* is denoted $\mathrm{SPW}^{\mathrm{sup}}(A)$.

Example 1. For the NFA A_1 given in Fig. 1:

- $\mathrm{SPW}(A_1, ab) = 2$, complete computations $\{(0, 1, 0), (0, 1, 2)\}$
- $\mathrm{SPW}(A_1, aaaa) = 1$, complete computations $\{(0, 1, 0, 1, 0)\}$
- Generally, $\mathrm{SPW}(A_1, (ab)^x) = x + 1$, $x \in \mathbb{N}$ □

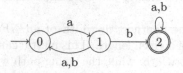

Fig. 1. NFA A_1

In fact, Goldstine et al. [6] have defined 'ambiguity' as the number of complete computations, which coincides with our notion of string path width. The string path width can be viewed as a blend between ambiguity and tree width in the sense of the following lemma. Since string path width counts only complete computations while tree width counts all computations, the string path width of an NFA A on a string w will always be at most the tree width of A on w.

Lemma 1. *Consider an NFA* $A = (Q, \Sigma, \delta, q_0, F)$ *and let* $w \in \Sigma^*$.

(i) $\mathrm{da}(A, w) \leq \mathrm{SPW}(A, w) \leq \mathrm{tw}(A, w)$.
(ii) *If* A *has no undefined transitions, that is,* $\delta(q, b) \neq \emptyset$ *for all* $q \in Q$, $b \in \Sigma$,
then $\mathrm{SPW}(A, w) = \mathrm{tw}(A, w)$.
(iii) *If all states of* A *are final, then* $\mathrm{SPW}(A, w) = \mathrm{da}(A, w)$.

Since string path width is, in the sense of Lemma 1 (iii), a special case of degree of ambiguity, from algorithms and bounds for ambiguity we get corresponding results for string path width. This is established using the transformation of the following lemma. In general, the transformed automaton is not equivalent to the original. Note that Lemma 1 (ii) gives a correspondence between string path width and tree width, but this cannot be used in a similar way because the corresponding transformation changes the string path width of the NFA.

Lemma 2. *Given an NFA* $A = (Q, \Sigma, \delta, q_0, F)$, *we can construct in linear time an NFA* A' *such that* $\mathrm{da}(A', w) = \mathrm{SPW}(A, w)$ *for all strings* $w \in \Sigma^*$.

Using Lemma 2, and the results by Weber and Seidl [24], we get:

Corollary 1 [24]. *Let* $A = (Q, \Sigma, \delta, q_0, F)$ *be an NFA.*

(i) *In time* $O(|Q|^6 \cdot |\Sigma|)$, *a random-access-machine can decide whether or not* $\mathrm{SPW}^{\mathrm{sup}}(A)$ *is finite, and in the positive case,* $\mathrm{SPW}^{\mathrm{sup}}(A) \leq 5^{\frac{|Q|}{2}} \cdot |Q|^{|Q|}$.
(ii) *The growth rate of* $\mathrm{SPW}(A, \ell)$ *is either bounded by a constant, polynomial in* ℓ, *or exponential in* ℓ. *If the growth rate is polynomial, the degree of the polynomial can be decided in* $O(|Q|^6 \cdot |\Sigma|)$ *time.*
(iii) *It can be decided in* $O(|Q|^4 \cdot |\Sigma|)$ *time whether or not the growth rate of* $\mathrm{SPW}(A, \ell)$ *is exponential.*

Also, it is known that for a fixed k and a given NFA A it can be decided in polynomial time whether $\mathrm{da}^{\mathrm{sup}}(A)$ (and consequently whether $\mathrm{SPW}^{\mathrm{sup}}(A)$) is at least k, but the question for degree of ambiguity becomes PSPACE-complete if k is part of the input [3].

Next we introduce the depth path width of an NFA as the number of all complete computations of a given length. This metric can be viewed as a broader version of the string path width; while the string path width counts the number of computations on a specific string, the depth path width considers all strings of the same length.

Consider an NFA $A = (Q, \Sigma, \delta, q_0, F)$ and let $\ell \in \mathbb{N}$. The *depth path width* of A on strings of length ℓ is

$$\mathrm{DPW}(A, \ell) = \sum_{w \in \Sigma^\ell} \mathrm{SPW}(A, w).$$

The depth path width of the NFA A is defined as $\mathrm{DPW}^{\mathrm{sup}}(A) = \sup_{\ell \in \mathbb{N}}(\mathrm{DPW}(A, \ell))$.

Example 2. For the DFA $A_2 = (Q, \Sigma, \delta, q_0, F)$ given in Fig. 2:

- $\mathrm{DPW}(A_2, 1) = 2$, complete computations $(0,0)$ on a, $(0,1)$ on b.
- Generally, $\mathrm{DPW}(A_2, \ell) = \ell + 1$, $\ell \in \mathbb{N}$. □

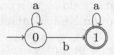

Fig. 2. DFA A_2

Directly from the definition it follows that for NFAs over a unary alphabet, the notion of depth path width coincides with string path width.

We give the necessary and sufficient conditions for an NFA to have unbounded depth path width. For this we use the correspondence between depth path width and the number of leaves in path trees (defined in Sect. 2).

Lemma 3. *Consider an NFA A and $\ell \in \mathbb{N}$. The value $\mathrm{DPW}(A, \ell)$ is equal to the number of leaves of the pruned path tree $T_{A,\ell}^p$.*

Intuitively, the conditions of Theorem 1 mean that q_1 and q_2 belong to a cycle and the state q_1 has another transition to a state q_3 such that the computations originating from q_3 are defined on infinitely many strings. Here q_3 may or may not belong to the same cycle as q_1 and q_2. If $q_2 = q_3$, then the alphabet symbols a and b must be distinct.

Theorem 1. *Consider an NFA $A = (Q, \Sigma, \delta, q_0, F)$. The depth path width of A is unbounded if and only if the following holds:*
There exist $q_1, q_2, q_3 \in Q$ and $a, b \in \Sigma$, where $q_2 \neq q_3$ or $a \neq b$, such that

(i) $q_2 \in \delta(q_1, a)$ and state q_1 is reachable from q_2, and,
(ii) $q_3 \in \delta(q_1, b)$ and the language of the NFA $A' = (Q, \Sigma, \delta, q_3, Q)$ is infinite.

Proof. First assume that conditions (i) and (ii) hold. Let C_1 be a computation from q_0 to q_1 (recall that we assume that NFAs have no unreachable states). Let C_2 be a cycle from q_1 back to q_1 that begins with the transition on a to q_2.

To show that $\mathrm{DPW}^{\mathrm{sup}}(A)$ is infinite, it is sufficient to show that for all $M \in \mathbb{N}$ there exists ℓ such that $\mathrm{DPW}(A, \ell) \geq M$. By condition (ii) there exists a path C_M having length $M \cdot |C_2|$ that begins in q_1 with the transition on b to q_3. Now A has M different computations of length $|C_1| + M \cdot |C_2|$:

$$C_1 \cdot C_2^i \cdot D_i, \quad i = 0, 1, \ldots, M - 1,$$

where D_i is an initial part of the path C_M having length $(M - i) \cdot |C_2|$. Note that the above are all distinct computations because the transitions from q_1 to q_2 on a and from q_1 to q_3 on b are distinct.

We sketch the proof in the "only if" direction: If $\text{DPW}^{\text{sup}}(A)$ is infinite, using Lemma 3 we see that the number of leaves of the pruned path tree $T^p_{A,\ell}$ can be chosen arbitrarily large for sufficiently large ℓ. When some state of A repeats on a path from the root to a leaf, we get a cycle and states satisfying conditions (i) and (ii).   □

The conditions of Theorem 1 yield a polynomial time algorithm to test whether the depth path width of an NFA is infinite.

Theorem 2. *If A is an NFA with m states over an alphabet Σ, we can decide in time $O(|\Sigma| \cdot m^5)$ whether or not the depth path width of A is infinite.*

Proof. Algorithm 1 checks the conditions of Theorem 1. Creating the copy of

---

Algorithm 1. Deciding if an NFA has infinite depth path width

---

1: Let $A = (Q, \Sigma, \delta, q_0, F)$ be an NFA where $|Q| = m$.
2: Create a copy of A and call it A', where all states of A' are final.
3: Create a distance matrix M, where $M[q, q']$ is the minimum distance from state $q \in Q$ to state $q' \in Q$.
4: infinityCondition = False
5: **for all** $q_1 \in Q$ **do**
6:     **for all** $q_2 \in \delta(q_1, a)$ **and** $q_3 \in \delta(q_1, b)$ such that $(q_2 \neq q_3$ **or** $a \neq b)$ **do**
7:         **if** $M[q_2, q_1] \neq \infty$ **then**
8:             Set initial state of A' to be q_3
9:             **if** $L(A')$ is infinite **then**
10:                 infinityCondition = True
11:             **end if**
12:         **end if**
13:     **end for**
14: **end for**
15: **return** infinityCondition

---

the NFA A takes $\Theta(m + |\delta|)$ time. Creating the adjacency matrix takes $\Theta(m^3)$ time and $\Theta(m^2)$ space using the Floyd-Warshall algorithm [5]. The two for all statements multiply the inner complexity by $\Theta(m^3)$, as there are m^3 triples of the form (q_1, q_2, q_3). Checking whether $L(A')$ is infinite takes $O(m + |\delta|)$ time using Tarjan's Strongly Connected Components algorithm [23]. So the worst-case runtime is $O(m + |\delta| + m^3 + m^3 \cdot (m + |\delta|))$ which simplifies to $O(|\Sigma| \cdot m^5)$.   □

4   Depth Path Width of Nearly Acyclic NFAs

We want to derive an upper bound for the finite depth path width of an m-state NFA. First we develop bounds for the depth path width measure of acyclic NFAs where the depth path width is naturally guaranteed to be finite.

Proposition 1. *Let A be an m-state unary aNFA. Then* $\mathrm{DPW}^{\mathrm{sup}}(A) \leq \binom{m-1}{\lfloor \frac{m-1}{2} \rfloor}$.

Note that the result of Proposition 1 indicates that the largest possible depth path width of an m-state aNFA is obtained by strings of length, roughly, m divided by two.

We now extend the result for arbitrary alphabet sizes.

Theorem 3. *Let A be an m-state aNFA. Then*

$$\mathrm{DPW}^{\mathrm{sup}}(A) \leq \sup_{\lfloor \frac{m-1}{2} \rfloor \leq \ell \leq m-1} k^\ell \cdot \binom{m-1}{\ell}.$$

The upper bound can be improved for acyclic DFAs (aDFA).

Corollary 2. *For an aDFA D with m states and k alphabet characters, the depth path width of D is at most k^{m-1}.*

It is easy to verify that an NFA A does *not* satisfy the conditions of Theorem 1 if and only if A does not have two non-equivalent cycles where one is reachable from the other. (Two cycles are equivalent if they are obtained from each other by a cyclical shift, see Sect. 2.) This condition forms the basis for the following definition.

Definition 1. *An NFA A is nearly acyclic (naNFA) if it does not have two non-equivalent cycles, C_1 and C_2, such that a state of C_2 is reachable from a state of C_1. An naNFA with a deterministic transition function is called a nearly acyclic DFA (naDFA).*

By Theorem 1, Definition 1 gives the most general class of NFAs that have finite depth path width. The influence of cycles that are reachable from one another is considered in a more general way by Msiska and van Zijl [16].

The limitation on the reachability between cycles implies a limitation on the number of (non-equivalent) cycles in a nearly acyclic NFA.

Lemma 4. *An m-state naNFA has at most $(m-1)$ cycles.*

The naNFAs with a maximal number of acyclic transitions and one self-loop on the initial state turn out to be useful for obtaining bounds for depth path width.

Definition 2. *An m-state initial self-loop maximal nearly acyclic NFA, an imax-naNFA, over an alphabet Σ has the set of states $\{0, 1, \ldots, m-1\}$ where 0 is the start state, there exists a transition on each alphabet symbol from i to j for all $0 \leq i < j \leq m-1$, and 0 has a self-loop.*

The transitions of an imax-naNFA are uniquely determined, except for the self-loop on the initial state, which can be on an arbitrary element of Σ. (If needed we could specify the symbol labelling the self-loop.) Also, for purposes of depth path width, the set of final states can be arbitrary. In Fig. 3 illustrating an m-state imax-naNFA, we use $m-1$ as the only final state.

We calculate the depth path width of imax-naNFAs as a function of the number of states and alphabet size.

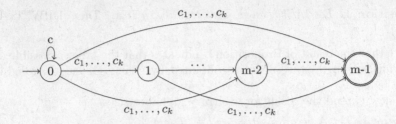

Fig. 3. An m-state imax-naNFA with alphabet $\{c_1, \ldots, c_k\}$.

Lemma 5. *An m-state imax-naNFA over a k-letter alphabet has depth path width $(k+1)^{m-1}$.*

Since acyclic DFAs are a special case of nearly acyclic DFAs, we can use the value acquired in Corollary 2 as a lower limit on the upper bound for the depth path width of an naDFA.

Theorem 4. *For $m \in \mathbb{N}$, there exists an m-state nearly acyclic DFA over a k-letter alphabet having depth path width k^{m-1}.*

Lemma 5 gives the depth path width of imax-naNFAs. From Lemma 4 we recall that an naNFA can have multiple cycles, however, it seems plausible that an m-state imax-naNFA could have maximal depth path width among all m-state naNFAs. This is established in the following lemmas.

Lemma 6. *Let A be an naNFA with (one or more) cycles of length at least two. Then there exists an naNFA A' with the same number of states over the same alphabet where all cycles are self-loops and $\mathrm{DPW}^{\mathrm{sup}}(A') \geq \mathrm{DPW}^{\mathrm{sup}}(A)$.*

Consider an m-state naNFA B where all cycles are self-loops. We can define an injective mapping from the set of computations of B having length ℓ to the length ℓ computations of an m-state imax-naNFA A. This then implies that the depth path width of B is at most that of A, and the observation is the basis for the following lemma.

Lemma 7. *Let A be an m-state imax-naNFA over alphabet Σ and let B be an m-state naNFA over Σ where all cycles are self-loops. Then $\mathrm{DPW}^{\mathrm{sup}}(B) \leq \mathrm{DPW}^{\mathrm{sup}}(A)$.*

Now we get a tight upper bound for the depth path width of an m-state naNFA.

Theorem 5. *If A is an m-state naNFA over a k-letter alphabet, then $\mathrm{DPW}^{\mathrm{sup}}(A) \leq (k+1)^{m-1}$. For each $m, k \geq 1$, there exists an m-state naNFA B_{imax} over a k-letter alphabet such that $\mathrm{DPW}^{\mathrm{sup}}(B_{\mathrm{imax}}) = (k+1)^{m-1}$.*

Proof. By Lemma 6, A can be converted to an m-state naNFA A' over the same alphabet without decreasing the depth path width where all cycles in A' are self-loops. Let B_{imax} be an m-state imax-naNFA over the same alphabet. Now

$$\mathrm{DPW}^{\mathrm{sup}}(A) \leq \mathrm{DPW}^{\mathrm{sup}}(A') \leq \mathrm{DPW}^{\mathrm{sup}}(B_{\mathrm{imax}}) = (k+1)^{m-1},$$

where the second inequality follows from Lemma 7 and the equality from Lemma 5. The equality also establishes the second claim of the theorem. $\square$

4.1   Languages Recognized by NaNFAs

Acyclic NFAs recognize the family of finite languages and, similarly, the nearly acyclic NFAs recognize a proper subfamily of the regular languages. The *density* of a language $L \subseteq \Sigma^*$ is defined as the function $d_L(\ell) = |L \cap \Sigma^\ell|$, $\ell \in \mathbb{N}$.

Proposition 2 (Shallit [21]). *The density of a regular language L over Σ is bounded, that is $d_L(\ell) \in O(1)$, if and only if L can be represented as a finite union of regular expressions xy^*z, where $x, y, z \in \Sigma^*$.*

The nearly acyclic NFAs recognize exactly the constant density languages.

Theorem 6. *A regular language L has constant density if and only if L is recognized by a nearly acyclic NFA.*

Proof. Suppose that $L \subseteq \Sigma^*$ is recognized by an m-state naNFA A. We show that $d_L(\ell) \leq m^3 \cdot |\Sigma|^m$ for all $\ell \in \mathbb{N}$. For $\ell \leq m - 1$ there is nothing to prove.

Consider then strings of length $\ell \geq m$. For each $w \in \Sigma^\ell$ accepted by A, fix one accepting computation C_w. Since A is nearly acyclic and $\ell \geq m$, the computation C_w must pass through exactly one cycle. Thus, we can write $w = w_{\mathrm{pref}}w_{\mathrm{cyc}}w_{\mathrm{suf}}$ where w_{cyc} is the maximal substring of w that in the computation C_w is "processed" by transitions of the cycle, and $|w_{\mathrm{pref}} \cdot w_{\mathrm{suf}}| \leq m - 1$. The number of strings of length at most $m - 1$ is upper bounded by $|\Sigma|^m$. In a string of length at most $m - 1$ the cycle can occur in at most m locations and, according to Lemma 4, A has at most m cycles and, furthermore, each cycle (equivalence class) can be started in at most m positions.[3] Once a particular cycle and its position in the "acyclic part" of the computation (consuming the prefix w_{pref} and suffix w_{suf}) are chosen, the length of the computation in the cycle is determined by the total length ℓ. Thus, the number of accepted strings of length ℓ is upper bounded by the constant $m^3 \cdot |\Sigma|^m$.

Conversely, if L has constant density then, by Proposition 2, L can be represented as a finite union of regular expressions of the form xy^*z, $x, y, z \in \Sigma^*$. An naNFA with one cycle recognizes xy^*z, and the languages recognized by naNFAs are clearly closed under union. $\square$

By considering unary regular languages it is easy to see that a constant density language can be recognized by an NFA that is not nearly acyclic. However, for DFAs, we get the implication also in the converse direction.

---

[3] This is a conservative upper bound chosen to keep the argument simple. If A were to have m cycles, the length of the cycles naturally could not be m.

Theorem 7. *Any DFA recognizing a constant density language must be nearly acyclic.*

As a corollary, we get that determinizing an naNFA must result in a nearly acyclic DFA. This could of course also be seen using a direct construction but it would require some effort.

Corollary 3. *Let A be an naNFA and let D be the DFA obtained from A using the subset construction. Then D is nearly acyclic.*

5 Conclusion

We have given an algorithm to decide whether the depth path width of an NFA is unbounded, and characterized automata with bounded depth path width as the class of nearly acyclic NFAs. We have given an upper bound for the finite depth path width of an m-state NFA over an alphabet of size k and shown that this bound is tight.

Nearly acyclic NFAs extend the class of acyclic NFAs that characterize the class of finite languages. A tight state complexity bound for determinizing acyclic NFAs is known [20]. From Corollary 3 we know that determinizing a nearly acyclic NFA always results in a nearly acyclic DFA. Establishing the worst-case size blow-up of determinizing a nearly acyclic NFA is a topic for future research. The size blow-up is at least as great as the exponential lower bound for determinizing unary (nearly acyclic) NFAs having cycles of different prime lengths [4].

Minimization of NFAs is PSPACE-complete [9] and remains NP-hard even for restricted subclasses of acyclic NFAs [1]. A linear time minimization algorithm for acyclic DFAs is given by Bubenzer [2] and incremental minimization techniques for acyclic NFAs have been considered e.g. by Lamperti et al. [14]. A topic for future work could be also to extend such methods for nearly acyclic NFAs.

Acknowledgments. Research supported by NSERC grant OGP0147224. Full version of the work can be found in [12].

References

1. Björklund, H., Martens, W.: The tractability frontier for NFA minimization. J. Comput. Syst. Sci. **78**(1), 198–210 (2012)
2. Bubenzer, J.: Cycle-aware minimization of acyclic deterministic finite-state automata. Discrete Appl. Math. **163**, 238–246 (2014)
3. Chan, T.-H., Ibarra, O.: On the finite valuedness problem for sequential machines. Theoret. Comput. Sci. **23**, 95–101 (1983)
4. Chrobak, M.: Finite automata and unary languages. Theoret. Comput. Sci. **47**, 149–158 (1986)
5. Cormen, T.H., Leiserson, C.E., Rivest, R.L., Stein, C.: Introduction to Algorithms, 3rd edn. MIT Press, Cambridge (2009)

6. Goldstine, J., Leung, H., Wotschke, D.: On the relation between ambiguity and nondeterminism in finite automata. Inform. Comput. **100**, 261–270 (1992)
7. Goldstine, J., Kintala, C.M.R., Wotschke, D.: On measuring nondeterminism in regular languages. Inform. Comput. **86**(2), 261–270 (1990)
8. Goldstine, J., Kappes, M., Kintala, C.M.R., Leung, H., Malcher, A., Wotschke, D.: Descriptional complexity of machines with limited resources. J. Univ. Comput. Sci. **8**(2), 193–234 (2002)
9. Holzer, M., Kutrib, M.: Descriptional and computational complexity of finite automata - a survey. Inform. Comput. **209**(3), 456–470 (2011)
10. Hromkovič, J., Seibert, S., Karhumäki, J., Klauck, H., Schnitger, G.: Communication complexity method for measuring nondeterminism in finite automata. Inform. Comput. **172**(2), 202–217 (2002)
11. Hromkovič, J., Schnitger, G.: Ambiguity and communication. Theory Comput. Syst. **48**(3), 517–534 (2011)
12. Keeler, C.: New metrics for finite automaton complexity and subregular language hierarchies. QSPACE. https://qspace.library.queensu.ca/handle/1974/15329
13. Kintala, C.M.R., Pun, K.Y., Wotschke, D.: Concise representations of regular languages by degree and probabilistic finite automata. Math. Syst. Theory **26**(4), 379–395 (1993)
14. Lamperti, G., Scandale, M., Zanella, M.: Determinization and minimization of finite acyclic automata by incremental techniques. Softw. Pract. Exp. **46**(4), 513–549 (2016)
15. Leung, H.: Separating exponentially ambiguous finite automata from polynomially ambiguous finite automata. SIAM J. Comput. **27**(4), 1073–1082 (1998)
16. Msiska, M., van Zijl, L.: Interpreting the subset construction using finite sublanguages. In: Proceedings of Prague Stringology Conference 2016, pp. 48–62 (2016)
17. Palioudakis, A., Salomaa, K., Akl, S.G.: State complexity of finite tree width NFAs. J. Automata Lang. Comb. **17**(2–4), 245–264 (2012)
18. Palioudakis, A., Salomaa, K., Akl, S.G.: Quantifying nondeterminism in finite automata. Ann. Univ. Bucharest Informatica **62**(2), 89–100 (2015)
19. Ravikumar, B., Ibarra, O.H.: Relating the type of ambiguity of finite automata to the succinctness of their representation. SIAM J. Comput. **18**(6), 1263–1282 (1989)
20. Salomaa, K., Yu, S.: NFA to DFA transformation for finite languages over arbitrary alphabets. J. Automata Lang. Comb. **2**(3), 177–186 (1997)
21. Shallit, J.: Numeration systems, linear recurrences, and regular sets. Inf. Comput. **113**(2), 331–347 (1994)
22. Shallit, J.: Second Course in Formal Languages and Automata Theory. Cambridge University Press, Cambridge (2009)
23. Tarjan, R.E.: Depth-first search and linear graph algorithms. SIAM J. Comput. **1**(2), 146–160 (1972)
24. Weber, A., Seidl, H.: On the degree of ambiguity of finite automata. Theoret. Comput. Sci. **88**(2), 325–349 (1991)
25. Yu, S.: Regular languages. In: Rozenberg, G., Salomaa, A. (eds.) Handbook of Formal Languages, vol. 1, pp. 41–110. Springer, Heidelberg (1997)

Square on Deterministic, Alternating, and Boolean Finite Automata

Ivana Krajňáková[✉] and Galina Jirásková

Mathematical Institute, Slovak Academy of Sciences,
Grešákova 6, 040 01 Košice, Slovakia
{krajnakova,jiraskov}@saske.sk

Abstract. We investigate the state complexity of the square operation on languages represented by deterministic, alternating, and Boolean
automata. For each k such that $1 \leq k \leq n-2$, we describe a binary language accepted by an n-state DFA with k final states meeting the upper
bound $n2^n - k2^{n-1}$ on the state complexity of its square. We show that
in the case of $k = n-1$, the corresponding upper bound cannot be met.
Using the DFA witness for square with 2^n states where half of them are
final, we get the tight upper bounds on the complexity of the square
operation on alternating and Boolean automata.

1   Introduction

Square is a basic unary operation on formal languages which is defined as
$L^2 = \{uv \mid u \in L \text{ and } v \in L\}$. It is known that if a language L is accepted
by a deterministic finite automaton (DFA) of n states, then the language L^2
is accepted by a DFA of at most $n2^n - 2^{n-1}$ states [7]. This upper bound was
proven to be tight in the binary case by Rampersad [8]. If the minimal DFA
for L has more than one final state, then this upper bound cannot be met. In
such a case the upper bound is $n2^n - k2^{n-1}$, where k is the number of final states
in the minimal DFA for L [10].

In this paper we study the state complexity of the square of languages
accepted by DFAs with more final states. Our motivation comes from the paper
by Fellah et al. [3] on alternating finite automata (AFAs). They provided an
upper bound $2^n + n + 1$ on the complexity of the square of a language represented by an n-state AFA. A language is accepted by an n-state AFA if and only
if its reverse is accepted by a DFA with 2^n states where 2^{n-1} of them are final
[1,3,5]. It follows that to prove the tightness of the upper bound $2^n + n + 1$, we
need to find a language represented by a DFA with half of the states final which
is hard for the square operation on DFAs.

Research supported by grant VEGA 2/0084/15 and grant APVV-15-0091. This work
was conducted as a part of PhD study of the first author at Comenius University in
Bratislava.

G. Pighizzini and C. Câmpeanu (Eds.): DCFS 2017, LNCS 10316, pp. 214–225, 2017.
DOI: 10.1007/978-3-319-60252-3_17

The problem seems to be interesting per se. Previously in [2], we tried to use Rampersad's binary witness for square [8] with k final states instead of original one. We were able to show the reachability of $n2^n - k2^{n-1}$ states in the subset automaton of an NFA for its square. However, to prove distinguishability a third letter was needed, so the binary case was left open. Surprisingly, in [2], we were unable to prove the tightness of the upper bound in the case of $n-1$ final states.

Here we solve both these open problems. We describe a binary language accepted by an n-state DFA with k final states meeting the upper bound $n2^n - k2^{n-1}$ on the state complexity of its square providing that $1 \le k \le n-2$. In the case of $k = n-1$, we prove that the corresponding upper bound $(2n+2)2^{n-2}$ cannot be met. To show it, we consider two cases. If the initial state is final, then we get the upper bound $(n+2)2^{n-2}$, and we show that it is tight in the binary case. If the initial state is not final, then the upper bound is $(n+3)2^{n-2}$ and is tight in the ternary case. The tight bound for binary languages is $(n+3)2^{n-2} - 1$ in this case. This solves the complexity of square on DFAs completely. The binary alphabet is optimal since it is known that in the unary case, the tight upper bound is $2n - 1$ [8].

Using these results we are able to describe a binary language accepted by an n-state AFA such that every AFA for its square has at least $2^n + n + 1$ states. This proves the tightness of the upper bound $2^n + n + 1$ given in [3]. We also consider Boolean finite automata (BFA) [1], and get the tight upper bound $2^n + n$ for the square on BFAs. To prove these results, we take the reversal of a language accepted by a DFA with 2^n states with half of them final meeting the corresponding upper bound for square on DFAs. Then this language is accepted by an n-state BFA, and we are able to prove that every BFA for its square has at least $2^n + n$ states. By more careful analysis of the number of final states in DFA for its square, we get the lower bound $2^n + n + 1$ for the square operation on AFAs. Our result can be extended for the concatenation operation just by concatenating two of our automata with different number of states. This provides an alternative proof of the tightness of the upper bound $2^m + n + 1$ for the concatenation operation on alternating automata with m and n states [4].

2 Preliminaries

Let Σ be a finite alphabet of symbols. Then Σ^* denotes the set of words over Σ including the empty word ε. A language is any subset of Σ^*. The concatenation of languages K and L is the language $KL = \{uv \mid u \in K \text{ and } v \in L\}$. The square of a language L is the language $L^2 = LL$. The cardinality of a finite set A is denoted by $|A|$, and its power-set by 2^A. The reader may refer to [9] for details.

A *nondeterministic finite automaton* (NFA) is a quintuple $A = (Q, \Sigma, \circ, I, F)$, where Q is a finite set of states, Σ is a finite non-empty alphabet, $\circ : Q \times \Sigma \to 2^Q$ is the transition function which is naturally extended to the domain $2^Q \times \Sigma^*$, $I \subseteq Q$ is the set of initial states, and $F \subseteq Q$ is the set of final states. The *language accepted by* A is the set $L(A) = \{w \in \Sigma^* \mid I \circ w \cap F \ne \emptyset\}$. For a symbol a, we say that (p, a, q) is a transition in NFA A if $q \in p \circ a$, and for a word w, we write $p \xrightarrow{w} q$ if $q \in p \circ w$. An NFA A is *deterministic* (DFA) (and complete) if $|I| = 1$ and $|q \circ a| = 1$ for each q in Q and each a in Σ. We write $p \cdot a = q$ instead of $p \circ a = \{q\}$ in such a case. The *state complexity* of a regular language L, $\mathrm{sc}(L)$, is the smallest number of states in any DFA for L.

Every NFA $A = (Q, \Sigma, \circ, I, F)$ can be converted to an equivalent DFA $A' = (2^Q, \Sigma, \cdot, I, F')$, where $R \cdot a = R \circ a$ for each R in 2^Q and a in Σ, and $F' = \{R \in 2^Q \mid R \cap F \neq \emptyset\}$. We call the DFA A' the *subset automaton* of the NFA A. The subset automaton may not be minimal since some of its states may be unreachable or equivalent to other states.

A *Boolean finite automaton* (BFA) is a quintuple $A = (Q, \Sigma, \delta, g_s, F)$, where Q is a finite non-empty set of states, $Q = \{q_1, \ldots, q_n\}$, Σ is an input alphabet, δ is the transition function that maps $Q \times \Sigma$ into the set $\mathcal{B}_n$ of Boolean functions with variables $\{q_1, \ldots, q_n\}$, $g_s \in \mathcal{B}$ is the initial Boolean function, and $F \subseteq Q$ is the set of final states. The transition function δ is extended to the domain $\mathcal{B}_n \times \Sigma^*$ as follows: For all g in $\mathcal{B}_n$, a in Σ, and w in Σ^*, we have $\delta(g, \varepsilon) = g$; if $g = g(q_1, \ldots, q_n)$, then $\delta(g, a) = g(\delta(q_1, a), \ldots, \delta(q_n, a))$; $\delta(g, wa) = \delta(\delta(g, w), a)$. Next, let $f = (f_1, \ldots, f_n)$ be the Boolean vector with $f_i = 1$ iff $q_i \in F$. The language accepted by the BFA A is the set $L(A) = \{w \in \Sigma^* \mid \delta(g_s, w)(f) = 1\}$.

A Boolean finite automaton is called *alternating* (AFA) if the initial function is a projection $g(q_1, \ldots, q_n) = q_i$. For details, the reader may refer to [1,3,5,6,9]. The Boolean (alternating) state complexity of L, $\mathrm{bsc}(L)(\mathrm{asc}(L))$, is the smallest number of states in any BFA (AFA) for L. It is known that a language L is accepted by an n-state BFA (AFA) if and only if the language L^R is accepted by an 2^n-state DFA (with 2^{n-1} final states). We state it in the next two facts.

Fact 1 (cf. [3] Theorem 4.1, Corollary 4.2 and [5], Lemma 1). *Let L be a language accepted by an n-state BFA (AFA). Then the reversal L^R is accepted by a DFA of 2^n states (of which 2^{n-1} are final).*   □

Corollary 2. *If L is a regular language, than $\mathrm{bsc}(L) \geq \lceil \log(\mathrm{sc}(L^R)) \rceil$ and $\mathrm{asc}(L) \geq \lceil \log(\mathrm{sc}(L^R)) \rceil$.*   □

Fact 3 (cf. [5], Lemma 2). *If L^R be accepted by a DFA A of 2^n states, then L is accepted by an n-state BFA. If L^R be accepted by a DFA A of 2^n states of which 2^{n-1} are final, then L is accepted by an n-state AFA.*   □

3   Square on DFAs

Let us begin with the precise method of construction an NFA for the square of some languages accepted by a minimal DFA with n states.

Construction 4. (DFA $A \to$ NFA N for $L^2(A)$)
Let $A = (\{q_0, q_1, \ldots, q_{n-1}\}, \Sigma, \cdot, q_0, F_A)$ be a minimal DFA. We construct NFA $N = (\{q_0, q_1, \ldots, q_{n-1}\} \cup \{0, 1, \ldots, n-1\}, \Sigma, \circ, I, F_N)$ as follows:

(a) take A and add a copy of A with the state set $\{0, 1, \ldots, n-1\}$;
(b) for each symbol a and each state q_i with $q_i \cdot a \in F_A$, add transition $(q_i, a, 0)$;

(c) the set of initial states of N is $I = \{q_0\}$ if $q_0 \notin F$, and $I = \{q_0, 0\}$ otherwise;
(d) the set of final state of N is $F_N = \{j \in \{0, 1, \ldots, n-1\} \mid q_j \in F_A\}$.

Proposition 5 (Upper Bound). *Let L be a language with $\mathrm{sc}(L) = n$, and let the minimal DFA for L have k final states. Then $\mathrm{sc}(L^2) \leq n2^n - k2^{n-1}$.*

Proof. Let L be accepted by DFA $A = (\{q_0, q_1, \ldots, q_{n-1}\}, \Sigma, \cdot, q_0, F_A)$ and let $|F_A| = k$. Construct an NFA N for L^2 as described above. Since A is deterministic, every reachable subset in the subset automaton of N is in the form of $\{q_i\} \cup S$, where $S \subseteq \{0, 1, \ldots, n-1\}$. Furthermore, if q_i is a final state of A, then $0 \in S$ because of the used construction. It follows that subsets containing a final state of A and missing 0 are unreachable. Hence the subset automaton of N has at most $n2^n - k2^{n-1}$ reachable states. □

Notice that the upper bound given by above proposition is maximal if $k = 1$, and it is $n2^n - 2^{n-1}$ in this case. The binary witness language meeting this bound was presented by Rampersad in 2006 [8].

Theorem 6 [8, Theorem 1]. *For every integer $n \geq 3$, there exists a DFA M with n states such that the minimal DFA accepting the language $L^2(M)$ has $n2^n - 2^{n-1}$ states.* □

Unfortunately, the square of Rampersad's automaton with k final states does not meet the upper bound on the state complexity in the general case. Here we provide the binary witness automaton with k final states that meets the upper bound $n2^n - k2^{n-1}$.

Theorem 7. *Let $n \geq 3$ and $1 \leq k \leq n-2$. Then there exists a minimal n-state DFA A with k final states defined over a binary alphabet such that every DFA for $L(A)^2$ has at least $n2^n - k2^{n-1}$ states.*

Proof. Let us take n-state DFA $A = (\{q_0, q_1, \ldots, q_{n-1}\}, \Sigma, \cdot, q_0, F_A)$ with k final states shown in Fig. 1. Notice that q_0 and q_1 remain non-final with every k in this DFA and there are two cycles; one on a, $(q_0, q_1, \ldots, q_{n-1})$, of length n and the second on b, $(q_2, q_3, \ldots, q_{n-1})$, of length $n - 2$.

Let us build an NFA N for $L(A)^2$ as in Construction 4. An example of NFA N if $n = 6$ and $k = 2$ is shown in Fig. 2.

We observe that there are only two types of states reachable in the subset automaton of N:

- $\{q_i\} \cup S$, where $S \subseteq \{0, 1, \ldots, n-1\}$ and $0 \leq i \leq n - k - 1$;
- $\{q_i, 0\} \cup S$, where $S \subseteq \{1, \ldots, n-1\}$ and $n - k \leq i \leq n - 1$.

We denote this family of sets as $\mathcal{R}$. We can see that in $\mathcal{R}$ there are exactly $(n - k)2^n + k2^{n-1} = n2^n - k2^{n-1}$ sets. Our goal is to show that the sets in $\mathcal{R}$ are reachable and also pairwise distinguishable in the subset automaton of N for $L(A)^2$.

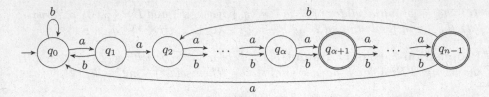

Fig. 1. A witness DFA A with k final states meeting the bound $n2^n - k2^{n-1}$, where $\alpha = n - k - 1$.

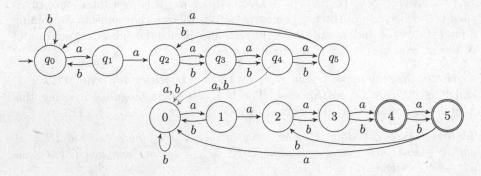

Fig. 2. NFA N for square of $L(A)$, if $n = 6$ and $k = 2$.

Let us start with reachability. We use mathematical induction by number of elements in set/state. The sets with one and two elements are reachable, because:

$$\rightarrow \{q_0\} \xrightarrow{a} \{q_1\} \xrightarrow{a} \cdots \xrightarrow{a} \{q_{n-k-1}\} \xrightarrow{a} \{q_{n-k}, 0\},$$

$$\{q_{n-k}, 0\} \xrightarrow{b} \{q_{n-k+1}, 0\} \xrightarrow{b} \cdots \xrightarrow{b} \{q_{n-2}, 0\} \xrightarrow{b} \{q_{n-1}, 0\},$$

$$\{q_{n-1}, 0\} \xrightarrow{a} \{q_0, 1\} \xrightarrow{b} \{q_0, 0\},$$

$$\{q_0, 1\} \xrightarrow{a} \{q_1, 2\} \xrightarrow{b} \{q_0, 3\} \xrightarrow{b} \{q_0, 4\} \xrightarrow{b} \cdots \xrightarrow{b} \{q_0, n-1\} \xrightarrow{b} \{q_0, 2\},$$

$$\{q_0, (j - i) \bmod n\} \xrightarrow{a^i} \{q_i, j\} \text{ for } i = 0, 1, \ldots, n - k - 1 \text{ and } j = 0, 1, \ldots, n - 1.$$

Assume now that every set in $\mathcal{R}$ with t elements is reachable. We show that then every set in $\mathcal{R}$ of size $t + 1$ is reachable. Let $S = \{q_i, s_1, s_2, \ldots, s_t\}$ be our desired set in $\mathcal{R}$ of size $t + 1$, where $q_i \in Q$ and $0 \leq s_1 < s_2 < \cdots < s_t \leq n - 1$. We deal with three cases:

(1) We show the reachability of sets of the second type, so let $n - k \leq i \leq n - 1$ and therefore $s_1 = 0$. We can write i as $i = \alpha + \beta$, where $\alpha = n - k - 1$ and $0 \leq \beta \leq k$, so our desired set is $S = \{q_{\alpha+\beta}, 0, s_2, s_3, \ldots, s_t\}$.

Let $s_2 = 1$, and take the set $\{q_{\alpha+\beta-1}, 0, s_3 - 1, \ldots, s_t - 1\}$, which is in $\mathcal{R}$ and is reachable because it has t elements. Then we have

$$\{q_{\alpha+\beta-1}, 0, s_3 - 1, \ldots, s_t - 1\} \xrightarrow{a} \{q_{\alpha+\beta}, 0, 1, s_3, \ldots, s_t\} = S.$$

Let $s_2 \geq 2$ and take the set $\{q_\alpha, s_2 \cdot b^{n-1-\beta} - 1, \ldots, s_t \cdot b^{n-1-\beta} - 1\}$, which is in $\mathcal{R}$ and is reachable because it has t elements. Then we have

$$\{q_\alpha, s_2 \cdot b^{n-1-\beta} - 1, \ldots, s_t \cdot b^{n-1-\beta'} - 1\} \xrightarrow{a} \{q_{\alpha+1}, s_2 \cdot b^{n-1-\beta}, \ldots, s_t \cdot b^{n-1-\beta}\}$$

$$\xrightarrow{b^{\beta-1}} \{q_{\alpha+\beta}, 0, s_2 \cdot b^{n-2}, \ldots, s_t \cdot b^{n-2}\} = \{q_{\alpha+\beta}, 0, s_2, \ldots, s_t\} = S.$$

(2) Next we show the reachability of sets of the first type in the next two steps. Let $i = 0$. We distinguish between three cases of s_1.

Firstly let $s_1 = 0$. We start from the set reached previously in (1) to achieve S in case of $s_2 = 1$ by $\{q_{n-1}, 0, s_3 - 1, \ldots, s_t - 1, n - 1\} \xrightarrow{a} \{q_0, 0, 1, s_3, \ldots, s_t\} = S$. Otherwise, if desired $s_2 \geq 2$, we reach S using previously reached set

$$\{q_0, 0, 1, s_3 - s_2 + 1, \ldots, s_t - s_2 + 1\} \xrightarrow{a} \{q_1, 1, 2, s_3 - s_2 + 2, \ldots, s_t - s_2 + 2\}$$

$$\xrightarrow{b^{n-2}} \{q_0, 0, 2, s_3 - s_2 + 2, \ldots, s_t - s_2 + 2\} \xrightarrow{b^{s_2-2}} \{q_0, 0, s_2, \ldots, s_t\} = S.$$

Secondly let $s_1 \geq 1$. Then the set $S' = \{q_{n-1}, 0, s_2 - s_1, \ldots, s_t - s_1\}$ is reached in (1). If $s_1 = 1$, then $S' \xrightarrow{a} S$, otherwise $s_1 \geq 2$, and $S' \xrightarrow{aab^{n-2}b^{s_1-2}} S$.

(3) Let $1 \leq i \leq n - k - 1$. Now we can reach the remaining sets of the first type using sets achieved in (2) like this $\{q_0, (s_1 - i) \bmod n, \ldots, (s_t - i) \bmod n\} \xrightarrow{a^i} \{q_i, s_1, \ldots, s_t\} = S.$

Let us continue with proving distinguishability of reached sets. Note that in N we have

$$\{n - 1\} \xrightarrow{b} \{2\} \xrightarrow{a} \{3\} \xrightarrow{b^{n-2}} \{3\} \xrightarrow{ab^{n-2}} \{4\} \xrightarrow{ab^{n-2}} \cdots \xrightarrow{ab^{n-2}} \{n - 1\}.$$

This means that the word $w = b(ab^{n-2})^{n-3}$ is accepted from the state $n - 1$. Let us read w from a different state t, $2 \leq t \leq n - 2$. First we have $t \circ b \in \{3, 4, \ldots, n - 1\}$. Next $\{3, 4, \ldots, n - 1\} \circ (ab^{n-2})^{n-3} = \{0\}$, so w is not accepted from t. Similarly, reading w from $\{0, 1\}$ results in the set $\{0\}$, thus w is not accepted from $\{0, 1\}$ either. Moreover, w is not accepted from $\{q_i\}$, because $\{q_i\} \circ w \subseteq \{q_j, 0\}$, where either $j = 0$ if $i < n - 1$, or $j = n - 1$ if $i = n - 1$. Therefore w is accepted by N from and only from the state $n - 1$. Notice that each state t in $\{1, 2, \ldots, n - 1\}$ has exactly one in-transition on a going from the state $t - 1$, so the word $a^{n-1-t}w$ is accepted by N only from state t, $0 \leq t \leq n - 2$. It follows that two sets $\{q_i\} \cup S$ and $\{q_j\} \cup T$ in $\mathcal{R}$ are distinguishable if $S \neq T$.

Now consider two distinct subsets $\{q_i\} \cup S$ and $\{q_j\} \cup S$ in $\mathcal{R}$. Without loss of generality, we have $0 \leq i < j \leq n - 1$. We will discuss three cases:

(1) Let $i = 0$ and $j = 1$. Then

$$\{q_0\} \cup S \xrightarrow{(ab^{n-2})^{n-2}} \{q_0, 0\} \xrightarrow{a} \{q_1, 1\} \xrightarrow{a^{n-k-1}} \{q_{n-k}, 0, n - k\},$$

$$\{q_1\} \cup S \xrightarrow{(ab^{n-2})^{n-2}} \{q_{n-1}, 0\} \xrightarrow{a} \{q_0, 1\} \xrightarrow{a^{n-k-1}} \{q_{n-k-1}, n - k\}.$$

Now we can distinguish these sets because they differ in the element from the second automaton copy.

(2) Let $i = 0$ and $j \geq 2$. Then

$$\{q_0\} \cup S \xrightarrow{b^{n-1-j}a} \{q_1\} \cup S_1,$$

$$\{q_j\} \cup S \xrightarrow{b^{n-1-j}a} \{q_0\} \cup S_1'.$$

If the subsets S_1 and S_1' are the same, then we continue as in (1), otherwise we continue as in case of $S \neq T$.

(3) Let $i \geq 1$. Then

$$\{q_i\} \cup S \xrightarrow{a^{n-j}} \{q_{i+(n-j)}\} \cup S_1,$$

$$\{q_j\} \cup S \xrightarrow{a^{n-j}} \{q_0\} \cup S_1'.$$

Similarly as in (2), if the subsets S_1 and S_1' are the same we continue as in (1) or (2), otherwise we continue as in case of $S \neq T$.   □

3.1   Square if $|F| = n - 1$

Recall that the automaton in the proof of Theorem 7 must have at least two non-final states. We show that for every language L accepted by an n-state DFA $A = (Q, \Sigma, \cdot, q_0, F)$ with a single non-final state, the state complexity of L^2 never meets the upper bound set in Proposition 5. In particular, we show:

(a) if $q_0 \in F$, then $\mathrm{sc}(L^2) \leq (n+2)2^{n-2}$ and this bound is tight if $|\Sigma| \geq 2$;
(b) if $q_0 \notin F$, then $\mathrm{sc}(L^2) \leq (n+3)2^{n-2}$ and this bound is tight if $|\Sigma| \geq 3$.

First, we consider the case of $|F| = n - 1$ and $q_0 \in F$.

Lemma 8. *Let $n \geq 3$ and let L be a regular language accepted by an n-state DFA $A = (Q, \Sigma, \delta, q_0, F)$ with $n - 1$ final states, where $q_0 \in F$. Then $\mathrm{sc}(L^2) \leq (n+2)2^{n-2}$, and this bound is tight if $|\Sigma| \geq 2$.*

Proof. The formula for the upper bound is based on the observation that q_0 is initial and also accepting in A, so the initial state in the subset automaton for $L(A)^2$ is $\{q_0, 0\}$. It follows that for every $i \in \{0, 1, \ldots, n-1\}$ if $\{q_i\} \cup X$ is reachable, then $i \in X$. So we consider the following family $\mathcal{R}$ of possible sets in the subset automaton for $L(A)^2$:

$$\begin{aligned}\mathcal{R} = &\{\{q_0, 0\} \cup X \mid X \subseteq \{1, 2, \ldots, n-1\}\} \ \cup \\ &\{\{q_1, 1\} \cup X \mid X \subseteq \{0, 2, 3, \ldots, n-1\}\} \ \cup \\ &\{\{q_i, 0, i\} \cup X \mid 2 \leq i \leq n-1, X \subseteq \{1, 2, \ldots, n-1\} \setminus \{i\}\}.\end{aligned}$$

This family consists of $(n+2)2^{n-2}$ sets. Hence $\mathrm{sc}(L^2) \leq (n+2)2^{n-2}$. To prove the tightness of this upper bound, we introduce the DFA A shown in Fig. 3 and we show that every DFA for $L(A)^2$ has at least $(n+2)2^{n-2}$ states. Notice that A has the same structure as the DFA in the Fig. 1, so the proof continues similarly as the proof of Theorem 7.   □

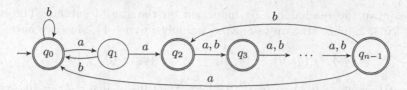

Fig. 3. A witness DFA A with $n-1$ final states meeting the bound $(n+2)2^{n-2}$, where $q_0 \in F$.

Now we consider the case where $|F| = n - 1$ and $q_0 \notin F$.

Lemma 9. *Let $n \geq 3$. Let L be a regular language accepted by an n-state DFA $A = (Q, \Sigma, \cdot, q_0, F)$, where $|F| = n - 1$ and $q_0 \notin F$. Then $\mathrm{sc}(L^2) \leq (n+3)2^{n-2}$, and the bound is tight if $|\Sigma| \geq 3$. The bound $(n+3)2^{n-2} - 1$ can be met by a binary language.*

Proof. We start with the upper bound. Suppose we have constructed an NFA N from the DFA A as described in Construction 4. Consider the corresponding subset automaton of N. We first show that two distinct subsets of this automaton, $\{q_i\} \cup S$ and $\{q_j\} \cup S$, where $\{i, j\} \subseteq S$ are equivalent. If a word w is rejected from state $\{q_i\} \cup S$ then $s \xrightarrow{w} 0$ for each element s in S. It follows that w is rejected from $\{q_j\} \cup S$ because $\{q_j\} \cup S \xrightarrow{w} \{q_0, 0\}$. Likewise, if w is rejected from $\{q_j\} \cup S$ then w is rejected from $\{q_i\} \cup S$. Excluding these equivalent subsets gives us the family $\mathcal{R}$ of $(n+3)2^{n-2}$ reachable and pairwise distinguishable subsets of the subset automaton of N, which is:

$$\mathcal{R} = \{\{q_0\} \cup X \mid X \subseteq \{0, 1, \ldots, n-1\}\} \ \cup$$
$$\{\{q_i\} \cup X \mid X \subseteq \{0, 1, \ldots, n-1\}, 0 \in X, i \notin X\}.$$

To prove the tightness of this upper bound, we introduce the DFA B shown in Fig. 4 and we show that every DFA for $L(B)^2$ has at least $(n+3)2^{n-2}$ states. Construct an NFA N for the square of $L(B)^2$ as described in Construction 4. Let us show that each set in $\mathcal{R}$ is reachable in the subset automaton of N and that all these sets are pairwise distinguishable.

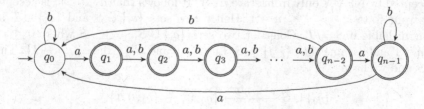

Fig. 4. A binary DFA B with $\mathrm{sc}(L^2(B)) = (n+3)2^{n-2} - 1$.

We prove the reachability by induction on the size of subsets. The basis, where $|S| \leq 2$, holds true up to one set, namely $\{q_0, n-1\}$, since we have

$$\rightarrow \{q_0\} \xrightarrow{a} \{q_1, 0\} \xrightarrow{b} \{q_2, 0\} \xrightarrow{b} \cdots \xrightarrow{b} \{q_{n-2}, 0\} \xrightarrow{b} \{q_0, 0\},$$

$$\{q_{n-2}, 0\} \xrightarrow{a} \{q_{n-1}, 0, 1\} \xrightarrow{b} \{q_{n-1}, 0, 2\} \xrightarrow{b} \cdots \xrightarrow{b} \{q_{n-1}, 0, n-2\} \xrightarrow{b} \{q_{n-1}, 0\},$$

$$\{q_{n-1}, 0\} \xrightarrow{a} \{q_0, 1\} \xrightarrow{b} \{q_0, 2\} \xrightarrow{b} \cdots \xrightarrow{b} \{q_0, n-2\}.$$

We deal with $\{q_0, n-1\}$ later. Now assume that each set in $\mathcal{R}$ of size t is reachable. Let $S = \{q_i, s_1, s_2, \ldots, s_t\}$ be a set of size $t+1$. Consider several cases.

(1) Let $i = 1$, so $s_1 = 0$. Then $\{q_0, s_2 - 1, \ldots, s_t - 1\} \xrightarrow{a} \{q_1, 0, s_2, \ldots, s_t\}$, where the former set of size t is reachable by induction hypothesis.

(2) Let $1 \leq i \leq n-2$, so $S = \{q_i, 0, s_2, s_3, \ldots, s_t\}$.

If $s_2 = 1$, then $\qquad\qquad\qquad\qquad \{q_{i-1}, 0, s_3 - 1, \ldots, s_t - 1\} \xrightarrow{a} S$.

If $s_2 \geq 2$ and $s_t \leq n-2$, then $\qquad\quad \{q_{i-1}, 0, s_2 - 1, \ldots, s_t - 1\} \xrightarrow{b} S$.

If $s_2 \geq 2$ and $s_t = n-1$, then $\quad \{q_{i-1}, 0, s_2 - 1, \ldots, s_{t-1} - 1, n-1\} \xrightarrow{b} S$.

This induction step with case (1) as the basis proves case (2) by induction on i.

(3) Let $i = n-1$, so $S = \{q_{n-1}, 0, s_2, s_3, \ldots, s_t\}$. Consider two cases of s_t.

If $s_t \leq n-2$, then $\qquad\qquad \{q_{n-2}, 0, s_3 - s_2, \ldots, s_t - s_2\} \xrightarrow{ab^{s_2-1}} S$.

If $s_t = n-1$, then $\quad \{q_{n-2}, 0, s_3 - s_2, \ldots, s_{t-1} - s_2, n-2\} \xrightarrow{ab^{s_2-1}} S$.

The starting set is reachable by induction on t in both cases.

(4) Let $i = 0$, so $S = \{q_0, s_1, s_2, \ldots, s_t\}$. We consider four cases of s_1 and s_t:

If $s_1 = 0, s_t \leq n-2$, then $\qquad \{q_{n-1}, 0, n-1, s_3 - s_2, \ldots, s_t - s_2\} \xrightarrow{ab^{s_2-1}} S$.

If $s_1 = 0, s_t = n-1$, then $\{q_{n-1}, 0, n-1, s_3 - s_2, \ldots, s_{t-1} - s_2, n-2\} \xrightarrow{ab^{s_2-1}} S$.

If $s_1 \geq 1, s_t \leq n-2$, then $\qquad\qquad \{q_{n-1}, 0, s_2 - s_1, \ldots, s_t - s_1\} \xrightarrow{ab^{s_1-1}} S$.

If $s_1 \geq 1, s_t = n-1$, then $\qquad \{q_{n-1}, 0, s_2 - s_1, \ldots, s_{t-1} - s_1, n-2\} \xrightarrow{ab^{s_1-1}} S$.

The starting sets are considered in case (3).

This proves reachability. To prove distinguishability, notice that the word b^n is accepted by NFA N only from state $n-1$. It follows that $a^{n-1-t}b^n$ is accepted only from state t, $0 \leq t \leq n-1$. Hence two sets $\{q_i\} \cup S$ and $\{q_j\} \cup T$ are distinguishable if $S \neq T$. Consider two sets $\{q_i\} \cup S$, $\{q_j\} \cup S$ where $0 \leq i < j \leq n-1$ and assume that $\{i, j\} \not\subseteq S$. Let $i = 0$ and $S \subseteq \{0, 1, \ldots, n-1\}$. Then $j \notin S$ and we have

$$\{q_0\} \cup S \xrightarrow{a^{n-1-j}b^n} \{q_0, 0\} \xrightarrow{a} \{q_1, 0, 1\},$$

$$\{q_j\} \cup S \xrightarrow{a^{n-1-j}b^n} \{q_{n-1}, 0\} \xrightarrow{a} \{q_0, 1\},$$

where the resulting states differ in state 0. If $i \geq 1$, then we use a^{n-j} to get the case above.

Up to now, we reached all sets in $\mathcal{R}$ except for $\{q_0, n-1\}$. This set remains unreachable because of the inability to reach it by a nor b from other state. Hence $\mathrm{sc}(L^2(B)) = (n+3)2^{n-2} - 1$. To reach the set $\{q_0, n-1\}$, we add one more symbol to B. We define the transitions on the symbol c as follows:

$$\delta(q_0, c) = q_0; \quad \delta(q_i, c) = q_{i+i} \text{ if } 1 \leq i \leq n-2; \quad \delta(q_{n-1}, c) = q_0.$$

Denote the resulting DFA over $\{a, b, c\}$ by C. Then in the corresponding subset automaton for $L^2(C)$ the set $\{q_0, n-1\}$ is reachable from $\{q_0, n-2\}$ by c. Thus $\mathrm{sc}(L^2(C)) = (n+3)2^{n-2}$. □

As a corollary of the two lemmas above, we get the next result.

Corollary 10. *Let $n \geq 3$ and L be a language over Σ accepted by an n-state DFA in which $n-1$ states are final. Then $\mathrm{sc}(L^2) \leq (n+3)2^{n-2}$, and this bound is tight if $|\Sigma| \geq 3$. The bound $(n+3)2^{n-2} - 1$ is met by a binary language.* □

We tested the state complexity of square on all binary automata with 3, 4 and 5 states where the initial state is the only non-final state. But we did not find any binary automaton with the state complexity of its square greater than $(n+3)2^{n-2} - 1$. The following result shows that this lower bound is tight for every $n \geq 4$ on a binary alphabet.

Theorem 11. *Let $n \geq 4$ and L be a binary language accepted by an n-state DFA in which $n-1$ states are final. Then $\mathrm{sc}(L^2) \leq (n+3)2^{n-2} - 1$, and this bound is tight.*

Proof Idea. We already showed the witness language with $\mathrm{sc}(L^2) \geq (n+3)2^{n-2}-1$ in Lemma 9. It remains to show that the upper bound $(n+3)2^{n-2}$ cannot be met in binary case.

The reason of missing the upper bound by one was not reaching the $\{q_0, n-1\}$ in the subset automaton for the square in the first place. So to find a harder DFA for square than B in Fig. 4 we need to reach all possible distinguishable states. We found out that our desired automaton must have certain transitions to reach them. For example, transitions on a must form a permutation and transitions on b are exactly as in DFA B in Fig. 4. But these certain transitions plus our original restrictions for this case counteract our effort to distinguish these states. It follows that if some subset automaton for the square has $(n+3)2^{n-2}$ reachable states, many of them are equivalent. Thus the state complexity $(n+3)2^{n-2} - 1$ is the best that we can do. □

3.2 Square on Unary DFAs

To complete the overview about the square operation on deterministic automata we should not forget unary alphabets. We refer to the paper by Rampersad [8] once again. Notice that the complexity of square in this case is exponentially smaller than in the binary case.

Theorem 12 [8, Theorems 3 and 4 with $k = 2$]. *Let L be a unary language with $\mathrm{sc}(L) = n$. Then $\mathrm{sc}(L^2) \leq 2n - 1$ and the bound is tight.*

4   Square on AFAs and BFAs

Fellah et al. in [3, Theorem 9.3] showed that if a language K is accepted by an m-state AFA and a language L is accepted by an n-state AFA, then the language KL is accepted by an AFA of at most $2^m + n + 1$ states. It follows that $2^n + n + 1$ is an upper bound for the square on AFAs. Here we use our results from the previous section to prove tightness of this upper bound. For the square on BFAs, we get the tight upper bound $2^n + n$. Recall that $\mathrm{asc}(L)$ is the smallest number of states in any AFA for L and $\mathrm{bsc}(L)$ is defined analogously.

Theorem 13 (Square on AFAs). *Let $n \geq 2$. Let L be a regular language over Σ with $\mathrm{asc}(L) = n$. Then $\mathrm{asc}(L^2) \leq 2^n + n + 1$, and the bound is tight if $|\Sigma| \geq 2$.*

Proof. From given upper bound from [3, Theorem 9.3] we know that $\mathrm{asc}(L^2) \leq 2^n + n + 1$. For tightness, let L^R be the language accepted by the DFA A defined in the proof of Theorem 7 with 2^n states where half of the state are final, that is, $k = 2^{n-1}$. By Fact 3, L is accepted by AFA with n states. Using Theorem 7 we know that $\mathrm{sc}((L^R)^2) = 2^n 2^{2^n} - 2^{n-1} 2^{2^n - 1}$. By Corollary 2, $\mathrm{asc}(L^2) \geq \lceil \log(\mathrm{sc}((L^R)^2)) \rceil = 2^n + n$.

Suppose for a contradiction that L^2 is accepted by an AFA with $2^n + n$ states. By Fact 1, the language $(L^2)^R$ is accepted by a $2^{2^n + n}$- state DFA with $2^{2^n + n - 1}$ final states. It follows that the minimal DFA for $(L^2)^R$ has at most $2^{2^n + n - 1}$ final states. However, the minimal DFA for the language $(L^2)^R$ has $2^n 2^{2^n} - 2^{n-1} 2^{2^n - 1} = 2^{n-1} 2^{2^n} + 2^{n-1} 2^{2^n - 1}$ states, where $2^{n-1} 2^{2^{n-1}} + 2^{n-1} 2^{2^{n-1} - 1}$ of them are non-final. Thus the number of final states in the minimal DFA for $(L^2)^R$ is $2^{n-1}(2^{2^n} + 2^{2^n - 1}) - 2^{n-1}(2^{2^{n-1}} + 2^{2^{n-1} - 1})$, and since $n \geq 2$, we get

$$2^{n-1}(2^{2^n} + 2^{2^n - 1}) - 2^{n-1}(2^{2^{n-1}} + 2^{2^{n-1} - 1}) =$$
$$2^{2^n} 2^{n-1}(1 + \frac{1}{2} - \frac{1}{2^{2^{n-1}}} - \frac{1}{2^{2^{n-1}+1}}) >$$
$$2^{2^n + n - 1}(1 + \frac{1}{2} - \frac{1}{4} - \frac{1}{4}) = 2^{2^n + n - 1}.$$

Hence the minimal DFA for $(L^2)^R$ has more than $2^{2^n + n - 1}$ final states, a contradiction. It follows that $\mathrm{asc}(L^2) \geq 2^n + n + 1$.   □

Theorem 14 (Square on BFAs). *Let $n \geq 2$. Let L be a regular language over Σ with $\mathrm{bsc}(L) = n$. Then $\mathrm{bsc}(L^2) \leq 2^n + n$, and the bound is tight if $|\Sigma| \geq 2$.*

Proof. The upper bound follows from the upper bound $2^m + n$ on the complexity of the concatenation operation on BFAs [5, Theorem 4]. Let L^R be a language accepted by DFA A from Fig. 1 with 2^n states and one final state. By Fact 3, L is accepted by an n-state BFA. We are able to determine the state complexity of $(L^R)^2$ using Theorem 7: $\mathrm{sc}((L^R)^2) = 2^n \cdot 2^{2^n} - 2^{2^n - 1}$. By Corollary 2,

$$\mathrm{bsc}(L^2) \geq \lceil \log(2^n \cdot 2^{2^n} - 2^{2^n - 1}) \rceil = 2^n + n.$$

□

5   Conclusions

We studied the state complexity of the square of languages represented by deterministic, alternating, and Boolean finite automata. First, for each k such that $1 \leq k \leq n - 2$, we showed that the upper bound $n2^n - k2^{n-1}$ on the square of languages represented by n-state DFAs with k final states is tight in the binary case. Then we analysed the case of $n - 1$ final states, where we proved that the bound $(2n + 2)2^{n-2}$ cannot be met. We provided the tight upper bound $(n + 2)2^{n-2}$ for the case when the initial state is final and we found a binary witness. When the initial state is the only non-final state, we obtained the upper bound $(n + 3)2^{n-2}$ with a ternary witness. In the binary case we proved that the tight upper bound is $(n + 3)2^{n-2} - 1$.

Finally, we used our results on the square on DFAs to describe binary witness languages meeting the upper bounds $2^n + n + 1$ and $2^n + n$ for square on alternating and Boolean finite automata, respectively. Our results can be extended for the concatenation operation just by concatenating two of our automata with different number of states. This provides an alternative solution for the open problem stated by Fellah et al. in [3].

References

1. Brzozowski, J.A., Leiss, E.L.: On equations for regular languages, finite automata, and sequential networks. Theor. Comput. Sci. **10**, 19–35 (1980). http://dx.doi.org/10.1016/0304-3975(80)90069-9
2. Čevorová, K., Jirásková, G., Krajňáková, I.: On the square of regular languages. In: Holzer, M., Kutrib, M. (eds.) CIAA 2014. LNCS, vol. 8587, pp. 136–147. Springer, Cham (2014). http://dx.doi.org/10.1007/978-3-319-08846-4_10
3. Fellah, A., Jürgensen, H., Yu, S.: Constructions for alternating finite automata. Int. J. Comput. Math. **35**(1–4), 117–132 (1990). http://dx.doi.org/10.1080/00207169008803893
4. Hospodár, M., Jirásková, G.: Concatenation on deterministic and alternating automata. In: Bordihn, H., Freund, R., Nagy, B., Vaszil, G. (eds.) NCMA 2016, vol. 321, pp. 179–194. Österreichische Computer Gesellschaft, books@ocg.at (2016)
5. Jirásková, G.: Descriptional complexity of operations on alternating and boolean automata. In: Hirsch, E.A., Karhumäki, J., Lepistö, A., Prilutskii, M. (eds.) CSR 2012. LNCS, vol. 7353, pp. 196–204. Springer, Heidelberg (2012). doi:10.1007/978-3-642-30642-6_19
6. Leiss, E.L.: Succint representation of regular languages by boolean automata. Theor. Comput. Sci. **13**, 323–330 (1981)
7. Maslov, A.N.: Estimates of the number of states of finite automata. Soviet Math. Doklady **11**, 1373–1375 (1970)
8. Rampersad, N.: The state complexity of L^2 and L^k. Inf. Process. Lett. **98**(6), 231–234 (2006). http://dx.doi.org/10.1016/j.ipl.2005.06.011
9. Sipser, M.: Introduction to the Theory of Computation. Cengage Learning, Boston (2012)
10. Yu, S., Zhuang, Q., Salomaa, K.: The state complexities of some basic operations on regular languages. Theor. Comput. Sci. **125**(2), 315–328 (1994). http://dx.doi.org/10.1016/0304-3975(92)00011-F

A Pumping Lemma for Ordered Restarting Automata

Kent Kwee and Friedrich Otto[✉]

Fachbereich Elektrotechnik/Informatik, Universität Kassel, 34109 Kassel, Germany
{kwee,otto}@theory.informatik.uni-kassel.de

Abstract. While stateless ordered restarting automata accept exactly the regular languages, it is known that ordered restarting automata with states accept some languages that are not even growing context-sensitive. In fact, the class of languages accepted by these automata is an abstract family of languages that is incomparable to the (deterministic) linear languages, the (deterministic) context-free languages, and the growing context-sensitive languages with respect to inclusion, and the emptiness problem is decidable for these automata. These results were derived using a Cut-and-Paste Lemma for ordered restarting automata that is based on Higman's theorem. Here we extend the arguments used in that proof to actually derive a real Pumping Lemma for these automata. Based on this Pumping Lemma, we then prove that the finiteness problem is also decidable for these automata, and that the only unary languages these automata accept are the regular ones.

Keywords: Restarting automaton · Ordered rewriting · Pumping lemma · Finiteness problem

1 Introduction

The *ordered restarting automaton* (ORWW-automaton for short) was introduced in [9], where its deterministic variant was extended into a device for recognizing picture languages. An ORWW-automaton (for words) has a finite-state control, a tape with end markers that initially contains the input, and a window of size three. Based on its state and the content of its window, the automaton can either perform a *move-right step*, a *rewrite/restart step*, or an *accept step*. While the deterministic variant of the ORWW-automaton characterizes the regular languages, it has been observed that the nondeterministic variant is more expressive. In fact, the nondeterministic ORWW-automaton and the languages it accepts have been studied in some detail in [6], where it is shown that the class of languages accepted by ORWW-automata forms an abstract family of languages, that is, it is closed under union, intersection (with regular sets), product, Kleene star, inverse morphisms, and non-erasing morphisms (see, e.g., [3]). However,

© IFIP International Federation for Information Processing 2017
Published by Springer International Publishing AG 2017. All Rights Reserved
G. Pighizzini and C. Câmpeanu (Eds.): DCFS 2017, LNCS 10316, pp. 226–237, 2017.
DOI: 10.1007/978-3-319-60252-3_18

it is neither closed under complementation nor under reversal. Further, it is incomparable to the (deterministic) linear, the (deterministic) context-free, and the growing context-sensitive languages with respect to inclusion, as it contains a language that is not even growing context-sensitive, while on the other hand, it does not even include the deterministic linear language $\{\, a^m b^m \mid m \geq 1 \,\}$. In addition, it was shown that the emptiness problem is decidable for ORWW-automata. Several of these results were derived from a Cut-and-Paste Lemma for ORWW-automata that is based on Higman's Theorem [2].

Here we continue the study of nondeterministic ORWW-automata, where we are particularly interested in the expressive capability of ORWW-automata and their algorithmic properties. The Cut-and-Paste Lemma of [6] states that, for each ORWW-automaton M, a non-empty factor can be cut from the *suffix* of each sufficiently long word accepted by M such that the resulting shorter word is accepted by M, too. Thus, in comparison to the Pumping Lemma for regular languages (see, e.g., [3]), the Cut-and-Paste Lemma just covers the case of pumping with exponent zero. Here we also present a real Pumping Lemma for ORWW-automata that takes care of the case of pumping with positive exponents. However, in contrast to the Cut-and-Paste Lemma, which applies to the suffix of a sufficiently long word, the Pumping Lemma applies to the *prefix* of a sufficiently long word. Then, based on both these lemmas, we show that finiteness is decidable for ORWW-automata, and we show that each unary language that is accepted by an ORWW-automaton is necessarily regular.

This paper is structured as follows. In Sect. 2, we introduce the ORWW-automaton and restate the known results on the class of languages it accepts. Then, in Sect. 3, we present the announced Pumping Lemma, which is derived from Higman's theorem similar to the Cut-and-Paste Lemma. In Sect. 4, we give two applications of this lemma by showing that finiteness is decidable for ORWW-automata and that all unary languages that are accepted by ORWW-automata are necessarily regular. The paper closes with Sect. 5, which summarizes our results in short and states a number of open problems.

2   Definitions and Known Results

An *ordered restarting automaton* (ORWW-automaton) is a one-tape machine that is described by an 8-tuple $M = (Q, \Sigma, \Gamma, \rhd, \lhd, q_0, \delta, >)$, where Q is a finite set of states containing the initial state q_0, Σ is a finite input alphabet, Γ is a finite tape alphabet such that $\Sigma \subseteq \Gamma$, the symbols $\rhd, \lhd \notin \Gamma$ serve as markers for the left and right border of the work space, respectively,

$$\delta : (Q \times ((\Gamma \cup \{\rhd\}) \cdot \Gamma \cdot (\Gamma \cup \{\lhd\}) \cup \{\rhd \lhd\})) \to 2^{(Q \times \mathsf{MVR}) \cup \Gamma} \cup \{\mathsf{Accept}\}$$

is the *transition relation*, and $>$ is a *partial ordering* on Γ. The transition relation describes three different types of transition steps:

(1) A *move-right step* has the form $(q', \mathsf{MVR}) \in \delta(q, a_1 a_2 a_3)$, where $q, q' \in Q$, $a_1 \in \Gamma \cup \{\rhd\}$, and $a_2, a_3 \in \Gamma$. It causes M to shift the window one position to

the right and to change from state q to state q'. Observe that no move-right step is possible, if the window contains the symbol $\lhd$.

(2) A *rewrite/restart step* has the form $b \in \delta(q, a_1 a_2 a_3)$, where $q \in Q$, $a_1 \in \Gamma \cup \{\rhd\}$, $a_2, b \in \Gamma$, and $a_3 \in \Gamma \cup \{\lhd\}$ such that $a_2 > b$ holds. It causes M to replace the symbol a_2 in the middle of its window by the symbol b and to restart, that is, the window is moved back to the left end of the tape, and M reenters its initial state q_0.

(3) An *accept step* has the form $\delta(q, a_1 a_2 a_3) = $ Accept, where $q \in Q$, $a_1 \in \Gamma \cup \{\rhd\}$, $a_2 \in \Gamma$, and $a_3 \in \Gamma \cup \{\lhd\}$. It causes M to halt and accept. In addition, we allow an accept step of the form $\delta(q_0, \rhd \lhd) = $ Accept.

If $\delta(q, u) = \emptyset$ for some state q and a word u, then M necessarily halts, when it is in state q with u in its window, and we say that M *rejects* in this situation. Further, the letters in $\Gamma \smallsetminus \Sigma$ are called *auxiliary symbols*.

If $|\delta(q, u)| \leq 1$ for all q and u, then M is a *deterministic ORWW-automaton* (det-ORWW-automaton), and if $Q = \{q_0\}$, that is, if the initial state is the only state of M, then we call M a *stateless ORWW-automaton* (stl-ORWW-automaton) or a *stateless deterministic ORWW-automaton* (stl-det-ORWW-automaton), as in this case the state is actually not needed.

A *configuration* of an ORWW-automaton M is a word $\alpha q \beta$, where $q \in Q$ is the current state, $|\beta| \geq 3$, and either $\alpha = \lambda$ (the empty word) and $\beta \in \{\rhd\} \cdot \Gamma^+ \cdot \{\lhd\}$ or $\alpha \in \{\rhd\} \cdot \Gamma^*$ and $\beta \in \Gamma \cdot \Gamma^+ \cdot \{\lhd\}$; here $\alpha\beta$ is the current content of the tape, and it is understood that the window contains the first three symbols of β. In addition, we admit the configuration $q_0 \rhd \lhd$. By $\vdash_M$ we denote binary relation that M induces on the set of configurations, and $\vdash_M^*$ is the reflexive transitive closure of this relation. A *restarting configuration* has the form $q_0 \rhd w \lhd$; if $w \in \Sigma^*$, then $q_0 \rhd w \lhd$ is also called an *initial configuration*. Further, we use Accept to denote the *accepting configurations*, which are those configurations that M reaches by an accept step.

Any computation of an ORWW-automaton M consists of certain phases. A phase, called a *cycle*, starts in a restarting configuration, the head is moved along the tape by MVR steps until a rewrite/restart step is performed and thus, a new restarting configuration is reached. If no further rewrite operation is performed, any computation necessarily finishes in a halting configuration – such a phase is called a *tail*. By $\vdash_M^c$ we denote the execution of a complete cycle, and $\vdash_M^{c*}$ is the reflexive transitive closure of this relation. It can be seen as the *rewrite relation* that is realized by M on the set of restarting configurations.

An input $w \in \Sigma^*$ is accepted by M, if there is a computation of M which starts with the initial configuration $q_0 \rhd w \lhd$ and which ends with an accept step. The language consisting of all input words that are accepted by M is denoted by $L(M)$. Further, by $\mathcal{L}(\text{ORWW})$ we denote the class of all languages that are accepted by ORWW-automata.

As each cycle ends with a rewrite operation, which replaces a symbol a by a symbol b that is strictly smaller than a with respect to the given ordering $>$, each computation of M on an input of length n consists of at most $(|\Gamma| - 1) \cdot n$ cycles. Thus, M can be simulated by a nondeterministic single-tape Turing machine in time $O(n^2)$.

The following technical result has already been used in [6] without stating or proving it explicitly. As below we will use it again, we present it in some detail.

Lemma 1. *For each ORWW-automaton M, there exists an ORWW-automaton M' that accepts the same language as M, but that performs accept steps only at the left sentinel.*

Proof. Let $M = (Q, \Sigma, \Gamma, \rhd, \lhd, q_0, \delta, >)$ be an ORWW-automaton. To obtain the automaton $M' = (Q', \Sigma, \Gamma', \rhd, \lhd, q'_0, \delta', >')$, we take $Q' = Q$, $q'_0 = q_0$, and $\Gamma' = \Gamma \cup \{*\}$, where $*$ is a new symbol. Further, we extend $>$ to $>'$ by taking $a >' *$ for all $a \in \Gamma$. Finally, we define the transition relation δ' of M' as follows, where $a \in \Gamma \cup \{\rhd\}$, $b \in \Gamma$, $c \in \Gamma \cup \{\lhd\}$, and $q \in Q$:

$$
\begin{aligned}
\delta'(q_0, \rhd\lhd) &= \delta(q_0, \rhd\lhd), \\
\delta'(q, abc) &= \delta(q, abc), & \text{if } \delta(q, abc) \neq \mathsf{Accept}, \\
\delta'(q, abc) &= \{*\}, & \text{if } \delta(q, abc) = \mathsf{Accept}, \\
\delta'(q, ab*) &= \{*\}, \\
\delta'(q_0, \rhd * d) &= \mathsf{Accept} & \text{for all } d \in \Gamma \cup \{\lhd, *\}.
\end{aligned}
$$

Obviously, M' performs an accept step only at its left sentinel. The automaton M' can simulate M step by step until M accepts, in which case M' writes the letter $*$. In the following cycles, whenever M' detects an occurrence of the symbol $*$, it copies this symbol to its left-hand neighbour. It follows that $L(M) \subseteq L(M')$. On the other hand, if M' accepts on input w, then it can do so only because it has been able to simulate an accepting computation of M on input w, as the first $*$-symbol can only be produced by M' on reaching a configuration in which M would accept. Thus, $L(M) = L(M')$ holds.   □

While nondeterministic ORWW-automata are quite expressive as we will see below, the deterministic variants are fairly weak.

Theorem 2 [5,11].

(a) *For each det-ORWW-automaton $M = (Q, \Sigma, \Gamma, \rhd, \lhd, q_0, \delta, >)$, there exists a stateless det-ORWW-automaton $M' = (\Sigma, \Gamma', \rhd, \lhd, \delta', >')$ such that $L(M') = L(M)$ and $|\Gamma'| = |Q| \cdot |\Gamma|^2 + 2 \cdot |\Gamma|$.*
(b) *For each DFA $A = (Q, \Sigma, q_0, F, \varphi)$, there is a stl-det-ORWW-automaton $M = (\Sigma, \Gamma, \rhd, \lhd, \delta, >)$ such that $L(M) = L(A)$ and $|\Gamma| = |Q| + |\Sigma|$.*
(c) *For each stl-det-ORWW-automaton M with an alphabet of size n, there exists an NFA A of size $2^{O(n)}$ such that $L(A) = L(M)$ holds.*
(d) *For each $n \geq 1$, there exists a regular language $B_n \subseteq \{0, 1, \#, \$\}^*$ such that B_n is accepted by a stl-det-ORWW-automaton over an alphabet of size $O(n)$, but each NFA for accepting B_n has at least 2^n states.*

Lemma 3 (Cut-and-Paste Lemma) [6].
For each ORWW-automaton M, there exists a constant $N_c(M) > 0$ such that each word $w \in L(M)$, $|w| \geq N_c(M)$, has a factorization $w = xyz$ satisfying all of the following conditions:

$$
\text{(a) } |yz| \leq N_c(M), \quad \text{(b) } |y| > 0, \text{ and (c) } xz \in L(M).
$$

In addition, the constant N_c can be determined from M effectively.

Theorem 4 [6]. $\mathcal{L}(\mathrm{ORWW})$ *is closed under union, intersection, product, Kleene star, inverse morphisms, and non-erasing morphisms, but it is neither closed under the operation of reversal nor under complementation.*

Using the Cut-and-Paste Lemma it is easily seen that the deterministic linear language $\{a^m b^m \mid m \geq 1\}$ is not accepted by any ORWW-automaton. On the other hand, there exists a language that is accepted by an ORWW-automaton, but that is not even growing context-sensitive. Thus, we have the following incomparability results, where DLIN denotes the *deterministic linear languages*, that is, those languages that are accepted by deterministic one-turn pushdown automata, LIN is the class of *linear languages*, CFL and DCFL are the classes of context-free and deterministic context-free languages, CRL is the class of *Church-Rosser languages* [8], and GCSL is the class of *growing context-sensitive languages* [1].

Corollary 5. *The language class* $\mathcal{L}(\mathrm{ORWW})$ *is incomparable to the language classes* DLIN, LIN, DCFL, CFL, CRL, *and* GCSL *with respect to inclusion.*

Also from the Cut-and-Paste Lemma the following decidability result follows.

Theorem 6 [6]. *The emptiness problem for ORWW-automata is decidable.*

The following result was given without proof in [6], pointing out that the construction for the deterministic case (see Theorem 2 (c)) can be extended accordingly. In fact, a simpler construction is presented in [7].

Theorem 7 [6]. *Let* $M = (\Sigma, \Gamma, \triangleright, \triangleleft, \delta_M, >)$ *be a stl-ORWW-automaton. Then* $L(M)$ *is a regular language.*

3   A Pumping Lemma for ORWW-Automata

Here we derive our main result, the Pumping Lemma for ORWW-automata.

Definition 8. *Let* $M = (Q, \Sigma, \Gamma, \triangleright, \triangleleft, q_0, \delta, >)$ *be an ORWW-automaton. The transition relation* δ *can be presented by a set of five-tuples of the form* (q, a_1, a_2, a_3, o), *where* $q \in Q$, $a_1 \in \Gamma \cup \{\triangleright\}$, $a_2 \in \Gamma$, $a_3 \in \Gamma \cup \{\triangleleft\}$, *and* $o \in \Gamma \cup Q \cup \{\mathsf{Accept}\}$. *Here a tuple* (q, a_1, a_2, a_3, q') *with* $q' \in Q$ *represents the move-right transition* $(q', \mathsf{MVR}) \in \delta(q, a_1, a_2, a_3)$, *a tuple* (q, a_1, a_2, a_3, b) *with* $b \in \Gamma$ *represents the rewrite/restart transition* $b \in \delta(q, a_1, a_2, a_3)$, *and a tuple* $(q, a_1, a_2, a_3, \mathsf{Accept})$ *represents the accept transition* $\delta(q, a_1, a_2, a_3) = \mathsf{Accept}$. *We introduce an alphabet* Ω *the letters of which are in 1-to-1 correspondence to these five-tuples.*

Let $w \in L(M)$ *and let* C *be an accepting computation of* M *on input* w. *With each integer* i, $1 \leq i \leq |w|$, *we associate a word* $\sigma_i^C \in \Omega^*$ *that corresponds to the sequence of operations that* M *executes within the computation* C *at position* i, *that is, when the* i-*th letter is in the middle of the window. Let*

$\sigma_i^C = t_{j_1} t_{j_2} \dots t_{j_s}$, where $t_{j_r} \in \Omega$ for all $1 \leq r \leq s$. If $t_{j_r} = (q_1, a_1, a_2, a_3, o_1)$ and $t_{j_{r+1}} = (q_2, b_1, b_2, b_3, o_2)$, then $a_1 \geq b_1$, $a_2 \geq b_2$, and $a_3 \geq b_3$. In addition, if $o_1 = q' \in Q$, that is, it represents a move-right operation, then $a_2 = b_2$, and if $o_1 = b \in \Gamma$, that is, it represents a rewrite/restart operation, then $a_2 > b = b_2$. Now the pattern $\tau_i^C \in \Omega^*$ is the word that is obtained from σ_i^C by condensing consecutive identical letters into a single letter.

Observe that it is only MVR operations that may be condensed.

Example 9. Consider the following accepting computation C of an ORWW-automaton M:

$$q_0 \triangleright aaa \triangleleft \vdash_M q_0 \triangleright a_1 aa \triangleleft \vdash_M \triangleright q_0 a_1 aa \triangleleft \vdash_M \triangleright a_1 q_0 aa \triangleleft$$
$$\vdash_M q_0 \triangleright a_1 aa_1 \triangleleft \vdash_M \triangleright q_0 a_1 aa_1 \triangleleft \vdash_M \triangleright a_1 q_0 aa_1 \triangleleft \vdash_M \text{Accept}.$$

This computation consists of two cycles and an accepting tail that are described by the following sequences of operations:

$$c_1 = (q_0, \triangleright, a, a, a_1),$$
$$c_2 = (q_0, \triangleright, a_1, a, q_0), (q_0, a_1, a, a, q_0), (q_0, a, a, \triangleleft, a_1),$$
$$c_3 = (q_0, \triangleright, a_1, a, q_0), (q_0, a_1, a, a_1, q_0), (q_0, a, a_1, \triangleleft, \text{Accept}).$$

For the first position, we thus get the sequence of operations

$$\sigma_1^C = (q_0, \triangleright, a, a, a_1)(q_0, \triangleright, a_1, a, q_0)(q_0, \triangleright, a_1, a, q_0),$$

which yields the pattern $\tau_1^C = (q_0, \triangleright, a, a, a_1)(q_0, \triangleright, a_1, a, q_0)$, while for the second position we get the sequence of operations

$$\sigma_2^C = (q_0, a_1, a, a, q_0)(q_0, a_1, a, a_1, q_0) = \tau_2^C.$$

For the third position we have $\sigma_3^C = (q_0, a, a, \triangleleft, a_1)(q_0, a, a_1, \triangleleft, \text{Accept}) = \tau_3^C$.

For two patterns τ_1^C and τ_2^C, we write $\tau_1^C \sqsubseteq \tau_2^C$ if τ_1^C is a *scattered subword* of τ_2^C, that is, if $\tau_1^C = \omega_1 \omega_2 \dots \omega_m$ for some $\omega_1, \omega_2, \dots, \omega_m \in \Omega$, then there are words $y_0, y_1, \dots, y_m \in \Omega^*$ such that $\tau_2^C = y_0 \omega_1 y_1 \omega_2 y_2 \dots y_{m-1} \omega_m y_m$. The next lemma is the main step towards the proof of the Pumping Lemma.

Lemma 10. *Let $M = (Q, \Sigma, \Gamma, \triangleright, \triangleleft, q_0, \delta, >)$ be an ORWW-automaton that accepts at the left sentinel, let C_{xz} be an accepting computation of M for the input xz, and let C_{uv} be an accepting computation of M for the input uv. If the pattern $\tau_{|u|}^{C_{uv}}$ of the computation C_{uv} at position $|u|$ is a scattered subword of the pattern $\tau_{|x|}^{C_{xz}}$ of the computation C_{xz} at position $|x|$, that is, $\tau_{|u|}^{C_{uv}} \sqsubseteq \tau_{|x|}^{C_{xz}}$, and if these two patterns contain the same rewrite operations, then $xv \in L(M)$.*

Proof. We construct an accepting computation C' for the input xv from the given computations C_{xz} and C_{uv}. The sequences of cycles $(C_1, C_2, \dots, C_\alpha)$ of C_{xz} and $(D_1, D_2, \dots, D_\beta)$ of C_{uv} are considered as working lists that are used for constructing the cycles of C' that have their rewrite operations in the prefix x or

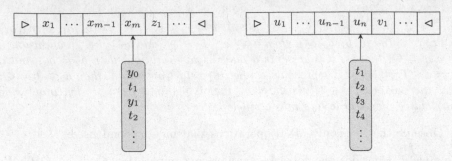

Fig. 1. The inputs xz and uv with the patterns $\tau_{|x|}^{C_{xz}}$ (left) and $\tau_{|u|}^{C_{uv}}$ (right)

in the suffix v of the input xv, respectively. As $\tau_{|u|}^{C_{uv}} \sqsubseteq \tau_{|x|}^{C_{xz}}$, these patterns can be written as $\tau_{|u|}^{C_{uv}} = t_1 t_2 \ldots t_r$ with $t_1, t_2, \ldots, t_r \in \Omega$ and $\tau_{|x|}^{C_{xz}} = y_0 t_1 y_1 \ldots y_{r-1} t_r y_r$ for some $y_0, y_1, \ldots, y_r \in \Omega^*$ (see Fig. 1). As both patterns contain the same rewrite operations, the factors $y_0, y_1, \ldots y_r$ only consist of MVR operations.

For constructing the computation C' on input xv, we start by taking C' to be the empty sequence of cycles. Now we consider the cycles of C_{xz} one after another (see Fig. 2).

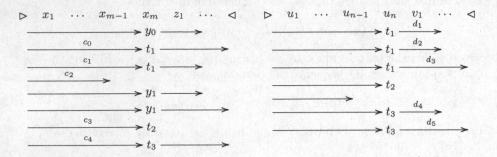

Fig. 2. The cycles of the computations C_{xz} (left) and C_{uv} (right). Each line represents a cycle, where the operation executed at the last position of x (left) or u (right) is displayed. The arrows labelled c_i represent initial parts of cycles executed within the prefix of the tape initially containing x (left), and the arrows labelled d_j represent final parts of cycles executed within the suffix of the tape initially containing v (right)

Let C_i be the cycle currently considered.

- If C_i is a *short cycle*, that is, a cycle that executes a rewrite step within a proper prefix of x, then we just append it to C' (see the cycle c_2 in Fig. 2).
- If C_i contains a rewrite operation at position $|x|$, then this operation corresponds to the letter t_l for some $1 \leq l \leq r$. Again we append this cycle to C' (see the cycle c_3). As both patterns contain the same rewrite operations, which must occur in the same relative order in both patterns, we see that the rewrite operation t_l can also be executed at this point in the computation C'.

- If C_i is a cycle that executes a rewrite step within the suffix z of xz, then this cycle contains a MVR operation at position $|x|$. If this operation does not correspond to one of the letters $t_1, t_2, \ldots, t_r$ in the pattern $\tau_{|x|}^{C_{xz}}$, we skip this cycle without appending it to C'.
- Finally, let C_i be a cycle that executes a rewrite step within the suffix z of xz, but the MVR operation executed at position $|x|$ corresponds to the letter t_l for some $1 \le l \le r$. By c_0 we denote the prefix of the cycle C_i up to position $|x| - 1$. Further, let $D_{i_1}, D_{i_2}, \ldots, D_{i_\nu}$ be all those cycles of C_{uv} that contain the MVR operation t_l at position $|u|$, and for all $1 \le j \le \nu$, let d_j be the suffix of the cycle D_{i_j} that starts with the operation t_l at position $|u|$. We now combine the prefix c_0 of C_i with the suffix d_j of D_{i_j} for all $1 \le j \le \nu$ (see c_0 and d_1, d_2, d_3 in Fig. 2). As the same operation t_l is applied in the cycle C_i at position $|x|$ as in the cycles $D_{i_1}, D_{i_2}, \ldots, D_{i_\nu}$ at position $|u|$, we see that $c_0 d_1, c_0 d_2, \ldots, c_0 d_\nu$ is a sequence of possible cycles of M. We append this sequence of cycles to C'.
- Any further cycle C_{i+s}, $s \ge 1$, that also executes a MVR operation at position $|x|$ which corresponds to the letter t_l of the pattern $\tau_{|x|}^{C_{xz}}$, is skipped (see c_1 in Fig. 2).

Figure 3 illustrates the result of the construction above. Finally, the computation C' is completed by attaching the accepting tail computation from C_{xz} to it. Recall that M accepts with the left sentinel in its window. It is now easily seen that C' is an accepting computation of M for the input xv.   □

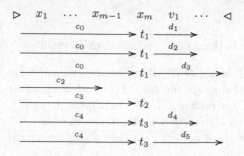

Fig. 3. The computation C' for input xv

Next we consider a special case of the above lemma.

Lemma 11. *Let $M = (Q, \Sigma, \Gamma, \triangleright, \triangleleft, q_0, \delta, >)$ be an ORWW-automaton that accepts at the left sentinel, let $w \in L(M)$, let C be an accepting computation of M for the input w, and let $1 \le i < j \le |w|$ be indices such that $\tau_i^C(w) \sqsubseteq \tau_j^C(w)$ and these two patterns contain the same rewrite operations. Then w can be written as $w = xyz$, where $|x| = i$ and $|y| = j - i$, such that $xyyz \in L(M)$. In fact, there exists an accepting computation C' for $xyyz$ satisfying $\tau_i^{C'}(xyyz) = \tau_j^{C'}(xyyz)$.*

Proof. If we choose $x_1 = xy$, $y_1 = z$, $u_1 = x$, and $v_1 = yz$, we can apply Lemma 10 to the factorizations $w = xyz = x_1y_1$ and $w = xyz = u_1v_1$. Thus, we obtain an accepting computation C' of M for the input $x_1v_1 = xyyz$. From the construction of C' in the proof of the above lemma we see that the patterns $\tau_i^{C'}(xyyz)$ and $\tau_j^{C'}(xyyz)$ coincide.   □

Finally, we need the following notion that has already been considered in [10] under the name of *det*-MVR$_1$-*form* for general restarting automata.

Definition 12. *An ORWW-automaton* $M = (Q, \Sigma, \Gamma, \rhd, \lhd, q_0, \delta, >)$ *is said to have* deterministic MVR operations *if, for all* $q \in Q$ *and all* $a, b, c \in \Gamma \cup \{\rhd, \lhd\}$, $\delta(q, abc)$ *contains at most a single MVR operation.*

Lemma 13. *For each ORWW-automaton* $M = (Q, \Sigma, \Gamma, \rhd, \lhd, q_0, \delta, >)$, *there exists an ORWW automaton* M' *with deterministic MVR operations that accepts the same language as* M. *If* M *accepts at the left sentinel, then so does* M'.

Proof. Using a variant of the well-known powerset construction, the ORWW-automaton M' can be defined as $M' = (2^Q, \Sigma, \Gamma, \rhd, \lhd, \{q_0\}, \delta', >)$, where, for all $\emptyset \neq S \subseteq Q$ and all $a, b, c \in \Gamma \cup \{\rhd, \lhd\}$,

$$T_{(S,abc)} = \{ q \in Q \mid \exists s \in S : (q, \mathsf{MVR}) \in \delta(s, abc) \}, \text{ and}$$

$$\delta'(S, abc) = \begin{cases} \mathsf{Accept}, & \text{if } \exists s \in S : \delta(s, abc) = \mathsf{Accept}, \\ \left(\bigcup_{s \in S} \delta(s, abc) \cap \Gamma\right) \cup \{(T_{(S,abc)}, \mathsf{MVR})\}, & \text{if } T_{(S,abc)} \neq \emptyset, \\ \left(\bigcup_{s \in S} \delta(s, abc) \cap \Gamma\right), & \text{if } T_{(S,abc)} = \emptyset. \end{cases}$$

□

The next lemma is the second technical main result.

Lemma 14. *Let* M *be an ORWW-automaton with deterministic MVR operations that accepts at the left sentinel. From* M *a constant* $N(M) > 0$ *can be computed such that, for each* $w \in L(M)$ *satisfying* $|w| \geq N(M)$ *and each accepting computation* C *of* M *on input* w, *there are indices* $1 \leq i < j \leq |w|$ *such that* $\tau_i^C(w) \sqsubseteq \tau_j^C(w)$ *and these patterns contain the same rewrite operations.*

Proof. Let $M = (Q, \Sigma, \Gamma, \rhd, \lhd, q_0, \delta, >)$ be an ORWW-automaton with deterministic MVR operations that accepts at the left sentinel, and let $n = |\Gamma|$. Further, let $w \in L(M)$ and let C be an accepting computation of M on input w. The MVR operations executed at a position $1 \leq k \leq |w| - 1$ only depend on the prefix of length $k + 1$ of w. As M has deterministic MVR operations, the MVR operation that can be executed at position k is uniquely determined by that prefix, if it exists at all. For this reason a different MVR operation can become applicable at position k only if that prefix has been modified by a rewrite operation. This, however, can happen at most $(k + 1) \cdot (n - 1)$ times. Therefore, the pattern $\tau_k^C(w)$ contains at most $(k + 1) \cdot (n - 1) + 1$ MVR operations. Additionally, it contains at most $n - 1$ rewrite operations. Therefore, $\tau_k^C(w)$ has length at most $(k + 1) \cdot (n - 1) + n + 1 = k \cdot (n - 1) + 2n$. Finally, we extend each pattern $\tau_k^C(w)$ into the word $\eta_k^C(w) = a_k \tau_k^C(w) s_k$ where a_k is the input letter at position k and s_k is the final letter produced by C at position k. Higman's theorem [2] (see, also [4,12]) implies there exists a computable constant $N(M)$ such that, if $|w| \geq N(M)$, then there are indices $1 \leq i < j \leq N(M)$ such that $\eta_i^C(w)$ is a scattered subsequence of $\eta_j^C(w)$. This means that $a_i = a_j$ and $s_i = s_j$, and that $\tau_i^C(w)$ is a scattered subsequence of $\tau_j^C(w)$. As in both positions the letter $a_i = a_j$ is rewritten into the letter $s_i = s_j$, and as each rewrite operation at position i occurs in $\tau_i^C(w)$ and therewith also in $\tau_j^C(w)$, we see that $\tau_i^C(w)$ and $\tau_j^C(w)$ contain exactly the same rewrite operations.   □

Now we can state and prove the announced Pumping Lemma.

Theorem 15 (Pumping Lemma). *For each ORWW-automaton M there exists a computable constant $N_p(M) > 0$ such that each word $w \in L(M)$, $|w| \geq N_p(M)$, has a factorization $w = xyz$ satisfying all of the following conditions:*

(a) $|xy| \leq N_p(M)$, (b) $|y| > 0$, *and* (c) $xy^m z \in L(M)$ *for all* $m \geq 1$.

Proof. Let M be an ORWW automaton. By Lemma 1 we may assume that M only accepts at the left sentinel. Further, by Lemma 13, we can convert M into an equivalent ORWW-automaton M_1 that is MVR-deterministic and that only accepts at the left sentinel. Then Lemma 14 implies that a constant $N_p(M)$ can be computed such that, for each $w \in L(M_1) = L(M)$ satisfying $|w| \geq N_p(M)$, and each accepting computation C of M_1 on input w, there are indices $1 \leq i < j \leq N_p(M)$ such that $\tau_i^C(w) \sqsubseteq \tau_j^C(w)$ and these patterns contain the same rewrite operations. Hence, by Lemma 11, w can be factored as $w = xyz$ such that $|xy| \leq N_p(M)$, $|y| > 0$, $xyyz \in L(M_1) = L(M)$, and $\tau_{|x|}^{C'}(xyyz) = \tau_{|xy|}^{C'}(xyyz)$, where C' is the accepting computation of M_1 for input $xyyz$ that is obtained from the computation C. Using Lemma 11 repeatedly we obtain that $xy^m z \in L(M_1) = L(M)$ holds for all $m \geq 1$.   □

4   Applications of the Pumping Lemma

In [6] we have used the Cut-and-Paste Lemma to prove that emptiness is decidable for ORWW-automata. Here we show that also finiteness is decidable for ORWW-automata using both, the Cut-and-Paste Lemma and the Pumping Lemma.

Theorem 16. *The following* finiteness *problem is decidable:*
INSTANCE: An ORWW-automaton M.
QUESTION: Is the language $L(M)$ finite?

Proof. Let $M = (Q, \Sigma, \Gamma, \rhd, \lhd, q_0, \delta, >)$ be an ORWW-automaton, let $N_c(M)$ be the corresponding constant from the Cut-and-Paste Lemma for M, and $N_p(M)$ be the corresponding constant from the Pumping Lemma for M. We claim that

$L(M)$ is finite iff it does not contain any word w such that $N_p(M) \leq |w| \leq N_p(M) + N_c(M)$.

Indeed, if $L(M)$ contains a word w such that $N_p(M) \leq |w| \leq N_p(M) + N_c(M)$, then the Pumping Lemma tells us that $L(M)$ is infinite. Conversely, if $L(M)$ is infinite, then it contains a word w of length at least $N_p(M)$. Assume that w is the shortest word with these properties. If $|w| \leq N_p(M) + N_c(M)$, then there is nothing to prove. On the other hand, if $|w| > N_p(M) + N_c(M)$, then we can apply the Cut-and-Paste Lemma to w, which yields a factorization $w = xyz$ such that $|yz| \leq N_c(M); |y| > 0$, and $xz \in L(M)$. Thus, $|w| > |xz| = |w| - |y| \geq |w| - N_c(M) > N_p(M)$, which contradicts our choice of w. Hence, we see that $L(M)$ is infinite iff it contains a word w such that $N_p(M) \leq |w| \leq N_p(M) + N_c(M)$.   □

The next result, which is also derived from the Pumping Lemma, shows that ORWW-automata only accept unary languages that are regular.

Theorem 17. *For each ORWW-automaton M, if the language $L(M)$ is unary, then it is already regular.*

Proof. Let M be an ORWW-automaton with input alphabet $\Sigma = \{a\}$, and let $\alpha = N_p(M)$ be the constant from the Pumping Lemma for M. For all integers c and d satisfying $0 \leq d < \alpha!$ and $0 < c \leq \alpha$, we let $S_{d,c} \subseteq \mathbb{N}$ be defined as follows:

$$S_{d,c} := \{ n \geq \alpha \mid n \equiv d \mod \alpha! \text{ and } a^{n+c \cdot i} \in L(M) \text{ for all } i \in \mathbb{N} \}.$$

By definition $\{ a^n \mid n \in S_{d,c} \} \subseteq L(M)$ for all pairs (d, c). On the other hand, if $a^n \in L(M)$ for some $n \geq \alpha$, then there exists an integer $d, 0 \leq d < \alpha!$, such that $n \equiv d \mod \alpha!$. By the Pumping Lemma there also exists an integer $c, 0 < c \leq \alpha$, such that $a^{n+c \cdot i} \in L(M)$ for all $i \in \mathbb{N}$. Hence, it follows that $n \in S_{d,c}$.

If $S_{d,c} \neq \emptyset$, it can be represented as the linear set $S_{d,c} = \{ \min(S_{d,c}) + i \cdot \alpha! \mid i \in \mathbb{N} \}$. Therefore, if $\psi : \Sigma^* \to \mathbb{N}$ denotes the Parikh mapping defined by $a^n \mapsto n$ $(n \geq 0)$, then

$$\psi(L(M)) = \{ n < \alpha \mid a^n \in L(M) \} \cup \bigcup_{d,c} S_{d,c},$$

which shows that $\psi(L(M))$ is a semi-linear subset of $\mathbb{N}$. Thus, it follows that $L(M)$ is indeed a regular language.   □

Actually, it can be shown that a regular expression can be determined for the language $L(M)$ of an ORWW-automaton M that has a unary input alphabet.

5   Concluding Remarks

We have established a Pumping Lemma for ORWW-automata that nicely complements the Cut-and-Paste Lemma for these automata presented in [6]. Observe that the Cut-and-Paste Lemma tells us that we can cut from the suffix of a sufficiently long word, while the Pumping Lemma tells us that we can pump within the prefix of a sufficiently long word. This effect is clearly demonstrated by the language $L = \{\, a^m b^n \mid m \geq n \,\} \in \mathcal{L}(\text{ORWW})$ [6], as from a word $a^m b^m \in L$, where m is a sufficiently large integer, the Cut-and-Paste Lemma yields a word of the form $a^m b^{m-i}$, and the Pumping Lemma gives words of the form $a^{m+c \cdot i} b^m$. From the Pumping Lemma we have then derived the solvability of the finiteness problem for ORWW-automata and the fact that the only unary languages accepted by these automata are the regular ones.

However, there still remain many open questions. For example, is it true that ORWW-automata only accept languages that are semi-linear? Further, given an ORWW-automaton M and a regular language R (for example, through a DFA), it can be checked whether $L(M)$ is contained in R, as this is the case iff $L(M) \cap R^c$ is empty. However, it is still open whether the converse inclusion (that is, is R contained in $L(M)$) can be checked. A special case is the *universality problem*, that is, given an ORWW-automaton M with input alphabet Σ, is $L(M)$ all of Σ^*? Finally, one may ask whether ORWW-automata yield more succinct representations for unary languages than deterministic ORWW-automata.

References

1. Dahlhaus, E., Warmuth, M.: Membership for growing context-sensitive grammars is polynomial. J. Comput. Syst. Sci. **33**, 456–472 (1986)
2. Higman, G.: Ordering by divisibility in abstract algebras. Proc. Lond. Math. Soc. **2**, 326–336 (1952)
3. Hopcroft, J.E., Ullman, J.D.: Introduction to Automata Theory, Languages, and Computation. Addison-Wesley, Reading (1979)
4. Karandikar, P., Schnoebelen, P.: Generalized Post embedding problems. Theory Comput. Syst. **56**, 697–716 (2015)
5. Kwee, K., Otto, F.: On some decision problems for stateless deterministic ordered restarting automata. In: Shallit, J., Okhotin, A. (eds.) DCFS 2015. LNCS, vol. 9118, pp. 165–176. Springer, Cham (2015). doi:10.1007/978-3-319-19225-3_14
6. Kwee, K., Otto, F.: On the effects of nondeterminism on ordered restarting automata. In: Freivalds, R.M., Engels, G., Catania, B. (eds.) SOFSEM 2016. LNCS, vol. 9587, pp. 369–380. Springer, Heidelberg (2016). doi:10.1007/978-3-662-49192-8_30
7. Kwee, K., Otto, F.: Nondeterministic ordered restarting automata (2017, Submitted)
8. McNaughton, R., Narendran, P., Otto, F.: Church-Rosser Thue systems and formal languages. J. Assoc. Comput. Mach. **35**, 324–344 (1988)
9. Mráz, F., Otto, F.: Ordered restarting automata for picture languages. In: Geffert, V., Preneel, B., Rovan, B., Štuller, J., Tjoa, A.M. (eds.) SOFSEM 2014. LNCS, vol. 8327, pp. 431–442. Springer, Cham (2014). doi:10.1007/978-3-319-04298-5_38
10. Mráz, F., Plátek, M., Procházka, M.: On special forms of restarting automata. Grammars **2**, 223–233 (1999)
11. Otto, F.: On the descriptional complexity of deterministic ordered restarting automata. In: Jürgensen, H., Karhumäki, J., Okhotin, A. (eds.) DCFS 2014. LNCS, vol. 8614, pp. 318–329. Springer, Cham (2014). doi:10.1007/978-3-319-09704-6_28
12. Schmitz, S., Schnoebelen, P.: Multiply-recursive upper bounds with Higman's lemma. In: Aceto, L., Henzinger, M., Sgall, J. (eds.) ICALP 2011. LNCS, vol. 6756, pp. 441–452. Springer, Heidelberg (2011). doi:10.1007/978-3-642-22012-8_35

Concise Representations of Reversible Automata

Giovanna J. Lavado[✉] and Luca Prigioniero[✉]

Dipartimento di Informatica, Università degli Studi di Milano, Milano, Italy
{lavado,prigioniero}@di.unimi.it

Abstract. We present two concise representations of reversible automata. Both representations have a size which is comparable with the size of the minimum equivalent deterministic automaton and can be exponentially smaller than the size of the explicit representations of corresponding reversible automata. Using those representations it is possible to simulate the computations of reversible automata without explicitly writing down their complete descriptions.

1   Introduction

Reversibility is a fundamental principle in physics: in thermodynamics a transformation is reversible if, after occurring, it can be inverted in order to recover the original state of the system. In the study of computations, reversibility means that each elementary step can be inverted, thus recovering the previous state of the system. In other words, every configuration must admit at most one predecessor. As shown by Landauer, the irreversibility in computation leads to heat dissipations [8], while Toffoli proved that it is ideally possible to build sequential circuits with zero internal power dissipation [12]. This observation suggested to study reversible computations in which there is no loss of information.

Reversibility has been studied on various computational models. In the case of general devices as Turing machines, Bennet proved that each machine can be simulated by a reversible one [1], while Lange, McKenzie, and Tapp proved that each deterministic machine can be simulated by a reversible machine which uses the same amount of space [9]. As a corollary, in the case of a constant amount of space, this implies that each regular language is accepted by a *reversible two-way deterministic finite automaton*. Actually, this result was already proved by Kondacs and Watrous [5]. In the case of *one-way* automata, the situation is different[1]. The class of languages accepted by *reversible automata* is a proper subclass of the class of regular languages. For example, the regular language a^*b^* cannot be accepted by any reversible automaton [11], even if multiple initial states are allowed. Classical automata, namely automata with a single initial state and a set of final states, have been considered in the works by Holzer, Jakobi, and Kutrib [3,6,7]. In particular, in [3] the authors gave a characterization of regular

---

[1] From now on, we will consider only *one-way* automata. Hence we will omit to specify "one-way" all the times.

© IFIP International Federation for Information Processing 2017
Published by Springer International Publishing AG 2017. All Rights Reserved
G. Pighizzini and C. Câmpeanu (Eds.): DCFS 2017, LNCS 10316, pp. 238–249, 2017.
DOI: 10.1007/978-3-319-60252-3_19

languages which are accepted by reversible automata. This characterization is given in terms of the structure of the minimum deterministic automaton, i.e., the smallest deterministic automaton accepting the language under consideration. Furthermore, they provide an algorithm that, in the case the language is acceptable by a reversible automaton, allows to transform the minimum deterministic automaton into an equivalent reversible automaton, which in the worst case is exponentially larger than the given minimum automaton. In spite of that, the resulting automaton is minimal, namely there are no reversible automata accepting the same language with a smaller number of states. However, it is not necessarily unique, in fact there could exist different reversible automata with the same number of states accepting the same language. Further results concerning minimality and reducibility for reversible automata have been proved in [10].

Due to the above mentioned exponential state gap between deterministic automata and equivalent reversible automata, an explicit representation of a minimal reversible automaton can be exponentially larger than the representation of the corresponding minimum deterministic automaton. However, the minimal reversible automaton produced by the construction in [3] is obtained by creating copies of some parts of the minimum automaton. So, its transition table contains repeated patterns. Thus, it is interesting to investigate whether it is possible to obtain a concise representation of it, by avoiding to repeat those patterns. This is the aim of this paper, where we present two concise representations of reversible automata, which can be used to simulate reversible computations without explicitly writing down the description of the reversible automaton.

The first representation is based on a parameter β which is equal to the maximum number of incoming transitions with a same letter in each state of the given deterministic automaton A. Given β and A it is possible to simulate the computations of a reversible automaton A' equivalent to A, without explicitly representing it. The drawback of this simple representation is that even when the given automaton A is minimum, the simulated reversible automaton A' is not necessarily minimal. This motivates us to search a different concise representation, which exploits a result shown in [10]. The authors have proved that all the minimal reversible automata accepting a language have the same "state structure", in the sense that for each state q of the minimum deterministic automaton they should contain exactly the same number $c(q)$ of states equivalent to q. The second representation is given by the minimum deterministic automaton A accepting the language under consideration and such function c. We prove that, using such representation, it is possible to simulate the behaviour of a minimal reversible automaton equivalent to A without explicitly representing it. Both representations have polynomial size with respect to the size of the given deterministic automaton A and require a precomputation (of the parameter β and of the function c, respectively) which can be performed in polynomial time.

2   Preliminaries

In this section we recall some basic definitions and results useful in the paper. For a detailed exposition, we refer the reader to [4]. Given a set S, let us denote by $\#S$ its cardinality and by 2^S the family of all its subsets. Given an alphabet Σ, $|w|$ denotes the length of a string $w \in \Sigma^*$ and ε the empty string.

A *deterministic automaton* is a tuple $A = (Q, \Sigma, \delta, q_I, F)$, where Q is the set of *states*, Σ is the *input alphabet*, $q_I \in Q$ is the *initial state*, $F \subseteq Q$ is the set of *accepting states*, and $\delta : Q \times \Sigma \to Q$ is the partial *transition function*. The function δ can be extended to words in a standard way. The *language accepted* by A is $L(A) = \{w \in \Sigma^* \mid \delta(q_I, w) \in F\}$. The *reverse* transition function of A is the function $\delta^R : Q \times \Sigma \to 2^Q$, with $\delta^R(p, a) = \{q \in Q \mid \delta(q, a) = p\}$. A state $p \in Q$ is *useful* if p is *reachable*, i.e., there is $w \in \Sigma^*$ such that $\delta(q_I, w) = p$, and *productive*, i.e., if there is $w \in \Sigma^*$ such that $\delta(p, w) \in F$. When the set of states Q is finite, the automaton A is said to be a deterministic *finite* automaton (DFA). In this paper we only consider automata with all useful states.

We say that two states $p, q \in Q$ are *equivalent* if for all $w \in \Sigma^*$, $\delta(p, w) \in F$ exactly when $\delta(q, w) \in F$. Two automata A and A' are said to be *equivalent* if they accept the same language, i.e., $L(A) = L(A')$. By *minimal automaton* (in a certain family of automata) we mean an automaton with a minimal number of states. When the minimal automaton is unique (e.g., for the family of all DFAs accepting a certain regular language) we call it *minimum*.

A *strongly connected component* (SCC) C of a DFA $A = (Q, \Sigma, \delta, q_I, F)$ is a maximal subset of Q such that in the transition graph of A there exists a path between every pair of states in C. We introduce the relation $\prec$ on the set of SCCs of A, such that, for two such components C_1 and C_2, $C_1 \prec C_2$ when no state in C_1 can be reached from a state in C_2, but a state in C_2 is reachable from a state in C_1. As usual, if $C_1 \prec C_2$ or $C_1 = C_2$ we write $C_1 \preceq C_2$. It can be verified that $\preceq$ is a partial order.

Given a DFA $A = (Q, \Sigma, \delta, q_I, F)$, a state $r \in Q$ is said to be *irreversible* when $\#\delta^R(r, a) > 1$ for some $a \in \Sigma$, otherwise r is said to be *reversible*. The DFA A is said to be *irreversible* if it contains at least one irreversible state, otherwise A is *reversible* (REV-DFA). As pointed out in [7], the notion of reversibility for a language is related to the computational model under consideration. In this paper we only consider DFAs. Hence, by saying that a language L is *reversible*, we refer to this model, namely we mean that there exists a REV-DFA accepting L. The following result presents a characterization of reversible languages:

Theorem 1 [3, Theorem 2]. *Let L be a regular language and $M = (Q, \Sigma, \delta, q_I, F)$ be the minimum DFA accepting L. Then, L is accepted by a REV-DFA if and only if there do not exist useful states $p, q \in Q$, a letter $a \in \Sigma$, and a string $w \in \Sigma^*$ such that $p \neq q$, $\delta(p, a) = \delta(q, a)$, and $\delta(q, aw) = q$.*

According to Theorem 1, a language L is reversible exactly when the minimum DFA accepting it does not contain the *forbidden pattern* consisting of two transitions on a same letter a entering in a same state r, with one of these transitions arriving from a state in the same SCC as r. An algorithm to convert a minimum DFA M into an equivalent REV-DFA, if any, was obtained in [3]. Furthermore, the resulting REV-DFA is minimal.

3   A Simple Concise Representation

In this section we present our first concise representation. Let us start with a construction for simulating a DFA by an equivalent REV-DFA, in which we use the information about the maximum number of incoming transitions with respect to a same letter in the irreversible states.

Let $A = (Q, \Sigma, \delta, q_I, F)$ be a DFA with all useful states and let β be the maximum number of transitions on a same letter incoming in a state of Q, i.e., $\beta = \max\{\#\delta^R(q, a) \mid q \in Q, a \in \Sigma\}$. We observe that $\beta > 1$ if and only if A is irreversible. We define the following automaton with infinitely many states $A_\infty = (Q', \Sigma, \delta', q'_I, F')$, where $Q' = Q \times \mathbf{N}$, $q'_I = \langle q_I, 0 \rangle$, $F' = F \times \mathbf{N}$ and the transitions are defined as follows: let $\delta(q, a) = p$ and $\delta^R(p, a) = \{q_{j_1}, \ldots, q_{j_k}\}$, $k \geq 1$ for $q, p \in Q$, $a \in \Sigma$. For $x \geq 0$:

$$\delta'(\langle q, x \rangle, a) = \begin{cases} \langle p, x \rangle & k = 1 \\ \langle p, x\beta + i - 1 \rangle & \text{otherwise} \end{cases} \tag{1}$$

where $i \in \{1, \ldots, k\}$ is such that $q = q_{j_i}$.

Notice that, if $\delta'(\langle q, x \rangle, a) = \langle p, y \rangle$ then $x \leq y$. Roughly speaking, the idea of the construction is to use the second component of the states in A_∞ as label in order to distinguish different copies of a state reached from an irreversible transition in A. The formula used for the second component allow us to obtain this goal, as we will prove in Theorem 2.

We denote by A' the automaton obtained by restricting A_∞ to useful states. We prove that A' simulates A and that it is finite if and only if A does not contain the forbidden pattern.

Theorem 2. *Let $A = (Q, \Sigma, \delta, q_I, F)$ be a DFA and $A' = (Q', \Sigma, \delta', q'_I, F')$ be the automaton obtained by applying the above construction to A, restricted to useful states. Then: (a) $L(A') = L(A)$, (b) A' is reversible.*

Proof.(a) It is enough to observe that each state $\langle q, x \rangle \in Q'$ is equivalent to $q \in Q$.

(b) We have to prove that for each $a \in \Sigma$, $\langle \bar{q}_1, x_1 \rangle \neq \langle \bar{q}_2, x_2 \rangle$ implies that if both $\delta'(\langle \bar{q}_1, x_1 \rangle, a)$ and $\delta'(\langle \bar{q}_2, x_2 \rangle, a)$ are defined then they are different. Observe that $\delta'(\langle \bar{q}_i, x_i \rangle, a)$ ($i \in \{1, 2\}$) can be undefined only if $\delta(\bar{q}_i, a)$ is undefined. We consider the following cases:

- If $\bar{q}_1 = \bar{q}_2$ and $x_1 \neq x_2$ then $\delta(\bar{q}_1, a) = \delta(\bar{q}_2, a) = p$ for some $p \in Q$, otherwise M would be nondeterministic. Let $\delta^R(p, a) = \{q_{j_1}, \ldots, q_{j_k}\}$, $k \geq 1$. Then there exists i such that $\bar{q}_1 = \bar{q}_2 = q_{j_i}$. Considering (1), $\delta'(\langle \bar{q}_1, x_1 \rangle, a) = \langle p, y_1 \rangle$ and $\delta'(\langle \bar{q}_1, x_2 \rangle, a) = \langle p, y_2 \rangle$. If $k = 1$ then $y_1 = x_1$ and $y_2 = x_2$, otherwise $y_1 = x_1\beta + i - 1$ and $y_2 = x_2\beta + i - 1$. Since $x_1 \neq x_2$ we get $y_1 \neq y_2$. Hence, $\langle p, y_1 \rangle \neq \langle p, y_2 \rangle$.
- If $\bar{q}_1 \neq \bar{q}_2$ and $\delta(\bar{q}_1, a) = p_1 \neq \delta(\bar{q}_2, a) = p_2$ then, in A' the states $\delta'(\langle \bar{q}_1, x_1 \rangle, a) = \langle p_1, y_1 \rangle$ and $\delta'(\langle \bar{q}_2, x_2 \rangle, a) = \langle p_2, y_2 \rangle$ are different regardless of the values of y_1 and y_2.

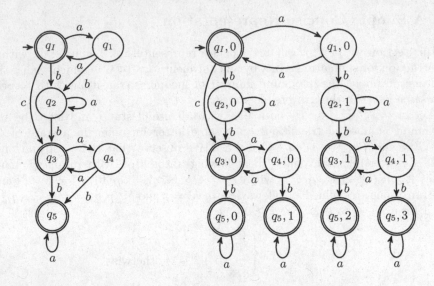

Fig. 1. A DFA where $\beta = 2$ and an equivalent REV-DFA

– If $\bar{q}_1 \neq \bar{q}_2$ and $\delta(\bar{q}_1, a) = \delta(\bar{q}_2, a) = p$, let $\delta^R(p, a) = \{q_{j_1}, \dots, q_{j_k}\}$, with $k > 1$. Then, there exist i, i', with $i \neq i'$ such that $\bar{q}_1 = q_{j_i}$ and $\bar{q}_2 = q_{j_{i'}}$. Considering (1), $\delta'(\langle \bar{q}_1, x_1 \rangle, a) = \langle p, y_1 \rangle$ and $\delta'(\langle \bar{q}_2, x_2 \rangle, a) = \langle p, y_2 \rangle$, where $y_1 = x_1\beta + i - 1$ and $y_2 = x_2\beta + i' - 1$. In the case $x_1 = x_2$, since $i \neq i'$, we get $y_1 \neq y_2$. In the case $x_1 \neq x_2$, and supposing, without loss of generality, $x_1 > x_2$, we get $\beta x_1 \geq \beta x_2 + \beta$, and hence $\beta x_1 > \beta x_2 + \beta - 1 \geq \beta x_2 + i' - 1$ (notice that $i' \leq \beta$). Then $y_1 = x_1\beta + i - 1 \geq x_1\beta > x_2\beta + i' - 1 = y_2$. This implies that $\langle p, y_1 \rangle \neq \langle p, y_2 \rangle$.

Hence, $\delta'(\langle \bar{q}_1, x_1 \rangle, a) \neq \delta'(\langle \bar{q}_2, x_2 \rangle, a)$. This allow us to conclude that A' is reversible. □

Theorem 3. *The automaton $A' = (Q', \Sigma, \delta, q'_I, F')$ obtained by applying the above construction to a DFA $A = (Q, \Sigma, \delta, q_I, F)$ is infinite if and only if A contains the forbidden pattern.*

Two examples related to the previous construction are shown in Figs. 1 and 2, where $\beta = 2$. Let us apply the construction to transform the DFA shown in Fig. 1 through an equivalent REV-DFA. Given for instance $\delta(q_3, b) = q_5$, we have $\delta^R(q_5, b) = \{q_3, q_4\}$, $k > 1$ and $i = 1$. Then $\delta'(\langle q_3, 1 \rangle, b) = \langle q_5, 2 \rangle$. Now we apply the same construction to the DFA in Fig. 2. Given for instance $\delta(q_1, b) = q_2$, we have $\delta^R(q_2, b) = \{q_I, q_1\}$, $k > 1$ and $i = 2$. Then $\delta'(\langle q_1, 0 \rangle, b) = \langle q_2, 1 \rangle$. This time taking $\delta(q_2, a) = q_3$, we have $\delta^R(q_3, a) = \{q_1, q_2\}$, $k > 1$ and $i = 2$. Then $\delta'(\langle q_2, 1 \rangle, a) = \langle q_3, 3 \rangle$. Actually, the simulation of a computation on a string does not require the explicit construction of the automaton A'. In fact, once we have β the computation of the automaton can be obtained, using the transition table of A and (1). For instance on aba we have the following steps: $q'_I \xrightarrow{a} \langle q_1, 0 \rangle \xrightarrow{b} \langle q_2, 1 \rangle \xrightarrow{a} \langle q_3, 3 \rangle$.

Notice that the second components in the states having a same q are not necessarily consecutive numbers, in the sense that, it is possible to have some gaps in the numbering as illustrated in Fig. 2 (states of the form $\langle q_3, x \rangle$ in the automaton on the right).

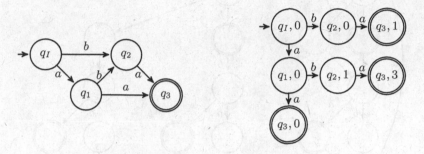

Fig. 2. A DFA where $\beta = 2$ and an equivalent REV-DFA

We point out that the automaton A' can be simulated without explicitly constructing its transition table. Indeed to simulate A' it is enough to know the value of β, which can be computed from the transition table of A, and to follow the transitions of A applying (1) to compute the states reached by A'. So, a concise representation of A' is given by the value of β and the automaton A. We will discuss later in this section how to compute β and how much the value of the second component of a state of A' can be large.

Even when applied to a minimum DFA, the above construction produces a REV-DFA which is not necessarily minimal as illustrated in Figs. 3 and 4: in Fig. 3 a minimum DFA M and an equivalent minimal REV-DFA (obtained by applying the algorithm in [3]) are shown. Notice that the minimal REV-DFA contains five states which are equivalent to q_7. Instead Fig. 4 shows the REV-DFA A' obtained by the above construction (notice that $\beta = 3$). In particular, A' contains six states equivalent to q_7.

In Theorem 3 it has been stated that when a DFA A does not contain the forbidden pattern, the automaton A' obtained by applying the above construction is finite. Furthermore, by Theorem 2, A' is reversible and, as already observed, not necessarily minimal. Hence, it is interesting to know what is the maximum value of the second component in a state of A'. In order to give a bound we will use the following lemmata.

Lemma 4. *If a DFA A contains less than two reversible states, then it contains the forbidden pattern.*

Lemma 5. *Let $A' = (Q', \Sigma, \delta', q'_I, F')$ be the automaton obtained by applying the above construction to a DFA $A = (Q, \Sigma, \delta, q_I, F)$ which does not contain the forbidden pattern. Given $w \in \Sigma^*$ and $q = \delta(q_I, w)$, consider $q_0, q_1, \ldots, q_m \in Q$, $a_1, a_2, \ldots, a_m \in \Sigma$ such that $w = a_1 \cdots a_m$, $q_0 = q_I$, $q_m = q$, and $q_i = \delta(q_{i-1}, a_i)$, for $i = 1, \ldots, m$. Then $\delta'(q'_I, w) = \langle q'_I, x \rangle$, where $\beta^{k-1} \leq x < \beta^k$, and $k = \#\{i \in \{1, \ldots, m\} \mid \#\delta^R(q_i, a_i) > 1\}$.*

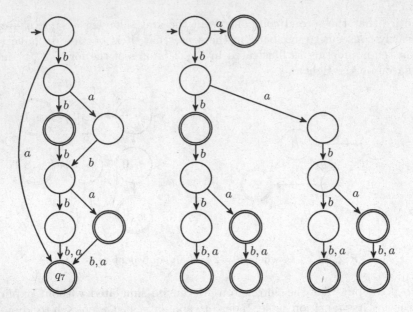

Fig. 3. A minimum DFA and an equivalent minimal REV-DFA

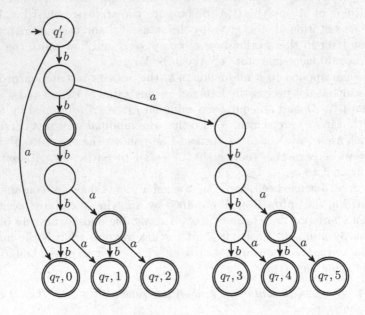

Fig. 4. A nonminimal REV-DFA obtained from the minimum DFA in Fig. 3

As a consequence of Lemma 5, the value of the second components of states of A' is smaller than β^k, where k is the maximum number of irreversible states that on a path from the initial state are reached by "irreversible transitions". Considering Lemma 4, we obtain:

Corollary 6. *If a* DFA *A does not contain the forbidden pattern, then the maximum value of the second component of a state of A' obtained by applying the above construction to A is smaller than $\beta^{\#Q-2}$.*

Observe that, the maximum value of the second component in a state of A' is reached when in each irreversible state r of A, the maximum number of incoming transitions for a same letter a is equal to β, i.e., $\#\delta^R(r,a) = \beta$. Two examples have been shown in Figs. 1 and 2. The DFA on the left of Fig. 2 has a path from q_I to q_3 reading the string $w = aba$ containing all irreversible states.

We also observe that β has an important role in the construction, so we believe useful to outline how β can be computed. Given a DFA $A = (Q, \Sigma, \delta, q_I, F)$ containing only useful states, we assume that δ resides in a transition table T of size $\#Q \cdot \#\Sigma$. The key observation is that a state is irreversible with respect to a symbol when it occurs more than one time in a column of T. Hence, the problem can be reduced to find the maximum number of occurrences of a state in a column of T, that requires time $\mathcal{O}(\#Q)$ for each symbol. So, the overall time is $\mathcal{O}(\#Q \cdot \#\Sigma)$, which is linear in the cardinality of Q when the alphabet is fixed.

4   Another Concise Representation

The drawback of the representation described in Sect. 3 is that the reversible automaton is not necessarily minimal. In this section we give a different representation which avoids such problem. To state it, some properties related to minimal REV-DFAs are useful. In [3] it has been observed that there are reversible languages having several nonisomorphic minimal REV-DFAs, while in [10, Lemmas 2 and 3] the following result has been proved:

Lemma 7. *Let $M = (Q, \Sigma, \delta, q_I, F)$ be the minimum* DFA *accepting a reversible language L. Then there exists a function $c : Q \to \mathbf{N}$ such that for each state $q \in Q$, in any* REV-DFA *equivalent to M there are at least $c(q)$ copies of q, and in any minimal* REV-DFA *equivalent to M there are exactly $c(q)$ copies of q. Furthermore, if $p, q \in Q$ are in the same* SCC, *then $c(p) = c(q)$.*

As a consequence of Lemma 7, all the minimal REV-DFAs accepting L have the same "state structure", in the sense that they should contain exactly $c(q)$ states equivalent to the state q of M.

Here we present an easy way to compute the value of $c(q)$, for each $q \in Q$, that is summarized in Algorithm 1. The algorithm firstly transforms the transition graph of M by decomposing it in SCCs, replacing each SCC by a single state, and linking with an edge two SCCs $\mathcal{C}'$ and $\mathcal{C}''$, with $\mathcal{C}' \neq \mathcal{C}''$, if there exist two states $p \in \mathcal{C}'$ and $q \in \mathcal{C}''$ such that $\delta(p,a) = q$ for some symbol a. This is summarized in line 1. After that, the obtained acyclic graph $\mathcal{S}_M$ can be sorted in topological order ($\preceq$, line 2). For further details about these constructions see, for example, [2, Chap. 23].

Then, all $c(q)$ are computed by analyzing the SCCs in topological order in the following way (lines 3–9): when a SCC $\mathcal{C}$ is considered, first of all the algorithm

Algorithm 1. Computation of $c(p)$ for each $p \in Q$.

1: Let $\mathcal{S}_M$ be the graph representing the SCCs of the transition graph of M
2: Let $\mathcal{L}_{\mathcal{S}_M}$ be the list of the SCCs of M sorted by topological order $\preceq$
3: **for all** SCCs $\mathcal{C} \in \mathcal{L}_{\mathcal{S}_M}$ **do**
4:     max_c $\leftarrow 1$
5:     **for all** states $q \in \mathcal{C}$ **do**
6:         **for all** letters $a \in \Sigma$ **do**
7:             max_c $\leftarrow$ max$\{$max_c$, \sum_{p \in \delta^R(q,a) \setminus \mathcal{C}} c(p)\}$
8:     **for all** states $q \in \mathcal{C}$ **do**
9:         $c(q) \leftarrow$ max_c
10: **return** c

---

computes for each state $q \in \mathcal{C}$ the maximum number of transitions on a same symbol a entering in q from SCCs different from $\mathcal{C}$, where a transition from p to q is *counted* $c(p)$ times, i.e., the algorithm computes $\sum_{p \in \delta^R(q,a) \setminus \mathcal{C}} c(p)$, for all $q \in Q$ and $a \in \Sigma$ and stores the maximum of all such values (lines 5–7). This value is assigned as $c(q)$ to each $q \in \mathcal{C}$ (lines 8–9). Note that, analyzing the SCCs in topological order, the value of $c(p)$ is used for all the states p in the set $\delta^R(q,a) \setminus \mathcal{C}$ when the algorithm is going to compute $c(q)$, for $q \in \mathcal{C}$. Obviously, for each state q in the first SCC $\mathcal{C}_{q_I}$, $\delta^R(q,a) \setminus \mathcal{C}_{q_I} = \emptyset$.

If M does not contain the forbidden pattern, then for each $q \in \mathcal{C}_{q_I}$, $c(q) = 1$ and the set $\delta^R(r,a) \setminus \mathcal{C}_{q_I}$ is empty for any $r \in \mathcal{C}_{q_I}$. As a consequence, the instruction at line 7 does not produce any increment of *max_c* for any state in the SCC under consideration.

It is easy to see that Algorithm 1 works in polynomial time: it is well known that operations at lines 1 and 2 require time $\mathcal{O}(\#V + \#E)$, where V and E are, respectively the set of vertices and the set of edges of the graph under consideration. So, in our case, the time for compute $\mathcal{S}_M$ and $\mathcal{L}_{\mathcal{S}_M}$ is $\mathcal{O}(\#Q)$. From line 3 to 9 the algorithm analyzes, the incoming transitions to each state q. This can be done in time $\mathcal{O}(\#Q)$ assuming that Σ is fixed. So, the Algorithm 1 uses $\mathcal{O}(\#Q)$ time.

The following property will be useful for the construction:

Lemma 8. *Let* $\delta^R(p,a) = \{q_{j_1}, \ldots, q_{j_k}\}$, $k \geq 1$, $p, q_{j_1}, \ldots, q_{j_k} \in Q$, *and* $a \in \Sigma$. *Then* $\sum_{h=1}^{i-1} c(q_{j_h}) + x < c(p)$, *for* $i = 1, \ldots, k$, $0 \leq x < c(q_{j_i})$.

We are now ready to present the construction which leads to our second concise representation. Let $M = (Q, \Sigma, \delta, q_I, F)$ be a minimum DFA accepting a reversible language L. We define the following DFA $A' = (Q', \Sigma, \delta', q_I', F')$, where $Q' = \{\langle q,x \rangle \mid q \in Q, 0 \leq x < c(q)\}$, $q_I' = \langle q_I, 0 \rangle$, $F' = \{\langle q,x \rangle \mid q \in F, 0 \leq x < c(q)\}$, and the transitions are defined as follows: let $\delta(q,a) = p$ and $\delta^R(p,a) = \{q_{j_1}, \ldots, q_{j_k}\}$, $k \geq 1$ for $q, p \in Q$, $a \in \Sigma$. Then:

$$\delta'(\langle q,x \rangle, a) = \langle p, \sum_{h<i} c(q_{j_h}) + x \rangle, \tag{2}$$

where $i \in \{1, \ldots, k\}$ is such that $q = q_{j_i}$ and $0 \leq x < c(q)$.

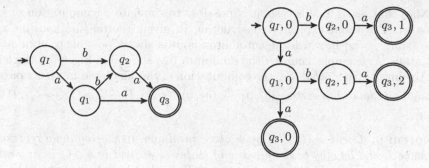

Fig. 5. A DFA and an equivalent minimal REV-DFA

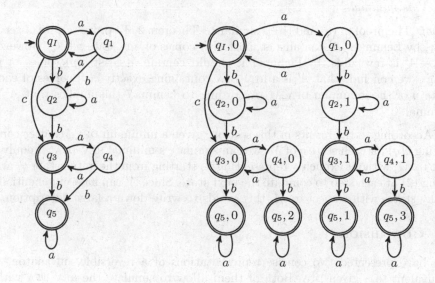

Fig. 6. A DFA and an equivalent minimal REV-DFA

Notice that by Lemma 8, this function δ' is well defined. We will prove that A' is a minimal REV-DFA equivalent to M.

Two examples related to the construction are shown in Figs. 5 and in 6. Let us apply the construction to the minimum DFA M in Fig. 5. The topological order $\preceq$ of the SCCs of M clearly is $q_I \preceq q_1 \preceq q_2 \preceq q_3$ and the number of copies $c(q)$ of a state $q \in Q$ follows the sequence of Fibonacci [3, Example 9]. In particular, $c(q_I) = c(q_1) = 1$, $c(q_2) = 2$, $c(q_3) = 3$. Given for instance $\delta(q_1, b) = q_2$, $\delta^R(q_2, b) = \{q_I, q_1\}$, then $\delta'(\langle q_1, 0\rangle, b) = \langle q_2, c(q_I) + 0\rangle = \langle q_2, 1\rangle$. Now we apply the construction to the minimum DFA M in Fig. 6. Consider the following number of copies $c(q)$: $c(q_I) = c(q_1) = 1$, $c(q_2) = c(q_3) = c(q_4) = 2$ and $c(q_5) = 4$. For instance, given $\delta(q_4, b) = q_5$, $\delta^R(q_5, b) = \{q_3, q_4\}$, we have $\delta'(\langle q_4, 0\rangle, b) = \langle q_5, c(q_3) + 0\rangle = \langle q_5, 2\rangle$.

Note that, even in this case, it is possible to simulate a computation of the REV-DFA A' without explicitly constructing it: given a letter and knowing the state $\langle state, index \rangle$ in which the automaton is, it is always possible to obtain the next state. As example, consider the minimum DFA showed in Fig. 6, (on the left) and the input string $abbab$. So, the computation of the simulated REV-DFA passes through the following states: $\langle q_I, 0 \rangle \xrightarrow{a} \langle q_1, 0 \rangle \xrightarrow{b} \langle q_2, 1 \rangle \xrightarrow{b} \langle q_3, 1 \rangle \xrightarrow{a} \langle q_4, 1 \rangle \xrightarrow{b} \langle q_5, 3 \rangle$.

Theorem 9. *Let $M = (Q, \Sigma, \delta, q_I, F)$ be a minimum DFA accepting a reversible language L and let $c(q)$ be the number of states equivalent to $q \in Q$ in any minimal REV-DFA equivalent to M. Let $A' = (Q', \Sigma, \delta', q_I', F')$ be the DFA obtained by applying the construction to M, then: (a) $L(A') = L$, (b) A' is reversible, (c) A' is minimal.*

Proof. The proof of (a) and (b) is similar to Theorem 2. To prove (c), we observe that, by Lemma 8, A' contains at most $c(p)$ copies of any state $p \in Q$. However since A' is reversible, by Lemma 7 it should contain at least $c(p)$ copies of p. Hence we conclude that A' is a REV-DFA containing exactly $c(p)$ copies of each state p of the minimum DFA M. According to Lemma 7 this implies that A' is minimal.   □

According to the results in this section, given a minimum DFA M, after computing $c(q)$ for each state q of M, we can simulate a minimal REV-DFA A' equivalent to M, without explicitly representing it, starting from the initial state q_I' and using (2) at each step to compute the next state. Since A' can have exponentially many states with respect to M, this avoids to write down a large description.

5   Conclusion

We have presented two concise representations of a reversible automaton A' equivalent to a given DFA. Both of them allow to simulate the REV-DFA without explictly writing down its transition table which, in the worst case, can be exponentially larger. The first representation in Sect. 3 requires an easy precomputation of a parameter β, but the obtained automaton is not necessarily minimal. Instead, the second representation in Sect. 4 requires the more involved precomputation of the function c, but the obtained automaton is minimal. Both precomputations can be done in polynomial time.

Even when the REV-DFA A' obtained from a minimum DFA A in the first representation is not minimal, its size is not too far from the size of a minimal REV-DFA in the following sense. In Lemma 5 we gave an upper bound of the maximum value of the second component in a state of A', i.e., β^{k_p}, where k_p is the maximum number of irreversible states on a path in A from the initial state q_I to p. Since A' is reversible we have $c(p) \leq \beta^{k_p}$ (Lemma 7). Furthermore, in the path at least two copies of each irreversible state should be created to obtain a reversible automaton. Then, $2^{k_p} \leq c(p) \leq \beta^{k_p}$. This implies that A' has a polynomial number of states with respect to the number of states of A if and only if each minimal REV-DFA equivalent to A has a polynomial number of states.

Acknowledgements. We are indebted with the anonymous referees for valuable suggestions.

References

1. Bennett, C.: Logical reversibility of computation. IBM J. Res. Dev. **17**(6), 525–532 (1973)
2. Cormen, T.H.: Introduction to Algorithms. MIT Press, Cambridge (2009)
3. Holzer, M., Jakobi, S., Kutrib, M.: Minimal reversible deterministic finite automata. In: Potapov, I. (ed.) DLT 2015. LNCS, vol. 9168, pp. 276–287. Springer, Cham (2015). doi:10.1007/978-3-319-21500-6_22
4. Hopcroft, J.E., Ullman, J.D.: Introduction to Automata Theory, Languages and Computation. Addison-Wesley, Boston (1979)
5. Kondacs, A., Watrous, J.: On the power of quantum finite state automata. In: FOCS, pp. 66–75. IEEE Computer Society (1997)
6. Kutrib, M.: Aspects of reversibility for classical automata. In: Calude, C.S., Freivalds, R., Kazuo, I. (eds.) Computing with New Resources. LNCS, vol. 8808, pp. 83–98. Springer, Cham (2014). doi:10.1007/978-3-319-13350-8_7
7. Kutrib, M.: Reversible and irreversible computations of deterministic finite-state devices. In: Italiano, G.F., Pighizzini, G., Sannella, D.T. (eds.) MFCS 2015. LNCS, vol. 9234, pp. 38–52. Springer, Heidelberg (2015). doi:10.1007/978-3-662-48057-1_3
8. Landauer, R.: Irreversibility and heat generation in the computing process. IBM J. Res. Dev. **5**(3), 183–191 (1961)
9. Lange, K., McKenzie, P., Tapp, A.: Reversible space equals deterministic space. J. Comput. Syst. Sci. **60**(2), 354–367 (2000)
10. Lavado, G.J., Pighizzini, G., Prigioniero, L.: Minimal and reduced reversible automata. In: Câmpeanu, C., Manea, F., Shallit, J. (eds.) DCFS 2016. LNCS, vol. 9777, pp. 168–179. Springer, Cham (2016). doi:10.1007/978-3-319-41114-9_13
11. Pin, J.-E.: On reversible automata. In: Simon, I. (ed.) LATIN 1992. LNCS, vol. 583, pp. 401–416. Springer, Heidelberg (1992). doi:10.1007/BFb0023844
12. Toffoli, T.: Reversible computing. In: Bakker, J., Leeuwen, J. (eds.) ICALP 1980. LNCS, vol. 85, pp. 632–644. Springer, Heidelberg (1980). doi:10.1007/3-540-10003-2_104

State Complexity of Unary SV-XNFA
with Different Acceptance Conditions

Laurette Marais[1,2(✉)] and Lynette van Zijl[1]

[1] Department of Computer Science, Stellenbosch University,
Stellenbosch, South Africa
[2] Meraka Institute, CSIR, Pretoria, South Africa
laurette.p@gmail.com

Abstract. Unary self-verifying symmetric difference automata were
introduced in [1], with an upper bound of $O(2^n)$ and lower bound of
$2^{n-1} - 1$ for state complexity. Implicit in the interpretation of self-
verifying acceptance for the symmetric difference case was the assumption that no state could be both an accept state and a reject state.
We present another interpretation of acceptance more aligned to the
equivalence of symmetric difference automata to weighted automata over
GF(2), where states that both accept and reject are allowed, and we give
a tight bound of $2^{n-1} - 1$ for state complexity for both interpretations
of acceptance.

1 Introduction

In [1] we showed how the concepts of symmetric difference finite state automata
(XNFA) and self-verifying acceptance (SV) could be combined, resulting in self-
verifying symmetric difference finite automata (SV-XNFA). We also provided an
upper bound of $O(2^n)$ on state complexity for n-state SV-XNFA in the unary
case, as well as a lower bound of $2^{n-1} - 1$. XNFA are useful in practice, with
applications in, for example, cryptography [2], and succinctly recognize groups
of languages that cannot be recognized succinctly by NFAs [3]. SV-NFAs are
interesting *per se* [4], and so we present a comparison between SV-NFAs and
SV-XNFAs.

It is customary for XNFA states to reflect the parity of the symmetric difference operation with the requirement that any state in the equivalent deterministic automaton (XDFA) contain an odd number of final XNFA states [5].
For SV-XNFA, we extended this to both the accepting state set F^a and the
rejecting state set F^r, requiring that an SV-XDFA state contain an odd number
of either of the two final state sets, but not both. The implicit assumption was
that an SV-XNFA state must itself either accept or reject or do neither, which
is consistent with self-verification for union automata [4] and automata theory
in general, where any particular state usually cannot both accept and reject.

In this paper we examine this implicit assumption more closely. We call the
interpretation of SV-XNFA acceptance where it is required that $F^a \cap F^r = \emptyset$

© IFIP International Federation for Information Processing 2017
Published by Springer International Publishing AG 2017. All Rights Reserved
G. Pighizzini and C. Câmpeanu (Eds.): DCFS 2017, LNCS 10316, pp. 250–261, 2017.
DOI: 10.1007/978-3-319-60252-3_20

disjunctive acceptance and we define so-called GF(2)-acceptance, where we allow $F^a \cap F^r$ to be non-empty. The result is that a final state may be an accept state, a reject state, or it may be both, and we show the implications of this interpretation in Sect. 3. We present various results for SV-XNFA for each of these forms of acceptance, finally showing that $2^{n-1} - 1$ is indeed a tight bound for the state complexity of both forms of acceptance.

2 Preliminaries

Definition 1. *An SV-XNFA with disjunctive acceptance is an SV-XNFA as defined in [1], i.e. a 6-tuple $N = (Q, \Sigma, \delta, Q_0, F^a, F^r)$, where Q, Σ, δ and Q_0 are defined as for XNFA, and F^a and F^r are the accept states and reject states, respectively, with the following requirement: for each input string w in Σ^*, there exist an odd number of paths ending in accept states, and zero or an even number of the paths ending in reject states, or vice versa. This is consistent with the parity acceptance typically applied to XNFA. Furthermore, $F^a \cap F^r = \emptyset$.*

The transition function $\delta : Q \times \Sigma \to 2^Q$ (where 2^Q represents the power set over Q) can be extended to strings in the Kleene closure Σ^* of the alphabet:

$$\delta^*(q, w_0 w_1 \ldots w_k) = \delta(\delta(\ldots \delta(q, w_0), w_1), \ldots, w_k).$$

For convenience, we write $\delta(q, w)$ to mean $\delta^*(q, w)$.

The choice of F^a and F^r for a given SV-XNFA N is called an *SV-assignment* of N. An SV-assignment where either F^a or F^r is empty, is called a *trivial SV-assignment*. Otherwise, if both F^a and F^r are nonempty, the SV-assignment is *non-trivial*. An SV-assignment that results in a language that is not the empty language or the universal language is called an *interesting SV-assignment*. For a detailed introduction to unary SV-XNFA, the interested reader is referred to [1].

XNFA have been shown to be equivalent to weighted automata over the finite field (Galois field) of two elements, or GF(2) [5,6]. Let $N = (Q, \Sigma, \delta, Q_0, F)$ be a unary XNFA with n states and $\Sigma = \{a\}$. We can represent the transition function $\delta : Q \times \Sigma \to 2^Q$ as an $n \times n$ matrix M over GF(2) whose (p, q)-th entry represents the weight (1 or 0) of the transition from p to q. Such a matrix has a characteristic polynomial $c(X) = \det(XI - M)$, where I is the identity matrix. Note that in [1] we used column vectors to represent the transitions from one state to another. In this paper we use row vectors as described, because it allows for a more intuitive presentation of the matrix and vector multiplication that follows. However, the results are identical, since any matrix and its transpose have the same characteristic polynomial.

We encode the initial states Q_0 as a vector of length n of elements in GF(2), namely $v(Q_0) = [q_{0_0} \ q_{0_1} \ \cdots \ q_{0_{n-1}}]$, where $q_{0_i} = 1$ if $q_i \in Q_0$ and $q_{0_i} = 0$ otherwise. Similarly, we encode the final states as an n-length vector, $v(F) = [q_{F_0} \ q_{F_1} \ \cdots \ q_{F_{n-1}}]$. We abuse notation by letting $\delta : Q \times \Sigma \to 2^Q$ (a function to sets of states) and $\delta : Q \times \Sigma \to \mathbb{Z}_2^n$ (a function to vectors of length n over GF(2)) depending on the context. Then the weight of a word w_k of length k is given by

$$\Delta(w_k) = v(Q_0) M^k v(F)^T.$$

In fact, $v(Q_0)M^k$ is a vector that encodes the XNFA states reachable from the initial states after reading k letters, or equivalently, it encodes the XDFA state that is reached from the initial state after reading k letters. That is, $\Delta(w) = \delta(w)v(F)^T$.

The important advantage of this interpretation is the fact that one can perform a change of basis on the transition matrix and initial and final state vectors of an XNFA to produce an equivalent XNFA. This ability is essential in, for example, minimisation algorithms for XNFA [6].

Let $N' = (Q, \Sigma, \delta', Q_0', F')$ be an XNFA, with transition matrix $M' = A^{-1}MA$ for some non-singular $n \times n$ matrix A, and let Q_0' and F' be such that $v(Q_0') = v(Q_0)A$ and $v(F')^T = A^{-1}v(F)^T$. Then

$$\begin{aligned}
\Delta'(w_k) &= v(Q_0')(M'^k)v(F')^T \\
&= v(Q_0)A(A^{-1}MA)^k A^{-1}v(F)^T \\
&= v(Q_0)(M^k)v(F)^T \\
&= \Delta(w_k).
\end{aligned}$$

Now, if we require for SV-XNFA that F^a and F^r be disjunct, a similar change of basis where $v(F'^a)^T = A^{-1}v(F^a)^T$ and $v(F'^r)^T = A^{-1}v(F^r)^T$ would not necessarily result in an equivalent SV-XNFA, since the resulting F'^a and F'^r might not be disjunct. Given M' and Q_0', it might be possible to choose another F'^a and F'^r that are disjunct so that the result is an SV-XNFA, but it is not immediately clear that such a choice would always be possible nor that the language would be preserved [7].

This brings us to the interpretation of SV-XNFA acceptance that excludes the requirement that F^a and F^r be disjunct. The result is that any SV-XNFA state is allowed to be both an accept and a reject state, or one or neither, as long as the SV-condition is met, i.e. that every word is either explicitly accepted by the automaton or explicitly rejected, but not both. We call this GF(2)-acceptance, since it is consistent with the interpretation of XNFA as weighted automata over GF(2) because a change of basis results in an equivalent XNFA (see Sect. 3).

Definition 2. *An SV-XNFA with GF(2)-acceptance is an SV-XNFA as defined in [1], i.e. a 6-tuple $N = (Q, \Sigma, \delta, Q_0, F^a, F^r)$, where Q, Σ, δ and Q_0 are defined as for XNFA, and F^a and F^r are defined as in the disjunctive acceptance case, but without the requirement that $F^a \cap F^r = \emptyset$.*

Note that an SV-assignment for disjunctive acceptance is also an SV-assignment for GF(2)-acceptance, but the reverse is not necessarily true, since the latter may involve assigning some states to both F^a and F^r.

2.1 Unary XNFA: Matrices and Polynomials Over GF(2)

Unary XNFA have been shown to be equivalent to linear feedback shift registers (LFSRs) [3]. We now give some relevant results from [2] relating LFSRs, and hence unary XNFA, to matrices and polynomials over GF(2).

Any $n \times n$ matrix M over GF(2) has a characteristic polynomial $c(X) = \det(XI - M)$. On the other hand, every polynomial $c(X)$ over GF(2) is the characteristic polynomial of some matrix M of the form shown in Fig. 1. M is said to be the companion matrix of $c(X)$. The following theorem further relates matrices and polynomials over GF(2).

$$M = \begin{bmatrix} 0 & 1 & 0 & \cdots & 0 \\ 0 & 0 & 1 & \cdots & 0 \\ \vdots & \vdots & & \vdots & \vdots \\ 0 & 0 & & \cdots & 1 \\ c_0 & c_1 & \cdots & c_{n-2} & c_{n-1} \end{bmatrix}$$

$$M' = \begin{bmatrix} A_1 & 0 & \cdots & 0 \\ 0 & A_2 & \cdots & 0 \\ \vdots & \vdots & \vdots & \vdots \\ 0 & 0 & \cdots & A_m \end{bmatrix}$$

Fig. 1. Companion matrix of $c(X)$

Fig. 2. Block diagonal matrix of companion matrices

Theorem 1 [2]. *Every matrix M over GF(2) is similar to a matrix M' of the form shown in Fig. 2, where each of the submatrices A_i is a companion matrix of a polynomial that is irreducible over GF(2) or of a power of a polynomial that is irreducible over GF(2), and the 0's are 0 submatrices of appropriate sizes.*

Each $c(X)$ over GF(2) is associated with a certain cycle structure. Specifically, the properties of the characteristic polynomial of a unary XNFA N allow conclusions about the possible length of the cycle of states of its equivalent XDFA N_D (see [1] in particular, as well as for example [2,3,8]). The choice of initial states for an XNFA determines which cycle in its polynomial cycle structure is the equivalent XDFA.

We say that a matrix M has an SV-assignment if some XNFA with M as its transition matrix has an SV-assignment.

In the rest of this paper, we consider only unary SV-XNFA with non-singular matrices, whose cycle structures do not include transient heads, i.e. states that are only reached once before a cycle is reached. By Lemma 1 of [1], this means that we only consider matrices with a characteristic polynomial $c(X) = X^n + c_{n-1}X^{n-1} + \ldots + c_1 X + c_0$ that does not have X as a factor, and hence $c_0 = 1$.

2.2 Unary XNFA: Linear Recurrences Over GF(2)

Since the structure of an XDFA is cyclic, for any state d_k of the XDFA that is reached after k letters have been read, there is some integer l so that, if $v(d_k) = v(Q_0)M^k$ for some k, then $v(d_k) = v(Q_0)M^{l+k}$. That is, l is the length of the cycle to which d_k belongs. This means that given any $v(d_k) = v(Q_0)M^k$ for some k, $v(d_{k-i}) = v(Q_0)M^{k-i}$ is well-defined.

We introduce the notion of linear recurrences with respect to XNFA to provide more information about how XDFA states occur together in a cycle. A linear recurrence over a finite field has a characteristic polynomial [9]. Specifically, the polynomial $c(X) = X^n + c_{n-1}X^{n-1} + \ldots + c_0$ characterises the linear recurrence $s_t = c_{n-1}s_{t-1} + c_{n-2}s_{t-2} + \ldots + c_0 s_{t-n}$. Let $c(X)$ be the characteristic polynomial of

1. a transition matrix M for an n-state XNFA N,
2. a linear recurrence over GF(2), namely $s_t = \Sigma_{i=1}^{n} c_{n-i}s_{t-i}$.

Let $\bar{s}_t = [s_{t_0}\ s_{t_1}\ \ldots\ s_{t_{n-1}}]$ be a vector of length n of elements in GF(2). Then,

$$[s_{t_0}\ s_{t_1}\ \ldots\ s_{t_{n-1}}] = c_{n-1}[s_{t_0-1}\ s_{t_1-1}\ \ldots\ s_{t_{n-1}-1}] +$$
$$c_{n-2}[s_{t_0-2}\ s_{t_1-2}\ \ldots\ s_{t_{n-1}-2}] + \ldots + \tag{1}$$
$$c_0[s_{t_0-n}\ s_{t_1-n}\ \ldots\ s_{t_{n-1}-n}].$$

That is, $\bar{s}_t = c_{n-1}\bar{s}_{t-1} + c_{n-2}\bar{s}_{t-2} + \ldots + c_0\bar{s}_{t-n}$.

Let $\bar{s}_0 = v(Q_0)$. The linear recurrence and the behaviour of the XNFA are both characterised by $c(X)$, so $\bar{s}_1 = v(Q_0)M$. In general $\bar{s}_k = v(Q_0)M^k$. We therefore have

$$\begin{aligned}
v(d_t) &= v(Q_0)M^t \\
&= \bar{s}_t \\
&= c_{n-1}\bar{s}_{t-1} + c_{n-2}\bar{s}_{t-2} + \ldots + c_0\bar{s}_{t-n} \\
&= c_{n-1}v(Q_0)M^{t-1} + c_{n-2}v(Q_0)M^{t-2} + \ldots + c_0 v(Q_0)M^{t-n} \\
&= c_{n-1}v(d_{t-1}) + c_{n-2}v(d_{t-2}) + \ldots + c_0 v(d_{t-n}).
\end{aligned} \tag{2}$$

Therefore, $d_t = \bigoplus_{i=1}^{n} c_{n-i}d_{t-i}$.

2.3 Notation

In this paper we let $\bar{s}_i$ refer to either the vector representing some set of states, or the set of states themselves, depending on the context. We use the symbol $\oplus$ and its sigma notation equivalent $\bigoplus$ to denote the boolean XOR operation when applied to boolean ones and zeroes, and the symmetric difference set operation when applied to sets, and specifically sets of states.

3 Main Results

This section presents results on SV-XNFA with both disjunctive acceptance and GF(2)-acceptance. We start by giving an example, to which we will refer back in the rest of the section, as various notions are discussed.

Example 1. Let N be an SV-XNFA with $Q_0 = \{q_0\}$, $F^a = \{q_0, q_1\}$ and $F^r = \{q_2, q_3\}$ and with its transition matrix being the companion matrix M for the polynomial $c(X) = X^4 + X^3 + X^2 + 1$ given in Fig. 1. Let the matrices A and M' (also shown in Fig. 3) be related to M in the sense that $M' = A^{-1}MA$. For now we only say that N' and N'' are SV-XNFA derived from N (both have M' as their transition matrix), and their equivalent XDFA's are given in Figs. 5 and Fig. 6, respectively, with a double edge indicating an accept state and a thick edge indicating a reject state.

$$M = \begin{bmatrix} 0 & 1 & 0 & 0 \\ 0 & 0 & 1 & 0 \\ 0 & 0 & 0 & 1 \\ 1 & 0 & 1 & 1 \end{bmatrix} \qquad A = \begin{bmatrix} 1 & 0 & 0 & 1 \\ 0 & 1 & 1 & 0 \\ 0 & 1 & 1 & 1 \\ 0 & 1 & 0 & 1 \end{bmatrix} \qquad M' = \begin{bmatrix} 0 & 1 & 0 & 0 \\ 1 & 0 & 0 & 1 \\ 1 & 1 & 1 & 0 \\ 0 & 0 & 1 & 0 \end{bmatrix}$$

Fig. 3. Example 1: matrices M, A and M'

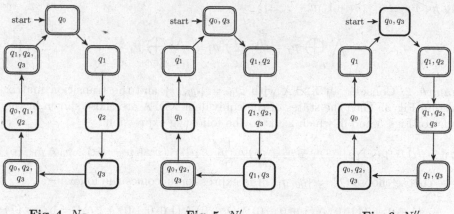

Fig. 4. N_D **Fig. 5.** N_D' **Fig. 6.** N_D''

Our first lemma provides a way to determine, given any cycle, whether an SV-assignment is possible.

Lemma 1. *Let $(d_1, d_2, ..., d_m)$ be a cycle representing an XDFA where $d_i \subseteq Q$ for $1 \leq i \leq m$, and Q is the set of states of the equivalent XNFA. Given either disjunctive acceptance or GF(2)-acceptance, the cycle has an SV-assignment if and only if for some some choice of $Q^F \subseteq Q$, where $p_j = 1$ for all $q_j \in Q^F$ and $p_j = 0$ otherwise, then*

$$\bigwedge_{i=1}^{m} \bigoplus_{q_j \in d_i} p_j = 1 \tag{3}$$

Proof. The expression in Eq. 3 can only evaluate to 1 if every XDFA state d_i contains an odd number of XNFA states that result in a value of 1. This means that for some choice of Q^F, an odd number of its elements must be present in every XDFA state. For disjunctive acceptance, Q^F represents those XNFA states that must be assigned to either F^a or F^r for the cycle to have an SV-assignment.

For GF(2)-acceptance, Q^F represents those XNFA states that must be assigned to either F^a or F^r but not both for the cycle to have an SV-assignment. That is, every XDFA state must contain an odd number of states that contribute to the count of either F^a or F^r but not both, so that one but not both of the counts sum to an odd number. $\qquad\square$

Since $p \wedge p = p$, we also have the following corollary.

Corollary 1. *For* $0 \leq k \leq m$,

$$\bigwedge_{i=1}^{m} \bigoplus_{q_j \in d_i} p_j = \bigwedge_{i=1}^{m} \bigoplus_{q_j \in d_i} p_j \wedge \bigoplus_{q_j \in d_k} p_j. \tag{4}$$

We assign some index $l > m$ *to a repeated state and generalise in the following way for any* $L \subseteq \{m+1, m+2, ...\}$:

$$\bigwedge_{i=1}^{m} \bigoplus_{q_j \in d_i} p_j = \bigwedge_{i=1}^{m} \bigoplus_{q_j \in d_i} p_j \wedge \bigwedge_{l \in L} \bigoplus_{q_j \in d_l} p_j. \tag{5}$$

Example 2. Consider an XNFA with $Q_0 = \{q_0, q_3\}$ and the transition matrix given in Fig. 3. Then the states of the equivalent XDFA are those shown in the cycles of Figs. 5 and 6, which leads to the following expression:

$$(p_0 \oplus p_3) \wedge (p_1 \oplus p_2) \wedge (p_1 \oplus p_2 \oplus p_3) \wedge (p_1 \oplus p_3) \wedge (p_0 \oplus p_2 \oplus p_3) \wedge p_0 \wedge p_1. \tag{6}$$

If we choose choose $Q^F = \{q_0, q_1\}$, the expression becomes the following:

$$(1 \oplus 0) \wedge (1 \oplus 0) \wedge (1 \oplus 0 \oplus 0) \wedge (1 \oplus 0) \wedge (1 \oplus 0 \oplus 0) \wedge 1 \wedge 1 = 1. \tag{7}$$

We can assign $F^a = \{q_1\}$ and $F^r = \{q_0\}$, and for now we only note that it is an SV-assignment given either disjunctive acceptance or GF(2)-acceptance. Figure 6 corresponds to this choice of final states.   □

Example 3. Consider again the XNFA and equivalent XDFA in Example 2. The characteristic polynomial of M is $c(X) = X^4 + X^3 + X^2 + 1$, so state transition behaviour is characterised by $s_t = s_{t-1} + s_{t-2} + s_{t-4}$. Let $\bar{s}_t = \{q_1, q_2\}$, then

$$\begin{aligned} \bar{s}_{t-1} + \bar{s}_{t-2} + \bar{s}_{t-4} &= \{q_0, q_3\} \oplus \{q_1\} \oplus \{q_0, q_2, q_3\} \\ &= \{q_1, q_2\} \\ &= \bar{s}_t. \end{aligned}$$

□

The following two lemmas shed more light on linear recurrences in XDFA cycles.

Lemma 2. *The RHS (right hand side) of the linear recurrence* $s_t = c_{n-1}s_{t-1} + c_{n-2}s_{t-2} + ... + c_0 s_{t-n}$ *of a polynomial* $c(X) = X^n + c_{n-1}x^{n-1} + ... + c_1 x + c_0$ *has an odd number of terms if* $X + 1$ *is a factor of* $c(X)$ *and an even number otherwise.*

Lemma 3. *Let* d_1 *be any state in an XDFA cycle of an equivalent XNFA with state set* Q *and let the cycle be characterised by the linear recurrence* $s_t = \sum_{i=1}^{n} c_{n-i}s_{t-i}$. *Let* $\sigma_1 = \bigoplus_{q_j \in d_1} p_j$ *for some choice of* $Q^F \subseteq Q$ *so that*

$p_j = 1$ if $q_j \in Q^F$ and $p_j = 0$ otherwise. Furthermore, let $T \subseteq \{2, ..., n\}$ be the set of indices such that $d_1 = \bigoplus_{k \in T} d_k$. Then

$$\sigma_1 = \bigoplus_{k \in T} \sigma_k. \tag{8}$$

In the case where the cycle length $m \leq n$, it is possible that $d_{1-i} = d_{1-j}$ for some i, j. We assign to the l-th duplicate of a state d_k (including any occurrences of d_1 itself) the index $lm + k$, referring to it as d_{lm+k}.

Theorem 2. *An XNFA N with characteristic polynomial $c(X) = X^n + c_{n-1}x^{n-1} + ... + c_1x + c_0$ has no SV-assignment, given either disjunctive acceptance or GF(2)-acceptance, if $X + 1$ is not a factor of $c(X)$.*

Proof. From the discussion in Sect. 2.2, we know that the state transition behaviour of N is described by $s_t = c_{n-1}s_{t-1} + c_{n-2}s_{t-2} + ... + c_0s_{t-n}$.

That is, in its equivalent XDFA N_D, each state is the $\oplus$-sum of some number of states in its cycle. Consider any cycle of N_D and let d_1 be any state in the cycle. Let $\mathbb{T} = \{2, ..., n\}$ and let $T_1 \subseteq \mathbb{T}$ be the set of indices so that

$$d_1 = \bigoplus d_i, i \in T_1.$$

If $m > n$, we use Eq. 3 from Lemma 1 as well as Lemma 3 to determine if the cycle has an SV-assignment. Since Lemma 1 applies to both disjunctive and GF(2)-acceptance, the rest of the proof applies similarly.

$$\bigwedge_{i=1}^{m} \bigoplus_{q_j \in d_i} p_j = \bigwedge_{i=1}^{m} \sigma_i$$

$$= \sigma_1 \wedge \bigwedge_{i \in T_1} \sigma_i \wedge \bigwedge_{i \in \mathbb{T} \setminus T_1} \sigma_i$$

$$= \bigoplus_{i \in T_1} \sigma_i \wedge \bigwedge_{i \in T_1} \sigma_i \wedge \bigwedge_{i \in \mathbb{T} \setminus T_1} \sigma_i.$$

If $m \leq n$, we let $K = \{i \in T_1 | i > m\}$ and use Eq. 5 from Corollary 1 and Lemma 3 in the following way:

$$\bigwedge_{i=1}^{m} \bigoplus_{q_j \in d_i} p_j = \bigwedge_{i=1}^{m} \bigoplus_{q_j \in d_i} p_j \wedge \bigwedge_{i \in K} \bigoplus_{q_j \in d_i} p_j$$

$$= \bigwedge_{i=1}^{m} \sigma_i \wedge \bigwedge_{i \in K} \sigma_i$$

$$= \sigma_1 \wedge \bigwedge_{i \in T_1} \sigma_i \wedge \bigwedge_{i \in \mathbb{T} \setminus T_1} \sigma_i$$

$$= \bigoplus_{i \in T_1} \sigma_i \wedge \bigwedge_{i \in T_1} \sigma_i \wedge \bigwedge_{i \in \mathbb{T} \setminus T_1} \sigma_i.$$

In both cases, if $c(X)$ does not have $X + 1$ as a factor, then by Lemma 2, $|T_1|$ is even. Therefore, $\bigoplus_{i \in T_1} \sigma_i \wedge \bigwedge_{i \in T_1} \sigma_i = 0$, and so the cycle does not have an SV-assignment. $\qquad \square$

Having shown that a characteristic polynomial with $X + 1$ is a necessary condition for a matrix to have an SV-assignment, we now prepare the ground for showing in Theorem 3 that it is also a sufficient condition. We first determine that performing a change of basis on an SV-XNFA always results in another SV-XNFA, albeit in different ways for disjunctive acceptance and GF(2)-acceptance.

Lemma 4. *Given GF(2)-acceptance, for any n-state XNFA N with transition matrix M, if N has an SV-assignment, then there is an N' with transition matrix M' that is similar to M, so that N' has an SV-assignment and N and N' accept the same language. Hence, if N has an (interesting) SV-assignment, then so does N'.*

Proof. If M' is similar to M, then $M' = A^{-1}MA$ for some non-singular $n \times n$ matrix A. We encode the initial states as the vector $v(Q_0) = [q_{0_0} \ q_{0_1} \ \cdots \ q_{0_{n-1}}]$, where $q_{0_i} = 1$ if $q_{0_i} \in Q_0$ and $q_{0_i} = 0$ otherwise. Similarly, we let $v(F^a) = [q_{a_0} \ q_{a_1} \ \cdots \ q_{a_{n-1}}]$ and $v(F^r) = [q_{r_0} \ q_{r_1} \ \cdots \ q_{r_{n-1}}]$, where q_{a_i} and q_{r_i} indicate membership to F^a and F^r respectively.

We define the following functions, where the SV-constraint is choosing F^a and F^r in such a way that $accept(N, a^k) \neq reject(N, a^k)$ for any k.

$$accept(N, a^k) = v(Q_0)(M^k)v(F^a)^T$$
$$reject(N, a^k) = v(Q_0)(M^k)v(F^r)^T$$

Now, we choose the initial states Q_0', and final states F'^a and F'^r so that $v(Q_0') = v(Q_0)A$, $v(F'^a)^T = A^{-1}v(F^a)^T$ and $v(F'^r)^T = A^{-1}v(F^r)^T$. Then

$$\begin{aligned}
accept(N', a^k) &= v(Q_0')(M'^k)v(F'^a)^T \\
&= v(Q_0)A(A^{-1}MA)^k A^{-1}v(F^a)^T \\
&= v(Q_0)(M^k)v(F^a)^T \\
&= accept(N, a^k)
\end{aligned}$$

and

$$\begin{aligned}
reject(N', a^k) &= v(Q_0')(M'^k)v(F'^r)^T \\
&= v(Q_0)A(A^{-1}MA)^k A^{-1}v(F^r)^T \\
&= v(Q_0)(M^k)v(F^r)^T \\
&= reject(N, a^k).
\end{aligned}$$

By assumption, F^a and F^r are an (interesting) SV-assignment for N, and so F'^a and F'^r are an (interesting) SV-assignment for N'. Furthermore, N and N' accept the same language. $\qquad \square$

Lemma 5. *Given disjunctive acceptance, for any n-state XNFA N with transition matrix M, if N has an SV-assignment, then there is an N″ with transition matrix M′ that is similar to M, so that N″ has an SV-assignment, but N and N″ do not necessarily accept the same language.*

Proof. We construct N'' so that $Q_0'' = Q_0'$ as in Lemma 4. However, we let $F''^a = F'^a \setminus F'^r$ and $F'''^r = F'^r \setminus F'^a$. That is, F''^a is the set of states that occur in F'^a but not in F'^r and vice versa for F'''^r, so that $F''^a \cap F'''^r = \emptyset$. Recall from Lemma 1 that for F'^a and F'^r to be an SV-assignment for GF(2)-acceptance, there must be some Q^F so that an odd number of XNFA states in each XDFA state are either accept or reject states but not both. F''^a and F'''^r are precisely those states, and so are an SV-assignment for disjunctive acceptance.

However, it is possible that $F'^a \subset F'^r$ or vice versa, and so it is possible that F''^a or F'''^r is empty even if F'^a and F'^r are non-empty. So although F''^a and F'''^r are an SV-assignment, clearly N'' does not necessarily accept the same language as N.   □

Example 4. Let N be the SV-XNFA with matrix given in Fig. 1. Then the equivalent XDFA N_D is the cycle as shown in Fig. 4. Note that in this cycle, both disjunctive acceptance and GF(2)-acceptance place the same constraints on possible SV-assignments, since the XNFA states each appear alone in XDFA states and therefore must accept or reject but cannot do both.

We use non-singular matrix A as shown in Fig. 1, and we perform two changes of basis: as described in Lemma 4 to get an XNFA N', and as described in Lemma 5 to get an XNFA N_D''. Both N' and N'' have transition matrix M' (Fig. 3). The equivalent XDFA N_D' with GF(2)-acceptance is the cycle as shown in Fig. 5, with $F'^a = \{q_1, q_3\}$ and $F'^r = \{q_0, q_3\}$. Note, for example, that the state $\{q_0, q_2, q_3\}$ accepts, because it contains an odd number of accept states, i.e. q_3, and an even number of reject states, i.e. q_0 and q_3. The XDFA N_D'' with disjunctive acceptance is shown in Fig. 6, with $F''^a = \{q_1\}$ and $F'''^r = \{q_0\}$.

The following lemma asserts the existence of SV-assignments for certain matrices.

Lemma 6. *Any matrix M that is a block diagonal matrix of companion matrices, with characteristic polynomial $c(X) = (X + 1)\phi(X)$, has an SV-assignment, given either disjunctive or GF(2)-acceptance.*

Theorem 3. *Given either disjunctive acceptance or GF(2)-acceptance, any matrix M with characteristic polynomial $c(X) = (X + 1)\phi(X)$ has an SV-assignment.*

Proof. By Theorem 1, M is similar to some block diagonal matrix M' with the companion matrices of factors of $c(X)$ on the diagonal. By Lemma 6, M' has an SV-assignment given either disjunctive or GF(2)-acceptance. Therefore, by Lemma 4 M has an SV-assignment given GF(2)-acceptance, and by Lemma 5 M has an SV-assignment given disjunctive acceptance.   □

The following theorem follows directly from Theorems 2 and 3.

Theorem 4. *Any matrix M has an SV-assignment given either disjunctive acceptance or GF(2)-acceptance, if and only if its characteristic polynomial has $X + 1$ as a factor.*

Along with Theorem 4, Lemma 7 and Theorem 5 that follow provide the grounds for concluding that $2^{n-1} - 1$ is a tight bound on the state complexity of unary SV-XNFA for both disjunctive acceptance and GF(2)-acceptance.

Lemma 7. *For an XNFA with a characteristic polynomial $c(X)$ with degree n that has $X + 1$ as a factor, the longest possible cycle has length $2^{n-1} - 1$.*

Proof. Suppose $c(X)$ has two irreducible factors, $\phi_1 = X + 1$ and ϕ_2, where ϕ_2 is an irreducible polynomial with degree $n - 1$. By Theorem 1 of [1], if ϕ_2 is primitive it has a single cycle of length $2^{n-1} - 1$, and together with $X + 1$ induces a cycle for $c(X)$ of the same length. If it is non-primitive it has cycles of length b where b is a factor of $2^{n-1} - 1$, inducing cycles of length b for $c(X)$ together with $X + 1$. Hence, the maximum cycle length is $2^{n-1} - 1$.

Now suppose that $c(X)$ has three irreducible factors, $\phi_1 = X + 1$, ϕ_2 of degree $k \leq n - 2$ and ϕ_3 of degree $n - k - 1$, with $k > n - k - 1$. Cycles of $c(X)$ induced together with $X + 1$ can only produce at most cycles of length $2^k - 1 < 2^{n-1} - 1$. Consider the cycle induced by ϕ_2 and ϕ_3. Since it will have greatest possible length if 2^k and 2^{n-k-1} are relatively prime, we assume this to be the case. The cycle induced has length $lcm(2^k - 1, 2^{n-k-1} - 1) = (2^k - 1) * (2^{n-k-1} - 1)$. That is,

$$(2^k - 1) * (2^{n-k-1} - 1) = 2^{n-1} - 2^k - 2^{n-k-1} - 1$$
$$< 2^{n-1} - 1.$$

Cycles of $c(X)$ are induced by pairs of factors of $c(X)$, and so if $c(X)$ had more irreducible factors, they would have smaller degree and so would induce even shorter cycles. Therefore, $2^{n-1} - 1$ is the longest possible cycle for a polynomial $c(X)$ of degree n that has $X + 1$ as a factor.   □

Theorem 5. *Given either disjunctive acceptance or GF(2)-acceptance, for any $n \geq 2$, there is a language $\mathcal{L}_n$ so that some n-state SV-XNFA accepts $\mathcal{L}_n$ and the minimal SV-XDFA that accepts $\mathcal{L}_n$ has $2^{n-1} - 1$ states.*

Proof. Theorem 7 of [1] gives a proof of the statement with regards to disjunctive acceptance. Since any SV-assignment for disjunctive acceptance is also an SV-assignment for GF(2)-acceptance, it is also a proof for the statement with regards to GF(2)-acceptance.   □

4   Conclusion

We have shown a close similarity between SV-XNFA with two different acceptance conditions, namely disjunctive acceptance and GF(2)-acceptance. In particular, they have the same state complexity bound of $2^{n-1} - 1$. Disjunctive acceptance shares a typical requirement of most other finite state automata, i.e. that a state cannot both accept and reject. However, for self-verification in unary XNFA, this removes the equivalence known between XNFA and weighted automata over $GF(2)$, since a so-called change of basis does not preserve the language. This has implications for operations such as minimisation, which depend upon it [6]. $GF(2)$-acceptance does preserve the equivalence, but results in the need for SV-XNFA states that both accept and reject. Whereas for disjunctive acceptance, neutral states are non-final, since they neither accept nor reject, $GF(2)$-acceptance introduces the notion of neutral final states that both accept and reject. While this is perhaps counter-intuitive, it allows for SV-XNFA that behave more predictably.

References

1. Marais, L., Zijl, L.: Unary self-verifying symmetric difference automata. In: Câmpeanu, C., Manea, F., Shallit, J. (eds.) DCFS 2016. LNCS, vol. 9777, pp. 180–191. Springer, Cham (2016). doi:10.1007/978-3-319-41114-9_14

2. Stone, H.S.: Discrete Mathematical Structures and their Applications. Science Research Associates, Chicago (1973)

3. Van Zijl, L.: Nondeterminism and succinctly representable regular languages. In: Proceedings of the 2002 Annual Research Conference of the South African Institute of Computer Scientists and Information Technologists. SAICSIT 2002, Republic of South Africa, South African Institute for Computer Scientists and Information Technologists, pp. 212–223 (2002)

4. Jirásková, G., Pighizzini, G.: Optimal simulation of self-verifying automata by deterministic automata. Inf. Comput. **209**(3), 528–535 (2011). Special Issue: 3rd International Conference on Language and Automata Theory and Applications (LATA 2009)

5. Vuillemin, J., Gama, N.: Compact normal form for regular languages as Xor automata. In: Maneth, S. (ed.) CIAA 2009. LNCS, vol. 5642, pp. 24–33. Springer, Heidelberg (2009). doi:10.1007/978-3-642-02979-0_6

6. Merwe, B., Tamm, H., Zijl, L.: Minimal DFA for symmetric difference NFA. In: Kutrib, M., Moreira, N., Reis, R. (eds.) DCFS 2012. LNCS, vol. 7386, pp. 307–318. Springer, Heidelberg (2012). doi:10.1007/978-3-642-31623-4_24

7. Van der Merwe, B.: Private communication (2017)

8. Dornhoff, L.L., Hohn, F.E.: Applied Modern Algebra. Macmillan Publishing Co., Inc., London (1978)

9. McEliece, R.J.: Finite Fields for Computer Scientists and Engineers, vol. 23. Springer Science & Business Media, Berlin (1987)

Reset Complexity of Ideal Languages
Over a Binary Alphabet

Marina Maslennikova[✉]

Ural Federal University, Ekaterinburg, Russia
maslennikova.marina@gmail.com

Abstract. We prove **PSPACE**-completeness of checking whether a given ideal language serves as the language of reset words for some automaton with at most four states over a binary alphabet.

Keywords: Ideal language · Synchronizing automaton · Reset word · Reset complexity · **PSPACE**-completeness

Introduction

Regular languages admit compact representations by different tools: deterministic and nondeterministic finite automata, syntactic monoids, regular expressions, etc. Each of these tools gives rise to the corresponding complexity measure of regular languages. Along with these general tools, there are more specific devices for representing regular languages from some special classes. One of such classes is formed by ideal regular languages. A language $I \subseteq \Sigma^*$ is called a *two-sided ideal* (or simply an *ideal*) if I is non-empty and $\Sigma^* I \Sigma^* \subseteq I$. In what follows we consider only languages which are regular, thus we drop the adjective "regular". Thus, the expression "ideal language" (or simply "ideal") always means a regular two-sided ideal language.

Let $\mathscr{A} = \langle Q, \Sigma, \delta \rangle$ be a *deterministic finite automaton* (DFA), where Q is the *state set*, Σ stands for the *input alphabet*, and $\delta: Q \times \Sigma \to Q$ is the totally defined *transition function* defining the action of the letters in Σ on Q. The function δ is extended uniquely to a function $Q \times \Sigma^* \to Q$, where Σ^* stands for the free monoid over Σ. The latter function is still denoted by δ. In the theory of formal languages the definition of a DFA usually includes the *initial state* $q_0 \in Q$ and the set $F \subseteq Q$ of *terminal states*. We use these ingredients when dealing with automata as devices for recognizing languages. A language $L \subseteq \Sigma^*$ is *recognized* by an automaton $\mathscr{A} = \langle Q, \Sigma, \delta, q_0, F \rangle$ if $L = \{w \in \Sigma^* \mid \delta(q_0, w) \in F\}$. We denote by $L[\mathscr{A}]$ the language recognized by the automaton $\mathscr{A}$.

A DFA $\mathscr{A} = \langle Q, \Sigma, \delta \rangle$ is called *synchronizing* if there exists a word $w \in \Sigma^*$ whose action leaves the automaton in one particular state no matter at which

The author acknowledges support by the Russian Foundation for Basic Research, grant no. 16-01-00795, the Ministry of Education and Science of the Russian Federation, project no. 1.3253.2017, and the Competitiveness Enhancement Program of Ural Federal University.

G. Pighizzini and C. Câmpeanu (Eds.): DCFS 2017, LNCS 10316, pp. 262–273, 2017.
DOI: 10.1007/978-3-319-60252-3_21

state in Q it is applied: $\delta(q, w) = \delta(q', w)$ for all $q, q' \in Q$. Any word w with this property is said to be *reset* for the DFA $\mathscr{A}$. For the last 50 years synchronizing automata have received a great deal of attention. For a brief introduction to the theory of synchronizing automata we refer the reader to the surveys [8, 10].

In the present paper we focus on some complexity aspects of the theory of synchronizing automata. We denote by $\mathrm{Syn}(\mathscr{A})$ the language of reset words for a given automaton $\mathscr{A}$. It is well known that $\mathrm{Syn}(\mathscr{A})$ is regular [10]. Furthermore, it is an ideal in Σ^*. On the other hand, every regular ideal language I serves as the language of reset words for some automaton. For instance, the minimal automaton recognizing I is synchronized exactly by I [4]. Thus synchronizing automata can be considered as a special representation of ideal languages. Effectiveness of such a representation was addressed in [4]. The *reset complexity $rc(I)$* of an ideal language I is the minimal possible number of states in a synchronizing automaton $\mathscr{A}$ such that $\mathrm{Syn}(\mathscr{A}) = I$. Every such automaton $\mathscr{A}$ is called a *minimal synchronizing automaton* (for brevity, MSA). Let $sc(I)$ be the number of states in the minimal automaton recognizing I. For every ideal language I, we have $rc(I) \leq sc(I)$ [4]. Moreover, for each $n \geq 3$, there exists a language I_n such that $rc(I_n) = n$ and $sc(I_n) = 2^n - n$ [4]. Thus the representation of an ideal language by means of a synchronizing automaton can be exponentially more succinct than the "traditional" representation via the minimal automaton. This resembles the well-known property of nondeterministic finite automata (for brevity, NFAs): for each $n \geq 3$, there is an n-state NFA $\mathscr{N}$ such that every DFA recognizing the same language as $\mathscr{N}$ has at least $2^n - 1$ states [6,7].

The following question arises: how hard is it to check that a given synchronizing DFA $\mathscr{B}$ is an MSA for a given ideal I (I is assumed to be given by a synchronizing DFA $\mathscr{A}$ with $\mathrm{Syn}(\mathscr{A}) = I$)? Another question related to the previous one is the following: how hard is it to verify the inequality $rc(I) \leq \ell$ for a given ideal I and a given $\ell \in \mathbb{N}$? The inequality $rc(I) \leq \ell$ means that there exists a synchronizing DFA $\mathscr{B}$ with at most ℓ states such that $\mathrm{Syn}(\mathscr{B}) = I$. The aforementioned questions are trivial for automata over a unary alphabet, thus in what follows we deal with alphabets that have at least two letters. The problem of checking the equality $\mathrm{Syn}(\mathscr{B}) = I$ is equivalent to the problem of checking the equality $\mathrm{Syn}(\mathscr{A}) = \mathrm{Syn}(\mathscr{B})$ for two given synchronizing automata $\mathscr{A}$ and $\mathscr{B}$. The complexity of the latter problem has been studied in [5]. It is well known that the equality of the languages recognized by two given DFAs can be checked in time polynomial of the size of automata. However, the problem of checking the equality of the languages of reset words of two synchronizing DFAs turns out to be **PSPACE**-complete [5]. Recall that the problem of checking the equality of languages recognized by two given NFAs is **PSPACE**-complete as well [9]. In this context we again find that synchronizing automata share some properties of nondeterministic finite automata.

We state formally the SYN-EQUALITY problem:

–*Input:* synchronizing automata $\mathscr{A}$ and $\mathscr{B}$.

–*Question:* is $\mathrm{Syn}(\mathscr{A}) = \mathrm{Syn}(\mathscr{B})$?

In [5] SYN-EQUALITY has been proved to be **PSPACE**-complete. In the present paper we provide a more transparent proof of **PSPACE**-hardness of this problem. In particular, it allows us to strengthen the result of [5] concerning the problem of evaluating the reset complexity of a given ideal language.

We state formally the RESET-INEQUALITY problem:

−*Input:* synchronizing DFA $\mathscr{A}$ over Σ, $\ell \in \mathbb{N}$.
−*Question:* is $rc(\mathrm{Syn}(\mathscr{A})) \leq \ell$?

In [5] RESET-INEQUALITY has been shown to be **PSPACE**-complete for $\ell = 3$ and enough large input alphabet (with at least five letters). In the present paper we significantly strengthen this result and prove that RESET-INEQUALITY, restricted to a binary alphabet, remains **PSPACE**-complete even for $\ell = 4$. Note that RESET-INEQUALITY is trivial for DFAs over a unary alphabet and, furthermore, RESET-INEQUALITY can be solved in polynomial of the size of $\mathscr{A}$ time for $\ell = 1$ and $\ell = 2$ in the general case [5]. Thus the only question that remains open concerns the complexity of RESET-INEQUALITY for $\ell = 3$ in the case of a binary alphabet.

The paper is organized as follows. In Sect. 1 we introduce some definitions and preliminary results. In Sect. 2 we provide a modified proof of **PSPACE**-hardness of SYN-EQUALITY. Section 3 contains the main result about **PSPACE**-completeness of the problem RESET-INEQUALITY in the case of a binary alphabet.

1   Preliminaries

A state s of a DFA $\mathscr{A} = \langle Q, \Sigma, \delta \rangle$ is said to be a *sink* if $\delta(s, a) = s$ for all $a \in \Sigma$. If the transition function δ is clear from the context, we write $q \cdot w$ instead of $\delta(q, w)$ for $q \in Q$ and $w \in \Sigma^*$. This notation extends naturally to any subset $H \subseteq Q$ by putting $H \cdot w = \{\delta(q, w) \mid q \in H\}$.

Recall that a word $u \in \Sigma^*$ is a *prefix* (*suffix* or *factor*, respectively) of a word w if $w = us$ ($w = tu$ or $w = tus$, respectively) for some $t, s \in \Sigma^*$. A reset word for a DFA $\mathscr{A}$ is called *minimal* if none of its proper prefixes nor suffixes is reset.

Due to [5, Corollary 1] we have the following proposition.

Proposition 1. *SYN-EQUALITY is in* **PSPACE**.

To prove that SYN-EQUALITY is a **PSPACE**-complete problem we reduce the following well-known **PSPACE**-complete problem to the complement of SYN-EQUALITY. This problem deals with checking emptiness of the intersection of languages recognized by DFAs from a given collection [2].

FINITE AUTOMATA INTERSECTION

−*Input:* given n DFAs $M_i = \langle Q_i, \Sigma, \delta_i, q_i, F_i \rangle$, for $i = 1, \ldots, n$.
−*Question:* is $\bigcap_i L[M_i] \neq \varnothing$?

Since FINITE AUTOMATA INTERSECTION is known to be **PSPACE**-complete even in the case of a binary alphabet, we may assume that $|\Sigma| = 2$, in particular, let Σ be $\{a, b\}$.

2 PSPACE-hardness of SYN-EQUALITY

The proof of **PSPACE**-hardness of SYN-EQUALITY is based on the same idea as the proof from [5]. However, our modified construction allows us to reduce the number of letters from 5 to 4. We provide a sketch of the proof of **PSPACE**-hardness for the sake of completeness.

Given an instance of FINITE AUTOMATA INTERSECTION, we can assume without loss of generality that each initial state q_i has no incoming edges and $q_i \notin F_i$. Indeed, excluding the case for which the empty word ε is in $L[M_i]$ we can always build a DFA $M_i' = \langle Q_i', \Sigma, \delta_i', q_i', F_i \rangle$, which recognizes the same language as M_i, such that the initial state q_i' has no incoming edges. This can easily be achieved by adding a new initial state q_i' to the state set Q_i and defining the transition function δ_i' by the rule: $\delta_i'(q_i', c) = \delta_i(q_i, c)$ for all $c \in \Sigma$ and $\delta_i'(q, c) = \delta_i(q, c)$ for all $c \in \Sigma$, $q \in Q_i$. Furthermore, we may assume that the sets Q_i, for $i = 1, \ldots, n$, are pairwise disjoint. Also we can suppose that any letter from Σ does not belong to $\bigcap_i L[M_i]$. Otherwise, we add a new initial state q_i'' to each M_i' and put $\delta_i(q_i'', c) = q_i'$ for all $c \in \Sigma$. This assumption will be of use in Sect. 3.

To build an instance of SYN-EQUALITY from the DFAs M_i, $i = 1, \ldots, n$, we construct a DFA $\mathscr{A} = \langle Q, \Delta, \varphi \rangle$ with $Q = \bigcup_{i=1}^{n} Q_i \cup \{s, h\}$, where s and h are new states not belonging to any Q_i. We add two new letters x and z to the alphabet Σ and let $\Delta = \Sigma \cup \{x, z\}$. The transition function φ of the DFA $\mathscr{A}$ is defined by the following rules:

$$\varphi(q, c) = \delta_i(q, c) \qquad \text{for all } i = 1, \ldots, n, \ q \in Q_i \text{ and } c \in \Sigma;$$
$$\varphi(q, x) = q_i \qquad \text{for all } i = 1, \ldots, n, \ q \in Q_i;$$
$$\varphi(q, z) = s \qquad \text{for all } i = 1, \ldots, n, \ q \in F_i;$$
$$\varphi(q, z) = h \qquad \text{for all } i = 1, \ldots, n, \ q \in Q_i \setminus F_i;$$
$$\varphi(h, c) = s \qquad \text{for all } c \in \Delta;$$
$$\varphi(s, c) = s \qquad \text{for all } c \in \Delta.$$

The resulting automaton $\mathscr{A}$ is shown schematically in Fig. 1. The action of letters from Σ on the states $p \in Q_i$ is not shown. Denote by G_i the set $Q_i \setminus (F_i \cup \{q_i\})$. All the states from the set G_i are shown as the node labeled by G_i. All the states from the set F_i are shown as the node labeled by F_i.

The constructed automaton is synchronizing, for example, by the word zz. It can be easily seen that by the definition of the transition function φ we get $\varphi(Q, w) \cap Q_i \neq \varnothing$ if and only if $w \in (\Sigma \cup \{x\})^*$. Consider the language

$$I = (\Sigma \cup \{x\})^* z \, \Delta^+.$$

From the observations above and the definition of φ we obtain Lemma 1.

Lemma 1. $\bigcap_{i=1}^{n} L[M_i] = \varnothing$ *if and only if* $\mathrm{Syn}(\mathscr{A}) = I$.

We omit the proof of Lemma 1 because of space constraints.

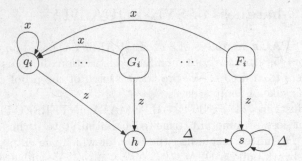

Fig. 1. Automaton $\mathscr{A}$

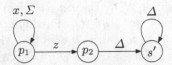

Fig. 2. Automaton $\mathscr{B}$

Now we build a 3-state automaton $\mathscr{B} = \langle P, \Delta, \tau \rangle$ (see Fig. 2). Its state set is $P = \{p_1, p_2, s'\}$, where s' is a unique sink state. It is easy to verify that I serves as the language of reset words for $\mathscr{B}$. Furthermore, I does not serve as the language of reset words for a synchronizing automaton of size at most two over the same alphabet Δ. So $\mathscr{B}$ is an MSA for I and $rc(\mathrm{Syn}(\mathscr{B})) = 3$.

Lemma 2. $\mathrm{Syn}(\mathscr{B}) = I$.

Finally, by Lemmas 1 and 2, we have the following claim.

Lemma 3. $\bigcap_{i=1}^{n} L[M_i] = \varnothing$ if and only if $\mathrm{Syn}(\mathscr{A}) = \mathrm{Syn}(\mathscr{B})$.

3   PSPACE-completeness of RESET-INEQUALITY

We have reduced the problem FINITE AUTOMATA INTERSECTION to the complement of SYN-EQUALITY. By construction of DFAs $\mathscr{A}$ and $\mathscr{B}$, we have $\Delta = \{z, a, b, x\}$. Now we are going to study the complexity of checking the inequality $rc(I) \leq \ell$ in the case of a binary alphabet. First we build DFAs $\mathscr{C} = \langle C, \{\mu, \lambda\}, \varphi_2 \rangle$ and $\mathscr{D} = \langle D, \{\mu, \lambda\}, \tau_2 \rangle$ over a binary alphabet $\{\mu, \lambda\}$ with unique sink states ζ_1 and ζ_2 respectively. It turns out that the constructions of $\mathscr{C}$ and $\mathscr{D}$ preserve the equality of reset languages. More precisely, $\mathrm{Syn}(\mathscr{A}) = \mathrm{Syn}(\mathscr{B})$ if and only if $\mathrm{Syn}(\mathscr{C}) = \mathrm{Syn}(\mathscr{D})$. Let $J = \mathrm{Syn}(\mathscr{C})$. We will prove that $rc(J) > 4$ if and only if $\bigcap_{i=1}^{n} L[M_i] \neq \varnothing$. It allows to obtain the desired result about **PSPACE-**completeness of RESET-INEQUALITY for a binary case alphabet.

In order to construct $\mathscr{C} = \langle C, \{\mu, \lambda\}, \varphi_2 \rangle$ and $\mathscr{D} = \langle D, \{\mu, \lambda\}, \tau_2 \rangle$ we apply a recoding technique which has been used in [1,3,5]. Namely, we define morphisms $h\colon \{\lambda, \mu\}^* \lambda \to \Delta^*$ and $\overline{h}\colon \Delta^* \to \{\lambda, \mu\}^* \lambda$ preserving the property of being a reset word for the corresponding automaton. Since the definitions of morphisms differ from those described in [5], we present them here. Let $d_1 = z$, $d_2 = a$, $d_3 = b$ and $d_4 = x$. We put $h(\mu^k \lambda) = d_{k+1}$ for $k = 0, \ldots, 3$ and $h(\mu^k \lambda) = d_4 = x$ for $k \geq 4$. Every word from the set $\{\lambda, \mu\}^* \lambda$ can be uniquely factorized by words $\mu^k \lambda$, $k = 0, 1, 2, \ldots$, whence the mapping h is totally defined. We also consider the morphism $\overline{h}\colon \Delta^* \to \{\lambda, \mu\}^* \lambda$ defined by the rule $\overline{h}(d_k) = \mu^{k-1} \lambda$.

Now we take the constructed above DFA $\mathscr{B} = \langle P, \Delta, \tau \rangle$ with the state set $P = \{p_1, p_2, s'\}$. We build $\mathscr{D} = \langle D, \{\mu, \lambda\}, \tau_2 \rangle$ with a unique sink state ζ_2.

We associate each state p_i of the automaton $\mathscr{B}$ with a 4-element set of states $P_i = \{p_{i,1}, \ldots, p_{i,4}\}$ of the automaton $\mathscr{D}$. Namely, the states $p_{i,2}, p_{i,3}, p_{i,4}$ are copies of the state p_i associated with $p_{i,1}$. The action of the letter μ is defined in the following way: $\tau_2(p_{i,k}, \mu) = p_{i,k+1}$ for $k \leq 3$, and $\tau_2(p_{i,4}, \mu) = p_{i,4}$. We put $D = P_1 \cup P_2 \cup \{\zeta_2\}$, where ζ_2 is a unique sink state. The action of the letter λ is defined by the rules:

- if $\tau(p_i, d_k) = s'$, then $\tau_2(p_{i,k}, \lambda) = \zeta_2$;
- if $\tau(p_i, d_k) = p_j$, then $\tau_2(p_{i,k}, \lambda) = p_{j,1}$.

The latter rule means that if there is a transition from p_i to p_j labeled by the letter d_k, then there is a transition from $p_{i,1}$ to $p_{j,1}$ labeled by the word $\mu^{k-1}\lambda$.

The DFA $\mathscr{C}$ is constructed in an analogous way. Figure 3 illustrates the automata $\mathscr{D}$ (left) and $\mathscr{C}$ (right). The actions of μ and λ are shown by solid and dotted arrows, respectively. For compactness, we do not show some transitions labeled by λ in $\mathscr{C}$. Nevertheless, the action of λ is defined on each state in $\mathscr{C}$. The resulting automata $\mathscr{C}$ and $\mathscr{D}$ have $4(|Q|-1)+1$ and 9 states respectively, where $|Q|$ is the cardinality of the state set of $\mathscr{A}$.

Lemma 4. $\mathrm{Syn}(\mathscr{A}) = \mathrm{Syn}(\mathscr{B})$ *if and only if* $\mathrm{Syn}(\mathscr{C}) = \mathrm{Syn}(\mathscr{D})$.

Proof. It is convenient to organize the DFA $\mathscr{D}$ as a table. The set P_i is called the *i-th column* of the set D. For each $k = 1, \ldots, 4$, the set $R_k = \{p_{1,k}, p_{2,k}\}$ is called the *k-th row* of the set D. The k-th row contains copies of all states corresponding to the k-th letter from Δ. The i-th column contains the state $p_{i,1}$ corresponding to the state p_i and its copies $p_{i,2}, p_{i,3}, p_{i,4}$. Each state from the i-th column maps under the action of μ to a state from the same column. For $k \leq 3$, the row R_k maps under the action of μ to the next row R_{k+1}. The 4-th row is fixed by μ, that is, $\tau_2(R_4, \mu) = R_4$. The state set D maps under the action of λ to a subset of $R_1 \cup \{\zeta_2\}$. The DFA $\mathscr{C}$ has the same properties.

Assume that $\mathrm{Syn}(\mathscr{A}) \neq \mathrm{Syn}(\mathscr{B})$. From the proof of Lemma 1 it follows that the word $w = xw'z$ with $w' \in \bigcap_i L[M_i]$ is reset for $\mathscr{A}$ and it is not reset for $\mathscr{B}$. Thus $\overline{h}(w) \in \mathrm{Syn}(\mathscr{C})$ and $\overline{h}(w) \notin \mathrm{Syn}(\mathscr{D})$. So $\mathrm{Syn}(\mathscr{C}) \neq \mathrm{Syn}(\mathscr{D})$.

Assume now that $\mathrm{Syn}(\mathscr{A}) = \mathrm{Syn}(\mathscr{B})$. We show that every minimal reset word of $\mathscr{C}$ is reset for $\mathscr{D}$ and every minimal reset word of $\mathscr{D}$ is reset for $\mathscr{C}$. Let u be a minimal reset word of $\mathscr{C}$. Any word $u \in \{\mu\}^*$ is not in $\mathrm{Syn}(\mathscr{C})$ since μ

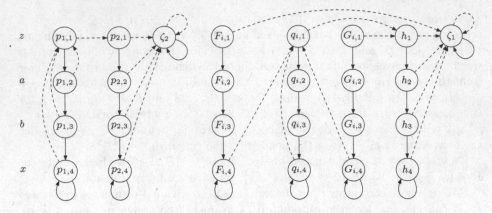

Fig. 3. The automata $\mathscr{D}$ (left) and $\mathscr{C}$ (right)

brings each column to its subset. Thus u contains some factor from $\{\lambda\}^+$. The automaton $\mathscr{C}$ possesses a unique sink state ζ_1. Hence $\mathscr{C}$ is synchronized to ζ_1. Furthermore, all transitions leading to ζ_1 are labeled by λ, and ζ_1 is fixed by μ and λ. Thus if u does not end up with λ, then it is not a minimal reset word. We have $u \in \{\lambda, \mu\}^*\lambda$, i.e., $u = u'\lambda$ for some $u' \in \{\lambda, \mu\}^*$. Let us note that λ^2 appears in u as a factor (otherwise, $u \notin \mathrm{Syn}(\mathscr{C})$). If the last letter of u' is λ and λ^2 is not a factor of u', then $u \notin \mathrm{Syn}(\mathscr{C})$. If λ^2 is a factor of u', then by the definition of the transition functions of $\mathscr{C}$ and $\mathscr{D}$ we have $u \in \mathrm{Syn}(\mathscr{C})$ and $u \in \mathrm{Syn}(\mathscr{D})$. So the inclusion $\mathrm{Syn}(\mathscr{C}) \subseteq \mathrm{Syn}(\mathscr{D})$ takes place. The opposite inclusion $\mathrm{Syn}(\mathscr{D}) \subseteq \mathrm{Syn}(\mathscr{C})$ is verified analogously.   □

Lemma 4 implies **PSPACE**-completeness of the problem SYN-EQUALITY restricted to a binary alphabet.

Theorem 1 *(Theorem 4, [5]). SYN-EQUALITY restricted to a binary alphabet case is* **PSPACE**-*complete.*

As a corollary, we immediately obtain the following statement.

Proposition 2 [5]. *Let ℓ be a positive integer number and $\mathscr{A}$ a synchronizing DFA. The problem of checking the inequality $rc(\mathrm{Syn}(\mathscr{A})) \leq \ell$ is in* **PSPACE**.

So we reduced FINITE AUTOMATA INTERSECTION to the complement of SYN-EQUALITY restricted to a binary case alphabet as follows. For an arbitrary instance of FINITE AUTOMATA INTERSECTION one may build the corresponding automata $\mathscr{C}$ and $\mathscr{D}$ over a binary alphabet $\{\lambda, \mu\}$ such that $\bigcap_{i=1}^{n} L[M_i] \neq \varnothing$ if and only if $\mathrm{Syn}(\mathscr{C}) = \mathrm{Syn}(\mathscr{D})$.

The set of all words synchronizing a fixed subset $H \subseteq D$ of the state set of $\mathscr{D}$ is defined as follows:

$$\mathcal{R}(H) = \{v \in \{\lambda, \mu\}^* \mid H \cdot v = \{\zeta_2\}\}.$$

Since ζ_2 is a unique sink state in $\mathscr{D}$, any reset word for $\mathscr{D}$ maps any subset of D to $\{\zeta_2\}$. Let us note that

$$\mathcal{R}(\{p_{2,1}\}) = \mathcal{R}(\{p_{2,2}\}) = \mathcal{R}(\{p_{2,3}\}) = \mathcal{R}(\{p_{2,4}\});$$
$$\mathcal{R}(\{p_{1,2}\}) = \mathcal{R}(\{p_{1,3}\}) = \mathcal{R}(\{p_{1,4}\}).$$

These equalities imply that the language of reset words of $\mathscr{D}'$ coincides with the language of reset words of $\mathscr{D}$ (see Fig. 4). Indeed, due to the equalities above we can merge states $p_{2,1}$, $p_{2,2}$, $p_{2,3}$, $p_{2,4}$ into a unique state p_2 and merge states $p_{1,2}$, $p_{1,3}$, $p_{1,4}$ into a unique state p_0. Solid arrows still denote the action of μ while dotted arrows stand for λ. In what follows we consider the DFA $\mathscr{D}'$ instead of $\mathscr{D}$.

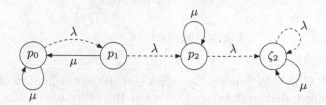

Fig. 4. The automaton $\mathscr{D}'$

A standard tool for finding the language of reset words of a given DFA $\mathscr{K} = \langle Q, \delta, \Sigma \rangle$ is the *power automaton* $\mathcal{P}(\mathscr{K})$. Its state set is the set $\mathcal{Q}$ of all nonempty subsets of Q, and the transition function is defined as a natural extension of δ to the set $\mathcal{Q} \times \Sigma$ (the resulting function is also denoted by δ), namely, $\delta(S, c) = \{\delta(q, c) \mid q \in S\}$ for $S \subseteq Q$ and $c \in \Sigma$. If we take the set Q as the initial state and singletons as final states in $\mathcal{P}(\mathscr{K})$, then we obtain an automaton recognizing $\mathrm{Syn}(\mathscr{K})$. It is easy to see that if all singletons are merged into a unique sink state s, the resulting automaton still recognizes $\mathrm{Syn}(\mathscr{K})$. Throughout the paper the term *power automaton* and the notation $\mathcal{P}(\mathscr{K})$ refer to this modified version.

Lemma 5. *Let* $J = \mathrm{Syn}(\mathscr{C})$. *The equality* $\bigcap_{i=1}^{n} L[M_i] = \varnothing$ *takes place if and only if* $rc(J) \leq 4$.

Proof. Let $\mathscr{E} = \langle P, \{\lambda, \mu\}, \gamma \rangle$ be an MSA for J. Assume that $\bigcap_{i=1}^{n} L[M_i] = \varnothing$. By Lemma 1 we get that $\mathrm{Syn}(\mathscr{A}) = \mathrm{Syn}(\mathscr{B}) = I$ with $I = (\Sigma \cup \{x\})^* z \Delta^+$. By Lemma 4 we have $J = \mathrm{Syn}(\mathscr{C}) = \mathrm{Syn}(\mathscr{D}')$. Let us note that $\lambda^3 \in \mathrm{Syn}(\mathscr{D}')$. Furthermore, $\lambda, \lambda^2 \notin \mathrm{Syn}(\mathscr{D}')$. It means that $P.\lambda^3 \subsetneq P.\lambda^2 \subsetneq P.\lambda \subsetneq P$. Hence $|P| \geq 4$. Therefore, $rc(J) \geq 4$. On the other hand, $\mathrm{Syn}(\mathscr{D}') = J$. Thus $\mathscr{D}'$ is an MSA for $J = \mathrm{Syn}(\mathscr{C})$, i.e., $rc(J) = 4$.

Let us assume now that $\bigcap_{i=1}^{n} L[M_i] \neq \varnothing$. We are going to show that $rc(J) > 4$ in this case. Let u be a minimal reset word for $\mathscr{C}$. By the arguments from the proof of Lemma 4 and by the construction of $\mathscr{C}$, one may note that u can be factorized as $u = u'\lambda$ for some $u' \in \{\mu, \lambda\}^+$. Also λ^2 is necessarily a factor of u. Moreover, by the definition of the transition function of $\mathscr{C}$ we have $\lambda^3 \in J$ while $\lambda, \lambda^2 \notin J$. From the arguments above it follows that every MSA for J has at least 4 states. Arguing by contradiction, let us assume that there exists a 4-state automaton $\mathscr{E} = \langle P, \{\lambda, \mu\}, \gamma \rangle$ with $\mathrm{Syn}(\mathscr{E}) = J$. Without loss of generality suppose that $P = \{0, 1, 2, 3\}$. We define the action of λ on the state set P. Since $\lambda^3 \in \mathrm{Syn}(\mathscr{E})$ and $\lambda, \lambda^2 \notin \mathrm{Syn}(\mathscr{E})$, there is a unique up to isomorphism way to define the action of λ on the states from the state set P (see Fig. 5).

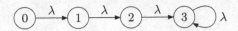

Fig. 5. The action of λ in $\mathscr{E}$

The word $\lambda^2\mu\lambda$ is in $\mathrm{Syn}(\mathscr{C})$, i.e., $\lambda^2\mu\lambda \in J$. By the definition of the action of λ in $\mathscr{E}$ we get that $\gamma(P, \lambda^2) = \{2, 3\}$. On the other hand, $\lambda^2\mu \notin \mathrm{Syn}(\mathscr{C})$, thus $\lambda^2\mu \notin \mathrm{Syn}(\mathscr{E})$. Hence $\{2, 3\}$ under the action of μ maps to a two-element subset which is translated by λ into $\{3\}$. So we need to guarantee the equality $\gamma(\{2, 3\}, \mu) = \{2, 3\}$. The action of μ at states 2 and 3 can be defined in two possible ways such that the last equality is true (see Fig. 6).

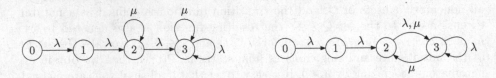

Fig. 6. The action of μ at states 2 and 3 in the DFA $\mathscr{E}$

Note that $\lambda\mu\lambda \notin \mathrm{Syn}(\mathscr{C})$. Therefore, $\lambda\mu\lambda$ is not a reset word for $\mathscr{E}$. Since we have $\gamma(\{1, 2, 3\}, \lambda\mu\lambda) = \{3\}$ for each variant from Fig. 6, the word $\lambda\mu\lambda$ should map the state 0 to a state different from 3. However $\gamma(0, \lambda) = 1$, thus 1 under the action of μ maps to either 0 or 1. All in all, for each variant from Fig. 6, we get two ways to define the image of 1 under the action of μ (see Fig. 7).

It remains to define the image of 0 under the action of μ. Let us note that $\mu^2\lambda^2 \notin \mathrm{Syn}(\mathscr{C})$. Since $\gamma(\{2, 3\}, \mu^2\lambda^2) = \{3\}$, one of the equalities, $\gamma(0, \mu) = 0$ or $\gamma(0, \mu) = 1$, is required to take place. Furthermore, we have $\gamma(\{1, 2, 3\}, \mu^2\lambda^2) = \{3\}$ in the third and forth variants from Fig. 7. It means that there exists the only possibility to put $\gamma(0, \mu) = 0$ for these variants. So we have six automata over the alphabet $\{\lambda, \mu\}$ shown in Fig. 8. It remains to check whether J could coincide with the set of reset words for one of these DFAs.

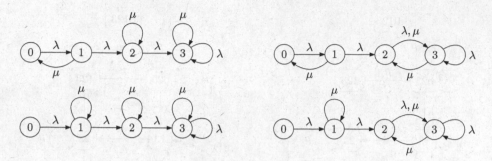

Fig. 7. Possible ways to define the action of μ at 1 in $\mathscr{E}$

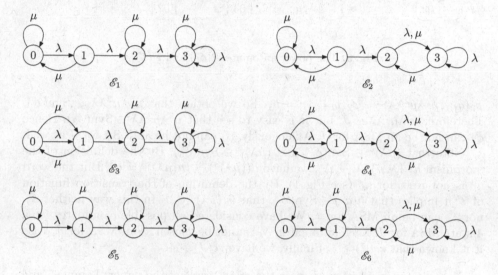

Fig. 8. Possible candidates for $\mathscr{E}$

The DFA $\mathscr{E}_1$ from Fig. 8 is isomorphic to $\mathscr{D}'$ for which we have $\mathrm{Syn}(\mathscr{D})' = \mathrm{Syn}(\mathscr{D})$. So $\mathrm{Syn}(\mathscr{E}_1) = \mathrm{Syn}(\mathscr{D})$. By the assumption $\bigcap\limits_{i=1}^{n} L[M_i] \neq \varnothing$, hence by Lemmas 1 and 4 we have $J = \mathrm{Syn}(\mathscr{C}) \neq \mathrm{Syn}(\mathscr{D})$. Therefore, $\mathscr{E}_1$ is not an MSA for J. For $\mathscr{E}_1$ and $\mathscr{E}_2$ the equality $\mathrm{Syn}(\mathscr{E}_1) = \mathrm{Syn}(\mathscr{E}_2)$ takes place. It can be easily checked by the construction of power automata $\mathcal{P}(\mathscr{E}_1)$ and $\mathcal{P}(\mathscr{E}_2)$ (see Fig. 9). It implies that $\mathscr{E}_2$ cannot be an MSA for J.

By the assumption $c \notin \bigcap\limits_{i=1}^{n} L[M_i]$ for all $c \in \Sigma$. It means that $b \notin L[M_j]$ or, equivalently, $\delta_j(q_j, b) \in Q_j \setminus F_j$ for some index j. Take the word xbz. By the definition of the transition function φ of $\mathscr{A}$ we have $\varphi(Q, xbz) = \{h, s\}$, so $xbz \notin \mathrm{Syn}(\mathscr{A})$. By the definition of the morphism $\overline{h} \colon \Delta^* \to \{\lambda, \mu\}^* \lambda$ we have $\overline{h}(xbz) = \mu^3 \lambda \mu^2 \lambda \lambda$. By the definition of the transition function φ_2 of $\mathscr{C}$ we get $\varphi_2(q_{j,1}, \mu^3 \lambda \mu^2 \lambda) = \varphi_2(q_{j,1}, \mu^2 \lambda) = p_{t,1}$, where $p_t = \delta_j(q_j, b)$ and $p_t \notin F_j$. Hence

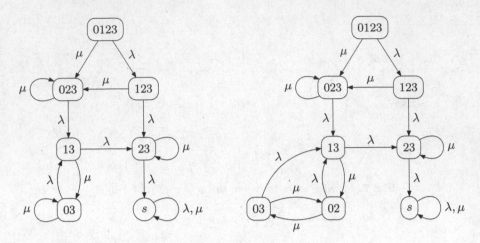

Fig. 9. The power automata $\mathcal{P}(\mathscr{E}_1)$ and $\mathcal{P}(\mathscr{E}_2)$

$\varphi_2(q_{j,1}, \mu^3 \lambda \mu^2 \lambda \lambda) = \varphi_2(p_{t,1}, \lambda) = h_1$. So we obtain that $\mu^3 \lambda \mu^2 \lambda \lambda \notin \mathrm{Syn}(\mathscr{C})$. Therefore, $\mu^3 \lambda \mu^2 \lambda \lambda \notin J$, but it is easy to see that $\mu^3 \lambda \mu^2 \lambda \lambda \in \mathrm{Syn}(\mathscr{E}_3)$. Hence $\mathscr{E}_3$ can not be an MSA for J. Analogously, $\mathscr{E}_4$ can not be an MSA for J as well.

Note that $(\mu\lambda)^3 \in \mathrm{Syn}(\mathscr{E}_5)$ and $(\mu\lambda)^3 \in \mathrm{Syn}(\mathscr{E}_6)$. By the definition of the morphism $h \colon \{\lambda, \mu\}^* \lambda \to \Delta^*$, we have $h((\mu\lambda)^3) = (h(\mu\lambda))^3 = a^3$. But the word a^3 is not reset for $\mathscr{A}$ (see Fig. 1). By the definition of the transition function of $\mathscr{C}$ it implies that $\overline{h}(a^3) \notin \mathrm{Syn}(\mathscr{C})$, that is $(\mu\lambda)^3 \notin J$. In this way neither $\mathscr{E}_5$, nor $\mathscr{E}_6$ can be an MSA for J. We have considered all possible candidates for a 4-state MSA for J. Each automaton $\mathscr{E}_i$ cannot be chosen as an MSA for J. Also it is known that $rc(J) \geq 4$. Finally, we have $rc(J) > 4$.   □

Now we are in position to state the main result of the paper. Lemma 5 and Proposition 2 imply the following theorem.

Theorem 2. *RESET-INEQUALITY restricted to a binary alphabet is* **PSPACE**-*complete for $\ell = 4$.*

References

1. Ananichev, D., Gusev, V., Volkov, M.: Slowly synchronizing automata and digraphs. In: Hliněný, P., Kučera, A. (eds.) MFCS 2010. LNCS, vol. 6281, pp. 55–65. Springer, Heidelberg (2010). doi:10.1007/978-3-642-15155-2_7
2. Kozen, D.: Lower bounds for natural proof systems. In: 18th Annual Symposium on Foundations of Computer Science, pp. 254–266. IEEE, New York (1977). doi:10.1109/SFCS.1977.16
3. Martygin, P.: Computational complexity of certain problems related to carefuuly synchronizing words for partial automata and directing words for nondeterministic automata. Theory Comput. Sci. **54**(2), 293–304 (2014). doi:10.1007/s00224-013-9516-6. In: Ablayev, F. (ed.), Springer

4. Maslennikova, M.I.: Reset complexity of ideal languages. In: Bieliková, M. (ed.) International Conference on SOFSEM 2012, vol. II, pp. 33–44. Institute of Computer Science Academy of Sciences of the Czech Republic (2012). arXiv:1404.2816
5. Maslennikova, M.: Complexity of checking whether two automata are synchronized by the same language. In: Jürgensen, H., Karhumäki, J., Okhotin, A. (eds.) DCFS 2014. LNCS, vol. 8614, pp. 306–317. Springer, Cham (2014). doi:10.1007/978-3-319-09704-6_27
6. Meyer, A.R., Michael, J.F.: Economy of description by automata, grammars, and formal systems. In: 12th Annual Symposium on Switching and Automata Theory, pp. 188–191. IEEE, New York (1971). doi:10.1109/SWAT.1971.11
7. Moore, F.R.: On the bounds for state-set size in the proofs of equivalence between deterministic, nondeterministic, and two-way finite automata. IEEE Trans. Comput. C–20(10), 1211–1214 (1971). IEEE, New York
8. Sandberg, S.: 1 homing and synchronizing sequences. In: Broy, M., Jonsson, B., Katoen, J.P., Leucker, M., Pretschner, A. (eds.) Model-Based Testing of Reactive Systems. LNCS, vol. 3472, pp. 5–33. Springer, Heidelberg (2005). doi:10.1007/b137241
9. Stockmeyer, L.J., Meyer, A.R.: Word problems requiring exponential time. In: Aho, A.V. (ed.) Proceedings of the 5th Annual ACM Symposium on Theory of Computing STOC 1973, pp. 1–9. ACM, New York (1973). doi:10.1145/800125.804029
10. Volkov, M.V.: Synchronizing automata and the Černý conjecture. In: Martín-Vide, C., Otto, F., Fernau, H. (eds.) LATA 2008. LNCS, vol. 5196, pp. 11–27. Springer, Heidelberg (2008). doi:10.1007/978-3-540-88282-4_4

2-State 2-Symbol Turing Machines with Periodic Support Produce Regular Sets

Turlough Neary[(✉)]

Institute of Neuroinformatics, University of Zürich and ETH Zürich,
Zürich, Switzerland
tneary@ini.phys.ethz.ch

Abstract. We say that a Turing machine has periodic support if there is an infinitely repeated word to the left of the input and another infinitely repeated word to the right. In the search for the smallest universal Turing machines, machines that use periodic support have been significantly smaller than those for the standard model (i.e. machines with the usual blank tape on either side of the input). While generalising the model allows us to construct smaller universal machines it makes proving decidability results for the various state-symbol products that restrict program size more difficult. Here we show that given an arbitrary 2-state 2-symbol Turing machine and a configuration with periodic support the set of reachable configurations is regular. Unlike previous decidability results for 2-state 2-symbol machines, here we include in our consideration machines that do not reserve a transition rule for halting, which further adds to the difficulty of giving decidability results.

1 Introduction

The search for Turing machines with small states-symbol products has received attention for a number of different variations of the model [2,8,12,13]. The variant that has received the most attention is what we call here the standard model [1,5,6,11] (single-tape Turing machines with the usual blank symbol and a specially reserved halt instruction). As one might expect if we generalise the standard model or the type of encoding it may use we can give machines with smaller state-symbol products. One generalisation used in the literature is to allow periodic support (an infinitely repeated word to the left of the input and another infinitely repeated word to the right). Universal machines that use such a generalisation are call weakly universal. Watanabe gave a number of small semi-weakly universal machines [13] (a repeated word only appears on one side of the input). Later, Cook [2] gave small weakly universal machines that simulate

This work is supported by Swiss National Science Foundation grant numbers 200021-153295 and 200021-166231. The author thanks the anonymous reviewers for their careful reading of the paper and their helpful comments.

G. Pighizzini and C. Câmpeanu (Eds.): DCFS 2017, LNCS 10316, pp. 274–286, 2017.
DOI: 10.1007/978-3-319-60252-3_22

the cellular automaton Rule 110, and these were improved upon in [7] to give weakly universal machines for the state-symbol pairs of $(6,2)$, $(3,3)$ and $(2,4)$.

For the standard model a number of authors have given lower bounds on the size of the smallest possible universal Turing machines by proving the halting problem decidable for machines with the following state-symbol pairs: $(2,2)$ [4,9], $(3,2)$ [10], $(2,3)$ (claimed by Pavlotskaya [9]), $(1,n)$ [3] and $(n,1)$ (trivial), where $n \geqslant 1$. Unfortunately, these results do not provide lower bounds relevant to the weak and semi-weak machines mentioned above, and while generalising the encoding can simplify the task of finding machines with smaller state-symbol products the task of giving decidability results becomes more difficult. In this work we give decidability results for 2-state 2-symbol machines with periodic support. Our main result is as follows:

Theorem 1. *Given an arbitrary 2-state, 2-symbol, single-tape Turing machine with periodic support, the set of reachable configurations from an arbitrary configuration is regular.*

This result implies the decidability of many questions for 2-state 2-symbol machines with periodic support such as (1) Will a computation halt? (2) Does word w appear on the tape during a computation? (3) Given a number x does a computation enter a repeating sequence of configurations of length x? The halting property in question 1 is the standard way of signaling the end of a computation in Turing machines. Each of the properties in (2) and (3) above have been used as a means to signal the end of a computation in universal machines [2,12]. The weakly universal machines in [2,7] use the appearance of a special word to simulate a halting Turing machine and so our results show that there exists no 2-state 2-symbol weakly universal machine that ends its computation in this way. Our proof does not assume that there is a transition rule reserved for halting which further adds to the difficulty when compared to previous decidability proofs for 2-state 2-symbol machines.

The layout of the paper is as follows: In Sect. 2 we explain notation and give some definitions including definitions for two types of computation, periodic and semi-periodic, and we then show that if a computation is periodic or semi-periodic the set of reachable configurations is regular. In Sect. 3 we reduce the number of cases to be considered leaving the cases only in Fig. 1 to be solved, and in Sect. 4 we solve the Fig. 1 cases to prove Theorem 1.

2 Turing Machines with Periodic Support

Definition 1. *A Turing machine with periodic support is a tuple $M = (Q, \Sigma, f, l, r)$. Here $Q = \{q_1, \ldots q_{|Q|}\}$ and Σ are the finite sets of states and tape symbols respectively, and $l, r \in \Sigma^*$ are the left and right blank words respectively, where $|r| > 0$ and $|l| > 0$. The transition function is of the form $f : Q \times \Sigma \to \Sigma \times \{L, R\} \times Q$.*

We write f as a list of transition rules. Each transition rule is a quintuple $(q_x, \sigma_1, \sigma_2, d, q_y)$, with initial state q_x, read symbol $\sigma_1 \in \Sigma$, write symbol $\sigma_2 \in \Sigma$, move direction $d \in \{L, R\}$ and next state q_y.

Definition 2. *A configuration c of a Turing machine with periodic support has the form $c = u\, \mathbf{q_x} \alpha\, v$ where q_x is the current state, the tape head is reading the symbol α, and the words $u, v \in \Sigma^*$.*

For a machine with periodic support, when the tape head moves to the right of v the word r is appended to the right of v and when the tape head moves to the left of u the word l is prepended to the left of u. When $l = r = 0$ we have the classic Turing machine with blank symbol 0. We write $c_1 \vdash c_2$ to denote that configuration c_2 is obtained via a single Turing machine computation step on c_1 and we write $c_1 \vdash^* c_t$ if there exists a sequence of 0 or more computations steps of the form $c_1 \vdash c_2 \vdash \ldots c_{t-1} \vdash c_t$. We say that c_t is *reachable* from c_1 and call $c_1 \vdash c_2 \vdash \ldots c_{t-1} \vdash c_t$ a computation sequence.

We label each Turing machine tape cell with an index. The cell with index i, which we will call cell i, has cell $i - 1$ immediately to its left and cell $i + 1$ immediately to its right. The position function $p(t)$ gives the index of the cell being read by the tape head at time t. The rightmost position up to time t is a cell index $P_r(t) = \max_{t' \leqslant t}(p(t'), p_r)$ and the leftmost position up to time t is a cell index $P_l(t) = \min_{t' \leqslant t}(p(t'), p_l)$, where p_l and p_r are respectively the leftmost and rightmost cells occupied by the input w.

Definition 3 (Periodic computation). *Let M be a Turing machine with periodic support. The computation of M is periodic if there is a sequence s of transition rules and a time t, such that sequence s is executed between times $t + i|s|$ and $t + (i+1)|s|$ for all $i \in \mathbb{N}$, where $|s|$ is the number of rules in s.*

Lemma 1. *If a computation is periodic, then $\{c_i | c_1 \vdash^* c_i\}$ is a regular set.*

Proof. After t time steps M has gone through a sequence of configurations $c_1 \vdash c_2 \vdash \ldots c_t$. There are two possible cases for the repeated sequence s, the sequence has either an equal or unequal number of left and right instructions. If there is an equal number of left and right instructions then after a further $|s|$ time steps we get $c_t, c_{t+1}, \ldots, c_{t+s}$ where c_t and c_{t+s} are identical. So in this case the set of configurations reachable from c_1 is the finite regular set $\{c_1, c_2, \ldots, c_{t+s-1}\}$.

If the number of left and right instructions in s are not equal, then we need only consider the case where there are more right than left instructions (as the case of more left than right instructions is symmetric). At time t we have a configuration $c_t = uu_1\, \mathbf{q_{x,1}} \alpha_1\, v_1$ such that the tape head visits the leftmost symbol in u_1 but does not revisit any symbol in u. Between times t and $t + s$ sequence s is executed giving the configuration sequence $c_t \vdash c_{t+1} \vdash \ldots c_{t+s}$ where $c_{t+i} = uu_i\, \mathbf{q_{x,i}} \alpha_i\, v_i$ for $0 \leqslant i < s$ and $c_{t+|s|} = uu'u_1\, \mathbf{q_{x,1}} \alpha_1\, v_1$. In configuration $c_{t+|s|}$ the words u_1 and v_1 must appear immediately to the left and right of the tape head position as the sequence of symbols read when executing s in the $|s|$ time steps following $c_{t+|s|}$ is identical to the sequence of symbols read in the $|s|$ time steps following c_t. Since the tape head will not visit any cell to the left of the leftmost symbol in u_1 when executing s the word u' is not revisited by the tape head and is not altered for the remainder of the computation. For each subsequent execution of s another u' is placed on the tape and so on iteration $j + 1$ of s we get a configuration sequence of the form $c_{t+|s|j} \vdash c_{t+|s|j+1} \vdash c_{t+|s|j+2} \vdash \ldots c_{t+|s|(j+1)}$ where $c_{t+|s|j+i} = u(u')^j u_i\, \mathbf{q}_{\mathbf{x},i}\alpha_i v_i$ and $0 \leqslant i < s$. So the set of configurations reachable from c_1 is the regular set $\{c_1, c_2, \ldots, c_t\} \cup u_i(u')^* u_i\, \mathbf{q}_{\mathbf{x},i}\alpha_i v_i$ where $0 \leqslant i < s$. $\qquad\square$

Lemma 2. *Let M be a 2-state, 2-symbol Turing machine with periodic support. If, when M is started on a configuration c_1, there exists an $m \in \mathbb{N}$ such that on more than $|r|2^{m+1}$ occasions the tape head of M is over a cell $P_r(t)$ and does not visit cell $P_r(t) - m$ after time t, then the set $\{c_i | c_1 \vdash^* c_i\}$ is regular.*

Proof. Let $uu'\, \mathbf{q}_{\mathbf{x}}\alpha v_r$ be a configuration at time t with $|u'| = m$ and the tape head over cell $P_r(t)$. If no cell to the left of $P_r(t) - m$ is visited after time t, then the future computation depends only on $u'\, \mathbf{q}_{\mathbf{x}}\alpha v_r$. By definition of $P_r(t)$ no cell to the right of the tape head's location at symbol α has yet been read and so v_r must be a suffix of r. As a result, there are only $|r|2^{m+1}$ possible values for $u'\, \mathbf{q}_{\mathbf{x}}\alpha v_r$. So, after $|r|2^{m+1}$ times where the tape head is over cell $P_r(t)$ and no longer visits cell $P_r(t) - m$, there are two times t_j and t_k that have the same value for $u'\, \mathbf{q}_{\mathbf{x}}\alpha v_r$. Since the future computation depends only on $u'\, \mathbf{q}_{\mathbf{x}}\alpha v_r$, the sequence of transition rules executed between times t_j and t_k are repeated ad infinitum. So from Lemma 1 the set $\{c_i | c_1 \vdash^* c_i\}$ is regular. $\qquad\square$

Using a similar argument to the one used in Lemma 2 we get Comment 1.

Comment 1. *Let M be a 2-state, 2-symbol Turing machine with periodic support. If, when M is started on a configuration c_1, there exists an $m \in \mathbb{N}$ such that on more than $|l|2^{m+1}$ occasions the tape head of M is over a cell $P_l(t)$ and does not visit cell $P_l(t) + m$ after time t, then the set $\{c_i | c_1 \vdash^* c_i\}$ is regular.*

Comment 2. *Let M be a Turing machine with periodic support. If M started on configuration c does not make at least 2 consecutive right moves an infinite number of times and at least 2 consecutive left moves an infinite number of times, then it either enters a loop or gives a computation of the type describe by Lemma 1 or Comment 1, and so the set of reachable configurations is regular.*

Definition 4 (Semi-periodic computation). *Let M be a Turing machine with periodic support. The computation of M is semi-periodic if there are $2x + 2$ sequences of transition rules, $s_r, s_l, e_1, e_2 \ldots e_x, h_1, h_2 \ldots h_x$, such that there is a time z where the sequence*

$$S = (s_r)^{i+1} e_1 (s_l)^{i+1} h_1 (s_r)^{i+1} e_2 (s_l)^{i+1} h_2 \ldots (s_r)^{i+1} e_x (s_l)^{i+1} h_x$$

is executed between times $t(i)$ and $t(i + 1)$ for all $i \in \mathbb{N}$, where $t(i) = z + \frac{(i^2+i)x}{2}(|s_r| + |s_l|) + i(|e_1 h_1 e_2 h_2 \ldots e_x h_x|)$, $f(s_r) = m$, $f(s_l) = -m$, $0 \leqslant f(e_i) < m$, $-m < f(h_i) \leqslant 0$, and $-m < f(S) \leqslant 0$ where $f(s) = $ (number of right instructions in sequence s) − (number of left instructions in sequence s). Also, for every instruction sequence y that is a prefix of s_l we have $f(y) \geqslant -m$, and for every instruction sequence y that is a prefix of s_r we have $f(y) \leqslant m$.

Lemma 3. *If a computation is semi-periodic, then $\{c_i | c_1 \vdash^* c_i\}$ is a regular set.*

Proof. At time $t(i)$ the sequence S is about to be executed by M for the $(i+1)^{\text{th}}$ time. The configuration at time $t(i)$ is given below on the left side of (1). From S in Definition 4 the execution begins with $(s_r)^{i+1}$, and so between times $t(i)+|s_r|k$ and $t(i)+|s_r|(k+1)$ we execute the sequence s_r, for $0 \leqslant k \leqslant i$. In Eq. (1) during the execution of each s_r the tape head does not move to the left of the word $u_{r,1}$ or to the right of the word $v_{r,1}$, and so since s_r has more right move than left move instructions we can use an argument similar to the one used in Lemma 1 to show that after k iterations of s_r ($|s^r|k$ time steps) the configuration on the right side of Eq. (1) is produced. Continuing on, the left side of Eq. (2) gives the configuration after i iterations of s_r, and one further iteration of s_r gives the configuration on the right. In the configuration on the right of Eq. (2) the word $v_{e_1,1} = v_{r',1}v_{e'_1}$, where $v_{r',1}$ is the length $|v_{r,1}|-m$ word that appears immediately to the right of the tape head after the last s_r in $(s_r)^{i+1}$ has executed (recall that each s_r shifts the tape head m cells to the right in the word $v_{r,1}$). The leftmost $(s_r)^{i+1}$ instruction sequence in S has now completed and so e_1, the next sequence in S, executes.

In Eq. (3) we show the $|e_1|$ times steps that complete the execution of e_1. Before we proceed we explain the presence of the word u'_1 (the length $f(e_1)$ prefix of u') that appears in the configuration on the right of Eq. (3). Immediately following the execution of e_1 we execute the sequence $(s_l)^{i+1}$, and as usual we give words $u_{l,1}$ and $v_{l,1}$ such that during the execution of each s_l the tape head does not move to the left of $u_{l,1}$ or to the right of $v_{l,1}$. From Definition 4 we know that executing e_1 shifts the tape head $f(e_1)$ cells to the right. So from Eq. (3) after the execution of e_1 (before the first s_l is about to execute) the tape head is at least $f(e_1)$ cells to the right of the rightmost u' subword in $(u')^{i+1}$. For every prefix y of s_l we have $f(y) \geqslant -m$ and so when executing s_l the tape head does not visit cells more than m positions to the left of its initial location when it began s_l. So since $|u'| = m$ and the initial tape head location is at least $f(e_1)$ cells to the right of the rightmost u', the leftmost $f(e_1)$ symbols in the rightmost u' (i.e. the prefix word u'_1) are not entered when executing the first s_l and so we have u'_1 to the left of $u_{l,1}$ in Eq. (3). Note that in Eq. (3) permitting the tape head to enter cells to the left of $u_{e_1,1}$ when executing e_1 will not effect the value of u'_1, as it is only possible to iterate s_l if u'_1 is a prefix of u' (see Eq. (4)) and so the prefix value of u'_1 is implied by the fact that $(s_l)^{i+1}$ is executed immediately after e_1.

$$u_{h'_1}u_{r,1}\,\mathbf{q_{r,1}}\alpha_{r,1}\,v_{r,1}(v')^i v_{e'_1} \quad \vdash^{|s_r|k} \quad u_{h'_1}(u')^k u_{r,1}\,\mathbf{q_{r,1}}\alpha_{r,1}\,v_{r,1}(v')^{i-k}v_{e'_1} \quad (1)$$

$$u_{h'_1}(u')^i u_{r,1}\,\mathbf{q_{r,1}}\alpha_{r,1}\,v_{r,1}v_{e'_1} \quad \vdash^{|s_r|} \quad u_{h'_1}(u')^{i+1}u_{e_1,1}\,\mathbf{q_{e_1,1}}\alpha_{e_1,1}v_{e_1,1} \quad (2)$$

$$u_{h'_1}(u')^{i+1}u_{e_1,1}\,\mathbf{q_{e_1,1}}\alpha_{e_1,1}v_{e_1,1} \quad \vdash^{|e_1|} \quad u_{h'_1}(u')^i u'_1 u_{l,1}\,\mathbf{q_{l,1}}\alpha_{l,1}v_{l,1}v_{e'_2} \quad (3)$$

$$u_{h'_1}(u')^i u'_1 u_{l,1}\,\mathbf{q_{l,1}}\alpha_{l,1}v_{l,1}v_{e'_2} \quad \vdash^{|s_l|k} \quad u_{h'_1}(u')^{i-k}u'_1 u_{l,1}\,\mathbf{q_{l,1}}\alpha_{l,1}v_{l,1}(v')^k v_{e'_2} \quad (4)$$

$$u_{h_1,1}\,\mathbf{q_{h_1,1}}\alpha_{h_1,1}v_{h_1,1}(v')^{i+1}v_{e'_2} \quad \vdash^{|h_1|} \quad u_{h'_2}u_{r,1}\,\mathbf{q_{r,1}}\alpha_{r,1}v_{r,1}v'_1(v')^i v_{e'_2} \quad (5)$$

$$u_{h'_n}u_{r,1}\,\mathbf{q_{r,1}}\alpha_{r,1}v_{r,1}v'_n(v')^i v_{e'_n} \quad \vdash^{|s_r|k} \quad u_{h'_n}(u')^k u_{r,1}\,\mathbf{q_{r,1}}\alpha_{r,1}v_{r,1}v'_n(v')^{i-k}v_{e'_n} \quad (6)$$

The execution of sequence $(s_l)^{i+1}$ as shown in Eq. (4) proceeds in a manner similar to that of $(s_r)^{i+1}$. The main difference is that s_l has more left move than right move instructions and so each successive s_l sequence begins m cells further to the left. Following the execution of $(s_l)^{i+1}$, the sequence h_1 is executed as shown in Eq. (5). In the configuration on the left of Eq. (5) the word $u_{h_1,1} = u_{h_1'} u_1' u_{l_1'}$, where $u_{l_1'}$ is the length $|u_{l,1}| - m$ word that appears immediately to the left of the tape head after the last s_l in $(s_l)^{i+1}$ has executed (recall each s_l shifts the tape head m cells to the left in the word $u_{l,1}$). The word v_1' that appears in the configuration on the right of Eq. (5) is the length $f(h_1)$ suffix of v' and its presence can be explained in a manner similar to that of u_1' in the previous paragraph. Continuing with the execution of sequence S, on the right side of Eq. (5) following the execution of h_1 the configuration is ready to allow the next $(s_r)^{i+1}$ sequence to execute. Note that unlike the configuration on the left of Eq. (1), the configuration on the right of Eq. (5) has the word v_1' to the left of $(v')^i$. This implies that $(v')^i$ is a prefix of $v_1'(v')^i$ as to execute $(s_r)^{i+1}$ we must have the word $(v')^i$ to the right of $v_{r_1,1}$. This prefix property holds for each v_j' word produced by executing a h_j sequence. Similarly all words of the form $(u')^i u_j'$ share a suffix that allows $(s_r)^{i+1}$ to execute, where u_j' is a word produced by executing an e_j sequence (see Eq. (3)). Returning to Eq. (5), at the right end of the configuration $v_{e_2'}$ is of the correct form to allow e_2 to execute at the end of the $(s_r)^{i+1}$ scan right, and following this we once again scan left with $(s_l)^{i+1}$ where $u_{h_2'}$ allows the execution of h_2. So the process of scanning right with $(s_r)^{i+1}$ and left with $(s_l)^{i+1}$ is repeated with the nth scan right given in Eq. (6). This continues until the sequence S is completed for the value i, whereupon S begins for $i+1$. The configurations for the nth iteration of S can be obtained from the configurations for the first iteration of S simply by increasing the number of u' and/or the number of v' words in each configuration. So the set of configurations reachable by M is the union of the finite set of configurations before the first iteration of S and the configurations indicated in Eqs. (1) to (6).   □

3   Reducing the Number of Cases Through Symmetries

There are 4096 possible 2-state 2-symbol machines and in this section we show how to reduce the number of cases to the 378 machines given in Fig. 1. Eq. (7) below gives the form of an arbitrary 2-state 2-symbol Turing machine where $\sigma_i \in \{0,1\}$, $d_j \in \{L,R\}$ and $q_k \in \{q_a, q_b\}$. In the sequel we denote each possible machine as a triple (Σ, D, Q) where $\Sigma = \{\sigma_1, \sigma_2, \sigma_3, \sigma_4\}$, $D = \{d_1, d_2, d_3, d_4\}$, and $Q = \{q_1, q_2, q_3, q_4\}$. Each Σ, D and Q has 16 possible values and here we show how to reduce the number of cases under consideration to 6, 7, and 9, respectively (see Tables 1 to 3). We do this by identifying symmetries using the notion of regular equivalent machines which we define below, and we also solve some of the simplest cases from Σ, D and Q.

$$q_a, 0, \sigma_1, d_1, q_1 \qquad q_a, 1, \sigma_2, d_2, q_2 \qquad q_b, 0, \sigma_3, d_3, q_3 \qquad q_b, 1, \sigma_4, d_4, q_4 \qquad (7)$$

Before we proceed we give some preliminary definitions and notation. Given a set with two elements $\{y, z\}$ we define $\overline{y} = z$ and $\overline{z} = y$. Given $w = w_0 w_1 \ldots w_m \in \{0,1\}^*$, we write $\overline{w} = \overline{w}_0 \overline{w}_1 \ldots \overline{w}_m$ to denote the word obtained by flipping each bit $w_i \in \{0,1\}$ in w. We define three functions g_{reverse}, $g_{\text{b-flip}}$ and $g_{\text{s-flip}}$ each of which map a configuration $c = u\,\mathbf{q_x}\alpha\,v$ to another configuration as follows

$$g_{\text{reverse}}(c) = \underline{v}\,\mathbf{q_x}\alpha\,\underline{u} \qquad g_{\text{b-flip}}(c) = \overline{u}\,\mathbf{q_x}\overline{\alpha}\,\overline{v} \qquad g_{\text{s-flip}}(c) = u\,\overline{\mathbf{q_x}}\alpha\,v$$

where if $w = w_0 w_1 \dots w_m$ then $\underline{w} = w_m w_{m-1} \dots w_0$.

Definition 5. *Given Turing machines M and M' with periodic support, we say that M and M' are regular equivalent if for every computation sequence $c_1 \vdash c_2 \vdash \dots c_t$ of M there is a computation sequence $g(c_1) \vdash g(c_2) \vdash \dots g(c_t)$ of M' and vice versa, where $g \in \{g_{\text{reverse}}, g_{\text{b-flip}}, g_{\text{s-flip}}\}$.*

Showing one direction of the equivalence is sufficient to prove that a pair of machines are regular equivalent as each function from g is its own inverse. Comment 3 follows from Definition 5 as regularity is closed under g, and used with Lemma 4 reduces the number of cases for Theorem 1.

Comment 3. *Let M be a Turing machine with periodic support such that the set of configurations reachable from any arbitrary configuraiton is regular. Then if Turing machines M and M' are regular equivalent, for every configuration of M' with periodic support, the set of configurations reachable for M' is regular.*

Lemma 4. *Let M be an arbitrary 2-state, 2-symbol Turing machine with periodic support. Then applying any one of the mappings in Eqs. (8) to (10) to all transition rules in M gives a regular equivalent Turing machine M'.*

$$f_{\text{d-flip}}(q_x, \sigma, \sigma', D, q_y) \to (q_x, \sigma, \sigma', \overline{D}, q_y) \tag{8}$$

$$f_{\text{b-flip}}(q_x, \sigma, \sigma', D, q_y) \to (q_x, \overline{\sigma}, \overline{\sigma'}, D, q_y) \tag{9}$$

$$f_{\text{s-flip}}(q_x, \sigma, \sigma', D, q_y) \to (\overline{q_x}, \sigma, \sigma', D, \overline{q_y}) \tag{10}$$

Proof. To prove this lemma we show that for each mapping on M given by Eqs. (8) to (10) there is a $g \in \{g_{\text{reverse}}, g_{\text{b-flip}}, g_{\text{s-flip}}\}$, such that for each computation sequence $c_1 \vdash c_2 \vdash \dots c_t$ of M there is a computation sequence $g(c_1) \vdash g(c_2) \vdash \dots g(c_t)$ of M' satisfying Definition 5 (recall that it is sufficient to prove only one direction of the equivalence). For each of the translations in Eqs. (8), (9) and (10) we set g to g_{reverse}, $g_{\text{b-flip}}$, or $g_{\text{s-flip}}$, respectively. For example, if we apply the translation in Eq. (8) to M, then for each computation sequence $c_1 \vdash c_2 \vdash \dots c_t$ of M there is a computation sequence $g_{\text{reverse}}(c_1) \vdash g_{\text{reverse}}(c_2) \vdash \dots g_{\text{reverse}}(c_t)$ of M'. Each of the three cases (i.e. applying Eqs. (8), (9) or (10)) can easily be verified using an inductive argument showing that if M gives $c_i \vdash c_{i+1}$ then M' gives $g(c_i) \vdash g(c_{i+1})$. $\square$

It is a straightforward matter to apply the mappings in Lemma 4 to the cases in Tables 1 to 3 to show that every case not given in the tables is regular equivalent to a case that is in the tables. Applying the mapping in (9) to machines for Σ_1, Σ_2, Σ_3 and Σ_4 gives machines for the Σ cases $(1,1,1,1)$, $(1,1,0,1)$,

$(1, 1, 1, 0)$ and $(1, 1, 0, 0)$ respectively[1]. Applying the mapping in (10) to Σ_2, Σ_3 and Σ_5 gives the Σ cases $(0, 1, 0, 0)$, $(1, 0, 0, 0)$, and $(1, 0, 0, 1)$ respectively, and applying the mapping (9) and then (10) to Σ_2 and Σ_3 gives cases $(0, 1, 1, 1)$ and $(1, 0, 1, 1)$ respectively. We have now shown that 9 of the 10 possible Σ values not given in Table 1 are regular equivalent to cases in the table, and now the only case not covered is $(0, 1, 0, 1)$. For $\Sigma = (0, 1, 0, 1)$ the read symbol is the same as the write symbol for each transition rule and so it never changes the tape contents. It follows that if machines for the case $(0, 1, 0, 1)$ enter the same cell more than twice they enter a loop and so computations for this case either loop or scan in one direction only never making 2 consecutive moves in the opposite direction and are thus covered by Comment 2.

Table 1. The 16 possible cases for the 4 read symbols in (7) reduced to 6 cases.

	Σ_1	Σ_2	Σ_3	Σ_4	Σ_5	Σ_6
$\sigma_1 =$	0	0	0	0	0	1
$\sigma_2 =$	0	0	0	0	1	0
$\sigma_3 =$	0	0	1	1	1	1
$\sigma_4 =$	0	1	0	1	0	0

Table 2. The 16 possible cases for the 4 move values in (7) reduced to 7 cases.

	D_1	D_2	D_3	D_4	D_5	D_6	D_7
$d_1 =$	L	L	L	R	L	L	L
$d_2 =$	L	L	R	L	L	R	R
$d_3 =$	L	R	L	L	R	L	R
$d_4 =$	R	L	L	L	R	R	L

Table 3. The 16 possible cases for the 4 next state values in (7) reduced to 9 cases.

	Q_1	Q_2	Q_3	Q_4	Q_5	Q_6	Q_7	Q_8	Q_9
$q_1 =$	q_a	q_b	q_a	q_a	q_b	q_b	q_b	q_b	q_b
$q_2 =$	q_b	q_a	q_b	q_b	q_a	q_a	q_b	q_b	q_b
$q_3 =$	q_a	q_a	q_a	q_b	q_a	q_b	q_a	q_a	q_b
$q_4 =$	q_a	q_a	q_b	q_a	q_b	q_a	q_a	q_b	q_a

Applying the mapping in (8) to cases D_1 to D_7 in Table 2 gives 7 regular equivalent cases. The remaining cases, (R, R, R, R) and (L, L, L, L), need not be included in Table 2 as they are covered by Comment 2.

The 16 possible cases for Q are reduced to the 9 given in Table 3 by omitting the 7 cases where $q_1 = q_2 = q_a$ or $q_3 = q_4 = q_b$. These 7 cases are not included in Table 3 as the behaviour for these cases is easily explained. To see this note that when we have $q_1 = q_2 = q_a$ state q_a is a trap state where if we enter q_a we never again enter state q_b and so from that point on the computation is essentially that of a 1-state 2-symbol Turing machine. Taking the case $q_1 = q_2 = q_a$, if the pair of transition rules for q_a both have the same write symbol (i.e. $\sigma_1 = \sigma_2$)

---

[1] Note that applying mapping (9) to machines of the form given by Eq. (7) also flips the read symbols and so applying it to $\Sigma = (\sigma_1, \sigma_2, \sigma_3, \sigma_4)$ gives $(\overline{\sigma_2}, \overline{\sigma_1}, \overline{\sigma_4}, \overline{\sigma_3})$ instead of $(\overline{\sigma_1}, \overline{\sigma_2}, \overline{\sigma_3}, \overline{\sigma_4})$.

or shift direction (i.e. $d_1 = d_2$), or if the write symbol is the same as the read symbol for both rules (i.e. $\sigma_1 = 0, \sigma_2 = 1$) then when the machine enters q_a the computation is periodic and from Lemma 1 this means that the set of reachable configurations is regular. For the remaining cases of $q_1 = q_2 = q_a$ we need only consider machines with the rules $q_a, 0, 1, R, q_a$ and $q_a, 1, 0, L, q_a$ as such machines are regular equivalent to all remaining cases for $q_1 = q_2 = q_a$. When in state q_a this machine scans right changing 0's to 1's until it reads a 1, and then it scans left changing 1's to 0's until it reads a 0, and this left scan right scan behaviour is repeated ad infinitum giving a semi-periodic computation. So from Lemma 3 the set of reachable configurations for machines with $q_1 = q_2 = q_a$ is regular. The same argument is applicable to the case $q_3 = q_4 = q_b$.

Legend — Location of each Q_i case within each (Σ_i, D_j) 3×3 block below:

Q_7	Q_8	Q_9
Q_4	Q_5	Q_6
Q_1	Q_2	Q_3

	D_1			D_2			D_3			D_4			D_5			D_6			D_7		
Σ_6	B	C	B	A	A	A	A	A	A	A	A	A	B	A	A	C	A	A	C	A	A
	B	C	B	A	A	A	A	A	A	A	A	A	C	A	A	C	A	A	B	A	A
	B	B	B	A	A	A	A	A	A	A	A	A	B	B	C	C	C	C	B	B	B
Σ_5	B	B	B	A	A	A	B	B	B	A	A	A	B	B	A	B	B	A	B	B	A
	B	B	B	A	A	A	B	B	B	A	A	A	B	A	A	B	A	A	B	A	A
	B	B	B	A	A	A	B	B	B	A	A	A	B	A	B	B	A	E	B	A	C
Σ_4	B	B	B	B	B	B	A	A	A	A	A	A	B	A	A	B	A	A	B	A	A
	B	B	B	B	B	B	A	A	A	A	A	A	C	A	C	B	A	C	E	A	B
	B	B	B	B	B	B	A	A	A	A	A	A	B	B	B	B	B	B	B	B	B
Σ_3	B	B	B	B	B	C	B	B	B	B	B	B	B	B	B	B	B	C	B	B	B
	B	B	B	C	B	C	B	B	B	B	B	B	C	B	B	C	B	C	B	B	B
	B	B	B	B	B	B	B	B	B	B	B	B	B	B	B	B	B	B	B	B	B
Σ_2	B	B	B	B	B	B	B	B	B	B	B	B	B	B	B	B	B	B	B	B	B
	B	B	B	C	B	B	B	B	B	B	B	B	B	B	B	B	B	B	C	B	B
	B	B	B	B	B	B	B	B	B	B	B	B	B	B	B	B	B	B	B	B	B
Σ_1	B	B	B	B	B	B	A	A	A	A	A	A	B	B	B	B	B	B	B	B	B
	B	B	B	C	B	B	A	A	A	A	A	A	C	B	B	B	B	B	C	B	B
	B	B	B	B	B	B	A	A	A	A	A	A	B	B	B	B	B	B	B	B	B

Fig. 1. An overview of the 378 cases given by Tables 1 to 3, which were obtained from the reduction in the number of cases given in Sect. 3. Each small square in the above figure represents a Turing machine. There is a 3×3 block of small squares for each (Σ_i, D_j) pair which gives the 9 possible values for Q_i. Letter A indicates a reduction to a symmetric case, B is for machines that have periodic computations, C is for machines that give semi-periodic computations, and E is for machines that are binary counters.

4   Solving Cases in Fig. 1

4.1   Case A: Reduce the Number of Cases Using Symmetries

From Comment 3 we know that if a pair of machines M and M' are regular equivalent we need only consider one of the two machines in our list of open cases. Table 4 shows that if the square in Fig. 1 for a machine (Σ_i, D_j, Q_k) contains an A then it is regular equivalent to another machine in the figure whose square does not contain an A. This means that we need not consider Case A machines because by solving the remaining cases each machine in Case A will be regular equivalent to a case that has been solved.

Table 4. Lemma 4 mappings that map each A case in Fig. 1 to a non-A case in Fig. 1. The mappings given on the left of each row are applied to the cases in that row to show that each case is regular equivalent to another case in Fig. 1. Here $Q' \in \{Q_1, Q_2, \dots Q_9\}$, $Q_m \in \{Q_2, Q_5, Q_6, Q_9\}$, $Q_l \in \{Q_6, Q_8, Q_9\}$, and $Q_p \in \{Q_5, Q_8, Q_9\}$. Keep in mind Footnote 1 when applying $f_{\text{b-flip}}$.

$f_{\text{s-flip}}$	(Σ_1, D_3, Q')	(Σ_1, D_4, Q')	(Σ_6, D_3, Q')	(Σ_6, D_6, Q_l)
$f_{\text{b-flip}}$	(Σ_5, D_2, Q')	(Σ_5, D_4, Q')	(Σ_5, D_5, Q_m)	(Σ_6, D_2, Q')
	(Σ_6, D_5, Q_5)			
$f_{\text{s-flip}}, f_{\text{b-flip}}$	(Σ_4, D_3, Q')	(Σ_4, D_4, Q')	(Σ_4, D_7, Q_p)	(Σ_6, D_4, Q')
$f_{\text{s-flip}}, f_{\text{d-flip}}$	(Σ_6, D_5, Q_l)	(Σ_6, D_7, Q_l)		
$f_{\text{b-flip}}, f_{\text{d-flip}}$	(Σ_5, D_6, Q_m)	(Σ_5, D_7, Q_m)	(Σ_6, D_6, Q_5)	(Σ_6, D_7, Q_5)
$f_{\text{s-flip}}, f_{\text{b-flip}}, f_{\text{d-flip}}$	(Σ_4, D_5, Q_p)	(Σ_4, D_6, Q_p)		

4.2   Cases B: Machines that Give Periodic Computations

In Fig. 1, if the square for a machine (Σ_i, D_j, Q_k) contains a B then the machine's computation is periodic. From Lemma 2 and Comment 1, periodicity can be proved by showing that a machine eventually scans right never again visiting cell $i - m$ after it visits cell i, or alternatively that the head scans left never again visiting cell $i + m$ after cell i. To achieve this we consider what happens after the tape head attempts to scan in the opposite direction after either $\geqslant 2$ consecutive right moves or $\geqslant 2$ consecutive left moves. Comment 2 allows us to consider only machines that make consecutive left moves and consecutive right moves. As an example of the above technique we show that after machine (Σ_5, D_6, Q_8) (given in (11)) makes 2 or more consecutive left moves it scans left for the rest of the computation never again visiting cell $i + 3$ after it visits cell i.

$$q_a, 0, 0, L, q_b \qquad q_a, 1, 1, R, q_b \qquad q_b, 0, 1, L, q_a \qquad q_b, 1, 0, R, q_b \qquad (11)$$

If the tape head is about to make a right move that follows $\geqslant 2$ consecutive left moves then either the configuration has the form given on the left of (12) or it has the form given on the left of (13) (where $\sigma'_i, \sigma'_{-i} \in \{0,1\}$). On the right of (12) we see that after 4 time steps the configuration has the same form as the configuration on the left side of (13) (so we need consider only the case in (13)). On the right of (13) we see that after 3 time steps the tape head is now reading σ'_{-1}, one cell to the left of its original position. If $\sigma'_{-1} = 0$ the tape head will move left again to make its second consecutive left move and so if we wish to make a right move in the future it will follow $\geqslant 2$ consecutive left moves and we will repeat the entire sequence of steps we have just described. Alternatively, if $\sigma'_{-1} = 1$ then we have the same case as the left side of (13) and the 3 steps in (13) are repeated. For both cases (12) and (13) the process repeats with the tape head moving left never visiting cell $i + 3$ after it has entered cell i, and so from Comment 1 the computation is periodic. The technique given here can be applied to all B cases in Fig. 1 to show that they have periodic computations.

$$\ldots \sigma'_{-2}\sigma'_{-1}\,\mathbf{q_a}1\,10\sigma'_1\sigma'_2\sigma'_3 \ldots \qquad \vdash^4 \qquad \ldots \sigma'_{-2}\sigma'_{-1}\,\mathbf{q_b}1\,01\sigma'_1\,\sigma'_2\sigma'_3 \ldots \qquad (12)$$

$$\ldots \sigma'_{-2}\sigma'_{-1}\,\mathbf{q_b}1\,01\sigma'_1\sigma'_2\sigma'_3 \ldots \qquad \vdash^3 \qquad \ldots \sigma'_{-4}\,\mathbf{q_b}\sigma'_{-1}\,011\sigma'_1\sigma'_2\sigma'_3 \ldots \qquad (13)$$

4.3   Cases C: Machines that Give Semi-periodic Computation

From the proof of Lemma 3 a semi-periodic machine operates by scanning right using a repeating sequence of rules that print a repeating pattern until some sequence of symbols is met on the tape that causes the machine to end the scan right, and following this the machine scans left printing out another repeating pattern until it meets another sequence of symbols on the tape that causes the scan left to end. The entire process is then repeated. The behaviour of the machine when ending a rightward scan depends on the sequence of symbols it reads when it ends the scan right. The scan length increases with each subsequent pass and the sequence of symbols that ends each scan is provided by the blank word that is repeated to the right of the input. Since there is only a finite number of positions at which a scan right can end in relation to the right blank word the behaviour of the machine at the end of scans to the right becomes periodic over time. This can be seen in Definition 4 and Lemma 3 where the first scan right ends with e_1, the second scan ends with e_2, the third with e_3, and so on until scan x which ends with e_x. Following scan x the process is repeated with e_1 ending the next scan right. The same is true for scans left with the sequence $h_1, h_2, \ldots h_x$ being repeated once for every x scans to the left. When a 2-state 2-symbol machine is executing a semi-periodic computation the patterns it prints during leftward and rightward scans have length $\leqslant 2$ and the behaviour at the end of left and right scans are repeated periodically as described above. For this reason it is straightforward to determine when a 2-state 2-symbol machine is executing a semi-periodic computation.

As an example let us consider the machine (Σ_6, D_6, Q_3) given in (14). It is easy to determine the behaviour of this machine just by looking at its instructions. The machine scans left in state q_a reading 0's and printing 1's to the tape until it reads a 1, then it scans right in state q_b reading 1's and printing 0's until it reads a 0, and then it begins another scan left in q_a. We now show how this behaviour matches the behaviour of the sequence S given in Definition 4. In the scans mentioned above the growth to the left depends on the position of 1's in the left blank word as each 1 terminates a scan left, and similarly the growth to the right depends on the position of 0's in the right blank word. Since the left and right blank words are repeated periodically the growth is periodic for some constant number of scans right, this constant is the x value in sequence S. We set sequences s_r and s_l so that $f(s_r) = m$ and $f(s_l) = -m$ (see Definition 4) where m is the growth over the x scans left and right during an iteration of S, and this means that during iteration i of S, scans right have the form $(s_r)^{i+1}$ and scans left have the form $(s_l)^{i+1}$. To account for the growth between successive left and right scans during a single iteration of S, we define each e_j and h_j so that the extra distance traveled between each successive execution of $(s_r)^{i+1}$ or $(s_l)^{i+1}$ during S is considered part of e_j or h_j. This completes our explanation of how to give the $2x+2$ sequence that define S in Definition 4. All the machines for Case C can be shown to be semi-periodic using similar analysis to that given above.

$$q_a, 0, 1, L, q_a \qquad q_a, 1, 0, R, q_b \qquad q_b, 0, 1, L, q_a \qquad q_b, 1, 0, R, q_b \qquad (14)$$

4.4   Cases E: Binary Counters

The two binary machines in Fig. 1 compute in a similar manner and so we will just look at machine (Σ_5, D_6, Q_3) given in (15). Below we show (Σ_5, D_6, Q_3) incrementing from 4 to 8. The left most 1 is not part of the number and the most significant bit is on the right. To increment a number the machine scans right in q_b changing 1's to 0's until it reads a 0 which it changes to a 1 and it then scans left in q_a until it reads a 1, which signals the beginning of the next increment. It is easy to see that when started on any configuration the set of configurations generated by this machine is regular as it generates all possible strings and the scans left and right that increment the number have a simple form. If the machine has periodic support then the set of reachable configurations remains regular. The repeated words on the left have no effect on the computation as the tape head can not move left over a 1. On the right when each blank words becomes part of the computation it effects the form of only a constant number of bits at the right end of the number and so the set of reachable configurations is regular.

$$\mathbf{q_a}1\,0010 \quad \vdash^2 \quad \mathbf{q_a}1\,1010 \quad \vdash^4 \quad \mathbf{q_a}1\,0110 \quad \vdash^2 \quad \mathbf{q_a}1\,1110 \quad \vdash^8 \quad \mathbf{q_a}1\,0001$$

$$q_a, 0, 0, L, q_a \qquad q_a, 1, 1, R, q_b \qquad q_b, 0, 1, L, q_a \qquad q_b, 1, 0, R, q_b \qquad (15)$$

References

1. Baiocchi, C.: Three small universal Turing machines. In: Margenstern, M., Rogozhin, Y. (eds.) MCU 2001. LNCS, vol. 2055, pp. 1–10. Springer, Heidelberg (2001). doi:10.1007/3-540-45132-3_1
2. Cook, M.: Universality in elementary cellular automata. Complex Syst. 15(1), 1–40 (2004)

3. Hermann, G.: The uniform halting problem for generalized one state Turing machines. In: Proceedings, Ninth Annual Symposium on Switching and Automata Theory (FOCS), pp. 368–372. IEEE Computer Society Press, October 1968
4. Kudlek, M.: Small deterministic Turing machines. TCS **168**(2), 241–255 (1996)
5. Minsky, M.: Size and structure of universal Turing machines using tag systems. In: Recursive Function Theory, Symposium in Pure Mathematics, vol. 5, pp. 229–238 (1962)
6. Neary, T., Woods, D.: Four small universal Turing machines. Fundam. Inform. **91**(1), 123–144 (2009)
7. Neary, T., Woods, D.: Small weakly universal Turing machines. In: Kutyłowski, M., Charatonik, W., Gębala, M. (eds.) FCT 2009. LNCS, vol. 5699, pp. 262–273. Springer, Heidelberg (2009). doi:10.1007/978-3-642-03409-1_24
8. Neary, T., Woods, D.: The complexity of small universal Turing machines: a survey. In: Bieliková, M., Friedrich, G., Gottlob, G., Katzenbeisser, S., Turán, G. (eds.) SOFSEM 2012. LNCS, vol. 7147, pp. 385–405. Springer, Heidelberg (2012). doi:10. 1007/978-3-642-27660-6_32
9. Pavlotskaya, L.: Solvability of the halting problem for certain classes of Turing machines. Math. Notes (Springer) **13**(6), 537–541 (1973)
10. Pavlotskaya, L.: Dostatochnye uslovija razreshimosti problemy ostanovki dlja mashin T'juring. Problemi kibernetiki, pp. 91–118 (1978). (in Russian)
11. Rogozhin, Y.: Small universal Turing machines. TCS **168**(2), 215–240 (1996)
12. Wagner, K.: Universelle Turingmaschinen mit n-dimensionale band. Elektronische Informationsverarbeitung und Kybernetik **9**(7–8), 423–431 (1973)
13. Watanabe, S.: 5-symbol 8-state and 5-symbol 6-state universal Turing machines. J. ACM **8**(4), 476–483 (1961)

State Complexity of Suffix Distance

Timothy Ng[✉], David Rappaport, and Kai Salomaa

School of Computing, Queen's University, Kingston, ON K7L 3N6, Canada
{ng,daver,ksalomaa}@cs.queensu.ca

Abstract. The neighbourhood of a regular language with respect to the prefix, suffix and subword distance is always regular and a tight bound for the state complexity of prefix distance neighbourhoods is known. We give upper bounds for the state complexity of the neighbourhood of radius k of an n state DFA (deterministic finite automaton) language with respect to the suffix distance and the subword distance, respectively. For restricted values of k and n we give a matching lower bound for the state complexity of suffix distance neighbourhoods.

1 Introduction

Distances between strings and languages are used in many applications [4,7,9, 10]. Perhaps the most commonly used distance, the Levenshtein distance (a.k.a. the edit distance), is defined in terms of the number of substitution, insertion and deletion operations needed to transform one string into another. The prefix distance [3,11] of strings x and y is the sum of the lengths of the suffixes of x and y after their longest common prefix. The suffix distance (respectively, the subword distance) of two strings is defined analogously in terms of the longest common suffix (respectively, subword) of the strings.

Calude et al. [2] have shown that additive quasi-distances preserve regularity in the sense that a neighbourhood of a regular language is always regular. The edit distance is the best known example of additive distances. However, not all regularity preserving distances are additive. The prefix, suffix, and subword distances are not additive, but are known to preserve regularity [3].

In general, since the 90's there has been much work on the state complexity of regular languages. Recent surveys on the descriptional complexity of regular languages include [5,6,12]. For regularity preserving distances an important question is to determine the state complexity of the distance, that is, what is the optimal size of a DFA (deterministic finite automaton) recognizing a neighbourhood of radius k of an n state DFA language. In the context of error correction this can be viewed also as the descriptional complexity of error detection [14]. The descriptional complexity of error systems has been considered from a different point of view by Kari and Konstantinidis [8]. They establish upper and lower bounds for the size of DFAs needed to recognize a given error system.

© IFIP International Federation for Information Processing 2017
Published by Springer International Publishing AG 2017. All Rights Reserved
G. Pighizzini and C. Câmpeanu (Eds.): DCFS 2017, LNCS 10316, pp. 287–298, 2017.
DOI: 10.1007/978-3-319-60252-3_23

A neighbourhood of a language recognized by a DFA A with respect to the prefix distance, roughly speaking, can be recognized by simulating the computation of A and, for each non-final state, keeping track of the shortest path (up to the radius of the neighbourhood) to a final state of A. Additionally, we just need a number of error states equal to the radius of the neighbourhood. This means that prefix distance is an "inexpensive" operation in terms of state complexity. A tight lower bound for the state complexity of prefix distance neighbourhoods is known both for general regular languages and for finite languages [15, 16].

On the other hand, suffix distance (and subword distance) neighbourhoods are considerably more "difficult", that is, more expensive in terms of state complexity, to recognize by a DFA because the computation has no way of knowing where the longest common suffix begins. This means that the computation has to be inherently nondeterministic and as can, perhaps, be expected the state complexity of the neighbourhood depends exponentially on the size of the original DFA and the radius of the neighbourhood.

This paper shows that the suffix distance neighbourhood of radius k of an n state DFA language over an alphabet of size $\ell \geq 2$ can be recognized by a DFA with $\frac{\ell^k - 1}{\ell - 1} + 2^n - 1$ states when $k < n$. If A recognizes a finite language, the upper bound for the state complexity of the neighbourhood is $\frac{\ell^k - 1}{\ell - 1} + k \cdot 2^{\lceil \frac{n}{2} \rceil}$. We give matching lower bound constructions both for general regular languages and for finite languages using a binary alphabet in the case when n is roughly equal to $2 \cdot k$. For $k > n$, we show that the suffix distance neighbourhood can be recognized by a DFA with $(k - n) + 2^{n+1} - 2$ states and give matching lower bound constructions for both general regular languages and finite languages over an alphabet of size $n+1$. We show also that for the class of suffix-closed languages, the neighbourhood is recognized by a DFA with at most $n + k + 1$ states and that this bound is tight for all $k \in \mathbb{N}$. Finally, we derive an upper bound for the state complexity of subword distance neighbourhoods but it remains open whether the bound is tight.

2 Preliminaries

We recall some basic definitions on regular languages and distance measures. For all unexplained notions on finite automata and regular languages the reader may consult the textbook by Shallit [17] or the survey by Yu [18]. A survey of distances is given by Deza and Deza [4].

In the following Σ is always a finite alphabet, the set of strings over Σ is Σ^* and ε is the empty string. The set of nonnegative integers is $\mathbb{N}_0$. The cardinality of a finite set S is denoted $|S|$ and the powerset of S is 2^S. A string $w \in \Sigma^*$ is a *subword* of x if there exist strings $u, v \in \Sigma^*$ such that $x = uwv$. If $u = \varepsilon$, then w is a *prefix* of x. If $v = \varepsilon$, then w is a *suffix* of x.

A *deterministic finite automaton* (DFA) is a tuple $A = (Q, \Sigma, \delta, q_0, F)$ where Q is a finite set of states, Σ is an alphabet, δ is a partial function $\delta : Q \times \Sigma \to Q$, $q_0 \in Q$ is the initial state, and $F \subseteq Q$ is a set of final states. We extend the transition function δ to a partial $Q \times \Sigma^* \to Q$ in the usual way. A DFA A is *complete* if δ is defined for all $q \in Q$ and $a \in \Sigma$.

A string $w \in \Sigma^*$ is *accepted* by A if $\delta(q_0, w) \in F$. The language recognized by A is $L(A) = \{w \in \Sigma^* \mid \delta(q_0, w) \in F\}$. Two states p and q of A are equivalent if $\delta(p, w) \in F$ if and only if $\delta(q, w) \in F$ for every string $w \in \Sigma^*$. A DFA A is *minimal* if each state $q \in Q$ is reachable from the initial state and no two states are equivalent.

A *nondeterministic finite automaton* (NFA) is an extension of a DFA where the transition function is allowed to be multivalued, that is, δ is a function $Q \times \Sigma \to 2^Q$.

Note that our definition of a DFA allows some transitions to be undefined, that is, by a DFA we mean an incomplete DFA. It is well known that, for a regular language L, the sizes of the minimal incomplete and complete DFAs differ by at most one. The constructions in this paper are more convenient to formulate using incomplete DFAs but our results would not change in any significant way if we were to require that all DFAs are complete. The (incomplete deterministic) *state complexity* of a regular language L, $\text{sc}(L)$, is the size of the minimal DFA recognizing L.

2.1 Distances and Neighbourhoods of Regular Languages

We recall definitions of the distance measures used in the following. Generally, a function $d : \Sigma^* \times \Sigma^* \to [0, \infty)$ is a *distance* if it satisfies for all $x, y, z \in \Sigma^*$, the conditions $d(x, y) = 0$ if and only if $x = y$, $d(x, y) = d(y, x)$, and $d(x, z) \leq d(x, y) + d(y, z)$. The *neighbourhood* of a language L of radius k with respect to a distance d is the set

$$E(L, d, k) = \{w \in \Sigma^* \mid (\exists x \in L)d(w, x) \leq k\}.$$

Let $x, y \in \Sigma^*$. The *prefix distance* of x and y counts the number of symbols which do not belong to the longest common prefix of x and y [3]. It is defined by

$$d_p(x, y) = |x| + |y| - 2 \cdot \max_{z \in \Sigma^*}\{|z| \mid x, y \in z\Sigma^*\}.$$

Similarly, the *suffix distance* of x and y counts the number of symbols which do not belong to the longest common suffix of x and y and is defined

$$d_s(x, y) = |x| + |y| - 2 \cdot \max_{z \in \Sigma^*}\{|z| \mid x, y \in \Sigma^* z\}.$$

The *subword distance* measures the similarity of x and y based on their longest common continuous subword and is defined

$$d_f(x, y) = |x| + |y| - 2 \cdot \max_{z \in \Sigma^*}\{|z| \mid x, y \in \Sigma^* z \Sigma^*\}.$$

The term "subword distance" is taken from Choffrut and Pighizzini [3]. However, "subword distance" has also been used for a distance defined in terms of the longest common noncontinuous subword [13].

It is known that neighbourhoods of regular languages with respect to the prefix, suffix and subword distance are always regular [3,15]. We refer to the size of the minimal DFA recognizing the radius k neighbourhood of an n state DFA language with respect to a distance X simply as the state complexity of distance X. Tight bounds for the state complexity of the prefix distance are known [15]. Optimal bounds for the size of an NFA recognizing a suffix distance, or subword distance, neighbourhood of a regular language are also known [15]. The bounds on the size of the NFAs imply the following upper bounds for deterministic state complexity of suffix distance and subword distance, respectively.

Proposition 1. *Suppose L is a regular language recognized by a DFA with n states and $k \in \mathbb{N}$. Then*

$$\mathrm{sc}(E(L, d_s, k)) \leq 2^{n+k} - 1 \quad \text{and} \quad \mathrm{sc}(E(L, d_f, k)) \leq 2^{(k+1)n+2k} - 1.$$

Finally, we define the function $\psi_A : Q \to \mathbb{N}_0$ to give the length of the shortest path from the initial state q_0 to the state q. Formally, ψ_A is defined by

$$\psi_A(q) = \min_{w \in \Sigma^*} \{|w| \mid \delta(q_0, w) = q\}.$$

Note that under this definition, $\psi_A(q_0) = 0$ for the initial state q_0.

3   State Complexity of Suffix Neighbourhoods

In this section, we consider the deterministic state complexity of suffix distance neighbourhoods. First, we construct a DFA for the neighbourhood of an n-state DFA of radius k with respect to the suffix distance d_s, when $k < n$ and then give a matching lower bound when $k = \lfloor \frac{n}{2} \rfloor$ for an n state DFA.

Proposition 2. *Let $n > k \geq 0$ and L be a regular language recognized by a DFA with n states over an alphabet Σ, with $|\Sigma| \geq 2$. Then there is a DFA recognizing $E(L, d_s, k)$ with at most $\frac{|\Sigma|^k - 1}{|\Sigma| - 1} + 2^n - 1$ states.*

Proof. Let L be recognized by the DFA $A = (Q, \Sigma, \delta, q_0, F)$ with $|Q| = n$. We construct a DFA $A' = (Q', \Sigma, \delta', q_0', F')$ that recognizes the neighbourhood $E(L, d_s, k)$. First, let us consider what it means if $w \in E(L(A), d_s, k)$. If w is in the neighbourhood, then this means that there exists a word x recognized by A such that $d(w, x) \leq k$. In other words, we can write $w = w'z$ and $x = x'z$ for words $w', x', z \in \Sigma^*$ such that $|w'| + |x'| \leq k$. However, when A' reads w, it is not known when such a common suffix z might begin. A common suffix may begin in each of the first k symbols of w, so A' must keep track of and compute all possible common suffixes that begin on each of the first k symbols of w.

We define the state set

$$Q' = \{0, \ldots, k\} \times 2^Q$$

and we define the initial state by $q_0' = (0, \{q \in Q \mid \psi_A(q) \leq k\})$. The set of final states is given by

$$F' = \{0, \ldots, k\} \times \{P \subseteq Q \mid P \cap F \neq \emptyset\}.$$

In other words, a state (i, P) of A' is final if and only if P contains a final state of A.

The state set consists of subsets of the original state set with a counter component. The operation of the machine begins by counting the first k steps of computation. On the ith step of the initial k steps, the machine reaches a state containing those states reachable from direct transitions from the set of states from the $(i-1)$th computation step and adds every state reachable from q_0 within $k - i$ steps and the counter component is incremented. After the kth computation step, no further steps need to be counted and the counter is no longer incremented since states are no longer added to the existing state sets.

The transition function δ' is defined for $a \in \Sigma$ by

- $\delta'((i, P), a) = (i + 1, X)$ for $0 \leq i \leq k - 1$, where X is defined as

$$X = \{\delta(p, a) \mid p \in P\} \cup \{q \in Q \mid \psi_A(q) \leq k - (i + 1)\},$$

- $\delta'((k, P), a) = (k, \{\delta(p, a) \mid p \in P\})$.

We now show that reading a word $w \in \Sigma^*$ reaches the state (i, P) if and only if there exists a word $x \in \Sigma^*$ such that $w = w'z$ and $x = x'z$ where $|w'| \leq i$, $|x'| \leq k - i$ and $\delta(q_0, x) \in Q$.

First, suppose that $\delta'(q_0', w) = (i, P)$. We write $w = w'z$ with $w', z \in \Sigma^*$ which may possibly be empty. By definition, $\delta'(q_0', w') = (|w'|, P')$ if $|w'| \leq k$ and P' contains all states q such that $\psi_A(q) \leq k - |w'|$. In other words, these are states $\delta(q_0, x')$ where $x' \in \Sigma^*$ is of length $\leq k - |w'|$. Choose q' to be one of these states and consider the state $\delta(q', z) = q$. Since $q' \in P'$ and $\delta'(q_0', w) = \delta'((|w'|, P'), z) = (i, P)$, we have $q \in P$. Thus, there exists a word $x = x'z$ such that $|x'| \leq k - i$ and $\delta(q_0, x) \in P$.

Now, conversely, suppose that for an input word $w = w'z$ with $|w'| \leq i$, there exists a word $x = x'z$ with $|x'| \leq k - i$ such that $q = \delta(q_0, x) \in P$. Since $|x'| \leq k - i$, let $q' = \delta(q_0, x')$ and we have $\psi_A(q') \leq k - i$. Then this means we have $\delta'(q_0', w') = (|w'|, P')$ with $q' \in P'$. Since $\delta(q', z) = q$, we have $\delta'((|w'|, P'), z) = (i, P)$ with $q \in P$ as desired.

Thus, $\delta(q_0', w) \in F'$ if and only if there exists $x \in L$ such that $|w'| + |x'| \leq k$ for $w = w'z$ and $x = x'z$.

However, not all $(k+1) \cdot 2^n$ states in $\{0, \ldots, k\} \times 2^Q$ are reachable. Note that for $i < k$, the only words that can be read to reach a state (i, P) are those of length exactly i. However, there are only $|\Sigma|^i$ words of length exactly i. Thus, the maximum number of reachable states for $0 \leq i < k$ is

$$\sum_{i=0}^{k-1} |\Sigma|^i = \frac{|\Sigma|^k - 1}{|\Sigma| - 1}.$$

Furthermore, the state $\emptyset \subseteq Q$ is unreachable. Thus, A' has at most $\frac{|\Sigma|^k-1}{|\Sigma|-1}+2^n-1$ reachable states. □

The statement of Proposition 2 assumes that the cardinality of the alphabet is at least two. For suffix distance neighbourhoods of unary languages we have the following bounds. We note that in the unary case the suffix distance coincides with the prefix distance and leave the easy proof for the reader.

Lemma 1. *Let A be an n state DFA over a unary alphabet and $k \in \mathbb{N}$. Then*

$$\mathrm{sc}(E(L(A), d_s, k)) \leq \begin{cases} n & \text{if } L(A) \text{ is infinite and } n > 2k, \\ \max\{1, n-k\} & \text{if } L(A) \text{ is infinite and } n \leq 2k, \\ n+k & \text{if } L(A) \text{ is finite.} \end{cases}$$

For every $n, k \in \mathbb{N}$ there exists an n state unary DFA A recognizing a finite language such that $\mathrm{sc}(E(L(A), d_s, k)) = n+k$. For values $n, k \in \mathbb{N}$ where $n > 2k$ there exists a unary DFA A with n states recognizing an infinite language such that $\mathrm{sc}(E(L(A), d_s, k)) = n$.

For a constant size alphabet, the bound of Proposition 2 is significantly better than the bound implied by known results on nondeterministic state complexity in Proposition 1. Next we show that, at least for some values of the radius k, the bound of Proposition 2 is tight.

Lemma 2. *Let $k = \lfloor \frac{n}{2} \rfloor$. Then there exists a DFA A_n with n states over a binary alphabet such that*

$$\mathrm{sc}(E(L(A_n), d_s, k)) \geq 2^k + 2^n - 2.$$

Proof. Let $A_n = (Q_n, \{a, b\}, \delta_n, 0, \{0\})$, shown in Fig. 1. □

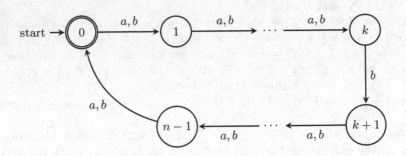

Fig. 1. The DFA A_n.

The following theorem then follows from Proposition 2 and Lemma 2.

Theorem 1. *Let $n > k$ and let L be a regular language recognized by an n-state DFA over an alphabet Σ with $|\Sigma| \geq 2$. Then a DFA recognizing $E(L, d_s, k)$ requires at most $\frac{|\Sigma|^k - 1}{|\Sigma| - 1} + 2^n - 1$ states. There is a family of DFAs with n states over a binary alphabet which reaches this bound when $k = \lfloor \frac{n}{2} \rfloor$.*

Now we will consider the case when the distance k is greater than the number of states n of the given DFA and give a matching lower bound.

Proposition 3. *Let $k > n > 0$ and L be a regular language recognized by a DFA with n states over an alphabet Σ with $|\Sigma| \geq 2$. Then there is a DFA recognizing $E(L, d_s, k)$ with at most $(k - n) + 2^{n+1} - 2$ states.*

Proof. Let $A = (Q, \Sigma, \delta, q_0, F)$ with $|Q| = n$. Then we follow the construction given in the proof of Proposition 2 to obtain the DFA $A' = (Q', \Sigma, \delta', q_0', F')$ that recognizes the neighbourhood $E(L(A), d_s, k)$ with $k > n$. We note that $\psi_A(q) \leq n$ for all $q \in Q$ and thus by the definition of the transition function, we have for $0 \leq i \leq k - n$ and all words w of length i, $\delta(q_0, w) = (i, Q)$. This gives us $k - n$ states. Then on the following n steps, we proceed as in the rest of Proposition 2. This suggests that there are at most $\frac{|\Sigma|^n - 1}{|\Sigma| - 1}$ states. However, in this case, there are far fewer states than this.

To consider how many states there are, we observe that the above bound requires that each word of length $i > k - n$ reaches a different state (i, P), giving us a total of $|\Sigma|^{i - (k-n)}$ states for each i. Then we must consider how many different subsets $P \subseteq Q$ are reachable. Recall that by definition, all states q with $\psi_A(q) \leq k - i$ are contained in P for (i, P). Thus, on step i, two states (i, P) and (i, P') both P and P' contain the subset $\{q \in Q \mid \psi_A(q) \leq k - i\}$. Then if P and P' are different, they must contain different subsets of the set $\{q \in Q \mid \psi_A(q) > k - i\}$.

Let j be the size of the set $\{q \in Q \mid \psi_A(q) > k - i\}$. Then in order for each word of length i to reach a different state, we must have $|\Sigma|^{i - (k-n)} \leq 2^j$ different subsets. This means that we must have at least $(i - (k - n)) \cdot \log_2 |\Sigma|$ states q with $\psi_A(q) > k - i$ on step i of a computation on A'. In other words, for each $1 \leq i \leq \max_{q \in Q} \psi_A(q)$, there are at least $\log_2 |\Sigma|$ states q with $\psi_A(q) = i$. However, since $k > n$, the number of states of A are further restricted by this condition.

Let $\ell = \max_{q \in Q} \psi_A(q)$. Then there are at most $k - \frac{n}{\log_2 |\Sigma|} + \frac{|\Sigma|^{\frac{n}{\log_2 |\Sigma|}} - 1}{|\Sigma| - 1}$ reachable states for words of length up to k. We observe that this is maximized when $|\Sigma| = 2$. That is, for any alphabet of size at least 2, the maximum is achieved when we have for each i exactly one state q such that $\psi_A(q) = i$. This gives us a maximum of $2^n - 1$ reachable states of the form (i, P) for $i < k$.

After the kth step of computation, there are $2^n - 1$ reachable states of the form (k, P) as usual. This gives us a total of at most $(k - n) + 2^{n+1} - 2$ states. □

We will show that the bound from Proposition 3 is reachable for a family of n state DFAs over an alphabet of size $n + 1$.

Lemma 3. *Let $k > n > 0$. Then there exists a DFA B_n with n states over an alphabet of size $n + 1$ such that*

$$\mathrm{sc}(E(L(A_n), d_s, k)) \geq (k - n) + 2^{n+1} - 2.$$

Proof. Let $B_n = (Q_n, \Sigma_n, \delta_n, 0, \{0\})$, shown in Fig. 2, with $\Sigma_n = \{a_0, a_1, \ldots, a_n\}$ and the transition function is defined by

$$\delta(i, a_j) = i + 1 \bmod n \quad \text{for all } 0 \leq i \leq n - 1, 0 \leq j \leq n, \text{ and } i \neq j.$$

$\square$

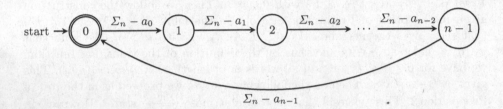

Fig. 2. The DFA B_n.

Proposition 3 and Lemma 3 can then be summarized in the following theorem.

Theorem 2. *Let $k > n$ and let L be a regular language recognized by an n-state DFA over an alphabet Σ with $|\Sigma| \geq 2$. Then a DFA recognizing $E(L, d_s, k)$ requires at most $(k - n) + 2^{n+1} - 2$ states. There is a family of DFAs with n states over an alphabet of size $n + 1$ which reaches this bound.*

3.1   State Complexity of Subword Distance

Now, we give an upper bound on the deterministic state complexity of subword neighbourhoods by giving a construction for a DFA for the neighbourhood of radius k with respect to the subword distance d_f. In the construction we again assume that the cardinality of the alphabet is at least two. For unary alphabets, the subword distance coincides with the suffix distance and a tight bound is obtained from Lemma 1.

Proposition 4. *Let $n > k \geq 0$ and L be a regular language recognized by a DFA with n states over the alphabet Σ with $|\Sigma| \geq 2$. Then there is a DFA recognizing $E(L, d_f, k)$ with at most $\frac{|\Sigma|^k - 1}{|\Sigma| - 1} + (k + 2) \cdot 2^{n \cdot (k+1)}$ states.*

The bound of Proposition 4 is significantly better than the bound implied by nondeterministic state complexity [14] (in Proposition 1) for a fixed alphabet Σ. However, we do not know whether the bound is the best possible.

4 State Complexity of Suffix Distance on Subregular Languages

Here, we consider the state complexity of neighbourhoods with respect to the suffix distance of languages which belong to subregular language classes. First, we consider neighbourhoods of finite languages.

Proposition 5. *Let $n > k \geq 0$ and L be a finite language recognized by a DFA with n states over a binary alphabet. Then there is a DFA recognizing $E(L, d_s, k)$ with at most $2^k + k \cdot 2^{\lfloor \frac{n}{2} \rfloor} - 1$ states.*

Proof. We use the construction for A' from the proof of Proposition 2. Observe that, as is the case for general regular languages, not all $(k + 1) \cdot 2^n$ states that are defined are reachable. Recall that the states of A' are pairs (i, P) where i is a counter from 0 to k and P is a subset of states of A and that a word w reaches a state (i, P) if and only if there exists a word $x \in \Sigma^*$ such that $w = w'z$ and $x = x'z$ where $|w'| \leq i$, $|x'| \leq k - i$ and $\delta(q_0, x) \in Q$. We also note that for $i < k$, any state (i, P) with $P \subseteq Q$ is reachable on a word of length exactly i. This gives us at most $\sum_{i<k} 2^i = 2^k - 1$ reachable states of the form (i, P) for $i < k$.

It remains to show how many states of the form (k, P) with $P \subseteq Q$ are reachable. Since P is a subset of the set of states of A, we would like to know how many different subsets P exist such that (k, P) is reachable. Since A recognizes a finite language, there exists at least one state q of A with $\psi_A(q) = i$ that is reachable on some string of length i and is not reachable on any string of length $j > i$.

Recall that A recognizes a finite language and in each state (k, P) of A', the set P is a subset of states of A. First, we observe that the above property does not hold for subsets $P \subseteq Q$ in states of the form (i, P) with $i < k$. To see this, we consider some i and observe that every state $q \in Q$ with $\psi_A(q) \leq k - i$ is in some subset P with (i, P) reachable for all $i < k$ by definition. Hence, why we can narrow our focus only to those states of the form (k, P).

Let (k, T) be a state that is reached on a word w of length k. Since A' is deterministic, there are up to 2^k possible such states.

Let $R_i \subseteq Q$ denote the set of states of A that are not contained in any state $P \subseteq Q$, where (k, P) is reachable on a word of length greater than $k + i$. In other words, R_i is the set of states of A which become unreachable in A on a word of length i. We note that R_i must contain at least one element, since A recognizes a finite language.

We write $T = R \cup S$, where $R \subseteq \bigcup_{0 \leq i \leq k} R_i$ and $S \subseteq Q \setminus R$. We have $|Q \setminus R| \leq n - k$, since $k < n$. From this, we can see that to maximize the number of states that are reachable, each R_i must contain at most one element. This gives us a total of 2^{n-k} possible subsets S.

Then for each set $T = R \cup S$ that is reachable on a word of length k, there is a state $T_i = (R \setminus \bigcup_{j=0}^{i} R_j) \cup S$ that is reachable on a word of length $k + i$ for $1 \leq i \leq k$. Since each R_i has one element, each subset S is contained in up to

k different subsets of Q that are reachable in A'. This gives $k \cdot 2^{\lfloor \frac{n}{2} \rfloor}$ possible subsets that can be reached on each string of length greater than k.

Thus, A' can have up to $\frac{|\Sigma|^k - 1}{|\Sigma| - 1} + k \cdot 2^{\lfloor \frac{n}{2} \rfloor} - 1$ states in total.   □

The statement of Proposition 5 assumes that the alphabet is binary. A tight bound is known from Lemma 1 also for finite languages.

Lemma 4. *Let* $k = \lfloor \frac{n}{2} \rfloor$. *Then there exists a DFA* C_n *with* n *states over a binary alphabet recognizing a finite language such that*

$$\mathrm{sc}(E(L(C_n), d_s, k)) \geq 2^k + k \cdot 2^{\lfloor \frac{n}{2} \rfloor} - 1.$$

Proof. Let $C_n = (Q_n, \{a, b\}, \delta_n, 0, \{n - 1\})$, shown in Fig. 3. We construct the DFA C'_n recognizing the neighbourhood by using the construction from Proposition 2.   □

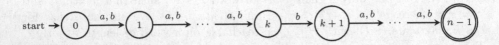

Fig. 3. The DFA C_n.

We can summarize the results of Proposition 5 and Lemma 4 as follows:

Theorem 3. *Let* L *be a finite language recognized by an* n-*state DFA over an alphabet* Σ *with* $|\Sigma| \geq 2$ *and* $k \leq n$. *Then a DFA recognizing* $E(L, d_s, k)$ *requires at most* $\frac{|\Sigma|^k - 1}{|\Sigma| - 1} + k \cdot 2^{\lfloor \frac{n}{2} \rfloor} - 1$ *states. There is a family of DFAs with* n *states over a binary alphabet which reaches this bound when* $k = \lfloor \frac{n}{2} \rfloor$.

Now, we show that if $k > n$, the lower bound coincides with the upper bound for regular languages.

Theorem 4. *Let* L *be a finite language recognized by an* n-*state DFA over an alphabet* Σ *with* $|\Sigma| \geq 2$ *and* $k > n$. *Then a DFA recognizing* $E(L, d_s, k)$ *requires at most* $(k - n) + 2^{n+1} - 2$ *states. There is a family of DFAs with* n *states over an alphabet of size* n *which reaches this bound.*

Proof. Let $D_n = (Q_n, \Sigma_n, \delta_n, 0, \{0\})$, shown in Fig. 4, with $\Sigma_n = \{a_0, a_1, \ldots, a_{n-1}\}$ and the transition function is defined by

$$\delta(i, a_j) = i + 1 \quad \text{for all } 0 \leq i < n - 1, 0 \leq j \leq n - 1, \text{and } i \neq j.$$

     □

Next, we consider the class of suffix-closed languages [1]. A language L is *suffix-closed* if $wx \in L$ implies $x \in L$. It is well known that the class of suffix-closed languages is a subclass of the regular languages. We will give a tight bound on the size of the DFA for neighbourhoods of suffix-closed languages with respect to the suffix distance.

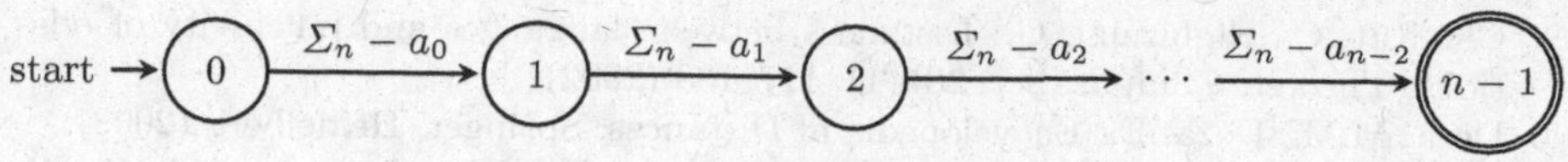

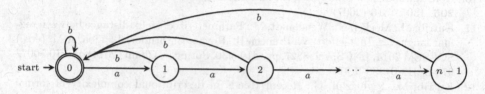

start → ⓪ $\xrightarrow{\Sigma_n - a_0}$ ① $\xrightarrow{\Sigma_n - a_1}$ ② $\xrightarrow{\Sigma_n - a_2}$ ⋯ $\xrightarrow{\Sigma_n - a_{n-2}}$ ⦿$(n-1)$

Fig. 4. The DFA D_n.

Theorem 5. *Let L be a suffix-closed language recognized by an n-state DFA. Then a DFA recognizing $E(L, d_s, k)$ requires at most $n + k + 1$ states. For each $n \in \mathbb{N}$ there exists an n-state DFA E_n recognizing a suffix-closed language such that the state complexity of $E(L(E_n), d_s, k)$ is $n + k + 1$ for all $k \in \mathbb{N}$.*

The DFA E_n is shown in Fig. 5.

start → ⦿0 → ① → ② → ⋯ → $(n-1)$

Fig. 5. The DFA E_n.

5   Conclusion

The state complexity of radius k prefix distance neighbourhoods of an n state DFA language depends linearly on n and on k [15]. As we have seen, the corresponding bounds for the suffix and the subword distance neighbourhoods depend exponentially on n and k and, furthermore, coming up with matching lower bounds is considerably more involved.

For suffix distance neighbourhoods where the radius k equals, roughly, half of the number of states n, we have given a matching lower bound construction based on a binary alphabet. However (and perhaps curiously), the construction does not seem to extend, at least not directly, for other values of the radius when $k < n$.

The precise state complexity of subword distance neighbourhoods remains open. We do not have a lower bound construction matching the upper bound of Proposition 4 for the state complexity of subword distance neighbourhoods.

References

1. Brzozowski, J., Jirásková, G., Zou, C.: Quotient complexity of closed languages. Theory Comput. Syst. **54**(2), 277–292 (2014)
2. Calude, C.S., Salomaa, K., Yu, S.: Additive distances and quasi-distances between words. J. Univers. Comput. Sci. **8**(2), 141–152 (2002)

3. Choffrut, C., Pighizzini, G.: Distances between languages and reflexivity of relations. Theoret. Comput. Sci. **286**(1), 117–138 (2002)
4. Deza, M.M., Deza, E.: Encyclopedia of Distances. Springer, Heidelberg (2009)
5. Gao, Y., Moreira, N., Reis, R., Yu, S.: A survey on operational state complexity. To appear in Computer Science Review, September 2015. arXiv:1509.03254v1 [cs.FL]
6. Holzer, M., Kutrib, M.: Descriptional and computational complexity of finite automata—a survey. Inf. Comput. **209**, 456–470 (2011)
7. Han, Y.-S., Ko, S.-K., Salomaa, K.: The edit distance between a regular language and a context-free language. Int. J. Found. Comput. Sci. **24**, 1067–1082 (2013)
8. Kari, L., Konstantinidis, S.: Descriptional complexity of error/edit systems. J. Automata Lang. Comb. **9**, 293–309 (2004)
9. Kari, L., Konstantinidis, S., Kopecki, S., Yang, M.: An efficient algorithm for computing the edit distance of a regular language via input-altering transducers. CoRR abs/1406.1041 (2014)
10. Konstantinidis, S.: Computing the edit distance of a regular language. Inf. Comput. **205**, 1307–1316 (2007)
11. Kutrib, M., Meckel, K., Wendlandt, M.: Parameterized prefix distance between regular languages. In: Geffert, V., Preneel, B., Rovan, B., Štuller, J., Tjoa, A.M. (eds.) SOFSEM 2014. LNCS, vol. 8327, pp. 419–430. Springer, Cham (2014). doi:10.1007/978-3-319-04298-5_37
12. Kutrib, M., Pighizzini, G.: Recent trends in descriptional complexity of formal languages. Bull. EATCS **111**, 70–86 (2013)
13. Lothaire, M.: Algorithms on words. In: Applied Combinatorics on Words. Encyclopedia of Mathematics and it's Applications, vol. 105. Cambridge University Press, New York (2005)
14. Ng, T., Rappaport, D., Salomaa, K.: State complexity of neighbourhoods and approximate pattern matching. In: Potapov, I. (ed.) DLT 2015. LNCS, vol. 9168, pp. 389–400. Springer, Cham (2015). doi:10.1007/978-3-319-21500-6_31
15. Ng, T., Rappaport, D., Salomaa, K.: State complexity of prefix distance. In: Drewes, F. (ed.) CIAA 2015. LNCS, vol. 9223, pp. 238–249. Springer, Cham (2015). doi:10.1007/978-3-319-22360-5_20
16. Ng, T., Rappaport, D., Salomaa, K.: State complexity of prefix distance of subregular languages. In: Câmpeanu, C., Manea, F., Shallit, J. (eds.) DCFS 2016. LNCS, vol. 9777, pp. 192–204. Springer, Cham (2016). doi:10.1007/978-3-319-41114-9_15
17. Shallit, J.: A Second Course in Formal Languages and Automata Theory. Cambridge University Press, Cambridge (2009)
18. Yu, S.: Regular languages. In: Rozenberg, G., Salomaa, A. (eds.) Handbook of Formal Languages, pp. 41–110. Springer, Heidelberg (1997)

The Quotient Operation on Input-Driven Pushdown Automata

Alexander Okhotin[1](✉) and Kai Salomaa[2]

[1] St. Petersburg State University, 14th Line V.O., 29B,
Saint Petersburg 199178, Russia
alexander.okhotin@spbu.ru
[2] School of Computing, Queen's University,
Kingston, ON K7L 2N8, Canada
ksalomaa@cs.queensu.ca

Abstract. The quotient of a formal language K by another language L is the set of all strings obtained by taking a string from K that ends with a suffix from L, and removing that suffix. The quotient of a regular language by any language is always regular, whereas the context-free languages and many of their subfamilies, such as the linear and the deterministic languages, are not closed under the quotient operation. This paper establishes the closure of the family of input-driven pushdown automata (IDPDA), also known as visibly pushdown automata, under the quotient operation. A construction of automata representing the result of the operation is given, and its state complexity with respect to nondeterministic IDPDA is shown to be $m^2 n + O(m)$, where m and n is the number of states in the automata recognizing K and L, respectively.

1 Introduction

Let K and L be formal languages over some alphabet Σ. Then, the right-quotient of K by L is the following formal language, denoted by $K \cdot L^{-1}$.

$$K \cdot L^{-1} = \{ u \mid \exists v \in L : uv \in K \}$$

The left-quotient operation is defined symmetrically.

$$L^{-1} \cdot K = \{ v \mid \exists u \in L : uv \in K \}$$

The family of regular languages is closed under quotient with *any* language: as shown by Ginsburg and Spanier [6], if K is a regular language, then the languages $K \cdot L^{-1}$ and $L^{-1} \cdot K$ are both regular, regardless of L. For formal grammars, Ginsburg and Spanier [6] showed that for every context-free language K and a regular language L, their quotients are again context-free. On the other hand, if both arguments can be any context-free languages, then their quotient need not be context-free: indeed, for $K = a\{ b^\ell a^\ell \mid \ell \geqslant 1 \}^*$ and $L = \{ a^m b^{2m} \mid m \geqslant 1 \}^*$,

© IFIP International Federation for Information Processing 2017
Published by Springer International Publishing AG 2017. All Rights Reserved
G. Pighizzini and C. Câmpeanu (Eds.): DCFS 2017, LNCS 10316, pp. 299–310, 2017.
DOI: 10.1007/978-3-319-60252-3_24

their quotient satisfies $K^{-1}L \cap b^* = \{ b^{2^n} \mid n \geqslant 1 \}$. Besides just the non-closure, it is known that every recursively enumerable set is representable as a quotient of two context-free languages [8].

For an important subfamily of grammars, the *LR(k) grammars*, which are equivalently defined by *deterministic pushdown automata* (DPDA)—it is known that they are closed under right-quotient with regular languages, but not closed under left-quotient with finite languages [5]. Another classical subfamily of *LL(k) grammars* is not closed under both right- and left-quotient with regular languages [18]. On the other hand, the family of languages recognized by pushdown automata with one stack symbol (the *one-counter languages*) is surprisingly closed under quotient [9].

This paper investigates the quotient operation for one of the most important subclasses of pushdown automata: the *input-driven pushdown automata* (IDPDA). These automata were introduced in the work of Mehlhorn [10] and of von Braunmühl and Verbeek [4], and are characterized by the following restriction: their input alphabet is split into three disjoint classes of symbols, on which the automaton must push one symbol onto the stack (left brackets), or must pop one symbol off the stack (right brackets) or may not touch the stack (neutral symbols). The model defined by Mehlhorn [10] was deterministic (DIDPDA); von Braunmühl and Verbeek [4] introduced its nondeterministic variant (NIDPDA) and presented a novel determinization construction. Furthermore, Mehlhorn [10] and von Braunmühl and Verbeek [4] presented efficient algorithms for simulating these automata.

Later, Alur and Madhusudan [1] reintroduced IDPDA under the name of *visibly pushdown automata* and pointed out their applications to verification; their work revived the interest in the model. One of the theoretical contributions of Alur and Madhusudan [1] is the study of the succinctness of description by input-driven automata. In particular, they proved that determinizing an n-state NIDPDA requires $2^{\Theta(n^2)}$ states in the worst case, and initiated a systematic study of their closure properties.

In the follow-up work, the state complexity of the main language-theoretic operations on IDPDA was determined. The precise number of states necessary to represent concatenation, Kleene star and reversal by deterministic IDPDA (DIDPDA) was later determined by the authors [14]. For Boolean operations, the state complexity results were obtained by Han and Salomaa [7] and by Piao and Salomaa [16]. Recently, the authors [15] established the closure of IDPDA under the edit distance operation. For more details on the descriptional complexity of input-driven automata, an interested reader is directed to a fairly recent survey paper [12].

This paper investigates the quotient operation on IDPDA. The main result is that the family of languages recognized by IDPDA is closed under the quotient. If both argument languages consist only of well-nested strings, then so does their quotient, and the construction of an IDPDA for that quotient is straightforward. In the general case, without the well-nestedness condition, the closure is established by a more involved construction: given a pair of NIDPDA with m and n

states, a construction of a $(3m + m^2 n)$-state NIDPDA recognizing their quotient is described in Sect. 3.

The rest of the paper establishes a close lower bound to this construction. The general plan of the lower bound argument, explained in Sect. 4, is to construct witness languages of a special form, so that the task of constructing them is basically a problem of finding witness NFA (nondeterministic finite automata) for the state complexity of a certain unconventional operation on languages. This operation has been named *palindromic quotient*, and the NFA state complexity problem for it is solved in Sect. 5. The results are adapted to NIDPDA in the final Sect. 6

2   Input-Driven Automata

The input alphabet of an *input-driven pushdown automaton* (IDPDA) [1,2,10] is split into three disjoint sets of *left brackets* Σ_{+1}, *right brackets* Σ_{-1} and *neutral symbols* Σ_0. If the input symbol is a left bracket from Σ_{+1}, then the automaton always pushes one symbol onto the stack. For a right bracket from Σ_{-1}, the automaton must pop one symbol. Finally, for a neutral symbol in Σ_0, the automaton may not use the stack. In this paper, symbols from Σ_{+1} and Σ_{-1} shall be denoted by left and right angle brackets, respectively $(<, >)$, whereas lower-case Latin letters from the beginning of the alphabet $(a, b, c, \ldots)$ shall be used for symbols from Σ_0. Input-driven automata may be deterministic (DIDPDA) and nondeterministic (NIDPDA).

Under the original definition used by Mehlhorn [10] and by von Braunmühl and Verbeek [4], input-driven automata operate on input strings, in which the brackets are *well-nested*. When an input-driven automaton reads a left bracket $(< \in \Sigma_{+1})$, it pushes a symbol onto the stack. This symbol is popped at the exact moment when the automaton encounters the matching right bracket $(> \in \Sigma_{-1})$. Thus, a computation of an input-driven automaton on any well-nested substring leaves the stack contents untouched.

For instance, in Fig. 1, the fragment of the computation beginning in the state q_4 and ending in the state q_{12} processes a well-nested substring $b<<cd>e>$, and therefore ends with the same stack contents as in which it began (in this case, the empty stack).

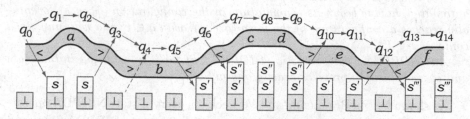

Fig. 1. A sample computation of an IDPDA on an ill-nested string.

The more general definition of input-driven automata proposed by Alur and Madhusudan [1] also allows *ill-nested* input strings, such as the whole string $<a>>b<<cd>e><f$ in Fig. 1. For every unmatched left bracket, the symbol pushed to the stack when reading this bracket is never popped, and remains in the stack to the end of the computation; in the figure, this is the case with the symbol s''' pushed in the state q_{12}. An unmatched right bracket is read with an empty stack: instead of popping a stack symbol, the automaton merely detects that the stack is empty and makes a special transition, which leaves the stack empty. The latter happens in the state q_3 in the figure, where the special transition upon an unmatched right bracket leads the automaton to the state q_4.

Definition 1 (von Braunmühl and Verbeek [4]; Alur and Madhusudan [1]). *A nondeterministic input-driven pushdown automaton (NIDPDA) over an alphabet $\widetilde{\Sigma} = (\Sigma_{+1}, \Sigma_{-1}, \Sigma_0)$ consists of*

- *a finite set Q of states, with set of initial states $Q_0 \subseteq Q$ and accepting states $F \subseteq Q$;*
- *a finite stack alphabet Γ, and a special symbol $\perp \notin \Gamma$ for the empty stack;*
- *for a neutral symbol $c \in \Sigma_0$, a transition function $\delta_c \colon Q \to 2^Q$ gives the set of possible next states;*
- *for each left bracket symbol $< \in \Sigma_{+1}$, the behaviour of the automaton is described by a function $\delta_< \colon Q \to 2^{Q \times \Gamma}$, which, for a given current state, provides a set of pairs (q, s), with $q \in Q$ and $s \in \Gamma$, where each pair means that the automaton enters the state q and pushes s onto the stack;*
- *for every right bracket symbol $> \in \Sigma_{-1}$, there is a function $\delta_> \colon Q \times (\Gamma \cup \{\perp\}) \to 2^Q$ specifying possible next states, assuming that the given stack symbol is popped from the stack (or that the stack is empty).*

A configuration is a triple (q, w, x), with the current state $q \in Q$, remaining input $w \in \Sigma^*$ and stack contents $x \in \Gamma^*$. Possible next configurations are defined as follows.

$$(q, cw, x) \vdash_A (q', w, x), \quad c \in \Sigma_0,\ q \in Q,\ q' \in \delta_c(q)$$
$$(q, <w, x) \vdash_A (q', w, sx), \quad < \in \Sigma_{+1},\ q \in Q,\ (q', s) \in \delta_<(q)$$
$$(q, >w, sx) \vdash_A (q', w, x), \quad > \in \Sigma_{-1},\ q \in Q,\ s \in \Gamma,\ q' \in \delta_>(q, s)$$
$$(q, >w, \epsilon) \vdash_A (q', w, \epsilon), \quad > \in \Sigma_{-1},\ q' \in \delta_>(q, \perp)$$

The language recognized by A is the set of all strings $w \in \Sigma^*$, on which the automaton, having begun its computation in the configuration (q_0, w, ϵ), eventually reaches a configuration of the form (q, ϵ, x), with $q \in F$ and with any stack contents $x \in \Gamma^*$.

An NIDPDA is deterministic (DIDPDA), if there is a unique initial state and every transition provides exactly one action.

As shown by von Braunmühl and Verbeek [4], every n-state NIDPDA operating on well-nested strings can be transformed to a 2^{n^2}-state DIDPDA. Alur and Madhusudan [1] proved that $2^{\Omega(n^2)}$ states are necessary in the worst case, and also extended the transformation to handle ill-nested inputs, with the resulting DIDPDA using 2^{2n^2} states.

For more details on input-driven automata and their complexity, the readers are directed to a recent survey [12].

3   Closure Under the Quotient

In this section, it is proved that the language family defined by input-driven automata is closed under the quotient operation.

For the class of regular languages, it is well-known that they are closed under quotient *with any language*. Indeed, if K is recognized by a deterministic finite automaton (DFA), then, from each state q of this DFA, it is the case or not the case that the DFA accepts some string from L beginning from q. Depending on this, q is relabelled as accepting or rejecting, and the resulting DFA recognizes exactly the quotient $K \cdot L^{-1}$.

Turning to input-driven automata, as long as all strings in L are well-nested, the same property still holds. That is, an n-state DIDPDA recognizing K can be transformed to an n-state DIDPDA recognizing the quotient $K \cdot L^{-1}$, simply by relabelling its states.

Given an arbitrary pair of NIDPDA, $\mathcal{A}$ and $\mathcal{B}$, the goal is to construct a new NIDPDA $\mathcal{C}$ that recognizes their quotient, $L(\mathcal{A}) \cdot L(\mathcal{B})^{-1}$. Whenever the automaton $\mathcal{A}$ accepts a string uv, and the other automaton $\mathcal{B}$ accepts the string v, the simulating automaton should therefore accept u. If none of the brackets in the u-part of uv match any brackets in the v-part, then the simulation proceeds like in the case of finite automata, without using any extra states. In the general case, the string u may have unmatched left brackets, v may have unmatched right brackets, and these brackets *match each other* in uv; thus, the computation of $\mathcal{A}$ may rely on the data transferred from u to v in the stack symbols. The simulating automaton $\mathcal{C}$ is given only u, with its unmatched left brackets, and while doing so, it has to guess the string v and imagine the computations of both $\mathcal{A}$ and $\mathcal{B}$ on this guessed v.

In the computation of $\mathcal{C}$ on u, these imaginary computations on v are traced *backwards*, so that whenever a left bracket ($<$) in u matches a right bracket ($>$) in v, the simulating automaton $\mathcal{C}$, upon reading u up to that left bracket, tracks the imaginary computations of $\mathcal{A}$ and $\mathcal{B}$ *that begin from the matching right bracket ($>$) in v and accept in the end of v*. As $\mathcal{C}$ finishes reading the string u, its imaginary computations on v are backtracked to their beginning at the boundary between u and v. Then, at this point $\mathcal{C}$ ensures that $\mathcal{B}$'s computation is in its initial configuration, whereas the actual simulated computation of $\mathcal{A}$ on u smoothly continues into the imaginary computation of $\mathcal{A}$ on v. Thus, $\mathcal{C}$ finally verifies that a string v and a computation on it that it has been guessing actually do exist; and accordingly $\mathcal{C}$ accepts u.

This idea is implemented in the following construction.

Lemma 1. *Let K be a language recognized by an NIDPDA $\mathcal{A}$ with the set of states P and with the pushdown alphabet Γ, and let L be another language recognized by an NIDPDA $\mathcal{B}$ with the set of states Q and with the pushdown alphabet Ω. Then, the quotient $K \cdot L^{-1}$ is recognized by an NIDPDA $\mathcal{C}$ with the set of states $(P \times \{0,1\}) \cup P \cup (P \times P \times Q)$ and with the pushdown alphabet $(\Gamma \times \{0,1\}) \cup \Gamma \cup \{\#\} \cup (\Gamma \times P \times Q)$.*

Proof (a sketch). At the **first phase** of the computation of $\mathcal{C}$ on an input string u, the simulation of the computations of $\mathcal{A}$ and $\mathcal{B}$ on its imaginary continuation v has not yet been started. This means that $\mathcal{C}$ assumes that all left brackets read so far are either going to have a matching right bracket in u, or are unmatched both in u and in v.

Thus, at the first phase, $\mathcal{C}$ simply simulates the operation of $\mathcal{A}$ on a prefix of u, while maintaining a single extra bit of data: whether the stack is empty or not. This is represented in states of the form (p, d), where $p \in P$ is the state of $\mathcal{A}$, and $d \in \{0, 1\}$, with $d = 0$ representing stack emptiness. While in these states, $\mathcal{C}$ uses stack symbols of the form (s, d), with $s \in \Gamma$ and $d \in \{0, 1\}$, which also carry the information on whether this stack symbol is at the bottom of the stack ($d = 0$). This allows the simulating automaton to enter a state of the form $(p, 0)$ upon popping the last symbol from the stack, and thus always be aware of its stack's emptiness.

Every time $\mathcal{C}$ reads a left bracket ($<$), it nondeterministically guesses whether this bracket has a matching right bracket ($>$) in v. If $\mathcal{C}$ guesses that this is not the case, it pushes the same stack symbol as $\mathcal{A}$ would push (that is, $\mathcal{C}$ pushes $(s, 0)$ or $(s, 1)$, if $\mathcal{A}$ would push s), and continues its computation in a state of the form $(p, 0)$ or $(p, 1)$. If later, while still at the first phase, $\mathcal{C}$ encounters a matching right bracket and pops that symbol, it again behaves as $\mathcal{A}$ would do, remaining in a state from $P \times \{0, 1\}$.

At some point, $\mathcal{C}$ may read a left bracket ($<$) and decide that it has a matching right bracket in v, so that $\mathcal{A}$ operating on uv would transfer some stack symbol s from the left bracket ($<$) to the right bracket ($>$). If this guess is correct, then this left bracket is unmatched in u, and thus $\mathcal{C}$ will never have a chance to pop the stack symbol it pushes at this moment; for that reason, it pushes a special stack symbol ($\#$) that will cause immediate rejection if it is ever popped. At the same time, $\mathcal{C}$ guesses the computations of $\mathcal{A}$ and $\mathcal{B}$ on a suffix of v containing the matching right bracket ($>$) and the neighbouring well-nested substrings, and enters the second phase of the simulation in a state from $P \times P \times Q$.

In the **second phase**, $\mathcal{C}$ uses triples of the form $(p, \widetilde{p}, \widetilde{q})$ as states, and, while reading the input string u from left to right, it also guesses an imaginary string v from right to left, along with the computations of $\mathcal{A}$ and of $\mathcal{B}$ on that imaginary string. According to this plan, the first component of each triple, $p \in P$, is the state of the ongoing simulation of $\mathcal{A}$ on the prefix of u read so far. The other two components are the states of $\mathcal{A}$ and $\mathcal{B}$ processing v. To be precise, the second component, $\widetilde{p} \in P$, is a state, beginning from which $\mathcal{A}$ accepts a suffix of v guessed in the course of this simulation, whereas $\widetilde{q} \in Q$ is a state of $\mathcal{B}$, beginning from which it accepts the same guessed suffix of v.

When $\mathcal{C}$ nondeterministically decides to move to the second phase along with reading a left bracket ($<$), it guesses $\mathcal{A}$'s and $\mathcal{B}$'s computations on the last suffix of the imaginary second part of the string. If $\mathcal{C}$'s stack is empty—that is, if $\mathcal{C}$ is in a state $(p, 0)$—then the last suffix of v is of the form $x{>}y$, where x is a well-nested string, the right bracket ($>$) following x is the one that matches the current left bracket ($<$) in u, and y is a concatenation of a *descending string* and an *ascending string* (that is, a concatenation of well-nested strings and right brackets, followed by well-nested strings and left brackets). All right brackets in y are then unmatched both in u and in the earlier part of v, and accordingly, $\mathcal{C}$ may enter any state $(p', \widetilde{p}, \widetilde{q})$ satisfying the following conditions:

1. upon reading this left bracket ($<$) in the state p, $\mathcal{A}$ pushes some stack symbol $s \in \Gamma$ and enters the state p';
2. the automaton $\mathcal{A}$, having begun its computation on $x{>}y$ in the state $\widetilde{p}$ and with s on the stack, accepts;
3. the other automaton $\mathcal{B}$, having begun its computation on $x{>}y$ in the state $\widetilde{q}$ and with the empty stack, accepts as well.

In the other case, if $\mathcal{C}$'s stack is not empty, and it is therefore in a state $(p, 1)$, the suffix of v is of the form $x{>}y$, where both x and y are well-nested, and the above three conditions remain the same.

Transitions of $\mathcal{C}$ in a state $(p, \widetilde{p}, \widetilde{q})$ are defined as follows. A right bracket ($>$) cannot be read in this state, and if it is encountered, $\mathcal{C}$ rejects.

Upon reading a neutral symbol $c \in \Sigma_0$, the simulation of $\mathcal{A}$ in the first component continues, while the last two components stay unchanged.

When reading a left bracket ($<$), the automaton $\mathcal{C}$ again has to guess whether this bracket has a matching right bracket ($>$) in v. In case it does, $\mathcal{C}$ pushes the stack symbol ($\#$) that will cause rejection if popped, and advances the simulation in all three components of the state in the same way as it did when entering the second phase. On the other hand, if $\mathcal{C}$ nondeterministically guesses that this left bracket ($<$) has a matching bracket in u, it suspends the simulation of $\mathcal{A}$ and $\mathcal{B}$ on the imaginary suffix v, pushing a triple $(s, \widetilde{p}, \widetilde{q})$ onto the stack, where s is the stack symbol in the ongoing simulation of $\mathcal{A}$ on u. Then, $\mathcal{C}$ enters a state $p' \in P$ and begins processing the current well-nested substring of u in the state from P, simulating only $\mathcal{A}$.

When this well-nested substring ends, $\mathcal{C}$ reads the matching right bracket ($>$) in u and pops the triple $(s, \widetilde{p}, \widetilde{q})$ from the stack. Then, it resumes the second phase of the simulation in the state $(p'', \widetilde{p}, \widetilde{q})$, where p'' is the next state in the ongoing simulation of $\mathcal{A}$ on u.

The precise correctness statement of the construction takes the following form. When the simulating NIDPDA, after having read a string $t{<}_1 u_1 \ldots {<}_h u_h \in \Sigma^*$, where t is any string, $u_1, \ldots, u_h$ are well-nested strings and $<_1, \ldots, <_h$ are unmatched left brackets in this string, is in a state $(p, \widetilde{p}, \widetilde{q})$ and has stack contents $(s_h, p_h, q_h) \ldots (s_1, p_1, q_1)$, this means that, **first**, there exists a computation of $\mathcal{A}$ on the string $t{<}_1 u_1 \ldots {<}_h u_h$ that pushes each symbol s_i on the corresponding left bracket $<_i$, and reaches the state p after reading $t{<}_1 u_1 \ldots {<}_h u_h$, and **second**, there exists a string of the form $v = v_h{>}_h \ldots v_1{>}_1 w$, where $v_1, \ldots, v_h$ are well-nested strings, ${>}_1, \ldots, {>}_h$ are right brackets and $w \in \Sigma^*$ is any string that has no matching right brackets ($>$) to any left brackets ($<$) in t, so that $\mathcal{A}$, having begun its computation on v in the state $\tilde{p}$, with the stack contents $s_h \ldots s_1$, after popping each right bracket ${>}_i$ will be in the corresponding state p_i, and will accept in the end, whereas $\mathcal{B}$, having begun its computation on the same string v in the state $\tilde{q}$ and with the empty stack, will be in the state q_i after each right bracket ${>}_i$, and will accept the string as well.

The correctness statement could be proved by induction on the length of the computation.

Finally, accepting states are of the form (p, p, q_0), that is, $\mathcal{A}$ finishes reading u in the state p, and $\mathcal{A}$ accepts v beginning in the state p, and also $\mathcal{B}$ accepts v beginning in the state q_0. Then, $\mathcal{C}$ recognizes exactly the desired quotient. $\qquad\square$

This proves the closure under right-quotient. Since the family of languages recognized by input-driven automata is closed under reversal (where, in the reversed string, left brackets become right brackets and vice versa [2]) the closure result also extends to the left-quotient operation.

Theorem 1. *The family of languages recognized by input-driven pushdown automata is closed under right-quotient and left-quotient.*

4   Plan for a Lower Bound Argument

The construction given in the previous section uses $3m + m^2 n$ states to represent the quotient, and it turns out that it cannot be much improved upon. A lower bound on the state complexity of the quotient of NIDPDA shall be proved using witness languages of the following general form.

Fix an alphabet of labels, Γ. The first language contains nested sequences of brackets with the matching brackets having identical labels; it is a subset of the following base language.

$$K_0 = \{\, {<}_{a_1} \ldots {<}_{a_m} {>}_{a_m} \ldots {>}_{a_1} \mid m \geqslant 0,\ a_1, \ldots, a_m \in \Gamma \,\}$$

All strings in the second language consist of right brackets ($>$), which are to be erased by the quotient operation. Thus, the second language is a subset of the following language.

$$L_0 = \{\, {>}_{a_m} \ldots {>}_{a_1} \mid m \geqslant 0,\ a_1, \ldots, a_m \in \Gamma \,\}$$

An automaton $\mathcal{A}$ recognizing a subset $K \subseteq K_0$ performs two tasks. First, upon reading each bracket ${<}_a$, it pushes the symbol a to stack, and upon reading a bracket ${>}_a$ it ensures that the symbol being popped is a; doing this task does not require any states. Second, it operates on the string as a DFA, ensuring that it belongs to a certain regular language.

The second automaton $\mathcal{B}$ recognizes a subset $L \subseteq L_0$ essentially as a DFA.

Then, the quotient $K \cdot L^{-1}$ contains a string of the form $<_{a_1} \ldots <_{a_m}$ if the whole string $<_{a_1} \ldots <_{a_m} >_{a_m} \ldots >_{a_1}$ is in K, whereas its second half $>_{a_m} \ldots >_{a_1}$ belongs to L.

In order to construct efficient witness languages of this form, it is convenient to reformulate them in terms of finite automata, and to consider a related state complexity problem for finite automata. Let every left bracket $(<_a)$ labelled with a symbol $a \in \Gamma$ be regarded as a symbol a, and let every right bracket $(>_a)$ be regarded as $\tilde{a}$, from a marked copy of the alphabet $\tilde{\Gamma} = \{\, \tilde{a} \mid a \in \Gamma \,\}$. Then the associated state complexity problem for finite automata over $\Gamma \cup \tilde{\Gamma} \cup \{\#\}$ is concerned with the complexity of the following *palindromic quotient* operation on languages with respect to NFAs.

$$\mathrm{PQ}(K, L) = \{\, a_1 \ldots a_m \mid a_1 \ldots a_m \# \tilde{a}_m \ldots \tilde{a}_1 \in K,\ \tilde{a}_m \ldots \tilde{a}_1 \in L \,\}$$

Lemma 2. *Let $K \subseteq \Gamma^* \# \tilde{\Gamma}^*$ and $L \subseteq \tilde{\Gamma}^*$ be any languages, and define the corresponding languages over the alphabet of brackets as follows.*

$$K' = \{\, <_{a_1} \ldots <_{a_m} >_{a_m} \ldots >_{a_1} \mid a_1 \ldots a_m \# \tilde{a}_m \ldots \tilde{a}_1 \in K \,\}$$
$$L' = \{\, >_{a_m} \ldots >_{a_1} \mid \tilde{a}_m \ldots \tilde{a}_1 \in L \,\}$$

Then:

1. *if K is recognized by an m-state NFA, then K' is recognized by an m-state NIDPDA;*
2. *if L is recognized by an n-state NFA, then L' is recognized by an n-state NIDPDA;*
3. *if $K' \cdot (L')^{-1}$ is recognized by an N-state NIDPDA, then $\mathrm{PQ}(K, L)$ is recognized by an N-state NFA.*

In particular, to prove the third part, one can directly transform an IDPDA recognizing the quotient $K' \cdot (L')^{-1}$ to an NFA recogizing the palindromic quotient $PQ(K, L)$ by eliminating all transitions by right brackets and by ignoring all symbols pushed to the stack upon reading left brackets.

5   The Lower Bound for NFA

In order to apply Lemma 2, the task is now to determine the state complexity of the *palindromic quotient* operation with respect to NFAs. The tools for doing this are well-known.

Definition 2 (Birget [3]). *Let $L \subseteq \Sigma^*$ and $S = \{(x_1, y_1), \ldots, (x_m, y_m)\}$, $x_i, y_i \in \Sigma^*$, $i = 1, \ldots, m$. The set S is a fooling set for L, if*

1. *$x_i y_i \in L$ for all $1 \leqslant i \leqslant m$,*
2. *$x_i y_j \notin L$ or $x_j y_i \notin L$ for all $1 \leqslant i < j \leqslant m$.*

The *nondeterministic state complexity* of a regular languate L, $\mathrm{nsc}(L)$, is the minimal number of states of any NFA recognizing L.

Lemma 3 (Fooling set lemma [3]). *If a regular language L has a fooling set of cardinality k, then $\mathrm{nsc}(L) \geqslant k$.*

For an alphabet Σ define $\widetilde{\Sigma} = \{\widetilde{a} \mid a \in \Sigma\}$. For a string $w = a_1 \cdots a_k$, $a_i \in \Sigma$, $1 \leqslant i \leqslant k$, let $\widetilde{w} = \widetilde{a}_1 \cdots \widetilde{a}_k$.

Consider an alphabet $\Omega = \Sigma \cup \widetilde{\Sigma} \cup \{\#\}$, where $\# \notin \Sigma \cup \widetilde{\Sigma}$. For $K, L \subseteq \Omega^*$ define

$$\mathrm{PQ}(K, L) = \{w \in \Sigma^* \mid w\#\widetilde{w}^R \in K, \ \widetilde{w}^R \in L\}.$$

The lower bound for the state complexity of the operation $\mathrm{PQ}(\cdot, \cdot)$ will be used for obtaining a lower bound for the state complexity of quotient of input driven languages. For this reason the alphabet is partitioned into sets Σ, $\widetilde{\Sigma}$ and $\{\#\}$ which play the roles of left brackets, right brackets and neutral symbols, respectively.

Lemma 4. *If A is an NFA with n states and B an NFA with m states, the language $\mathrm{PQ}(L(A), L(B))$ has an NFA with $n^2 \cdot m$ states.*

Proof. The language $\mathrm{PQ}(L(A), L(B))$ can be recognized by an NFA C operating as follows. On input $w \in \Sigma^*$, C simulates in parallel (i) a computation of A from a start state to a state q_1, (ii) a computation of A in reverse starting from a final state on the string $\widetilde{w}$, ending in a state q_2, and (iii) a computation of B from a final state in reverse on the string $\widetilde{w}$ ending in a state p. Thus, the states of C are triples (q_1, q_2, p) where q_1, q_2 are states of A and p is a state of B. A state (q_1, q_2, p) is accepting if A has a transition on $\#$ from q_1 to q_2 and p is a start state of B.

Now C has $n^2 \cdot m$ states and, by the choice of the final states, it is clear that $L(C) = \mathrm{PQ}(L(A), L(B))$. $\square$

Lemma 5. *Let $\Sigma = \{a, b, c\}$ and $\Omega = \Sigma \cup \widetilde{\Sigma} \cup \{\#\}$. For $n, m \in \mathbb{N}$ there exist regular languages K and L over the alphabet Ω with $\mathrm{nsc}(K) = n$ and $\mathrm{nsc}(L) = m$ such that*

$$\mathrm{nsc}(\mathrm{PQ}(K, L)) \geqslant n^2 \cdot m.$$

Proof. Define

$$K = \{u_1 \# u_2 \# \cdots \# u_\ell \mid u_i \in \Omega^*, \ |u_i|_a + |u_i|_{\widetilde{b}} \equiv 0 \mod n, \ i = 1, \ldots, \ell\},$$

$$L = \{v \in \widetilde{\Sigma}^* \mid |v|_{\widetilde{c}} \equiv 0 \pmod m\}.$$

Note that the definition allows some of the substrings u_i to be empty which means that the strings of K may begin or end with $\#$ and have consecutive occurrences of $\#$.

The language K is recognized by an NFA $A = (\Omega, Q, 0, 0, \delta)$ where $Q = \{0, 1, \ldots, n-1\}$ and the transitions of δ are defined by setting

1. $\delta(i, a) = \delta(i, \widetilde{b}) = i + 1$ for $i = 0, \ldots, n-2$, and $\delta(n-1, a) = \delta(n-1, \widetilde{b}) = 0$,
2. $\delta(i, b) = \delta(i, c) = \delta(i, \widetilde{a}) = \delta(i, \widetilde{c}) = i$ for $i = 0, \ldots, n-1$,
3. $\delta(0, \#) = 0$ and $\delta(i, \#)$ is undefined for $i = 1, \ldots, n-1$.

The automaton A is, in fact, an incomplete DFA having a cycle of length n where the cycle counts the sum of the numbers of symbols a and $\widetilde{b}$ modulo n. Transitions on $\#$ are defined only when the current sum has a value divisible by n. This means that A checks that in the substring between two occurrences of $\#$ the sum of the numbers of occurrences of a and $\widetilde{b}$ must be divisible by n and A recognizes exactly the language K.

It is clear that L has an NFA with a cycle of length m that simply verifies that the input is in $\{\widetilde{a}, \widetilde{b}, \widetilde{c}\}^*$ and counts the number of occurrences of symbols $\widetilde{c}$ modulo m.

For establishing the lower bound for the nondeterministic state complexity of $\mathrm{PQ}(K, L)$ we define

$$S = \{(a^i b^j c^k, a^{n-i} b^{n-j} c^{m-k}) \mid 0 \leqslant i, j \leqslant n - 1, \, 0 \leqslant k \leqslant m - 1\}.$$

The set S has cardinality $n^2 \cdot m$ and to prove the claim, by Lemma 3, it is sufficient to verify that S is a fooling set for $\mathrm{PQ}(K, L)$.

For any pair $(a^i b^j c^k, a^{n-i} b^{n-j} c^{m-k})$ of S we have $a^i b^j c^k \cdot a^{n-i} b^{n-j} c^{m-k} \in \mathrm{PQ}(K, L)$ because with $w = a^i b^j c^k a^{n-i} b^{n-j} c^{m-k}$ we have $w \# \widetilde{w}^R \in K$ and $\widetilde{w}^R \in L$ due to the observations that $|w|_a + |w|_{\widetilde{b}} = n$, $|\widetilde{w}|_a + |\widetilde{w}|_{\widetilde{b}} = n$ and $|\widetilde{w}|_{\widetilde{c}} = m$.

Next consider two distinct elements of S, $(a^i b^j c^k, a^{n-i} b^{n-j} c^{m-k})$ and $(a^r b^s c^t, a^{n-r} b^{n-s} c^{m-t})$, where $(i, j, k) \neq (r, s, t)$. Denote $w = a^i b^j c^k \cdot a^{n-r} b^{n-s} c^{m-t}$. If $k \neq t$, $w \notin \mathrm{PQ}(K, L)$ because $|\widetilde{w}|_{\widetilde{c}} \not\equiv 0 \mod m$. If $i \neq r$ then $|w|_a + |w|_{\widetilde{b}} = i + n - r \not\equiv 0 \mod n$ and, consequently, $w \# \widetilde{w}^R \notin K$ and $w \notin \mathrm{PQ}(K, L)$. Similarly, if $j \neq s$ then $|\widetilde{w}|_a + |\widetilde{w}|_{\widetilde{b}} = j + n - s \not\equiv 0 \mod n$ and again $w \# \widetilde{w}^R \notin K$.   □

6   The State Complexity of the Quotient

The results on the number of states in NIDPDA needed to represent the quotient are put together in the following theorem.

Theorem 2. *In order to represent the quotient of an m-state NIDPDA by an n-state NIDPDA, it is sufficient to use an NIDPDA with $3m + m^2 n$ states. In the worst case, it is necessary to use at least $m^2 n$ states.*

This gives the state complexity of $m^2 n + O(m)$.

If the goal is to construct a deterministic automaton, one possible solution is to determinize the constructed NIDPDA. However, that would produce as many as $2^{\Theta(m^4 n^2)}$ states. Previously, for some operations, such as the concatenation, a much more succinct direct construction of a DIDPDA was defined [14] using the idea of computing *behaviour functions* of the given DIDPDA [11]. Investigating whether there is a significantly better construction of a DIDPDA for a quotient of two DIDPDAs is left as an open problem. A possible starting point is the DFA state complexity of the *palindromic quotient* operation defined in this paper.

Another open problem concerns the state complexity of the quotient for the intermediate *unambiguous IDPDA* model [13].

Acknowledgement. The authors are grateful to the anonymous reviewers for many pertinent comments and suggestions; the implementation of some of them is deferred until the full version of this paper.

References

1. Alur, R., Madhusudan, P.: Visibly pushdown languages. In: ACM Symposium on Theory of Computing, STOC 2004, Chicago, USA, pp. 202–211, 13–16 June 2004
2. Alur, R., Madhusudan, P.: Adding nesting structure to words. J. ACM **56**, 3 (2009)
3. Birget, J.-C.: Intersection and union of regular languages and state complexity. Inf. Process. Lett. **43**, 185–190 (1992)
4. von Braunmühl, B., Verbeek, R.: Input driven languages are recognized in $\log n$ space. Ann. Discret. Math. **24**, 1–20 (1985)
5. Ginsburg, S., Greibach, S.A.: Deterministic context-free languages. Inf. Control **9**(6), 620–648 (1966)
6. Ginsburg, S., Spanier, E.H.: Quotients of context-free languages. J. ACM **10**(4), 487–492 (1963)
7. Han, Y.-S., Salomaa, K.: Nondeterministic state complexity of nested word automata. Theoret. Comput. Sci. **410**, 2961–2971 (2009)
8. Hartmanis, J.: Context-free languages and Turing machine computations. In: Proceedings of Symposia in Applied Mathematics, vol. 19, pp. 42–51. AMS (1967)
9. Latteux, M., Leguy, B., Ratoandromanana, B.: The family of one-counter languages is closed under quotient. Acta Inform. **22**(5), 579–588 (1985)
10. Mehlhorn, K.: Pebbling mountain ranges and its application to DCFL-recognition. In: Bakker, J., Leeuwen, J. (eds.) ICALP 1980. LNCS, vol. 85, pp. 422–435. Springer, Heidelberg (1980). doi:10.1007/3-540-10003-2_89
11. Okhotin, A.: Input-driven languages are linear conjunctive. Theoret. Comput. Sci. **618**, 52–71 (2016)
12. Okhotin, A., Salomaa, K.: Complexity of input-driven pushdown automata. SIGACT News **45**(2), 47–67 (2014)
13. Okhotin, A., Salomaa, K.: Descriptional complexity of unambiguous input-driven pushdown automata. Theoret. Comput. Sci. **566**, 1–11 (2015)
14. Okhotin, A., Salomaa, K.: State complexity of operations on input-driven pushdown automata. J. Comput. Syst. Sci. **86**, 207–228 (2017)
15. Okhotin, A., Salomaa, K.: Edit distance neighbourhoods of input-driven pushdown automata. In: Weil, P. (ed.) CSR 2017. LNCS, vol. 10304, pp. 260–272. Springer, Cham (2017). doi:10.1007/978-3-319-58747-9_23
16. Piao, X., Salomaa, K.: Operational state complexity of nested word automata. Theoret. Comput. Sci. **410**, 3290–3302 (2009)
17. Salomaa, K.: Limitations of lower bound methods for deterministic nested word automata. Inf. Comput. **209**, 580–589 (2011)
18. Wood, D.: A further note on top-down deterministic languages. Comput. J. **14**(4), 396–403 (1971)

Author Index

Printed in the United States
By Bookmasters